More

"A wonderful exciting chronicl... pendium of information."

"The amazing facts about that y... well researched and always fascinating. This reader was absorbed in the material."

—*West Coast Review of Books*

"From eyewitness accounts in newspapers and periodicals, Klingaman vividly reconstructs the details—the weather, the furniture, the fashions, the curious and adoring crowds, their personalities. . . . Like Frederick Lewis Allen's *Only Yesterday, 1919* is a compilation of facts which recreates the atmosphere of a time and place."

—*Charlotte Observer*

"The new age is brilliantly described in Klingaman's Prologue. . . . Truly 1919 was a busy year. Klingaman has caught the hectic excitement that ushered in the modern world."

—*Grand Rapids Press*

"[A] rich mosaic . . . 'The world broke in two in 1919,' stresses Klingaman; in dramatic detail he shows how it happened, and why."

—*Publishers Weekly*

"The world split apart in 1919, says William Klingaman in his monumental history. . . . Drawing on memoirs, diaries, journals and newspaper accounts, the author has woven a mosaic of the world in 1919 that is rich in sweep, color and drama. For historians and scholars, it is a treasure trove. Klingaman's lively and well-researched narrative ranges far and wide to capture the flavor of a troubled year. . . . Klingaman introduces an immense cast of characters—contemporary and future international shakers—in this sweeping panorama. . . . This is a masterpiece of historical narrative."

—*Springfield Union*

1919

THE YEAR OUR
WORLD BEGAN

William K. Klingaman

PERENNIAL LIBRARY

Harper & Row, Publishers, New York
Grand Rapids, Philadelphia, St. Louis, San Francisco
London, Singapore, Sydney, Tokyo

FOR JANET

Grateful acknowledgment is made for permission to use the following material:

Selections from the poems of W. B. Yeats, reprinted with permission of Macmillan Publishing Company from *The Poems of W. B. Yeats*, by W. B. Yeats, edited by Richard J. Finneran. Copyright 1924 by Macmillan Publishing Company, renewed 1952 by Bertha Georgie Yeats.

A hardcover edition of this book was published in 1987 by St. Martin's Press. It is here reprinted by arrangement with St. Martin's Press.

First PERENNIAL LIBRARY edition published 1989.

LIBRARY OF CONGRESS CATALOG CARD NUMBER 89-45099

ISBN 0-06-097251-3

89 90 91 92 93 FG 10 9 8 7 6 5 4 3 2 1

CONTENTS

PREFACE

The world broke in two in 1919. Like a ghost that lingered past the appointed hour, the nineteenth century—with its essential orderliness, its self-confidence, and its faith in human progress—had tarried until August 1914, when the major European powers suffered a collective attack of muddleheadedness that led directly to the senseless slaughter of millions of the best young men of a generation. Four and a half years later, as the world tried to pick up the pieces after the wrenching cataclysm of the Great War, it became apparent to many (but by no means all) contemporary observers that the last remaining vestiges of the old order had been swept away, and that mankind had entered a new age that was considerably less rational and less forgiving of human imperfections.

Those who had expected peace to usher in a better world found their hopes betrayed in 1919. The most famous of those who dared to dream, President Woodrow Wilson, ended the year broken in body and spirit. In one nation after another, 1919 brought nothing but disaster, discontent, and disillusionment. Beneath the surface, the forces of change that had been unleashed during the war already were being used by men such as Lenin, Adolf Hitler, Mohandas Gandhi, and Benito Mussolini to undermine the postwar settlement fashioned at the Paris Peace Conference. For the next two decades, the tension between these forces would make much of the world a very unhappy place, creating an atmosphere of bitterness and resentment that occasionally flared into violence; eventually it led civilization straight into a second world war that began in 1939.

Besides tracing the political and diplomatic developments of this chaotic and fascinating year, I have attempted to re-create the atmosphere of everyday life in 1919. In America, this was a time of low-cut gowns and disappearing waistlines, of suffragettes and the Great Red Scare, of police strikes, race riots, and prohibition. Charlie Chaplin, Douglas Fairbanks, and Mary Pickford ruled the world of cinema. Science was revolutionized when astronomers and mathematicians gathered the first physical evidence to support Albert Einstein's theory of relativity. Jack Dempsey won the world heavyweight boxing title, Sir Barton became the first horse to win the Triple Crown, and the Chicago White Sox earned themselves an eternal place in sports infamy by deliberately throwing the World Series.

Since all these characters went to such extraordinary lengths to provide me with colorful material, I decided I should at least try to fashion a dramatic narrative worthy of their efforts. Any reader expecting to find six hundred pages of tedious historical analysis herein will, I hope, be greatly disappointed. However, I would like to express my appreciation to my editor, Tom Dunne, for saving me from the worst excesses of an occasionally idiosyncratic writing style. I am also most grateful to Norman Graebner and the late Edward Younger for teaching me about the joys and the responsibilities of being a historian. Raymond Callahan and John Wells Gould, too, played a vital role.

To my family I owe more than I could ever say. My four-year-old son, Nicholas, helped me type this manuscript and has generously offered to share the responsibility for any errors herein.

Finally, I should point out that the epigraphs at the start of each section and chapter (with the sole exception of the Prologue) are drawn from the Book of Jeremiah; their author has graciously agreed to allow me to use them free of charge.

PROLOGUE

"The last day

of this

dreadful year."

—HARRY KESSLER,

In the Twenties

Early on a dark morning that was cold and raw even by London's dismal winter standards, five carriages departed Buckingham Palace. Despite the bleak weather, the royal carriages were open; the first carried King George V and his guest of the past five days, President Woodrow Wilson, the first American president ever to set foot in England. After a week of testimonial dinners and public adulation, Wilson was now concluding a tour that *The Times* of London believed to be "the most successful visit to England ever paid by the chief of another State." In the second carriage rode Mrs. Wilson, her umbrella raised, the Queen, and Princess Mary. The men, women, and girls who poured out of the underground stations and trudged along the city streets through the chilling drizzle to their jobs in the West End stopped to cheer politely when the procession passed. The crimson-clad royal footmen, outriders, and coachmen—each bedecked in a white wig and cocked hat, resplendent even under the mottled gray sky—stared straight ahead with no sign of emotion.

The Great War was over. It had ended with Germany's unconditional surrender and the armistice signed on November 11 in a railroad car in Compiègne Forest. There would be no more air raids over London, with terrified women shielding small children from death and praying for the signal of "all clear"; over a thousand British children now lay dead or wounded. There would be no more husbands and brothers and sons stumbling blindly across the shell-plowed fields of France, no more agonized waiting for a bullet in the trenches or a telegram in the homes. But since only a small part of the British Army had been demobilized by the end of the year, Wilson could still see numerous patches of khaki among the London crowd that morning; the women soldiers' uniforms, with either trousers or the short skirts that revealed a considerable expanse of stocking, shocked staid American visitors. Upon the city's walls and pillars, as high as a man's hand could reach, remnants of recruiting posters bearing urgent appeals from Lord Kitchener or the likeness of an embattled man at a gun somewhere on the Western Front now were turning gray and pale, barely visible through the veil of a winter's mist. On another street, out of Wilson's view, a disabled veteran was begging for money, playing music and displaying a sign: THIS IS THE WAY OUR GOVERNMENT REWARDS US FOR DOING OUR BIT.

If the stately royal procession looked beyond the weary soldiers and the decaying posters, beyond the preponderance of women among the commuters on their way to work and the continuing shortages of beer and orange marmalade in the pubs, it appeared that London had outwardly changed very little since August 1914. No one could tell for certain whether the country was heading forward into a new age—a Britain "fit for heroes to live in"—or only returning to the old familiar ways. The royal carriages came to a halt in front of Victoria Station.

Precisely at 9:00, the party walked to the platform by the President's special train, where they were greeted by a host of British political and military officials, the most prominent of whom was the Welsh wizard, Prime Minister David Lloyd George, the brilliantly opportunistic leader of the Liberal-Conservative coalition that had led the nation to victory. For its reward, Lloyd George's government had been given an overwhelming vote of confidence by the voters in the general election held several weeks earlier. (Harold Nicolson believed the electorate had also returned to Westminster "the most unintelligent body of public-school boys which even the Mother of Parliaments has known.") Certainly the nation was in a vindictive mood, applauding candidates' promises to "hang the Kaiser" and to squeeze Germany like a lemon "until you can hear the pips squeak." Lloyd George and Wilson would meet again in two weeks, at the peace conference in Paris.

The four then posed for photographs as a burst of flash powder caught their images for history: King George in a naval uniform, peering out stolidly from behind a neatly trimmed beard and full mustaches; Queen Mary dignified in a brown fur coat and dark hat with a blue feather; Mrs. Wilson in black furs and a violet velvet hat, looking perhaps a bit out of her league amid European royalty, carrying a bunch of violets given her in the waiting room; and Wilson in his familiar black coat, carrying a silk hat, his long thin face drawn and tired from the burdens imposed by war and peace and, most of all, by his own Calvinist conscience. The President shook hands warmly with his British hosts and began to board the train. He called back to his wife, who was still chatting enthusiastically with the Queen, to remind her that the train was starting to pull out of the station. As the train departed at 9:18 with a shrill whistle and a hiss of steam, the Irish Guards band played the American national anthem.

Put bluntly, King George was glad to see the last of Wilson. The whole affair had been a bother from the start, since it had forced the King to postpone his plans for a year-end holiday at Sandringham. Further, he had found the President quite unpleasant. "I could not bear him," King George confided to a friend. Wilson, he said, was "an entirely cold academical professor—an odious man." Lloyd George, who had the odd habit of judging a man by the shape of his head (Neville Chamberlain, for instance, was a "pinhead"), was more charitable in describing the President: "Wilson with his high but narrow brow, his fine head with its elevated crown and his dreamy but untrustful eye—the makeup of the idealist who is also something of an egoist."

In Germany, chaos. All aspects of the prewar imperial system seemed to be decaying or disappearing. Defeat, despair, and the deaths of nearly two million men had shattered the once-proud German military machine. Sailors mutinied and raised the red flag over their ships. Some disillusioned soldiers openly insulted their officers and joined with rebellious industrial workers to set up local government councils that requisitioned (i.e., stole) scarce food supplies for their own use. Many tired soldiers simply left their units and went home.

Germany's obsessive drive to achieve industrial supremacy in the years before the war had forced the country to import food for its cities in the best of times. Now, with the Allies occupying the Rhineland and blockading the northern coast, with the lands to the east devastated by war and revolution, and the nation's rail transportation facilities almost totally disorganized, food shortages became critical. One American correspondent walking the streets of Frankfurt found himself surrounded by small children begging him to ask President Wilson to send more bread and milk. A British physician declared that many of Frankfurt's children unquestionably were too weak to survive even an ordinary illness, much less influenza. An almost total shortage of milk on the open market was killing thousands of babies throughout Germany; even in the relatively prosperous area of Coblenz, an American investigation revealed that the mortality rate for children under five had nearly doubled since 1913. In Berlin, official monthly rations for one person included one and a half pounds of meat with bone, two-fifths of a pound of grain or cereal, and twenty-eight pounds of potatoes. Marmalade was made from beets, and coffee from ground plum pits, acorns, and fig leaves. At the first public costume ball held in Berlin in four years—dancing had been forbidden during the war—middle-class couples competed for the first prize of one pound of butter.

There was a government in Berlin, but no one was certain if it controlled anything beyond the few buildings it occupied. The Kaiser had abdicated under pressure on November 9, after his Chancellor had left him no choice in the matter by announcing the abdication prematurely to the cheers of a crowd of ten thousand discontented workers and soldiers in the capital. Now the leaders of the Majority Socialist party took the Kaiser's place. Friedrich Ebert, a former bartender whose orderly mind was better suited to the finite certainties of accounting than governing a disintegrating nation, sat alone in the Chancellor's office as the highest official in Germany. Ebert could not know if the remnants of the Imperial Army would remain loyal to his government. Outside, in the streets of Berlin, the radicals who had launched an abortive revolution in November continued to stir up unrest among the hungry and the cold, and the government did little to stop them. A delegate from Moscow encouraged German workers to join forces with their comrades to the east. Reports of Bolshevist uprisings in Bavaria and German Silesia at the end of December encouraged the atmosphere of disorder. For one American visitor, "the eight days I spent in Berlin more nearly resembled the successive grotesqueries of a movie show than a visit to what was formerly an orderly and strictly regulated metropolis."

And what of the ex-Kaiser? The former emperor of the Second Reich was a pathetic refugee at a castle in Holland, pacing up and down the corridors, playing the role of the Prince of Peace at a private Christmas Eve gathering, and now suffering from a high fever on New Year's Eve. To *The New York Times*, William II was "the most wretched of mortal men." Even his cousin, King George of England, believed him to be "the greatest criminal known for having plunged the world into this ghastly war which has lasted over four years and three months with all its misery." Count Harry Kessler held William personally responsible for Germany's tragedy:

HE WAS BOTH SHY AND INTEMPERATE, SCREAMING HIS HEAD OFF TO HIDE HIS EMBARRASSMENT. HIS BRUTALITY AND HIS CHEAP POSTURING WERE MEANS OF SELF-PROTECTION AND SELF-DECEPTION, A PURELY PERSONAL MATTER FOR WHICH ALL OF US ARE NOW PAYING THE PRICE BY WAY OF POLITICAL DESTRUCTION AND ECONOMIC RUIN. THIS RABBIT ROARING LIKE A LION WOULD BE HISTORY'S MOST RIDICULOUS MONSTER IF HIS PERFORMANCE HAD NOT RESULTED IN SUCH SUFFERING AND RIVERS OF BLOOD. THE MENDACITY OF HIS BEHAVIOUR UNDERMINED POLICY AND THE STATE, SUBSTITUTED SHAM AND SHOW FOR SOUND PRUSSIAN TRADITION, AND DISTORTED THE PERSPECTIVE OF ALMOST THE ENTIRE NATION.

William II's eldest son, the Crown Prince, vowed that the British and French would "never get me alive." The Imperial Palace in Berlin, its heavy iron doors shattered by the gunfire of the revolution, its ornate balconies and gardens in ruins, was sacked by looters who plundered the wardrobes and jewelry cases of the former Emperor and Empress. Police recovered some of the booty; silks, satins, furs, velvets, military decorations, and the dress uniforms of other nations that the Kaiser had worn on his official visits abroad all were scattered in disarray at police headquarters. On a writing table in the Kaiserin's private room at the palace lay an unfinished letter to one of her younger sons and a tear-off calendar bearing the date November 10. Among the confusion in the Kaiser's suite was found an old, often-patched uniform of a common soldier, who had left it behind after appropriating a royal outfit. In the same room, on a table, undisturbed, there stood the imperial collection of tin soldiers from nearly every European nation that had suffered casualties in the war.

President Wilson's train reached Dover at eleven o'clock. The President was greeted upon his arrival by the Mayor of Dover, the Lord Lieutenant of Kent, and a number of naval and military officers. Wilson stepped from the train and walked briskly past the Royal Fusiliers and a guard of blue-jackets from the British fleet while the band of the Buffs played the American national anthem. A sharp west wind was whipping the Channel into whitecaps. The crews of the Dover trawler patrol gave the President three hearty cheers as he and his party reached the pier. Wilson chatted with several American officers for a few moments, shook hands all around, and boarded the steamer transport ship *Brighton*.

At 11:20 the *Brighton* pulled out of Dover, bound for Calais. The old battery at Dover Castle fired a royal salute of twenty-one guns, while the band played "The Star-Spangled Banner" one more time. The President and Mrs. Wilson stood on the *Brighton*'s bridge, smiling and waving farewells to those on shore, though the wind carried away the words of the British sailors who had raised the American flag over their ships in honor of their guest. The unfavorable weather made it impossible for squadrons of aircraft to be in attendance as planned, but a flotilla of seven British destroyers escorted the President's ship to mid-Channel, where a guard of French destroyers took over.

During the trip across the Channel, Wilson relaxed with a group of American reporters on deck. His official duties over for a few moments, the President had changed into a fur overcoat and soft cap. Wilson told the reporters that his deerskin coat, with its collar of raccoon skin, had been made from animals killed by a friend of his in Georgia. The mention of coon hunting, the President said, brought to mind a story he had heard recently of a Negro soldier in France. When an officer asked him what he would do if he saw the German cavalry approaching, the Negro innocently replied, "I sure would spread the news through France." It was, the President hastened to add, just a story. As the ship neared the French shore, Wilson sighed. "Where now is my dress hat? I must go and get it."

The *Brighton* reached Calais at 12:40. After a brief reception by French officials, the President and Mrs. Wilson boarded a special train for Paris at one o'clock.

In Russia, civil war. The ruined Romanoff empire, John Dos Passos wrote, "lay across the eastern third of the hemisphere writhing in agony like a snake run over on the road." The Czar was dead. The Bolshevik forces of Lenin and Trotsky that had overthrown Kerensky's provisional government and seized power in November 1917 now controlled only an area about eight hundred miles in diameter, with the center of the circle in the Red capital of Moscow. But though they ruled less than 20 percent of Russia's landmass, they held the most vital regions, and the Bolsheviks had the added advantage of being the only effective and competent political force in the country. Their opponents were a diverse and querulous group of conservatives, Cossacks, and glory-seeking militarists, aided by Czech troops who happened to have been caught in Russia when Lenin made peace with Germany in March 1918. The Allies—France, Britain, and the United States—viewed the Bolshevik regime with varying degrees of fear and distrust, and each nation had sent troops into central or northern Russia to protect its own perceived interests against the Reds. But in the absence of any coordinated political or military strategy, these troops only added to the confusion.

The civil war was a characteristically Russian conflict, fought with grand movements made over distances of hundreds of miles to outmaneuver the enemy, fought by armies of nearly frozen men who often carried only the most primitive firearms, men who trudged mindlessly through the endless snow and ice and forests, stopping now and then to raid a village and perhaps receive a slow, halting ride in the freight car of a decrepit train. And then when the enemy finally appeared, there would be no mercy shown by either side. "Tens of governments and tens of armies sprang up on the vast spaces of the country wearing all the colors of the political spectrum, from Red to Southern," wrote General Denikin, one of the leaders of the White anti-Bolshevik forces. Denikin watched as the exhausted and apathetic Russian population "abandoned 'the defeated' and deserted to 'the victors' and with ease exchanged the red cockade for the tricolor triangle and back as though these were merely decorations on a uniform. All exertions of the Red, White, and Black leaders to attach national significance to the struggle failed."

From his vantage point in England, Winston Churchill saw Russia in late 1918 as "a very large country, a very old country, a very disagreeable country inhabited by immense numbers of ignorant people largely possessed of lethal weapons & in a state of extreme disorder." Western Europe was constantly bombarded with exaggerated reports of the Bolsheviks' destruction of all vestiges of civilized behavior in Russia's two largest cities, Moscow and Petrograd (the former imperial capital). *The Times* of London, for instance, informed its readers that "the real dictator of Petrograd is a woman of the name of Jacobleva, aged 22, who . . . surpasses all existing legends of cruelty." But the truth itself was more than bad enough. Petrograd: the dark broken streets, famine, deserted factories, closed shops, vacant houses, and always the cold. Moscow: ravaged by typhus and the Bolshevik reign of organized terror; starvation, bodies piled up like cords of firewood at the cemeteries when graves could not be dug in the frozen ground and when people no longer cared, and still the cold. A feeling of panic had begun to work upon the Bolsheviks by the end of 1918, for they had counted heavily upon a rising of kindred spirits in Central and Eastern Europe—and especially in Germany—to come to their support, but still they waited, alone, and isolated.

Directing this spectacle of social destruction from a small office in the Kremlin was Vladimir Ilyich Ulyanov, known by his pseudonym: Lenin. Although Lenin cared nothing for the outward trappings and show of authority, he took an almost demonic delight in the exercise of absolute power. Five telephones in his office and a host of telegraph machines in the corridor outside brought in the news from every military and political battlefront and sent out Lenin's orders in reply. On his desk, amid the clutter of several pairs of scissors, a mother-of-pearl paper knife, and souvenirs sent by admirers, sat a cast-iron figure of an ape sitting on a pile of books, pensively examining a large human skull. Affable and grinning with visitors, Lenin had already begun to rely more and more on the use of sheer terror to solidify Bolshevik control. Maxim Gorky, the most popular Russian writer of the day, recalled once sitting with Lenin at a concert, listening to a gifted Russian pianist play Beethoven's *Appassionata:* "I know of nothing greater than the *Appassionata,*" Lenin told Gorky. "I would like to listen to it every day. It is marvelous superhuman music. I always think with pride—perhaps it is naïve of me—what marvelous things human beings can do." Then, screwing up his eyes and smiling, Lenin added, rather sadly, "But I can't listen to music too often, it works on my nerves, makes me want to say kind, stupid things and pat the heads of people who, living in this vile hell, can create such beauty. But now one must not pat anybody's head—they might bite off your hand, and you have to beat them on the head, beat them without mercy, although we are ideally opposed to the use of force against anyone. Hm, hm, this is an infernally difficult job."

On his journey through the French countryside on the way to Paris, Wilson slept as the train passed by scenes of ruin and destruction caused by four years of brutal warfare on the Western Front. The names of the towns of northern France had been burned into the memories of the men who had huddled in the trenches day after day: St-Omer, Aubers, Lens, Vimy, Verdun, Amiens, Château-Thierry. The women at home would remember the names of the rivers where their husbands died: the Marne, the Aisne, the Yser, the Meuse.

A few miles to the east, as Wilson's state coach rolled easily through the bomb-shattered city of Amiens (the President roused himself briefly at this point halfway between Calais and Paris), lay the valley of the Somme, perhaps the most devastated region of all. Nearly 500,000 acres destroyed and the once-rich farmland ripped apart by trenches and shells. Villages cast down in ruins as if by earthquake, with only formless masses of bricks and dust left behind as proof they had ever existed. Rutted tracks remained where country lanes once had run; wounded trees, limbless and headless, loomed above the desolation like scaffolds; sometimes an entire forest had vanished. The valley was a skeleton without flesh, save for the bodies of half a million dead men ground up beneath the ceaseless bombardments. Stretching out to the horizon lay a sickening and monotonous legacy of waste that spoke of the decay that follows death, the ground sown with unexploded shells, the inevitable weeds wrapped around the rusted barbed wire, and empty trenches disintegrating in the rain. "The earth must have looked like this when first it cooled, and before there was life and all was void," wrote one British witness. "A wound [has] been inflicted which can never heal."

Women, children, and old men who had fled from the German offensive now returned to find their homes completely gone, along with all their tangible links with the past. Herbert Hoover, directing the American relief effort overseas, cabled his impressions back to the United States. "The destruction of some twenty principal towns and literally hundreds of villages renders the return of these refugees a stupendous problem. . . . They evade all official urgings [to delay their return] and the roads are a continuous procession of these pitiable bodies. Thousands of them reach their villages to find every vestige of shelter destroyed, and finally wander into the villages further back from the acute battle area, which are themselves already overcrowded to a heart-breaking degree." The German invaders, Hoover learned, also had brutally erased all traces of industry in the region, razing factories, flooding coal mines, blowing up railway lines. ("The German method of destruction was to bend every single rail by exploding a hand grenade under it, rendering it useless for all time.")

But Wilson never saw these things, for they were things he chose not to see. The President had resisted the repeated urgings of the French government to visit these devastated areas and their graveyards with acre upon acre of small white crosses because he felt the fearsome sights might affect his judgment at the forthcoming peace conference. "The French want me to see red," Wilson realized. And though he claimed that "I could not despise the Germans more than I do already," Wilson had come to Europe to restrain the French and British desire for revenge upon the despised Hun. (Rudyard Kipling, who had lost his only son in the war, believed the Germans were "a people with the heart of beasts"; to the otherwise gentle and charitable British Foreign Secretary, Arthur Balfour, "brutes they were, and brutes they remain.") But Wilson would save the Allies from themselves. He would be the new messiah, using American power—and his own personal prestige as the hope of the common people—to lead the world into a new age by rejecting the claims of emotion, selfish nationalism, and the age-old European reliance upon the balance of power and military force. He would devise instead a peace with justice, a peace based upon enduring moral principles as defined in his famous if occasionally vague Fourteen Points, a peace with a League of Nations embodying the forces of right to deter future aggressors.

President and Mrs. Wilson finally arrived in Paris at the Gare du Nord at seven o'clock that evening. Badly in need of a rest, Wilson had expressly requested that there be no formal reception at the station. But before the waiting automobiles could hurry them away to the Murat Palace, the dignified eighteenth-century stone mansion that served as the Wilson's home during their stay in Paris, a crowd recognized the President and pressed around the cordon of French hussars and American soldiers to give him yet another round of enthusiastic greetings. "*Vive Wilson!*" "*Vive les Etats-Unis!*"

Just as Wilson entered Paris, Premier Georges Clemenceau was boarding a train heading out of the city for a week's rest. He retreated to a small village on the Atlantic coast, to breathe the air of his native province in the west of France, to rest and prepare for the coming fight. Seventy-eight years old and a veteran of decades of intrigues, plots, and counterplots in the maelstrom of French political life, Clemenceau was the professional destroyer, known as "the Tiger," whose savage attacks had brought down government after government. He knew no fear and gave no quarter. Lloyd George, once more expressing his fascination with the shape of a man's cranium, described him thus: "Clemenceau, with a powerful head and the square brow of the logician—the head conspicuously flat topped, with no upper storey in which to lodge the humanities, the ever vigilant and fierce eye of the animal who has hunted and been hunted all his life." He had courageously defended Captain Alfred Dreyfus, and was an old and close friend of Claude Monet. The Tiger had taken control of the French government in November 1917 and guided his nation through the terrible German onslaught of the following spring, occasionally venturing out to the front lines himself to hurl insults at the enemy trenches. Clemenceau had seen the Prussians crush and burn France in 1870 and again in

1914. Alone in his room at night, suffering from insomnia, he made his plans to ensure that Germany was buried forever.

Clemenceau would let no one, and certainly not Wilson, interfere with those plans. "America is very far from Germany, but France is very near," he had reminded the world several days earlier, "and I have preoccupations which do not affect President Wilson as they do a man who has seen the Germans for four years in his country. There are old wrongs to be righted. . . . This must not begin again." The partisan French press, usually at each other's throats, were virtually united in their approval of Clemenceau's motto, "Never Again." On December 29, Clemenceau spoke in the Chamber of Deputies of Wilson's *"noble candeur,"* an ambiguous French phrase that could be interpreted as denoting either admirable honesty or the simplemindedness of the local village idiot. Colonel Edward House, Wilson's chief adviser and one of the few men the President truly trusted, sat in his Paris hotel room on New Year's Eve and confided to his diary that "coming on the heels of the English election . . . the situation strategically could not be worse."

In the United States, there was a buoyant spirit of optimism and faith in the future. Newspapers announced that January 1, 1919, would be "the dawn of a New Year and the dawn of a new era on earth." 1918 had been "a wonderful year in the annals of human progress," a year of tremendous advances for the forces of morality at home and abroad, and the country prayed that the new year would be "a champion joy-bringer" and "a year of jubilee." It was not surprising that this fulsome spirit seemed to ignore the realities of life in Europe: there had been no battles on American soil, no widespread famine, social upheaval, or political revolution; and even though nearly 50,000 American men had been killed and over 230,000 wounded in action, those numbers paled in comparison to the losses of every major European power. At the end of the year, the financial cost of the war to American taxpayers had reached $22,580 million, a stupendous figure by prewar standards, but again much less than the costs incurred by Britain and France.

Still, the nation would tolerate no delay in eliminating the constraints of wartime life. Holiday gift sales soared as pent-up emotions gained release, and a run on silk stockings developed in New York's finest department stores when exuberant husbands and boyfriends sought the most extravagantly frivolous items. One gentleman ordered eighteen pairs of black silk hose at eighteen dollars apiece (presumably for eighteen girl-friends), each pair to have embroidered upon it pictures of cats, dogs, elephants, and other animals. A pair of exceedingly fine-spun silk stockings with a front of Chantilly lace had been shown in a shop window and then withdrawn during the war on the grounds that the display of such luxury seemed inhuman while the fighting was still going on in Europe. Now a Broadway impresario purchased the stockings for $250. Stockings with pictures of mice, turkeys, lobsters, cupids, and the words "You're fresh" also sold well. It was a giddy time, a time for silliness.

Stock prices were up on December 31, and so were women's hemlines. Debates raged that winter over the proper dress for women. At the annual meeting of the Public Health Association in Chicago at the end of the year, Dr. Charlotte Throckmorton of Charlton, Iowa, claimed that the customary street dress of women was "offensive against decency," and that mothers should be chastised for allowing their daughters to defy pneumonia with only a lavaliere for protection. Another critic deplored the women who looked "ridiculous" in their thin blouses, "their lingerie too conspicuous and too scanty and their skirts much too short." Dr. Effie Lobdell of Chicago disagreed strenuously. Obviously a product of progressive thinking induced by life in the big city, Dr. Lobdell defended the diaphanous trend in women's wear; with fewer clothes to launder, she argued, women would keep their garments cleaner. She even went so far as to endorse the wearing of thin and scant clothing from a moral standpoint, since it left less to men's imaginations and prevented them from doing anything silly to satisfy their curiosity. A number of men in the audience heartily endorsed Dr. Lobdell's stand.

One major casualty of the war was booze. Aided by wartime pressures to conserve grain supplies, as well as by the association of beer-drinking with German culture in the popular mind, the prohibition movement had brought thirty-one states into the dry column by the end of the year. The water-wagon was the tank that would level every Prussian trench, sobriety the bomb that would blow Kaiserism to kingdom come. An emergency national prohibition measure was scheduled to become law on July 1, 1919, but the real battle now was over the constitutional amendment already approved by Congress and needing only affirmative votes from five more state legislatures before it became a reality. Montana, which had been supplying much of the bootleg liquor to Oregon, Idaho, and Washington, went dry at midnight, December 30. The previous afternoon, liquor stores throughout the state had sold up all their stocks and closed early. On December 31, Florida banned the importation of liquor into the state, the transport of liquor within the state, and of course all private distillation. Of all the forty-eight state legislatures, only New Jersey—notorious for its corrupt machine politics—seemed to stand in steadfast opposition to the amendment.

There were two major threats to American tranquility at the end of 1918, and naturally both of them came from Europe. One was the persistence of the Spanish influenza epidemic. More American soldiers, sailors, and marines had died of disease than in battle during the war, and civilian deaths in the United States from influenza would approach 500,000 before the epidemic abated. Newspapers were full of advertisements for products that would help ward off the dreaded flu: "You can't be too careful if you have a cold—treat it promptly with Father John's medicine." Obeying the terms of an old Russian superstition that a marriage in a graveyard between two people who had never met would help stop an epidemic, a couple of total strangers named Harry Rosenberg and Fanny Jacobs were wed in Philadelphia's Cobb Creek Cemetery. It didn't work. On New Year's Eve, influenza still raged through the city's Jewish district.

Philadelphia also witnessed a manifestation of the second cloud looming on the American horizon. It was a Red cloud, threatening a reign of terror by alien radicals and bolsheviks. At 10:45 on the evening of December 30, a bomb exploded at the home of Ernest T. Trigg, president of the Philadelphia Chamber of Commerce. Ten minutes later and three miles away, a three-story brick apartment house at 1139 North 41st Street, where Acting Superintendent of Police William B. Mills resided, was blown up, Mills being thrown from his bed into an adjacent corridor ten feet away. At 11:10, four miles farther away, the front of the house of State Supreme Court Justice Robert von Moschzisker, at 2101 Delancey Street, was torn out by a third bomb.

A crudely printed circular found near the explosions was addressed "To the exploiters, the judges, policemen, the priests, the soldiers. . . . Science triumphed over Torquemada's century. Anarchy will triumph over the present Torquemadas of our century. We have demanded the freedom of all political prisoners, freedom of press and speech. You have refused. We war against you." The following day, scores of detectives were sent out to question every person known to be identified with radical organizations in the city. Agents of army and navy intelligence, the Department of Justice, the Post Office, and the Shipping Board launched their investigations. Clues appeared to point to radicals from New York, or perhaps Chicago, or possibly the Pacific Northwest. The Home Defense Reserve was called into service to protect churches and the homes of city officials and wealthy Philadelphians on New Year's Eve. Captain Mills believed the bombings were "a part of the plot which the Bolsheviki are starting on a nation-wide scale. I think they started in Philadelphia, and that outbreaks may be expected any day and in any part of the country." In announcing that he would tolerate no further meetings of radical groups in Philadelphia, William H. Wilson, director of the Department of Public Safety, sternly declared that "this is America—not Russia."

Police arrested and held without bail Edward Moore, a fifty-six-year-old former hatmaker accused by the *Philadelphia Inquirer* of being "one of the city's most intractable revolutionists" for his association with such dangerous provocateurs as Eugene V. Debs and "Big Bill" Haywood. "We are holding him right here in the City Hall, incommunicado," Captain Mills told reporters. "I don't give a damn if he is being held without the advice of an attorney. I will even refuse him the rights of Habeus Corpus. This is no time for legal technicalities. They used brute force, and the police department, in hunting these criminals down, will resort to the same methods." "There is a lamppost for every Bolshevist who has taken part in these murderous and insane outrages," warned the chief postal inspector.

No more bombs exploded on New Year's Eve, although one seventeen-year-old boy was killed when a nervous Home Defense Reservist thought he heard a shot, stumbled, and accidentally discharged his own revolver into a crowd of young people on a sidewalk.

The Great Red Scare had begun.

New Year's Eve, London. The West End was densely packed with partygoers; theaters turned away hundreds of disappointed ticket seekers; long queues formed outside almost every restaurant; music blared from innumerable dances throughout the city; colonial troops collected in small groups in the street and sang their songs of home. An hour before the new year arrived, in Ave Maria Lane, Godliman Street, Dean's Court, and all the other little streets around St. Paul's Cathedral, British and foreign soldiers and sailors and WAACs gathered together laughing and dancing. A few minutes before midnight, all the street lamps went out, "and instantly we were back in that dark, mysterious London of war-time. You knew there were men crowded together in the street because of the movements of their glowing cigarettes, but you could scarcely see them. Instead, you saw that the lovely outline of St. Paul's . . . was lifting itself towards a starlit sky just as we have seen it so often—but not always with like tranquility—in the sombre years that are gone. . . . People were awed; their clamour stilled. The midnight hour boomed from the unlighted tower." Then came roars of cheering, a blaze of lights—and one last time the bugles sounded the signal "All Clear."

* * *

New Year's Eve, Berlin. There was dancing and champagne for the profiteers; although six hundred waiters from the city's major restaurants went
on strike promptly at eight o'clock, there was still more dancing and
champagne and confetti to frighten away the Bolsheviks. Around the floor
they glided in waltzes, the fox trot, the one-step and two-step, in hundreds
of cafés as Berliners celebrated the minutes of freedom left today, "which
perhaps to-morrow will be unable to guarantee him any more . . . the drink
before the drowning. . . . Never in Berlin has there been so much and such
furious dancing. Between dance time and street disturbances, between
confetti and red flags the couples glided in the New Year." Count Harry
Kessler, writing in his diary, was far too optimistic: "The last day of this
dreadful year. 1918 is likely to remain the most frightful date in German
history."

New Year's Eve, at an American military outpost in northern Russia. A
fur-clad American patrol walked through snow a foot deep in the desolate,
trackless forests in zero-degree weather. Doughboys from Detroit sat in icy
dugouts by a frozen river, unable to build a fire for fear of enemy snipers
and artillery. The lucky ones rode in sleighs over the frozen swamps and
were grateful for the presents brought by the Red Cross on Christmas Eve.
Eighty-six men were dead: nine in action, seven of wounds, three
drowned, two dead from accidents, and sixty-five from disease. "Another
thing. Are they really holding a separate war up here for our benefit? Just
because we were not in on the big doings in France is no reason why they
should run past the season series especially for us. We appreciate the
kindness, honor and all that, but, believe me . . . when we see ourselves on
outpost duty with one blanket and poncho, or sleeping in twenty-eight
inches of pure oozy mud which before we awaken turns into thin ice, it
makes us want to cry out and ask the universe what we have done to
deserve this exile."

New Year's Eve, the Vatican. Pope Benedict, in a message to America,
spoke of "those same principles which have been proclaimed by both
President Wilson and the Holy See, insuring for the world justice, peace
and Christian love. In this solemn moment, when a new era in the history
of the world is about to begin, we pray that the Almighty may shed His
light upon the delegates who are meeting in Paris to settle the fate of
mankind, and especially upon President Wilson as the head of the noble
nation which has written such glorious pages in the annals of human
progress."

* * *

New Year's Eve, Paris. The restaurants closed at 9:30; la Place de la Concorde stood vast and vacant in the small hours of the night, but the arc lamps glittered coldly on the captured German guns. In the countryside to the east, at an American military encampment near Verdun, Captain Harry S Truman of the 129th Field Artillery wrote a letter to his sweetheart, Bess Wallace, back in Missouri: "I have the helmet off the first dead Hun I ever saw and I reckon I'll keep that. That's about all I have that's worth keeping. . . . Two of my lieutenants went up to Douaumont the other day and found a helmet out in front of the fort with a skull in it. There was a hole right through iron, head, and all. There are some queer sights up in front of that old fort and also in front of forts Vaux and Tavannes. Except the Somme, it is the hardest-fought battlefield in France. . . . Tomorrow is New Year's and we are going to celebrate it by a few boxing bouts and wrestling matches. Maybe a basketball game or two if it isn't as muddy as usual and some races."

New Year's Eve, New York City. Times Square was strangely quiet, the celebration far more subdued than the riotous parties that had followed the Armistice in November. Hundreds of sailors and soldiers, many leaning on crutches, lined the sidewalks along Broadway, waiting to see if New Year's Eve in New York was as good as its reputation. Across from the Times Building, peddlers lined up by seven o'clock with their stocks of horns, rattles, confetti, and little black mustaches; many had used their savings to purchase vast quantities of novelties in hopes that partygoers would spend liberally, but by midnight horns had dropped from twenty-five cents to ten cents, and black mustaches had been withdrawn from the market. There were serious assaults upon restaurants' liquor supplies, the customers realizing that this could be the last wet New Year's Eve for a long time. When many of the city's waiters went on strike here as in Berlin, their places were taken by young women, Negroes, recently discharged servicemen, and even teamsters and longshoremen who "rose to the occasion with uncommon alacrity." At eleven-thirty the chimes of Trinity Church began to ring out, and a subdued crowd gathered in the rain-slicked streets of Broadway to listen: "Adeste Fideles" and "Columbia, the Gem of the Ocean." And then the voices of men in uniform joined in a chorus, singing the songs that had kept them company during the long lonesome nights: "Over There," "There's a Long, Long Trail a-Winding," "Keep the Homes Fires Burning," and finally, at midnight, "Auld Lang Syne."

* * *

New Year's Eve, Los Angeles. A spectacular parade of two hundred gaily decorated, illuminated automobiles began at Fourteenth and Figueroa at eight o'clock and proceeded through the city, vying for the first prize that would be awarded by four movie starlets. (A Packard won.) At a dinner party in the opulent Alexandria Hotel, Charlie Chaplin sold kisses for the Red Cross, with bids ranging from $50 to $250. Shortly before midnight in Pershing Square, there was a spectacular fireworks display featuring an hourglass that rose more than twenty feet into the air. At five minutes before the old year—the tired year, the shattered year—departed forever, the hourglass was ignited. A *Los Angeles Times* reporter witnessed the scene:

AT A GIVEN SIGNAL, THE MASSIVE PIECE FACING THE EAST IN A COMMAND-ING POSITION, FRONTING THE FOUNTAIN, WAS ILLUMINATED AND A JET OF FIRE, SYMBOLIC OF THE SAND OF TIME, BEGAN TO DROP FROM THE UPPER SECTION OF THE HOURGLASS AND DESCEND INTO THE LOWER BOWL. THE CROWD, NUMBERING NEARLY 10,000 PEOPLE, ASSEMBLED IN FRONT OF THE BIG PIECE AND MASSED OVER THE LAWN AND INTO HILL STREET, REMAINED IN MOMENTARY SILENCE, AND THEN, AS A NEAR-BY SIREN BEGAN TO SCREAM ITS MESSAGE THAT THE OLD YEAR WAS DYING, THE ONLOOKERS BROKE INTO A MIGHTY CHEER THAT SOUNDED WITH THE FORCE OF A CATARACT CRASHING AGAINST THE EAR.

And it was 1919.

ONE

THE DAYS
OF
VANITY

"Both the prophet

and the priest

go about into a land

that they know not."

1

"They are vanity,

and the

work of errors . . ."

In the first month of the new year, William Butler Yeats set down a troubling mystical vision of the approaching death of a civilization nearly twenty centuries old and the birth of a monstrous spirit that was slowly emerging to take its place. Long fascinated by a theory that history moves in grand, sweeping cycles measured in thousands of years, Yeats now witnessed the old order falling apart as events whirled further and further out of control:

> Mere anarchy is loosed upon the world,
> The blood-dimmed tide is loosed, and everywhere
> The ceremony of innocence is drowned;
> The best lack all conviction, while the worst
> Are full of passionate intensity.
>
> Surely some revelation is at hand;
> Surely the Second Coming is at hand.
> The Second Coming! . . .

Undaunted by the cold rain of a New Year's morning in Paris, Thomas Woodrow Wilson packed up his clubs and rode out to the famous fairways of St-Cloud golf course immediately after breakfast. Accompanied by Mrs. Wilson and his personal physician, Rear Admiral Cary T. Grayson (who had just ordered Wilson to take two full days' rest), the President enjoyed an hour of release from the cares of the world by chasing a small white ball all around the beautiful course.

Later in the day, Wilson met with Colonel House, still laid up with a bad cold, in House's hotel room. Wilson reviewed his recent progress through Britain, telling House that he had felt quite uncomfortable in the snobbish, old-boy public-school atmosphere of British politics. House chuckled over the inconvenience Wilson had caused his hosts, forcing them to postpone their holidays on the Riviera.

The first day, 1919: Lloyd George greeted the new year by visiting family and friends in his native North Wales, taking long walks, driving about his constituency, and holding interminable conversations about local Welsh politics; his Foreign Secretary, Arthur Balfour, was not going to be deprived of *his* holiday on the Riviera, and had just arrived in Cannes for a rest.

Clemenceau sat alone in the kitchen of the Hôtel Franc-Picard as the bleak winter sunlight first made its way into a tiny village in his native Vendée; after a peasant's breakfast dish of half porridge and half stew, he shuffled along the beach in a hooded oilskin coat, recognizable through the mist and the salt spray by his distinctive drooping white mustache.

While the statesmen took their rest and recreation, Europe continued its descent into anarchy.

"Europe is in revolution," warned the *Manchester Guardian*, "all its political landmarks removed, vast new forces released, all things in its political world in flux, the whole landscape in the present, the whole prospect in the future utterly changed. . . . there are indeed mighty forces now released whose sweep will surely extend even to these sea-girt isles . . . we are perhaps now only at the beginning of a new chapter in the world's history, poised, as it were, at one of its expectant moments."

"Mankind are on the march," wrote General Jan Christiaan Smuts. "You cannot say whither they are journeying." Born and raised in South Africa, Smuts was accustomed to seeing men trek into the distance with no clear idea of their ultimate objective. Wilson himself realized that "there was throughout the world a feeling of revolt against the large vested interests which influenced the world both in the economic and in the political sphere." But while the liberal Wilson preferred to attack social injustice through discussion and gradual reform, the world had grown impatient of delay; hence, as Wilson recognized, the attraction of Bolshevism for those thoroughly disgusted with the old regime.

In January, Budapest was "a city built over an active volcano." Following the overthrow of the Dual Monarchy of the Hapsburgs in the final days of the war ("The Revolution came and went with the elemental force and swiftness of a cyclone. In the space of five hours the whole fabric of the former Hapsburg Monarchy was swept away."), the old institutions of law and order had decayed throughout the diverse lands of the now-defunct Austro-Hungarian Empire. The Bolshevist epidemic had reached the virulent stage in Budapest, feeding upon the famine and the freezing weather; parents wrapped their children in newspapers to keep them warm.

Béla Kun, a former prisoner of war in Russia who had recently returned from Moscow as the leader of the Red faction in Hungary, plotted with the aid of Russian funds to capture control of the tottering government and capitalize upon every element of disorder. No one stood against the Reds because the people were simply too exhausted to care:

IN HUNGARY NO ONE DOES ANY WORK. THE PEASANT WILL NOT WORK. HE WORKED LAST YEAR, HE SAYS, FROM MORNING TO NIGHT, AND EVERYTHING HE HAD WAS TAKEN FROM HIM. THE DISBANDED SOLDIER WILL NOT WORK. HE HAS BEEN TOILING, HE SAYS, FOR FOUR YEARS FOR HIS COUNTRY, AND NOW IT IS UP TO HIS COUNTRY TO DO SOMETHING FOR HIM. THE SHOPKEEPERS STAND IDLE IN THEIR SHOPS, FOR THEY HAVE NOTHING TO SELL. THE UTMOST EFFORTS OF THE GOVERNMENT HAVE FAILED TO PRODUCE EVEN THE SEMBLANCE OF AN ARMY, IN SPITE OF THE HIGH PAY OFFERED. THE LAND, THE PEOPLE, EVEN THE VERY ANIMALS, ARE TIRED OUT. APATHY AND EXHAUSTION ARE EVERYWHERE.

"The plain fact is that great tracts of Europe are on the verge of starvation," confirmed the newly appointed British Food Controller. "In Serbia and Rumania the position is acute. In German Austria, rations have been reduced to 2½ pounds of flour of all kinds per week, 4 ounces of fats and 3½ ounces of meat. There are no potatoes." In Prague, the mayor had not eaten any meat for six weeks. (Authorities allowed a meat ration of three ounces per person per week, but it could never be found without resorting to illegal sources of supply.) For the past year and a half, milk in that city had been distributed only to nursing mothers, children under two, and the sick; now half the supply even for these catagories was not forthcoming. Since the Armistice, the bread ration in Prague had consisted of one and a half loaves per week of some vaguely grainlike substance that was "almost impossible to digest."

After detailed investigation of conditions in Central and Eastern Europe, Hoover's relief commission concluded that "there is a constant menace through the threatened spread of Bolshevism, especially in the cities." Crops were far below normal, any existing surpluses were rapidly being exhausted, and in many districts starvation was expected shortly if it was not already at hand. In the Baltic States, Hoover reported, "the food may last one or two months on a much reduced scale." In Yugoslavia, "the bread ration in many towns is three or four ounces. All classes are short of fats, milk and meat." In Vienna, "there are no coffee, sugar or eggs and practically no meat." Armenia was "already starving." In Poland, "the mortality in cities, particularly among children, is appalling for lack of fats, milk, meat and bread." "Revolution is the child of starvation," warned one British relief official, "and President Wilson has pointed out that the best way of stopping the onward sweep of Bolshevism is by food and not by force."

After a quiet New Year's dinner in the Murat Palace, Wilson left Paris for a triumphal tour through Italy.

"Garibaldi's Song of Italy," as interpreted by the recently married Enrico Caruso, topped the list of records released by the Victor Company in the United States to welcome the new year. Also available was the Zionist hymn "Hatkiva" ("Our Hope"), played by Zimbalist and Glück, which had special appeal for Americans interested in the movement to reestablish a Jewish homeland in Palestine. For those with more frivolous tastes, Olive Klein and the Orpheus Quartet offered their rendition of the dainty "A Little Birch Canoe and You," while on the flip side Elsie Baker performed "The Bluebird" with an enchanting flute obbligato.

The Second Coming: Wilson had departed France for Garibaldi's country at seven o'clock on the evening of January 1. Accompanying him in the eight-car royal Italian train were Mrs. Wilson, his thirty-two-year-old daughter Margaret, and Admiral Grayson. Once again the President had requested nothing more than an informal send-off, but when he arrived at the Gare de Lyon he found it decorated with hundreds of flowers, assorted greenery, and plush draperies in the colors of the Allied forces, plus a detachment of Italian *carabinieri*. French troops controlled the inevitable Parisian crowd, whose cheers for Wilson continued until he took his place in the salon car. "*Vive* France," Wilson called back politely.

When he awoke, the train was crawling slowly through steep mountain passes. (Not far away, all but six of the dogs kept by the monks of St. Bernard were dead. Ever since the special breed had first been brought to the monks' house of refuge in the Swiss Alps in the seventeenth century, the famous dogs had rescued thousands of travelers surprised by sudden snowstorms while crossing the mountains through the Great St. Bernard Pass. Now, for the first time in the history of the order, the great dogs were slaughtered for want of food.) Margaret Wilson caught her first glimpse of the snow-capped peaks of the western Alps at breakfast, and at ten-thirty that morning they crossed into Italy in bright sunshine. It was the first period of sustained sunshine Wilson had encountered since arriving in Europe several weeks before. The Duke of Lante, representing King Victor Emmanuel, greeted the President at the border town of Modane. Townspeople crowded around the station; then the train rolled southward through the Italian countryside while mountaineers and villagers swarmed down out of the green hills, waving flags and handkerchiefs under the blue sky. A brief reception followed at Turin in the afternoon, where Wilson was greeted by American flags flying next to the Italian tricolor everywhere throughout the city, then dinner at Genoa.

The train arrived in Rome at ten-twenty-five (five minutes ahead of schedule) on the morning of January 3. Victor Emmanuel, Queen Helena, the Duchess of Aosta, the Duke of Genoa, all the government ministers, and a battalion of assorted military officials received the presidential party at the station. After a short step across a red carpet, the triumphal procession through Rome began. Wilson and the king sat side by side in the first carriage, drawn by two horses traveling at a foot pace, with Queen Helena and Mrs. Wilson following behind in the next carriage. Mounted cuirassiers in brilliant uniforms escorted the dignitaries as faithful Secret Service agents Joe Murphy and Dick Jervis trailed the President closely in a taxicab. The Via Nationale was bedecked with flags and covered with golden sand, and portraits of Wilson filled the shop windows. The procession was accompanied by a continuous rumble of applause from the Romans along every street and in the Plaza del Quirinale. Low-flying airplanes (including one of the famous Caproni triplane bombers) dropped thousands of fresh flowers, and one pilot astounded the spectators by looping the loop above the housetops. Perhaps it was just a story that an Italian worker told his friends that he hoped the Pope would not die, because the omnipotent "Voovro Veelson" might then appoint a Protestant to rule the Vatican.

The only sour note in the day's proceedings came when Wilson was told that it was customary for visiting rulers to donate $10,000 for the city's poor. Wilson was, to put it mildly, taken aback by this revelation, and explained that the State Department had not authorized him to expend funds for official gifts during his stay in Europe. Any donations would have to come out of his own pocket; he had already spent nearly a thousand dollars on tips of twenty-five or fifty dollars to railroad porters, hotel attendants, and waiters, but a gift of this magnitude was obviously out of the question. Gossip about American miserliness failed to move the President.

Before setting foot in Italy, Wilson had decided that the incumbent

Italian government, with its brazenly imperialist outlook, was "quite incapable of taking a wide view of things." He objected especially to its demands for "almost the whole of the Dalmatian coast and practically all the islands of the Adriatic." Much of the Italian press supported the government's territorial goals on the grounds that many parts of the newly freed Balkan states were actually populated by citizens of Italian origin who wished to be reunited with their motherland. Benito Mussolini, editor of the newspaper *Popolo d'Italia,* had shouted on January 1 that "imperialism is the eternal, the immutable law of life." Wilson's advisers had pressed him to go to Italy to appeal to the Socialist opposition, to help put pressure on the government of Prime Minister Vittorio Emanuele Orlando (who had learned a smattering of English in preparation for the peace conference: "eleven o'clock," "I don't agree," and "goodbye") and Foreign Minister Baron Sidney Sonnino, who hid an unscrupulous character beneath an air of culture and high-mindedness.

Although Italy possessed an ancient culture, it was still a very young nation. Fewer than fifty years had passed since Rome had become the capital of a united Italy. A spectacular population explosion, from 11 million to 37 million people, had occurred between 1871 and 1914, straining the resources of the new country and leading to a tremendous increase in emigration, particularly to the United States. An 80-percent illiteracy rate plagued southern Italy. As a young man, Mussolini had grown up belligerent, vowing that "one day Italy will be afraid of me"; later, he would recall with shame the days of eating only *polenta*—maize flour cooked in water—for dinner. But the future Duce was still far better off than the thousands of Italian families who were constantly plagued by a desperate poverty and hunger. By January 1919, the food situation had grown so bad that the American Red Cross had to send relief shipments of spaghetti to southern Italy. The war had strengthened, at least temporarily, the hold of the old social order, and the working class remained lost in mystical dreams of justice and true democracy, lacking an effective leader or program.

Thus, Wilson appeared to the dreamers as the great deliverer, the man from the land to which their brothers and cousins had fled with such great hopes. And so the Italian government tried to keep Wilson so busy with ceremonial functions that he would have little time to make contact with opposition leaders or deliver any impassioned speeches—for Wilson was a magnificent and extraordinarily persuasive speaker—that might sway public opinion. Occasionally the tension broke through; when Roman officials visited Wilson at the United States Embassy in the Palazzo del

Drago, he commented sarcastically that even though the recent wave of immigration had made New York the largest Italian city in the world, he hoped Orlando's government was not going to claim *it*, too. And during his speech to the Italian Parliament, Wilson reminded the legislators that the recent war had destroyed empires that held people together against their will, and that such people—specifically the Balkan provinces of the former Austro-Hungarian Empire—must now be allowed to direct their own affairs themselves.

Otherwise, the President and Mrs. Wilson were overwhelmed with Italian hospitality. Their suite in the royal palace overlooked the magnificent garden where Renaissance popes had taken their daily walks amid centuries-old pines and cypresses. Wilson's bedroom was furnished with beautifully carved chairs and a bedstead covered with opulent Venetian embroidery, the walls hung with priceless tapestries depicting biblical episodes. Wilson would have been less than human if this regal splendor, combined with the adoration of the crowds, had not heightened his sense of self-importance.

Wilson, of course, was already certain that he personally represented the organized moral force of mankind. He was also a devout Calvinist. Nevertheless, while in Rome he could not avoid visiting the only other man on earth who could claim with equal justification to speak with the power of divine guidance. Before his audience with Pope Benedict XV on the afternoon of January 4, Wilson ascended to the great hill overlooking Rome and stood bareheaded beside the imposing monument to Garibaldi and the ruins of glories past, looking out over the splendor of the city with the sunlight glinting off the dome of St. Peter's and the green of the Vatican gardens, and in the distance the crumbling walls of the Colosseum and the columns of the Forum that had broken into fragments long, long ago. Then he descended and began another triumphal journey in an open touring car through the city's streets amid another shower of flowers.

The demonstrative reception, or possibly Wilson's Presbyterian prejudices, made him over thirty minutes late for his audience with His Holiness. The President entered the Vatican and was welcomed by the Swiss Guards in their multicolored uniforms designed by Raphael; his automobile crossed to San Damaso in the center of the Apostolic Palace, where a detachment of gendarmes heralded his presence with bugles. Emerging to a reception by virtually every available Vatican official, Wilson walked through hallways gorgeous with antique tapestries and priceless paintings. He greeted the Pope in the throne room, where two gilded armchairs awaited. Pope Benedict later told another American visitor that Wilson had talked of almost nothing else but his plans for a League of Nations during the course of their twenty-minute meeting. After indicating his support for the main outlines of Wilson's plan, His Holiness presented the President with a mosaic three feet wide and valued at $40,000, reproducing Reni's famous portrait of St. Peter's.

Then Wilson moved on to the American Protestant Episcopal Church in Rome, where he could breathe more freely. He had planned to make an appeal to the Roman public that evening from his balcony in the Quirinal Palace, to stir up opposition to Orlando's imperialistic goals, but Italian troops cordoned off the plaza and prevented any crowd from assembling to hear the President. Furious, Wilson lashed out at the government in the presence of the press corps. It was too late. Shortly after nine o'clock that evening, Wilson left Rome for Paris.

"We cannot undertake even to feed the starving people of Europe until at least a semblance of order has been established," warned *The New York Times*, "and we do not suppose anybody would hold that hunger must defer its satisfaction to await the convenience of statesmen going about the world's chief business in the leisurely manner hitherto observed. The Peace Conference must begin its work and at once."

2

"I beheld the earth . . ."

Like Yeats, Carl Sandburg (then the labor editor for the *Chicago Daily News*) believed that mankind stood at the dawn of a new age. The young poet's message to America in January 1919 discarded the past as completely irrelevant:

> I tell you the past is a bucket of ashes,
> I tell you yesterday is a wind gone
>   down, a sun dropped in the west,
> I tell you there is nothing in the world,
>   only an ocean of tomorrows, a sky
>   of tomorrows.

Sandburg's rejection of history and his unbounded optimism were characteristically American, but there were those across the ocean, like Captain Andrew Lang of the Royal Air Force, who shared his faith in the promise of a sky of tomorrows.

Strong gusts of wind swirled about Captain Lang as he strode across the field of the Martlesham Experimental Aeroplane Station on the morning of January 2. Awaiting him on the landing strip was a two-seat De Havilland biplane bomber equipped with a British-designed and -built 450-horsepower Napier engine. The hardbitten Australian pilot, who had first gained international fame by leading a motorcar expedition for his government across uncharted stretches of northern Australia in 1910, had neither taken a drink nor smoked a cigarette for weeks in preparation for this day. Lang climbed into the pilot's seat alongside the man who would serve as his observer, nineteen-year-old Lieutenant A. W. Blowes of Canada, an experienced fighter pilot in his own right who had brought down several

German airplanes over France during the war. At 11:30, the De Havilland took off into a gale and began to climb in big sweeping circles through the new year's sky.

Lang could not stay on course as the winds blew the light plane about like a leaf. Still, at every thousand feet of altitude, Lang took detailed readings of his engine's instruments, recording his observations on a board strapped to his right leg, glancing over the side occasionally to note his bearings. Blowes kept a close watch on the air-temperature gauge. At eight thousand feet the winds subsided, and Lang and Blowes found themselves far out at sea over the Yarmouth coast. The sun shone brightly above, and through the haze below Lang could see distant ships and occasionally a glimpse of the Thames.

As they passed ten thousand feet and continued to climb, the temperature began to drop precipitously. Both men were prepared for the cold, resembling nothing as much as the children of an overprotective mother who had bundled them up in so many layers of clothing that they were scarcely able to move. Each wore two pairs of silk socks under three pairs of stockings and thigh boots lined with lamb's wool; on top of thick underclothing and three sweaters and a Sidcot Arctic suit lined with fur, they each had a balaclava with a fur-lined cap, a muffler, and electrically heated gloves with gauntlets. Covering their eyes were goggles lined with cotton wool. Lang also had a small glass shield fitted on the plane to protect his right eye, but the gun that was still attached to the other side of the De Havilland had prevented the installation of a similar device for the left.

At twenty thousand feet, Blowes turned on the oxygen supply. Shortly thereafter, the oxygen frosted on Lang's goggles; when he took them off, his left eye watered, froze, and swelled. At 12:08:20 P.M., the plane reached 25,000 feet. Several minutes later, Blowes felt faint and turned up his oxygen supply an extra pound. Nothing happened; the force of the plane's intense vibrations had broken the main pipe connected to his oxygen bottle. Blowes scribbled a note to Lang informing him of his plight, but lost consciousness before he could pass the message along. Lang continued, unaware of his companion's condition.

At 27,000 feet the air grew turbulent and Lang virtually lost control of the plane. At 28,000 feet he noticed that his heating apparatus was working erratically. Still the plane continued to climb. Lang then began to suffer from a lack of oxygen himself and signaled to Blowes for more. Finally he glanced over and discovered that Blowes was unconscious. "It was most fortunate I was able to continue Lieutenant Blowes's work and take the atmospheric temperatures, without which the test would have been worthless," Lang later told a reporter.

Still Lang took the plane higher. As the barograph read 30,500 feet—nearly six miles high, in approximately seventy degrees of frost—the thin air could no longer push the small propellers attached to the oil and gasoline pumps. The engine sputtered and nearly died. Lang was forced to descend. Slowly, the engine gradually recovering, he dropped down over the sea. Blowes regained consciousness at 20,000 feet. Upon landing at Martlesham, the young Canadian was taken to a hospital with serious frostbite injuries to his hands and toes. Lang suffered from a frostbitten face and fingers. But they had accomplished their mission. They had gone higher than any man had ever gone before in an airplane, breaking the previous record of 29,800 feet set by an American pilot in September 1918.

On January 6, four days after his ordeal, British Army authorities placed Captain Lang under arrest for disclosing the details of his flight to the public without prior authorization from his superiors.

TROTZKY ARRESTS LENINE, Western newspapers announced hopefully, searching for a break in Bolshevik solidarity. But only Lenin's humanity was imprisoned. LENIN SEEN IN SPAIN, another headline trumpeted. But Lenin was not meant for the warmth and sun of Spain. Decades earlier, Count Tolstoy had given the Russian nation a terrified warning: "Beware of the Genghis Khan who rules by telephone."

Now mere anarchy was loosed—Lenin appeared as the murderous country doctor, with his spectacles and an old but neatly pressed suit, chewing thoughtfully on a lead pencil with a notebook open on his knee, listening to the complaints of a feverish and freezing nation. A delegation of peasants sat in Lenin's office in the Kremlin, rubbing their hands together to keep warm. Lenin barely noticed the cold anymore. "There's no wood," he told them, "we have to economize." When the peasants returned home, they sent him a load of kindling. Lenin and his wife welcomed guests for tea and black bread in their apartment, and everyone shared the only two teaspoons in the household.

Trotsky wore a black leather uniform and rode a special armored train—Marx's "locomotive of history," they called it, with converted Pullman cars equipped with the ammunition of modern propaganda: library, radio station, telephones to the Kremlin, printing press, electric power generator, and restaurant—arriving without warning at the front in Siberia, steaming across the southern plains, coming to punish and cajole and beat Russia over the head without mercy, and always to push the Revolution forward, as if it were powered by the force of Trotsky's will.

Still, the Allies could not agree on a policy to deal with the Bolsheviks. In fact, they could never even agree on what really was happening behind the borders of the former Romanoff dominions. "We were never dealing with ascertained, or, perhaps, even ascertainable facts," mourned Lloyd George. "Russia was a jungle in which no one could say what was within a few yards of him."

Rats. Reports from agricultural districts throughout Britain indicated that the nation's rat population had increased tremendously during the recent war. Even before 1914, the old methods of control practiced by gamekeepers and professional rat-catchers—trapping, ferreting, and poisoning—had begun to lose much of their efficacy, but even these efforts had been largely suspended for the past four years. With each pair of adult rats capable of producing 880 hungry offspring each year, the rodent population of Britain had reached an estimated 40 million by January 1919, and damage to foodstuffs approached £15,000 sterling, not to mention the gnawing attacks upon docks and warehouses.

The Food Controller had issued a Rats Order in August 1918, directing local authorities to take all necessary measures to destroy the prolific creatures, and some county councils had instituted bounties for every dozen dead rats brought to them. Yet much more needed to be done to bring the plague under control. Lloyd George's government thus decided to import an expert adviser with considerable experience in killing rats on the Continent.

"Liberate Eddie Moore or you will get yours." Scrawled in the script of a nearly illiterate person—but written on good quality paper—this message was mailed to police headquarters; the signature read, "Black Hand."

Q.: Detective Lieutenant Scanlon, do you believe that Edward Moore was in fact the man who placed the bombs around Philadelphia on the evening of December 30?

A.: There is every evidence that the prisoner knows something about the explosion.

Q.: What clues have you found to link Moore with the crimes?

A.: Among the junk in Moore's house at 3533 North Water Street were nearly two hundred letters from conscientious objectors and aliens interned at various camps throughout the United States, and a .32-caliber automatic pistol with two loaded clips. We believe that Moore is a professional agitator who has been on the payroll of Socialist organizations for quite a while.

Q.: How about you, Mr. Moore? Just what do you know about this bomb plot?

A.: I don't know a thing except what I read in the newspapers.

Four days after his arrest, Moore was released on the grounds that there was absolutely no concrete evidence that he was involved in the bombings in any way. (Police officials would not return his letters, however.) New York detectives who had hurried to Philadelphia to help track down the perpetrators held a lengthy conference with their local counterparts and then went home empty-handed. Philadelphia authorities admitted that the theory that Bolsheviks or IWW members were responsible for the bombings was "not at all clear," and that the bombs actually might have been planted by gangsters. The police quietly abandoned the case, explaining lamely that recent rainstorms had made it difficult to do any serious detective work in the case.

Not to be deterred in their search for Red suspects, federal agents surrounded Philadelphia's Broad Street Station and arrested three more radicals—two of them as they stepped off an express train from New York, and the other as he stood waiting for his compatriots. Ivan Korsky, Solomon Hurowitcz, and Joseph Bauracz (the last allegedly an old acquaintance of Leon Trotsky) were "night birds of anarchy," suspected of involvement in the recent bombing attacks, and federal sources claimed that their apprehension had "probably frustrated a conspiracy by Bolsheviki organizations, which aimed at the destruction of the City Hall and other municipal buildings." They were considered suspicious primarily because one of the three was dressed in a gray overcoat of medium length with a black fur collar, and a soft felt hat. The feds claimed that investigators in Chicago had told them that this outfit represented the official disguise adopted by Bolshevik operatives. Justice Department agents grilled the three men for several hours, and then released them, too.

Still the search continued for Reds. BOLSHEVIK GROWTH ALARMS U.S. AGENTS; LIST 2000 "RED" AGITATORS IN PHILADELPHIA AND OTHER CITIES— LENINE AND TROTZKY FOLLOWERS HAVE $500,000. Terming the spread of Bolshevism in the United States "alarming," New York State's deputy attorney general announced that his department had uncovered evidence that secret Soviet agents had reached New York City with a fund of nearly half a million dollars for propaganda and recruitment purposes. Justice Department agents acknowledged that they possessed a card index of two thousand "Red" agitators in the major metropolitan centers of the country, and estimated the number of passive Bolshevik sympathizers in New York alone at nearly 500,000.

Unsettled by the war and the spread of radicalism in Europe and Russia, still under the spell of nationalistic emotions encouraged by wartime propaganda, and alarmed at the recent wave of immigrants from Central and Eastern Europe who chose to retain much of their native culture even after their arrival in the United States, a great many otherwise rational Americans were perfectly ready to believe that flocks of foreign anarchist agents were hard at work undermining the structure of American society. Proposed remedies ranged from the deportation or imprisonment of undesirable aliens to the "Americanization" movement that sought to ban the teaching of foreign languages in public or parochial schools. Others sought to bar any further immigration from Russia into the United States, so that no more "mental disease carriers . . . tainted with the Bolshevik distemper" could threaten American values.

In Los Angeles, the city council passed an ordinance prohibiting the display or possession of a red flag, except in museums or theaters where it obviously did not represent an endorsement of Bolshevik ideals.

Waiters continued their strike in Berlin. Just as Harry Kessler was about to order dinner at a fashionable restaurant, a deputation of waiters walked in, stopped everything, and presented the manager with an ultimatum: he could accept the strikers' demands within ten minutes, or else his business would be shut down. Five minutes later, the manager surrendered. "The strikers, with red tabs stuck in their hats and carrying a red flag, left. Blackmail completed, we could return to the matter of food. Many places have already been shut, others attacked and wrecked. This afternoon a party of Roman Catholics together with some Protestants stormed the Religious Affairs Ministry in order to haul out the Minister. We are returning to the days of strong-arm law. The Executive is wholly powerless."

Berlin: "one of the prime breeding places of Evil," as witnessed by Ben Hecht, who was then an enterprising young correspondent for the *Chicago Daily News* assigned to cover German affairs. Several decades later, Hecht recalled that

ALL THE INHUMANITY I NOTE AS HISTORY, I SAW IN GERMANY IN 1918 TO 1920, EXCEPT THAT I SAW IT THEN WITH A YOUTHFUL DELIGHT FOR THE PREPOSTEROUS. POLITICAL ZANIES, QUIBBLERS AND ADVENTURERS—MINDLESS AND PARANOID—PERFORMED AROUND ME IN THAT TIME IN GERMANY AS IF I HAD BLUNDERED INTO A SIDE-STREET GRAND GUIGNOL PLAYHOUSE.

I HAD NO NOTION THAT ITS HUMORLESS AND MACABRE ATMOSPHERE WAS
TO BECOME THE AIR OF THE WORLD. . . . OUR PRESENT SHOUTING UP OF
FALSE BOOGIEMEN, OUR CYNICAL DEALINGS WITH ENEMIES, OUR SECRET
BETRAYALS OF OUR FRIENDS ARE ALL IN THE TALE WHICH THE GERMANY
OF 1919 DRAMATIZED FOR ME. I WAS A YOUTH OF TWENTY-FOUR WHEN
I ENTERED GERMANY. WHEN I EMERGED FROM IT MY YOUNG CYNICISM
HAD LOST MUCH OF ITS GRIN.

Berlin for Hecht was a group of homosexual aviators, delicately per-
fumed and elegantly monocled and usually in the embrace of cocaine or
heroin, who made love to one another openly in an officers' club and then
departed in the early hours before dawn for a tryst in a mansion belonging
to one of them; sometimes the lovers were accompanied by several dark-
eyed, wide-mouthed, aristocratic-born nymphomaniacs with burns and
cuts up and down their sides. Berlin was ten-year-old girls with heavily
rouged faces parading after midnight along the pavements of the Friedrichstrasse, wearing the short dresses of small children.

In Munich, a toolmaker named Anton Drexler and a two-bit journalist,
Karl Harrer, formed the German Workers' Party (*Deutsche Arbeiterpartei*,
or DAP) on January 5. For the moment, it was merely a shell of a political
organization, one of many right-wing parties founded in an effort to restore German national pride. The man who would later join the party and
raise it to international prominence was then only a guard at a quiet
prisoner-of-war camp in a small town near the Austrian frontier. Checking
the passes of everyone who wished to enter or leave the camp, Adolf Hitler
stood and thought and waited.

The Chicago White Sox dumped Clarence "Pants" Rowland and hired a
new manager, William "Kid" Gleason. Star second baseman Eddie
"Cocky" Collins enthusiastically declared that "in view of the fact that
Gleason has been made chief skipper of the Sox, I would not change places
on any club with anyone in the American League. By this I mean to say
that the White Sox look to me as the best bet for 1919 in the American
League."

Indeed, the Sox also had a reliable veteran backstop in future Hall-of-
Famer Ray "Cracker" Schalk and ace pitcher Eddie "Eddie" Cicotte, ready
for another run at the pennant. But the star of the Chicago show was
undoubtedly "Shoeless Joe" Jackson, one of the best pure hitters of all time.
Stories of Jackson's supposed illiteracy were widely repeated; staring at a
menu in a restaurant, he would wait until someone else ordered, and then

tell the waiter, "I'll have what he's having." Whether the stories were true or not, Jackson was extremely sensitive about the matter. Once when he hit a triple in an opposing team's stadium, a fan yelled out to him, "Hey, Joe, can you spell 'cat'?" Jackson glanced over, spat tobacco juice in the general direction of the heckler, and called back, "How about you, big shot—can you spell 'shit'?"

Having won the pennant in 1917 (the Boston Red Sox, with ace pitcher Babe Ruth, finished first in the war-shortened 1918 season), the White Sox had to be considered a very strong choice for the upcoming 1919 campaign.

A bucket of ashes lay on the sidewalk in front of the White House. At four o'clock in the afternoon of New Year's Day, militant suffragettes, furious over President Wilson's effusive praise of democracy abroad at a time when women were still denied the right to vote in many parts of the United States, had lit a "watchfire of freedom" in a ceremonial urn directly across from the entrance to the Executive Mansion. They vowed to keep the fire burning until the Senate joined the House of Representatives and approved the Susan B. Anthony amendment to establish women's suffrage as a constitutional right. (Although fifteen states allowed women to vote in all elections, the rest presented a bewildering array of restrictions: women could vote only in presidential elections in some states, but only in local elections in others, or only in primaries or on bond questions or matters of school management. In twelve states, including Pennsylvania, Maryland, Missouri, and Indiana, women could not vote at all.)

Mrs. Lawrence Lewis, who had brought with her from Philadelphia several branches of a tree growing in Independence Square beneath the Liberty Bell, began to drop copies of Wilson's recent European speeches into the fire. As the last document was destroyed, the female sentinels unfurled a banner accusing the President of being a "false prophet of democracy." This was too much for the soldiers and roughneck boys who had joined the crowd of generally unsympathetic spectators to taunt and jeer at the women. "Out wit' de fire, out wit' de fire," chanted one seventeen-year-old tough. A dozen men in uniform surrounded the banner and hid it from view while an army captain stepped in front of the crowd and called for three cheers for Woodrow Wilson, "the world's leader of democracy and the best friend the women of America ever had"—the latter half of which assertion was certainly debatable.

Later that evening, a small riot began when soldiers attempted to put out the fire with chemicals and succeeded only in strengthening the blaze. The suffragettes were knocked down and dragged around the streets, their banners torn and ripped apart, the urn smashed. Undaunted, several women managed to rekindle another fire in one of the large urns in Lafayette Park. Momentarily outmaneuvered, the Washington police charged across Pennsylvania Avenue to the new scene of action. They arrested five women, including National Woman's Party Chairman Alice Paul, for violating park regulations. After several hours, the women were released without bail and told to appear in the police court the following morning. (They had no intention of doing so.) Reduced to burning torches, the remaining members of the depleted suffragette battalion continued their vigil on the cold sidewalk in front of the White House, shivering under the rain, sleet, and snow, their noses turning crimson in the bitter winter wind. Another special urn was on its way, along with wood sent in from various parts of the nation. "It is inconceivable that any such puerile performances as they stage could help the cause of suffrage," wrote one critic, who believed that the cause of women's suffrage was moving ahead steadily despite the militants' antics. "The truth is that were it not for the fact that they seem to get 'the goat' of bone-headed police officials almost at regular intervals, they would be treated in accordance with the value of their efforts—which, as said before, is zero."

For several days after the New Year's Day melee, persistent sleet and drizzle kept things quiet along Pennsylvania Avenue. But on the evening of January 3, as Wilson lay sleeping peacefully among the ancient treasures of the Quirinal Palace in Rome, a crowd of soldiers on leave and schoolboys launched another attack upon the militant suffragettes and their watchfires. Once again the women were dragged into the street, their banners torn, and their new stone urn smashed. Police stood nearby and watched, but did not interfere.

A few women then lit torches from the watchfire embers still smoldering on the sidewalk, and started a bonfire on the sidewalk itself. Unfortunately, the pavement soon became overheated and buckled, causing a powerful, bomblike report (tourists several blocks away were convinced the White House was under bombardment by alien Reds) and scattering flames across the street. This time the police came running over and put out the blaze, but not before the suffragettes managed to relight their torches.

On January 6, six members of the National Woman's Party watchfire brigade were sentenced to jail terms ranging from five to ten days for refusing to pay their fines. They promptly began a hunger strike in the District jail. At the end of five days, several of the suffragettes were so ill and weak that authorities decided to release them all. Stirred by the women's dedication, reinforcements from across the country arrived in Washington to take part in the vigil.

*　*　*

On a frigid day in early January, William Hohenzollern, former Kaiser of the German Empire, arose early, enjoyed a massage from one of his soldier attendants, smoked the first cigarette in a chain that would extend throughout the day until bedtime, and sat down to a simple breakfast with his wife. Then came a shave and a trim of his neat, newly grown iron-gray beard by Otto Kruger, the barber who had served him faithfully for ten years. In inclement weather William spent the rest of the morning pacing up and down the damp corridors of Amerongen Castle for exercise. If sunshine broke through the clouds in the dismal Holland winter sky, he would don a great gray fur cloak for a walk around the castle grounds, pausing to admire the rose gardens, watching the Rhine steadily rise to flood the meadows surrounding the estate, and then watching the skaters who crowded the outer moat when it froze. And William himself of course was always watched (for his own protection) by a detachment of guards who refused, for security reasons, to let him walk in the nearby woods. All visitors to the castle and all new arrivals in the neighboring village were interrogated immediately by detectives. While the ex-Emperor toured the enclosed grounds, every opening in the castle walls was closed up with thick straw curtains to prevent any outsider from seeing him at close range. But those who observed him from a distance saw a man who looked to be "perhaps fifteen years older than when he crossed the frontier of Holland," scarcely recognizable to those who had met him when he first came to Amerongen two months before. The famous upturned mustache now turned down into his short Vandyke beard.

Daily, the winter routine continued with a quiet lunch with his wife (William himself drank only water with every meal), and afternoons were spent with the letters and telegrams that his Court Chamberlain permitted him to see. These usually contained nothing more than family news: the former Crown Prince was living in virtual isolation on the island of Wierengen; William's fourth son had just taken a job with the Benz Motor Company. When healthy, William could spend the rest of the day indulging in his favorite form of exercise from the years before the war—sawing and chopping wood. Among the baggage he had brought across the frontier was a massive case weighing several hundred pounds, full of the tools he needed for his hobby. He never tired of shattering the logs handed to him by servants (each log had already been sawed three-quarters through), and he waited impatiently while his aides gathered up the splintered sticks. Holland's coal shortage required everyone to burn wood for heat that winter, and on a good day William could chop enough to supply every fireplace in the castle. Chopping ever harder and faster, not looking up, swinging his good arm while the withered one hung uselessly at his side, sweating profusely despite the damp cold, pounding the sharp edge into the next log and the next. Then a sharp draft caught him in a corridor of the castle and a chill shook his body; there would be another bout with fever tonight.

Back in Washington, Senator McKellar of Tennessee urged that William be tried for the murder of each and every man who died in the war: "If he is found guilty, he should be hanged as any other common murderer is hanged." Senator Lawrence Sherman of Illinois: "William Hohenzollern should be sent to St. Helena, as Napoleon was." Senator Edwin Johnson of South Dakota: "Get the Kaiser out of Holland and put him at every-day labor, such as work in the streets of the cities, the balance of his days, as a living example to the rulers of all countries and to plutocracy generally." "I think the Kaiser should be executed," insisted Senator H. L. Myers of Alabama. "I think it should be done without a trial. There is no need for a trial. . . . Armed forces of the United States and the Entente Allies should capture the Kaiser and execute him by decree of the Peace Council."

Late on the evening of January 5, an automobile containing several Americans, including ex-Senator Luke Lea of Tennessee and a half-dozen army officers, approached the castle in Amerongen. Lea handed Count Bentinck, whose family owned the estate, an ostensibly official pass stating that he and his associates were proceeding to Holland under a special mandate of the American government. (Actually, Lea later admitted that his real intention was to give the Kaiser a free ride to Paris and hand him to President Wilson as a belated Christmas present.) Bentinck told Lea to wait and carried to the Kaiser the request for an interview. William replied that he would not see them unless they were formal representatives of the American government. Just as Bentinck brought William's answer to Lea, Dutch soldiers on motorcycles suddenly roared into the courtyard. Lea and his friends departed precipitously and sped away toward the French frontier in their car. Several days later, an airplane of unknown nationality, flying very high, circled over the castle.

And what of Germany? Among the Allied delegations arriving in Paris, a consensus was emerging that they could not simply exterminate the entire German nation of seventy million people (although some French officials liked to say that there were twenty million Germans too many); that Germany would have to pay vast indemnities to the Allies to make up for the ravages of war, and that the German people must therefore be allowed to go back to work; and that there must be a stable government in Berlin, or else all of Western Europe might be infected with Bolshevism, just as Russia had infected Eastern Europe. "The practical danger is a recrudescence of [German] imperialism on the one side, and the growing menace of Bolshevism on the other. . . . Either extreme will be disastrous to the Allies."

3

"A wonderful and horrible

thing is

committed in the land . . ."

Berlin, Saturday, January 4. The forces of German working-class radicalism, known as the Spartacus League (after the gladiator-slave who had led a revolt against Roman oppression twenty centuries before), held yet another of their daily antigovernment demonstrations through the city streets. For the past eight weeks, ever since the Kaiser had fled to Holland, the unsteady government of the Socialists had displayed an unseemly reluctance to challenge these would-be revolutionaries. While the Spartacists marched defiantly through Berlin, Minister of War Gustav Noske took President Ebert to the suburban town of Zossen, thirty-five miles outside of the capital, and proudly displayed four thousand troops, well-armed and parading in neat formation, all pledged to defend Ebert's beleaguered government. "Real soldiers," declared Ebert in amazement. "Don't worry," Noske said. "Everything is going to turn out all right now." These volunteers were the first Freikorps ("free company") units placed at the government's disposal; by the first week of January, restless career army officers, driven by a desire to rebuild an effective German fighting force, had already assembled a dozen Freikorps outfits across the country. Emboldened by this revelation of effective military support for the regime, Ebert's government finally moved against the Spartacists late that evening by dismissing Berlin Police Commissioner Emil Eichhorn, the left-wing radical who had appointed himself commissioner immediately after the Kaiser's abdication. Eichhorn, however, refused to give up his office; instead, he armed his supporters from the arsenal of rifles, machine guns, and hand grenades stored at police headquarters in Alexanderplatz, and sat back to await the fight.

Berlin, Sunday, January 5. Eichhorn's refusal to resign left the government momentarily paralyzed, unable to respond effectively to radical provocations. Spartacist irregulars still seemed to dominate the capital. The decorations at the Brandenburg Gate—laurel wreaths, red streamers and banners, and the slogan PEACE AND FREEDOM—strung up to celebrate the return of troops into the city from the front, silently mocked the government's feeble, halfhearted efforts to preserve its authority. Spartacists collected in Siegesallee and held a mass demonstration against Eichhorn's dismissal. At five o'clock in the afternoon, police headquarters remained in the hands of Eichhorn and the Spartacists. Many bitter, disillusioned soldiers in gray field uniforms were among the mob protecting the building from government troops. Long rows of windows, too, were crowded by soldiers with red armbands. The Bolshevik theorist who led the Spartacists, Dr. Karl Liebknecht—dark-eyed, quick-moving, short and slender, with a thin black mustache—now openly declared that the time was right for the final Revolution. Speaking first from an open motorcar and then from the balcony of police headquarters, Liebknecht told the crowd in Alexanderplatz that "the proletariat must be armed. . . . The soldiers, together with the armed proletariat, must do everything to prevent the removal of Eichhorn."

Liebknecht spoke slowly and expressively, with the air of a pious clergyman who was certain that he and only he held the key to his audience's salvation. He stood as a shadowy figure on the balcony, with the rooms behind him in total darkness. The crowd, desperate for any fresh ideals in which they could invest their faith, roared its approval when he finished, applauding and waving red flags and tossing their hats in the air. To Harry Kessler, Liebknecht resembled a priest leading his listeners into the service of the new and diabolical Russian religion—Bolshevism—that threatened all of twentieth-century Europe, just as Muhammad's disciples had poured into Christendom from the East in the seventh century. The old, broken order confronted Liebknecht and his followers with bayonets, but with few ideas or hopes or dreams of its own.

Berlin, Monday, January 6. The German capital fell into a state of complete anarchy as civil war began in earnest. Spartacist soldiers controlled a great number of public buildings; all the banks were barricaded. Thousands of armed workers and government supporters crowded the streets in uneasy proximity. Two processions met at eleven o'clock at the corner of Siegesallee and Viktoriastrasse. Both were made up of shabbily dressed artisans and girls from the factories waving red flags, but one band shuffled along chanting antigovernment slogans while the other cursed the Spartacists. Bystanders could feel the tension ready to overflow into violence. "Down with Ebert!" "Down with Liebknecht!"

Armed conflict began at two o'clock, as Berlin was racked by the sound of machine-gun fire. Liebknecht appeared to be everywhere, exhorting his followers and organizing his troops for the final battle. Later that afternoon, the Ministry of Foreign Affairs stood empty. All the clerks and officials had fled to safety. Only government troops remained behind the windows. Shots rang out for no apparent reason. At a quarter after five there was the sound of shooting outside the Kaiserhof hotel. Soldiers shouted to each other on the pavement below and then scampered across the cold puddles in the glistening street. Finally all was quiet.

"Damn the Bolshevists!" Ten minutes later more machine guns blasted forth, accompanied by artillery and hand grenades, as if this were a full-scale battle on the Western Front. Suddenly, at six-thirty, the soldiers in the Wilhelmplatz cried, "All unarmed persons get away! The Spartacides are approaching to attack!" The rebels were indeed approaching, several battalions of them, armed with guns. Bystanders pushed their way through the flying crowd to find shelter inside a convenient office building. Two seconds later a terrible fusillade began and lasted about five or ten minutes. It seemed as if everything was over when suddenly there was the thunder of a field gun. One single shot was fired, but it had the effect of restoring a deathly silence for a few seconds. That evening the Wilhelmplatz was strewn with dead and wounded; Berlin resembled nothing more than the chilling emptiness of a no-man's-land. HUNDREDS SHOT DEAD IN BERLIN STREETS; BIG GUNS USED TO CHECK REVOLUTIONISTS. "There is shouting all the time," Harry Kessler wrote in his diary. "Berlin has become a witches' cauldron wherein opposing forces and ideas are being brewed together. Today history is in the making and the issue is not only whether Germany shall continue to exist in the shape of the Reich or the democratic republic, but whether East or West, war or peace, an exhilarating vision of Utopia or the humdrum everyday world shall have the upper hand." Hundreds fled from the city in the darkness.

In the quiet hours before dawn on the sixth day of January, Theodore Roosevelt died in his sleep at his home on Sagamore Hill in Oyster Bay, Long Island. President, soldier, cowboy, hunter, author, conservationist, explorer, and historian, Roosevelt was the most beloved American of his generation. Woodrow Wilson appealed to the public's mind and conscience; Roosevelt appealed to men's hearts. From the time he began his political career as a New York State assemblyman, through his service as Federal Civil Service Commissioner, Police Commissioner of New York, Assistant Secretary of the Navy, colonel of the Rough Riders, Governor of New York, Vice-President, and finally in his two terms as President,

Roosevelt had consistently stressed one theme above all others: the gospel of public and private duty that came straight from the universal conscience of mankind. "My problems have been moral problems," he once said, "and my teaching has been plain morality." Americans remembered the huge grin, the waving arms, the flashing eyeglasses. "His country did well to be proud of him," said *The Times* of London. "He was not an original thinker, he was not a very profound thinker, but he was one of those thinkers whose thoughts became acts because they were eminently the thoughts of a man." In accordance with his wishes, Roosevelt was buried as a plain American citizen in the village cemetery near his home, after a simple ceremony attended by his family and a few friends.

Roosevelt's death was unexpected, and threw the Republican Party into something of a quandary, because most political analysts believed that he would have been the Republican nominee for President in 1920. He had recently regained the allegiance of party regulars—if not the hidebound Old Guard, which still detested him for his attacks on big business—who had held little love for him after the disastrous split of 1912, when Roosevelt ran as the progressive Bull Moose candidate against Wilson and the regular Republican candidate Taft, and opened the door of the White House to the Democrats. There were no men of truly outstanding stature left in the party at the national level. Instead, *The New York Times* now heard "insistent talk" in favor of Senator Warren G. Harding of Ohio: "Among radicals and regulars the same feeling was expressed. Harding in one day appeared to have jumped into a prominent place in the consideration of possibilities."

Roosevelt and Wilson had never been on very good terms. Their basic social philosophies were antithetical. Wilson saw the aggressive side of the human character and tried to deny it by raising man above himself; Roosevelt saw the same aggressiveness and welcomed it as a powerful weapon to be used in the fight for social justice. Roosevelt was seldom shocked by the dark side of human behavior. Once he appointed an old Rough Rider comrade, Ben Daniels, as federal marshal of Arizona. Senator George F. Hoar, a man of proper New England morality, was scandalized.

"Mr. President," Hoar asked in horrified tones, "do you know anything about the character of this man Daniels whom you have appointed to be marshal of Arizona?"

"Why, yes, I think so," Roosevelt answered. "He was a member of my regiment."

"Do you know," announced Hoar impressively, "that he has killed three men?"

Roosevelt appeared completely taken aback. "You don't mean it."

"It is a fact," Hoar affirmed solemnly.

The President pounded his fist on the table indignantly. "When I get hold of Daniels," he said, "I will read him the riot act. He told me he'd only killed two."

Several weeks before he died, Roosevelt denounced Wilson's peace plans. The congressional elections of November 1918, which Wilson had sought to make a referendum on his foreign policy and which had resulted in Republican majorities in both the House and the Senate, represented for Roosevelt a complete and emphatic repudiation of the President. (Actually, they were no such thing, as most of the congressional contests turned on local and regional issues rather than on international affairs.) "Mr. Wilson and his Fourteen Points and his four supplementary points and his five complementary points and all his utterances every which way," Roosevelt commented sarcastically, "have ceased to have any shadow of right to be accepted as expressive of the will of the American people."

Wilson received the news of his longtime adversary's death while the royal train was stopped at the Modena station on the Franco-Italian border, on the trip back to Paris. Arthur Krock, then a newspaper correspondent trailing behind the presidential tour through Europe, watched from the platform as a French messenger gave the telegram to Wilson's valet, who then entered the compartment where the President sat in plain view. Krock, who was unaware of what was in the message, watched as Wilson opened and read the telegram. "The first expression on his face struck me as extraordinary. As I reconstructed this (after I learned what the message was—that Colonel Roosevelt was dead), Wilson's first expression was that of anyone at news that his most powerful adversary has forever left the lists: a kind of spontaneous relaxation. But Wilson's next expression was a distinctly sad one."

On the journey north from Rome, Wilson had stopped at Genoa to visit the monument to Christopher Columbus. Caught in a torrential downpour, the President stood bareheaded in the rain while he laid a wreath at the base of the statue, and then made a few brief remarks amid the soaked and torn decorations and the flagstaffs snapped in half by the wind: "Being free, America desires to show others how they may also share in the freedom of the world." On to Milan, the heart of intellectual and industrial Italy, where working men and women poured into the streets to welcome the prophet of democracy. "The thoroughfares were choked with humanity," wrote one observer, "and the President's motorcar was forced to crawl and edge its way through with the greatest difficulty and in constant danger of running the citizens down." Wilson stood on the balcony of the palace, leading a band and throwing kisses with both hands to the adoring crowd, the magnificent *alpini* soldiers parading before him; he graciously bestowed a personal greeting upon an invalid Italian general confined to a wheelchair. The celebration continued with a dinner at La Scala (an event to which Mussolini had wangled an invitation), followed by a gala performance of *Aïda*; from the royal box where he and Mrs. Wilson sat, the President assured the audience that "I cannot find words to express to you all that my grateful heart feels for the moving reception that the great people of Milan have given me. *Viva l'Italia!*" In Turin, the ancient capital of the Kingdom of Sardinia and the dominions of the house of Savoy, more than a thousand mayors of cities and towns in the Piedmont came from the hills, the valleys, and the fields—some traveling over Alpine glaciers to reach Turin—each man wearing a tricolored sash as a badge of office. Wilson had a smile and handshake for them all, and several mayors bowed and kissed his hand in return. A stirring Wilsonian speech about peace with justice aroused the assembled multitude, but meanwhile a few men circulated among the crowd, handing out Roosevelt's critique of the Fourteen Points. The President then received an honorary degree from the university, responding with a simple and moving speech of gratitude to the students there. The audience stood and cheered as Wilson shed his customary reserve and playfully donned a blue student cap. "How young and virile he looked as he stood there," recalled Mrs. Wilson admiringly, caught up in the excitement of what she called her "Cinderella role" in the triumphal European procession.

But a British observer sounded an ominous warning: "Looking back on President Wilson's short stay in Italy, the main fact that impresses itself on me is not what the President thinks, or says, or would do, but what he symbolizes to the people, what they expect from him." And it was a heavy burden of expectations and hopes Wilson had raised.

At ten o'clock on the morning of January 7, an exhausted Wilson returned quietly to Paris. Against Admiral Grayson's medical advice, he began almost immediately a round of conferences with his advisers. Clemenceau had arrived in the city earlier the same day. Lloyd George still lingered in Britain.

"Waiting for peace in Paris these days," complained a disgruntled American correspondent, "is not an occupation one would choose on account of its exhilarating attractions. Peace making has taken on the elusive qualities of the will-o'-the-wisp.... The grand quest of world peace is as far from realization as is perpetual motion or the philosopher's stone.

Thus hope deferred maketh the heart sick." "The wolf," warned Herbert Hoover, "is at the door of the world."

Finally the French government set January 18 as the date of the first formal session of the Paris Peace Conference. As Clemenceau knew well, it was the anniversary of France's surrender to Germany in 1871.

Fed by the winter rains and snow, the Seine began to rise inexorably above its banks.

Berlin, Tuesday, January 7. At ten o'clock the rattle of machine guns broke the morning silence. Three hours later there was total chaos, a sea of bewildered humanity in the squares and streets. An American correspondent watching the melee described the Spartacists as "typical proletarians, some of whom affect an even more dilapidated appearance than is naturally their own." Rumors enveloped the city: there would be a Spartacist attack on the Chancellor's palace soon; the government was expecting reinforcements of thousands of reliable veteran troops; Field Marshal Paul von Hindenburg himself had arrived to oversee the government strategy. The one certainty was that Eichhorn still ruled supreme at police headquarters. Meanwhile, Minister of Defense Gustav Noske drew up his own bloody plans to destroy the Spartacists, who were fortifying their fortress in the stables south of the imperial palace. At four in the afternoon more rifle fire was heard from the direction of the Brandenburg Gate. At a street corner, shots were exchanged while a few yards away a barrel-organ was playing a mocking tune. "Get out of the way, you civilians!" A fearful panic ensued, women shrieking and fainting and people running heedlessly hither and thither. Fortunately the firing ceased in a few seconds, but twenty people were left dead or wounded in the street.

Confusion and terror reigned unchallenged. Even in the darkness, crowds remained milling about restlessly, listening to impromptu speeches. From time to time hand grenades were thrown into a streetcorner gathering, and revolvers were fired wildly, but so dense were the crowds that a hundred feet away people could not tell what was going on. (There was a rumor that several more government regiments were en route to the city from Potsdam.) Now and then in the squares of the city a shot set off a general melee and sent people rushing to the entrances of the subway or trying to force open the doors of houses. Americans in the luxurious Hotel Adlon averted assault by hoisting the Stars and Stripes on the flagpole. At nine o'clock, people in their homes could still hear the chatter of machine-gun fire in front of their doors. Near one in the morning there was an exchange of pistols in the streets, and more rifle fire an hour later.

* * *

Berlin, Wednesday, January 8. Utter disorganization and lawlessness. Early in the morning all the Berlin trams ceased to run, as did the state railways. Some parts of Berlin were without light and water. Wilhelmstrasse was impassable. There was a huge gun in front of the Chancellery. Along Unter den Linden near the Tiergarten, life seemed to go on as before: pedestrians strolled about, street vendors shouted and barrel-organs played, shops and cafés served their patrons. Then suddenly a machine gun atop the Brandenburg Gate opened fire into the Tiergarten crowd. Shrieks came from the wounded as they fell and everyone else fled in terror.

Masses of people gathered in front of the Chancellery building. Someone called out, "Liebknecht is coming!" A droshky containing Liebknecht and three companions arrived. Cries of "Down with Liebknecht! Seize him! Away with the dog!" were mingled with shouts of "Long live Liebknecht!" Meanwhile, the droshky driver apathetically allowed the mob to pull him off the box and take the reins and whip from him. Liebknecht appeared as he always did, emaciated, high-strung, electric. He motioned up and down with his hand for silence, but no one paid attention. The confusion grew worse, and while the people argued among themselves, Liebknecht, with his droshky waving its red flag, disappeared.

In the evening, Spartacists cordoned off a number of primary streets. Suddenly the cry went up, "Back! Back! There is to be fighting here." The crowd scattered precipitately left and right into Friedrichstrasse, and while armed men threatened one another, onlookers heard the cries of itinerant vendors hawking candies at a mark a packet, cigars and cigarettes, or the evening newspapers. In the distance, one of these street merchants tootled on a flute; from a neighbouring café came applause rewarding the efforts of a comedian. Bullets struck the rain-drenched streets from every side; the dull banging of hand grenades sounded with distressing regularity. Many people dropped while trying to reach safety.

Along Mauerstrasse, a crowd of people came running for their lives; a series of detonations followed them. Spartacists were firing from the Ministry of War. Several persons fell, among them an old man and a young girl. A passerby asked a sailor to help to carry the girl away. Blood was streaming from her as she lay in the street. They lifted her up and carried her to a forsaken horse omnibus.

Berlin, Thursday, January 9. The weather was delightful, a portent of the springtime to come. The government declared a full-scale state of siege. Troops loyal to the Ebert regime arrived from Potsdam; scores of army officers in Berlin placed themselves at the disposal of Herr Noske. Government soldiers dispersed street meetings with bayonets and rifle butts. The rebels, meanwhile, formed their own provisional government under the title of the Revolutionary Committee. "Nobody who has not witnessed it can possibly form the slightest picture of the awful confusion existing here," wrote a British journalist. At almost every street corner in the central part of the city there were violent confrontations and wild shooting. Berlin became a city of hastily improvised fortresses, some held by the government and some by the Spartacists, with artillery thundering and machine guns sputtering night and day, and now and then brief interruptions of minutes or a half hour at best. Loss TWENTY TIMES AS BIG AS IN FIRST REVOLT LAST NOVEMBER, proclaimed *The New York Times*.

Artillery boomed through the streets as Spartacists once again renewed their attempts to seize the Chancellor's palace but were driven back. The government entrusted its life to battle-hardened soldiers just back from the front; these veterans entered upon their work in a grim, deadly, business-like fashion. Although many Majority Socialists did not really trust the Freikorps officers because of their previous loyalty to the former Kaiser, once the government had elected to crush the insurrection by force, it really had no other reliable weapons.

Now the battle raged most fiercely around the Tageblatt Newspaper Building. Rebels fired from behind barricades made of bales of newspapers. The Spartacists had stocked every one of their buildings with machine guns and, with the connivance of the city police under Eichhorn, had accumulated enormous quantities of hand grenades, which they now rained upon the unprotected government soldiers in the streets below. Immense crowds watched the progress of operations from safe street corners until government troops dispersed them roughly. An estimated two hundred people lay dead from the fighting of the past week.

The government forbade all processions and ordered its troops to shoot to kill. Ebert announced, "The Government is taking all necessary measures to destroy this domination of frightfulness and prevent its return. You will not have to wait long for these decisive measures. Have patience for yet a little while." During the night there was more desultory shooting, then the clattering of horsedrawn carriages along the pavement. In the darkness, no one could recognize who anyone was.

In Paris, the Seine continued to rise more rapidly than predicted, often more than twelve inches a day. No supplies could reach the capital by river; navigation was at a complete standstill. The Samartine Baths sank off the Pont Neuf and were lashed by steel cables to the bridge to keep them from being carried downstream. The railroad to the Gare des Invalides was submerged. The stone Zouave who guarded the Pont d'Alma stood in icy water up to his waist. (In the disastrous flood of 1910, the river had risen to his neck.) Bakeries and flour mills were flooded, tram service disorganized; thousands were driven from their homes, popular restaurants in Champigny-sur-Marne were underwater, the Gare d'Orsay closed down, hotels were deprived of heat and light. Crowds lined the banks of the Seine to watch its swelling; some resourceful Parisians took advantage of the impending disaster by casting fishing lines into the swirling current.

Henry White, one of the five American Peace Commissioners (along with Wilson, House, Secretary of State Lansing, and General Tasker Bliss) took time to send a cable to Senator Henry Cabot Lodge:

FEEL I SHOULD NO LONGER DELAY LAYING BEFORE YOU CONDITION WHICH HAS BEEN GRADUALLY FORCING ITSELF UPON OUR DELEGATION AND WHICH NOW DOMINATES ENTIRE EUROPEAN SITUATION ABOVE ALL ELSE; NAMELY, STEADY WESTWARD ADVANCE OF BOLSHEVISM. IT NOW COMPLETELY CONTROLS RUSSIA AND POLAND AND IS SPREADING THROUGH GERMANY. ONLY EFFECTIVE BARRIER NOW APPARENTLY POSSIBLE AGAINST IT IS FOOD RELIEF, AS BOLSHEVISM THRIVES ONLY ON STARVATION AND DISORDER. . . . IT IS TOO LATE I FEAR TO STOP BOLSHEVISM IN RUSSIA AND POLAND, BUT THERE IS STILL HOPE OF MAKING GERMANY, ROUMANIA AND CERTAIN OTHER AREAS EFFECTIVE BARRIERS.

En route to Europe in December, Wilson had forbade any more American correspondents from entering Germany or Russia. Oswald Garrison Villard, editor of the *Nation*, believed Wilson's edict was intended to keep from the American public the fact that the war blockade was still being enforced and that "old men and women and children were daily dying in Germany for lack of adequate food. . . . The godly Presbyterian from the White House also could not be induced to make a public stand against this indefensible cruelty to noncombatants; the screw of starvation was kept turned in order to compel the vanquished to sign whatever treaty might be drafted."

An American special mission sent to investigate conditions in Germany cabled its findings to Wilson and his colleagues in Paris:

ESPECIALLY IN BERLIN, BUT ALSO IN MUNICH, THE PEOPLE ON THE STREETS SHOW MARKED SIGNS OF INSUFFICIENT NUTRITION. THE CHILDREN HAVE AN ANAEMIC AND DELICATE APPEARANCE COMPARED WITH TWO YEARS AGO, AND THE OLDER PEOPLE ALSO SHOW SIGNS OF EMACIATION AND

LACK OF STRENGTH. . . . THE BREAD IS VERY POOR AND MEAT RATION, ½ LB. PER WEEK, INCLUDING BONES, INSUFFICIENT. THE POTATO CROP, AC- CORDING TO PERSONAL STATEMENTS WHICH WERE MADE TO ME, WAS MUCH WORSE THAN HAS BEEN ADMITTED IN THE PAPERS. THE SYSTEM OF FOOD DISTRIBUTION HAS ALMOST COMPLETELY BROKEN DOWN AND THE RESULT HAS BEEN THAT THE RICH ARE OFTEN ABLE TO OBTAIN SUFFICIENT SUPPLIES BY PAYING EXORBITANT PRICES AND BY UNDERHAND METHODS OF ALL KINDS, WHICH ARE NOW EMPLOYED WITHOUT HESITATION. . . . THE INFANT MORTALITY IS SAID TO BE TERRIBLE, AND IN GENERAL I WAS TOLD THAT 800 MORE DEATHS OCCUR DAILY THROUGHOUT GERMANY THAN WAS THE CASE BEFORE THE WAR. DEATHS WERE NOT DIRECTLY DUE TO STARVATION, BUT TO WASTING DISEASES CAUSED BY MALNUTRITION.

The chief of the special mission added that the Spartacus movement drew its strength largely from "the serious food and economic situation, resulting in hunger, disease, and unemployment; a nervous collapse, due in the first place to defeat, and in the second to under nutrition; . . . [and] the fact that they are in control of large sums of money obtained principally from Russian sources."

In the Kremlin, Lenin paced restlessly around his tiny office, waiting for the latest news from Berlin on the progress of the German revolution he had encouraged, hoping that it signaled the start of a full-scale uprising throughout Europe. But in Berlin the Minister of the Interior was one of the few who realized that Bolshevism was not in fact the greatest danger to his government: "To him the greater danger appeared to be from the Right, not for the present but in the long run, for he believed the reaction which was not showing its head now would emerge sooner or later. . . . The people were so used to the Hohenzollerns and to militarism that it would at best be a difficult matter to destroy the sentiment entirely."

While chaos reigned in Berlin and the old and the very young were being starved, Paris began to regain its outward appearance of gaiety. Jewelry shops did an enormous business, and American officers on leave wined and dined their favorite prostitutes in expensive cafés. Professor Charles Seymour of Yale, a member of the American peace delegation, wrote that the combination of excessive eating and lack of exercise was making him "fat as a seal. Actually I don't know what to do, my trousers and waistcoat are getting so tight." Expeditionary forces had been raised in Burgundy and Bordeaux to rescue wine supplies from the cellars in those regions, and several special trainloads of wine were on their way for the relief of Paris.

And the Seine continued to rise.

* * *

Berlin, Friday, January 10. Loyal troops, their faces impassive under steel helmets, recaptured several police buildings from the Spartacists, although Eichhorn himself escaped. The government's order to open fire upon any unofficial demonstrations had accomplished its purpose; for most of the day, the city's streets remained relatively empty. Machine guns and hand grenades cleaned out several Spartacus strongholds. The numbers of government forces kept rising steadily. In an effort to starve the citizenry into supporting the uprising, Spartacists kept large parts of Berlin without bread or water. A band of rebels mistook an American movie camera team filming the scene from a rooftop for a machine-gun nest. Women with shopping bags on their arms accompanied a Spartacist procession late in the day, in hopes that the rebels might decide to plunder some shop along the way. As the parade advanced, street vendors precipitated themselves upon it with baskets of Bavarian malt bonbons, a cure for hoarseness. This had an electrifying effect on the marchers, all of whom had shouted themselves hoarse, and large baskets of the pleasant remedy were quickly sold out. An American correspondent saw an innocent-looking van loaded with sewing machines, but also carrying machine guns, hand grenades, and rifles.

Sleep was hard to come by that evening. All night long, machine guns rattled, rifles were fired, hand grenades exploded, and shouted orders mingled with the sounds of modern warfare. Harry Kessler noted that nothing in particular was attained by all of this; the shooting, he observed, was notable chiefly for its extreme nervousness. With every passing day, Berlin came to resemble more closely a theater of war in which some 100,000 fighting men were locked in combat with one another, while the 3,500,000 people who constituted the remainder of the population remained warily outside the struggle.

Berlin, Saturday, January 11. By now the Ebert government had definitely regained the upper hand in the capital, although fighting continued in many sectors. In the morning a two-hour battle raged between Spartacists armed with machine guns, barricaded in several newspaper buildings, and government troops with seven-centimeter field guns in the streets and on the rooftop of the Patent Office. The Spartacists refused to surrender unconditionally, whereupon they were battered into submission by gas bombs and mine-throwers. There were a few tremendous detonations, shattering all the windows in the neighborhood. An enormous cloud of dust arose, and the whole front of one building collapsed on the sidewalk, burying some Spartacist machine guns and their crews. A white flag on a long pole was extended from the ruins.

The city's workers now became seriously alarmed at the defeat of the proletarian forces by the government with the aid of the army and the bourgeoisie. One Berliner who had witnessed the conflict from the start described the eerie impression made by the shelled Leipzigerstrasse:

THE LIGHTLESS FAÇADES OF THE HOUSES TOWERED EVEN MORE HUGELY IN THE DARKNESS. AT STREET-CORNERS PEOPLE COULD BE SEEN TAKING COVER BECAUSE UNCERTAIN WHAT TO DO. AT EVERY CROSSING A SMALL, MURKY, SHAPELESS THRONG DITHERED BEFORE THE EMPTY BUT FIRE-RAKED STREETS AS ON THE EDGE OF A CHASM. TRAMS WITH THEIR LIGHTS EXTINGUISHED RAN THEIR ROUTES AT FULL SPEED, THROWING OFF ELEC-TRIC SPARKS WHICH CRACKLED LIKE FIREWORKS AND WERE BRIEFLY RE-FLECTED IN THE WET, GLISTENING ROADWAY. . . . MANY WERE NOT PREPARED TO TAKE THE RISK OF USING THE TRAMS AND STAYED STUCK IN DOORWAYS. THIS DUMB PANIC IN A TANGLE OF STREETS TURNED INTO A BATTLEFIELD WAS ONE OF THE MOST WEIRD SCENES THESE REVOLUTION-ARY DAYS HAVE PRESENTED.

Berlin, Sunday, January 12. Sooner than even the most optimistic govern-ment supporters had expected, the power of the Spartacists was broken. Reporters discovered to their astonishment that many of the captured rebel machine-gun crews were women. Cleaned out of police headquarters and all other major buildings in the city, the rebels were reduced to waging a guerrilla war from the rooftops, firing indiscriminately upon soldiers and civilians below. In suppressing the revolt, government troops had also killed their share of civilians (much as the Kaiser's army had in Belgium during the war just ended). Passersby and vehicles were sniped at by both sides. According to a semiofficial statement, over one thousand harmless pedestrians had been killed or wounded in the streets within the past week. Between the total darkness that prevailed and the constant checks and searches by government troops, it took over two hours to walk a distance usually covered in half an hour.

Berlin, Monday, January 13. The battle was over. Liebknecht and his comrades were in flight or in hiding. The center of the city was held by government troops with rifles, bayonets, hand grenades, machine guns, heavy artillery, flamethrowers, tanks, howitzers, and armored cars. Nu-merous columns of infantry marched along Potsdammerstrasse to the Tiergarten. Unwilling to take any chances on a renewal of the fighting, the government began arresting all suspicious persons and confiscating all arms and ammunition. Government soldiers shouted orders at innocent pedestrians: "Don't proceed any further or you might get shot." A shot discharged anywhere brought forth volleys of Freikorps bullets in response. The story was told of several Spartacist propagandists captured as they tried to flee across a rooftop, unable to run fast enough because they were carrying their precious typewriters with them.

"The Government has chosen to crush a non-reactionary movement by all the arts of sanguinary warfare," wrote the *Manchester Guardian*'s Berlin correspondent. "In fact, it looked ominously like a second mobilisation, and the regiments marching with full equipment into Berlin today betrayed something of the sinister enthusiasm of August 1914. . . . Today's events profoundly changed the whole aspect of German politics. . . . The formidable military machine, which seemed to be crushed for ever, has risen again with astounding rapidity. Prussian officers are stalking the streets of Berlin, soldiers marching, shouting and shooting at their command." Harry Kessler warned that "it will be a terrible thing if, for lack of any desire to bring it about, all this destruction and suffering does not prove to be the birth-pangs of a new era and it turns out that nothing better than a patchwork job can be done. . . . Today the band of the Republican Defence Force played *Lohengrin* among the splintered glass in the courtyard behind the badly battered main gate of Police Headquarters. A large crowd collected in the street, partly to see the damage and partly to hear *Lohengrin.*"

Scores of Spartacus men were shot down after surrendering, and others were disposed of with rifle butts. A sixteen-year-old boy who dared to shout "Long live Liebknecht!" had his skull smashed with a rifle. In Bertolt Brecht's play *Drums in the Night*, a drunk in the corner of Glubb's Gin Mill sang:

> All my brothers now are dead, yes, dead,
> I've come through alive, I don't know how.
> In November I was Red, yes Red.
> But it's January now.

When government troops finally located Karl Liebknecht and Rosa Luxemburg—the Polish Bolshevik and humanist who had helped lead the Spartacist revolution, even though she knew its time had not yet come— they roughly forced the rebel leaders into an interrogation chamber in the

Eden Hotel. Soldiers standing outside sealed off the streets around the hotel. After a brief and desultory confrontation, Liebknecht was taken out by a side entrance, where Private Otto Runge promptly clubbed him twice over the head with a rifle butt. Throwing Liebknecht into a waiting car, six officers drove a short distance, stopped the car, pushed their prisoner into the street, and shot him dead. Rosa Luxemburg, defenseless and already crippled by a chronic hip injury, was beaten senseless by her captors. "I shall never forget how they knocked the poor woman down and dragged her around," a hotel chambermaid recalled. Private Runge clubbed Rosa, too, and she was thrown dead or unconscious into a second car. Lieutenant Kurt Vogel then put a pistol to her head and blew her brains out. Her lifeless body was tossed into a nearby canal. The next day the officers and men who had participated in the murders gathered for a celebration at the Eden.

Official reports stated that Liebknecht had been shot while trying to escape en route to Moabit Prison, and that Luxemburg had been attacked and dragged from the government's protective custody by a hostile mob. Lenin may have mourned for Liebknecht, but not for Luxemburg, who had consistently and sentimentally opposed his use of terror to further the ends of the Bolshevik revolution in Russia. *The New York Times* shed no tears for either of the murdered rebels: "Regrettable as is the manner of death, the work of private violence, not the law, that came to Dr. Liebknecht and Rosa Luxemburg, it was to be expected, and does a summary, if irregular, justice to the fomenters of robbery, murder, and anarchy."

"Wir sind alle Todten auf Urlaub." Late in 1918, sitting in one of the seemingly endless chain of prisons to which she had been condemned in a lifetime of political protest, Rosa Luxemburg had written, "We are all dead men on furlough."

4

"In vain shall

thou make thyself fair;

thy lovers

will despise thee . . ."

A stellar vaudeville bill captivated audiences at the Hippodrome Theater in Los Angeles. The harmonies of the Four Farmerettes formed the main attraction, ably supported by the winsome talents of Florence Lester ("The Whistling Girl"), and the Kafka Trio with their whirlwind iron-jaw act. There were an estimated 907 vaudeville houses—plush red seats, stained-glass and art deco windows, and gold braid everywhere—still drawing appreciative audiences in the United States, and employing nearly nine thousand performers. It was not an easy life, nor was it a particularly law-abiding segment of the population; according to testimony before a federal commission, about 90 percent of the nation's vaudevillians were "only about four days ahead of the sheriff."

In Britain, Lord John Sanger's menagerie was preparing to embark on its usual spring tour. The circus's performances had, of course, been severely curtailed during the war, since most of the staff had been placed on active service. (The elephants spent the duration "working on the farm.") Bob Pender's troupe of acrobats and clowns, perennially one of Britain's most popular stage attractions, was already touring from one town to the next, always on the move. Pender's company included an earnest young man who was about to celebrate his fifteenth birthday; dancing, tumbling, walking on stilts, Archie Leach loved every moment of his life in the spotlights. Movie audiences would love Archie even more in years to come; to them he would be known as Cary Grant.

On the afternoon of January 14, Harold Nicolson received his first audience with Woodrow Wilson. Nicolson, a member of the British peace

delegation in Paris, accompanied Arthur Balfour (recently returned from
the beaches of Cannes) to the Murat Palace, where he found troops and
police pickets saluting every dignitary in sight. "Wilson is much guarded,"
Nicolson noted dryly. For two and a half hours Nicolson and his colleagues waited in a glass-roofed gallery, staring at a statue of Napoleon in
Egypt, while Balfour, Lloyd George, and Andrew Bonar Law conferred
with Wilson. Mrs. Wilson strolled past, carrying a massive bunch of mimo-
sas in her arms, her high heels clicking on the parquet floor. After a while
Nicolson began reading the *Irish Times*. An old butler began putting out
the lights, one by one.

Finally the door opened and the four old men emerged. "Oh! Dear me!"
Balfour exclaimed. "Have you been waiting all this time? I never realized!"
Turning to Wilson, Balfour introduced Nicolson as "a young man who
could have told us all we wanted."

"What we wanted," explained Wilson, "was the exact figure of the
Germans who would be annexed by Italy if they got the Brunner [sic]
frontier. Now can you tell us that?" Nicolson said he did not have the exact
figures, but it should be about 240,000. "Or was it not 250,000?" Wilson
interrupted. Nicolson replied that he had been going to say 245,000. "Well,
a matter of thousands, anyway," Wilson concluded.

Wilson then asked Nicolson for similar figures for the port city of
Fiume. Eager to impress, Nicolson asked whether the President wanted the
population of the suburbs included. "Yes," Wilson replied, "there is a
suburb called Ashak or something." *Susak*, Nicolson corrected. After a
pause to scrabble about in his briefcase, Nicolson produced the statistics.
"So I thought," nodded Wilson. "And the line between Fiume and Ashak
is a small one." A mere rivulet, Nicolson confirmed; the two places could
not be separated. "So I gather," Wilson added. "But the Italians tell me that
if one tries to pass from Fiume to Ashak one is certain to be murdered."
Nicolson began to demur, but the President cut him off. "Waal! I guessed
he was talking through his hat. Well, good night to you gentlemen. Good
night, Mr. Balfour." And this, wrote Nicolson in his diary, was what was
known as "giving expert advice."

On the way downstairs, Balfour apologized for keeping Nicolson waiting. "To tell the truth," Balfour admitted, "the last half hour we have only
been discussing whether Napoleon and Frederick the Great could be called
disinterested patriots." Nicolson politely asked what their conclusion had
been. "Oh—I forget the conclusion."

Wilson seemed to Nicolson to be younger in person than his photographs made him appear. "One does not see the teeth except when he

smiles, which is an awful gesture: broad shoulders and a narrow waist: his shoulders are out of proportion to his height; so is his face (not the head itself, but the surface from ear to chin). His clothes are those of a tailor's block: very neat and black and tidy: striped trousers: high collar: pink pin. A southern drawl."

"Anyhow I had the most pleasant dream last night and my oh how I did hate to wake up. Of course I was in the U.S.A. parading down some big main street and I met you and there was a church handy and just as casually as you please we walked inside and the priest did the rest, and then I thought we were in Paris and I woke up in a Godforsaken camp just outside of old ruined Verdun. You've no idea how often and constantly that last part is a daydream with me. It seems that Sam is never, never going to take us home so that priest can be met."

Captain Harry Truman had no patience for the leisurely pace of peace-making, or for the complexities of international diplomacy. (He liked to say that as far as he was concerned, the Czechs could elect the King of the Lollipops to rule over them if they so desired.) Like most American dough-boys, he just wanted to go home—in his case, to marry young Bess Wallace. A shortage of transport ships was keeping American troops in France throughout the winter, bored and frustrated. "It is a myth that our men love the French and vice versa," wrote Charles Seymour from Paris. "I think the sooner we get our troops home the better for our national relations." Seymour believed that American troops objected primarily to "the dirtiness of the poorer French country houses," and were "sore at the way they have been overcharged (largely their own fault for they wouldn't learn the money)." The French, in turn, were sore at the relatively well paid American soldiers for bidding up the price of almost everything in sight. "I have heard lots of men discuss the reasons but none of them differed on the fact that we and the French ('Frogs' the doughboys call them) do not get on. Where our men come in contact with the English," added Seymour, "they get on even less; on the other hand we get on very well with the Scotch and the Australians."

In mid-January, Truman received orders to move to a town that he described as a "dirty, little old French village." He wrote to Bess: "It's my opinion we'll stay there until Woodie gets his pet peace plans refused or okayed. For my part, and I'm sure every A.E.F. [American Expeditionary Force] man feels the same way, I don't give a whoop (to put it mildly) whether there's a League of Nations or whether Russia has a Red government or a Purple one, and if the President of the Czecho-Slovaks wants to pry the throne out from under the King of Bohemia, let him pry but send us home. . . . For my part I've had enough *vin rouge* and frogeater victuals to last me a lifetime."

British troops, some of whom had sweated in the trenches for over four years, were even more eager to return home. In the time-honored tradition of obtuse British Army command decisions, however, Lloyd George's government had developed a perverse demobilization scheme that seemed to have been deliberately designed to antagonize the greatest number of people. Instead of discharging first the men who had served the longest time, the army gave top priority to "key men" who had held essential jobs in civilian life. From the standpoint of national economic welfare, there was some justification for such a policy; but there was little if any defense for the subsequent decision that only men with firm promises of employment would be discharged in the immediate future. Since those who had joined most recently were also the ones most likely to have job offers still waiting for them, this pronouncement was instantly greeted with ugly scenes of insubordination and riots at numerous British military encampments.

Nearly twelve thousand Tommies in the camps at Folkestone and Dover demonstrated against returning to France in the first week of January. When men at the Army Service Corps depot at Kempton Park formed a "soldiers' council" and announced their intention to ally themselves with local workers' groups, images of the post-Armistice chaos in Germany flashed through the minds of British military officials. Soldiers in lorries demonstrated near Whitehall with the slogans, "We want civvie suits." "We won the war. Give us our tickets." "Promises are not pie crust." Winston Churchill, who took office as Secretary of State for War on January 9, received an intimate look at the crisis on his first day on the job when a crowd of insubordinate soldiers demonstrated outside his window. He directed his officers to "arrest the mutineers," but trouble continued in British camps in France, Palestine, Flanders, Greece, and Mesopotamia.

The most serious uprising occurred in Calais, where five thousand men demanded to be sent home at once. Infantry troops formed a soviet, and the Army Service and Royal Army Ordnance Corps men went on strike. No mention of the extent of these mutinous activities reached the public. Field Marshal Douglas Haig recommended that several of the ringleaders be executed. Churchill overruled Haig on the grounds that execution should be reserved for occasions when a soldier's cowardly or criminal conduct endangered the lives of his comrades. The disturbances abated after Churchill issued new orders basing demobilization firmly upon length of service, but lingering doubts about the reliability of the remaining troops made it impossible for Lloyd George even to consider any new military adventures in Russia or anywhere else for the moment. Still, the men who had been discharged were not necessarily better off than those who had to stay in the service a little while longer.

The Soldier's Return, Part One. At the Thames Police Court, a corporal in the army asked the magistrate's advice with respect to his wife, who had borne an illegitimate child during his absence in France. "I am afraid your case is only one of many," the magistrate replied, "and the only advice I can give you is to divorce her. There is a process by which persons who are not well off can get a divorce from women who have sinned. If you go into the office you can obtain the necessary papers telling you how to proceed. I am sorry for you."

The Soldier's Return, Part Two. When Henry Delahay returned home on Christmas leave from his service abroad in the British Army (France, the Dardanelles, Salonika, Serbia, Palestine, and Egypt; twice wounded), he discovered that his wife had become a drunkard and had had an illegitimate child. Two of his own children had died. Delahay found her in a pub, but when he offered to buy her a drink and "let bygones be bygones," she threatened to throw the beer in his face. When the landlord tried to calm him down, Delahay threw a glass at him. Mr. Montagu Sharpe, the magistrate at Middlesex Sessions, told Delahay that he understood how he felt, but he still should not have attacked the publican. "I am afraid," Mr. Sharpe concluded, "there will be a great many cases of men coming home and finding that things have not gone as they ought to have gone."

The Soldier's Return, Part Three. Police throughout Britain reported a startling increase in crimes of violence in and around London and other cities following the Armistice. According to a highly placed Scotland Yard official, the increase was chiefly noticeable "in areas where large numbers of troops are stationed or are spending their leave." It was not merely a matter of men with time on their hands getting into trouble. In overcoming a recruit's reluctance to stab another man in the stomach, the army had concurrently removed many of the barriers that had kept him from committing violent crimes. It was part of the unavoidable price of war that now had to be paid.

* * *

Other loose habits of military life persisted. Following his demobilization early in 1919, Robert Graves noticed that "I still had the Army habit of commandeering anything of uncertain ownership that I found lying about; also a difficulty in telling the truth—it was always easier for me now, when charged with any fault, to lie my way out in Army style." Graves discovered that he also continued "stopping cars for a lift, talking without embarrassment to my fellow-travellers in railway carriages, and unbuttoning by the roadside without shame, whoever might be about. Also, I retained the technique of endurance: a brutal persistence in seeing things through, somehow, anyhow, without finesse, satisfied with the main points of any situation. But," Graves added proudly, "at least I modified my unrestrainedly foul language."

At seven o'clock on the morning of January 16, reporters climbed off a revenue cutter in New York City harbor and boarded the transport ship *Belgic*, full of American soldiers returning from France. The reporters showed the doughboys copies of the morning newspapers, which carried reports of the impending victory of the prohibition movement. By the time the *Belgic* docked, Nebraska had become the thirty-sixth state to ratify the proposed measure, and prohibition had become a constitutional reality in the United States. "Good night, isn't there any booze left?" asked one incredulous doughboy. "Isn't there even any cognac here?" "Say, what is this about the country going dry? Is that straight?" "I'm going back to France 'toot sweet.'" Liquor stores throughout Manhattan reported that their normal volume of business more than doubled that day.

Church bells rang throughout the nation. "The rain of tears is over," the flamboyant evangelist Billy Sunday declared. "The slums will soon be a memory. We will turn our prisons into factories, our jails into storehouses and corn cribs. Men will walk upright now, women will smile, children will laugh, hell will be for rent. If any State fails to ratify the amendment the star in the flag that represents it should be draped in mourning." Not every cleric was quite as joyful at the news. Cardinal Gibbons of Baltimore had opposed total prohibition because he feared that the manufacture of sacramental wine essential to the celebration of the Catholic Mass would be curtailed along with recreational alcoholic beverages. Moreover, the cardinal warned that enforcement of the law would lead the government to invade the privacy of people's homes, "which up to now all men have agreed is a sacred, holy place."

The triumph of the American prohibition movement (which had begun in earnest in the decade before the Civil War) owed a great deal to the development of novel techniques for the mobilization of public opinion on a nationwide scale to achieve a political goal. Dry forces—effectively led by the superbly organized and well-financed Anti-Saloon League—had worked first in the small country towns and villages in the South and Midwest, drumming up support for their movement among church and community leaders, who then pressured their political representatives to support local prohibition measures. Gradually the grassroots movement spread throughout the nation; when a prohibition bill came up before Congress, league officials would alert their members, and an avalanche of anti-liquor telegrams descended upon Capitol Hill. When Congress passed the Sheppard prohibition amendment in December 1917, submitting the constitutional question to the states, it gave dry forces seven years to persuade the necessary thirty-six state legislatures to approve the measure. It took only thirteen months.

Prohibition did not represent the victory of a small, humorless, puritanical minority imposing its will unfairly upon its neighbors. The movement clearly enjoyed widespread popular support, especially in non-urban areas. By the beginning of 1919, there were 2,546 dry counties in the nation, and only 351 wet ones. Public opinion was swayed in favor of prohibition primarily by a distaste for the new wave of immigrants from Central and Eastern Europe, whose drinking habits distressed many middle-class Americans; by a desire to avoid wastefulness in wartime (the successful prohibition of liquor in the armed services seemed to be a powerful endorsement for the constitutional amendment); and by the Progressive wish to uplift man by improving his environment, which would also enhance industrial efficiency (no drunks falling down on the job). Many citizens believed that prohibition would also check the power of corrupt political machines, which bought votes and loyalty with booze. The constitutional amendment would become effective on January 16, 1920, twelve months from the date of its ratification, but the wartime prohibition measure was already scheduled to go into effect on July 1, unless Wilson stopped it by declaring the army demobilized.

Few doubted that prohibition would have a powerful effect upon the nation's behavior. For one thing, the federal government stood to lose hundreds of millions of dollars in tax revenues. The movie industry cheerfully predicted that theaters would replace saloons as the primary source of cheap entertainment for American men. Many restaurant owners were less sanguine about their future; "If the country goes dry," announced "Joe" of the Black Cat in Greenwich Village, "I get out. Oh, yes, it is as bad as that. I close up. . . . Take the wine away from Greenwich Village and where is the village?" More ominous was the possibility that the use of hard drugs would increase when prohibition became effective. The head of the New York Health Department claimed that there already were between 50,000 to 100,000 habitual users of drugs in the city, and that the habit was spreading rapidly among all classes of society. A survey of thirty-three chemists' shops in New York—less than 2 percent of the total in the city—revealed that the extraordinary quantity of 2,638 ounces of cocaine, heroin, and morphine had been sold in those shops alone in December 1918.

The attorney for the New York State Brewers' Association predicted that "national prohibition will instantaneously make hundreds of thousands of violators and evaders of the law and as many more hypocrites." Clearly, effective enforcement had to be the next goal of the dry forces, and it was already obvious that it was not going to be an easy task. Ever since individual states began banning liquor within their borders, whiskey-smuggling operations had displayed a constantly increasing level of ingenuity. Two well-dressed Southern gentlemen persuaded a couple of New York truckers to load ten sealed cases—each bearing the label of a prominent brand of mustard—onto a ship bound for Virginia. Unfortunately, one of the cases fell onto the pier and broke open, scattering bottles and demijohns over the concrete pavement. Within two minutes a small-scale riot erupted as the crowd fought for the precious whiskey. Police eventually restored order, but the mustard men could not be found. Federal authorities were more successful in using a U-boat chaser, complete with underwater listening devices, to locate and overtake a booze-laden launch off the Louisiana coast. That haul netted a shipment of whiskey valued at $15,000.

Yeats's vision of the spirit of the dawning age concluded with the image of a grotesque shape stirring slowly to life:

> . . . somewhere in sands of the desert
> A shape with lion body and the head of a man,
> A gaze blank and pitiless as the sun,
> Is moving its slow thighs, while all about it
> Reel shadows of the indignant desert birds.
> The darkness drops again; but now I know
> That twenty centuries of stony sleep
> Were vexed to nightmare by a rocking cradle,
> And what rough beast, its hour come round at last,
> Slouches towards Bethlehem to be born?

* * *

In Paris, on the eve of the Peace Conference, the Seine finally began to recede, but expectations were rising. Children played in the parks, kicking their footballs and sailing their boats. This was a city "gashed to its very soul," with pockmarked buildings where the bombs had landed—especially around the Eiffel Tower, a favorite German target. Every corner house had signs directing pedestrians to shelter from the air raids; sandbags still covered Napoleon's tomb; profiteers and extortionists seemed to be everywhere; for those lucky enough to find them, there were freezing rooms available in hotels; less fortunate souls were forced to wander about the streets at night, searching for any place to sleep; women everywhere wore mourning. Envoys in exotic costumes came from every corner of the earth, hoping to plead their case to the three men—Wilson, Lloyd George, and Clemenceau—who would strive to shape the future. The shadow of death loomed over the nineteenth century, ghosts of empires and states now dead who could only prolong the twilight before fading into the black night forever. The weariness of the world was hidden by a forced gaiety and sumptuous all-night banquets, by an oppressive intensity of life at a fever pitch; but behind it all was the haunting knowledge that the clock was ticking away the life of civilization as men had known it for over a hundred years. And so the people looked to three men for wisdom, three men who could only deflect the currents of time while working under impossible conditions, amid "stones crackling on the roof and crashing through the windows, and sometimes wild men screaming through the keyholes."

In the deadly white silence of the fields on the Western Front, the corpses of men who had been heroes while they lived still lay where they had fallen, under the mist of a soft rain.

TWO

THE DAYS
OF
GREAT RAIN

"And they shall drink,

and be moved,

and be mad. . . ."

5

"I will get me

unto the great men,

and will speak unto them . . ."

Vaslav Nijinsky stared at the audience. Behind the Asiatic eyes, the most violently creative mind in the history of dance teetered on the edge of insanity. His audience sat entranced, hypnotized by the intensity of the dancer's gaze. For nearly thirty minutes, Nijinsky stared.

Then he began to move. Standing upon a huge cross of black and white velvet, Nijinsky stretched out his arms as if to protect himself, opened his arms in welcome, raised them in prayer, then let them fall as if broken. "Now I will dance you the war, with its suffering, with its destruction, with its death. The war which you did not prevent and so you are also responsible for." And then he was dancing, dancing against death, dancing on the edge of the abyss of unimaginable terrors in his mind, in the nightmares of those who watched, in the memories of the world.

His wife, Romola, watched with horror; earlier that day he had told her that his performance would be "my marriage with God." Nijinsky had not danced in public since October 1917, and this private recital in a hotel ballroom in his adopted home of St. Moritz would be his last. Twenty-nine years old, the Russian who had liberated and revolutionized the ballet in his athletic, often jarring performances with the Ballet Russe in the years before the war now danced the dance of Man trapped by forces he could not comprehend. "It was tragic," Romola recounted; "his gestures were all monumental, and he entranced us so that we almost saw him floating over corpses." Whirling and spinning, the steel muscles struggling against the steel machines of war, transporting imaginations to the front, where men ran and fell and in their anguish rose only to fall again, the terror and the incessant pain, the eternal spirit leaping to escape the inevitable blows landing again and again and again, and finally the peace of exhaustion. Tea was served after the last dance.

"I want to live a long time," Nijinsky confided to his diary that evening. "My wife loves me very much." But he complained that those who had seen him dance "were afraid of me, thinking I wanted to kill them. I did not. I loved everybody but nobody loved me and I became nervous and excited: the audience caught my mood. They did not like me, they wanted to go away. . . . I wanted to go on dancing but God said to me: 'Enough.' I stopped."

On the afternoon of Saturday, January 18, a weak winter sun turned the swollen Seine to molten gold as a crowd began to gather in front of the French Foreign Office: a massive, long, low gray building on the broad, shaded Quai d'Orsay. Atop the columns at the entrance to the Pont Alexander III—the tangible symbol of Franco-Russian friendship in another time—gilt eagles shone above the river. Behind the Seine lay the Place de la Concorde, the great square where the guillotine had done its efficient work during the Reign of Terror over a century earlier, and where American doughboys now amused themselves by hiding behind captured German artillery and throwing snowballs at French girls. American flags there and throughout the city still flew at half-mast in honor of Colonel Roosevelt. Farther in the background, the sun glinted off the dome of Les Invalides, the tomb of Napoleon Bonaparte, the man who once had so terrorized Europe for over a decade that the continent's statesmen actually sat down at the Congress of Vienna in 1815 and talked and drew up a peace settlement instead of making war upon each other.

At 2:30, limousines began discharging passengers at the Foreign Office, amid fanfares of trumpets for the dignitaries. There were still plenty of khaki uniforms among the spectators, and gendarmes in blue capes with hands on sword hilts pacing the streets and courtyards. Deep blue ranks of poilus with steel helmets made a passageway from the street to the foot of the stairs. French Foreign Minister Stephen Pichon (accompanied by Louis Klotz, the Minister of Finance, whom Clemenceau liked to describe as "the only Jew in France who can't count") arrived early to greet his guests. There followed the delegations of the smaller nations, the Japanese, the Siamese, Indian nobility wearing turbans, and Prince Faisal of the Hedjaz in his black robe and flowing gold-banded headdress. (When the first list of representatives for the opening session had been drawn up, Arabia was entirely excluded, apparently because the British simply forgot about it.) Despite the national flags on the hoods of the automobiles, the crowd recognized only a few of the arrivals.

Wilson arrived at 2:50, a tall, rigid figure greeted by salutes and cheers.

Clemenceau received a similar reception. "He looks calm, the old one," a French soldier said of the Tiger. "He was like that when I saw him in Champagne, right at the very front. A shell burst twenty yards away, and he never turned a hair—just threw his head back and looked right ahead of him." At 2:58, President Poincaré, the rotund French chief of state, arrived in a large black limousine, strode up the staircase and greeted Clemenceau, and the two passed through the door together. The crowd outside began to drift away, pausing only to admire the cars parked along the avenue. "Well, they've made a start at last," muttered an elderly Parisian woman in a plain black dress. "Now let's hope they end it quickly, so that my boy can come home again, and we can all make a new start."

Inside, the representatives of every major nation—except Germany, the defeated, and Russia, the outcast—and dozens of minor states gathered in small groups, Peru talking with China, Australia with Arabia, Italians in frock coats chatting with anyone who would listen to their claims. All had gathered in the conference room, formerly known as the Clock Room for the ugly ornate timepiece residing in the mantelpiece, now renamed the Salon de la Paix, with its heavy crimson and deep cream-colored draperies that blocked most of the afternoon sunlight from the five large windows that overlooked the Seine. A thick red carpet cushioned the feet of the delegates, and above four great crystal chandeliers hung from the white and gold frescoed ceiling bordered by dancing Cupids. Around the edges of the room stood chamberlains, waiters in exquisite dress suits, servants in fine livery. For the first time in history, a gathering of men would attempt to decide the fate of the entire world. This made the room rather crowded. Reporters were allowed to watch the proceedings from an adjoining salon, but they soon spilled out into the conference room and, with a disregard for diplomatic decorum, began talking to some of the delegates. Shortly before three o'clock, everyone sat down. . . .

On January 18, 1871, in Louis XIV's absurd Hall of Mirrors in Versailles, the elderly King William of Prussia had been proclaimed Kaiser Wilhelm I, German Emperor. William, Crown Prince Frederick, Bismarck, Moltke, and a panoply of Prussian generals and nobles had assembled for a religious service. After the sermon, the King read a patent establishing the empire, and Bismarck prayed, "May God grant us and our successors ever to be increasers of the German empire, not by warlike conquests, but with the graces and gifts of peace for the national well-being, for freedom and civilization." The Grand Duke of Baden led the cheers for the new Kaiser. (Both William and Bismarck viewed the whole ceremony as a preposterous charade, but a necessary formality to cement German unity; "as midwife," Bismarck wrote, "I several times most urgently wished I was a bomb to go off and blow the whole edifice to pieces.") Five weeks later, Bismarck sat in his apartments in the Rue de Provence in Versailles and forced Louis-Adolphe Thiers as the envoy of a defeated France to sign a humiliating treaty surrendering all of the province of Alsace and most of Lorraine, to submit to a German victory parade through Paris, and to pay a staggering indemnity of 5 billion francs in less than four years. Two hundred years earlier on the same day, the Kingdom of Prussia had been founded. . . .

Poincaré entered the chamber precisely at three o'clock. Everyone stood up. The French president was conducted to a crimson and gilt armchair—Wilson had the other gilt chair, everyone else having to be content with ebony and bright crimson leather armchairs—at the head of a horseshoe-shaped table covered with the traditional green baize of diplomacy. In front of each delegate was a gloriously oversized blotting pad, an ashtray, and a box of matches. Three cameras had been set up in a corner, and the delegates braced themselves for a burst of flash powder, but it never came, and the cameras eventually disappeared as mysteriously as they had appeared. With Wilson standing at his right, Poincaré immediately began to read his opening address in a monotone: "You hold in your hands the future of the world. . . ." Lloyd George was supposed to be on Poincaré's left, but one of his subordinates in the British delegation got his schedules crossed, and the Prime Minister did not arrive until Poincaré had been speaking for fifteen minutes.

The consensus was that it was a most dull speech. Several British delegates, searching for something to do, noticed that Wilson was wearing old-fashioned high-buttoned shoes. After Poincaré concluded at 3:25, everyone sat down again, and the official interpreter, Professor Etienne Mantoux ("disguised," wrote one British reporter, "as a bearded British subaltern"), translated the speech into English. Then Poincaré rose (everyone else stood up again) and left the room, waddling around the table and shaking each delegate's hand on his way out. (Everyone sat down again.) As the faint notes of bugles outside the building began to call soldiers to assembly, Clemenceau rose and suggested that a permanent chairman for the conference be elected. Wilson nominated the Tiger, paying effusive tribute, in his Southern accent, to Clemenceau's virtues. (More bugles from the troops outside announced Poincaré's departure.) Lloyd George, who meanwhile had been handed a note saying that he would have to make a speech seconding Clemenceau's nomination, did so gracefully. In response to this shower of Anglo-American praise, Clemenceau simply nodded and said, *"Merci."* In the only humorous moment of the day, Mantoux translated Lloyd George's description of Clemenceau—"the Grand Young Man of France"—as "the Grand Old Man of France." Clemenceau and Lloyd George immediately protested the translation. It was four o'clock. The gathering dusk outside left the chamber in semidarkness.

Suddenly the lights in the chandeliers flashed on to a chorus of *aaahs* from the delegates around the table. Following a unanimous vote on his election as chairman, the Grand Young Man took over the conference, moving briskly through the rest of the formalities. *"Y a t'il d'objections? Non? Adopté."* ("Like a machine gun," Nicolson said.) Only when Clemenceau declared the meeting adjourned did a Chinese delegate on the left inside corner of the table set down his pencil, having studiously recorded nearly every word of the entire session. The delegates pushed their chairs back, and there were more handshakes all around. One intrepid young American reporter from a Western newspaper put on his overcoat and derby and placed a large Bismarck cigar in his mouth and began to mingle with the delegates, asking them impertinent questions. Jules Cambon, former French ambassador to Washington, turned to a member of the British delegation and cynically predicted that the end result of the whole conference would be simply *"une improvisation."*

Another small crowd had gathered outside to watch the statesmen depart. Clemenceau descended the stairs in a casual, matter-of-fact way, a simple bowler hat on his bald head. Arthur Balfour accompanied him down the steps. The elegant British Foreign Secretary, who was dressed considerably better than Clemenceau, apologized for wearing a top hat. "I was told," said Balfour, "that it was obligatory to wear one." "So," Clemenceau replied, "was I."

Wilson's departure was more ceremonial, as a number of officials came out first to make sure that the car really was ready before the President was allowed to emerge from the Foreign Office.

Beneath the surface, of course, all was not sweetness and harmony. Ralph Pulitzer, publisher of the *New York World*, wrote from Paris that

THE ALLIED GOVERNMENTS ARE SUFFERING ALL THE VICISSITUDES OF VIC- TORY. THE SOLIDARITY OF A COMMON DANGER HAS DEPARTED. THE JOINT INSTINCT OF SELF-PRESERVATION HAS GIVEN PLACE TO CONFLICTING AIMS OF SELF-AGGRANDIZEMENT. THE VANITIES, CUPIDITIES, AND PUGNACITIES WHICH MASQUERADE AS NATIONAL ASPIRATIONS ARE SEETHING BENEATH THE SERENITY OF THE QUAI D'ORSAY. IF THE PEACE CONFERENCE IS

ALLOWED TO REMAIN A CONFERENCE BETWEEN GOVERNMENTS INSTEAD OF
BETWEEN PEOPLES IT IS APT TO DEGENERATE INTO A SATURNALIA OF
STATESMANSHIP WHICH WILL CROWN A WAR TO END WAR WITH A PEACE
TO END PEACE.

To Oswald Garrison Villard, who had observed the start of the first day's
proceedings and then left in disgust, the whole scene was "artificial and
even repellent":

WHENEVER I LOOKED INTO THE CONFERENCE ROOM I COULD ONLY SEE
THAT OF ALL THE MILLIONS OF MOTHERS AND WIVES WHO HAD GIVEN OF
THEIR BELOVED THERE WAS NOT ONE PRESENT; NOT ONE OF THE PRIVATE
SOLDIERS WHO HAD BORNE THE BRUNT OF THE FIGHTING AND HAD POURED
FORTH MOST OF THE BLOOD, AND NO SINGLE REPRESENTATIVE OF THE
MASSES WHO HAD PAID THE PRICE OF THE STUPIDITIES, THE FOLLIES, THE
BLUNDERS, AND THE CRIMES OF THE STATESMEN AND THE GENERALS THERE
ASSEMBLED. THE VICTORS, YES, BUT NONE OF THE VICTIMS UNDER THEIR
OWN FLAGS. HOW COULD ANY THINKING MAN EXULT OR SEE IN THIS
GATHERING THE DAWN OF A NEW WORLD AND OF PERPETUAL PEACE?
GREAT TERRITORIES INVOLVING THE LIVES OF MILLIONS OF BLACK MEN
WERE TO BE TURNED OVER TO NEW MASTERS, YET THERE WAS HARDLY A
DARK SKIN VISIBLE. WORST OF ALL, FOR THE FIRST TIME IN MODERN
HISTORY, A GREAT PEACE WAS TO BE WRITTEN WITHOUT A SINGLE REPRE-
SENTATIVE OF THE DEFEATED PEOPLES IN THE COUNCIL CHAMBER.

Only Woodrow Wilson, Villard believed, stood as a barrier to an unstable peace of stupidity and selfishness and revenge, and the editor of the
Nation had no illusions that the President would be able to hold out alone.

Valentine's Day, Part One. Amid all the pompous songs of martial triumph
and homecoming that topped the popularity charts in early 1919, there was
one simpler and more honest record that perhaps best captured the sweet,
heartfelt sentiment of the times: Nora Bayes's rendition of the ever-popular
"My Barney Lies Over the Ocean Just the Way He Lied to Me."

There was no way the Peace Conference would ever complete its work if
every session were held in public, with delegates posturing and reporters
gawking, nor could it make swift progress if representatives of three dozen
nations were permitted to debate and decide every issue. Wilson had
promised "open covenants openly arrived at" in his Fourteen Points, but

the circuslike atmosphere of the opening day's session was not what he had in mind. Instead, the five major powers—France, Britain, Italy, the United States, and Japan (whose delegates kept their sights firmly focused upon their prime objective: the former German economic concessions in northern China)—at once began to hold separate private sessions as the Council of Ten, with the president or prime minister and the foreign secretary from each delegation present. Even this proved too unwieldy, however, and eventually Wilson, Clemenceau, Lloyd George, and Orlando decided to constitute themselves the Council of Four.

Since the members of the Council were quite ignorant of the details of most of the issues upon which they would pass judgment, they called in their expert advisers for information on each day's topic. (The experts soon learned to sit immediately behind their chiefs, prompting them when someone made an absurd statement, and handing them maps and statistics to explain the subject under discussion.) Smaller powers were admitted to the inner sanctums of power only when their vital interests were being considered, and then only to present their case—not to have a voice in the decisions. Wilson usually listened politely and attentively to everyone; Clemenceau was often impatient and prone to make insulting witticisms. "I must say," recorded Nicolson, "that Clemenceau is extremely rude to the small Powers: but then he is extremely rude to the Big Powers also." In the course of a discussion about Czechoslovakia's borders, the Tiger brusquely cut off a speaker who had been waiting half a day for his opportunity to plead his case: "O, we'll appoint a special commission and you can talk to them for a couple of hours. Now we had better have a cup of tea." Once when a Japanese delegate was making a point, Clemenceau leaned to a colleague and said in a stage whisper, *"Qu'est-ce qu'il dit, le petit?"*

Lloyd George also had the distracting habit of carrying on a continuous round of comments in an undertone during presentations to the Council. Charles Seymour found him to be "really the best fun of these conferences; very alert, not knowing much about things in exact terms. . . . He reminds me of a very businesslike bird. He is much shorter and fatter than I had realized." Unabashed in his ignorance of technical details ("Now is it Upper or Lower Silesia we're giving away?" "What! You mean to tell me that the President of the United States cannot declare war? I never heard that before."), Lloyd George had absolutely no shame when it came to evading the obligations of conscience or truth; if he began arguing a case and found that the facts did not support him, he simply shifted to the other side. After one particularly obfuscatory oration, Clemenceau turned in frustration and asked aloud, "But is he *for* or is he *against?*" Orlando usually had little to say unless the subject involved Italy's boundaries.

Clemenceau and Lloyd George were wiser and wilier by decades of experience in what Lloyd George called the "tangled and thorny jungle" of Old World diplomacy—"for ages the favourite hunting ground of beasts of prey and poisonous reptiles springing and creeping on their victims"—and some observers feared that in these secret conferences, without the presence of the press to publicize their cynical dealings, they would devour Wilson as an innocent lamb among the wolves. "That settles it," declared the progressive Kansas newspaperman William Allen White when he learned that the conference's business would be done behind closed doors. "That finishes the conference and Wilson. Lloyd George and Clemenceau will now take him upstairs into a private bedroom and fool him to death." (According to Villard, White actually used a much less elegant word than "fool.")

But White was wrong. At the very least, Wilson held his own in the daily give-and-take with his European counterparts. If Wilson failed to achieve his goals, the problem lay not in the President's alleged naïveté or ignorance, but in the utter impossibility of strictly applying his moral sentiments to the intricately intertwined issues which the conference had to decide. In Lloyd George's words, Wilson eventually discovered "a truth which has so often baffled all of us in life: that our greatest difficulties come not so much from deciding whether we should follow the dictates of a clear principle or not, but in choosing the particular principle which is most applicable to the facts or in ascertaining accurately the particular facts upon which the principle is to be shaped. . . . He found that he could not measure accurately with his rigid yard-stick timber gnarled and twisted by the storms of centuries." It was all very well to speak of "self-determination," but how did one determine whether a village along the Adriatic coast wished to be part of Italy or Yugoslavia? Once the conference gave its blessing to the existence of a state, did it have an obligation to ensure the economic viability of that nation, even if it meant handing over territory whose people wished to be part of another country? Should Poland be given a German city to provide the Poles with an outlet to the sea? Did France deserve Germany's coal-rich Saar Valley as compensation for the brutal destruction of French coal mines by the German army during the war? Should Italy be permitted to annex non-Italian territories to provide her with defensible frontiers? Would Wilson allow the British Empire to swallow up former German colonies in return for Lloyd George's support of other Wilsonian goals? Clemenceau's earlier comment now appeared prophetic: "God gave us the Ten Commandments and we broke them. Wilson gives us the Fourteen Points. We shall see."

Remarkably, considering their vanities and their philosophical differences, the Big Three got along rather well on a personal level—for the moment, anyway. Tempers flared occasionally, of course; at one meeting when Clemenceau repeatedly accused Lloyd George of misstating the facts, the Welshman seized him by the collar and an onlooker heard muttered talk about a duel. And Clemenceau delighted in offering bon mots to puncture Wilson's pious pretensions. "Lloyd George believes himself to be Napoleon," he told a friend, "but President Wilson believes himself to be Jesus Christ." Lloyd George seems to have enjoyed watching his two colleagues circle each other warily: "Clemenceau followed [Wilson's] movements like an old watchdog keeping an eye on a strange and unwelcome dog who has visited the farmyard and of whose intentions he is more than doubtful."

6

"Behold, the noise of the bruit is come,

and a great commotion

out of the north country . . ."

Influenza was ravaging the island paradise of Tahiti. The plague had come to Tahiti in one of the white man's steamships several months earlier, and by mid-December more than one-seventh of the native population lay dead. The island's governor had urgently requested assistance from his superiors in France; the French government passed the message along to the U.S. State Department; the State Department turned the appeals over to the American Red Cross, which decided that nothing could be done. It would take a supply ship six weeks to reach Tahiti from San Francisco, and besides, no ships would be heading that way for another two months, and by that time the epidemic probably would have run its course. But still the dying continued on the enchanted island. The two doctors on Tahiti, one of whom was the American consul, had long ago exhausted their medical supplies. Nearly 20 percent of the native population had perished by late January. The older generation was almost completely wiped out. The island was a charnel house. No easy laughter, no songs in the valleys. On a volcanic ridge burned great funeral pyres upon which the bodies were thrown every night and every day.

Russia was a Red plague, the menacing shadow that doggedly followed the diplomats and experts in Paris no matter how they strove to ignore it. The riddle, the sphinx, the enigma. Germany was no such problem; Germany was a known quantity, a power-hungry nation with conventional (albeit extraordinarily ambitious) territorial and economic goals, a rogue tiger that simply needed to have its claws drawn. But Russia and the Bolshevist plague—how did one deal with the largest country in the world when it was almost totally disorganized and infected with a bacillus that threatened the stability of every other civilized state? "The Bolshevik danger was very great at the present moment," warned Clemenceau in a council meeting on January 21 in Pichon's office. "Bolshevism was spreading. It had invaded the Baltic Provinces and Poland, and that very morning they had received very bad news regarding its spread to Budapest and Vienna. . . . If Bolshevism, after spreading in Germany, were to traverse Austria and Hungary and so reach Italy, Europe would be faced with a very great danger. Therefore, something must be done against Bolshevism."

Something must be done, but what? Sir James Headlam-Morley, the British Foreign Office historian and a member of the British delegation in Paris, noted in his diary that whenever Wilson, Clemenceau, and Lloyd George sat down to discuss the peace settlement, "everything inevitably leads up to Russia. Then there is a discursive discussion; it is agreed that the point at issue cannot be determined until the general policy towards Russia has been settled; having agreed on this, instead of settling it, they pass on to some other subject."

Wilson and Lloyd George were convinced that military intervention was no longer a viable policy. "One of the things that was clear in the Russian situation," Wilson argued, "was that by opposing Bolshevism with arms they were in reality serving the cause of Bolshevism. The Allies were making it possible for Bolsheviks to argue that Imperialistic and Capitalistic Governments were endeavoring to exploit the country and to give the land back to the landlords, and so bring about a reaction." When Baron Sonnino obdurately insisted that additional Allied troops be sent to aid the White Russian forces, Lloyd George countered by asking what contributions America, France, and Italy might be willing to make in terms of fighting men. Wilson, Clemenceau, and Orlando all agreed. None.

Every evening Lenin drove out to the children's school in the woods of Sokolniki, a suburb of Moscow, to visit his wife, Krupskaya. She had been sent out of the city in hopes that rest and fresh air might restore her deteriorating health, and the cure appeared to be working. The snow banked high along the streets muffled the sound of the car as Lenin's chauffeur neared Sokolniki in the Sunday twilight. Lenin sat in the backseat with his sister and a bodyguard.

They heard a shout: "Stop!" The chauffeur stepped on the gas and swerved to avoid the man who had jumped in front of the car.

Ahead, Lenin saw that a half-dozen sailors armed with revolvers were standing in the middle of the road; someone shouted, "Halt! Stop the car!" Lenin ordered the driver to comply. One of the bandits grabbed Lenin's arm and pulled him out of the car. The other passengers followed. Two guns were pointed at Lenin's head. The chauffeur, with his pistol cocked, decided that Lenin probably would be killed in a shoot-out, and so he, too, left the car peacefully. Not recognizing the man they had stopped, the thugs stole Lenin's wallet, overcoat, portfolio, watch, and the Browning automatic pistol he carried.

"Don't you know who this is?" cried his sister, Maria Ulyanova. "He is Lenin! Where are your warrants?"

"We don't need papers," came the brusque reply. "We have a right to do this."

They took the car and left Lenin stranded by the side of the road. When he and his comrades reached the Sokolniki Soviet building, the guard at first refused to admit Lenin without seeing his identity card (which had been in the stolen wallet). Finally they were allowed to telephone the Kremlin for a car to take them to Krupskaya's school. Lenin joined the children in the festivities around the fir tree, but the presents he had brought them were lost with the car.

He decreed that the culprits would be severely punished, but Cheka guards found the abandoned automobile later that evening. Beside it, there was bloody snow beneath a policeman and a Red Army soldier who had been shot to death. No one ever found the bandits.

"Forget your fireplaces; the fires have gone out," were the words to the latest song in Moscow. On trains bound for no one knew where, hundreds of thousands of refugees lived in boxcars and moved from freightyard to freightyard. Baggage racks were highly prized sleeping places. Other trains were encrusted with human beings clinging to the outsides, hanging on to the engines, fenders, or couplings. No one knew how they survived the cold; and perhaps many did not. Others slept on the floors of railroad stations. Typhus slaughtered thousands every month; when officials cleared the peasants out of the Central Railway Station in Moscow to clean it, they found the bodies of five typhus victims that had been lying for days among the crowd. There was no medicine and little soap or even boiling water with which to combat the disease, owing to the lack of fuel. Malnutrition made Muscovites easy targets, and in Petrograd it was worse. Authorities reportedly ordered those with terminal cases to be killed in an effort to stem the spread of disease.

Chaos and the cold ruled everywhere, with greater power than the Czar had ever enjoyed or the Bolsheviks had yet attained. The elite of the old regime stood on street corners and sold their clothes to buy food. Snow drifts cut off all shipments of flour to Moscow at the end of January. Women journeyed three hundred miles to the frontier to purchase sugar;

there were stocks of food throughout Russia, but the total disorganization of transport kept it from the starving. The supply of electricity to factories was cut off to conserve fuel. People were worn out, cheerless, and hopeless. Soldiers returning from prisoner-of-war camps in the west trudged through the snow with feet bound in rags because they had no boots, or only rough shoes made from hollowed-out logs. "Our chief characteristic is that we are tired," a Russian writer confided to a friend in the West, "tired of looting, tired of killing, tired of fighting and tired of wandering from pillar to post." The mother superior of a convent outside of Moscow told her story to an American correspondent:

"One day, one of my nuns came to me and said the Bolsheviki were downstairs, eating the dinner we had prepared for the poor, and wanted to arrest me. I put on my robe and walked down calmly into the big dining-room. Why, some of those Bolsheviki were local boys whom I had known as children. I walked up to them and said: 'Here I am: arrest me.' But they were ashamed, and said it was all a mistake, and went away. But the next morning they took the son of a priest and shot him. I don't know why."

To the east, where the Don River flowed through central Russia, the civil war continued through the "terrifying still, short days. . . . The villages lay like the untrodden, virgin steppe," wrote the novelist Mikhail Sholokov.

IT WAS AS THOUGH ALL THE DONSIDE DISTRICTS HAD DIED, AS THOUGH A PESTILENCE HAD LAID WASTE THE DISTRICT SETTLEMENTS. AND IT WAS AS THOUGH CLOUDS HAD COVERED ALL THE DON REGION WITH THEIR BLACK, OPAQUE WINGS, SPREADING SILENTLY AND TERRIBLY, UNTIL A WIND SHOULD SEND THE POPLARS BENDING TO THE EARTH, A DRY, CRASHING PEAL OF THUNDER SHOULD BURST AND MARCH TO CRUSH AND SHATTER THE WHITE FOREST BEYOND THE DON, TO SEND THE SAVAGE STONES LEAPING FROM THE CHALKY HILLS, AND ROAR WITH THE DESTRUCTIVE VOICE OF THUNDER. . . .

IN THE EVENING THE RED-HOT SHIELD OF THE MOON AROSE FROM BE-YOND THE ROOTS OF THE NAKED FOREST. IT MISTILY SOWED THE BLOODY SEEDS OF WAR AND INCENDIARY FIRE OVER THE SILENT VILLAGES. AND IN ITS MISERABLE, FADED LIGHT AN INARTICULATE ALARM WAS BORN IN THE HEARTS OF MEN. THE ANIMALS FIDGETED ANXIOUSLY; THE HORSES AND BULLOCKS COULD NOT SLEEP AND WANDERED ABOUT THE YARDS UNTIL DAWN. THE DOGS HOWLED BALEFULLY, AND THE COCKS BEGAN TO CROW ONE AGAINST ANOTHER LONG BEFORE MIDNIGHT. THEIR STIRRUPS AND

WEAPONS CLATTERING, AN INVISIBLE MOUNTED ARMY MIGHT HAVE BEEN
MARCHING DOWN THE LEFT BANK OF THE DON, THROUGH THE DARK
FOREST AND THE GREY MIST.

W. D. Childs, the longtime chief representative of the Western Union
Telegraph Company in Russia, was dead of starvation in Petrograd.

Lloyd George was appalled. "What happened in the ruthless struggle
between Red and White in Siberia, in Southern Russia and in the Ukraine,
is too ghastly to perpetuate in the memory of man. It is an agony to dwell
upon the details of horror enacted in these orgies of hate. Hell was let loose
and made the most of its time."

But Lloyd George's political life had been one long paean to the spirit
of compromise. Perhaps, he thought optimistically, if the Peace Conference invited the Bolsheviks and the White Russian leaders to sit down and
reason together, some form of settlement might emerge. Lloyd George
originally suggested a meeting in Paris, but Clemenceau refused to have
any murderous Bolshevik officials in *his* city. Wilson then recommended
that the Russian factions meet elsewhere, on neutral ground. The site
finally chosen was Prinkipo, the largest island in a chain known as the
Princes Islands, in the Sea of Marmara, near Constantinople. Centuries
ago, the islands had been a place of exile for members of the Byzantine
nobility who had fallen into disfavor. Now they sheltered an enormous
number of dogs recently exiled from Turkey when the government had
decided to reduce the mainland's canine population.

Wilson selected William Allen White as one of the two American
delegates to the Prinkipo Conference. White, who admitted that he was
"abysmally ignorant" of the issues at stake, and could speak no languages
except "United States and Red Cross restaurant French," was willing at
least to decide for himself whether the Bolsheviks were as black as they
were painted. "If the Bolsheviki had got something worthwhile to develop
in the form of government," he declared, "they ought to have the opportunity to do so without interference. If they have not got anything they'll
go on the rocks soon enough." That attitude made White probably one of
the most open-minded men in Paris in the late winter of 1919.

Jules Vedrines had been unable to sleep the previous night. He feared not
death, but the Paris police. In fact, when the thick morning fog refused to
lift, he had a fleeting notion that the authorities had gotten wind of his
scheme and were deliberately manufacturing an artificial smokescreen to
keep him on the ground. The fog began to disappear shortly after noon,

however, and at 12:42 Vedrines took off from the aerodome at Issy.

The famous French ace's wartime exploits, which included downing German planes and landing Allied secret agents behind enemy lines, had won him the Military Medal and War Cross with numerous stars. Before the war, Vedrines had won numerous marathon air races, including the Circuit of Europe, and had flown from Paris to Madrid in twelve hours— fighting with eagles, so it was said, when crossing the Pyrenees. He was a fearless but unscientific pilot, barely able to read a map. Now he was out of uniform, dressed in a civilian knickerbocker suit with helmet and goggles, flying a small, prewar Caudron III biplane with an antiquated eighty-horsepower revolving Rhone engine. Suddenly there was a fog bank straight ahead, encircling the Eiffel Tower. Vedrines prayed. He ran out of the fog over the Seine.

Coming in low over the Louvre and the boulevards and the housetops along the Rue Scribe, the plane terrified spectators who had been enjoying their quiet Sunday noon meal on the terraces of nearby cafés. Pulling up to avoid a huge sign above the houses, then shutting off his engine and plunging down again, Vedrines flew only a few feet above the balustrade surrounding his target. At 12:45, three minutes after takeoff, Jules Vedrines landed his plane upon the rooftop of a vast dry-goods store known as the Galeries Lafayette in the ninth *arrondissement*, one of the busiest commercial sections of Paris. Since the roof was only thirty yards long and just a few feet wider than the wingspan of the aircraft, and since it was considerably hemmed in by advertising signs, the effect of Vedrines's feat was much like dropping the plane into a hole. The plane was damaged, but Vedrines was unharmed.

Having won a 25,000-franc prize for being the first airman to land on a roof in the city, Vedrines immediately announced his plans to fly from Paris to Rome as soon as weather permitted, and then to fly around the world, going eastward. He estimated it would take him three to four months to complete a tour of the globe, but he argued that "it is perfectly feasible, given the nerve and sufficient backing." Of course the French government, Vedrines scoffed, would never finance the trip. "Why, don't you know they'll take sixteen francs off me as it is for breaking regulations by landing in the city precincts?"

Sunday in Paris. Airplanes landing on roofs; choirs singing in Notre Dame and St-Etienne; slow, wandering walks through the narrow streets of the old city; a vermouth cassis at the Café du Panthéon; *La Bohème* at the Opéra Comique.

Sunday in Berlin. Elections for the National Assembly that would meet in February and draft a constitution for the new German Republic; city walls plastered with election posters, the streets strewn with political leaflets; gray government automobiles flitting nervously between the Chancellery and the Foreign Office; government troops with weapons prominently displayed massed around the polling places to prevent Spartacists from disturbing the elections. But the radicals were too intimidated—for the moment—to cause any trouble. Voting proceeded without excitement or enthusiasm. It was the first German national election in which women were eligible to vote, and whole families, including small children, cooks, old women, and nurses, stood patiently in line and quietly made their choices. "As undramatic as any natural occurrence," reported Harry Kessler, "like a rainy day in the country."

Underground, discontent continued to grow. At the same time, the army consolidated its thinly veiled grasp upon power. "Berlin is lucky to be spared the proletarian dictatorship," wrote the correspondent of *The Times*, whose reports from Berlin showed no love of Spartacism. "We have, however, in its place a military dictatorship, worse than the population has ever known before." One prominent Berliner who had supported the suppression of the Spartacist revolt a week earlier complained to the Berlin Soldiers' Council that the Freikorps soldiers "have been raging like Huns in Berlin, and the destruction they wantonly worked is worse even than anything the German armies performed in Belgium or France. Nobody can accept responsibility for the armed troops who now terrorize Berlin."

Heavily armed troops patrolled the city streets unceasingly. Field guns remained in strategic positions in public squares. At certain checkpoints everyone had to submit to a close search; women, who had been known to carry rounds of cartridges under their cloaks, were not exempt. The election turned out to be a solid victory for Ebert's Social Democrats and other centrist parties, but it remained an open question whether Ebert could extricate himself and his colleagues—lurching from one crisis to the next, able to halt the threatened collapse only at the point of a bayonet—from the meshes of the reviving German military machine.

Everywhere the nation seemed to be going on strike. Miners throughout Germany's coalfields struck to protest the killing of Liebknecht and Luxemburg by government troops. As Ebert, Philipp Scheidemann, and the rest of the big guns of the government gathered at the Chancellor's Palace late on the afternoon of January 22 to devise a coherent plan to prevent further disorders, they were suddenly plunged into total darkness. Fourteen hundred municipal electrical workers wanting higher wages had walked off their jobs without warning. Berlin came to a standstill. Telephones were out, tramcars stopped dead in the middle of the streets; the cavernous government office buildings stood deserted and immobilized, hotels and theaters and restaurants were all black except for a few candles here and there (nimble diners fled in the darkness before their bills were presented). Panic pressed in among the commuters heading home on the subways. In the overcrowded hospitals, surgeons were able to keep their patients alive only because they had learned to deal with unexpected disasters during four bloody years of war. It was all much more effective in dislocating the life of the city than the Spartacist violence.

Three days later, the funeral procession for Karl Liebknecht began at noon. The government had instructed its troops to cordon off the entire center of the city, and masses of soldiers, machine guns, and artillery were deployed at strategic points to keep the proletariat marchers from entering the more prosperous sections of Berlin. To prevent people from coming in from the suburbs to take part in the ceremony, subway trains passed six successive downtown stations. The streets were completely devoid of onlookers when the procession made its way toward the dreary eastern sector of the city. Nine black wagons carried thirty-three black coffins of victims of the recent uprising. Nearly forty thousand people joined in the procession. Liebknecht's coffin was covered with a fiery red ribbon, the wagon driven by a coachman in an old faded gray field uniform. It took three hours to reach the Friedrichsfelde cemetery, where one vast common grave had been prepared for all the dead Spartacists. Liebknecht's body was interred first, as his wife and two sons looked on. After a few words, the other bodies followed, and the gathering then quietly dispersed.

On the occasion of the Kaiser's sixtieth birthday on January 27, Amerongen Castle was buried under a deluge of flowers. (Each shipment was first carefully checked for hidden explosives by a steward.) Two entire rooms in the Kaiser's apartment were filled with bouquets. Flowers from German schoolgirls, expressions of sympathy from some of his bolder former subjects, whispers of allegiance from others.

"For centuries," wrote one conservative German newspaper on that auspicious occasion, "the German people dreamed of a secret Kaiser arising some day to unite all the German tribes. Now we live in a Socialist republic, but the old German colors, black, white and red, are still dear to us. We again dream of that secret Kaiser. . . . We meet the present sham government and sham power with our belief in Kaiserism and empire, and wait for the day when the German nation will be restored to it."

All the prisoners had gone from the camp in the small town by the

Austrian border, and so Adolf Hitler returned to the barracks in Munich and waited for his new orders.

"I am going to ask for a figure in my contract for next season which may knock Mr. Frazee silly, but nevertheless I think I am deserving of everything I ask." Babe Ruth, the reigning American League home-run champion and star left-handed pitcher who had led the Boston Red Sox to the World Series in 1918, obviously was not going to come cheap for the 1919 campaign. On the other hand, Harry Frazee, owner of the Red Sox (and a Broadway impresario with an impressive string of flops), claimed that he was not going to give away the store just to sign the Babe. "I've had actors just like Babe," Frazee bravely told reporters. "They'll swear they are through with the show, that they will leave it flat, but it would take a squad of marines to keep them out of the theater and off the stage." Perhaps. But when Ruth visited Frazee's office on January 21, he told the owner what it would take to sign him (namely, the nearly unheard-of sum of $15,000), and turned around and left without discussing the matter further.

Ruth was the most famous reluctant star that winter, but he had plenty of company. The war had played havoc with the 1918 season, with many players drafted into the service, and others, like Shoeless Joe Jackson (whom Ruth described as "the most natural and graceful hitter who ever lived"), leaving the game temporarily to work for the defense effort in shipyards or munitions plants. The owners had unilaterally decided to shorten the 1918 season, releasing their players after 140 games and refusing to pay them for the rest of the year (September 2 to October 13) as stipulated in their contracts. A number of ballplayers—including the fiery Tyrus Raymond Cobb, who reportedly was asking for $20,000 for the 1919 season—got the revolutionary idea that their releases made them free agents, able to bargain with any club they wished. The owners, of course, refused to accept such logic; besides, they had already reached an informal understanding that each club would respect every other team's players and not bid for their services.

But that wasn't all. At their meeting in mid-January, the National League owners decided to try to roll back what they considered to be the outrageous salaries of prewar days by establishing a salary cap for the eight teams in the senior circuit. By a vote of 6 to 2, the owners instituted a salary limit of $11,000 per team per month, a figure that would have slashed some players' salaries severely. (Under this radical and unprecedented plan, the average player's monthly salary would have been $523.) When the American League failed to follow suit, the National League owners soon publicly rescinded their plan, but suspicions lingered among major-leaguers that some form of a season-long salary cap remained in force behind the scenes in both leagues. In further austerity moves, baseball's magnates decided to continue with a 140-game schedule in 1919, and to limit rosters to twenty-one men.

Baseball had a much more serious problem brewing, however. On January 30, National League president John Heydler held a hearing on charges that Hal Chase, the Cincinnati Reds' first baseman, had violated Section 40 of the League Constitution: "Any person who shall be proven guilty of offering, agreeing, conspiring or attempting to cause any game of ball to result otherwise than on its merits under the playing rules, shall be forever disqualified by the President of the league from acting as umpire, manager or player, or in any other capacity in any game of ball participated in by a league club."

There had been rumors over the past year that Chase had been involved in unsavory betting schemes on major-league games. Cincinnati's manager, Christy Mathewson, believed the rumors had enough substance that he suspended Chase indefinitely in August 1918. Never missing a chance to save a bit of extra money, the club cut off his salary. Chase had always been one of the freer spirits in the game, refusing to take baseball or anything else very seriously, causing dissension on nearly every team he joined. One of his former managers said Chase had "a corkscrew mind." If he had not always been an excellent hitter, and probably the finest fielding first baseman in baseball, he would have been long gone.

It was the first case since the early days of the professional game that linked a major-league player to gambling. The hearing went on for more than five hours. On February 5, Heydler cleared Chase of the charges (even though he was almost certainly guilty), on the grounds that all of the evidence against him was more or less unsubstantiated hearsay and probably the result of careless talk by Chase and others. Nevertheless, Heydler issued a stern warning: "Any player who, during my tenure as President of the National League, is shown to have any interest in a wager on any games played in the league . . . will be promptly expelled from the National League. Betting by players will not be tolerated."

Despite the ruling, Cincinnati had had enough of Chase's flaky behavior, and traded him to the New York Giants, where his ability to work the hit-and-run consistently made him a most valuable part of manager John McGraw's offensive arsenal. The Redlegs had now cleared out most of the old cliques that had caused so much discord on the club in the past, and with their new manager, Pat Moran, were ready to start the 1919 season with far greater team harmony.

7

"Though thou clothest thyself with crimson,

though thou deckest thee

with ornaments of gold . . ."

At La Scala, where Wilson had enjoyed the adoration of the Milanese crowd in the first week of the new year, Benito Mussolini planned his own raucous demonstration. On a cold night when a thick fog shaded reality and aroused the atavistic aggressive impulses of the vicious and psychotic, a pack of *arditi* stood in the center of the square, by the statue of Leonardo da Vinci. These were the violent commandos of the Italian army ("a bomb in each hand and a knife between the teeth"), now cast aside by the politicians, forced to search for a purpose in peacetime and an outlet for the murderous emotions bred into them by their country. Carrying black flags with a skull and crossbones, wearing daggers in their belts, and bearing on their chests medals and more medals for killing—these were men who took no prisoners.

These now were Mussolini's latest love. Inside the hall, the anti-imperialist politician Leonida Bissolati was to speak in favor of the League of Nations. Mussolini and the arditi marched arrogantly into La Scala with the sole purpose of disrupting the meeting. Even before Bissolati came on stage, the hall was full of shouted insults and threatening gestures. Mussolini, with his shaved, heavy head, standing in a box surrounded by bodyguards, watched the fever rise as Bissolati began to speak of the bitterly contested territorial question. An Italian journalist recorded the chaos:

> FOR A FEW MINUTES BISSOLATI WAS ALLOWED TO GO ON, SEEMINGLY UNDISTURBED BY THE CONFUSED MURMUR OF THE HALL. THEN AT A GIVEN MOMENT, AS IF AN INVISIBLE BATON HAD GIVEN THE SIGN, THE INFERNAL SYMPHONY BEGAN. SQUEAKS, SHRIEKS, WHISTLES, GRUMBLES, NEARLY HUMAN, AND ALL THE THINKABLE COUNTERFEITS OF THE WILD PACK'S HOWLING, MADE UP THE BULK OF THE SOUND WAVE. . . .

Now suddenly Bissolati recognized Mussolini in the chorus: that unmistakable voice, disheartiningly wooden, peremptorily insistent, like the clacking of castanets.

He turned his head to the friends who were nearest to him and said in a low voice: *"Quell'uomo, no!"*—"I will not fight with that man!"

Mussolini attempted to follow the demonstration with a speech of his own, but was howled down by shouts that he had sold out to the big industrialists.

A week later, Mussolini and the absurdly romantic poet and half-blind ace army pilot Gabriele D'Annunzio endorsed a pro-imperialist counter-rally at La Scala. Writing in Mussolini's *Popolo d'Italia*, D'Annunzio outlined his vision of Italy's future: "And what peace will in the end be imposed on us, poor little ones of Christ? A Gallic peace? A British peace? A star-spangled peace? Then, no! Enough. Victorious Italy—the most victorious of all the nations—victorious over herself and over the enemy—will have on the Alps and over her sea the Pax Romana, the sole peace that is fitting."

Nevertheless, Italy continued to suffer from inflation, strikes, hunger, the consolidation of economic control by huge industrial concerns, and unemployment (most of all among the forgotten and bitter demobilized soldiers). All this fed Mussolini's appetite for power, for he sided with every discontented man, no matter the cause. Over it all he sounded his love for an Italy that had never existed except in his mind, an Italy now seemingly demoralized and betrayed by Socialists, German spies, and Russian agitators, who Mussolini believed had thrown the nation "into an awful spiritual crisis." He accused President Wilson, "who could not comprehend Italian life or history," of unconsciously aiding these traitors with his talk of a peace without victory. As Mussolini lay awake in silent meditation at night, he came to realize that "we had no dam to stop this general decay of faith, this renunciation of the interests and destiny of a victorious nation." And so he would take up arms against the returning beast of decadence.

Valentine's Day, Part Two. Los Angeles was no stranger to bizarre murder mysteries, but this was one of the best. The basic facts of the matter were undisputed: Frank Gibbons had been a Pullman conductor who had suffered from an advanced case of tuberculosis. His wife, Gertrude (who was technically a bigamist, never having obtained a divorce from her first husband), admitted that she had purchased a quantity of potassium cyanide from a drugstore near their home at 220 South Bonnie Brae Avenue with the intention of giving it to Gibbons. Mrs. Gibbons did, in fact, provide her husband with cyanide capsules. On December 15, 1918, Frank Gibbons died.

When police arrested Gertrude Gibbons two days later, she admitted everything. Her explanation was that her husband had been despondent over his declining health, that he had agreed to the scheme, and that he had accepted the cyanide from her with a full understanding of what it was.

But then prosecutors—and the defense—were astonished to learn that the results of the postmortem were inconclusive. Two prominent toxicologists found traces of cyanide in Gibbons's body, but a number of other medical experts were unable to detect any trace of the poison, and the coroner and autopsy surgeon both were prepared to testify that Gibbons had died of a pulmonary hemorrhage. Not surprisingly, Mrs. Gibbons's attitude brightened considerably upon hearing the news. The county's case against her had seemed airtight and, according to its experts, still was; but now the defense could argue persuasively that there had been no murder at all. "Those familiar with the case," reported the *Los Angeles Times*, "say that Mrs. Gibbons herself does not know the truth any more than anyone else. She firmly believed that Gibbons died from the cyanide she gave him, and was the most surprised person of all when Professor Maas [of the University of Southern California] reported no cyanide present in the viscera."

On January 16, the Los Angeles County grand jury refused to indict Mrs. Gibbons, and the following day she was released from jail. During the thirty days of her incarceration, Gertrude had studied philosophy, and now decided that she would change her name and embark upon a teaching career. "I want to teach people to be happy. I have enough money to last me for a while, then I shall take up this work, and try to be forgotten by going somewhere where no one knows me." There were no reports that she planned to return to her first husband, who presumably remained in good health.

The American delegation to the Peace Conference was housed at the Hôtel Crillon; everything seemed comfortable enough, although it was a bit difficult adjusting to the idiosyncracies of Gallic technology. Charles Seymour reported that he had

AN AWFUL TIME WITH THE FRENCH ELEVATOR, GOING UP; I AM ALWAYS SCARED STIFF WHEN THEY START ONE OFF ALONE, AND KEPT FIGURING WHAT I SHOULD DO IF IT DIDN'T STOP. THEN IF YOU PLEASE IT *DIDN'T* STOP

WHEN IT SHOULD; I SAW MYSELF BEING CRUSHED AGAINST THE ROOF, AND
HASTILY PUSHED ALL THE BUTTONS IN SIGHT; THE RESULT WAS A SUDDEN
STOP BETWEEN FLOORS. I PUSHED ANOTHER BUTTON AND DROPPED
TWENTY FEET; THEN ON TRYING ANOTHER I SOARED WAY OVER MY FLOOR
AND WITHIN TWO FEET OF THE ROOF. FINALLY I GOT EXPERT AND WITH
TREMBLING KNEES EMERGED ONTO TERRA FIRMA.

The khaki uniforms of Kansas farmboys, New York streetcar conductors, and Chicago department store clerks gave a touch of reality to the
theatrical decorations of the Crillon: immense mirrors in the halls, pink
brocaded silk on the walls, gold-leaf molding, white enameled woodwork.
Every morning at ten-thirty during the early weeks of the conference,
reporters filed into the hotel's antechamber to receive a briefing from
Secretary of State Lansing, General Bliss, and Henry White. But the
briefings gave no important news, for Lansing, Bliss, and White had no
substantive information to give. Wilson had frozen them out, preferring
to keep all negotiations in his own hands. (White and Bliss were, however,
invited to accompany the President to the opera for a performance of
Castor and Pollux.)

No matter; there were better things to do than listen to Lansing equivo-
cate and evade questions. Judging from their journals, the Americans who
spent the winter of 1919 in Paris were preoccupied with sex and food as
well as peace. There seemed to be at least as many prostitutes as delegates
in the city: Frenchwomen who had lost their husbands and lovers (over a
million and a half Frenchmen had died in the war, and nearly two million
more were mutilated or tubercular); middle-class French girls who no
longer had a job when the defense factories shut down, and had not been
trained for any sort of career. "Some of the hotels were open houses of
assignation," Oswald Villard clucked disapprovingly. Nor were all of the
whores French. One Canadian Red Cross nurse repeatedly lost her way in
the Hôtel Continental and found herself in the room of a strange man by
mistake nearly every day. "So sorry," she murmured sweetly, and then sat
down on the bed and refused to leave. An American woman journalist
reportedly "said no to nobody in uniform in Paris." American army authorities, recognizing their helplessness in the circumstances, refused to
enforce military regulations against such conduct. Villard once found
himself in a train compartment, sitting opposite two young American
officers in company with "two of the worst-looking prostitutes imaginable.
Their tawdry finery was filthy—as if they had literally lain in the gutter.
... Arrived in Paris the officers showed their leaves, bundled the women
into a taxi, and disappeared."

Getting into the spirit of things, French officials rented a gorgeously vulgar palace, the Maison Dufayel, where they entertained American press representatives with dinners and receptions. The owner of the mansion had been obsessed with the female form; one saw sculptures and paintings of naked women everywhere: bending over doorways and windows, spreading over fireplaces, standing on the posts to greet visitors at the top and bottom of every staircase. "It was a forest of obtrusive nudity," noted William Allen White, "and it became known to the American press delegation as 'The House of a Thousand Teats.' " When Balfour lunched at the mansion, he was seen to gaze with amiable surprise at the figures on the ceiling.

While waiting—and waiting—for something newsworthy to happen, or for the Big Three to provide details of what was going on behind the scenes, reporters made the rounds of the best restaurants of Paris, eating (almost) everything French cuisine had to offer: "I balked at snails but Bill got them down without a quiver." Food prices were high, of course, which wrought a severe hardship on the working population of Paris, but the Americans always seemed to have enough cash to get by handsomely. (Charles Seymour reported that the clothes in Paris cost about twice as much as they did in the States, "but they look better.")

Occasionally one of the other nations would host a party as a public-relations gesture, to drum up support for their particular diplomatic objectives. The most memorable affair was an elaborate dinner given by the Chinese for the foreign press, a night that lived long in the gustatory memories of those who attended. It began at eight o'clock. After every course was completed, the correspondents kept expecting the Chinese to announce the presumed purpose of the meeting, to explain their side of their struggle with Japan over control of Shantung Province. A half-dozen most gracious Chinese gentlemen who spoke perfect English chatted pleasantly with the reporters, but were far too polite to speak directly of the issues pending in the conference. Food was still being served as midnight came and went; wanting to repay their hosts' generosity, the reporters lingered for a while after the meal was over in the early-morning hours, but eventually they began to make their apologies and slip away. William Allen White staggered home, sober but very full, along about the crack of dawn: "I was the last American to leave, and I never learned—and no one ever learned—the purpose of that dinner. The Chinese were just that polite. Moreover, I had to be on hand at noon the next day to a most formal and gorgeous luncheon given by the Mexicans. . . ."

* * *

It was a cold, wet winter in Paris, with more snow than expected. Within the city, away from the glitter, hundreds of children were dying for lack of milk. "The shortage of milk is so great," reported a prominent Paris physician, "that the hospitals are ordered to prescribe for economical, not medical reasons a water and vegetable soup diet. We have been compelled to diminish the milk rations of infants from one to two years old, with the result that these children diminish in weight."

For those who were not dazzled by the artificial splendor of the conference, it appeared merely as a gathering of elderly gentlemen in bowler hats very much afraid of catching cold, traveling to and from the Quai d'Orsay in closed limousines ("as rarely seen on foot as Roman cardinals") to avoid being soaked to the skin. They may have been the destroyers of thrones and the creators of a new heaven and earth, or they may have been old men playing at a formerly familiar game that had unaccountably become a riddle. Dull gray skies, gray wet streets, and the gray Seine rising once again.

Outside the city, American doughboys shivered through January and February in the small towns of France and western Germany. Captain Truman and his two lieutenants shared a pair of rooms: "One of them has a fireplace in it like old man Grimm tells about in his fairy tales. You build a fire in the center and sit inside the fireplace to keep warm. Out in the room it's about freezing all the time. The old lady we stay with is very good to us, cooking *pommes de terre frites,* or French fried potatoes, and stewed Belgian hare. She's very careful that we don't burn our candles two at a time. They are our own but are so expensive in France that she doesn't like to see them wasted. All French women are thrifty."

Again and again, American soldiers voiced their preference for the clean, neat towns of western Germany over the dirty, disorderly French villages. They joked that you could always tell the most prominent citizen of a French town by the height of the manure pile in front of his house. The fact that the fertilizer was located directly by the front entrance exasperated the doughboys no end. The smell and the flies in hot weather sometimes proved too much; one pile became so offensive than an American officer had his men pour creosote all over it, whereupon the village authorities complained that he had ruined their water supply, which now tasted unmistakably of oil. For their part, French civilians considered Americans to be rude, arrogant, insensitive to French wartime losses, ignorant of French culture, and disgustingly prone to drunkenness.

There were fewer complaints about Germany. Ralph Pulitzer spoke with one American MP stationed in Treves who declared, "Gee! This is a swell town! Some change from France. This reminds me of my home town. It's so clean and orderly. They wash the streets four times a day, and the houses are the same way. They ain't no dirt and they ain't no smells. Give me Germany every time." Army regulations forbade fraternization with the civilians, and some German priests warned the young girls of their parish to beware the American gigolos, but there was still a certain amount of socializing. Certainly the American boys "were guests and not conquerors," noted William Allen White after a tour of the Rhine Valley. "The hosts and the guests were as polite to each other as a basket of chips." Local civilians could even learn a new sport if they watched Captain Hamilton Fish's team from the Fourth Division defeat their 42nd Division rivals, 6–0, in a snowy and muddy field just north of Coblenz. (Fish's team was heavily favored to win the American Third Army football championship.)

Ensconced in his headquarters in a magnificent home high above the road overlooking the Rhine, General Douglas MacArthur held court. Clean-shaven, with a finely chiseled profile, thirty-eight years old and six feet tall, wearing a ragged brown sweater and civilian pants, adored by his staff, worshiped by his men (and still a bachelor), MacArthur impressed White tremendously: "I had never before met so vivid, so captivating, so magnetic a man. He was all that Barrymore and John Drew hoped to be. And how he could talk!" He talked to White of the German people he had met, the common folk, how they had had war crammed down their throats, and were now truly sick of fighting and of everyone who favored war. And the German army, MacArthur argued, had become so demoralized so rapidly that it was not going to pose a threat to anyone for quite a while.

One group of Americans that would *not* be traveling to Paris that winter was the advance guard of the militant suffragette movement. When their watchfire demonstrations in front of the White House failed to draw public opinion or the Senate in the desired direction, representatives of the National Woman's Party embarked upon a tour of the United States on a train they called the Democracy Limited. (Their critics derisively labeled it the Prison Special.) The suffragettes' avowed intention was to wreak their vengeance upon obdurate senators and "to make it clear to the people that the Administration is responsible for the fact that American women are forced to endure imprisonment in their effort to secure the passage of the [suffrage] amendment." *The New York Times* recognized an ominous trend in the use of these tactics that smacked of "limited democracy, a democracy modified by terrorism," where single-interest pressure groups such as the NWP or the Anti-Saloon League—well-stocked with persistence, implacability, and cash—would always succeed in imposing their views upon others.

From coast to coast, from the Great Lakes to the Gulf of Mexico, the suffragettes planned to hold meetings in every large city through which the train passed. Brandishing their motto, "From Prison to People," the highlight of each gathering would be films showing the indignities inflicted upon the Washington demonstrators by police (SUFFS PLANNING HORROR SPECIAL); then, live and in person, the former inmates themselves would appear (MILITANTS TO STAR JAILBIRDS THROUGH COUNTRY), still wan and emaciated from their hunger strikes (PALE PICKETS' EXHIBIT TO GET EVEN WITH WILSON).

To obtain international publicity, the NWP had also planned to send four delegates to Paris to picket the Peace Conference whenever Wilson was present, to post a suffragette guard outside the Murat mansion, and to light suffrage watchfires in the French capital. Two of the appointees had been refused passports earlier in the year, but Miss Clara Wold of Portland, Oregon, and Miss Mildred Morris of Denver, Colorado—both veterans of the White House demonstrations—almost made it out of the country before the State Department realized who they were. Posing as reporters researching stories on industrial conditions affecting women in France and England, Wold and Morris were apprehended just before they sailed for Europe. In their luggage they carried purple banners with gold lettering; the inscriptions, in French and English, read: "President Wilson is deceiving the world when he appears as the prophet of democracy. He is responsible for the disfranchisement of millions of Americans. We in America know this. The world will find him out"; and "An autocrat at home is a poor champion of democracy abroad." In response to these irreverent sentiments, a conservative pressure group known as the National Association Opposed to Woman Suffrage sent a petition to the Senate asking it to include the NWP and other radical suffragette organizations in its official investigation of Bolshevist activities in America.

Meanwhile, the suffrage amendment came up for another vote in the Senate. Ever since it had first been introduced (and soundly defeated, 16 to 34) in the Senate in 1887, the measure had steadily gained support. In its last try in October 1918, it had fallen just two votes shy of the two-thirds majority required for passage. The largest single stronghold of opposition remained the Southern Democratic bloc, in part because the boys from Dixie believed women's suffrage could upset their carefully balanced arrangements to preserve white rule throughout the South.

On the day before the scheduled vote, the militants again distinguished themselves by parading from their headquarters in Jackson Place through downtown Washington to the White House, seventy-five stern and determined women, waving the American flag, carrying that most precious relic, the watchfire urn, and holding aloft their purple, gold, and white banners. When they reached the White House, Sue White and Gabriel Harris, two NWP stalwarts, consigned an effigy of President Wilson (two feet tall and looking like "a huge doll stuffed with straw") to the flames. Through the smoke, White declared that Wilson "has forgotten, or else he never knew, the spirit of true democracy." As the inevitable impassioned oratory poured forth from the militants standing at the White House fence, members of the metropolitan and military police, aided by the ever-vigilant local chapters of the Boy Scouts, rounded up the demonstrators and bundled about sixty of them into patrol wagons. Naturally, the women refused to post bail; the twenty-five who were sentenced to five days in the District jail promptly announced they would begin another hunger strike.

Despite warnings from former presidential nominee William Jennings Bryan that opposition to women's suffrage would cripple the Democratic Party in the north, eighteen Democratic Senators joined eleven Republicans in opposing the amendment (twenty-four Democrats and thirty-one Republicans voted in favor of it). It fell one vote short. "It is not the women, it is the nation that is dishonored," declared a disappointed Carrie Chapman Catt, president of the more moderate National American Woman Suffrage Association. Suffragette leaders vowed to try once again when the new Sixty-sixth Congress convened in the spring.

Other women seemed to feel they had more pressing concerns. For the New York City Federation of Women's Clubs, meeting in the Hotel Astor, the burning issue of the day was the descent of fashion into perilous extremes of indecency, a trend that was "having a most demoralizing effect upon the youth of the country." The Federation accordingly went on record in opposition to "low-cut evening frocks and those without corsages"; it also passed resolutions against lynching and in favor of shelters to protect subway ticket sellers from the cold, and a rainbow flag for the League of Nations, and a model playground in New York as a memorial to Colonel Roosevelt. "It is the way of this world of sin," noted one bemused observer, "to say that Puritans in petticoats never hate a mode in which they have the faintest hope of looking becomingly arrayed."

While the Women's Clubs debated décolletage, working women who hoped they had left the sheltered life of a housewife behind forever wondered what would happen to their jobs when the men finally came marching home. Employers were understandably reluctant to refuse to give a veteran his old job back, and if some businesses tried to find other positions for the women who had filled in so admirably during the war, still the opportunities for gainful employment began a sharp and inevitable decline. But tens of thousands of American women had taken a giant step forward during the war, and those who had experienced the joys of a full pocketbook and the comfort of a regular paycheck without begging for a stipend from a spouse would not gladly surrender their financial independence if they had any choice in the matter. "There has resulted from the war a new birth for women of the entire world," announced an official of the U.S. Labor Service, "an escape from a former serfdom of which they were only subconscious before, but which now that they have tasted of this new freedom, they will be loath to go back to."

For those women who did remain at their jobs, there were fledgling institutions such as the Haven Day Nursery in New York, where for ten cents a day (supplemented by voluntary contributions), the children of the surrounding Irish- and Italian-American neighborhood were cared for from half-past seven in the morning until six at night. A carefully planned diet, sanitary conditions—healthy children were sent to live at the nursery when other family members contracted influenza—a great deal of individual attention, and instruction by a Montessori teacher provided the children with the sort of care they could never have received otherwise.

British women also faced the loss of their jobs as the pace of demobilization increased. An official government white paper disclosed that between 1914 and 1918 more than 1,500,000 women had taken over jobs formerly held by men, primarily in the fields of industry and commerce. By the end of the war, women represented over a third of the British work force. The increases in some fields were startling. In July 1914, there had been only 1,500 women employed in British banks; four years later the number had risen to more than 37,000. Railroad companies that had employed 12,000 women before the war now had 65,000 on their payrolls.

But in the winter of 1919, thousands of British women were being dismissed every week. The majority of trade unions made no effort to help them keep their jobs; in fact, many unions called upon the government to establish legal restrictions to keep women out of their industries. The government had employed female clerks during the war only as a matter of dire necessity, and it quickly discharged thousands of them as soon as the men returned. What would happen to the waitresses, the munitions workers, the telegraph messenger girls in blue serge uniforms and shiny straw hats, the postwomen, the bus conductors, the "farmerettes"? What would happen to the war widows whose husbands had died or been disabled by the war, the women who were now the sole breadwinners for their families, the hundreds of thousands of women who now had no hope of marriage and who needed jobs to support themselves and provide for their old age? At meetings of the National Federation of Women Workers, demonstrators carried placards demanding HANDS OFF OUR JOBS, and proclaiming that OUR MACHINES FED THE GUNS, and INJUSTICE BREEDS DISCONTENT; speakers urged the adoption of a women's charter insisting upon the right to work at suitable jobs with at least a measure of dignity, the right to a living wage, and the right to a reasonable amount of leisure time, "time to think and play, and do things."

But it was all to little avail. The Home Office admitted that women had proved themselves capable of filling skilled jobs that had hitherto been reserved for men and had "displayed unexpected readiness for work which at first sight seemed highly unsuitable for them," and it offered a pious wish that the experience of wartime might open up fresh fields of employment for women. Few concrete recommendations were forthcoming, however, especially at a time when many men were also searching for jobs; veterans nearly always received preference, and by the end of the year nearly a million women had been dismissed. Many of those still employed had returned to the old traditional positions, such as domestic service. Looming over those women who were able to retain their jobs was the specter of sharply decreased wages, now that the pool of available labor was expanding again.

A meeting of Liverpool magistrates in late January petitioned the Home Office to take strong action to arrest the spreading evil of drinking methylated spirit. Medical officials reported that an alarming number of women in the city's poorer districts had taken to drinking the mixture, "a vicious spirit practically composed of alcohol," from six to ten times stronger than ordinary whiskey. It was this very potency, however, that made it so popular, and it was quite easy to obtain; merchants in oil and paint shops could not refuse to sell methylated spirit prepared for commercial purposes to any customers who assured them they needed it for painting. Not even the introduction of coloring matter or paraffin, which made the mixture more difficult to drink, prevented users from consuming it. The physical and psychological effects were not pleasant; many women became frantic soon after drinking the spirit and eventually went insane.

Following a drinking bout with two female companions, the thirty-five-year-old wife of a railroad porter in Notting Dale died of alcoholic poisoning and bronchial pneumonia. The two survivors admitted that drinking methylated spirit was a common practice among the women in their neighborhood.

8

"Clouds are gathering on the horizon which give deep concern to every one who can read the weather, though as yet they be no bigger than a man's hand." This prescient warning came from *The Times* of London, in a discussion of the industrial situation in Britain. "The public, who are in a frivolous mood, will do well to take heed lest they be caught unawares in a heavy storm."

The storm broke first in Belfast, where shipyard workers had gone out on strike for a forty-four-hour week. On Monday, January 27, municipal electrical and gas employees seeking similar concessions walked off their jobs. Electric power was cut by 90 percent. The city's tramway service naturally stopped dead, and workers throughout the city that morning were forced to trudge through a heavy snowfall to get to work. When the girls who staffed Belfast's linen manufacturing establishments reached their workrooms and found that their sewing machines lacked electric power, they had to turn around and slog home through the slush. Clerks shivered in unheated offices; restaurants had no gas to cook hot meals for lunch; streets were unlighted; churches abandoned their services, or else parishioners worshiped by the light of candles stuck in beer bottles. Gravediggers employed in the city cemeteries decided to strike in sympathy with the shipyard workers, as did the wardens and nurses of a local asylum (allegedly with the hearty concurrence of the inmates). The strike committee appeared to govern Belfast from the humble environs of Artisans' Hall. Any city resident who used more than one candle in his home at night was considered disloyal to the strikers, and risked having his house stoned in retaliation. "Belfast is like a dead city . . . a city of candles."

In Glasgow on the same day, all the principal industries were "struck to a man" as a general strike began to enforce demands for a forty-hour week (a scheme intended to reduce the unemployment that demobilization was expected to bring). Rousing speeches exhorted the faithful at mass union demonstrations and a red flag was raised on the municipal flagpole. The strikers conveyed their demands to the Lord Provost, who promised to transmit the government's reply at noon on Friday, January 31. Alarmed by the prospect of a Spartacist-Bolshevik uprising in a city that had long been a troublesome labor spot, the government called up reinforcements and stationed troops around the outskirts of the city. (The local garrison, apparently under some suspicion of harboring a fair measure of sympathy with the strikers, was kept in its barracks.)

Shortly before noon on Friday morning, a crowd began to gather in George Square near the City Chambers, with many arriving behind brass bands and pipers and drummers. Space soon was at a premium; demonstrators climbed up onto statues and into trees, or sprawled over pavements and grass plots. The assemblage remained orderly until a scuffle broke out between strikers and policemen around a trolley car. Then the police swung into action with a truncheon charge, knocking down anyone—men and women alike—who stood in their way. The crowd responded in a similar spirit of goodwill. As the scene began to take on the appearance of a full-scale riot, Sheriff Alastair Oswald Morison Mackenzie (KC), accompanied by the chief constable, emerged and began to read the Riot Act. While performing his duty, Mackenzie was struck on the hand by a piece of broken glass, someone snatched the Riot Act and made off with it, and a thrown bottle landed upon the head of the chief constable, J. V. Stevenson. The government then escalated the conflict by calling out a detachment of mounted police, and another baton charge chased the demonstrators from the square. Fifty or sixty people in the front lines were hit repeatedly; one policeman deliberately clubbed a fifteen-year-old boy, who fell stunned on his face, and John Forrest, a moulder, later testified that he was struck while endeavoring to pick up an old woman who had fallen. Still recovering from a head wound from the first police charge, a pattern-maker named Archibald Stevenson was approached menacingly by another policeman. Fortunately, the policeman stopped when Stevenson plaintively asked, "Do ye no' think I've got enough!"

Retreating up North Frederick Street, the crowd appropriated new ammunition in the form of bottles of lager beer and aerated water, with which they showered the police. Jewelry and confectioner's shops were looted, and two dozen tramcars were overturned. To stop the melee, several of the strike leaders who had been arrested for inciting to riot appeared on a balcony and appealed for calm. Within the next several days, ten thousand troops with fixed bayonets and full battle regalia, accompanied by five tanks, poured into Glasgow to guard strategic points throughout the city. Machine guns and trench mortars encircled George Square. Soldiers stood posted upon the roofs of buildings nearby. Conventional opinion in London deplored the unseemly behavior of the rabble (i.e., the strikers), and the three ringleaders of the unions—William Gallacher, David Kirkwood, and "the Jewish tailor" Emanuel Shinwell—were roundly condemned and accused of Bolshevik tendencies. "The proceedings in Belfast and Glasgow," intoned *The Times* solemnly, "contain plain intimations of a deliberate intention to terrorize the public and make ordinary life impossible, with the ultimate intention of creating disorder and violence, out of which a state of things similar to that in Russia and elsewhere may arise." (At this point it should be noted that Kirkwood sat as a member of Parliament from 1922 to 1951, at which time he was made a baron; Shinwell served in the post–World War II Labour cabinets, first as minister of fuel and power, and later as war secretary and minister of defense; and Gallacher, an avowed Communist, sat as an MP for West Fife from 1935 to 1950. As one of Glasgow's town councilors later confirmed, "We are all disposed to treat Gallacher from the humorous standpoint.")

A visitor from America was less sanctimonious than *The Times*. He saw Glasgow's laboring people, "pale, hollow-chested, poorly clad, haggard-faced—the third and fourth generation of factory hands—and the terrible slums they inhabit. We in America have nowhere reached, as yet, this specialization in physical deterioration." These were the used and discarded products of nineteenth-century liberalism, free competition, and laissez-faire economics.

Siegfried Sassoon, the English poet who covered the Glasgow disorders as a correspondent for a socialist newspaper, was appalled by what he found in a walk through the slums of the city: "I had thought of slums as wretched and ramshackle, but had imagined them mitigated by some sort of Dickensian homeliness. These courts and alleys were cliff-like and cavernous, chilling me to the bone. The few unfortunates who scowled at us from doorways looked outlawed and brutalized. Here the thought of comfort never came, and there was a dank smell of destitution. Cold as the stones we trod was the bleak inhumanity of those terrible tenements."

On February 3 the scene shifted to London when the city's subway motormen suddenly walked out on strike. The precipitating cause of the strike appeared appallingly insignificant to many observers: having recently been granted an eight-hour working day, the motormen insisted that they still be given the traditional breaks—ten minutes for tea or smokes and a half hour for meals—that they had enjoyed as part of the nine-hour days they had previously worked. The government agreed that they could take time off for refreshments, but that they still had to work an actual eight hours. The union said no, the eight hours must include break time. Unfortunately, the agreement that had established the eight-hour standard was, at best, a model of imprecision on this point. Impatient of further discussion and refusing to wait for the explicit approval of their union officials, the railwaymen took matters into their own hands and struck.

In large measure, this was all part of the general weariness with wartime tensions and restrictions that pervaded Britain that winter. Now that the war was done with, the public no longer wished to put up with crowded transportation facilities, continued food rationing, low stocks of coal, inadequate supplies of new clothing, and apartment shortages. Petty irritations rubbed nerves raw, and mere pinpricks produced drastically disproportionate reactions.

Combined with this generalized anxiety was the fear of widespread unemployment if industrial expansion did not keep pace with demobilization; a million people were out of work by mid-February, and four million men more would be released from military service over the next several months. There was a growing assertiveness on the part of the younger generation of the labor movement, the men who had played a vital role in winning the war, and who believed they should now be rewarded accordingly. Working men and women wanted respect, an intangible but hardly unattainable goal; they would no longer be content to be merely "hewers of wood and drawers of water." This sentiment, with its air of rebelliousness, was not entirely novel or unexpected. In the several years before 1914, a wave of violent strikes had swept over Britain, part of a widespread discontentment with the lingering presence of the more unpleasant and outdated aspects of Victorian culture. The war had prevented this reaction from continuing to a conclusion; as George Dangerfield has aptly observed, "It was as if some vivid organism had struggled out of its chrysalis, only to be smashed in August 1914 by a universal thumb." In 1919 the organism revived, and some therefore considered a rash of disruptive strikes an inevitable part of the postwar readjustment. "What did you expect? We shall not realize for ten years all we went through in the war," an Englishman explained to a *New York Times* correspondent. "Strikes were inevitable, and it is lucky it is not Summer time." At the end of January there were 105 continuing strikes throughout Great Britain.

As a symbol of the new postwar power and aggressiveness of the British working class, the Labour Party formed the largest single opposition group in the new Parliament that convened in February. It was a Parliament that has always had a rather distasteful reputation, largely because of the character of its Conservative members. Stanley Baldwin, who would serve as Prime Minister off and on for nearly half of the next two decades, described this gathering as a group of "hard-faced men who look as though they had done well out of the war," and Austen Chamberlain believed them to be "a selfish, swollen lot." Lloyd George's Conservative-Liberal coalition held 484 seats in the House of Commons to Labour's 59, and only 26 for the Asquith branch of the Liberal Party (which never recovered from the disastrous split of 1916 between Herbert Asquith and Lloyd George, or from the inability of classic Liberal philosophy to come to grips with the irrational spirit of the new century). Never again would the Liberal Party approach a majority in the Commons; one perceptive historian has likened it to the Whig Party in the 1840s, which Disraeli described as "absolutely forlorn . . . spoken of as a corpse, it was treated as a phantom." From now on the Left belonged to the Labourites, and although the road would be long to an effective government of their own, they had already become "a separate, distinct, and individual force in British politics" that scared the wits out of both older parties.

When the London Underground motormen walked out, hundreds of thousands of commuters who had not known about the strike when they left their homes in the suburbs that morning were forced to make their way to work as best they could. A mad scramble for spaces on tramcars and omnibuses followed all along the affected Tube routes. Many left their jobs early that afternoon to improve their chances of getting a ride home, but in the late hours of evening crowds of unlucky pedestrians could still be seen slipping and sliding their way across the thin layer of frozen snow that covered the city streets. There was more of the same the next morning; in fact, it was worse, for engineers on the district rail lines joined the Underground strikers, adding several hundred thousand more desperate commuters to the pretty mess. Buses were full by seven o'clock. Shopgirls, clerks, and businessmen stood in tiresome queues in the damp cold for hours vainly trying to catch a ride, and finally decided to join the processions marching down Oxford Street, Piccadilly, Haymarket, and the Strand, sometimes not arriving at their jobs until noon. Soldiers passing through the city to rejoin their units had to walk across London from one railroad station to the next, carrying their equipment and heavy kitbags with them. Members of the Royal Automobile Club volunteered their cars ("Free Transport for Tired Workers") for emergency service. Antiquated carts, lorries, dilapidated cabs, anything that had wheels were pressed into service, but still it was not nearly enough. A new four-inch snowfall on

February 5 did not improve matters at all. Nor did the strike of eight thousand waiters and hotel servants, which forced restaurants to close up entirely or offer only meager imitations of their regular menus. ("Look here, we can get lunch here, can't we?" "Well, sir, you can try." "I'm afraid it's cold beef again today, gentlemen.") Even the local physicians got into the act, holding a mass meeting in Hyde Park and only narrowly rejecting a motion to form a regular registered trade union themselves. It really was the most demoralizing time for Londoners since the bombardments of air-raid week, back in September 1917.

Patience began to wear thin. The only consoling thought was that it would all have been worse in foggy weather. *The Times* called the strike "a definite revolutionary agitation which aims at disorder and anarchy." Like the electrical workers' strike in Berlin, the job action showed just how vulnerable urban society had become to the disruptive actions of a handful of men. The government, which had refused to intervene in the Belfast and Glasgow disputes on the grounds that they were private matters between the workers and their employers, decided that things were quite different when the crisis struck close to home. The Cabinet spent several days in a dither about what to do: "We are in chaos in England as regards these strikes," reported Lord Alfred Milner, "which under Lloyd George's regime are being dealt with by every sort of man and every sort of department, each acting on a different principle from the others." Finally the War Department eased the pressure by mobilizing over a thousand military motor lorries driven by volunteers from the Royal Army Service Corps garages. Passengers were packed thickly into every available square inch of space on the trucks and jounced along the war-worn city streets. "On the whole," advised one veteran straphanger, "it is advisable to 'hang' all the way, for motor-lorries can play strange tricks, especially when the journey is a 'non-stop' and efforts are being made to reach the City in twenty minutes."

But the last straw for the government came when members of the Electrical Trades Union threatened to cease work at six o'clock on the evening of February 6 and "plunge London into darkness" if the Cabinet did not intervene in the Glasgow dispute. Taking advantage of King George's presence in London to call a Council meeting, and acting on the theory that cutting off the lighting supply to a metropolis such as London was tantamount to creating a riot, the Cabinet promulgated a new regulation under the Defence of the Realm Act, whereby any electrical worker who stopped work without notice, or anyone who incited a worker to do so, was subject to six months' imprisonment and/or a fine of one hundred pounds. In addition, troops were detailed to stand by to assist if necessary in the operation of power stations. By the way, British voters wondered, what was Mr. Lloyd George doing in France at a time like this, and when was he going to do something about these bloody Bolshevist strikers?

The Prime Minister had remained in Paris until now, but as it became clear that his colleagues were unable to cope with the succession of labor troubles, the master conciliator hurried back to London on the evening of February 8. He was not in a particularly good mood; when a reporter asked him how things were going at the Peace Conference, Lloyd George snapped, "Well," and that was all.

He promptly began a round of meetings with his Cabinet ministers and the Board of Trade, and railway union officials were told to stand by for further discussions.

Facing a government obviously determined to prevent any disruption of the city's power supply, the electrical workers reconsidered their threat to strike. In a temporary settlement, the Tube motormen were granted permission to take unofficial brief breaks "for the satisfaction of their bodily wants, which, of course, includes the taking of refreshment," with no corresponding additions to their eight-hour day. Meetings with Belfast unions resulted in a compromise granting a slightly shorter work week. Only in Glasgow did strikers fail to gain any significant concessions. On February 12 the unions' Joint Committee urged workers in that city to return to their jobs and wait for more propitious times.

For the moment, all was calm again. But behind the jerry-built façade of industrial peace, the Triple Alliance of miners, railwaymen, and transport workers began to formulate their demands for the next national confrontation.

Valentine's Day, Part Three. Mr. Austin Flint Gibbons (apparently no relation to the late Frank Gibbons) filed his answer to his wife's suit for a trial separation. Mrs. Gibbons (Anna Olga) had charged him with mistreating her, but Austin claimed that precisely the opposite was true.

The happy couple had been wed on December 16, 1916; the very next day she allegedly struck him. Before they parted, Gibbons said, she had kicked him in the face; hit him with a poker; thrown a porcelain swan at him; struck him three times in the face on June 25, 1917; thrown a briefcase at him; struck him with a clenched fist on Easter Sunday 1918; thrown a cup and saucer at him; struck him over the arm with a hand mirror, cutting him, on New Year's Eve 1916; thrown a large plaster statue at him; struck him across the side of the head from behind with an umbrella; and attacked him with a broomstick.

* * *

From his vantage point in Paris as he watched the Peace Conference procrastinate its way through January and early February, Oswald Villard wondered how long it would be before French unions launched their own series of strikes. "Heaven knows I wish they would strike," he wrote home. "It is enough to make an anarchist out of anybody to see the world in such hands. The calm way they go on carving up Europe without consulting the Russians, Germans, Austrians, Hungarians, etc., is beyond words. No one knows where it will end. The Poles and Czechoslovaks, Italians, and others have about as much idea of making this a better world and ending war as the cows in New Jersey."

Colonel House complained that the Council of Ten was "not getting anywhere, largely because of the lack of organization." Another cause of the glacial pace of negotiations was the insistence of Wilson, Clemenceau, Lloyd George, and Orlando to hear and decide questions about which they knew little or nothing; "geography, ethnography, psychology, and political history were sealed books to them," complained a British expert. Nicolson wrote home describing the "desultory and unconvincing" nature of the proceedings. "The Big Ten or the Big Five, as they are alternatively called, decide important questions *in camera* and on what seems a wholly empirical and irresponsible basis. They seldom take the trouble to notice the facts and arguments prepared for them by their staffs. . . . We have not really got to grips as yet and all this delay is merely the reflection of Council indolence and jealousy. When practical questions *do* come up for judgment they will be decided in a hurry. . . . Damn! Damn! Damn!" Wilson and Lloyd George drove and chipped and putted at the Montmartre golf course, fenced off for the private use of the distinguished guests of the French Republic. Tennis matches between the American and British delegations occupied the covered tennis courts at Auteuil. Winston Churchill, eager for military intervention against the Bolsheviks in Russia, suddenly appeared at the conference one day. "Halloa!" called a friend. "Have you come to hurry us up?" "No," Churchill answered, "I have come to get myself an army."

A meeting of the Council of Ten at the Quai d'Orsay: Outside Pichon's small office, where the secret conferences are held, about twenty experts and interested parties sit in the main waiting room. Wilson's personal detective is sprawled in a chair reading *A Bed of Roses*. Then the door opens into the council room. A high domed ceiling, heavy chandelier, lots of oak with carvings of cupids over the doorway, a simple fireplace, two Empire commodes, electric lights, a luxurious carpet with a swan border, copies of Marie de Médicis paintings from the Louvre, two large windows that look out onto the garden below. As the afternoon light fades behind the green silk curtains, the lights are turned on gradually one after another. It is very warm and quiet and extremely stuffy. Clemenceau sits at a plain table in the center of the room in his black skullcap, wearing as usual the gray suede gloves that cover the eczema on his hands, heavy eyebrows hiding his half-closed eyes, his face expressionless or wearing, in Harold Nicolson's apt phrase, "the half-smile of an irritated, sceptical and neurasthenic gorilla" until someone mentions a subject of vital interest and then he leans forward with eyes open very wide, and utters more insulting comments. "The worst of Clemenceau," wrote Nicolson in his diary, "is that he is so terribly audible."

Behind Clemenceau sits Mantoux, the interpreter who never stoops to merely rendering speeches into another language, but throws himself into the translation with fervor equal to if not greater than that of the original speaker. To Clemenceau's right are the Council members; Lloyd George is late again today, but who can blame him? As the meeting wears on, Balfour stretches out his long legs, crosses them, yawns, and rests his head on the back of his chair. Italian Foreign Minister Sonnino falls asleep, and when he awakens scowls menacingly at the Yugoslav delegation that has been invited to speak today. Wilson gets pins and needles and begins to pace up and down the soft carpet, kicking his boots to wake up his feet, and then goes and sits down for a few minutes among the Yugoslavs. Maps are passed around. After a speaker finishes, Wilson politely murmurs "Hear! Hear!" and silently claps his hands. A resolution is made to refer the matter under discussion to an expert committee. "*Objection? Adopté,*" Clemenceau rattles off before anyone can speak. Then it is time for lunch.

Little was achieved by anyone, save for the League of Nations committee, which did most of its work in the evenings. Wilson, in fact, was putting in eighteen-hour days, and his temper began to fray. He complained of the difficulty of weaving all the threads of peace into a coherent pattern; he resented the time spent traveling to and from the Quai d'Orsay; he abandoned exercise; he grew tired of hearing of the sacrifices France had made during the war, snapping that it wouldn't change the settlement if all France were one big shell hole; he seldom laughed at his wife's little stories and her impressions of his colleagues.

The greatest excitement during the somnolent first month came when the Parisian press, in an effort to intimidate Wilson into softening his opposition to French claims against Germany, stepped up its attacks on the President's lofty principles. Outraged, Wilson responded with a threat to move the conference to Geneva. And so it went, until Lloyd George left for London, and Wilson made his plans to return to the United States in mid-February for the adjournment of Congress.

Was the Paris conference to be a reprise of the Congress of Vienna, where the delegates had seemed preoccupied with the latest dances and idle flirtations? Vienna, the magical city on the Danube, the city that had known Johann Strauss, Emperor Franz Joseph, Sigmund Freud, Gustav Mahler, and Anton Bruckner . . .

In February 1919, Vienna was icebound, freezing to death. Virtually no coal entered the city. At five o'clock in the afternoon, all shops closed their shutters and the main thoroughfares around the Opera stood deserted. Nor was it any warmer inside the houses. One could walk through the dirty streets on the outskirts of the city after dark for two hours and see not a single window reflecting the warm glow of a fireplace. Wretchedly fed men and women crouched weakly against a wall for shelter from the vicious wind, or stood in long lines for hours in the snow, waiting for a bowl of barley soup. An American military observer reported a 90-percent infant mortality rate in Vienna: "Germany and Austria are smoldering volcanoes which starvation will put in eruption." Women and children marched past the government buildings, crying "Food! Food! Food!" over and over again. Desperate soldiers begged in the streets. Factories closed for lack of fuel, and unemployment spiraled out of control.

Supplies designated for Vienna lay rotting in railyards throughout Europe, victims of the chaotic state of transportation. Bridges and trestles lay in ruins, and the few trains that ran were stuffed full of men and women smuggling food. Politicians closed borders as dozens of local wars broke out among the former states of the Austro-Hungarian Empire. "The emancipated races of Southern Europe," wrote Lloyd George, "were at each other's throats in their avidity to secure choice bits of the carcasses of dead empires. . . . The resurrected nations rose from their graves hungry and ravening from their long fast in the vaults of oppression. They were like Athelstane, in *Ivanhoe*, who rose from his bier with the insatiable cravings of famine raging in his whole body. Like him they clutched at anything that lay within reach of their hands—not even waiting to throw off the cerements of the grave and array themselves in the apparel of living nations." For any among the Allies who suspected that the news from Vienna was exaggerated, Marshal Foch, the venerated French military chief, confirmed that "in Austria, especially, the population is certainly in a state bordering upon famine."

Fugitives from the conflicts along the borders poured into Vienna. There were thousands of Jews fearing pogroms, along with hundreds of thousands of returning soldiers who found their way into the city, thereby increasing the population by more than a million over the levels of 1914 and exacerbating the overcrowding, the unemployment, and the hunger. Vienna's confidence in the future had evaporated, replaced by a dull fatalism.

American military representatives sent their reports back to Hoover: "Hell has been to.this place. It is still here. Twenty-five per cent of the children in this town have died in the last two months." And, "We can count food in calories but we have no way to measure human misery."

A Swiss doctor visited an institution for destitute children, filled to five times its normal capacity. "The appearance of the children was terrible: their heads looked disproportionally big (owing to their stunted bodies), black rings round their eyes, the eyelids red and ulcerated." Infants were given one-half liter of milk a day and a syrup made from boiled-down turnips; children over the age of one were fed on turnips and cabbage. No coffins were available for the children who died ("the lucky ones"), but boxes were used for the bodies whenever available. The Swiss doctor wept.

On the unfashionable side of the river, a café was open from seven o'clock in the morning to eight in the evening. It was always busy and crowded. Patrons had to pay to get in, but inside there were boots, matches, and candles spread out on tables and available for purchase—at extravagant prices, of course. And there was bread. Through the thick, dark air one could see and smell loaves of all kinds of bread. Upon one table there was even muslin underwear that wealthy customers could put on (in a dark corner) before leaving. Although the dingy walls were hung with police notices forbidding any black-market trade in cafés, a good-natured policeman walked up and down outside and ignored what was going on. Once a man who scampered away with six loaves of bread hidden under his coat—a month's ration for a family of four, if they could ever find it or afford it—dropped his booty on the pavement, and the policeman stooped to help him pick the loaves up again. You could find anything you needed at the profiteering café, except perhaps a cup of coffee.

To the north, no flour had reached Prague for the past two weeks. The seemingly insoluble transport problems exacerbated the gravity of the situation in a city where refugees from a multitude of invasions had doubled the population in two months after a long and devastating war. "Factories are stopped, houses unheated, the streets dark, the shops shut at sundown, and there is no public safety." A British doctor visited the bourgeois sections of the city:

I SAW YOUNG GIRLS EMACIATED TO THE BONE, ILL OF VARIOUS MALADIES, BUT PRINCIPALLY OF LACK OF PROPER FOOD. THEIR PLACE WOULD NATURALLY BE IN HOSPITAL, BUT IN PRAGUE THE VAST EXTENT OF MISERY PRECLUDES FURTHER RECEPTION IN HOSPITAL OF ANY EXCEPT EXTREME CASES. I SAW MEN TRYING TO WORK BY SHEER WILL POWER, THEIR MUSCLES NO LONGER SUPPORTING THE TASK. . . . I SAW FAMILIES WITH EIGHT OR NINE CHILDREN IN ONE ROOM, LIVING ON BLACK BREAD AND IMITATION COFFEE FURNISHED BY THE STATE. . . .

ONLY IN ONE INSTANCE DID I SEE ANYTHING THAT SUGGESTED LINEN OR COTTON CLOTH. THAT WAS IN A TINY ROOM IN WHICH DWELT A MOTHER AND EIGHT CHILDREN. ITS GLASS DOOR HAD ONE PANE MISSING, BUT EVERYTHING WAS SCRUPULOUSLY CLEAN AND IN ORDER, AND ON THE BED A SNOW-WHITE SHEET AS THE ONLY COVERING—A RELIC OF PAST WELL-BEING.

Budapest witnessed street battles between the Bolsheviks—including striking miners and discharged soldiers—and government troops. Rumania was dying of cold, hunger, and disease; perhaps ten percent of the population was dead. Stocks of seed corn for Rumania still awaited shipment in France, Great Britain, and America, although the harvesting of crops was supposed to begin in July. One of Hoover's men believed Rumanians to be "the most starved looking lot of people I have seen in Europe. The women and children for the most part are without shoes and stockings, everyone had patched ragged clothes. . . . All of them complained that their children had died for lack of food. . . . I visited many homes or hovels. . . . I found no food. . . . Cattle, pigs, even dogs are about half their normal weight. . . ."

Allied informants warned that if the clever men in Paris allowed the situation in Central Europe to drift on much longer, the bottom might drop out of the whole situation. Then all the discussions and expert commissions and hearings and negotiations would have been nothing more than an academic exercise in pious aspirations.

"Of course," conceded Charles Seymour, "the Conference is working under difficulties far greater than those of the Congress of Vienna, for conditions in Central Europe are in such a state of flux, to say nothing of Russia. . . ."

On the shores of the Gulf of Dvina shivered the Arctic city of Archangel, the main military base of the Allies in northern Russia. There were five thousand American troops stationed in Archangel in February 1919, most of whom daily cursed the fates (and the politicians) that had landed them there. They complained that the wind whistling across the Dvina River reminded them of the *Twentieth Century Special* passing Podunk; one sarcastic doughboy from Michigan said, only half-jokingly, that Archangel was so tough that the people were outnumbered three to one by ugly half-breed dogs, and the peasants had to build fires around the cows before they could milk them. The only color in the city in the dead of winter came from the gigantic frescoes of the Last Judgment emblazoned on the walls of the onion-domed cathedrals.

Since the temperature often dipped to forty-five degrees below zero or worse, the standard American military uniform in the Archangel sector consisted of a heavy sheepskin coat, fur cape and mittens, white cowls as camouflage in the snow, moosehide moccasins, a fur parka, and the famous thick winter boots known as "mukluks." The British Army had commissioned Sir Ernest Shackleton, the noted Arctic explorer, to devise a special diet for the Allied troops; the food was rich in fats to maintain body heat and energy, and dried fruit helped fill the gap left by an almost complete lack of fresh vegetables. The Red Cross did its best to help, sending books, playing cards, ukeleles, mandolins, footballs, wigs, greasepaint, and Bibles to help the men pass the dead hours during the long winter nights, but morale kept sinking lower and lower nonetheless.

Along the battlefront that ranged across an arc four hundred miles wide, supplies were moved by sleighs drawn by shaggy little ponies with jingling bells around their necks, driven single-file over the tundra and across primitive roads cut through pine forests. The trick was to avoid falling into the unfrozen swamps that could swallow up a man in minutes. It was a remarkably picturesque and brutal war. American and British soldiers would advance across mile after endless mile of depressing, dreary forests of fir to capture a group of concrete blockhouses; then the Bolshevik artillery would drive them back, and the game would start all over again further down the line. Meanwhile, the peasants huddled in their log huts or the lonely white churches topped with five blue towers, perfectly content to leave the fighting to the foreigners outside. There were unconfirmed reports that the Bolsheviks were employing German gas shells, and the bodies of a number of dead American soldiers were retrieved with their heads and limbs mutilated by repeated blows of an axe.

A correspondent of the *Chicago Tribune* spent two months in northern Russia and came back with a tale of bungled opportunities. "The North Russia allied expedition," he reported, "has developed into a pitiful failure. It has failed to inspire confidence and loyalty and give real assistance to

Russia. It has become a cesspool of jealousy, hatreds, mistakes, and shattered illusions. The different allies distrust each other and the Russians distrust the entire expedition." Heavy-handed intervention in local political affairs, especially by British military officials, had embittered the civilian population; poorly trained Allied soldiers who had no idea why they were fighting and who wanted desperately to go home (after all, the war was over everywhere else) took out their frustrations on the Russian peasants and made insubordinate threats to their own officers that reportedly bordered upon mutiny; and the peasants themselves much preferred the Bolsheviks, who at least gave them a bit of land of their own, to the oppressive old regime represented by the White armies. "Here in the north, in a district that never was violently Bolshevist, where the Allies had many friends at the start, and where since the first days there have been unlimited opportunities to advance confidence and gain respect, here with everything their own way, the Allies have failed utterly."

By intervening with only a relative handful of troops, the Allies had become entangled in a protracted internal Russian political and military struggle that showed no signs of coming to a clear resolution in the near future. Given the popular pressures for demobilization, the governments could hardly send vast numbers of new troops to Archangel. Senator Hiram Johnson of California led the congressional criticism of Wilson's confused Russian policy. He accused the President of abandoning five thousand American boys who were "making a valiant stand against overwhelming odds in all of the severity of an arctic winter, suffering untold privation and hardship and fighting a war which had never been sanctioned or declared by the American people." Johnson promised that there would be "a heavy reckoning some day for those who have been responsible for this wicked and this useless course in Russia. And the heaviest responsibility, the wrong which can never be atoned, is the shedding of American blood in Russia. . . . I would not give one American life in Russia for all the Bolsheviki spawned by centuries of tyranny and mad with the lust of a ruthless ephemeral power."

But there were powerful conservative forces, especially in Britain and France, that continued to call for military action to destroy the Bolshevik menace. So, for the time being, the war continued across the Arctic wasteland, where shells exploding upon the frozen ground spread their destructive force twice as far as they would under normal conditions. And day after day came the report from Allied headquarters: "The situation is unchanged in all sectors."

* * *

Valentine's Day, Part Four. Irving I. Bloomingdale had had enough. A member of the famous Bloomingdale Brothers mercantile family, Irving was being sued by his wife, Rosalie B. Bloomingdale, for an additional $1,000 per month in alimony; she was already receiving $2,000 per month. Irving told the New York State Supreme Court that Rosalie was not entitled to the additional income because she was a spendthrift with an utter disregard for the value of money. For instance, he claimed that while she was taking golf lessons at White Sulphur Springs, she had bought a Tiffany watch and used it as a tee. When one of their sons was born, Irving had bought her a $3,000 watch; she had angrily called it a "niggardly" present and exchanged it for one costing $5,000. Further, she had allegedly accumulated considerable debts from playing cards. Whenever he had complained to her about her spending habits, Irving added, Rosalie had thrown tantrums and drowned his criticisms "in a torrent of abuse." And besides, Mr. Bloomingdale concluded, he objected to her friendship with several other men, including her golf instructor at White Sulphur Springs.

9

"And the right

of the needy

do they not judge . . ."

Bound for Karachi in a Handley-Page airplane nicknamed "Old Carthusian" on the last leg of a journey that began at Martlesham Aeroport on December 13, Major A. S. MacLaren and his party encountered stiff headwinds after leaving Baghdad, reducing their speed to fifty miles per hour. Three miles out to sea, off the Baluchistan coast, one cylinder of the port engine blew out, and MacLaren and his copilot, Captain Halley, were compelled to make an emergency landing on the beach. A gunboat was dispatched from Karachi to assist them if they should wish to dismantle the plane and discontinue their mission, but after considerable deliberation MacLaren opted instead to continue the flight by lightening the machine— taking off all spare parts and the wireless, and reducing the petrol supply and the crew to a bare minimum—and by tuning the remaining three Rolls-Royce engines to their highest pitch. Naturally they retained their prize passenger, General McEwan, who was on his way to take up a Royal Air Force command in the East.

After a one-mile run along the hard beach, the plane managed to take off, but a short while later two of the engines momentarily gave out when the wind vanes flew off the gasoline pumps. Caught over an especially rocky section of coastline, MacLaren was understandably reluctant to land. The crew began pumping by hand. Thirty-five miles from Karachi, a fracture in one of the oil lines disabled the rear starboard engine. MacLaren pushed the remaining two engines, barely avoiding stalling the plane, for the last leg of the journey. He landed safely in Karachi only slightly behind schedule.

Several days later, General McEwan departed for Delhi by train.

Seattle: "the hot-bed of IWW insurrection on the Pacific Coast", according to *The New York Times*. Before the war, the International Workers of the World, the most widely known and widely despised radical labor organization in America, had gained its greatest following among the miners, lumberjacks, and migrant workers of the Pacific Northwest. Left-wing labor leaders had called "lightning strikes" in the Seattle area during the war, and their militancy carried over into the immediate postwar era; on January 16, a demonstration by five hundred workers protesting the conviction of forty-six IWW members on charges of attempting to obstruct the American war effort had been dispersed by twenty mounted police supported by five automobiles containing police armed with carbines; behind these had come a platoon of police with clubs. So when 25,000 shipyard workers in the city walked off their jobs on January 21 demanding higher wages, Seattle's Central Labor Council voted to support the job action with a general strike that would close the city down completely.

Middle-class Americans were terrified. Could this be the start of the Bolshevik revolution in the United States? The federal government had encouraged a conciliatory attitude toward unions during the war, in return for organized labor's dedication to the war effort. But now many businessmen wanted to turn the clock back and dispense with such dangerous notions as collective bargaining. At the same time, many American workers, like their compatriots in Britain, expected to maintain and improve upon their wartime gains. What they did not expect was a concerted effort by employers to roll back wages in the face of continuing increases in the cost of living.

Seattle was the first full-scale test of American labor's power in 1919. At 10:00 A.M. on February 6, the first general strike in the nation's history began. Longshoremen defied their international union officials and voted to join the strike; four out of five theatrical employees' unions walked out; janitors in schools, elevator operators in office buildings, truck drivers, streetcar men, barbers, newsboys and newspaper typesetters, waiters, all went on strike in sympathy with the shipyard workers. Schools closed, restaurants stood empty, and newspapers stopped publication. Culinary union members opened twelve soup kitchens to feed the strikers (twenty-five cents) and anyone else (thirty-five cents) looking for a hot meal. Patrons stood in long lines and were served in military-mess fashion, although a lack of eating utensils on the first day forced some to use pocket knives or pointed sticks to handle their food (beef stew or spaghetti, bread, and coffee). Downtown Seattle lay deserted that evening. There were no streetcars and few automobiles; theaters and store windows were dark. Those city residents who owned a decrepit old car or an antique buggy (with a horse, of course) brought it out of retirement. Central Labor

Council officials offered to preserve order through their own police force, but Mayor Ole Hanson was not about to give the workers any such wedge with which to usurp his authority.

Instead, Hanson called for the army, and Secretary of War Newton Baker gave it to him. Before the strike was twenty-four hours old, eight hundred troops (accompanied by Hanson riding in an automobile draped with the American flag) had taken up their positions throughout downtown Seattle. Two more battalions and a machine-gun company stood ready in Tacoma, thirty-six miles away. Hanson hired one thousand extra police and threatened to add ten thousand more, warning the unions that "any man who attempts to take over control of municipal government functions here will be shot on sight." There were rumors that workers had made enormous purchases of thumbtacks, which they planned to strew across streets to thwart motorcycle policemen.

The next day more troops poured into the city. "We have 1,500 police officers, 1,500 Regulars from Camp Lewis, and will get the services, if necessary, of every soldier in the Pacific Northwest to protect life, business, and property," Hanson proclaimed. At one police station stood a large truck carrying a machine gun, with sandbags built up around its edges and army veterans ready to fire upon any strikers bold enough to approach. A single streetcar guarded by heavily armed soldiers and bearing large placards that read U.S. MAIL ran along the municipal line on Fourth Avenue. Authorities were on the lookout for Leon Ridowsky, a.k.a. Leon Green, the alleged ringleader of the labor extremists.

Hanson, army authorities, and the press all agreed that the strike was a Red plot to establish a Bolshevik beachhead in America. The distribution of revolutionary handbills with the captions "Russia Did It!" and "Rise, workers, and show your power!" did nothing to discourage the notion that the action was more a rebellion against the government than a strike over economic issues. "The sympathetic revolution was called in the exact manner as was the revolution in Petrograd," Hanson declared. Representative Royal Johnson of Washington charged that the strike leadership included "a great array of Slovinskis and Ivan Kerenskys and names of that sort," and called for a four-year suspension of immigration into the United States. The *Los Angeles Times* discerned that "only four of the strike committee which has seized Seattle by the throat are Americans. Most of the remainder are Bolsheviki of the most radical Russian type." The normally rational *Baltimore Sun* termed the strike "an attempted Bolshevik revolution—an attempt to start a conflagration which . . . could bring the United States to the condition of Russia where anarchy, assassination, starvation, and every calamity that can oppress a people is rioting," and it urged that the government continue deporting anarchists back to Russia.

Hanson's belligerent stand against the strikers made him a national hero overnight. His desk was covered with great bouquets of flowers from grateful Seattle citizens and hundreds of letters and telegrams from supporters in cities across the nation, who applauded the way he met radicalism head-on and "punched it in the jaw." Prior to 1919, Hanson had had a checkered career; in fact, he had had several checkered careers. The son of Norwegian parents who had emigrated to the United States, Hanson had driven a covered wagon across the West sixteen years before. After a brief stay in Santa Barbara as an itinerant photographer ("I knew little or nothing about taking pictures," Hanson confessed), he had landed in Seattle, where he worked as a real-estate salesman, an investment broker, and a grocery storekeeper before he ran as the Progressive candidate for the Senate in 1914. He had broken with Seattle's leftist community when it snubbed him for another spot on the ticket; forsaking his image as a champion of the underdog to become a fierce defender of the establishment, Hanson was nominated for mayor by the city businessmen's organization. Voters had chosen him over an extreme radical, and now, at age forty-three, thin and restless, with a wavy thatch of prematurely gray hair (and the father of eight children, including two girls named Lloyd George Hanson and Eugene Field Hanson), Ole Hanson made the most of his rendezvous with immortality.

By February 8, 75,000 workers had joined the strike, but they were facing machine guns and soldiers with fixed bayonets as well as the imminent deadline of Hanson's threat to place the operation of essential utilities under the control of the federal government. Over the next two days, the movement quickly disintegrated as strikers began returning to their jobs. On February 10, the general strike committee voted to abandon the strike officially at noon the following day. Mayor Hanson crowed over his victory; the revolution, he proclaimed, "never got to first base, and it never will if the men in control of affairs will tell all traitors and anarchists that death will be their portion if they start anything."

To prevent similar uprisings in the future, Hanson urged the Washington state legislature to require loyalty tests of all city and state government employees ("The employee in a public utility department has no more right to strike than the surgeon has to lay down his knife and let the patient die," he said) and recommended that the government "arrest, try and punish all leaders in this conspiracy. . . . The city authorities have quelled this rebellion. It is now the government's duty to punish. The whitewash brush must not be used."

The 25,000 shipworkers in whose name the general action was called had gained nothing and remained out on strike.

Watching as the unrest spread through the working classes and the soldiers still in khaki from Archangel to Budapest to Milan to Berlin to Paris to London and Seattle, Charles Seymour discerned the outlines of the chasm that separated 1919 from 1914: "An enormous revolution has taken place here in the past few months. Socialists of the kind we feared a few years ago are now reactionaries and we might as well acknowledge the fact. If we want a lasting peace and one undisturbed by Bolshevism we have got to combine with the moderate socialists. . . . It is foolish to blink at the fact and if the Conference tries to, its work will be swept away in a couple of years."

As the drama in Seattle played itself out, a train filled with fifty-four "undesirable aliens" in two heavily guarded tourist sleeping cars left the city bound for New York. For the past year, federal immigration authorities had been investigating radical labor activities in the Pacific Northwest, and these men (and one woman) had been stamped as "IWW leaders and troublemakers" and designated for deportation. Forty of them came from the Seattle area; three allegedly had played a role in provoking the general strike. All were being sent back to their native lands: a few to England, half a dozen to Russia, most to Scandinavia.

"The procedure against United States enemies of this type is simple," said an official with the train. "Just two hours before the Seattle strike was called we gathered forty agitators into the cars with everything cleared away between them and the middle of the Atlantic Ocean." Twenty-four of the prisoners were charged with belonging to "an organization which advocates the unlawful destruction of property" (i.e., the IWW), nine were described as anarchists, four were ex-convicts, two were "diseased," three had allegedly violated the white slavery laws, and the rest were deemed likely to become public charges. The Honorable Anthony Caminetti, U.S. Commissioner General of Immigration, told reporters that about six thousand aliens would be deported, most because they were insane or otherwise a burden upon the public treasury. (Caminetti, incidentally, had also gained popular renown for his endorsement of "Nuxated Iron," a potion that purportedly created "red blood, strength and endurance." "Despite his 64 years," the advertisement proclaimed, Caminetti "is today more active and alert than many a younger man.")

Aboard the train, the crowded berths were littered with red flags, strike placards, and IWW banners. Many of the men killed time by playing cards. The one woman wore an old fur coat and a black sailor hat, and sat silently by a window while she watched the guards pace up and down the aisles. Fifty-four pairs of handcuffs were stashed under a blanket for use in an emergency, but a guard cheerfully reported that "we don't need the cuffs now. What we need is a number of good gags. This is a musical gang. They sing foreign songs for hours. Some of 'em wake up in the night to do it."

Arriving in New York early on the morning of February 11, the prisoners (many of whom carried canvas carpetbags but lacked overcoats against the cold) were taken by boat to Ellis Island. Shortly after they left the dock at Hoboken, a scuffle broke out, and several radicals ended up with bruises and cuts on their faces and bodies from the guards' clubs and pistol butts. For the time being, immigration authorities refused to allow anyone—especially attorneys—to visit the prisoners while they awaited transportation back to Europe.

In Washington, official outrage mounted over testimony that seemed to reveal widespread Red infiltration of America. Vice-President Thomas R. Marshall attacked foreign radicals as "anarchists and wild-eyed theorists," and promised that "if I had my way all such who have naturalization papers would be deprived of them and all others would be driven from the country." A Senate Judiciary Subcommittee chaired by Senator Overman of North Carolina made a neat segue from investigating pro-German propaganda in wartime to uncovering pro-Bolshevik activities in peacetime. One witness from army intelligence told Overman's committee that he had discovered a vast network of anarchist and subversive intellectuals, including numerous professors in American colleges and universities. The list contained names such as Oswald Garrison Villard, Jane Addams, Chancellor David Starr Jordan of Stanford University, and former U.S. Commissioner of Immigration Frederick G. Howe.

To keep more foreign radicals from entering the country, Representative John L. Burnett of Alabama introduced a bill to ban virtually all immigration into the United States for four years, on the grounds that "the time has come when we should begin cleaning house in the United States. The people are in the right temper for it, and it can be done more easily and thoroughly now than ever before." Fearing an influx of foreign workers fleeing depressed conditions in Europe, organized labor endorsed the bill, but the *Los Angeles Times* magnanimously supported the right of aliens to seek refuge in America. Who else, the editors asked, would do the "hard, grueling, rough, dirty, back-breaking work that is especially repugnant to the American notion of living? . . . The economy of production calls for Chinese and Mexican performance of unpleasant jobs that the American workman may be supplied with the more ambitious tasks for which his higher intelligence has fitted him."

Throughout the nation, the reaction against radicals began to grow more and more hysterical. Chicago police raided IWW headquarters and arrested twenty-nine people who were fingerprinted, photographed, and then released after being advised in no uncertain terms to "get a job or get out of town." In Zane Grey's new novel, *The Desert of Wheat*, IWW agitators served as a convenient source of villany.

At 3:00 P.M. on the afternoon of February 6, in the Court Theater in the quaint old town of Weimar, 160 miles southwest of Berlin, the new German National Assembly officially began its efforts to establish a federal government and write a republican constitution. Ebert and his colleagues had chosen Weimar—center of German classical culture, where Goethe and Schiller had lived, and where Franz Liszt had conducted the premiere of Wagner's *Lohengrin*—over Berlin as the seat of the national legislature partly because they wished to conjure up memories of a nonaggressive German nationalism, partly because they wished to placate the southern German states, and partly because they feared Spartacist efforts to disrupt the Assembly. They could and did control Weimar much more completely than Berlin; several divisions of infantry, along with artillery and cavalry contingents, were dispatched to Weimar and surrounded the town. Mounted troops constantly patrolled the streets. No one could enter Weimar without a special pass; all accredited government and press representatives were given a bewildering array of color-coded cards: one gave your room assignment, others told you where to take your meals (a different card for each meal), and still others allowed you to purchase sugar, butter, bread, and marmalade. ("The entire arrangement is a characteristic German system," wrote one American correspondent, "and it seems to work excellently except for the annoyance of keeping track of so many cards.")

Hours before the Assembly began its deliberations, a well-dressed crowd shuffled along the sidewalks through the slushy snow to gain admittance to the opening session. Once inside, they saw that the theater had been transformed into a credible imitation of a legislative chamber. Writing desks for the legislators (of whom thirty-four were women) replaced the orchestra chairs; the upper circle and gallery were reserved for the press and spectators, and local dignitaries occupied the dress circle. On a special platform upon the stage sat the presiding officer in the old Reichstag presidential chair, an enormous high-backed leather throne emblazoned with the German eagle. The stage was nearly buried in masses of red, pink, and white carnations and long lines of lilies of the valley, "the general effect produced being frankly rather like that of an English harvest thanksgiving service," reported *The Times* of London.

Ebert, dressed in a plain black frock coat, made his opening remarks: "We have done forever with princes and nobles, by the grace of God. . . . Militarism has been dethroned. . . . In reliance upon President Wilson's Fourteen Points Germany laid down her arms. Now give us the Wilson Peace, to which we have a claim. . . . We warn our opponents not to drive us to the uttermost. Hunger is preferable to disgrace and deep privation is to be preferred to dishonor." Ebert was duly elected President of the German Republic. He named Philipp Scheidemann as Chancellor and Gustav ("the Bloodhound") Noske as Minister of Defense. The castle bell duly tolled to celebrate the occasion, but schoolchildren did not line the streets to cheer Ebert, nor did he receive the promised guard of honor as he left the Assembly. Even the delegates did not seem overly enthusiastic about their new President or his Cabinet; one delegate was heard to mutter, "Well, anyhow, Ebert and Scheidemann are better than anarchy and chaos." Indeed, there were no truly charismatic popular figures to be found in Weimar. Ebert's wife reported that they celebrated the election with a few friends and a bottle of wine: "A few telegrams of congratulations arrived and some letters, and somebody sent a beautiful basket of flowers. That was all."

In one of Berlin's largest movie theaters, a picture of Ebert, encircled by a wreath, was thrown onto the screen with the caption "Germany's First President." The band played a few strains of a patriotic air, and the projectionist waited for the audience's response. But the only sound was that of people shuffling for their hats and coats. The projectionist next showed an advertisement for a corset shop.

Former Berlin Police Commissioner Eichhorn reportedly was hiding in Brunswick under the protection of the local leftist regime. Tension continued throughout Germany between the left-wing Soldiers' Councils and the regular army officers. Hindenburg was raising a new force of volunteers—promising five marks a day, good food, and new uniforms—to defend the eastern borders from the Bolshevik menace that endangered the Fatherland. Middle-class Berliners still made way and saluted when members of the Hohenzollern family passed.

A member of the United States Medical Reserve Corps reported to American officials in Paris that Germany was still starving. "There are no eggs, no milk and only half a pound of beet sugar for each person a month. Shop girls have lost from ten to forty-five pounds in weight, while everyone shows a lack of vitality. I found children going to school shod with paper sandals or with cloth shoes to which wooden soles had been attached. No one knows the composition of the black, gritty bread that is being issued in limited quantities. Tuberculosis is increasing and skin diseases due to lack of nourishment and lack of soap are prevalent. The Germans who overran France should be punished and permitted to starve," he concluded, "but not the women and children. Hungry men and women do not make good neighbors." Another American observer told of seeing scores of children in Berlin with great sores upon their bodies from lack of proper nutrition. He said that a former high German government official had called his attention to the suffering children, and asked why America was not sending food to prevent such a calamity. "This unrest may be dormant in Berlin now," he warned, "but it will spring up again there and elsewhere if food does not get into Germany quickly."

And Berlin continued to dance on the edge of a pit. The Palais de Danse was filled every night with smartly dressed patrons drinking expensive champagne and dancing under the great colored lights; the sound of rifles crackled in the slums nearby; packets of money were thrown upon illegal roulette tables; half-frozen workers who could not obtain coal for their homes huddled around the public fires that blazed in huge square braziers in the Unter den Linden; the icy winds blew in from Russia; and arc lamps shone brilliantly upon long stretches of ice on the Lietzensee and Deer Park, throwing grotesque shadows from the skaters who glided to the sounds of music until late into the night.

Wilson may not have been everyone's ideal Valentine, but French schoolgirls found him tremendously appealing nonetheless. "He smiles all the time," wrote one adoring mademoiselle. "He has long cheeks and a big chin without any beard. That is so little children may have all the more place to kiss him." Another smitten young student declared, rather inexplicably, that she "would like to be the daughter of the concierge of President Wilson." But they were all surpassed by the fervor of one eleven-year-old who voiced her deepest hope: "I wish that President Wilson would never die."

Wilson had no illusions about his own mortality, but he believed a part of him would live on—forever, he hoped—in his most cherished accomplishment: the creation of a League of Nations. The League would be the foundation of the entire peace settlement; he knew that the Peace Conference could never hope to settle permanently every international dispute within the space of a few months in 1919, or to placate every national or economic interest that pleaded its case to the Council of Ten. With the League in place, more mundane questions, such as territorial boundaries, could always be adjusted peacefully in the years to come; without the League, there was no hope that any settlement could last long before being ripped apart by the losers, those who had failed to gain their objectives or who had been completely shut out by the victors at Paris.

So Wilson spent long hours in that first month at Paris in a labor of love, working with House and Lord Robert Cecil of Britain and General Smuts of South Africa to draft a constitution for the League. Admiral Grayson, still concerned about the strain on Wilson's delicate health, finally ordered his patient to take a complete day of rest on the first Sunday in February, forbidding the President even to attend church services. At one point Wilson asked to have his "secretary" sent up to his room; British delegates who heard of the request conjured up images in their minds of a shapely young lady taking dictation upon the President's knee; instead, a battered old typewriter was dispatched to Wilson's chambers. (This was the sort of behavior that led the British to deem Wilson "a queer old bird.") But veteran Wilson-watchers knew that when he locked himself up alone with that typewriter, he was struggling to express his most intimate personal thoughts.

On February 14, Valentine's Day, a military guard of honor greeted Wilson as he arrived at the Foreign Office on the Quai d'Orsay for another plenary session of the Peace Conference. Inside—in the same chamber with the same overwrought clock where the conference had been called to order four weeks earlier—all the delegates were already assembled, awaiting Wilson's entrance. A heavy fog rolled in through the high windows overlooking the Seine. Clemenceau greeted the President and called the meeting to order at three-thirty. Wilson rose and began to speak. He spoke of the work the League of Nations commission had achieved; he spoke of the constitution—the Covenant, with all the quasi-religious connotations that word carried for a devout Calvinist—which the commission had fashioned, a Covenant that, according to Wilson, remained open to change if it could be improved in any way. "The best report I can make is to read the document itself." And so he did, for thirty-five minutes.

Then Wilson spoke of what the creation of a League of Nations meant to the world: "It is definite as a guarantee of peace. It is definite as a guarantee against aggression. It is definite against a renewal of such a cataclysm as has just shaken civilization. . . . Men are looking eye to eye and saying: 'We are brothers and have a common purpose. We did not realize it before, but now we do realize it, and this is our covenant of friendship.' " And for Wilson the League was as precious as a child and needed just as much loving care to ensure that it fulfilled its promise. "A living thing is born and we must see to it what clothes we put on it." Meanwhile Mrs. Wilson, smuggled in by Grayson and hidden (not very successfully) in an armchair behind a curtain in back of the delegates' table, beamed with almost maternal pride as she watched her husband's triumph. "It was a great moment in history and as he stood there—slender, calm and powerful in his argument—I seemed to see the people of all depressed countries—men and women and little children crowding round and waiting upon his words."

As Wilson finished, having spoken for an hour, the clock stood at four-thirty. Delegates who believed in Wilson's mission (including Colonel House) had tears in their eyes. House passed the President a note: "Dear Governor, Your speech was as great as the occasion—I am very happy—EMH." Wilson sent a reply: "Bless your heart. Thank you from the bottom of my heart. WW." When the session adjourned at seven o'clock, Wilson hurried to his waiting limousine and sank back into the cushions as he wearily removed the ever-present silk hat. His wife asked if he was tired. "Yes, I suppose I am," he replied, "but how little one man means when such vital things are at stake." Then he returned to the Murat to prepare for the journey he would begin that evening, first to Brest and then aboard the *George Washington*, the liner that would take him home for several weeks to attend to domestic business before Congress adjourned.

Some thought the conference now had already successfully completed the most dangerous phase; with the Covenant in place, all the other questions could be negotiated through the usual give-and-take of diplomacy. Clemenceau was not convinced. Just a few days earlier, he had told an Associated Press reporter that the war had not necessarily yet been won: "It would perhaps be more accurate to say that there is a lull in the storm. . . . Although Germany had been beaten militarily and had been largely disarmed, there still remained a chaotic but fruitful Russia from which great help may be drawn by the Teutons." Clemenceau would not be satisfied with a League of Nations empowered only with the moral force of organized world opinion as protection against a resurgent German military power, nor would the editors of the popular French newspaper *Le Journal*. "While all are speaking of fraternization and eternal peace, the French people cannot lose sight of reality," *Le Journal* warned, especially "reality in the vicinity of 70 million humiliated Germans shuddering under merited punishment." Reality also meant half of Europe in chaos. Now Wilson would be away from Paris for four weeks; Lloyd George already was in London arbitrating the latest labor disputes; Orlando had to return to Rome to deal with another in the never-ending series of Italian Cabinet crises; and Clemenceau himself was facing increasing domestic criticism.

Wilson dined alone with his wife and his achievement that evening. House and Lansing stopped by to wish him well, and at 9:05 the presidential party drove away in their automobiles, accompanied by a detachment of the Republican Guard. At the Invalides railway station, the usual array of red carpets, flowers, plants, flags, and a company of infantry with a band greeted the Americans, and an array of French dignitaries, including Clemenceau and Poincaré, bade Wilson bon voyage. A French railway executive presented Mrs. Wilson with a massive bouquet of orchids. As the train left Paris at 9:20, Wilson leaned out of a window and shouted, *"Au revoir."*

He arrived at Brest at ten-thirty the following morning in a thick fog and persistent drizzle. He would share the *George Washington* with an excited group of several thousand doughboys, most of whom had spent the previous day peering over the railings of the ship in hopes of catching a glimpse of the President. Before Wilson arrived, local businessmen had given the *George Washington*'s captain a present for the President: a magnificent Quimper platter that had originally been fashioned for the World's Fair of 1878. Assistant Secretary of the Navy Franklin Delano Roosevelt nearly upstaged Wilson when he got to the harbor after his boss and hurriedly boarded the ship. An American woman presented the President with a bouquet; he grinned and bowed in reply. Mrs. Wilson received flowers of her own from a French official. There was little ceremony except handshaking with local military and civic officials as Wilson walked past a battalion of American soldiers standing at attention along the path from the railroad siding to the dock. A French marine band played the obligatory stanzas of "The Star-Spangled Banner." All ships in the harbor raised the American flag. Wilson made a brief speech thanking the French people for their hospitality. The crowd that had been watching the scene in the harbor from the city's highest walls since early in the morning gave the President a resounding cheer in response. Wilson took a few moments to speak with several Americans ("There's some of me still left," he declared) who had turned out for the ceremony. To steel baron Charles M. Schwab, who had recently arrived on a visit to France, he told the story of the optimist who fell out of a twelfth-story window; as he passed by the fifth floor he shouted, "I'm all right so far."

Standing on the quay, Wilson beckoned to his wife that it was time to go, and helped her down the stairs and into the gunboat that would take them to the *George Washington*. All traffic in the harbor stopped as Wilson rode out to the liner. An escort of French cruisers would take the *George Washington* to the open sea, where American vessels headed by the *New Mexico* would take over. There was a thunder of twenty-one-gun salutes.

As the gunboat began to pull away from the dock, Wilson stood and smiled and waved his hat to the crowd. Before the boat had gone twenty yards, the President had disappeared into the mist. Still Wilson continued to stand and smile and wave.

At last he stopped.

THREE

THE DAYS OF
THE SHADOW
OF DEATH

"The young men

shall die by

the sword;

their sons and daughters

shall die by famine . . ."

"How long shall

the land mourn . . ."

Late in February of 1919, Georgie Hyde-Lees Yeats was delivered of a daughter. Watching over his wife and child at the old Norman tower he had purchased several years earlier near Ballylee in western Ireland, William Butler Yeats wrote out a verse for the infant Anne: "Once more the storm is howling, and half hid / Under this cradle-hood and coverlid / My child sleeps on. . . ."

His daughter slept on unaware of the storms on the Atlantic and in the hearts and minds of men during that bitter winter, and Yeats, who knew the world she had entered, offered a prayer for her happiness. "I have walked and prayed for this young child an hour," he wrote,

> And heard the sea-wind scream upon the tower,
> And under the arches of the bridge, and scream
> In the elms above the flooded stream;
> Imagining in excited reverie
> That the future years had come,
> Dancing to a frenzied drum,
> Out of the murderous innocence of the sea. . . .

By early 1919, the sun had begun to set upon the British Empire, although that fact was hidden from most Englishmen, and particularly from the government in London. The war had not been kind to imperial pretensions, sweeping aside the Second Reich and the decayed and tottering edifices of the Russian, Ottoman, and Austro-Hungarian empires. But the British Imperium survived, and the Conservative-dominated Parliament returned in the khaki election of December 1918 had no intention of letting any vital pieces of the Empire slip away quietly now that peace had come.

That same election, however, witnessed a complete revolution in Irish politics. Seventy-three of the 105 Irish parliamentary seats were won by candidates of Sinn Fein (pronounced "Shin Fain" and meaning "Ourselves" in Gaelic). The Sinn Fein movement had emerged in the years immediately before the war as a revival of Irish nationalism and culture; its objectives and philosophy were generally expressed in rather nebulous terms influenced heavily by ancient Celtic mythology, and it was not, at first, a violent revolutionary movement at all. But because of this lack of precise definition, by 1914 the name had come to be applied to nearly every sort of rebellious Irish activity.

In the spring of 1916, thinking to sabotage the British war effort at a time when the stalemate on the Western Front had begun to produce a deepening sense of desperation in England, a group of determined but decidedly impractical Irish patriots had launched a rising in Dublin on Easter Monday by seizing the General Post Office and a half-dozen other prominent buildings. Quite naturally, the British Army wasted no time in blasting half of downtown Dublin to smithereens to oust the rebels from their strongholds. When the insurrection ended in ignominious defeat less than a week later, the general reaction in Ireland was that the rebel leaders were fools and worse for having brought down British wrath upon the entire country and jeopardizing recent progress toward limited Home Rule status. Displaying their usual heavy-handedness in Irish affairs, however, the army and the government in Whitehall managed to turn the irresponsible rebels into martyrs by staging a series of secret military trials and carrying out fourteen cold-blooded executions over a ten-day period. Those like Yeats who had derided the pretentiousness of the rebel leaders now knew that the situation had "changed, changed utterly: A terrible beauty is born."

The Easter Rising and its aftermath produced a striking psychological change in Ireland, making anything less than independence from Britain— independence now, not fifty years down the road—appear totally inadequate. Hence the Sinn Fein tidal wave in the December 1918 elections (one of the successful Sinn Fein candidates was the Countess Markievicz, née Constance Gore-Booth, the first woman ever elected to Parliament). And if direct military action seemed an unattractive option for Irish nationalists in early 1919, then they would follow a more peaceful but no less vigorous course: the duly elected Members of Parliament would refuse to take their seats in London and would instead set up their own parliament in Dublin to govern Irish domestic affairs.

So, on the dreary and drizzling afternoon of January 21, the first Dail Eireann (Assembly of Ireland) had convened in Dublin to issue Ireland's Declaration of Independence: "Now, therefore, we, the elected Representatives of the ancient Irish people in National Parliament assembled, do, in the name of the Irish nation, ratify the establishment of the Irish Republic and pledge ourselves and our people to make this declaration effective by every means at our command." (Of course, the declaration was not intended to be an announcement of the birth of a new nation, but a reaffirmation of the ancient Irish right of independence that had been temporarily suppressed for seven centuries by the English tyrant.)

Although a crowd of about a thousand curious onlookers stood outside the Mansion House to observe the historic proceedings, there really was not very much to see or hear. Only twenty-seven of the seventy-three Sinn Fein MPs attended the proceedings, most of the rest being lodged in British prisons for various seditious speeches or activities. And although the roll was called in English, the Dail's proceedings after that were almost all in Gaelic—carefully rehearsed and memorized—which virtually none of the audience or the deputies understood. Fortunately for the sake of posterity, the Irish Declaration of Independence was read (with everyone standing) first in Gaelic, then in French, and finally in English. Then came a message to the free nations of the world (also read in three languages) requesting their support and demanding to put forth the Irish case at Paris. The Dail appointed three delegates to the Peace Conference, but since two of them were in jail at the moment (including Eamon de Valera, a veteran of the 1916 Rising whose death sentence had been commuted), it seemed something of an empty gesture. As the session ended, one observer muttered darkly, "Fools. What good is a revolution without an army? What good is an Island without a navy?"

Nevertheless, the fuse had been lit. The Dail proceeded to set up a system of local councils and courts to replace the King's writ throughout most of the island. A random campaign of terrorism began; on the same day the Dail convened, two members of the Royal Irish Constabulary who were guarding a cartload of gelignite in Solloghodbeg, County Tipperary, were ambushed and killed by a squad of masked Irish Volunteers. Lloyd George's government responded by placing the county under the Crimes Act, which imposed a regime not unlike that in the occupied cities of Germany: all meetings were prohibited, no one was allowed outdoors after 7:00 P.M. without a permit, no letters could be sent or received except through the censor, and more troops arrived to enforce the regulations. In a less deadly fashion, Sinn Fein representatives ranged throughout Ireland forcing the cancellation of hunting meets on the grounds that the enjoyment of such sport was immoral while true Irish patriots wasted in English prisons.

On February 3, De Valera and two Sinn Fein associates effected a dramatic escape from Lincoln Jail through the use of a spare key smuggled in from the outside, and the three fugitives disappeared into the English countryside. The break electrified Dublin, and when the Dail named a new government in the spring, it chose De Valera as president of the new republic. Realizing that it had little to gain except aggravation and embarrassment from the continued incarceration of the Sinn Fein deputies, the government finally decided to release them gradually.

Those Irish nationalists who took seriously Woodrow Wilson's speeches on the right of self-determination for small nations hoped that he would look favorably upon their claims at Paris. In the United States, Irish-Americans mobilized their political power in support of the Dail. Cardinal Gibbons proclaimed that "Ireland wants freedom to breathe the air of heaven. She wants freedom to stretch her brawny and sinewy arms. She wants freedom to develop the riches of her soul. She wants freedom to carve out her own destiny." (She also wanted American money, and the Irish Race Convention that met in Philadelphia in mid-February pledged $1.25 million for the cause of Irish freedom. Since the convention also agreed that a state of war existed between Ireland and England, it was not difficult to discern the uses to which the funds would be put.) The entire Democratic House delegation from Massachusetts urged the President to take steps at the Peace Conference to bring "justice, freedom and right for Ireland." And a New Jersey judge who had spent his own time in a British jail with the Irish nationalist Charles Parnell several decades earlier wondered aloud: "Can it be possible that after delivering speeches that were incentives to Irish rebellion, and after declaring again and again that no people should be obliged to live under a sovereignty it objects to, that President Wilson was saying one thing while meaning another?"

Yes, as a matter of fact, it *was* quite possible. Wilson may have sympathized with Irish claims, and he certainly recognized the value of Irish-American votes for the Democratic Party and his administration, but he also understood that Great Britain would never extend independence to Ireland under anything save extreme duress. And he was not foolish enough to expend diplomatic capital upon such a quixotic quest when a vastly more important objective (the League of Nations) required him to play all the trumps he held.

So Wilson refused the Lord Mayor's invitation to visit Dublin and receive the freedom of the city, and he refused to meet with any Irish delegation in Paris. For the time being, the Irish were left to their own not-inconsiderable resources.

* * *

Six million had died in India from influenza in the last three months of 1918. The epidemic still raged, its ravages supplemented by an outbreak of cholera. There was widespread famine from a failure of the rains, shortages of fodder endangered the cattle supply, and prices in early 1919 soared a hundred percent above the already high levels of 1917. For the masses of India, barely one step above a subsistence diet in the best of times, it was a devastating series of blows.

On the political front, agitation for independence had slowed during the war, but the All-India National Congress that met at the end of 1918 resumed the campaign by reaffirming its previous demands for increased self-government and a declaration of Indian rights. British opinion scoffed at such native pretensions, smelling a Bolshevik plot behind Indian demands for independence. The fact was that the nationalist movement was still almost exclusively the property of a small group of educated Indians, with no leader who could effectively command the loyalties of the masses across the nation. Nevertheless, in the spirit of the times, the Congress appointed three delegates to journey to Paris to put India's case before the Peace Conference. One of the three was a young, London-educated attorney who had returned in 1915 from a twenty-two-year stay in South Africa, where he had helped mobilize resistance within the Indian community to that country's discriminatory policies. A severe attack of dysentery prevented him from traveling any great distances in the early months of 1919, but as he slowly recovered, Mohandas Karamchand Gandhi completed his own unique plan to restore Indian dignity and obtain justice from the British.

Dignity and justice for formerly subject peoples were commodities much sought after by diplomats in Paris in February 1919, and two of the most earnest petitioners were Emir Faisal, third son of Sherif Hussein and prince of the Hejaz, and Dr. Chaim Weizmann, president of the English Zionist Federation. The dark and delicately mysterious Faisal was, by all accounts, one of the most dramatic and picturesque figures at the Peace Conference. Clad in an elegant white flowing headdress and gold-embroidered white coat, openly displaying a golden scimitar and a jewel-encrusted revolver, glowering at mere mortals with his dark eyes and running a long finger over his pointed black beard, he looked to one American observer to be "what he doubtless is—a son of Mars, Oriental version." Secretary of State Lansing, after hearing Faisal speak before the Council of Ten, wrote that "his voice seemed to breathe the perfume of frankincense." And everywhere Faisal went, Colonel Thomas Edward Lawrence, his British friend and interpreter (although Faisal could speak perfectly good colloquial English and French when he wished) was sure to follow.

The fair-haired Lawrence, a thirty-year-old former Oxford history student who, with Feisal, had organized and led the wartime Arab revolt against the Turks, was in Paris to see to it that the British government kept its promises to grant national sovereignty to the Arabs in the wake of the dissolution of the Ottoman Empire. From time to time, Harold Nicolson would come upon Lawrence in his whispering robes, gliding along the corridors of the Hotel Majestic, "the lines of resentment hardening around his boyish lips: an undergraduate with a chin." Faisal wanted an independent Arab nation—though he was perfectly willing to allow either Britain or the United States to be given a temporary mandate to oversee Arabian affairs—and he insisted that the state's boundaries include Syria, a land to which he felt entitled since his forces had, after all, conquered Damascus in the last months of the war. "The Arabs have long enough suffered under foreign domination," Faisal proclaimed. "The hour has at last struck when we are to come into our own again."

The British government, eager for a friendly and stable power to the east of Suez, were willing to grant his claims. The French, however, had their own plans for Syria, and the secret Sykes-Picot treaty of 1916 that divided certain Ottoman territories between the Allies appeared to give British sanction to French objectives. Accordingly, Clemenceau's government dismissed Faisal as nothing more than a British puppet and sought to placate him with gifts (including a damascened sporting rifle) and honors (the Croix de Guerre). To complicate matters further, Wilson naturally argued that all previous undertakings and agreements had been invalidated after both Britain and France had accepted his Fourteen Points as a basis for the peace settlement, and that the conference only had to ascertain the wishes of the people involved—a difficult task at best, in this instance.

Wilson had met with Faisal before leaving Paris and reportedly had been quite impressed: "Listening to the Emir I think to hear the voice of liberty, a strange and, I fear, a stray voice, coming from Asia." Another voice, and not a stray one by any means, was coming from the Zionists who wished to obtain the conference's blessings for a national home in Palestine. They had already received a qualified endorsement from the British government in a letter from Arthur Balfour to Lord Rothschild in November 1917. (Balfour had been careful to obtain the personal approval of President Wilson before he dispatched the letter.) The Balfour Declaration eventually took on immense symbolic significance for both the Zionist and Arab causes; in its original context, it was largely a tactical wartime ploy to obtain support for the Allied effort from Jews in Russia and the United States and to encourage the small bands of Zionist military forces (the Jewish Legion) already in Palestine. After the war, Britain continued to favor Zionist settlement in the Holy Land as another buffer to French expansionist aims. Beyond the exigencies of international politics, however, the notion of a Jewish homeland also held a definite appeal for a number of British and American statesmen on the grounds of sentiment and disinterested justice.

Palestine in early 1919 was a desolate and dispirited land of brown grass, yellow scrub-covered hills, rat holes, and orphans. The orthodox Jewish community in Jerusalem seemed to be living a thousand years in the past; when Weizmann had visited the city during the war, he had been appalled to discover that it was nearly impossible to find a Jew who could do some simple plumbing or even type a letter. After centuries of Ottoman rule, Jerusalem itself was a miserable, filthy medieval town, short of water (save for the drainage from rooftops collected in dirty cisterns under the houses, and the germ-infested liquid dispensed from leather sacks hung upon the backs of native water carriers), with roads stretching out in the distance to nowhere, lacking any effective civilian government and housing a multitude of quarreling sects of three different religions. It was, Weizmann admitted, "a land crying out for such simple things as ploughs, roads and harbours." That was one reason for the recent influx of money from the United States and immigrants from Europe who wished to restore the splendor of the promised land. David Ben-Gurion had already been in Palestine for thirteen years, and Golda Meir (then Golda Meyerson) was contemplating emigration from Milwaukee: the stirring rhetoric at the first convention of the American Jewish Congress in Philadelphia in the winter of 1919 inspired Mrs. Meyerson to write to her husband Morris, "I tell you that some moments reached such heights that after them one could have died happy."

For the moment, Zionist representatives such as Weizmann and Rabbi Stephen Wise claimed that they did not want an independent separatist state reserved exclusively for Jews, but rather "a place where our widely scattered people may be at home." Faisal and Lawrence were willing to grant them a place in Palestine, on the assumption that Jewish capital could help develop the land while allowing the Bedouin to maintain their traditional culture outside the limited areas of Jewish settlement, although every time Faisal made a pronouncement on the matter he said something slightly different from his previous statements. To buttress the idealistic dreamer Weizmann, U.S. Supreme Court Justice Louis Brandeis dispatched the intensely tough-minded Felix Frankfurter to Paris, where he was joined by a young attorney named Benjamin V. Cohen (later one of the prime architects of the New Deal in the 1930s) and Judge Julian Mack, president of the Zionist Organization of America. The organization had recently launched a $3-million fund drive for the reconstruction of Palestine—to build hospitals, roads, and schools, and to establish an effective system of local government. By mid-February, nearly $2 million had already been pledged, and the Zionist Society of Engineers was sending a mission to Palestine to survey the land and prepare plans for its development.

On the sand dunes outside the Arab city of Jaffa, sixty Jewish families had begun several years earlier to build a new city known as Tel Aviv. And to protect the still-tiny *yishuv*—the Jewish community in Palestine—there was already a self-defense organization known as Halshomer, one of whose members was the difficult and fiercely dedicated Ben-Gurion.

11

"My wound is grievous . . ."

Emile Cottin arose early on the morning of February 19. Scattered about his room in a small hotel in the Parisian suburb of Montrouge were an assortment of cheaply printed anarchist pamphlets and an edition of the complete writings of Auguste Comte. Cottin took out the Browning automatic pistol he had purchased from a demobilized soldier for thirty-five francs and loaded a full clip of cartridges, placing two more clips in his pocket. He aimed and fired a practice shot, striking and shattering a looking glass upon a wall. Then Cottin put on a yellow mackintosh and left his room and walked into Paris.

He was not leaving much behind—a job at a furniture maker's shop in the Faubourg St-Antoine. Twenty-three years old, pale, with long, dirty blond hair, "Milou" Cottin had no close friends. He had been invalided out of the army, and sentenced three times for inciting French soldiers to disobey their commanders. Once he had been arrested at a meeting of radicals for shouting "Death to Clemenceau!" but the authorities had not taken him seriously and had let him go. He knew exactly where to go this morning: he had been there several days in a row, to make certain his timing was absolutely accurate.

Cottin entered the Passy quarter of the city, where Benjamin Franklin had lived during his stay in Paris a century and a half before. He saw the police guards in front of the small, unpretentious house of his quarry; it was, he thought, a very simple house for such a famous man, and very ugly, but the Premier had consistently refused to move into his official residence. Across the street, in the window of an old curiosity shop, sat a stuffed tiger.

Retreating quietly to mingle with the Parisian housekeepers on their morning rounds to purchase the day's vegetables, Cottin hid himself behind a circular iron public urinal on the pavement by the wide Boulevard

Delessert, around the corner from the Rue de Franklin, and waited.

Clemenceau had followed his normal routine that morning, arising between five and six to the sound of cockcrow, taking a small breakfast, then exercising to prepare his seventy-seven-year-old body for the rigorous tasks that lay ahead that day. At 8:45 he emerged from his house in the narrow Rue de Franklin and climbed into a black limousine. The soldier-chauffer eased the car into traffic and headed toward the river; once he had turned onto the boulevard, it would be a straight drive to the War Office, where Clemenceau had scheduled a ten o'clock meeting with Balfour and Colonel House. But first the car had to slow down to make the turn, in front of and barely three feet from the *pissoir* where Cottin was hiding.

At 8:50 the Premier's car reached the corner. As it pulled onto the boulevard, Cottin leaped out and fired. In that split second, Clemenceau recognized Cottin as the man he had seen hiding in the shadows near his house the night before. The first shot splintered the windshield by the driver's head. By now they had passed the assassin, but Cottin stepped into the street and fired three more bullets into the back of the limousine, then ran after it, firing until the magazine was empty.

Believing that the danger had passed with the first shot, Clemenceau leaned forward to inspect the damage and thought, "Clumsy fellow; he's going to miss me." He felt a violent and painful shock as the second shot struck him in the back. The other bullets pierced the back window; one grazed the gendarme accompanying Clemenceau, and the rest passed harmlessly through the car. The officer jumped out and fired several shots at Cottin without hitting him. The driver immediately wheeled the car around and sped back to Clemenceau's house. "My adversaries are really poor shots," the Premier muttered to himself. "They are exceedingly clumsy."

When the limousine arrived back at the Rue de Franklin, a soldier who had witnessed the incident opened the door and found Clemenceau still leaning forward and bent down, shaken but calm. As he stepped out of the car, the Premier passed a bloodstained hand across his face, making it appear as if a bullet had grazed his head. He started off by himself to walk to the front door, but a number of bystanders came rushing up to help him. "Yes, I am slightly touched," he told them, "but it is not serious this time." The blood already had stained his shirtfront and was trickling down the left sleeve, turning the gray glove on his left hand dark brown. Leaning on the shoulder of one of his servants, Clemenceau walked up one flight of stairs to his bedroom and sat down in an armchair to wait for a doctor. His household staff fluttered about him and some began to cry. He waved his hand to dismiss the severity of the wound: *"Ce n'est rien."*

Cottin, meanwhile, had stopped running after the car and stood still in the middle of the boulevard after emptying his pistol. He threw the gun down in the street. As it dawned upon the customers of the butcher shops, fishmongers, and patisseries that lined the sidewalk that the Premier had been attacked, a number of them rushed toward the assassin. A seventeen-year-old barber's assistant, who had thought at first that the shots came from American soldiers firing into the air, as was their wont, ran after Cottin ("As I ran, I was greatly puzzled as to what to do with him once I reached him"), and began kicking and punching him. Others joined in the melee, women who had just come from the hairdressers beating Cottin with their umbrellas; believing that he was a foreign agent, the crowd began shouting, "Death to the Bolshevik!" A storekeeper named Raoul Dreyfus, unaware of what had happened, tried to restrain the mob from beating Cottin to death. They then turned upon Dreyfus, attacking him and his shop and screaming, "Accomplice! Anarchist! Down with the Jews!" When the police arrived they rescued and arrested both Cottin and Dreyfus.

At the police station, Cottin declared that he had tried to kill Clemenceau "to get rid of the man who is preparing another war." Insisting that the Premier was the enemy of humanity, Cottin proclaimed himself "an integral anarchist, a friend of men, not excepting the Germans, and a friend of humanity and fraternity." The police concluded that his brain had become overheated from a steady diet of anarchistic literature.

Outside Clemenceau's house, the street was blockaded with motorcars. Refusing to believe that the assailant was a Frenchman, the Parisians who had gathered around kept shouting, "This is a Russian!" Poincaré arrived at nine-thirty and Marshal Foch at ten. "I have dodged bigger ones than that at the front," Clemenceau told the Marshal. Major Dreyfuss from the Army Medical Service gave the Premier first aid until two surgeons from the University of Paris arrived to inspect the wound. An X-ray revealed that the bullet had lodged near Clemenceau's lung, but the location of the wound and the victim's advanced age convinced the surgeons that it would be safer to leave the bullet where it was than to try to remove it.

Balfour was in Colonel House's office when he heard that Clemenceau had been shot. "Dear dear," he murmured, "I wonder what that portends?" (Just as though someone had spilled a cup of tea, an observer noted.) "I don't know," replied House, "but we must find out." He grabbed Balfour by the arm and hurried him into a car. From Britain and the United States came the expected expressions of outrage and sympathy. "Horrified at dastardly attempt on your life," wired Lloyd George from London, "but felicitate you, France, and Allies on your escape from serious injuries. Looking forward to seeing you at Peace Conference in few days." "I am shocked to hear of the dastardly attack made upon you this morning," wrote King George. The U.S. State Department assured the French government that the "Government and people of the United States are shocked beyond measure and deeply moved at hearing of the criminal attempt on the life of M. Clemenceau, whose fearless devotion as a leader of his people has won for him in this country universal admiration and respect." Even the *North German Gazette* admitted that "the Paris criminal has done no service to the cause of peace. Clemenceau's enmity to the German people is no reason for not branding the attempt on his life as an execrable crime." The Pope sent his blessing; Clemenceau, with his usual irreverent good humor, replied by sending his blessing to the Pope.

Inevitably the attempted assassination created a wave of public sympathy for Clemenceau. Locked in combat with the Tiger over the fundamental character of the peace treaty with Germany, this clearly was not what Wilson needed at that moment.

In Paris, the dressmakers' showrooms were beginning to regain their prewar appearance, but prices were higher than ever. The new styles showed short skirts, wide enough to permit dancing and trimmed to look even wider, with short sleeves, and generally employing two types of material: one flimsy and one substantial, such as crepe and serge, or silk and mousseline de soie. Stripes were popular; vivid colors were returning for spring, but the glittering materials of last season already were considered commonplace and passé. In fact, one expert predicted that various neutral shades and simple black and white would remain the most popular hues in France. New hats were appearing every week; this week it was a soft little straw toque in gray or black and white.

On the day Clemenceau was shot, the *George Washington* was out of wireless communication with the rest of the world for nearly twenty-four hours. Passing through heavy seas, her naval escorts had fallen away one by one. The *New Mexico*, the pride of the fleet and the only electrically driven battleship in the U.S. Navy, stripped a turbine engine and had to drop back. The rest of the destroyer flotilla was forced to slow and leave the line when the weather turned rough. The *George Washington* continued on alone. From Washington, Secretary of the Navy Josephus Daniels ordered the *Denver* to go out and meet the President's ship.

The first few days out of Brest had seen fair weather, allowing Wilson to recover his strength after the exertions of Paris. Although Grayson continued to prescribe rest—especially after virtually the entire Secret Service contingent aboard contracted influenza—Wilson received wireless messages from Colonel House in their own secret code, keeping the President fully informed on the latest developments at the conference. Always the League of Nations dominated the President's thoughts and conversation: at lunch with Assistant Secretary Roosevelt and his wife, Eleanor, Wilson announced gravely that the United States must join the League, "or it will break the heart of the world for she is the only nation that all feel is disinterested and all trust." To Washington, Wilson cabled a request to meet with the foreign relations committees of Congress at the White House on February 26. He also asked that they withhold comment on the League Covenant until he had explained it to them in person; Wilson told three congressman traveling with him that "he was sure he could convince Congressional leaders that there were no fundamental objections." A number of Republicans ignored him and began denouncing "the evil thing with the holy name" as soon as they could find a reporter to listen. Senator Henry Cabot Lodge of Massachusetts, the cold and proud man who would chair the Senate Foreign Relations Committee when the new Congress convened, declined comment on the Covenant until he had more time to study it.

Every morning, Wilson attended the ship's chapel services. In balmy weather the presidential party and the troops on board shed their overcoats and enjoyed the sunshine on deck. Once the ship struck rough winds, however, almost everyone went below decks; Wilson surrendered only once, when the waves and salt spray dashed over the bridge and drenched him as he watched his destroyer escort plunging about in the rolling seas. A boat drill complete with bugles and calls to abandon ship interrupted one presidential breakfast, and Wilson and his wife stood dutifully by their assigned boat while the exercise ran its course. A minstrel show staged by the crew one evening ended in near disaster when a sailor who played the part of a chorus girl came down into the audience and threw his hairy arms around the presidential neck and even chucked Wilson under his square Presbyterian chin. Franklin Roosevelt saw Wilson's face turn to ice: it was a look that FDR never forgot.

Escaping the ice of northern Russia and accompanying the presidential party on board the *George Washington* was Ambassador David Francis, retiring as envoy to Russia and returning home for the first time in two years. In a series of briefings during the voyage, Francis gave Wilson a firsthand account of the chaos that raged throughout that unhappy country. He spoke, of course, of the incredible outrages stemming from "a reign of terror instituted by the Bolsheviki." But what Francis told Wilson concerned far more than Mother Russia alone. "I think it is impossible to restore peace in Europe with chaos prevailing in Russia," he warned. "In fact, with Germany practically uninjured industrially, I am persuaded that if peace is negotiated with Bolshevik rule continuing in Russia, Germany in twenty years will be stronger than she was at the beginning of the war. . . . If this turns out, Germany, instead of having been defeated, will have gained a victory."

Wilson on the high seas; Lloyd George in London; Clemenceau in bed with a bullet in his body. In Paris, things were getting more rather than less difficult. A rift had been growing among the Allies; Sir James Headlam-Morley told a friend that "I think it is a good thing that Wilson has gone away; it is extraordinary to hear from those who have heard his speeches at the Conference how very strong a feeling of distrust and opposition he creates. . . . There is no doubt a very nasty feeling arising between the French and the Americans, and there have been awkward incidents which of course are kept very secret." Harold Nicolson, too, noticed that the French feeling against Wilson and the League was growing: "They loathe the League of Nations." After one month of negotiations, Wilson had his League, Lloyd George had his mandate for Britain to administer the best portion of the former German colonies, and Clemenceau had the diplomatic credits he would cash in for French security when Wilson and Lloyd George returned. But Italy had not yet received the conference's blessings for the territories it desired so ardently, and Orlando was growing desperate for a victory to bolster his Cabinet's power in Rome.

What especially irked the British and Americans about Italy's imperialistic claims was the willingness of her delegation to advance them by using any devious means that came to hand. "What swine these people are," Balfour once spat in disgust. Nicolson confessed that he could not understand the Italian attitude: "They are behaving like children, and sulky children at that. They obstruct and delay everything—and evidently think that by making themselves disagreeable on every single point they will force the Conference to give them fat plums to keep them quiet." In truth, Orlando was caught between the imperialists at home and Wilson's idealistic insistence upon the principle of self-determination; as Nicolson later explained, "the attempt to combine the fifteenth with the thirtieth century would, in the best of circumstances, be liable to lead to some misconception of motive. And Paris of 1919 was not the best of circumstances."

But beyond Italian obstructionism, the diplomats and committees of experts at Paris were oppressed most of all by a sense that the task they had undertaken was nearly impossible to complete. They felt that precious time was slipping away even as they knelt over their huge detailed maps spread out upon the thick carpets in hotel rooms, as they read their reports sinking under the weight of massive compilations of statistics, as they drew the boundaries that were not merely lines on a map but the hopes and fears of flesh-and-blood men and women. Somewhere, something was going terribly wrong; Nicolson believed that "there is a definite inarticulate human element behind it all somewhere, and somewhere there must be a definite human desire behind all these lies and lies." Vicious pogroms against Jews were provoked by greedy, land-grabbing Poles emboldened by the defeat of Germany and the disabling of Russia; Czech statesmen grimly declared, "Give us the coal mines and we'll take care of the population"; 20 percent of the babies in Hungary were born dead, and 40 percent died within a month of birth. Lies and lies, and the shadow of the truth behind the lies. And every midnight another precious day was gone.

Painting the portraits of the great men of the conference, Sir William Orpen finally obtained Wilson's consent to be included in the anteroom group that included Clemenceau, Lloyd George, Orlando, Balfour, Foch, Pershing, Haig, Faisal, the Maharajah of Bikanir, and a Japanese representative to be named later. . . .

As February drew to a close, the New York Yankees had signed only three regulars. Like most of the other major-league clubs, the Yankees were planning to improve their profit sheet by taking fewer players to spring training and slashing the salaries of those who made the team. "We are not worrying about the players," announced Colonel T. L. Huston, co-owner of the Yankees, even though the club looked to be notoriously weak in the outfield again this year. "When the opening day comes we will have a ball club in the field and a good one, too. Any business that pays out more than it takes in season after season cannot live, and that is what this club has been doing. Baseball," Huston vowed, "will have to be put on a strictly business basis and the sooner the better. It's about time the players learned something about the business end of this game."

One player who was learning about business was Boston's Babe Ruth, who still had not come to terms with Red Sox owner Harry Frazee. Barred by the terms of his contract from becoming a prizefighter to earn extra cash, the Babe was investigating the possibility of purchasing the New Bedford roller polo franchise as an investment. In Chicago, Kid Gleason revealed to no one's surprise that the White Sox had offered Shoeless Joe Jackson a new contract, hoping that he and his teammates would desert the defense shipyards and return to the diamond now that the war was over. "I want Jackson and the other players back with me," Gleason said. "I shall make every inducement to have them return." Not to worry; they were on their way. As the start of spring training inched closer, one of the ex-shipyard men, Claud "Lefty" Williams—the crafty southpaw Gleason was counting on for a twenty wins or more—signed his 1919 contract with the White Sox, as did veteran third baseman George "Buck" Weaver ("If there is one thing Weaver would rather do than eat, it is play baseball") and young shortstop Charles "Swede" Risberg.

Disgusted with the sham and pompous show of the Peace Conference proceedings at Paris, Oswald Villard packed his bags and headed for Berne and the socialists' International Conference ("The Second Internationale"). There he found ninety-one delegates, mostly from Western and Central Europe, debating, without ceremony or formality, the future of the world. "There is not a lackey, not a uniform, not a decoration nor title. . . . There are no long lines of automobiles before the building, no waiters in dress suits to serve tea, no gilt, no braid, no candelabra!" The liberal Villard was delightfully impressed.

By all odds, one of the most impressive men in Berne in February 1919 was Kurt Eisner, the gentle president of Bavaria, erstwhile drama critic and student of philosophy, and the only head of a government attending the conference. A balding, bespectacled Jew from Galicia whose thick, slightly reddish beard and long hair flowing back over his collar gave him the appearance of a quintessential absentminded German professor, Eisner had gained fame and jail sentences for his brilliant journalistic work on behalf of peace and labor before and during the war. His unyielding advocacy of radical socialism and his unquestioned integrity had earned him the leadership of the leftist forces in Bavaria in late 1918; when the last members of the ruling Wittelsbach family fled Bavaria in alarm and comic disarray in the face of popular demonstrations against the dynasty in November (Ludwig III's automobile ran off the road while heading south out of Munich and became mired in the wintry muck of a potato field), Eisner immediately assumed power and established a republic. He insisted that only a thoroughgoing economic revolution could safeguard the future of the German republic, although he was willing to proceed quite slowly to avoid violent opposition. "In these days of senseless, brutal murder," Eisner wrote in his first proclamation of November 8, 1918, "we have the greatest abhorrence for all bloodshed. Let every human life be sacred." Not surprisingly, then, he opposed the Ebert-Noske policy of armed suppression of the Spartacist revolts, believing quite correctly that it represented the revival of militarism in Germany. To his admirers, Eisner was a prophet; to the bourgeoisie of hidebound, tradition-ridden Catholic Bavaria, he was an impudent upstart; to the reactionary upper class, he was a devil who threatened the very foundations of order and civilization.

Worse, he now became a traitor. When his turn came to speak to the gathering at Berne on February 4, Eisner (dressed, according to British Labour Party leader Ramsay MacDonald, "in afternoon tea-party garb") began by frankly admitting Germany's guilt for instigating the war, and he personally named William Hohenzollern as the one man most to blame for the bloodshed and atrocities. In the smoke-filled air, over the silence of the astounded audience, Eisner's soft, calm, and measured voice condemned all aspects of Prussianism, including Germany's vicious treatment of French civilians and military prisoners during the war, and called upon the government at Weimar to help rebuild the devastated regions of France. The next day, facing an upsurge of opposition to his government at home, Eisner departed by train for Munich. A friend congratulated him on his courage in making the speech; "*In neun Tagen wird's mit mir aus,*" Eisner replied with great sadness. "In nine days I shall be finished."

Several days later, Villard himself boarded a train ("a wreck, the cars dirty, with broken windows and torn seats") bound for Munich. On the morning of his arrival in the city, six hundred sailors entered Munich and attempted a reactionary coup. Watching the street fighting around the railway station, Villard understood that four years of brutal warfare "had not been without their effect in accustoming all classes to the method of attaining their ends by violence." He saw the Bavarian Supreme Court, of which his father had been a member, its stonework bullet-chipped and shell-battered, its ornamental sculpture mutilated. He ate lunch at his hotel and knew that the poorer classes could not even afford the paltry fare he was served: "incredible coffee which tasted like straw—nothing else. The soup was tepid water slightly flavored; there were some things I could not identify which passed for vegetables; and there was the Ersatz which went by the name of bread."

After spending a morning investigating the situation at the Food Bureau, Villard realized that the official daily ration "would not keep a chicken alive"; worse, there would be absolutely no food in Munich in three months unless the Allies lifted their blockade. And Villard comprehended the death of the old world when he visited his elderly aunt, whom he had not seen since before the war: "I was the same, but she! War, suffering, and undernourishment had taken their toll. This pitifully thin, trembling, almost tottering woman hardly suggested the extraordinarily erect, vigorous, distinguished aristocrat who was my aunt, the one who was always beautifully gowned, always equal to any situation, whose title *Excellenz* seemed not a title but a description. The world she loved and adorned had crashed. She who had known royalty and courts was now like a pitiful child confused."

On the morning of Friday, February 21—two days after the attempt on Clemenceau's life—Villard walked to the Landtag, the Bavarian parliament, to witness the opening meeting of the first democratic assembly in that nation's history. While Villard wedged his way into the standing-room-only press gallery, Kurt Eisner, having suffered defeat in the recent elections, was on his way from the Foreign Ministry to submit his resignation to the Landtag to make way for the formation of a new government. He was not terribly distressed at the prospect; he had, he told friends, always been more comfortable in opposition anyway. Eisner's secretary accompanied him. Inside, a fellow correspondent pointed out the important personages below to Villard. "Now they are all here except Kurt Eisner."

Then a young man, very pale, walked up to the platform. It was Eisner's secretary. Before he could speak, a soldier burst into the press box. "Kurt Eisner is murdered!" he shouted. The eyes of the delegates stared, at first uncomprehending. "Kurt Eisner has been shot!" And the soldier held up the bloody eyeglasses of the dead man as proof. Cries of "Shame!" and "Adjourn! Adjourn!" filled the hall. "You'd better get away," one reporter told his wife. "Things are likely to happen here."

On Prannerstrasse, Count Anton Arco Valley, a young aristocrat and lieutenant in the Prussian Guards, had stepped to within a few yards of Eisner, and, shouting, "Down with the revolution, long live the Kaiser," shot him twice in the back of the head. Eisner died instantly. They took his body and laid it in the porter's lodge in the Foreign Office building.

When the Landtag reassembled, a butcher named Alois Lindner walked in through a side door, raised his arm, and shot point-blank at the Minister of the Interior, Herr Auer—a dedicated foe of the Spartacists and lately a vocal critic of Eisner's regime. Ironically, Auer was shot while he was in the midst of a speech condemning Eisner's murder. An officer who tried to apprehend Lindner was shot dead. Then firing began from the galleries.

Another deputy and a clerk were killed; people fled the building on their hands and knees. "I have seen terrible things and witnessed two attempts to assassinate kings," one correspondent testified, "but I never saw anything like the panic and terror and flight and the general promiscuous shooting." Villard had been standing outside the building when the second round of attacks began; as he waited by the doorway, the ashen-faced Lindner came out and pointed to Villard and told the soldiers around him, "There's another chap we ought to get." Two soldiers hustled Villard to safety, and the rest allowed the butcher to escape.

As news of Eisner's murder spread throughout the city, Munich stopped. (With allowances for minor local variations, the sight of a modern city on strike was much the same everywhere: Berlin, Belfast, Seattle, Munich. Streetcars disappeared, shops pulled down their heavy shutters, telephone and telegraph services suddenly were out of order, cabs and cars vanished, the afternoon newspapers failed to appear, restaurants closed.) The Council of Workmen, Soldiers, and Peasants proclaimed a three-day general strike and urged the proletariat to protect the revolution. Long processions of gaunt workingmen in the streets vowed to get even with the aristocrats who had slain Eisner. Twenty prominent local citizens were seized and shut up in a hotel and told they would all be lined up and shot if any more assassinations took place. Sheets of white paper that drifted down from airplanes declared that everyone in the city must be indoors by seven o'clock that evening; sheets of crimson paper announced the consequences of a state of siege: anyone on the streets after seven would be shot. Red flags were hoisted everywhere and flew at half-mast. That night machine-gun fire rattled through the heavy winter air. "Comrades! Don't shoot. This building is in the hands of the Councils."

The next day, supplies came into the city for the government soldiers, who forced their way into homes and requisitioned all the arms they could find. Workingmen over twenty years of age were given weapons, and the bourgeoisie was disarmed. Cars with red flags and placards calling for "Revenge for Eisner" patrolled the streets. Resolutions to the workers' Council called for the immediate establishment of a Bavarian Soviet. Prince Joachim, sixth son of the ex-Kaiser, had been living in Munich under the name of Count Merz; he and his wife were forced onto a train and taken to Prussia under escort.

Upon the spot where Eisner fell, women and children came and left small handfuls of flowers and men removed their hats in respect (those who did not were beaten). On Tuesday, February 25, the city stopped again for Eisner's funeral. There was a great solemn procession, with masses of flowers and black-draped portraits of Eisner; airplanes flew above in tribute; military bands played dirges. At the service in the cemetery chapel there were no prayers, no religious rites, but civil authorities forced the Catholic churches to ring their bells for an hour in honor of Eisner, the man responsible for separating the Bavarian church and state. After a few brief eulogies, the body was taken away for cremation. At the end, the family and government officials rode home in the royal carriages of the Wittelsbachs, the same coaches from which Eisner himself had earlier removed all the royal crests and silver trappings.

Munich remained calm. The general strike ended, but the state of siege continued. No officer of the *ancien regime* dared appear on the streets in uniform. Coal was nearly nonexistent, and hundreds of thousands of unemployed workers wandered through Bavaria. Villard cabled to Hoover and Colonel House in Paris that unless the Allies put food into Munich soon, there would be Bolshevism in Bavaria by the middle of April. Meanwhile, the various socialist factions that Eisner had united for a brief moment began to fall out among themselves. And at the other end of the city, the middle class watched with mounting uneasiness as the old world receded further into the distance.

During his brief stay in Berne, Eisner had spoken to Ramsay MacDonald of "the torn and disrupted social fabric in the centre of Europe, and how the long delays in letting the people know what were to be the terms of peace and in getting the wheels of society to go round again were playing havoc with order, defeating all attempts to establish authority, and dividing the countries into conspiracies of revengeful reaction and agitations of purposeless revolution." Eisner had spoken, MacDonald recalled, "as one whose mind was clouded and troubled." And upon hearing of Eisner's death, MacDonald added his own warning to the men in Paris:

A RECKLESS LACK OF DIGNITY AND SANITY IN POLICY, A DRAGGING ON OF THE PARIS PRELIMINARIES, A CONTINUANCE OF THE BLOCKADE, AN INDULGENCE IN BEDLAM THREATS AGAINST THE NEW DEMOCRACIES AS INHERITORS OF THE INIQUITIES OF THE OLD MONARCHIES—THESE AND SUCH THINGS ARE A METHOD OF PUNISHING GUILTY ENEMIES BY INVOLVING THEM AND OURSELVES IN COMMON RUIN. SPARTACISM IS REVIVED, SCHEIDEMANN WILL BE DRIVEN FARTHER TO THE RIGHT AND MAY BE DISPLACED BY A REVOLUTIONARY GOVERNMENT OF UNSETTLEMENT, A CLEAR DIVISION INTO EXTREMES WILL TAKE PLACE, AND MEN IN THE MIDDLE WILL BE CRUSHED OR SILENCED.

On the evening before Eisner died, demonstrations by four thousand unemployed and a thousand Communists shook Budapest, producing wild shooting by police and civilians and leaving scores wounded.

Living quietly in the army barracks in Munich, Adolf Hitler was given the mindless but time-consuming task of examining hundreds of old gas masks to determine whether they were still in working order. He spent most of his evenings at the opera, only occasionally attending the meetings of the local Soldiers' Councils. For now, Hitler took no part in the drama unfolding before his eyes in Bavaria.

WILLIAM BUTLER YEATS'S PRAYER FOR HIS DAUGHTER:

In courtesy I'd have her chiefly learned;
Hearts are not had as a gift but hearts are earned
By those that are not entirely beautiful;
Yet many, that have played the fool
For beauty's very self, has charm made wise,
And many a poor man that has roved,
Loved and thought himself beloved,
From a glad kindness cannot take his eyes.

On the morning after Cottin's attack, Clemenceau slept until eight o'clock, an extraordinarily late hour for him. "I am a lazy man," he told Sister Theoneste, the nurse who had been summoned to attend the Tiger. "That is the first time in twenty years that I have been so late getting up." Sister Theoneste had nursed Clemenceau after a previous operation, and was widely believed to be the only woman in France who could handle him. Even so, hers was not an easy task. Clemenceau repeatedly threw off the old army blanket that covered him and got out of his armchair when he should not (the wound would not allow him to lie down). He constantly talked too much, and drove his doctors to despair by sleeping from 9:00 P.M. to midnight and then beginning a full work schedule in the middle of the night. Clemenceau also took great delight in teasing Sister Theoneste with his unconventional views on organized religion. Once he told her that he had dreamed he had walked to the gates of heaven, where he saw Saint Peter standing guard as usual. Saint Peter was chatting with an old woman outside the gate, and the woman was obviously distressed. Clemenceau overheard the conversation:

"I fear you cannot come in," Saint Peter told her. "In extremis, you failed to confess."

"But death came so suddenly," the poor woman cried, "there was no time to find the village priest."

"I am sorry, but there are the regulations."

At that point Clemenceau intervened and suggested that Saint Peter call one of the priests already in heaven to the gates and have him administer the sacrament to the old woman. Saint Peter glared at Clemenceau for impudently daring to meddle in divine affairs, but finally called a messenger—Clemenceau thought it was one of the seraphim—and with a barely disguised lack of patience said, "Go fetch me a priest."

In a few moments the messenger returned and whispered something to Saint Peter, who responded with a look of total disbelief and sent the angel off again. Finally, after a long, long time, he came back and gave Saint Peter his message.

"Well, well," said Clemenceau, who was getting rather tired of waiting.

"Well," Saint Peter replied, shaking his head sadly, "it seems there are no priests at all in heaven." And he slammed the door.

Clemenceau asked Sister Theoneste what this dream could possibly mean. Unruffled, she replied that if Monsieur le President would only say his prayers as he should, Saint Peter would not keep him waiting outside the gate. Then, in an aside to a friend, she added, "He is such good company and such a good man that perhaps they will let him in anyhow. At least I hope so; and that hope I never fail to include in my prayers."

Clemenceau had even less use for doctors, whom he called "a gang of jackasses," than for priests. He had been trained as a physician himself in his misspent youth, and jokingly confessed to having committed numerous murders—not in wartime, but during his practice of medicine in Montmartre. He insisted on helping them to draw up the daily bulletins to the press on his medical condition. "I am better," he assured one of his doctors, "but it is not your fault. It is my good nature which has produced it." Despite their cautionary warnings, he ventured out into his garden to enjoy the springlike weather several days after the attack. Observers noted the drawn look of his face, the skin paler than usual, the eyes deeper under the famous bushy eyebrows, and a dark stubble of beard; but they also recognized the inevitable skullcap worn at a rakish angle over the left ear, and the everpresent gray suede gloves.

After investigators raided the homes and meeting places of known Bolsheviks and anarchists in Paris in search of evidence that Cottin was involved in an elaborate radical plot—he wasn't—they came to get Clemenceau's account of the assassination attempt. The interview lasted only twenty-five minutes. The Premier pretended that it had all been an "accident," and that Cottin's abominable marksmanship went far toward explaining why France had had such a difficult time winning the war: "We have just won the most terrible war in history, yet here is a Frenchman who at point-blank range misses his target six times out of seven. Of course the fellow must be punished for the careless use of a dangerous weapon and for poor marksmanship. I suggest that he be locked up for about eight years, with intensive training in a shooting gallery."

On the afternoon of February 26, after his usual lunch of soup, vegetables, a baked apple, and mineral water, Clemenceau emerged to the cheers of a large crowd and took a two-hour drive to Versailles and back. The next day he was back at work at the Ministry of War. Of course, Clemenceau suffered more than he let on; despite his spartan habits and decades of a relatively abstemious existence, his seventy-seven-year-old body could not take such a violent shock without a serious reaction. Increasingly he turned over his responsibilities to his subordinates, and the heavy-lidded eyes closed in sleep during conferences and meetings even more frequently than before. At times his wound could be diplomatically convenient. When Baron Sonnino came to complain about Italy's treatment at the hands of the Allies, Clemenceau groaned and announced that he was in terrible pain. "It feels like an Italian stiletto," he whispered to a friend. But still, after all the jokes, the work of the Peace Conference had suffered a further, damaging delay.

Narrow-chested, high-waisted, close-fitting suits for men were out, proclaimed the International Custom Cutters' Association. "The man we must fit today is not the same fellow physically for whom we made clothes before this war began," announced the association's chairman. "The rigorous army training has given him a broad, deep chest and straight back. The great majority of our customers are now athletic men and we must design our clothes to fit him and must do away with all narrow, stooping styles." The National Association of Merchant Tailors predicted that for summertime wear, silks, linens, and other delicate fabrics would replace the usual flannels. Just to show how far innovation had already come, one New York exhibitor at the tailors' convention dared to introduce a tradition-shattering double-breasted dinner jacket; while everyone agreed it was an artistic triumph, obviously it could be worn only by the slimmest of men.

As far as the returning doughboys were concerned, however, the most important consideration in civilian clothes was color—any bright color to alleviate the sartorial boredom of months wearing nothing but khaki. Scotch plaids became immensely popular, and suits in stripes that resembled a futurist painting of Mount Vesuvius; green and blue and gray socks, white socks with black clocks and black socks with white clocks. Any merchant stuck with a stock of khaki-colored merchandise couldn't give it away. "The war is over," one young veteran declared. "Why should I go around looking like an undertaker, just because I served in the army? Me for 'glad rags' just as soon as I can put aside my uniform."

From the National Association of Men's Straw Hat Manufacturers of America, however, came an ominous warning of impending shortages for the coming season. The association's members had not expected the Armistice to come as quickly as it had, and now they would be unprepared to meet the demand for straw hats (a good, serviceable model cost about $2.50 or $3.00) if summer arrived early.

From Scott to Zelda:

> DARLING HEART AMBITION ENTHUSIASM AND CONFIDENCE I DECLARE EVERYTHING GLORIOUS THIS WORLD IS A GAME AND WHILE I FEEL SURE OF YOU LOVE EVERYTHING IS POSSIBLE I AM IN THE LAND OF AMBITION AND SUCCESS AND MY ONLY HOPE AND FAITH IS THAT MY DARLING HEART WILL BE WITH ME SOON.

Considered one of the most completely expendable men in the American armed forces, F. Scott Fitzgerald was the second man discharged from his unit at Camp Sheridan. On February 22 he sent a wildly optimistic (and, as it turned out, quite unrealistic) telegram from New York to his "Darling Heart," Zelda Sayre, in Montgomery, Alabama. Fitzgerald hoped to land a good-paying position that would enable him to marry his sweetheart as soon as possible. But after several newspapers turned him down, he found himself composing trolley-car cards for the Barron Collier advertising agency at a salary in the general neighborhood of one hundred dollars a month. The stories he wrote in the evenings in his room at 200 Claremont Avenue (close by Columbia University) earned nothing but rejection slips; during the early months of 1919, Fitzgerald wrote nineteen stories and received an estimated 122 rejections. Still he wrote faithfully to Zelda every day as he had promised, although her replies to him grew less and less frequent as spring approached.

12

"The prophet that hath a dream,

let him tell a dream . . ."

Another wireless message, this one from the *George Washington:* All well, weather moderating.

While the President was steaming home, Secretary of War Newton Baker released the text of a letter the administration had sent to the Senate and House military affairs committees, confirming that orders had been given to withdraw American troops from northern Russia "at the earliest possible moment that conditions in the spring will permit." Given the weather and logistical difficulties, the earliest possible moment probably meant sometime in June. In the meantime, two additional companies of American engineering troops, another 720 men, had been ordered to Archangel to facilitate the withdrawal and to assist British authorities in sending reinforcements to Murmansk by putting the local railroad in reasonably efficient condition. The United States now had 161 officers and 4,764 men in northern Russia. As the weather began to turn warmer (up to thirty degrees below zero), Bolshevik artillery and infantry attacks increased in frequency and intensity. Allied troops were forced to sleep in double-insulated boxcars, and wounded soldiers were placed in sheepskin-lined bags, with hot-water bottles packed around them, to be evacuated via sleds pulled by reindeer or Canadian dog teams. The monotonous pattern was to retreat, retreat, and then advance again. There were now 191 Americans dead and 252 wounded, and insomnia remained the most common complaint of the living. One weary doughboy sent home a tale that was all too common:

TWO WEEKS AGO THIS MORNING, A BOLSHEVIK ARTILLERY OF SIX 18-POUNDERS SHELLED OUR VILLAGE FOR TWO HOURS. THEN 500 INFANTRY-MEN ADVANCED ON AN OUTPOST. EIGHT MEN OUT OF FORTY GOT AWAY.

IT WAS 32 DEGREES BELOW ZERO AND IT WAS AT LEAST AN HOUR BEFORE
WE COULD GET OUT TO PICK UP THE WOUNDED. SOME OF THEM FROZE
THEIR HANDS AND ARMS TO THE ELBOWS. WE GOT THE WOUNDED IN UNDER
HEAVY FIRE, AND SENT THEM TO THE REAR. OUR HOSPITAL WAS SHELLED
AND BURNED. . . .

IN THE MEANTIME THEY HAD CUT THE COMMUNICATION BACK OF OUR
BASE. AT 2:30 A.M. WE EVACUATED THE BASE, MARCHED 36 MILES WITH-
OUT A STOP. RESTED OVERNIGHT AND DAY AND WERE ON THE GO AGAIN.
MARCHED ALL NIGHT AND TOOK UP A NEW POSITION. UP TO THIS POINT
WE HAD MARCHED 98 MILES. LOST ALL OUR EQUIPMENT. . . .

Out of the heavy weather and back in communication with the mainland,
all seemed well aboard the President's ship (the continuing influenza epidemic notwithstanding) until the afternoon of February 23, when the
George Washington approached the Massachusetts coast. Wilson had chosen Boston as his port of landing, partly because he had never made a
formal visit to the city since taking office, and partly—despite official
denials—because this was the home ground of Senator Henry Cabot
Lodge.

That afternoon, however, a thick fog and heavy rain made it impossible
to see any ground more than a few yards away. While running for the
Boston light by dead reckoning, the *George Washington* and its new destroyer escort, the *Harding*, lost their bearings at about three o'clock.
Suddenly the *Harding*'s lookout discovered land—straight ahead lay the
beach of Thatcher Island, Cape Ann—and the destroyer gave five quick
blasts on its whistle and made a quick turn across the bow of its companion.
Since the wind was landward, the sound of the whistle was carried away
from the President's ship, but a deck officer saw the five jets of steam and
signaled full speed astern. As the ship quivered and trembled in the churn-
ing water, Wilson (reportedly with a copy of the League Covenant stuffed
into his overcoat pocket) jumped from his chair to see what was the matter.
Surveying the scene through a sudden snow squall, Franklin Roosevelt
offered his expert opinion, based upon his experience as a sailor in the area,
that they were somewhere near Marblehead. When visibility improved,
another passenger with binoculars spied his summer cottage and announced that he was prepared to sail off for home in a breeches buoy.
Although many of the troops on board were so unconcerned that they
remained in the ship's movie theater belowdecks during the entire incident,
one excited doughboy shouted, "I don't care if it is the beach. It's the good
old U.S.A., whatever it is, and I say 'hurrah for it.' "

The *George Washington* backed away and finally navigated its way into Boston harbor early that evening. Wilson and his entourage remained on board overnight, preparing for the ceremonies of welcome planned for the following morning. Federal and city officials were also making their preparations—for the tightest security net ever thrown over a presidential appearance in the United States. Earlier that day a force of Secret Service operatives, aided by detectives and the New York City Police Department bomb squad, had raided a shabby building at 1722 Lexington Avenue in New York and arrested fourteen members of a Spanish radical organization. Authorities found the rooms filled with seditious literature (it was in Spanish and the police didn't understand a word of it, but it certainly *looked* seditious); there was also a picture of Karl Liebknecht on a wall, and in another room a suspicious-looking (albeit dismantled) "complicated machine," which government agents suspected was designed for the manufacture of homemade bombs. A simultaneous raid in Philadelphia netted ten more Cubans and Spaniards. The Justice Department initiated the raids on the basis of information supplied by an undercover agent that two radicals from each major city in America had been selected to meet in New York at a "national murder conference," where they would draw lots to select one or more of their number to assassinate President Wilson during his Boston appearance. Officials kept searching for links between the recent bomb outrages in Philadelphia and these members of "the Spanish branch of the IWW," but they never discovered any bombs meant for Wilson. For the moment the authorities simply held the radicals (most of whom were cigarmakers) without bail until they decided what charges to bring against them.

So when Wilson stepped out onto Commonwealth Pier at 11:42 on the suddenly sunny morning of February 24 ("Wilson weather," they called it), he was surrounded by security precautions: aircraft overhead, submarine chasers and torpedo-boat destroyers and riflemen in fishing boats in the water, fifty mounted policemen at the head of the procession, a mounted troop of the Massachusetts Guard as an escort, soldiers and sailors in a double row on each side along the length of the pier, sharpshooters with high-powered rifles stationed on the roofs of buildings, and more soldiers watching from other vantage points. On every street along the route from the pier to the Copley-Plaza Hotel—a distance of nearly three miles—rows of federal and state troops, aided by nine hundred policemen, stood shoulder to shoulder and tried to keep people away from the President, although in the narrow Boston streets it still would have been possible for an outstretched hand to touch him. Wilson and his wife, both muffled in fur coats, rode in the first car, along with Governor Calvin Coolidge and Mayor Peters; Franklin Roosevelt and his wife were relegated to the fifth car in the procession, but Eleanor still saw enough of the streets "packed with people wildly shrieking" to convince her that "I never saw a better crowd or more enthusiasm."

The city had declared a holiday and closed the schools, so there were indeed masses of people—official estimates ran as high as 500,000—lining the procession route, straining to get a glimpse of Wilson. Small boys swarmed over the numerous Boston monuments and climbed into trees to see; women stood at windows and waved handkerchiefs. Wilson seemed genuinely glad to be back in America, looking tanned and fit from his rest at sea, standing and grinning and waving his silk hat and nodding his head up and down and shaking every hand that came within reach. The parade proceeded through Summer Street, Dewey Square, Winter Street, and Tremont, passing four hundred wounded doughboys in seats of honor, then headed up the steep hill of Park Street. The only incident that marred the occasion was the arrest of twenty-two militant suffragettes who took up their positions in front of the reviewing stand opposite the State House and refused police orders to move on. Although the militants refrained from carrying out their threat to burn copies of Wilson's speeches on Boston Common, there were the standard white, purple, and gold banners (MR. PRESIDENT, HOW LONG MUST WOMEN WAIT FOR LIBERTY?), but no overt hostility by either the demonstrators or the police, and the women went quietly off, clutching their suffragette sashes, to the Joy Street station, where they refused to post bail. Most of them also refused to pay their five-dollar fines for loitering and were thereupon sent to Charles Street Jail, where they refused to give their names and were each accordingly registered as "Jane Doe." (Within a week, a mysterious gentleman calling himself "E. J. Howe" had, without their consent or knowledge, paid the fines of all except one suffragette, whose husband threatened to obtain a court injunction if anyone paid her fine. Angered that they had been deprived of the publicity of an extended jail stay, but unable to remain any longer in their cells, the last remnant of the Boston battalion of militants hopped into an automobile and sped away to fight another day.)

Unperturbed by the militants' activities, Wilson was hurried from his parade car into the Copley-Plaza for a lunch that of course included Boston baked beans. Inside, Eleanor Roosevelt found herself seated next to Governor Coolidge; despite her valiant efforts, she could not induce him to say a single word during the entire meal. After lunch, Wilson received a delegation from the nonmilitant Massachusetts Woman's Suffrage Association and assured them of his "warm regards and sympathy." Then the party was off to Mechanics Hall, the largest auditorium in the city, where an audience of eight thousand awaited Wilson's first public message to America since the Peace Conference had begun.

Wilson entered the hall at 2:44. Receiving an enthusiastic welcome, the President sat down and leaned back with one leg swung comfortably over the other. After a minute of applause, someone called for three cheers for Woodrow Wilson; the President rose and bowed repeatedly, and the crowd responded with another round of clapping and whistling. A reporter from *The New York Times* noted that Wilson looked quite pleased with the reception: "There was a got-back-home twist to his famous smile, and he looked and acted like a man who had been among strangers a long time and was now getting his first look at the home folks." The famous Irish tenor John McCormack sang two verses of "The Star-Spangled Banner," Mayor Andrew Peters made an introductory speech, and Governor Coolidge extolled the virtues of Massachusetts' 26th Division; Coolidge spoke, according to the *Times* reporter, "in the clear, incisive twang which we have come to expect from New England statesmen, with the pause after each word, and the two gestures, one consisting of parting the two hands before the speaker as if he were swimming, and the other of raising the right arm high in the air." A soldier in the audience led everyone in singing "The Battle Hymn of the Republic" (the words to which were apparently unknown to most of the crowd) and "Onward Christian Soldiers" (which seemed more familiar and which elicited an enthusiastic vocal performance from the President), and then Wilson rose for his speech.

Wilson's advisers had been wondering whether the President would choose to conciliate senatorial critics of the League Covenant or meet them head-on. Since his speech was almost completely extemporaneous, they did not know what he would say until he said it. Wilson began mildly, assuring his listeners that "in some respects during the recent months I have been very lonely indeed without your comradeship and counsel," admitting that the complex work of the Peace Conference appeared from a distance to be progressing slowly ("from day to day in Paris," he added, "it seems to go slowly," too), and reminding them of the vision, the dream that inspired American doughboys through the bitterness and destruction of the Great War.

Then he launched the counterattack that would last for nearly twelve months; "the Old Man," as some irreverent spirits in Washington called Wilson, had clearly decided to go to the mat. America had entered the war to help forge a new world, Wilson insisted, and any peace treaty that ignored the spirit of the new age would be nothing more than a "modern scrap of paper" that would last no more than a generation. "Any man who resists the present tide that runs in the world will find himself thrown upon a shore so high and barren that it will seem as if he has been separated from his human-kind forever." Leaning over the podium, his face set in tense lines and his right hand firmly clenched, Wilson declared that "any man who thinks that America will take part in giving the world any such rebuff and disappointment as that does not know America. I invite him to test the sentiment of the nation." Hearty applause. Then came the biggest demonstration of the day, when the President proclaimed, "I have fighting blood in me, and it is sometimes a delight to let it have scope, but if it is a challenge on this occasion, it will be an indulgence." He scorned "those narrow, selfish, provincial purposes which seem so dear to some minds that have no sweep beyond their nearest horizon," and, at the end, Wilson fervently expressed his thorough confidence in the ultimate triumph of the forces he represented: "I have no more doubt of the verdict of America in this matter than I have of the blood that is in me."

The crowd cheered, the President waved, and then he and Mrs. Wilson departed by train for Washington, where a small army of workmen had just given the White House a thorough spring cleaning.

FEBRUARY 27, 1919

DEATH CAME UNEXPECTEDLY—FOR I WANTED IT TO COME. I TOLD MYSELF I DID NOT WISH TO LIVE. I DID NOT LIVE LONG. I WAS TOLD I WAS MAD. I THOUGHT I WAS ALIVE, BUT WASN'T GIVEN ANY PEACE. . . . I DO NOT WANT PEOPLE TO LAUGH AT ME AND HAVE DECIDED NOT TO DO ANYTHING. GOD TELLS ME NOT TO DO ANYTHING ELSE, ONLY TO WRITE DOWN MY IMPRESSIONS. I WILL WRITE. I WANT TO UNDERSTAND MY WIFE'S MOTHER AND HER HUSBAND. I KNOW THEM WELL, BUT I WANT TO BE SURE.

Romola Nijinsky's mother and father took it upon themselves to have their son-in-law committed to a public institution. He would be rescued by Romola and placed in a more suitable private sanitarium, but on February 27 he was communicating with the world for one of the last times. It was the last entry in his diary, and the only one that bore a date. For the next thirty-one years, Vaslav Nijinsky lived in and out of sanitariums, in and out of the world of so-called rational thought and behavior.

I WANT TO GO TO PARIS, BUT I AM AFRAID I WILL BE TOO LATE. . . . IT IS PAST ONE O'CLOCK AND I AM STILL AWAKE. PEOPLE OUGHT TO WORK DURING THE DAY BUT I WORK AT NIGHT. . . . I WANT TO CRY BUT GOD ORDERS ME TO GO ON WRITING. . . . MY CHILD SEES AND HEARS EVERYTHING AND I HOPE THAT SHE WILL UNDERSTAND ME. I LOVE KYRA. MY LITTLE KYRA FEELS MY LOVE FOR HER, BUT SHE THINKS TOO THAT I AM ILL, FOR THEY HAVE TOLD HER SO. . . . SOON I WILL GO TO PARIS AND CREATE A GREAT IMPRESSION— THE WHOLE WORLD WILL BE TALKING ABOUT IT. . . . MY SOUL IS ILL. MY SOUL, NOT MY MIND. THE DOCTORS DO NOT UNDERSTAND MY ILLNESS. . . . I SUFFER, I SUFFER. . . . I AM A MAN, NOT A BEAST. I LOVE EVERYONE, I HAVE FAULTS, I AM A MAN—NOT GOD. I WANT TO BE GOD AND THEREFORE I TRY TO IMPROVE MYSELF. . . . I AM A PART OF GOD, MY PARTY IS GOD'S PARTY. I LOVE EVERYBODY. I DO NOT WANT WAR OR FRONTIERS. THE WORLD EXISTS. I HAVE A HOME EVERYWHERE. I LIVE EVERYWHERE. I DO NOT WANT TO HAVE ANY PROPERTY. I DO NOT WANT TO BE RICH. I WANT TO LOVE. . . . I AM MAN. I AM MAN. GOD IS IN ME. I AM IN GOD. I WANT HIM, I SEEK HIM. I WANT MY MANUSCRIPTS TO BE PUBLISHED SO THAT EVERYBODY CAN READ THEM. . . . I AM A SEEKER, FOR I CAN FEEL GOD. GOD SEEKS ME AND THEREFORE WE WILL FIND EACH OTHER.

GOD AND NIJINSKY,
SAINT MORITZ-DORF,
VILLA GUARDAMUNT
FEBRUARY 27, 1919

And in the world of 1919, who could say with truth that he knew who was sane and who was mad? For instance:

Captain Konrad Hetzler, a German Army engineer, had been surveying the German-British boundary in Papua, New Guinea, when war broke out in August 1914. Rather than face the prospect of combat, Captain Hetzler shed his uniform and, wearing only a waistband, fled into the bush and lived with a tribe of cannibals for four years. Upon learning of the Armistice, he retrieved his clothes from their hiding place and returned to civilization. Arriving in Sydney with a considerable tan under his German uniform, he was arrested and interned.

* * *

Lieutenant Ormer C. Locklear of the U.S. Army became the world's first aviator to leap from one airplane to another while flying at top speed. He accomplished this feat by swinging head-down from the lower wing of one biplane, and then dropping to the upper wing of another plane as it passed underneath.

Official statistics revealed that there had been 215 murders reported in New York City in 1918. "What an appalling record!" lamented one out-of-town newspaper. "It indicates the fact that human life is very cheap in the great city." Another 1,189 throughout the state had been killed by automobiles in 1918; in the first month of 1919, forty-nine New York City residents had already died in auto accidents. One explanation of the increasing rate of automobile fatalities came when an official investigation of the records in the office of the Secretary of State of New York revealed that driving licenses had been given to "insane people, drug addicts, criminals, and habitually intoxicated people."

The United States government took 200,000 artillery shells filled with poison gas—mostly chloropicrin (which induced vomiting) and mustard gas (an irritant and quite effective blistering agent)—from a storage facility in Baltimore and towed them out to sea. They were dumped in 1,500 feet of water between sixty and one hundred miles from shore. The shells were disposed of because their containers had started to leak, and although the rest of the chemical arsenal was ultimately slated for a similar fate, the army intended to keep a substantial amount of gas on hand for the time being—just in case.

"One had only to open a newspaper," announced Lord Henry Bentinck in Parliament, "to see that at the present moment all the peoples east of the Rhine, not only Germany but Russia, Rumania, Austria, and Bohemia, are in danger of starvation." In Prague, meat, rice, coffee, and tea had completely disappeared. Milk was nearly nonexistent (only three pints remained to feed five infants in one hospital), soap was impossible to find; no leather, no wool or cotton to make clothes. The mortality rate among children under fourteen years old in the city had risen to the incredible figure of 40 percent over the past year; among childbearing women, it had increased from 3 to 34 percent. In a Czech mining town, 116 out of 165 children born in 1918 had already died of tuberculosis. "Our children die, the conditions are desperate," cried a desperate relief official. "Austria said if she must lose Bohemia she will lose it as a corpse." Austrian troops had removed all the railway freight cars they could take as they retreated; now Italian troops were blockading the border to enforce Italy's demands for the locomotives and wagons that remained. The American commission sent to investigate conditions in Montenegro found families scratching in the ground to find roots to eat. In Bucharest, families existed on sauerkraut, onions (if they were fortunate), and marmaliga, a mixture of corn flour and water that resembled "the food ordinarily given in America to poultry." Five Red Cross canteens and six city-operated kitchens fed 8,500 people daily: wives, widows, children and orphans of Rumanian soldiers, and crippled soldiers who could get themselves to the food. An American correspondent found a ring of mud huts around the capital, and within Bucharest entire families lived in windowless rooms six by ten feet: "I found the children dressed in shirts. They had neither drawers, shoes, nor stockings. Two barefoot children, living with their barefoot mother, had not eaten for twenty-four hours. There was no wood in the house and no money to buy bread. The children lay upon the bed sick from cold and hunger."

To the north and west, 90 percent of the merchandise in many German millinery and women's clothes shops consisted of black hats and mourning clothes because of the terrible rate of infant mortality. Despite vicious opposition from die-hard nationalists at home, groups of English women responded to desperate pleas and sent thousands of rubber nipples to Germany to keep more babies from starving to death. A survey by Berlin medical societies of conditions throughout Germany brought forth a reply from one hospital: "Our inmates are all dead." The official ration for children under six in Germany now included one-half ounce of fats a week and less than five ounces of meat. A veteran British journalist who toured the hospitals of Cologne reported with despair that "although I have seen many horrible things in the world, I have seen nothing so pitiful as these rows of babies feverish from want of food, exhausted by privation to the point that their little limbs were like slender wands, their expression hopeless, and their faces full of pain." Yet France still refused to lift the blockade or help feed Germany; every cent of available German funds, the French government insisted, had to be used to rebuild the devastated areas of France.

Winston Churchill, the British Secretary of State for War and Air:

AT THE PRESENT MOMENT WE ARE BRINGING EVERYTHING TO A HEAD IN GERMANY: WE ARE HOLDING OUR MEANS OF COERCION IN FULL OPERATION OR IN IMMEDIATE READINESS FOR USE. WE ARE ENFORCING THE BLOCKADE

WITH RIGOUR, WE HAVE STRONG ARMIES READY TO ADVANCE AT THE
SHORTEST NOTICE. GERMANY IS VERY NEAR STARVATION. ALL THE EVI-
DENCE I HAVE RECEIVED FROM OFFICERS SENT BY THE WAR OFFICE ALL
OVER GERMANY SHOWS, FIRST OF ALL, THE GREAT PRIVATIONS WHICH THE
GERMAN PEOPLE ARE SUFFERING; AND SECONDLY, THE DANGER OF A COL-
LAPSE OF THE ENTIRE STRUCTURE OF GERMAN SOCIAL AND NATIONAL LIFE
UNDER THE PRESSURE OF HUNGER AND MALNUTRITION. NOW IS THERE-
FORE THE MOMENT TO SETTLE. TO DELAY INDEFINITELY WOULD BE TO RUN
A GRAVE RISK OF HAVING NOBODY WITH WHOM TO SETTLE, AND OF HAVING
ANOTHER GREAT AREA OF THE WORLD SINK INTO BOLSHEVIST ANARCHY.
THAT WOULD BE A VERY GRAVE EVENT.

Under the circumstances, the definition of sanity appeared to be very
much up for grabs.

The legacy of war, as the *Nation* saw it: "Too many men have been taught
the use of deadly weapons, too many soldiers have learned the advantage
of indirect attack, to make the world very safe for either democracy or
autocracy at present. Certain monsters have an unhappy way of turning
against their Frankensteins."

Chaim Weizmann and his colleagues were summoned to appear before the
Council of Ten on the afternoon of February 27. The Council had been
discussing several unrelated minor matters before they asked the Zionists
to enter Pichon's office at the Quai d'Orsay; as Weizmann's delegation
entered, Clemenceau, still feeling considerably weakened, stood up and put
on his new fur coat and left. The Zionists then put before the council their
claim to "their historic rights to Palestine, the land of Israel, where, in
ancient times, the Jewish people had created a civilisation which had since
exercised an enormous influence on humanity." They asked that the Jewish people be allowed to establish a National Home in Palestine, and that
Great Britain be awarded a mandate to govern the land as the representative of the League of Nations. Weizmann argued that Palestine could
absorb considerable Jewish immigration because it was extremely under-
populated at the moment; neighboring Lebanon's population density was
more than ten times that of Palestine. Moreover, the Jews of Eastern
Europe were suffering extreme hardships: partly from organized pogroms,
and partly from widespread famine and pestilence that struck hardest at the
most enfeebled classes of society—in many cases, the Jews. Weizmann
himself claimed to speak "in the name of a million Jews who, staff in hand
were waiting the signal to move."

As the afternoon wore on, the members of the Council became restless; one decided that it was "a fine chance for a nap" and dozed off during a lengthy speech in Hebrew by one of the Zionist representatives. Finally, Lansing asked Weizmann the crucial question: Did the words "Jewish National Home" mean that the Zionists intended to establish an autonomous Jewish government? Weizmann said no; at least not right away. "The Zionist organization did not want an autonomous Jewish Government, but merely to establish in Palestine, under a mandatory Power, an administration, not necessarily Jewish, which would render it possible to send into Palestine seventy to eighty thousand Jews annually." It also requested permission to build Jewish schools to teach Hebrew, and thereby gradually build up a nationality that would be as Jewish as the French nation was French and as Great Britain was British. Later, Weizmann added, "when the Jews formed the large majority, they would be ripe to establish such a Government as would answer to the state of the development of the country and to their ideals."

No formal decision was rendered at that time, and after the Zionist delegation withdrew, the Council proceeded instead to discuss whether the Aaland Islands should be given to Sweden or Finland. But Balfour sent out his secretary to congratulate Weizmann on his presentation, and several days later André Tardieu, an intimate of Clemenceau who had sat in for the Tiger in the Council that day, told reporters that "there is not the slightest difference of opinion among the great powers on the establishment of a Zionist state nor on giving Great Britain the mandatory." Weizmann professed himself gratified with the reception afforded his pleas, and repeated again and again that nothing would be done in Palestine at present to prejudice the civil and religious rights of existing non-Jewish communities: "We do not aspire to found a Zionist State. What we want is a country in which all nations and all creeds shall have equal rights and equal tolerance. . . . For two thousand years we have known what it means to be strangers. We Jews know the heart of the stranger: are we likely to deal out oppression?"

In Washington, a delegation from the American Jewish Congress, led by Judge Julian Mack and Rabbi Stephen Wise, spent an hour with Wilson in his second-floor study at the White House and came away with the President's promise to support a Zionist home in Palestine. "As for your representations touching Palestine," the official White House statement read, "I have before this expressed my personal approval of the declaration of the British Government regarding the aspirations and historic claims of the Jewish people in regard to Palestine. I am, moreover, persuaded that the allied nations, with the fullest concurrence of our own government and people, are agreed that in Palestine shall be laid the foundations of a Jewish Commonwealth."

Lawrence and Faisal, however, continued to vacillate in their public statements regarding Palestine, Faisal especially hedging on his earlier expressed support of Jewish immigration into the Holy Land. To calm the Zionists' fears—at least for the duration of the Peace Conference—Lawrence sat down in a Paris hotel room with Frankfurter and Weizmann and drafted a public letter, released under Faisal's signature and ostensibly addressed to Frankfurter, affirming the Arab people's "deepest sympathy" for the Zionist movement and its proposals to the Council of Ten. "We will do our best," Faisal/Lawrence blithely declared, "in so far as we are concerned, to help them through; we will wish the Jews a most hearty welcome home." In private conversations with Allied officials, Lawrence and Faisal were less sanguine about a future that included millions of Jewish immigrants dominated by the "very militant spirit" displayed by recent Jewish settlers in Palestine. They made it quite clear that in their opinion, "if the views of the radical Zionists, as presented to the Ten, should prevail, the result will be ferment, chronic unrest, and sooner or later civil war in Palestine."

From Rome, Pope Benedict chimed in with his opposition to either an autonomous Jewish or Arab state in Palestine. "It would be a great grief to the Holy See," the pontiff announced, "if in Palestine the preponderating position were given to infidels, and a still greater grief if the holy places were given to a non-Christian power."

Not far from the spot in Weehauken, New Jersey, where Aaron Burr had shot and killed Alexander Hamilton in a duel 115 years earlier, Jack Dempsey signed a contract to meet reigning heavyweight champion Jess Willard in a bout not to exceed forty rounds, to be scheduled for sometime in July 1919. The twenty-three-year-old Dempsey, a rough-hewn slugger who had come out of the West swinging with both hands at anything that stood in his way, had accumulated an impressive string of knockouts in his brief career. As the consensus top-ranked contender, Dempsey was guaranteed a purse of $27,500 and one-third of the movie revenues from the fight. The giant Willard, a former horse trader and the man who had ended mainstream America's long search for a "Great White Hope" by defeating the "uppity" black champion Jack Johnson in Havana on April 5, 1915, received a guaranteed $100,000 for the fight with Dempsey, as well as a one-third share of his own of the movie receipts. Despite the initial public adoration following the Johnson fight, Willard had been an extraordinarily unpopular champion in the past three years, partly because he had refused to volunteer for military service during the war (so had Dempsey; both men had to face accusations of being "slackers"), and partly because he had defended his title only once, in a mismatch against Frank Moran in 1916. He had become known as the "idleweight champion"; in fact, there were few worthy challengers for Willard during the war, and so he had toured with Buffalo Bill's Wild West Show to pick up several thousand dollars here and there, and then sat back on his farm in Kansas, gathering fat and waiting for a decent bout.

No one was quite sure how good Willard really was. He had killed a fighter named Bull Young in California in 1913, and he had beaten Johnson after plenty of other white fighters had gone down before the black man's relentless attack. But rumors persisted that the Havana fight had been fixed, that it had been decided that Johnson had held the crown long enough, and a black champion was no good for the future of boxing. Johnson himself told reporters in March 1919 that he had agreed to throw the Willard bout in return for a promise by federal authorities to clear up the "trouble" (a conviction on charges of violating the Mann Act) that had forced him to flee the United States. Still, Willard enjoyed a marked advantage over Dempsey in height, weight, and reach. Tex Rickard, the fight's promoter, had been reluctant to give Dempsey a shot at the title because of the size differential; "Every time I see you," he told Dempsey early in 1919, "you look smaller to me."

A number of boxing aficionados, however, realized that if anyone could cut Willard down to size, it would be Dempsey with his vicious, slashing style of fighting. One sportswriter who acknowledged that the challenger was "a stripling compared to Willard" nevertheless admiringly described Dempsey as "a whirlwind of the ring. He can box if he desires, but he prefers to maul. He rushes to close quarters, swings and hooks for the head and drives straight with both hands to the body." Before the serious training started, Dempsey took the opportunity to earn some extra money (reportedly about a thousand dollars a week) by embarking on a six-week tour of the vaudeville circuit, giving brief speeches and exhibiting his pugilistic skills on the same bill with "The Seashore Flirts" (featuring the enticing terpsichorean talents of the devastating Sultana). Meanwhile, Rickard had to find a suitable site for the bout. It wasn't easy. Most states forbade prizefighting in 1919; it was a misdemeanor even to sign a contract for a fight in New York, which is why Dempsey and Rickard had met in a ferry house in Weehauken. As February drew to a close, Rickard was still searching.

13

"Everyone that passeth

thereby shall be astonished . . ."

While fight fans awaited the Willard-Dempsey bout with growing anticipation, another, even more primitive battle was scheduled for Madison
Square Garden: Ed "Strangler" Lewis vs. Wladek Zbyszko, in a free-for-all
heavyweight championship wrestling match. The last time these two had
met in New York, Lewis won a technical victory when the "Polish Prince"
was disqualified on a foul. The Strangler vowed that this time he had a
foolproof plan for victory. Certainly the fans couldn't lose; if neither man
won decisively, everyone would get his money back. (And if anyone really
believed the promoters would ever refund his money, he probably also
believed that professional wrestling matches weren't fixed.)

Conventional opinion in Britain and the United States continued to decry
"the disappearing evening bodice." One British critic pointed out that a
similar fashion came into vogue following the Napoleonic Wars and the
Congress of Vienna in 1815, and that women had died like flies from lung
and throat troubles shortly thereafter. While the low necklines of Queen
Victoria's court admittedly had been "becoming to those who possess, as
the majority of British women do, well-formed busts and arms and white
skins," the bodice of current fashion threatened to drop off entirely.

In New York, Mrs. James Griswold Wentz, president of the Woman's
Republican Club and acting chairman of the Decent Dress Committee,
announced that she and her colleagues had divided the city into districts,
each of which would be patrolled by a member of the committee to watch
window displays and protest against the public exhibition of gauzy lingerie
and waistless evening gowns. (The committee was laboring under the
assumption that decent women did not look at such sights, and that men
would only be adversely affected by these immodest displays.) "I under-

stand the French gowns which are coming in are to be worse than any we
have had yet," declared Mrs. Wentz sadly, "but I don't know how they
can be." The current fashion, she added, was "demoralizing to our very
young girls, and it will demoralize our young men who are coming home
from France."

WILLIAM BUTLER YEATS'S PRAYER FOR HIS DAUGHTER:

My mind, because of the minds that I have loved,
The sort of beauty that I have approved,
Prosper but little, has dried up of late,
Yet knows that to be choked with hate,
May well be of all evil chances chief.
If there's no hatred in a mind
Assault and battery of the wind
Can never tear the linnet from the leaf.

Still weakened from his recent illness, Mohandas Gandhi could not have
been more demoralized had the entire Decent Dress Committee appeared
before him stark naked. Gandhi was appalled by newspaper reports that
the government of India intended to ratify legislation incorporating the
July 1918 recommendations of the Rowlatt Committee—an investigative
body chaired by an English magistrate, Sir Sidney Rowlatt, that had
weighed mountains of documentary evidence (some obtained by means of
searches that would not have been tolerated in England) and alleged
confessions regarding wartime seditious activities throughout India. Concerned that nationalist agitation might increase after the war, and convinced of the existence of a Bolshevik plot to instigate revolt in India,
British officials moved in February and March 1919 to replace the temporary secret tribunals and newspaper censorship with permanent repressive
legislation. The two Rowlatt bills gave virtually unlimited power to the
central government to make and enforce its own definition of conspiracy,
to try accused conspirators *in camera* and without counsel or juries, and
to deny appeals to those found guilty.

   This was a cause to bring Gandhi directly into Indian national politics
for the first time. The Rowlatt recommendations, Gandhi wrote, "seemed
to me to be altogether unwarranted by the evidence published in its report,
and were, I felt, such that no self-respecting people could submit to them."
The nationalist Congress of India bitterly criticized the bills; almost every
native member of the Imperial Indian legislative council, including the

moderates, declared himself opposed; and the most influential young Indian Moslem leader, Muhammad Ali Jinnah, proclaimed that any government enacting such a law during peacetime had forfeited its claim to be called a civilized government.

Gandhi urged the Viceroy, Lord Chelmsford, in private and public letters not to approve the Rowlatt bills; for the first and last time, he attended the proceedings of the Indian legislature as it discussed the measures. All in vain: "You can wake a man only if he is really asleep," Gandhi later confirmed; "no effort that you may make will produce any effect upon him if he is merely pretending sleep. That was precisely the Government's position. . . . Its decision had already been made." And so Gandhi initiated his first nationwide *satyagraha*, the tactic he had employed so successfully in South Africa and on a local level in India during the war.

Satyagraha, "fidelity to truth," was a process of protest by "self-purification" developed personally by Gandhi. It emphasized the inner thought and motivation of the protestor by calling for a campaign of self-inflicted suffering, nonviolence, and civil disobedience performed in a spirit of love for the enemy. A satyagraha, properly carried out, would uplift both the protestor and the opponent, producing on all sides a recognition of the justice of the cause. Hatred had no place in such a movement. Clearly there was an element of mysticism involved, for Gandhi believed that the failure of a satyagraha resulted not from the cruelty or stubbornness of an enemy, but from a lack of self-discipline on the part of the satyagrahi themselves.

In February, then, Gandhi embarked on a tour across India to arouse interest in his campaign. Since he was still too weak to stand and speak, an associate read Gandhi's speeches condemning the Rowlatt bills as "evidence of a deep-seated disease in the governing body [that] must be met by passive resistance," calling upon his audiences to sign a pledge in support of the satyagraha. The movement proved an immediate popular success, and even *The Times* of London, no fainthearted supporter of British imperialism, granted that "Mr. Gandhi's sincerity and honesty are beyond doubt." But the movement also appeared to have strengthened Britain's resolve to enact the repressive legislation; one official vowed that the government would never yield to any passive resistance movement, although it did accept an amendment limiting the life of the measures to three years. On March 18, the Rowlatt Anarchical and Revolutionary Crimes Bill was approved as Chelmsford steadfastly and with a straight face denied that the legislation was a slur on India's good name. Jinnah promptly resigned from the Viceroy's Council, and Gandhi pondered his next move.

* * *

It mattered not at all to the infamous (and as yet undiscovered) influenza virus whether its victim was British or Indian, rich or poor. During one week in February, London and its suburbs reported 974 deaths from the latest wave of the flu epidemic; Liverpool added another 188, and Manchester 130. An unusually prolonged period of cold, wet, raw weather combined with the added exposure to the elements during the transport strike in London to weaken much of the population and encourage the spread of the virus. Physicians found that this wave, unlike previous manifestations, struck primarily at adults between twenty and fifty years of age, rather than at the very young or the very old, and was often accompanied by pneumonia.

Many medical experts urged their patients to increase their intake of whiskey to soften the impact of the disease; local authorities released additional quantities of spirits from their stocks (alcoholic beverages had been tightly rationed during the war) to accommodate authentic prescriptions. Although temperance forces in Britain stoutly denied the therapeutic value of whiskey, nurses from Red Cross hospitals were supplied with small quantities of liquor for the patients on their rounds. Others praised the value of fresh air and daily physical exercise as more efficacious means of prevention. Across the Atlantic, the president of Washington's West Side Tennis Club proudly announced that none of his club's members had died of influenza, thus demonstrating the value of a regular turn on the courts as a preventative. Additional evidence came from Sing Sing, where no one had died—of the flu, at least—since the warden had instituted a strict regimen of sterilizing the cells, with plenty of sunshine and fresh air for everyone. All of the 106 prisoners who had caught the disease had been cured through prompt treatment and enforced rest; of course, they were hardly in a position to refuse the doctor's orders.

"The Shape is the Important Feature; whether the woman be small, medium or large, you will find good lines and genuine comfort in a Warner Rust Proof Corset. WARNER'S RUST PROOF: Guaranteed Not to Rust, Break or Tear."

Britain in the late winter of 1919: as the dominance of khaki in the West End gradually faded with the approach of spring, Piccadilly and Bond Street filled with young men in smart, well-creased clothes with bright ties and gay spats and boutonnieres. Nearly one million men and women were officially recorded as unemployed. "Isn't it awful," E. M. Forster wrote to

Siegfried Sassoon, "how all the outward nonsense of England has been absolutely untouched by the war—still this unbroken front of dress-shirts and golf." Anyone who knew the score spoke not rapidly as his parents had, but in a slow, throaty manner that made *yes* sound like "yaas" and *suppose* like "spawse" and *square* like "squawre." The high wages and higher prices of wartime continued into peacetime. British society, said Robert Graves, was no longer divided between the governing and the governed classes as before the war, but between those who had seen battle ("the Fighting Forces") and those who had remained at home ("the Rest"). Advertisements urged a return to prewar comfort and prewar daintiness as if August 1914 had been the summit of human bliss and the future something to be avoided or at least ignored. To visitors it appeared that almost half of the men in England were crippled or scarred or twisted—the reality becoming somehow even more shocking when the men were dressed in civilian clothes, or when they tried to pull themselves aboard a moving bus. Joseph Conrad compared the government's efforts to promote industrial peace and harmony between capital and labor (when the mere conciliation of interests was barely possible) to "people laying out a tennis court on a ground that is already moving under their feet." The installation of automatic telephones throughout London meant that one would no longer hear the familiar request, "Number, please," when one picked up the receiver. A government commission found that the most important household innovation from the housewife's point of view was the availability of cheap electricity. Hundreds of thousands of women had learned that "their hands are capable of something besides handling babies or doing housework." Black and navy serge suits with white pinstripes were the rage, as was short hair for women, and short skirts and wool or cotton stockings. Government offices posted notices requesting occupants not to stoke the fire after 3:00 P.M. unless they intended to stay after 5:00 P.M. There was an unprecedented drop in population as the number of deaths in the last quarter of 1918 exceeded the number of births for the first time since civil registration had begun in 1836 (the drop being largely due to the lowest birthrate on record, the effects of influenza, and an increase in infant mortality, the latter especially among bastard children; 37,000 children were born out of wedlock in England and Wales each year, and 20 percent of them died before their first birthday). More beer was on the way to alleviate discontent in industrial towns; the prices of cheese and fish were falling, and restrictions on tea and bacon had been removed, but beef and sugar remained still in short supply, and there was no jam available at all for fruit tarts. On the other hand, the Oatmeal Restriction Order had been revoked. Margarine and butter were also plentiful, and Lloyd George declared to a friend that "personally, I would sooner have butter than meat. If I can get plenty of good butter, I can do without meat quite well." The popular Princess Patricia married Commander Alexander Ramsay, RN, in Westminster Abbey before King George and Queen Mary. The government locked away Bolshevik agitators in Brixton Prison, and police raided the headquarters of "The People's Russian Information Bureau" in Fleet Street. Nearly 327,000 soldiers had been pensioned from disability. The Red Hats were gone as Cambridge escaped from its military occupation and the undergraduates returned to see shop windows once again full of blue and black gowns, white fur hoods, the brilliant stripes of obscure club ties, and ashtrays and little wooden shields and tobacco jars adorned with the arms of colleges. The smart set frowned on the traditional practice of introductions at dances, and the boy scout clubs entered their second decade of service. And tourists constantly complained about the shortage of coal in hotels in London: "The other day, on what Londoners call only a reasonably misty day, when I blew into my unheated room, in my unheated hotel, in my unheated metropolis of London, I swear by all the gods of Mark Twain that so thick lay the fog in my room I had difficulty in distinguishing the bed from the wardrobe until I bumped my shins on the former; and I began to brush my teeth with my saving brush. . . . You could have used me for a baseball bat—I was that frozen."

Demobilization continued, but slowly. By the end of February, nearly two million men still remained in the army. Discontent among the impatient soldiers occasionally flared into open rebellion. On Tuesday evening, March 4, khaki-weary Canadian soldiers (many of whom had been in France for four years), who were temporarily quartered in Kinmel Park Camp at Rhyl, Wales, while they awaited embarkation for home from nearby Liverpool, began a full-scale insurrection upon learning that their transport would not be forthcoming on the promised schedule, and that some relatively recent conscripts were being sent home on the few ships that were available. A few radicals—aided by beer looted from the officers' stores—fanned the sparks of discontent; a red flag was raised and someone shouted, "Come on, the Bolsheviks!" The first night the damage was limited mostly to food and liquor supplies and the women's auxiliary quarters, where the rioters broke in and, in an orgy of curiosity and loneliness, carried off every item of feminine apparel they could find. The next day the authorities called in the cavalry to restore order but instructed the troops not to shoot. Someone ignored the order and indiscriminate firing began on both sides, leaving five dead and twenty-one injured. An army official was flown in on Thursday and promised the men that their grievances would be heard and the rate of discharge stepped up; that stopped the immediate disturbance, but the incident left the War Office shaken and wary. Meanwhile, Secretary Churchill, never one to understate the need for a strong peacetime force, told Parliament that he needed to keep at least 900,000 men in uniform, and accordingly asked for a service budget of nearly £500 million for 1919.

On the labor front, Lloyd George had decided to convene a national industrial conference to recommend policies on a nationwide level to replace the piecemeal day-to-day expedients hitherto employed. Such an overall solution seemed essential in light of the growing sentiment within the ranks of labor in favor of nationalization of key industries, including coal, railways, and electrical supply, to ensure that they were being run as efficiently as possible and that excess profits were not being earned at the expense of wages. When the conference opened on February 27 with some five hundred labor delegates and three hundred of the principal employers of the country present, the general tone of the proceedings was surprisingly subdued and moderate. Lloyd George concluded the one-day session with a call for national unity: "Some months ago, in the darkest hours of the war, I appealed to the whole British people to hold fast. Now I appeal to you employers and employed to hold together." Then the conference adjourned to await the specific recommendations of a joint committee it had appointed to study industrial problems.

Meanwhile, the Triple Alliance of miners, railwaymen, and dockers, a combination representing a million and a half workers, began making threatening noises. The miners voiced their grievances most loudly, calling for nationalization of the coal mines and a share in their management, a 30-percent increase in wages, and a six-hour day. Strike ballots gave the union an overwhelming majority—615,164 to 105,082—in favor of a strike to begin March 15. Lloyd George's government had no intention of supporting the miners' demands, since the end result would have been a sharp increase in the price of coal and industrial products, but neither could the nation afford a prolonged strike in the mines during that winter of scarce fuel. The Cabinet therefore asked Parliament to appoint a commission to inquire into the conditions prevailing in the coal industry and to recommend a settlement of the dispute. The commission was to consist of three representatives of the miners' unions, three mine owners, three industrialists, and three economists (including Sidney Webb).

To persuade labor that this endeavor was on the up-and-up, Sir John Sankey—one of the judges of the King's Bench and a former advocate for South Wales miners during his years in private law practice—was chosen as chairman. The unions agreed to postpone their strike until March 31 to await the preliminary recommendations of the Sankey Commission regarding wages, the miners' notoriously poor housing conditions, and nationalization. They could not know that behind the obvious sincerity of Justice Sankey lay the government's intention to use the commission—and the National Industrial Conference—to play for time, to delay until the passions of the immediate postwar period had cooled and labor had lost its fervor for radical proposals.

In the late winter of 1919, Britain was torn between its desire to return to a "normal" peacetime existence (which was impossible) and its vision of a plentiful and just society worthy of the terrible sacrifices of war (which was highly unlikely, given the miserly mood of Parliament). Lloyd George himself was trapped between his own Liberal prejudices and a reliance upon the Conservative element in his parliamentary coalition. His political dilemma was exacerbated by his well-documented tendency to try any expedient to solve Britain's problems for today, while keeping his sights tightly focused on his one overriding objective—to remain in power. And there were warnings of more dangerous storms ahead: Conservative MPs were demanding outrageous indemnities from Germany; the government had lost a by-election at West Leyton; there was widespread discontent at the unexpectedly high cost of Churchill's military budget (which, *The New York Times* reported, "has left electors wondering whether [they] really have won the war or whether it is only that [they] have lost the peace"); humanitarian opposition to the blockade of Germany continued to mount; and everyone was growing increasingly impatient at the seemingly endless delay in obtaining peace at Paris.

WILLIAM BUTLER YEATS'S PRAYER FOR HIS DAUGHTER:

And may her bridegroom bring her to a house
Where all's accustomed, ceremonious;
For arrogance and hatred are the wares
Peddled in the thoroughfares.
How but in custom and in ceremony
Are innocence and beauty born?
Ceremony's a name for the rich horn,
And custom for the spreading laurel tree.

Russia in the late winter of 1919: hordes of peasants sacked elegant country houses, slashing priceless paintings, digging their axes into the rich, polished wood of pianos, using elegantly bound books and ornate furniture for firewood; Maxim Gorky watched as a Peasant Congress quartered in the Winter Palace deliberately desecrated precious porcelain vases with human waste: "Two revolutions and a war have supplied me with hundreds of cases which reveal this lurking, vindictive tendency in people to smash, mutilate, ridicule, and defame beautiful things." Petrograd's water supply was so contaminated that it had to be boiled before drinking, but since there was no fuel for a fire, the citizens burned their useless fuel ration cards instead to heat the water. Severe cold cracked the water pipes of houses, rendering all indoor plumbing useless. There was never any soap, and public baths were strictly rationed; but the bathhouses were infested with lice anyway. Muscovites passed the nights in almost total darkness because there was only enough electric power to turn on the lights when the Cheka came to arrest enemies of the Revolution. Lenin's face wrinkled with laughter, for he knew that the Revolution would succeed no matter what he or anyone else might do. There were no new clothes anywhere. "Until every man has one room," warned a revolutionary slogan, "no man has a right to two." The cold made it impossible to sleep. An old man drove a sleigh piled high with the bones of dead horses, cracking his whip to keep away the crows that always came back to tear at the flesh remaining on the bones. The blue glow from the few street lights in Petrograd shone dully on the frozen streets, with great piles of snow bordering the walks. People spoke of "dinner" and said "I have dined" merely for the pleasant sound of the words, but still they were always hungry. The Bolsheviks provided free lunches and free books for the schoolchildren in the cities, and country houses were requisitioned as homes for poor or orphaned children. Piles of ammunition and barbed wire and heaps of rubbish sat high inside the Kremlin walls; in the Church of St. Nicholas in Moscow, the ikons of the Evangelists and the Resurrection were broken and thrown down; the east wall had been destroyed by shells, and the entrance to the church where the relics lay had been used as an outhouse, but the altar remained unharmed. On a large crucifix by the north wall of the Church of the Twelve Apostles in the Kremlin, the outstretched hands of Christ had been broken off, the figure gashed with sharp bits of brick, and oil poured over it, causing red spots to appear. There was an astounding rise in the number of theaters and popular interest in theatrical productions throughout the country. A Russian-American sociology professor living in Petrograd complained that "our existence was filled with queues; queues for bread and salt, queues for herrings and tobacco, queues for 'coffee' and gruel, queues for registering our address, as we had to once a month, queues for any official certificate we might require, queues for everything imaginable. . . . The real scientific definition of Communism, based on experience, is queues, endless queues." Suicides were on the rise. Full rations had been ordered for the Red Army to encourage enlistment. The cost of dog meat and cat meat kept going up. The Terror filled the yards of the Cheka and the land along the railroads with corpses. World revolution now seemed somehow less important than the urgent need to get bread to Moscow. Russia's birthrate was cut in half. Isolation forced the nation further and further back into primeval conditions. Despite the rumor in the West, the Soviet government had not nationalized all women between the age of seventeen and forty-five and legalized free love. And two workmen argued the essential political question: "If only it were not for the hunger . . . ." "Yes, but will that ever change?"

Close by Lenin's Kremlin apartment, in a small room smothered in red decorations (with red draperies and a red floor) in the old shell-battered Courts of Justice that dated back to the late eighteenth century when the magnificently voracious Catherine the Great had ruled Russia, an irregular band of thirty-five men and women gathered on March 3. Banners in various languages proclaimed the purpose of the meeting—"Long Live the Third International"—although it was still a secret from the rest of the country and of course from the rest of the world. At the end of the room, on a raised platform, sat Lenin, his cold gray eyes half smiling, half contemptuous. This was his congress, these were his delegates, hand-picked as "representatives" of the Communist movement to the nations of the civilized world. Actually, all but five were either Russian government officials or else simply foreign radicals visiting Russia who had been drafted by the Russian Central Committee to fill places at the gathering. Among the former was Trotsky, with his fierce black eyes, wild hair, huge forehead, and carefully manicured nails. He was by far the best dressed of all the Soviet leaders, resplendent in his leather coat, military breeches, and fur hat with the crimson star of the Red Army on its front.

Lenin opened the meeting with the patently absurd statement that the Revolution and the Soviet system had "triumphed not only in backward Russia, but also in Germany, the most advanced nation in Europe, and in Britain, the oldest of the capitalist countries." Others followed with a babble of speeches in diverse languages and dialects (German was used whenever possible, as the language most delegates understood), but Lenin was clearly in control, dominating the congress by the force of his personality the way a teacher with a birch rod controlled his schoolboys.

After the reports of battles already won in the Ukraine and the confident predictions of ultimate military victory within Russia, after the exaggerated reports of Bolshevik advances throughout Europe amid the chaos and decay of capitalism, the delegates overwhelmingly decided that they constituted the Third International—later known as the Comintern—the heir to the two previous worldwide socialist associations founded in the nineteenth century, which had in fact rested upon far greater popular foundations. This was a direct challenge to the legitimacy of the Second International, which had recently heard Eisner's remarkable speech in Berne; this was a declaration from Moscow that the tide had passed over the sands of mere socialist rhetoric. Despite the ramshackle nature of the Comintern in March 1919, the proclamation provided Lenin with a theoretical claim to sovereignty within the Communist movement that he could employ in his efforts to direct the course of Bolshevik revolutions outside Russia.

On the final day of the session, the congress met in the Kremlin's Great Theater, where crowds assembled to get a glimpse of the proceedings. To Arthur Ransome, the English writer of children's books and histories who had journeyed to Moscow for a firsthand view of the Revolution as a correspondent for the *Manchester Guardian*, the scene was an overwhelming demonstration of Lenin's personal popularity: "It was a long time before he [Lenin] could speak at all, everybody standing and drowning his attempts to speak with roar after roar of applause. It was an extraordinary, overwhelming scene, tier after tier crammed with workmen, the parterre filled, the whole platform and the wings. A knot of workwomen were close to me, and they almost fought to see him, and shouted as if each one were determined that he should hear her in particular."

Outside, it was so cold you had to rub snow on your nose to keep it from getting frostbitten.

The International adjourned on March 6. Two days later, another sort of delegation arrived in Moscow from Paris. This was the Bullitt mission, a quasi-official commission headed by William Christian Bullitt, special assistant in the U.S. State Department and a member of the American Peace Conference delegation, secretly dispatched by Colonel House and Lloyd George to meet privately with Lenin and determine the conditions, if any, under which the Russian civil war could be ended and normal relations restored with the West. The idea of such informal discussions had recommended itself to Wilson and Lloyd George after the French had sabotaged the Prinkipo proposal by encouraging conservative Russian representatives in Paris to refuse to treat with the Bolsheviks; hence, the French were now deliberately kept uninformed of Bullitt's mission. In fact, Lloyd George later flatly denied that he had approved the project, but Bullitt had in his possession a note from the Prime Minister's private secretary outlining his preconditions for reopening diplomatic contact with the Soviet Union.

The twenty-eight-year-old Bullitt, a wealthy Philadelphian who later married Louise Bryant (the widow of the radical author John Reed), and who returned to Moscow in 1933 as the first United States Ambassador to the Soviet Union, took with him several assistants and the noted muckraking journalist Lincoln Steffens, who had been attending the Paris Peace Conference as a correspondent. They were welcomed by the Soviet officials in Moscow; to the latter the mission represented an opportunity to escape from the bleeding effects of the blockade and to preempt further Allied support of the White military forces. After a week of negotiations, Bullitt and Lenin concluded a draft agreement calling for a cessation of hostilities within Russia, an end to the Allied blockade, the withdrawal of Allied troops, and an end to military aid to the Whites, combined with amnesty for the Russians who had supported the White forces and the reestablishment of regular channels of communication between Russia and the West. Both parties were under the impression that if the men at Paris formally put this proposal to the Soviet government, it would be accepted. Unfortunately, as George Kennan has pointed out, Bullitt unwisely had painted his superiors into a corner by negotiating a specific document that now they either had to accept or reject in its entirety: "By taking cognizance of the document, they would obviously place themselves in a position where they could only take it or leave it. Any alteration in its text at the Allied end would have given the Soviet government formal grounds for refusing to accept it." At the moment, however, Bullitt believed he had made a breakthrough that might solve the Russian riddle and allow peace at least a slight chance in the new world being shaped in Paris.

During their discussions, Bullitt had found Lenin "a most striking man—straightforward and direct, but also genial and with a large humor and serenity." Steffens, who had been encouraged by Colonel House to obtain his own informal impressions about Russian diplomatic objectives, finally had a chance to meet with Lenin after Bullitt had completed the official negotiations. Stepping into Lenin's private office, Steffens saw a quiet man clad in old clothes: "An open, inquiring face, with a slight droop in one eye that suggested irony or humor, looked into mine." After an exchange of pleasantries, Steffens asked whether Lenin could give any assurances that the Terror would soon cease.

Lenin jumped to his feet. "Who wants to ask us about our killings?" The men at Paris, Steffens replied.

"Do you mean to tell me," Lenin cried incredulously, "that those men who have just generaled the slaughter of seventeen millions of men in a purposeless war are concerned over the few thousands who have been killed in a revolution with a conscious aim—to get out of the necessity of war and—and armed peace?" Then, after the explosion, Lenin calmed down. "But never mind, don't deny the terror. Don't minimize any of the evils of a revolution. They occur. They must be counted upon. If we have to have a revolution, we have to pay the price of revolution."

The Terror, Lenin argued, kept the contented (and therefore dangerous) people from scuttling the ship of the Revolution: "The absolute, instinctive opposition of the old conservatives and even of the fixed liberals has to be silenced if you are to carry through a revolution to its objective." And had the Revolution achieved its objectives? Lenin took a piece of paper and drew a straight line with his pencil. "That's our course, but"— and he added a crooked line off to the side—"that's where we are. That's where we have had to go, but we'll get back here on our course some day."

When the party reached Helsinki on the return trip, Bullitt excitedly rushed to cable his proposed agreement to Paris. Arthur Ransome came out with Bullitt and Steffens, but before leaving Russia he discussed the future of the Soviet government with an expatriate American who had become a high-ranking official in Petrograd. How long could the Bolsheviks hold out against the blockade and civil war, Ransome asked? Back came the reply: "We can afford to starve another year for the sake of the Revolution."

"Destruction upon

destruction is cried . . ."

Speed the peace treaty and lift the blockade. Pope Benedict appealed to the Allied powers, urging them to conclude peace quickly with Germany. The Vatican claimed to have reliable information that the social and economic situation in Germany was so grave that the pontiff feared the establishment of a Bolshevist state there. The only way to avoid such an outcome, Pope Benedict believed, was peace now, and a peace that would not humiliate the German people.

Speed the peace treaty and lift the blockade. Colonel Henry W. Anderson, head of a joint civilian-military American commission to aid the Balkan states, reported that "all the Balkan peoples just now are in a state of moral exhaustion and demoralization brought about by the terrible privations they have had to undergo through war and revolution." The country that needed help most, according to Anderson, was Rumania: "The Germans have taken everything there—food, clothing, and household utensils. Small children can be seen walking the streets in bitter cold with only flimsy stuff to cover them, their limbs black and blue with cold. There are fifty thousand orphans in Rumania."

Speed the peace treaty and lift the blockade. Sir William Beveridge, British representative on the inter-Allied commission investigating conditions in Austria, Hungary, and Czechoslovakia, found that the dismemberment of the Austro-Hungarian Empire into separate, antagonistic nations had produced economic chaos. Coal was scarce; normal lines of transport had completely broken down. Everywhere they went, Beveridge reported, people expressed a fear of Bolshevism arising from the misery:

To prevent a collapse of social order comparable to what has occurred in Russia, the Allies must practically, if not formally,

TREAT THE WAR WITH AUSTRIA AS CONCLUDED, AND HELP POSITIVELY IN RECONSTRUCTION THERE, NOT BECAUSE THE HUNGARIANS OR GERMAN-AUSTRIANS DESERVE SPECIAL CONSIDERATION OR HAVE ANY CLAIM TO AVOID SUCH SUFFERINGS AS BEFELL NORTHERN FRANCE OR BELGIUM, BUT BECAUSE THEY ARE SO COMPLETELY SMASHED THAT WARTIME STANDARDS OF INHUMANITY ARE NO LONGER APPLICABLE AND BECAUSE THE FURTHER SPREAD OF DISORDER IN EUROPE IS A DANGER TO ALLIED COUNTRIES THEM-SELVES.

Speed the peace treaty and lift the blockade. Frank Vanderlip, a prominent American banker, in Paris after a tour through Europe, reported, "America was once told there might be peace without victory. What we have is victory without peace. Production has ceased, and unless production can be speedily resumed, one's imagination cannot comprehend the chaos which may ensue. . . . The first essential step is fixing the terms of peace. The danger from delay cannot be overestimated."

Speed the peace treaty and lift the blockade. Hunger is the parent of revolution, warned the *Manchester Guardian* on March 2,

AND WHATEVER PROMOTES HUNGER PROMOTES REVOLUTION. THAT IS PRE-CISELY THE PROCESS IN WHICH WE ARE NOW ENGAGED. WE ARE NOT ONLY MAINTAINING THE BLOCKADE OF GERMANY, WE HAVE INCREASED ITS STRINGENCY. . . . OF COURSE IF THE OBJECT BE TO INFLICT THE MAXIMUM OF SUFFERING ON GERMANY, TO RUIN HER INDUSTRIES AS SHE HAS RUINED SOME OF THOSE OF BELGIUM AND OF FRANCE, AND TO KILL OFF THE OLD AND THE VERY YOUNG, AS SHE ALSO HAS IN SOME CASES BEEN GUILTY OF DOING, THAT MAY BE A RUDE KIND OF JUSTICE, ALSO ON A PRE-CHRISTIAN MODEL. BUT THEN GOOD-BYE TO INDEMNITIES. GOOD-BYE ALSO TO THE HOPE OF ORDER IN CENTRAL EUROPE. WELCOME TO REVOLUTION AND TO THE DISSOLUTION OF SOCIETY OVER A LARGE PART OF EUROPE.

Speed the peace treaty and lift the blockade. Angered by the dispiriting delay, Secretary of State Robert Lansing (the nominal head of the American peace delegation in Wilson's absence) told American and French journalists at a March 11 International Press Club reception in Paris that common sense demanded peace and the provisioning of Germany:

EAST OF THE RHINE THERE ARE FAMINE AND IDLENESS, WANT AND MISERY. POLITICAL CHAOS AND OUTLAWRY HAVE SUPPLANTED THE HIGHLY ORGA-NIZED GOVERNMENT OF IMPERIAL GERMANY. SOCIAL ORDER IS BREAKING

DOWN UNDER THE DIFFICULTIES OF DEFEAT AND THE HOPELESSNESS OF THE
FUTURE. LIKE THE ANARCHY WHICH FOR YEARS MADE AN INFERNO OF
RUSSIA, THE FIRES OF TERRORISM ARE ABLAZE IN THE STATES OF GER-
MANY. OVER THE RUINS OF THIS ONCE GREAT EMPIRE THE FLAMES ARE
SWEEPING WESTWARD. IT IS NO TIME TO ALLOW SENTIMENTS OF VEN-
GEANCE AND OF HATRED TO STAND IN THE WAY OF CHECKING THE ADVANCE
OF THIS CONFLAGRATION, WHICH WILL SOON BE AT THE GERMAN BORDERS
AND THREATENING OTHER LANDS. WE MUST CHANGE THE CONDITIONS ON
WHICH SOCIAL UNREST FEEDS AND STRIVE TO RESTORE GERMANY TO A
NORMAL, THOUGH IT BE A WEAKENED, SOCIAL ORDER. . . . WE OUGHT TO
MAKE, WE MUST MAKE, PEACE WITHOUT DELAY, AND SHIPS LADEN WITH
FOOD MUST ENTER THE HARBORS OF GERMANY.

It was the first time a top-level American official had depicted so clearly
the gulf that separated the United States from France on the treatment of
Germany, but it would not be the last. Lansing's warning followed an
especially dramatic and acrimonious meeting of the Council of Ten on
Saturday, March 8. Shortly after Lloyd George returned to Paris on the
evening of March 5, he was greeted by a telegram from General H.C.O.
Plumer, the Commander of the British Army of the Rhine, informing the
Prime Minister that his troops could no longer stand the spectacle of
women and children starving. That, for Lloyd George, was the breaking
point, and he would brook no longer any French arguments supporting
the murder of civilians:

SO FAR, NOT A SINGLE TON OF FOOD HAD BEEN SENT INTO GERMANY. THE
FISHING FLEET HAD EVEN BEEN PREVENTED FROM GOING OUT TO CATCH A
FEW HERRINGS. THE ALLIES WERE NOW ON TOP, BUT THE MEMORY OF
STARVATION MIGHT ONE DAY TURN AGAINST THEM. THE GERMANS WERE
BEING ALLOWED TO STARVE WHILST AT THE SAME TIME HUNDREDS OF
THOUSANDS OF TONS OF FOOD WERE LYING AT ROTTERDAM, WAITING TO
BE TAKEN UP THE WATERWAYS INTO GERMANY. THESE INCIDENTS CON-
STITUTED FAR MORE FORMIDABLE WEAPONS FOR USE AGAINST THE ALLIES
THAN ANY OF THE ARMAMENTS WHICH IT WAS SOUGHT TO LIMIT. THE
ALLIES WERE SOWING HATRED FOR THE FUTURE: THEY WERE PILING UP
AGONY, NOT FOR THE GERMANS, BUT FOR THEMSELVES.

Lloyd George then proceeded to read General Plumer's telegram to the
council: "The mortality amongst women, children, and sick is most grave,
and sickness due to hunger is spreading. . . . The continuance of those

conditions is unjustifiable." The general could not be responsible for his troops, he said, "if children were allowed to wander about the streets half starved. The British soldiers would not stand that, they were beginning to make complaints, and the most urgent demands were being received from them." Indeed, they were refusing to continue to occupy a territory in order to maintain the population in a state of starvation. And no one, Lloyd George assured the council, could claim that General Plumer was pro-German. Moreover, British military officials throughout Germany were reporting that the lack of food was daily increasing sympathy for the Spartacists: "As long as the people were starving they would listen to the arguments of the Spartacists, and the Allies by their action were simply encouraging elements of disruption and anarchy." It was like stirring up an influenza puddle next door, Lloyd George said, and "if Germany went, and perhaps Spain, who would feel safe? As long as order was maintained in Germany, a breakwater would exist between the countries of the Allies and the waters of revolution beyond." But once that breakwater was swept away, Lloyd George feared that France might be the next to go, and he trembled for his own country.

Colonel House, in Wilson's absence, agreed. Clemenceau did not.

Hell in Berlin.

The Bloodhound, Gustav Noske, the gaunt Minister of Defense, his large dark eyes hidden by tinted glasses, looked out over the city in the first week of March and saw the Spartacists—aided by workingmen and renegade marines from the People's Naval Division—launch one more round of violence against the Ebert-Scheidemann government amid the chaos created by hunger and the general strike. He decided to do away with the menace once and forever. Noske had dictatorial authority from Weimar to smash the rebels, and so to the commanders of the Freikorps—the vicious, semiautonomous bands of White Guards who nominally served the government but who were truly loyal only to their own individual commanders—went the orders from the Bloodhound: Shoot on sight anyone carrying arms without government authorization. Shoot on sight anyone violating the evening curfew. Shoot the unarmed prisoners taken to Moabit Prison.

Hell in Berlin.

The area around police headquarters and Alexanderplatz, one of the most populous parts of the city, was the scene of the fiercest fighting, until it resembled a wasted frontline village. Utter desolation reigned: skeleton houses in the cold daylight, bullet-riddled streets, walls blown away by artillery. No instrument of destruction tested during the war was withheld: gas shells were lobbed into insurgent strongholds; a column of fire rose above the housetops where flamethrowers had done their work; mines battered Spartacist strongholds; tanks and machine guns dispersed crowds of spectators. Thirty thousand steel-helmeted Freikorps troops marched into the city. Spartacist snipers fired upon Red Cross workers clearing corpses from the streets. The Kaiserstrasse was littered with dead and wounded. Government airplanes dropped huge bombs on the rebels holed up in the Royal Stables, and on a group of fifty idle onlookers whom the pilot mistook for rebels. Machine guns guarded the doorways of the big hotels, and at daybreak troops stalked through the city with artillery and flamethrowers. Howitzers threw shells that made holes nearly twenty feet deep. An armored car patrolled the streets carrying a placard with a white skull and crossbones at the top, bearing the message, "Attention! Warning! Stay in your houses! There is danger to life in the streets!" A blind organ-grinder was shot dead. In the side streets, groups of people stood looking vacantly at their ruined homes while children played in the shell craters and in the ankle-deep rubble of broken glass, pieces of paving stone, pulverized brick, and roof tiles. A pool of blood lay on the pavement in front of the Tietz department store. Government airplanes sliced through the darkness of night with magnesium flares that lit up rooftops to uncover Spartacist snipers. Four of Noske's soldiers were slain on the Kurfursten-damm near the spot where Rosa Luxemburg's body had been thrown into the canal. Berliners shuffled quietly through the morgues to identify rela-tives, looking at the naked bodies behind the glass windows; one woman in a leopardskin coat, her hair disheveled and bright red rouge on her cheeks, searched for her lover and trembled as she looked at each white face on the slabs until she found her sailor.

By March 7, every morgue in the city was filled to overflowing. The rebels' last stronghold was the suburb of Lichtenberg. The White Guards deliberately slowed their attack, gradually strangling the area with a steel cordon, drawing out the agony until they had killed everyone they could. A *New York Times* correspondent reported scores of innocent women and children slain. "They must all be killed," General von Luttwitz, the man in charge of the Berlin operations, told another American reporter. "I'm glad they are still fighting, for it gives us a chance to kill more of them."

A poster displayed a picture of a woman dancing with a skeleton: "Ber-lin, do you not see that it is Death that is your partner?"

"Take it from me," an American soldier stationed in Berlin wrote to the folks back home, "there's been shooting up around here that would have made Nick Carter's *Bleeding Heart* look like *Pilgrim's Progress.*" The Wolff Bureau, the leading German news agency, estimated that one thousand people lay dead or wounded; others put the death toll alone over eight hundred. Noske's terms: unconditional surrender.

Hell in Berlin. The executions in the city became notorious even in that brutal winter. Learning that a band of sailors suspected of rebel sympathies were due to come to headquarters on March 11 to receive their pay, Noske sent troops to occupy the building and wait for their arrival. When the sailors appeared, the government soldiers arrested them and, without asking any questions, promptly executed all twenty-four in the courtyard; some were shot with pistols at point-blank range while they begged on their knees for mercy. "Sheer gruesome murder," reported Harry Kessler in agonized despair. Later an American correspondent watched as guards herded ten white-faced Spartacist prisoners like cattle to Moabit. Six of the captives were boys hardly more than seventeen years old; one was a woman covered with mud, bleeding from the corners of her mouth. Rifles were too slow for the government firing squads; machines guns were far more efficient. One executioner reported that he had helped kill two thousand in one morning: "Units of twenty-five men, women and boys chained to one another were marched across the prison yard. Three machine guns opened fire on them and kept up the firing until the bodies had stopped moving." Ben Hecht stood outside the walls of Moabit on the sunny afternoon of March 11 and saw men of the Reinhardt Regiment, known for their ruthlessness in the service of the White Terror, march 220 prisoners—mostly workingmen, along with a few women—inside to their death as an organ-grinder played a merry tune nearby. Hecht heard the prisoners plead for mercy. Then came the sound of the machine guns: "They were shooting behind the walls of Moabit. The shooting continued. Above the sound of the guns came the cries of men. I could not distinguish the words. The cries changed to howling. The machine guns continued. I waited till the howling and the sputtering were both over. It had grown dark in the street. The sun was setting." The next day the German government ordered Hecht to leave the country by midnight "for reporting lies."

In the midst of the carnage and flames, the reckless orgy of dancing and gambling went on. Crimson handbills announced a grand masked ball at the largest café in Berlin, with prizes for the prettiest and the most original costumes; stakes of ten thousand marks were a common sight at the baccarat tables; Charlottenburg Opera House was crammed to its last seat; teenaged boys and old roués leered at their partners in the dance halls. "What on earth else is there to do," asked one bored man in a suburban café. "I can't work because there is no labor available. I can't sleep because I see ruin ahead for all of us. And the only way I can get through these awful days is to dance all night and try to sleep most of the day." Outside, street orators incited crowds against the Jews, and soldiers began to visit houses in the west end of the city to demand if there were any Jews living inside.

Villard had returned to Berlin in time to witness the last days of the Spartacist uprising. "The truth is," he wrote, "that these people are so deadened to killing by four years of war, and so enervated by starvation and long-drawn-out undernourishment, that most of them have lost the capacity to feel very deeply." And the hunger went on. When a horse was killed during the rioting, women and children pounced upon it and cut chunks of meat off the bones with kitchen knives. An observer with Herbert Hoover's mission saw a child suffering terribly from malnutrition who hid under his straw mattress all the bread he received, his dread of hunger stronger than the actual pain.

Friedrich Ebert, good-natured and sincere in his hopes for the future of his country, presided over the Terror, his dreams of social justice vanished in the deaths at Moabit and in the opposition of still-powerful German industrialists who feared the effects of socialization on their profits. Still, Ebert refused to resign his office; put a Socialist behind an official rolltop desk, the saying went, and he will hold on to his place as if the future of all civilization depended upon it. Ebert was lodged temporarily in the Bellevue Palace next to the Tiergarten while the former Ministry of the Prussian Court was being renovated for him. General Ludendorff returned from his self-imposed exile in Sweden and arrived at the Adlon Hotel in Berlin on March 16 to hold a series of interviews with officials left over from the days of William Hohenzollern; a week later he received enthusiastic ovations when he appeared in the streets, and stories circulated of a movement to convince the Allies that only Ludendorff could restore order and make Germany an effective bulwark against Bolshevism. Hindenburg had taken up residence at his new headquarters on the Polish frontier, where he was greeted by adoring masses singing "Deutschland Über Alles." Rumors of harsh peace terms from Paris sparked demonstrations in Berlin that turned into great popular expressions of sympathy for the Kaiser (often now no longer known as the "ex-Kaiser"). There were an estimated 800,000 army officers of the line and reserve from the war still in Germany in March 1919. The Assembly at Weimar had thus far failed to produce any legislation to indicate the advent of a radically new era or a new spirit; "its achievement during this time," wrote one British observer, "may be best characterised by saying it has wound up the German revolution and has gone a long way towards the restoration of the old regime."

Noske indignantly denied accusations that the German Junker military caste had recaptured power at the head of the so-called republican army: "Such apprehension is entirely groundless." But British and American observers were almost unanimous in declaring Ebert and Scheidemann—and Noske, too—mere puppets of the generals. A former university professor now serving with the American army watched the course of political developments in Germany and grew more and more convinced that while the German people felt "conquered, abased, and powerless, the feeling for revenge is burning and the war spirit is not dead but bides its time."

"You can starve us; you can drive us into Bolshevism," warned General Reinhardt, Prussian War Minister and one of the most powerful Freikorps commanders in Germany, "but you are playing a dangerous game." And from the somber red brick prison known as Amerongen Castle came the cry from a member of the Kaiser's entourage: "Germany will soon repent of having overthrown the monarchy. . . . There are still good patriots in Germany who will not allow her to become bankrupt."

At the opening of the Nine O'Clock Frolic on the roof of the New Amsterdam Hotel in New York City, Mrs. Ogden Mills created quite a stir when she wore an evening gown made entirely of gold tissue, with a scarf of the same material draped over her shoulders. Suddenly, in the early months of 1919, all the luxurious accoutrements of fashion that had been put away for the duration of the war were reappearing in high society. "Not in years have such beautiful jewels been seen as those which are being worn this season," testified *Vogue* magazine. Mrs. John Sanford, for instance, attended the opera in a soft, deep violet velvet gown accompanied by an intricate diamond corsage ornament and a diamond dog collar. Jeweled evening slipper buckles were still being worn extensively, sometimes in the Continental mode with a little black bow behind the buckles.

Wilson had returned to Washington on February 25 and immediately plunged into a hectic round of conferences about appointments, resolutions, and the Democratic Party's internal affairs. In the President's absence, Congress had been dawdling about, accomplishing nothing and quarreling about everything, much like a class of unruly schoolboys when the regular teacher is away. But now, overshadowing all the routine presidential paperwork of signing bills and making nominations, the burgeoning quarrel with Republican senators about the League of Nations loomed larger and larger. Wilson had never been known for a willingness to subtly cajole recalcitrant congressmen into supporting his policies; already, both he and a number of his senatorial opponents appeared quite unwilling to compromise, obstinately proclaiming their readiness to take their case to the people for a final decision.

At eight o'clock on the evening of February 26, the President and Mrs. Wilson entertained the members of the Senate Foreign Relations Committee (excluding Senators Borah and Fall, who declined Wilson's invitation) and the House Foreign Affairs Committee at a White House dinner. Mrs. Wilson sat next to Lodge at the dinner table, and in a most undiplomatic manner spoke to him of the marvelous reception her husband had received in Boston the other day. Such cheering from the crowds—oh, but then that's your home state isn't it, Senator Lodge? After the meal, the men adjourned to the East Room (Lodge gallantly escorted Mrs. Wilson, who made her apologies and retired), pushed the chairs into an oval, with Wilson at one end, and lit their cigars. Until 11:30 Wilson fielded questions and explained the League Covenant in general terms, and made his familiar arguments in favor of American membership. No, the League would not interfere with purely domestic questions such as immigration restrictions. No, the Covenant did not abrogate the Monroe Doctrine. No, the League probably would not force Britain to grant independence to Ireland. Yes, the League required the good faith and goodwill of every nation involved, if chaos was to be avoided.

After several hours, Senator Frank B. Brandegee of Connecticut bluntly announced, "Well, Mr. President, I do not see that this league will end wars."

"I never said that it would," Wilson reportedly replied. "I have not said that we had reached so utopian a state. What I have said is that such a league will reduce to a minimum warfare in the world." The League would encourage discussion before a resort to arms, the President added: "If there had been one week's discussion before the beginning of the European war it would not have occurred."

No one appeared to be much moved by any of this; Senator Brandegee later told the *New York Sun* that he felt "as if I had been wandering with Alice in Wonderland and had tea with the Mad Hatter." (Brandegee also childishly complained that Wilson really might have made more cigars available.) Another senator said that the President had treated them as if he were a very frigid Sunday-school teacher admonishing a class of wayward boys. In a private meeting with members of the Democratic National

Committee on February 28, Wilson described the senators who stood steadfast in their opposition to the League as "blind and provincial people." For the moment, Lodge contented himself with only a mildly sarcastic speech in the Senate two days after the dinner, but Washington is a poor city for secrets, and word soon got out that he was planning a dramatic counterstroke against the President. And so the galleries were packed with spectators leaning far over in their seats (more stood in the hallways and the stairways and even the elevators) to hear every word when Lodge entered the Senate chamber at 11:45 on the evening of March 3 with a piece of paper in his hand. After listening to the tedious debate about a finance bill for several minutes, Lodge rose and obtained the floor. "I only want to take a moment," he announced. Then, at two minutes after midnight, Lodge offered a round-robin resolution signed by thirty-seven senators opposing the League of Nations Covenant in its present form and calling upon the Paris Conference to conclude peace with Germany immediately. More senators who happened to be out of town at the moment, Lodge predicted, would add their signatures later. Democratic senators objected to consideration of the resolution, but Lodge had achieved his objective: the public—and the President—had been placed on notice that any treaty that included Wilson's precious League, without Republican-sponsored amendments, would not obtain the two-thirds majority in the United States Senate that it required for approval. "It is a notice to the President and the Paris Conference," said one prominent senator later that morning. "It is definite notice that the incoming Senate will not ratify a treaty which surrenders the Monroe Doctrine and subjects all or many of the important problems which we consider of our own concern to a council of foreign powers with the right to enforce their dictates upon us, when we consider that such dictation is in violation of the Constitution of the United States."

Wilson had spent his ten days in Washington completing three months' worth of official business—possibly the most hectic and tiresome period of his presidency thus far—working late into the night and arriving at his desk early in the morning, and the fatigue showed clearly on his face when he finally was able to escape from his office on the afternoon of March 3 for a brisk walk with his wife among the downtown matinee crowds and homeward-bound commuters. Stopping several times to speak to wounded soldiers, he attracted such a following that traffic became impeded and police finally had to disperse the crowd.

Immediately following the adjournment of Congress the next morning, the President and Mrs. Wilson boarded a train at Union Station to take them to New York, where Wilson was scheduled to make a speech at the Metropolitan Opera House that evening before embarking upon the return trip to Paris. Along the way, they stopped for an hour in Philadelphia to visit Wilson's new grandson, Woodrow Wilson Sayre, born a few days earlier and now resting comfortably in a private room next to his mother (Wilson's youngest daughter by his first wife) at Jefferson Hospital. The baby's nurse insisted that young Woody was "the sweetest and best behaved baby ever born," but when the President saw him he had his eyes closed and his mouth wide open. "With his mouth open and his eyes shut," Wilson told the nurse, "I predict that he will make a Senator when he grows up."

The presidential party arrived in New York at 8:15 P.M. Driving through the city standing in an open car, with even more massive police protection along the route than in Boston, Wilson saw a crowd whose size was second only to the frenzied celebration that had greeted the news of the Armistice. He saw his wife waving with his white muffler, which had fallen from his hands as he acknowledged the cheers. He did not see the two hundred suffragettes who scuffled with city police at 14th Street and Sixth Avenue ("Brutes!" "That policeman hit me!" "Someone kicked me!" "Give 'em hell, give 'em hell!" "Call yourselves ladies?" "The butchers! They have knocked a woman down!" "Hasn't the President got enough to take care of without being bothered by bunch of nuts?"), and who later charged the police with brutality. Upon entering the Met, Wilson stood before an enthusiastic but well-behaved (for New York) audience of five thousand, listened to a rousing rendition of "Over There" (Wilson kept time to the music with a slight swaying of his head) and "The Star-Spangled Banner" sung by Enrico Caruso, heard a ringing approval of the League by Wilson's predecessor in the White House—and now a genial Republican elder statesmen—William Howard Taft, and finally an introduction by Governor Al Smith. Now Wilson would show Lodge how much the Senate's round-robin resolution had moved him: not at all. America must join the League; it *would* join the League. "The great tides of the world do not give notice that they are going to rise and run," Wilson proclaimed, "they rise in their majesty and overwhelming might, and those who stand in the way are overwhelmed. Now the heart of the world is awake, and the heart of the world must be satisfied. . . . I do not mean to come back until it's over over there, and it must not be over until the nations of the world are assured of the permanency of peace." The senatorial criticisms of the Covenant had made no impression upon him, Wilson claimed, for those men were ignorant of the "great pulse of the heart of the world." He accused Lodge and his cohorts of preaching "a doctrine of careful selfishness, thought out to the last detail. I have heard no counsel of generosity in their criticism. I have heard no constructive suggestion.

I have heard nothing except 'Will it not be dangerous to us to help the world?' It would be fatal to us not to help it." After Wilson ended his forty-two minute speech, there were cheers and a shouted question, "What about Ireland?" Then the band broke into a spirited rendition of "Dixie," and the President retired, exhausted, to a private room to meet with a delegation of Irish-Americans. He had little encouragement for them; while he might sympathize with their cause, there really was little he could do to pressure Britain on the matter. At 1:15 A.M., he and Mrs. Wilson walked out on Pier 4 at Hoboken and boarded the *George Washington* ("Home again," Wilson sighed). The ship had been scrubbed and freshly painted, and equipped with a new wireless transmitter with a radius of 1,100 miles. The presidential party was scheduled to sail for France at 8:15 the next morning.

There was little pomp or ceremony when the ship steamed out of port early on March 5, far less formality than when Wilson had sailed for Europe for the first time in December. No band played "The Star-Spangled Banner" when the presidential flag was broken out at the masthead; Mrs. Wilson was still asleep in her cabin, surrounded by dozens of bouquets of roses, and was not to be disturbed. Doughboys on an incoming troopship cheered the President as they passed. Wilson smiled and bowed in return. Admiral Grayson briefed the press on the President's medical condition: "He is tired, of course, but in fine shape physically and mentally. In Paris they think he is made of steel. They can't understand how he could keep up working all day and far into the night, as he did the last two weeks he was there."

WILLIAM BUTLER YEATS'S PRAYER FOR HIS DAUGHTER:

Considering that, all hatred driven hence,
The soul recovers radical innocence
And learns at last that it is self-delighting,
Self-appeasing, self-affrighting,
And that its own sweet will is Heaven's will;
She can, though every face should scowl
And every windy quarter howl
Or every bellows burst, be happy still.

On the evening of March 13, on a night bright with moonlight that cast a white glow upon the man's face, President Wilson stepped onto French ground once again near the mud flats of Brest. He was a tired man and a sick man.

FOUR

THE DAYS OF DARKNESS

"And the shepherds

shall have no

way to flee . . ."

15

"For I heard

the defaming of many,

fear on every side . . ."

The Cabinet of Dr. Caligari, Part One. Between 1913 and 1919, the young German film industry enjoyed a period of tremendous expansion as the number of movie theaters in the country jumped from twenty-eight to 245. Although the Kaiser's government had established a virtual monopoly on movie production during the later years of the war for propaganda purposes, Ebert's Cabinet opted to return the industry to a purely private basis, permitting budding movie moguls to produce whatever they and the public desired. Much of the early output focused upon—what else?—sex (*Lost Daughters, Hyenas of Lust,* and the more than slightly unconventional *A Man's Girlhood*), but there were other filmmakers with more serious artistic pretensions.

Early in 1919, a pair of antiauthoritarian poets—an Austrian named Carl Mayer, whose personal experiences had filled him with a deep-seated distrust of the psychiatric profession, and Hans Janowitz, a Czech who still remembered an eerie murder he thought he had witnessed before the war—joined forces to write a story of madness and murder.

Das Cabinet des Dr. Caligari, directed by Robert Wiene, and featuring Werner Krauss as the infamous doctor, Conrad Veidt as the Somnambulist, and Lil Dagover as the Girl, purported to be "a tale of the modern reappearance of an eleventh-century myth involving the strange and mysterious influence of a mountebank monk over a somnambulist." When our story opens, a young man (later identified as Francis) is sitting on a bench, telling his tale of horror to a friend. It all began, Francis said, in his hometown of Holstenwall—which, in the movie, becomes a distorted, crazy-quilt vision of slanted buildings, warped walls, and tilted windows, all pierced by bizarre zigzag lines and shapes. One day a fair came to Holstenwall, bringing with it an odd old man with spectacles and white hair sticking wildly out from beneath his top hat: Dr. Caligari himself.

When the good doctor applies for a permit to set up his booth at the fair, an arrogant town clerk calls him a fool and a faker, and denies his request. Another official gives him the permit, but that night the obstreperous clerk is found murdered, the first in a series of strange and mysterious (to the local police, if not to the audience) killings. The next day, Francis and his friend Alan go to the fair and enter Dr. Caligari's tent, where the doctor is preparing to awaken a somnambulist named Cesare, who has been asleep for twenty-five years. Caligari opens his "cabinet" (actually a long wooden box that bears a striking resemblance to a coffin), and there stands Cesare: a tall, powerfully built man with sunken eyes, nostrils that flare as menacingly as nostrils can possibly flare, and a cruel, presumably red mouth. Caligari then proudly announces that the mysterious Cesare can predict the future, and he invites questions from the audience.

Alan jumps up. "How long shall I live?" he asks naïvely.

Cesare gives an excellent impression of a ghoul about to devour his prey. "The time is short. You die at dawn."

Alan laughs (the more fool he), but sure enough, that night he is attacked and murdered in his bed. Cesare then goes back to sleep in the cabinet of Dr. Caligari.

Hearing the awful news of his friend's death, Francis runs to the police, crying, "There is something frightful in our midst!"

Wilson had managed to catch up on his sleep on the return voyage from New York to Brest (between shuffleboard matches with his wife), but he could never truly rest while his League was threatened by enemies at home and in Paris. He had seen the desperate hope in the eyes of the people lining the streets in the nations of Europe, he knew how much they depended on him and him alone to bring them a peace that would keep them and their descendants from being the pawns sacrificed in yet another round of human destruction. "I have ridden along the streets of European capitals and heard cries of the crowd, cries for the League of Nations," Wilson had said in New York. He had heard cries that came "from people whose hearts said that something by way of a combination of all men everywhere must come out of this. As we drove along country roads weak old women would come out and hold flowers up to us. Why should they hold flowers up to strangers from across the Atlantic? Only because they believed that we were the messengers of friendship and of hope, and these flowers were their humble offerings of gratitude that friends from so great a distance should have brought them so great a hope. It is inconceivable that we should disappoint them, and we shall not." No compromise, no surrender.

But now a new obstacle stood in Wilson's path. Colonel House, the trusted adviser and confidante, surprised the President by traveling to Brest in person to give Wilson a first-hand report of what had transpired at the conference during his absence. Adjourning to a private compartment on the train to Paris, Wilson and House conferred for several hours. When House finally left, after midnight, Mrs. Wilson opened a door and saw her husband standing and silently holding out his hand. "The change in his appearance shocked me. He seemed to have aged ten years." This, Edith Wilson later came to believe, marked the beginning of Wilson's decline and final collapse. Unaware for the moment of the gravity of his plight, she grasped his outstretched hand and, weeping, asked him what was the matter. He gave a sad and bitter smile. "House has given away everything I had won before we left Paris."

In order to speed up the work of the conference, House told Wilson, he and Balfour had agreed to the drafting of a preliminary peace treaty based largely upon the stiff Armistice renewal terms imposed on Germany by Marshal Foch and the Supreme War Council; unfortunately for Wilson, the so-called preliminary treaty would include all the hard issues of French security upon which he had decided to take a firm stand against Clemenceau: boundaries, limitations on the size of the German army and navy, and indemnities. Worst of all, it did *not* include any provision for a League of Nations. Wilson knew that if a treaty with Germany were signed without any mention of a League, it would be difficult at a later time to compel his Allied colleagues—preoccupied with their own pressing domestic concerns—to concentrate their attention on the Covenant again. And once written, the terms of preliminary treaties had a persistent habit of perpetuating their existence and appearing virtually unchanged in the final draft.

Reconstructing the events of the past month in his mind, the President concluded bitterly that House had yielded point after point under Clemenceau's persistent prodding and flattery until there was nothing left. "Bursting with indignation," Mrs. Wilson later recalled, "I stood holding my husband's hand. Before I got myself together, he threw back his head. The fight of battle was in his eyes. 'Well,' he said, 'thank God I can still fight, and I'll win them back or never look these boys I sent over here in the face again.' " Wilson liked to say he had a single-track mind, and now he set out to prove it.

Physically weakened by a persistent cold and sore throat caught while sitting in a draft for several hours watching movies in the *George Washing-*

ton's theater (against Admiral Grayson's advice), and by the nagging discomfort of teeth hastily and apparently improperly filled by a Washington dentist during the hectic sojourn in the States, the President arrived in Paris at noon on March 14. Poincaré and Clemenceau met him at the Gare des Invalides; Wilson congratulated the Tiger upon his narrow escape from death. "My hide is too thick for a little piece of lead to do me any harm," Clemenceau replied. After Wilson and his entourage sped away from the station in their fleet of official automobiles, the President's first stop was his new residence, a three-story house on the Place des Etats-Unis selected by the French government for its proximity to both the Hôtel Crillon and Lloyd George's flat, which stood only a few yards away, at 23 Rue Nitot, and which now displayed an American flag draped over its balcony to welcome Wilson. (The lease had run out on the Murat palace, and apparently there had been some difficulty in renewing it. Besides, the Murat had been far too large for Wilson's taste, and Wilson suspected all the French servants there of being Clemenceau's spies.) The owner of this charming residence, a writer named Francis de Croisset, had moved out the previous week to make room for the presidential presence. It was smaller than the Murat, but still imposing: a massive railing stood between the house and the street; big double doors in the gate, flanked by red-and-white striped sentry boxes that looked like Jack-in-the-boxes, allowed automobiles to drive into the courtyard; five large double windows on each floor provided an excellent view of the city (and from the small garden at the side one could see the Eiffel Tower, wearing a blue and gray mist like a scarf around its throat); and upstairs was a sunken bathtub— which excited Mrs. Wilson no end—with gold faucets and overhead a chandelier adorned with birds of many colors.

Then at three o'clock Wilson met with Clemenceau, Lloyd George, and House at the Crillon, making it quite clear that he had no intention of acquiescing in any deals struck behind his back. Instead, he wanted to return to where nearly every important issue had stood when he left Paris on February 15. Lloyd George, who had come back across the Channel from London the week before, was furious. After the meeting he complained to Lord Riddell that "we shall never get a settlement if we continually re-open what has been decided." The conference at the Crillon had achieved nothing, Lloyd George declared with considerable disgust: "Wilson talked for an hour about the League of Nations and his ideals, but we did nothing practical. The position is serious." To his private secretary and mistress, the lovely Frances Stevenson, Lloyd George confided that Wilson could think and talk of nothing but the League; "everything must hang on to that for him to take any interest in it." Not that Lloyd George had distinguished himself, either, since his return. The Welshman had managed to alienate Clemenceau once again; angered at what he considered to be British double-dealing on the reparations and Rhineland issues, Clemenceau told Poincaré (while they were waiting at the station for Wilson's train to arrive) that he was going to dig in his heels: "I won't budge. I will act like a hedgehog, and wait until they come to talk to me. I will yield nothing. We will see if they can manage without me. Lloyd George is a trickster. . . . I don't like being double-crossed. Lloyd George has deceived me. He made me the finest promises, and now he breaks them."

The next day, Wilson petulantly refused to attend the scheduled meeting of the Supreme War Council, excusing himself by saying he had not had time to read and ponder the papers outlining the proposed terms of peace with Germany. Instead, he called his press chief, Ray Stannard Baker, and instructed him to distribute a release denying rumors that there might be a peace treaty without the League. Baker thus obediently announced that the conference's earlier decision that the League would be an integral part of any settlement was "of final force" as far as the President was concerned, and would not be overturned. On the sixteenth, Wilson was so fatigued from overwork, from trying to catch up on a month's work in a few days, that he remained in bed until noon, and then reviewed the military and naval terms one more time with House in the afternoon. Then he took a ride with his wife to St-Germain. Incredibly, the conference was now not only not moving forward; it was actually starting to go backward. . . .

Meanwhile, the situation in Central and Eastern Europe continued to deteriorate. Poland was raising an army of 350,000 men to defend the far-flung frontiers it claimed for itself, frontiers that included the port city of Danzig, for centuries a vital German trading center and one of the most aggressively pro-German cities in Europe. Poland's Premier, Ignace Jan Paderewski, the internationally acclaimed concert pianist who had turned his talents to politics, defended his government's unilateral military actions by conjuring a nightmarish vision of a German-Soviet entente capable of dominating Eastern Europe in the absence of a strong Polish state. Then, just as the first substantial Allied food shipments began to arrive in the former territories of the Austro-Hungarian Empire, Herbert Hoover—one of the few men at Paris capable of getting anything done properly and promptly—announced he intended to resign his position as head of the Allied relief effort in July to return to private business. "It appears that things are not going quite smoothly in Paris," lamented the *Manchester Guardian* with marked understatement. "Day by day it is becoming more apparent that to make peace is a harder thing than to make war."

Stung when the Yugoslavs ousted an official Italian military mission from the town of Laibach in disputed territory, Italy closed down the Adriatic coast, instituting a blockade that prevented supplies from reaching either Yugoslavia or the Czechs. The United States responded by threatening to cut off relief shipments of food to Italy if the blockade were not lifted immediately. The Yugoslavian delegation in Paris asked that Wilson arbitrate their territorial dispute with Italy. Italy refused to cooperate, and, to emphasize its displeasure with its newly independent neighbor, suspended the repatriation of Yugoslavian prisoners captured from the Austrian army. Yugoslavia thereupon began to mobilize its military forces. It was all degenerating into a wretched street brawl.

At Madison Square Garden, the largest crowd since the days before the war came to witness the epic struggle between Strangler Lewis and Wladek Zbyszko. Numerous judges, bankers, and businessmen left their Fifth Avenue clubs and pushed through the thousands of disappointed ticket-seekers outside to take their places in the boxes. There were hundreds of women in the audience, screaming themselves hoarse; "There has seldom, if ever, been so much enthusiasm at a sporting event in the history of the old arena," said one veteran ring buff. The bout began at 9:14. The two men mauled each other for a while, then Lewis—the pride of Lexington, Kentucky—tossed Zbyszko to the mat so hard that the rafters of the Garden shook in reply. The battle seesawed back and forth for another thirty minutes, until the Strangler ensnared his foe in one of his trademark headlocks. The Pole's face turned red, his eyes bulged as Lewis maintained his deadly, viselike hold (the crowd loved it), until Zbyszko finally screwed up enough strength to curl up his legs and break away with a mighty kick. Then Wladek obtained a toe-hold on the Strangler, producing a look of excruciating pain on Lewis's face as the Kentuckian writhed and squirmed on the mat in agony. Alas, try as he might, Zbyszko could not detach his opponent's big toe from his foot, and Lewis finally emerged, limping but whole.

As the match passed the ninety-minute mark, the action heated up. First came another grueling headlock; Zbyszko broke from the Strangler's clutches and put on a scissors hold; Lewis tore himself free and responded with a crotch hold, at which point the crowd went wild; the Pole replied by kicking Lewis through the ropes and out of the ring; then came a game of leapfrog and yet another headlock by the Strangler. After a minute and a half, the "Polish Prince"—clearly at the end of his rope—summoned every last reserve of energy and struggled to a half-erect position; grabbing Lewis about the body, he gave a desperate heave, lifted him up, and threw him to the mat like a sack of meal. (The crowd gasped in amazement.) The Strangler lay in a heap on his back, an exhausted and beaten man. Zbyszko pinned Lewis's shoulders down for the count precisely one hour, thirty-four minutes, and thirty-six seconds after the match began.

If no one dared to call the austere Henry Cabot Lodge "Strangler," still the Massachusetts senator and his round-robin resolution had thrown the President against the ropes and immensely complicated Wilson's task at Paris. Not only did the resolution damage the President's authority as a spokesman for American popular sentiment, but, more important, it raised the specter of American withdrawal from international politics and a return to isolationism once the peace treaty had been written. Not surprisingly, this prospect strengthened the French delegation in its determination to obtain physical and financial guarantees against future German aggression. French diplomats nodded their heads with the wisdom of Gallic cynicism: you see, they said, we told you we could not rely on Wilson's high-sounding ideals to protect us from the Boches.

Since Clemenceau and his colleagues had never really believed in the League as a substitute for more concrete guarantees, Wilson's difficulties with the Senate caused only a minor adjustment—a stiffening of resolve —in French diplomatic strategy; but Britain was caught in a bit of a quandary. Never wholeheartedly enthusiastic about active involvement in the political and military affairs of the Continent during peacetime, some British diplomats now began to question seriously how deeply they should commit their nation if the United States abandoned Europe. Arthur Balfour hoped it would never come to that. "I may say that an immense responsibility rests upon the American people," he told British correspondents after learning of Lodge's opposition to the League Covenant. "They have come into the war. Their action has had a profound importance. Their service to mankind in this crisis will make a great page in their history. But that service is only half accomplished if they do not take a share in the even more responsible labors of peace." The editor of the independent conservative journal *The Observer* was even more emphatic when he wrote, "Do Americans fully realize what is going to happen in this age of flight, that the Atlantic will cease to be a barrier, and how the United States will now be involved in European affairs quite as much as England and

France? If America withdraws now she will kill the hopes of civilization, and throw Europe into the melting pot again. I cannot believe this round robin [resolution] is the last word."

The Cabinet of Dr. Caligari, Part Two. While Francis tells his frightful tale to the police, Dr. Caligari plots his next outrage. Propping up Cesare in his cabinet, the doctor strengthens his protégé for the night's festivities by spoon-feeding him a disgusting (but apparently nutritious) bowl of gruel. Then, under cover of darkness, Cesare steals off to the house of Francis's girlfriend. Entering through a window, he spies our unsuspecting heroine lying on her bed; he watches her breast rise and fall in the rhythmic motion of deep sleep; he raises his dagger to plunge it into her white skin. No. Wait just a moment now. Something is stirring within Cesare, behind that manic countenance. It turns out to be lust.

Picking up the girl, who by this time is wide awake and struggling to preserve her virtue if not her dignity, Cesare departs by a window and starts a madcap dash over the picturesque rooftops of Holstenwall. Alerted by their daughter's screams, the girl's parents and the rest of the household set off in pursuit. Before reaching Caligari's hut, however, Cesare's strength begins to flag (not enough gruel, and the girl was heavier than he expected), and after crossing a bridge he drops the girl to the ground, where she is found shaken but unharmed by her rescuers. Fleeing an angry mob of townspeople, Cesare stumbles on, until he at last loses his balance and falls from the top of a high wall.

Learning of the attempted assault, Francis (who always seems to be about one step behind the action) confronts Caligari. The doctor flees; Francis follows. Through the city streets they run, until Caligari finds sanctuary behind the walls of a lunatic asylum. Francis enters and finds a white-coated doctor strolling in the courtyard: Have they a patient named Caligari here? The name does not ring a bell, the doctor replies, but then only the director of the institute is allowed to reveal the names of patients. Would Francis like to speak with him? Francis unsuspectingly gives an affirmative nod. (Ah, will he never learn?) Ushered into the director's office, our hero sees, seated behind the director's desk—Dr. Caligari himself! Staggering backward in fright and astonishment, Francis beats a hasty retreat.

French objectives at the Peace Conference: the return of the provinces of Alsace and Lorraine; detachment of the west bank of the Rhine from Germany and the establishment of an independent Rhenish republic as a "buffer" state, and/or Allied military occupation of the Rhineland; annexation of the coal-rich Saar Valley despite the obvious German sympathies of its inhabitants; astronomical German reparations payments of which France would receive the lion's share as compensation for the destruction wrought by the Hun armies; severe limitations on the size of the German army; the surrender of the German fleet to the Allies; and, farther to the east, the construction of a *cordon sanitaire* of strong Eastern European states to hem in the Bolsheviks in Moscow. If Britain and the United States would pledge themselves to a military alliance with France against Germany, Clemenceau would modify these terms, but the early returns from the conference indicated that the Atlantic powers were preparing to retreat into a policy calling for (in the words of a cynical French editor) "as few engagements as possible, hands as free as possible [and] a gelatinous League of Nations substituted for solid alliances."

While the Tiger yielded to no one in his dogged pursuit of French security, it had become obvious by the middle of March that the old Clemenceau, the agile negotiator, had been slowed by Cottin's shot. After all, said Lloyd George, shaking his head sadly, no man of seventy-seven could be shot in the lungs with impunity. The Prime Minister realized that Clemenceau was not the man he had been six months ago. "The old boy has lost his power of coming to decisions," Lloyd George told Riddell. "He is overcome by the torrent of Wilson's eloquence. It seems to paralyze him." Still, much of France—and especially the young people—retained their affection for the father of victory. When students paraded through the streets of Paris on Shrove Tuesday wearing costumes of flowers, with artists' ties in their school colors, they proudly carried at the head of their procession a large cardboard tiger.

A deputation of ten schoolgirls from the Lycée Jules-Ferry visited Clemenceau at the Ministry of War to express their thankfulness at his recovery and to give him a present: a gold pen (crafted by the same artist who was forging the sword to be offered Marshal Foch by the city of Paris) with which to sign the peace treaty. "You see," explained one proud young lady, "one cannot give the Prime Minister a commonplace pen, a pen that anyone could buy with money." As the girls trooped bravely past the helmeted poilus on guard, past the grim and resolute army officials, they came at last to the Prime Minister's door. Clemenceau emerged from his dark green study—where the walls were hidden by huge maps studded with small colored flags—and held out his hands in welcome. Beneath the black skullcap perched like a military bonnet, above the strongly cut features that looked more than ever as if they were cut out of ivory, the Tiger's small black eyes began to mist over as he beheld the schoolgirls. Geneviève Hild, the fourteen-year-old daughter of a Paris barrister, read him a tribute from the class, praise for the man who had "assured the victory of Right and given back to eternal France the luster of her ancient glory." The old man was overcome. "I thank you. You are dear and good little girls," he told them. "I have children and grandchildren; it is a grandfather who is speaking to you, and he is very touched by your thought. Yes, I will sign the Peace Treaty with your pen, and I will do everything in order that this Treaty may be just and lasting, so that you, my children, may not have to endure the agony and the suffering which have, alas, been the sad lot of your mothers. And now, whether you like it or not, I must kiss you." And he did. As they left, Marshal Foch was on his way into Clemenceau's office. The marshal graciously drew back, bowed, and gave a sharp military salute to the future of France.

Emil Cottin, meanwhile, had been sentenced to death by a French tribunal. To a courtroom jammed with spectators, the prosecution described the assassin as "a poisonous flower which has grown up in the soil of anarchy"—a characterization to which Cottin objected, shouting that his accusers were pretty poisonous themselves. "Rarely," continued the government's report, "has a crime been accomplished with more sustained premeditation, more mature design and more implacable tenacity, with a certainty of method which it seemed would infallibly lead to a fatal result." The Premier's overcoat and waistcoat, complete with bullet holes, were introduced as evidence, although Clemenceau had let them go only reluctantly and insisted that they be returned as soon as possible. "While clothes are so expensive," the Tiger growled, "I am not going to indulge in the luxury of a new overcoat just because a fool shot a few holes in my old coat." (Clemenceau later refused a Paris museum's request that he donate the coats for display.) Notably thin and pale during his trial, Cottin admitted that if he had escaped, he probably would have tried again to kill Clemenceau. Rejecting a tearful plea for mercy from Cottin's mother, the court returned its unanimous verdict after only ten minutes' deliberation.

France, four months after the Armistice: Amid the increasing activity in training stables, the government announced that horseracing would resume on May 5, the first meet to be held at St.-Cloud, and the Grand Prix set for June 29. Harry Truman, preparing for his return to the States, visited a cathedral at Bar-le-Duc and discovered that:

THEY HAVE BEAUTIFUL COSTUMES FOR THE PRIESTS AND CHOIRBOYS. ONE OLD PRIEST WHO TOOK UP THE COLLECTION HAD ON A LACE SKIRT THAT MOST ANY AMERICAN WOMAN WOULD TRADE HER HUSBAND FOR. THERE WAS ONE INDIVIDUAL WHOSE DUTIES AND POSITION I COULDN'T QUITE FATHOM. HE HAD ON A NAPOLEON BONAPARTE HAT WITH A WHITE PLUME RUNNING FROM END TO END OF IT. HIS UNIFORM WOULD MAKE A GREEK GENERAL JEALOUS AND HE HAD ON A RAPIER OR SWORD, I COULDN'T TELL WHICH. . . . ONE LITTLE OLD KID WAS SURE AN EXPERT AT SWINGING THE INCENSE POT. IF THE MAIN PRIEST HAD EVER BACKED UP WHILE THAT POT WAS WORKING HE'D HAVE BEEN BRAINED SURE.

Passing through the ruined villages of the French countryside, American Red Cross officials saw families "standing in the doorways of houses which have for their roofs nothing but a sheet of canvas which sags under the weight of the snow. Smoke curls up from a hole in the ground, and investigation of its source discloses a family of four huddled about a fire in the cellar of a completely wrecked home. The children wear old blankets, and the parents work and sleep in a ragged patchwork of costumes." Other less fortunate children remained in a deep state of psychological shock from the sights they had witnessed during the war.

Auto tours through southern France were, in the current phrase, "napoo"—not permitted—but delegates to the Peace Conference amused themselves on their days off by touring the battlefields of the Western Front and searching for souvenirs. "There are considerable dumps of both German and French munitions," wrote Charles Seymour:

WE PICKED OUT BRAND NEW FUSES FROM THE BOXES, MRS. BOWMAN SAYING THEY WOULD BE LOVELY PLAYTHINGS FOR THE CHILDREN! WE LATER LEARNED THAT THE SMALLER ONES HAD FULMINATE OF MERCURY AND THE LARGER ONES TNT CAPS. . . . THE GROUND IS LIKE THE SURFACE OF THE MOON THROUGH A TELESCOPE, SIMPLY A MASS OF SHELL-HOLES, MERGING INTO EACH OTHER, WITH THE SUBSOIL CHURNED UP. . . . WE HAD LUNCH JUST OPPOSITE FORT MALMAISON. IT WAS WITHOUT EXCEPTION THE MOST DESOLATE SPOT I EVER VISITED; FOR MINUTES AT A TIME ABSOLUTE DEAD SILENCE, NOT A BIRD OF ANY KIND; ONLY THE REPORTS OF SHELLS OR HAND GRENADES WHICH ARE BEING FIRED BY THE ANNAMITES, WHO ARE JUST BEGINNING TO CLEAN UP.

The destruction of the French industrial machine and the nation's transport system; the increased percentage of aged people in the French population and the concomitant popularity of pessimistic and cautious attitudes among the public; the cry, "Germany must pay!" and the hope that Britain and the United States would forgive France her war debts; and the belief that the dismemberment of Germany would render France invulnerable for all time.

Back in Paris, the spring did not come, the cold exacerbated by the continuing coal shortage. The daily cost of living was nearly double that of London or New York; relief was provided only when the government opened barracks in the most populous and poorest quarters of the city and sold foodstuffs directly to consumers, attracting lines of women standing hatless in the cold, their hair disheveled; finally, when their turn came, the women neglected vegetables and asked instead for the full quota of two pounds of fat. Outside the Théâtre Française, billboards announced the production of a little-known Victor Hugo comedy entitled *Shall They Eat?* All the cafés in the Latin Quarter closed at ten-thirty sharp. A well-known Parisian comedienne sued another actress for calling her a "Boche" and won a $200,000 libel judgment. Observing the children (and adults) climbing over the captured German artillery guns in the Place de la Concorde, an enterprising photographer set up shop and did a land-office business in portraits of Parisians and visitors (often whole families in their best clothes) in front of the howitzer of their choice. . . . The Métro was so crowded that people were expressly warned against the perils of hatpins. Fontainebleau was overflowing with British staff cars and khaki uniforms: "Quite a lot of people are having the Sunday afternoon off," noted an amused American reporter. Versailles, where the Peace Conference would repair for its final formal deliberations, remained for another long month nothing more than one of the most popular Sunday resorts of the capital, where American doughboys played baseball near the legendary Hall of Mirrors, much to the consternation of the natives.

Attending a dinner at the Ritz one evening, Harold Nicolson found himself chatting with Marcel Proust, who made a rather poor first impression on the British diplomat: "white, unshaven, grubby, slip-faced." Proust was waiting for his latest work, *A l'Ombre des Jeunes Filles en Fleurs*, to wend its way through the seemingly interminable publication process, and was spending the winter correcting proofs and trying to fend off the seemingly never-ending chills that were always lurking in unheated hallways to destroy his fragile health. After dinner with Nicolson, Proust donned his fur coat—his usual protection against drafts—and a pair of white kid gloves, and sat huddled up, drinking two cups of black coffee sweetened with chunks of sugar. "Yet," Nicolson marveled, "in his talk there is no affection. He asks me questions. Will I please tell him how the Committees work? I say, 'Well, we generally meet at 10.0, there are secretaries behind. . . .' 'Mais non, mais non, vous allez trop vite.' " Start over again, Proust begged Nicolson. You take the official car, you arrive at the Quai d'Orsay, you walk up the stairs, you enter the room . . . and then? "Precisez, mon cher, precisez." So Nicolson told him everything: "The sham cordiality of it all: the handshakes: the maps: the rustle of papers: the tea in the next room: the macaroons. He listens enthralled, interrupting from time to time—'Mais precisez, mon cher monsieur, n'allez pas trop vite.' " Proust's presence was something of a coup for the hostess, for he was notoriously fussy about the conditions under which he would consent to attend a dinner. To another friend who proposed a party in his honor, Proust replied, "If your house is warm, and if all the windows are closed in the dining room, but more particularly in the room where you go afterwards, I shall do my best to come to dinner. . . . I am not on any special diet, I eat everything and I drink everything, I don't think I like red wines but I like all sorts of white wines, as well as beer and cider."

16

"Thou hast filled me

with indignation . . ."

Sitting beside the pilot in a twin-engine Handley-Page bomber, the Prince of Wales was enjoying himself immensely. After taking off from Cricklewood Aerodome thirty minutes ago on his first airplane flight as a civilian, he and three friends (including Lady Joan Mulholland, seated in the machine-gunner's cockpit in front) had been treated to a bird's-eye view of London, turning to and fro again and again over the City and the West End, circling above St. Paul's Cathedral at fifteen hundred feet. David had a jolly good time picking out landmarks: Buckingham Palace, Fleet Street, and the Houses of Parliament. To demonstrate the plane's stability—and to make the flight a bit more memorable—RAF Lieutenant Carruthers, the pilot, exchanged places in midair with one of his passengers, Admiral Mark Kerr (also a qualified flier). Upon landing half an hour later, the prince graciously said he had had a very wonderful flight and would like to go up again in a four-engine plane sometime soon (after all, Prince Albert was actually taking flying lessons, but then Bertie was not the heir to the British throne—not yet, anyway), and he listened attentively while Carruthers explained the mechanical complexities of the machine. As David stood on the landing strip at Cricklewood, Andrew Bonar Law passed by overhead, bound for Paris.

For the charming and cynical Conservative chieftain Bonar Law, Lord Privy Seal and leader of the House of Commons, the Royal Air Force shuttle between London and Paris had become quite routine. He could confer with Lloyd George in Paris at 10:30, hop on a Handley-Page or De Havilland 4 an hour later, arrive at Hendon at 1:55, and be sitting in his study in Downing Street by 2:15. The shuttle service had been established back in January to facilitate the passage of officials and correspondence between the Peace Conference and Whitehall. Every morning, weather reports were telephoned to the RAF detachment a few miles outside Paris from stations along the route: if conditions were favorable, the flights began immediately; if not, men and dispatches were sent via the morning boat train. Average time for the 250-mile journey was two and a half hours, though the record—set by a solo pilot—was a mere eighty minutes.

But the news Bonar Law brought to the Prime Minister on this occasion was not particularly welcome. There was a Conservative revolt brewing in Parliament over the issue of indemnities. Elected on the strength of extravagant campaign promises to "make the Germans pay," hundreds of MPs were becoming alarmed at the "sinister rumors" from Paris that Lloyd George would be willing to base indemnities not upon a calculation of the war's total direct and indirect cost to Britain, but upon Germany's capacity to pay. What, they wondered aloud, had practical considerations such as that to do with anything? Moreover, the first by-election since the opening of Parliament, a campaign in the presumably safe district of West Leyton, had resulted in a wholesale shift of votes that swamped the coalition government's candidate and returned an independent Liberal instead. Political commentators who professed to see cracks appearing in the imposing façade of Lloyd George's coalition were given additional evidence when the government lost a second by-election in Central Hull, a contest occasioned by the death of Sir Mark Sykes—an extremely able and well-liked government servant who unfortunately has become known to posterity primarily for his role in negotiating the infamous Sykes-Picot treaty. "Give them Hull!" cried Asquith's Liberals, but at 23 Rue Nitot, the Welsh Wizard was not unduly concerned. "My ship may be in danger, but it is still floating pretty securely," he announced cheerfully to Riddell. In fact, in one sense Lloyd George welcomed the election results, for they provided him with additional leverage in his struggle to move his hidebound Tory allies out of the nineteenth century.

British objectives at the Peace Conference: substantial indemnities from Germany to repay the cost of the war, but not enough to wreck the intricately balanced system of international commerce upon which British prosperity depended so greatly; mandates for the administration of former German colonies in Africa and the Far East; the elimination, insofar as possible, of the sources of future conflicts on the European continent— which meant that France could not be permitted to carve up Germany like a stuffed capon, or to bolster Poland and Rumania excessively at the expense of Hungary or Russia; and the elimination of the German navy as a threat to British supremacy on the high seas. While France wished to appropriate the German fleet and employ it for French maritime purposes, Great Britain and the United States—already well equipped with commercial and military vessels—preferred to sink as many German ships as possible.

Dissatisfied with the slow progress of negotiations, Lloyd George refused his Cabinet's urgent request to make another quick trip across the Channel for more meetings on the continuing crisis with the Triple Alliance unions, and decided instead to call his lieutenants together for an intensive weekend of work at Fontainebleau. The Prime Minister vowed to find a way through the deadlock, "to put in the hardest forty-eight hours' thinking I have ever done. The Conference is not going well, and I must try to pull things together." Once that was done, it would be far easier to deal with the unions. Lloyd George was convinced that industrial peace and prosperity in England and throughout Europe depended upon the speedy conclusion of the discussions at Paris: "There is a sense of disquiet throughout the world. Nobody is settling down. . . . Everybody wants to know what is going to happen."

The question of indemnities was proving especially troublesome. British financial experts calculated Germany's bill at about $90 billion; France was stubbornly demanding $200 billion. More dispassionate American studies indicated that Germany could pay no more than $25 billion to $30 billion. (Upon first learning of the Allied proposals for indemnities, Colonel House had confided to his diary that "I thought the British were as crazy as the French but they seem only half as crazy which still leaves them a good heavy margin of lunacy.") Of course, each nation also had its own scheme to divide up the reparations booty to obtain the maximum share.

At least Lloyd George had finally convinced his French allies that Germany needed food *now*. Negotiations with German representatives at Brussels had produced an agreement by which Germany would surrender its merchant fleet in return for food from the Allies. The food would be supplied at a price, of course: $55 million in gold for starters. So preparations were begun for the immediate shipment of two hundred and seventy thousand tons of foodstuffs, including wheat, bacon, rye flour, oatmeal, rice, margarine, and beans. Two additional shiploads were sent up the Elbe to Czechoslovakia. But Hungary—Hungary was another matter.

On Saturday, March 22, as Lloyd George and his team assembled at Fontainebleau to plan their strategy to resolve the outstanding issues of the conference, events in Budapest provided them with an irrefutable argument in favor of urgency.

* * *

A bitter message from Budapest: "The Government has resigned in circumstances requiring a change in policy." Pressured by Allied military
demands to surrender vast chunks of territory to Rumania, Czechoslovakia,
Yugoslavia, and Serbia, Hungary was simultaneously confronted with
grave food shortages, rampant unemployment, and industrial stagnation
growing out of the near-total absence of coal and raw materials (attribut-
able primarily to the continuing Allied blockade). The situation was
inflamed further by the disorganization wrought by the sudden demobilization of the nation's military forces and the breakdown of its transportation system. Finally the government of Count Michael Karolyi threw in
the towel. Charging that the Paris Peace Conference "has secretly decided
on the military occupation of almost all of Hungary," a public statement
issued in Karolyi's name—he never signed the statement, but neither did
he disavow it—concluded that "in the face of this Peace Conference decision, I, the Provisional President of the Hungarian People's Republic,
appeal to the world proletariat for assistance and transfer all power to the
proletariat of the Hungarian people."

Karolyi, one of the wealthiest men in Hungary and a dedicated and
idealistic liberal nationalist who had striven for years to free his country
from Austrian domination, had assumed the leadership of the new Hungarian republic upon the demise of the Hapsburg Empire in the last month
of the war. Unlike Ebert and Scheidemann in Germany, Karolyi and his
Socialist allies feared a reaction from the Right more than any Bolshevist
threat, and hence for a time they attempted to conciliate Béla Kun and his
leftist comrades. Karolyi also cast his political and diplomatic fate with the
Allies in the hope that Wilson's Fourteen Points were something more
than pious platitudes. The old regime against whom the Allies had warred
for four years had been swept away, he insisted; but now the Hungarian
republic required food and supplies to resume its normal economic life.

Those supplies were not forthcoming, however. (When Karolyi told the
Allied commander-in-chief in the Balkans, General Franchet d'Esperey,
that Hungary was desperately short of coal to operate its factories, the
general had playfully replied, "Why, use windmills then.") And the
boundary lines ostensibly established by the Armistice in November 1918
were constantly being shifted by the men in Paris, always at Hungary's
expense. The Peace Conference's decisions, reported one British observer,
"entirely frustrated the efforts of the Karolyi Government to introduce
order into the prevailing chaos, since it destroyed the foundation on which
these efforts were based. To build up any sort of stable government on such

a pile of ruins as the former Hapsburg Monarchy now presents would be no light task at any time, but it becomes an impossibility when the ruins are being perpetually shifted about."

The last straw came when the Allies, in the person of Colonel Vix, the chief of the French mission in Budapest, presented an ultimatum to Karolyi's government on March 20, calling upon Hungary to comply with yet another new boundary line established in Transylvania. No Hungarian government could accept the Allied note and survive, Karolyi informed Colonel Vix; surely this could only result in his government's fall and a Communist takeover. Vix's considered response was a gruff *"Das ist mir ganz egal"*: "I couldn't care less."

Hence the Socialists opted to invite Béla Kun to join them in a coalition government. An official delegation promptly betook itself to a cell in a Budapest jail to put the proposition to Kun, who was still recovering from a savage beating administered several weeks earlier by policemen who had objected to Bolshevik attacks upon their colleagues during the course of February's violent street demonstrations. The Socialists agreed to support a Bolshevik program, to name Kun foreign minister, and publicly to affirm Hungary's allegiance to Lenin's Third International. Their strategy was not difficult to discern: if Kun's government should fall—as it surely must—under the pressure of internal economic disintegration or Allied military actions, the Communists would have to shoulder most of the blame. By that time, they hoped, conditions might be more auspicious for the successful establishment of a purely Socialist regime.

Following the forced resignation of Karolyi (who blamed his government's failure upon the Allies' "blindness and malice"), Kun's Soviet regime assumed power on March 22, and immediately issued a plethora of proclamations promising an alliance with the Soviet government in Moscow: the establishment of Workers', Soldiers', and Peasants' Councils; the nationalization of large estates to provide adequate housing for the poor; an assault on food speculators and the seizure of hidden stocks of food; the abolition of titles and aristocratic privileges; the separation of church and state; the opening of theaters to the proletariat; and the introduction of programs designed to provide all children, rich and poor, legitimate or not, with the basic necessities of life (including free baths twice a week). There was no organized terror, no wholesale appropriation of foreign property, and virtually no bloodshed or violence in Budapest. The French and British military missions were detained for several days and then permitted to leave. Kun appeared determined to prove that a Communist coup need not result in the disorder of Lenin's Russia, and he hastened to assure the

Allies that a Bolshevist Hungary was not planning any new campaigns of conquest: "Our only object is to protect the common people and defend their soil and also the industries, which are the property of the proletariat."

This, then, was the fruit of the policies of Paris. The race between peace, poverty, and plunder had begun in earnest, and peace had already fallen behind. "We knew that conditions in Hungary were dangerous," lamented Charles Seymour, "but have been unable to get anyone here to take them seriously and send out either a mission or an Allied force to occupy Budapest. Now it is possibly too late." Upon hearing the news from Budapest, Nicolson worried that "we are losing the peace rapidly and all the hard work is being wasted. The [Council of] Ten haven't really finished off anything, except the League of Nations, and what does that mean to starving people at Kishineff, Hermannstadt and Prague? It is despairing."

The revolution in Hungary could only be interpreted as deliberate defiance of the Peace Conference's decisions, as a defeat for all the Allies' careful plans, and as one ominous consequence of the seemingly interminable delay caused by the hundreds of hours spent studying maps and statistics and debating boundaries. As one British general pointed out, Béla Kun rode into power on a wave of "despair dictated by hunger at present and uncertainty for the future." "There is no peace," *The Times* of London complained, "and there are no certain signs that even a provisional peace is at hand. The Hungarian revolution is the most startling of many reminders that while the Conference, with its committees and its sub-committees, its reports, its references, and its 'conversations,' continues to employ all the paraphernalia of antiquated diplomacy on a scale of unprecedented magnitude, the world is moving."

Lenin, of course, was ecstatic. Radio Budapest had called him at 5:00 P.M. on March 22; returning the call from the Moscow radio station twenty minutes later ("Lenin at the microphone. I want to speak to Comrade Béla Kun"), he was informed that the Hungarian Soviet Republic offered the Russian Soviet government an armed alliance against the enemies of the proletariat. (Actually, what Kun's government had in mind when it suggested an "armed alliance" was Russian military support against a threatened Allied invasion of Hungary.) While he was not yet willing to divert any scarce and precious troops from the civil conflict against the Russian Whites, Lenin obviously recognized the propaganda value of the latest turn of events in Budapest. "We are certain that this will be our last difficult half-year," he proclaimed to the Eighth Congress of the Russian Communist Party on March 23. "We are especially confirmed in this conviction by the news which was announced to the congress the other day, the news of the victory of the proletarian revolution in Hungary. . . . We have here, in addition to a victory of Soviet power, a moral victory for us . . . the dying beast of international imperialism . . . will perish and socialism will conquer the world."

From Germany, the Workers' and Soldiers' Councils cabled their congratulations to the Hungarian revolutionaries, while Ebert's government pointed hysterically to the no-longer-hypothetical Bolshevist threat in Eastern Europe as proof that the Allies needed a strong German state to resist further Soviet encroachment. The Czechs, too, used the events in Budapest to buttress their demands to the Allies for desperately needed food and raw materials. Meanwhile, a delegation from Hungary arrived in Munich to foment further confusion in that tortured city. In Vienna, where dogs and cats were now routinely stolen and sold for food, thousands marched in a demonstration through the city streets, shouting "Down with the capitalists!" and waving banners that read LONG LIVE THE HUNGARIAN COUNCIL REPUBLIC! Rumania's railroad system was a shambles, and from the Allies there came vast quantities of silk stockings and French perfume—but little food or clothing. George Creel, who had just returned from a tour of Eastern Europe after resigning his post as Wilson's wartime propaganda chief (officially the Chairman of the Committee on Public Information), predicted that "what happened in Hungary is going to happen soon in all those other countries unless something is done, and done quickly, to let them know where they stand. . . . No country, no Government, can stand this uncertain, indecisive period, especially when its factories are idle, its people starving and almost without clothing."

Faced with this challenge to their authority, a number of Allied officials in Paris—the French in particular and, surprisingly, Charles Seymour and some of the other experts on the Eastern European boundary commissions—favored military action against the Hungarian Soviets. (Back in Philadelphia, a reporter asked Princess Catherine Radziwill, who had once lived in the splendor of the Czar's court at St. Petersburg, what action the Allies should take in Hungary. "Intervention, intervention, intervention!" she insisted shrilly, fiercely stamping her foot to emphasize her point.) Ever since the Armistice, French troops had been stationed along the Hungarian-Rumanian border to enforce the victors' boundary decisions; at this time, they and reliable Rumanian forces were no more than 145 miles southeast of Budapest. The Rumanians were permitted to move forward to the Peace Conference's new line of demarcation, but no farther—for the present.

Wilson, informed by Secretary Lansing that the boundary decision that had precipitated the crisis might have been unjust to begin with, stood steadfast against military intervention. "It was important to avoid an excessively hard attitude which would push one country after another into Bolshevism," the President argued. "The same danger existed in Vienna; should we have to trace a line of demarcation [for Austria], Vienna might answer by throwing herself into Bolshevism. If such developments were to repeat themselves, there would be no one with whom to make peace. . . . [Wilson] was ready to converse with any rascal, provided what the latter proposed was acceptable and left his honor intact." Above all, Wilson believed, the Allies needed to clarify the situation before taking any decisive action. Kun was not yet guilty of the crimes charged to Lenin's Bolsheviks. The Kun regime, said Wilson, was "probably nationalist. It is a soviet government because that is the form of revolution which is in fashion; and there may well be different species of soviets." To make the American position perfectly clear, the War Department publicly confirmed that the demobilization of American troops was actually proceeding ahead of schedule, and would not be affected by the events in Hungary. In fact, instead of sending soldiers, the United States proposed sending pigs. Realizing that Hungary had lost possession of approximately 250,000 hogs through various boundary changes, Hoover's Relief Administration prepared to replace the animals to help allay the hunger in Budapest.

Lloyd George wholeheartedly supported Wilson's stand against intervention on the grounds that "one Russia was quite enough." At the end of March, Clemenceau finally relented and agreed to forgo military action for the present. Instead, the Allies decided to dispatch a high-level observer to obtain a firsthand view of the situation in Budapest without formally recognizing the Soviet regime. Lloyd George proposed South Africa's General Smuts; while it may have appeared to some "a curious business that a Welshman was sending a Dutchman to tell a Hungarian not to fight a Rumanian," as British General Sir Henry Wilson put it, Smuts nonetheless set off for Hungary by special train on the evening of April 1 with an entourage that included Harold Nicolson and an ample supply of army rations.

Above all else, the revolution in Hungary finally convinced the men in Paris that unless peace was soon restored, the world would slide further and further toward the maelstrom of hatred and chaos created by four years of war, further into the swirling turbulence that now threatened to engulf the civilization they thought they governed. Perhaps the shadow of Yeats's rough beast loomed just ahead.

And so, abandoning the formalities of the Council of Ten (and leaving the Japanese by the wayside), Wilson, Clemenceau, Lloyd George, and Orlando began their secret conferences as the Council of Four, to thrash out a final settlement among themselves.

When the Boston Red Sox boarded a boat for their spring training facility in Tampa, George Herman Ruth was not among the southbound party. The Babe had given owner Harry Frazee his demands ($15,000 for one year or $10,000 per season for three years), and he vowed to sit out the season rather than budge an inch. Frazee made vague threats to trade the most valuable player in baseball ("Yes, I'll trade Ruth if I can get what I want"), but few took him seriously. Boston fans sided with the Babe and talked of taking up a public subscription to pay Ruth's salary; "not since Mr. Parker invented the Parker House roll," declared one sportswriter, "has a man been so popular in cultured Beantown."

Finally, Frazee caved in and offered Ruth a multi-year contract close to what the slugger had demanded. By the first week of April the Bambino was back in mid-season form, bashing the ball almost to Petrograd and back. In an exhibition game against the Giants in Tampa, Ruth stepped to the plate, heaved his shoulders, shook himself all over, and smacked a hanging curve over the right-field wall and over the racetrack beyond. The boy who found the ball swore it came down covered with ice; old-timers said they had never seen anyone hit a ball that far.

Spring training always made everyone feel younger, and imbued normally rational old men with delusions of eternal youth. During his sojourn in Florida in March 1919, Colonel Jake Ruppert, co-owner of the Yankees, decided to try to capture time in a bottle. Visiting St. Augustine, Ruppert was introduced to an old natural spring that locals promoted as the fabled Fountain of Youth. Ruppert promptly guzzled eight quarts of its magical waters, and purchased dozens of filled flasks besides. He told a reporter that he planned to take the flasks back to New York with him and inject the water into the legs of his players at intervals during the 1919 season.

Try as they might, Americans in Paris just couldn't get their French hosts excited about baseball in the early spring of 1919; Grantland Rice believed this Gallic indifference stemmed from the fact that after four and a half years of war, Frenchmen were sick and tired of wearing any sort of steel helmets.

American objectives at the Peace Conference: a world at peace to permit the United States to pursue its own affairs without interruption from abroad, a stable world in which American industrial and agricultural products could find ready and profitable markets, and a democratic world to satisfy American ideals—and, not incidentally, because the extension of democracy abroad appeared most likely to promote peace and stability. The League of Nations was Wilson's chosen vehicle to achieve these goals. Despite the scornful dismissal of the League by French diplomats and Republican senators as nothing more than the naïve obsession of a mildly deranged Presbyterian dreamer, the Covenant was in fact the product of a rational, calculated strategy to safeguard vital American interests in an era when widespread and fundamental change wracked the world.

So when Wilson assigned nearly the entire American delegation in Paris to the task of revising the Covenant to meet senatorial objections while preserving the document's spiritual integrity, he was not simply wasting everyone's time. Nor, as Wilson reminded his critics, was the work of the Committee on the League of Nations the major stumbling block to the speedy conclusion of a peace treaty. Wilson himself refused to draft any amendments to the Covenant, perhaps because he found the whole process repugnant. "I am yielding to men, to the judgment of men, who have little knowledge or appreciation of the world situation, but who, alas! control votes," the President admitted. Although he far preferred to stand by the League Covenant's original text, he was willing to agree to an explicit acknowledgement of the Monroe Doctrine, to a clause excluding domestic matters from the League's jurisdiction (Western senators wanted to make certain that American immigration restrictions against a sudden influx of Asians remained intact), and to a recognition of any nation's right to withdraw from the League ten years after ratification. "These changes we shall put through" to save the League from total defeat, Wilson promised, "but I fear we will find that we have jumped out of the frying pan into the fire." And these amendments were as far as he chose to go to meet the opposition's demands.

The League, Hungary, the Rhineland, Italy, indemnities, the Saar, Russia—Wilson's days spun one upon the other as the issues intertwined and it all became ever more urgent to see the fight through, for he was the champion of the people and the spokesmen of the silent masses, and it was a heavy cross he bore. (Lloyd George and Clemenceau had no such burden; each had only to attend to his own nation's interests.) Wilson reduced the time prescribed by Admiral Grayson for relaxation, taking only a short walk with his wife or Grayson every day for exercise; all social events were canceled. Paranoia began to set in. Detectives watched over Wilson night and day, and even stood guard outside his bathroom. The meeting times of the Council of Four and the daily schedule of Wilson's movements no longer were published in Paris newspapers, to discourage the crowds which used to gather to watch the President arrive.

On March 23, Wilson ventured out to visit—for the first time—the devastated regions of the Western Front. When the President's car stopped for fuel at the small town of St.-Maxence, children and old women brought bouquets of flowers to him and his wife. There were five automobiles with Secret Service men in Wilson's entourage that day, but during the return trip to Paris late in the afternoon, another car, with a Red Cross insignia, cut into the procession. To close the line, the last car in Wilson's group speeded up, passed the stranger, and slowed down; the intruder in turn speeded up and passed two of the government cars. The race was on. One government car passed the Red Cross car and was again passed in return; then two of Wilson's cars passed the Red Cross car and it responded by passing both of them. Meanwhile, the unmarked car carrying Wilson and his wife, which always remained ahead of the mysterious interloper, kept going faster and faster. The driver of the Red Cross car finally gunned the engine and sped past the President's car at sixty miles an hour. For fifteen seconds the two cars were running side by side in the gloaming on that French country road, and Wilson could see his pursuers clearly. They turned out to be William Allen White, Ray Stannard Baker, and Ida Tarbell, the famous muckraking journalist, out for a picnic in the countryside, and completely unaware that they had been engaged in a game of tag with the Secret Service.

The Cabinet of Dr. Caligari, Part Three. That night, as the director sleeps, Francis and the doctors at the asylum sneak into his office and examine his papers. They find (to no one's surprise) numerous works on somnambulism, the director's special field of study. One book features an account of a renegade monk named Caligari, who, in the year 1093, visited the small towns of northern Italy, traveling with a somnambulist named Cesare whom he carried about in a rough wooden box. (An alarm begins to ring somewhere in the back of Francis's nimble mind.) Caligari, the narrative continues, "ordered his somnambulist, whom he had completely forced into his power, to carry out his adventurous plans . . . creating in town after town great panic by repeated occurrences of murder committed always under the same circumstances."

Checking the director's diary, the inquisitive crew finds that one morning around the middle of March a somnambulist was admitted to their asylum. The camera cuts to a shot of Caligari exulting over the sleeping form of the man who would become his Cesare. "Now nothing stands in the way of my long-cherished ambition. . . . I now shall soon know if this patient can be compelled to perform deeds he would shrink from in his normal waking state.

"Can he be made to commit *murder?* I must know—I will become Caligari!" Transported by the imminent gratification of his most diabolical primal urges, the director rushes outside. There he sees and hears one name repeatedly endlessly. Every wall of every warped building, every myopic bird and every twisted tree, every little breeze seems to whisper the name: "Caligari! Caligari! Caligari! Caligari! CALIGARI!"

REPORT OF THE INSPECTOR GENERAL OF PUBLIC SECURITY OF MILAN REGARDING BENITO MUSSOLINI, PREPARED FOR PREMIER ORLANDO:

PROFESSOR BENITO MUSSOLINI, BORN IN PREDAPPIO (FORLI) ON JULY 29, 1883; NOW RESIDING IN MILAN AT FORO BONAPARTE 38; REVOLUTIONARY SOCIALIST; HAS A POLICE RECORD; ELEMENTARY SCHOOLTEACHER QUALIFIED TO TEACH IN SECONDARY SCHOOLS . . .

BENITO MUSSOLINI IS OF STRONG PHYSICAL BUILD EVEN THOUGH HE HAS BEEN AFFLICTED BY SYPHILIS. HIS ROBUSTNESS ENABLES HIM TO WORK CONTINUOUSLY. HE RESTS UNTIL A LATE HOUR IN THE MORNING, LEAVES HIS HOME AT NOON, BUT DOES NOT RETURN AGAIN UNTIL 3:00 A.M., AND THOSE FIFTEEN HOURS, EXCEPT FOR A BRIEF PAUSE FOR MEALS, ARE DEVOTED TO NEWSPAPER AND POLITICAL WORK.

HE IS A SENSUAL TYPE, AND THIS IS REVEALED BY THE VARIOUS RELATIONSHIPS HE HAS CONTRACTED WITH WOMEN. . . . HE IS AN EMOTIONAL, IMPULSIVE TYPE, AND THESE CHARACTERISTICS CAUSE HIM TO BE SUGGESTIVE AND PERSUASIVE IN HIS SPEECHES, ALTHOUGH IT CANNOT BE SAID THAT HE IS AN ORATOR, EVEN THOUGH HE SPEAKS WELL.

BASICALLY HE IS A SENTIMENTAL TYPE—A FACT WHICH RESULTS IN SYMPATHY AND FRIENDSHIP FOR HIM. HE IS DISINTERESTED, GENEROUS WITH THE MONEY THAT HE HAS AVAILABLE, AND THIS HAS GIVEN HIM A REPUTATION FOR ALTRUISM AND PHILANTHROPY. . . .

HE IS VERY AMBITIOUS. HE IS MOTIVATED BY THE CONVICTION THAT HE REPRESENTS A SIGNIFICANT FORCE IN THE DESTINY OF ITALY, AND HE IS DETERMINED TO MAKE THIS PREVAIL. HE IS A MAN WHO DOES NOT RESIGN HIMSELF TO POSITIONS OF SECONDARY RANK. HE INTENDS TO RATE FIRST AND TO DOMINATE. . . .

Marzo è pazzo: March is mad.

On Sunday, March 23, as Woodrow Wilson was touring the battlefields of northern France and one day after Béla Kun's coup in Hungary, Benito Mussolini stood before a meeting of perhaps a hundred men—"the ones that came were not numerous," he admitted—in a small reception room belonging to the local Association of Merchants and Shopkeepers at Piazza San Sepolcro 9, in Milan. In the square below, a squad of armed arditi stood guard. This was the first general meeting of the Fascio Milanese di Combattimento, the Milanese Battle Fascio; this was the official birth of the Italian Fascist movement. Alarmed at the rising tide of industrial unrest throughout Italy (provoked by widespread unemployment and rampant inflation) and the concomitant growth of support for militant socialism (the Italian Socialist Party had recently voted to pledge its allegiance to Lenin's Third International), and maddened to distraction by the reports from Paris that portended defeat after defeat for his beloved Italian imperialist program, Mussolini had assembled a disparate band of dissatisfied veterans, futurists, anarchists, criminals, and retail clerks whose only common bond was their conviction that Italy's glorious destiny must be achieved by strength and force. The men who had gathered together to cheer Mussolini on this day and who now signed their names to Mussolini's program were the *sansepolcristi*, the Fascists of "the first hour." Those who sat in the front rows and applauded the loudest were appointed to the executive committee.

In the morning, Mussolini outlined the program for the nationwide "anti-party" he proposed to form. The old political parties, he charged, had grown "tawdry and insufficient—unable to keep pace with the rising tide of unexpected political exigences, unable to adjust to the formation of new history and new conditions of modern life." In their place he offered "to lay the foundation of a new civilization," to end the treason and corruption, to arrest the decay within Italy and the intrigue and avarice from abroad. The founding charter of the Fascio Milanese di Combattimento, as presented by Mussolini on March 23, 1919, included three main declarations: a readiness to give wholehearted support to the demands of war veterans' associations; vigorous insistence upon the acquisition of Adriatic territories, including Fiume and Dalmatia; and a pledge "to sabotage in every way the candidates of neutralists in all the various parties."

Nor was that all. Mussolini also called for the abolition of the Italian Senate, advocated universal suffrage, and urged the granting of workers' rights and economic democracy. And yet, he added nonchalantly, details of the Fascist program were unimportant at this moment. In fact, for Mussolini, details always were of little consequence; action and action alone was crucial for the Fascist movement: "We are dynamic, and we intend to take our rightful place, which must always be in the vanguard." As the old order withered and faded away, Mussolini envisioned the Fasci as "organs of creativity and agitation that will be ready to rush into the piazzas and cry out, 'The right to the political succession belongs to us, because we were the ones who pushed the country into war and led it to victory!' " After everyone else had left, a band of arditi stood in the room and raised their black banner and swore to kill and to die to defend their country. "I have the feeling," murmured Mussolini, "that in Italy the road to the replacement of the current system is open."

Certainly Italy presented Mussolini with an excellent opportunity for creating his own vicious brand of mischief in the late winter and early spring of 1919. Rome, Milan, and Genoa were shaken by a series of strikes by printers, dockworkers, and postal, telegraph, and telephone workers. Food remained in short supply; meat was virtually unavailable, and the quality of bread (already far inferior to French or even British bread) was cut once again to preserve the scarce stores of wheat. A severe coal shortage forced the Prefect of Rome to issue a decree limiting the consumption of gas to eight hours out of every day. Gabriele D'Annunzio—openly abetted by Sonnino's faction in the capital—continued his frantic, vitriolic attacks upon America, Great Britain, and France for denying Italy her just rewards on the Adriatic coast. Placards in the streets of Rome exhorted the *citadini* to arouse themselves against the despised Yugoslavs; on the cover of a popular Italian weekly appeared a full-page portrait of Wilson as the new Moses, brandishing two tablets with the Fourteen Points inscribed upon them. An Italian veteran, recently released from an Austrian prisoner-of-war camp and with no money at all, stood in the American YMCA, quietly asking for a postage stamp so he could notify his family in Naples that he was alive. And a warning came from a prominent Italian banker: "If Italy does not get what she wants, she will be forced straight into the arms of Germany." The crumbling Forum, the arch of Titus, and the rough stones of the Via Sacra symbolized the centuries of departed glory, when Rome represented the civilized world's ideal of militarism and conquest.

17

"Remember that

I stood before thee . . ."

Determined to win over his Montgomery belle, F. Scott Fitzgerald sent his mother's engagement ring to Zelda in Alabama. It gained her the attention she sought when she wore it to dances, but Zelda was getting a bit peeved with her suitor's constant long-distance declarations of eternal devotion. "Scott," she finally wrote, "you've been so sweet about writing—but I'm so damned tired of being told that you 'used to wonder why they kept princesses in towers'—you've written that verbatim, in our last six letters! It's dreadfully hard to write so much—and so many of your letters sound forced—I know you love me, Darling, and I love you more than anything in this world, but if it's going to be so much longer, we just *can't* keep up this frantic writing. . . ." Enclosed in the letter was a photograph of Zelda, inscribed for another one of her beaux.

A dispatch from Fort Yukon to Ottawa announced the safe return of Storker Storkerson and four companions to the northern coast of Alaska. Storkerson, a veteran Arctic explorer, had set out from Cross Island, Alaska, on an ice floe in March 1918, accompanied by twelve other men, eight sledges, and virtually no provisions. The purpose of the expedition was to test the theory that the currents in the polar basin would carry them to the west coast of Siberia. Over the next few weeks Storkerson sent back all but four of his men and most of the sledges. For eight months the remainder of the party drifted about in the Arctic Ocean, subsisting on the meat of seals and polar bears. Finally it became apparent that they would never reach Siberia via ice floe; instead, they had only been going around and around in an irregular circle, caught in a great eddying drift.

The American troops abandoned at Archangel might have been excused for thinking that they, too, were caught in a great eddy, moving around in circles and circles. Washington's announcement that the boys would be brought home as soon as the ice around Archangel broke up gave them hope that they might eventually see the good old U.S.A. again, but it also made them extremely reluctant to risk their necks in a fight that even the War Department seemed to acknowledge was not really worth it. Along the front lines, they were also subjected to a constant, demoralizing bombardment of Bolshevik propaganda. During the long winter nights, often separated from the Reds by only a seventy-five-yard-wide stream, the American garrisons could hear the enemy calling out, reminding them that the war with Germany was over, that their wives and sweethearts were waiting for them across the Atlantic, and what were they doing in northern Russia anyway? Back came the flippant responses from the American lines: "Can that stuff!" "What's eating you?" and other more graphically impolite army expressions. Large red banners with white letters urging the Yankees to go back home were hung in trees on the Bolshevik side of the river. Occasionally the doughboys would be serenaded by a Soviet accordion playing "Yankee Doodle." American officers even agreed to distribute Bolshevik literature and comic books among their men, hoping that it would at least provide a respite from the deadly boredom.

But on March 30, trouble arose when Company I of the 339th Infantry, scheduled to return to the front after a brief spell of rest (if not recreation) in Archangel, was ordered to fall out of its barracks and pack its sleds for the trip to the railroad station. The men refused to obey. The war in Europe had ended, they argued with considerable logic, and the United States was not at war with the Bolsheviks, so why should they put their lives in jeopardy? After a lengthy appeal by the regimental commander to their sense of army tradition—and to their own self-interest, for their failure to move might have placed the entire American defensive position in jeopardy—the men agreed to return part of the way, but not all the way, to the front lines. And if they did not soon receive official confirmation that all American troops would be withdrawn from Russia as soon as possible, they threatened to launch a general mutiny.

Understandably reluctant to publicize the incident, the War Department kept it quiet until an Associated Press correspondent broke the story, whereupon an army spokesman in Washington formally confirmed that the men would be withdrawn from Archangel by June at the latest: "Just as soon as we can we will get them out." Meanwhile, the presence of foreign troops on Russian soil was producing precisely the sort of nationalistic reaction Wilson had feared. Maxim Gorky, who, until this time, had been notoriously unenthusiastic about the Revolution, now swung around to support the Moscow government against the "wicked hypocrisy" of the

West. Ironically, Gorky cast Wilson as the villain in the Archangel drama, bitterly attacking the man "who only yesterday was the eloquent champion of peoples' autonomy and rights of democracy, and [who] is now equipping a powerful army to restore order in revolutionary Russia, where the people have already exercised their lawful right to take power into their own hands."

It seems not to have occurred to Allied military commanders in Russia, or at least not to have mattered to them, that the ice would break up first along the rivers south of Archangel, allowing the Red Army to bring its gunboats upstream before American and British ships could arrive from the north. As March brought a partial thaw, the Bolsheviks mounted a concerted offensive to try to push the Allied forces into the sea. Although there clearly was no cause for panic, British proponents of increased aid to the Whites exaggerated the danger to drum up public support for their schemes. Winston Churchill, who fervently believed that "of all tyrannies in history the Bolshevist tyranny is the worst, the most destructive, and the most degrading," led the anti-Soviet crusade. Undeterred by Lloyd George's obvious distaste for any large-scale intervention in Russia, Churchill—without Cabinet approval—sent British howitzers to White commanders and helped form a legion of British volunteers (maximum service, nine months; pay between twelve and thirteen pounds per month) to fight the Bolshies. On April 9 the advance guard of the British relief force bound for Archangel sailed from Tilbury on the *Prinz Heinrich*, a former German steamer. Most of the men were veterans, and the scenes of parting from wives and sweethearts reminded one observer "too much of the war we hoped was over to be at all cheerful. . . . It all seemed to be starting again."

And the civil war ground inexorably on. The White forces under Admiral Koltchak ("Supreme Ruler of Russia"), numbering 300,000 well-to-do peasants and counterrevolutionary Cossacks armed with rifles and sabers, held a line from Perm to Omsk and were now pressing forward in the Urals, but the tyranny of the White Terror led by Koltchak was also constantly creating new recruits for Bolshevism; the Red Army, now 1,800,000 strong (400,000 veterans in the frontline units) and supported by 150 armored cars, 450 dilapidated airplanes, and two battleships, conquered two-thirds of the Ukraine along with the region's rich stores of grain, coal, and minerals. As Churchill put it, "by rolling forward into fertile areas, like the vampire which sucks the blood from his victim, they gain means of prolonging their own baleful existence." Meanwhile, the troops of General Denikin ("Deputy Supreme Ruler"), generally regarded as the best of the White forces, stood along the line of the Don and swept down nearly to the Caspian Sea; both White and Red armies stuffed their prisoners with dynamite cartridges and then blew them up; General Yudenich, aided by bands of White Estonians, threatened Petrograd; and a force of fifty thousand Allied soldiers, including three French regiments, were forced to evacuate Odessa and leave the city to the Bolsheviks. "One day," recalled Grigori (later Marshal) Zhukov, "our regiment was detrained at a place called Yersho. I remember how the Red Army men who had been half-starved in Moscow jumped straight out of the goods wagons and rushed to the local market. They bought up big round loaves of bread and wolfed them down on the spot. Many were taken ill. That was quite understandable, for in Moscow they were getting only a quarter of a pound of bad quality bread a day and some cabbage soup cooked with horsemeat or salt fish."

Returning to Paris at the end of March with Lenin's tentative approval of a compromise settlement, William Bullitt found Wilson and his "single-track" mind preoccupied with more urgent concerns. Besides, Wilson said, he had a terrible headache and really could not receive Mr. Bullitt just now. Why didn't he give his report to Colonel House instead? Bullitt thus spent a day trying to persuade House and the other American peace commissioners to endorse the Moscow agreement, but with little success; House had already decided to support a project devised by Herbert Hoover that proposed to provide Russia with food in return for political concessions by the Soviets—a plan that stood no chance at all of acceptance by Lenin.

Frustrated, Bullitt went to Lloyd George, but there he received even less encouragement. Conservative members of Parliament had been asking embarrassing questions about a rumored Allied proposal to recognize the despicable Bolsheviks, and the headlines of Tory newspapers shrieked their horror at any suggestion of betrayal of the White cause. According to Bullitt, Lloyd George brandished a particularly noxious edition of the *Daily Mail* in front of him and asked, "As long as the British press is doing this kind of thing, how can you expect me to be sensible about Russia?" Government spokesmen solemnly announced in Parliament that no mission to Russia had received official blessing; several weeks later, Lloyd George himself washed his hands of the Bullitt agreement. "There was some suggestion," he told the Commons, "that a young American had come back from Russia with a communication. It is not for me to judge the value of this communication, but if the President of the United States had attached any value to it he would have brought it before the conference, and he certainly did not."

Lincoln Steffens believed that Lloyd George disavowed any knowledge of the Bullitt mission primarily because, having approved it without Clemenceau's knowledge, he did not wish to ruffle French feathers any more than necessary at a time of high tension in the Peace Conference's labors. Bullitt interpreted the rejection of his labors as a personal affront and never forgave Wilson. Steffens, who, after decades of life in the rough-and-tumble world of American journalism, was already irretrievably cynical about the integrity of statesmen, took it all more philosophically. At least the experience provided him with the opportunity to make perhaps his most famous utterance; when the American financier Bernard Baruch innocently asked, "So you've been over into Russia?" Steffens glibly replied, "I have been over into the future, and it works." In fact, Steffens was so pleased with his pronouncement that he repeated it incessantly for the rest of his stay in Paris. "Like the ancient mariner," William Allen White recalled, "Steffens was always stopping the wedding guests and telling them his Russian story until they beat their breasts in despair." Although his colleagues in the American press delegation respected Steffens immensely, they eventually got a little tired of hearing that same phrase repeated over and over again in the lobby of the Hôtel Crillon. So from time to time they would prod him with little darts of skepticism to raise his ire and lead him into ever more preposterous paeans of praise for the Soviet system. Once, White said, "near the climax of his story, to prove with a sentence the reality of his Utopia, he exclaimed, 'Gentlemen, I tell you they have abolished prostitution!' " Faced with this astonishing information, one of Steffens's tormentors held up his hand and cried, "My god, Steff! What did you do?" Steffens, never known as a libertine, blushed beet-red and hastily excused himself, much to the delighted cackles of his colleagues.

Back in the United States, the battle against the Bolsheviks received a powerful and timely boost from Wilson's nomination of A. Mitchell Palmer as Attorney General to replace Thomas Gregory, who was returning to his private law practice. Palmer, a forty-seven-year-old Pennsylvanian and a Quaker, had served three terms in Congress from 1909 to 1915, building up an impressive record of support for progressive legislation until he was defeated in a bid for Boise Penrose's Senate seat. After serving as liaison between Wilson's reelection campaign and organized labor, Palmer was appointed Alien Property Custodian in 1917; during his tenure in that office he gained considerable publicity by rousing Congress to investigate the pro-German wartime propaganda activities of William

Randolph Hearst. Now, upon becoming the newest member of Wilson's Cabinet in March 1919, the flamboyant and ambitious Palmer immediately declared his intention to ask Congress for enhanced powers to investigate and deport dangerous radicals of every ilk.

For those intimately involved in hunting down bewhiskered and unwashed Reds in America, Palmer's appointment came none too soon. Bolsheviks seemed to be crawling out of the woodwork everywhere. The *Washington Post* solemnly proclaimed that "Bolshevism in America is planning for the final struggle between organized society and anarchy." In Pittsburgh, federal agents seized ten Russian anarchists who allegedly had in their possession blueprints of a diabolical scheme to seize the local government arsenal and use the commandeered munitions to blow up every major industrial plant in western Pennsylvania. Six more Russian radicals were arrested in Toledo, Ohio, for having in their possession copies of the infamous "Little Red Book"—reportedly a Bolshevist handbook for violent social revolution. A raid on a Bolshevik nest at 133 East 15th Street turned up additional copies of the feared crimson book, and police took 164 suspected anarchists in for questioning. The prisoners, noted one observer who saw them enter the Criminal Courts Building, were "typical of those who gather at radical meetings in this and other cities. Some of them carried violin cases." All but four were released within twenty-four hours.

On Ellis Island, twelve of the alien radicals brought East on the "Red Special" and still awaiting deportation were set free; the government was finding it difficult to prove that men who couldn't read subscribed to the anarchistic principles espoused in IWW literature. Shocked by this display of official leniency, *The New York Times* argued that the path of safety "does not lie in mistaken gentleness. When there is doubt, not the alien IWW but the country should have the benefit of the doubt." Another member of the Ellis Island crew was reported to be not an alien at all, but a native of Cleveland (which was somehow considered to be more socially desirable). The Immigration Bureau persisted in prosecuting the rest of the prisoners, insisting that they were guilty of "many lawless things, such as attempting to set up a Soviet Government in the Northwest, of fomenting a strike [in Seattle] that nearly verged upon rebellion, and of seeking to turn the minds of newly arrived immigrants toward Bolshevism." A government spokesman added that the accused had proven that they remained unrepentant during their captivity by constantly singing radical songs. Defense attorneys replied that their clients were being harassed simply because they had dared to antagonize the powerful lumber interests in because they had dared to antagonize the powerful lumber interests in the Northwest with their labor organizing activities. Meanwhile, in another federal courtroom in New York, Judge John C. Knox granted a writ of habeas corpus for the fourteen Spaniards arrested in connection with the supposed plot against President Wilson's life; the judge added a rebuke to government prosecutors for holding the men so long without warrants or a court hearing. Meanwhile, another trainload of aliens rounded up in San Francisco and Oregon began the cross-country trip to Ellis Island.

Certainly there was no shortage of politicians willing to join Palmer on the Red-baiting bandwagon. Enjoying his new-found popularity as the defender of one-hundred-percent Americanism—one small town in Kentucky had already nominated him for President for 1920—Seattle Mayor Ole Hanson declared that the Bolshevik menace was "a peril we all must face and conquer. These alien enemies should not be tolerated. They should be deported as soon as they are found, or this nation will fail." (The Seattle shipyard strike had finally ended with the workers accepting precisely the same conditions they had rejected in January.) The Judiciary Committee of the United States Senate unanimously approved legislation to ban the display of red flags. The mayor of New York proposed to prohibit all meetings in the city "whose proceedings are conducted in a foreign language for the abuse of our government, or by or under the auspices of any person or persons who are not citizens of the United States." In Albany, the state assembly—acting on secret information that indicated that Bolshevik agitators with "heavy financial backing" were making rapid headway throughout New York—adopted a resolution authorizing $30,000 for a full-scale investigation to learn "the whole truth" about the radical movement in the state. Armed with "the most drastic anti-Bolshevik law in the United States," the governor of New Hampshire (of all places) vowed to "rake the State with a fine-tooth comb" to uncover the Reds who were rumored to be working in two or three centers within the state's borders. Vice-President Thomas R. Marshall, too, joined the chorus. If any naturalized citizen of the United States took up the Bolshevist cause, Marshall told a Rotary Club gathering in Phoenix, "I would take away his naturalization papers and send him to the farthest of the South Sea Islands."

It may be truly said of Marshall that the former governor of Indiana was one of the least notable nonentities ever to occupy the vice-presidential office. Wilson himself had been known to describe his two-time running mate as "a very small calibre man." Contemporary opinion seemed to agree; upon learning that President Wilson was going to be spending several months at the Peace Conference in Paris, Will Rogers wrote that "I was in favor of his going because I thought it would give us a chance to find out who was Vice President, But it Dident [*sic*]." Marshall was perhaps best known for his oft-quoted opinion that "what this country needs is a good five-cent cigar," and for his malapropisms, which earned him the undisputed title of "chief humorist of the administration" (for which he had little competition). Conscientiously fulfilling his ceremonial obligations as president of the Senate, Marshall had been listening attentively to a last-minute filibuster when the members of that body finally decided to adjourn on the morning of March 4. As the clock on the wall struck noon, Marshall declared in stentorian tones that the Sixty-Fifth Congress was hereby "adjourned *sine Deo*"—"without God." Asked if he didn't mean *sine die*, "without date," Marshall replied with lofty disdain, "I cannot interpret anything I announce from the chair."

"The slogan of Europe ought to be 'Get back to work,' " urged Herbert Hoover. "To a great extent the whole production is stopped. We are working on a wholly artificial basis. . . . We have got to have peace as early as possible, and then all our countries can go back to work." Finally the Allied blockade was lifted for Poland, Czechoslovakia, Rumania, and Austria, but not for Germany or Hungary. Still, the chaotic state of transport kept food and vital industrial supplies from the areas that needed them most. In Paris, the boundary commissions continued their seemingly interminable work, studying charts on which an inch of map represented a million inches of real ground, wondering if there was any sense to an exercise that resembled "putting brass rails on a ship that has already sunk." Mornings were filled with rain, and the spring withheld its favors. Lloyd George and Balfour enjoyed *Figaro* at the Opéra Comique. Young women strolling along the boulevards saw a French general with his gray hair parted precisely down the back of his head.

Wilson's deteriorating physical condition became the subject of considerable backroom gossip in the hotels and meeting places of Paris. The tic in his left cheek was more noticeable; he displayed symptoms of a personality too high-strung and nervous to continue for long. His confidence appeared to be gone. André Tardieu advised Colonel House that "it is of course a most delicate and difficult matter, but what we fear is that the President is near a physical breakdown and of course that would be a catastrophe for us all." Grayson pleaded with him to slow the pressure of work. "Give me time," Wilson replied. "We are running a race with Bolshevism and the world is on fire. Let us wind up this work here and then we will go home and find time for a little rest and play. . . ."

"I have sat at the feet of the tacticians and the strategists of the Supreme War Council both in Versailles and on the Places des Invalides, but the result is a crazy quilt," admitted one American observer. "Of one thing only am I convinced, and that is, even these wise men do not know all the answers."

Thursday, March 27. A compromise was proposed in the Council of Four to settle the fate of the Rhineland. Still refusing to detach the left bank of the Rhine from Germany, Lloyd George and Wilson agreed instead to offer a defensive treaty to Clemenceau: if Germany should, without provocation, attack France (or, more improbably, Great Britain or the United States), then the other two Allies would immediately send military and financial assistance to the victim. There was no way this treaty would ever get through the U.S. Senate, and Wilson probably knew it; certainly it appeared to contravene the principles of the New Diplomacy upon which the League of Nations would be founded. Nonetheless, Lloyd George made the offer (adding in a burst of exuberance a promise to build a Channel tunnel to bring British troops to the aid of France more quickly), and Wilson seconded the suggestion. Clemenceau was not impressed. "I think," confided Charles Seymour, "that the Conference is approaching the moment of crisis."

Friday, March 28. Clemenceau demanded the Saar Valley. Wilson reminded him that it had been and remained overwhelmingly German in sentiment; Clemenceau could not have it. Clemenceau demanded exorbitant reparation payments for France. Wilson objected to that, too. The Tiger bluntly accused the President of being pro-German. Stung, Wilson hinted that he might have to leave the conference if France remained obdurate. Clemenceau replied that he did not wish Wilson to go home, but that he would do so himself, and promptly stalked out of the room. ("A most unpleasant scene," Lloyd George's secretary, Frances Stevenson, recorded in her diary.) At lunch with Grayson, Wilson said little, but asked the doctor to join him as he rode about the Bois afterwards. Obviously shaken deeply by the morning's confrontation, Wilson remained silent during the ride, but just before he returned to the conference, he turned to Grayson and asked him to come into the room with him. "Those men this morning accused me of being pro-German. They have gone a step too far and I don't know what may happen."

Standing before Clemenceau, Lloyd George, and Orlando, Wilson spat out his words in a cold fury. He had never liked Germany, he said; he had never even been in Germany, he had never admired German methods of education, and no one in the room was less pro-German than he, and he resented Clemenceau's accusations. Wilson turned to Clemenceau:

AND YET YOU THIS MORNING TOLD ME THAT I SHOULD BE WEARING THE KAISER'S HELMET. AND WHY? BECAUSE I HAVE PROTESTED AGAINST LAY-ING A TAXATION UPON GERMANY WHICH WILL MAKE LIFE SO UNATTRAC-TIVE TO THE LITTLE CHILDREN AND THE CHILDREN YET UNBORN THAT EXISTENCE WOULD BE A RUNNING SORE AND DREAMS OF VENGEANCE AN OBSESSION. I AM NOT THINKING ONLY OF GERMANY. I AM THINKING ABOUT THE FUTURE OF THE WORLD. . . . WE ARE FACING A NEW WORLD WITH NEW CONDITIONS. WE ARE TRYING TO STABILIZE A WORLD THAT HAS BEEN THROWN INTO CHAOS.

Clemenceau moved to interrupt. "You sit down," Wilson hissed. "I did not interrupt you when you were speaking this morning." He was not thinking only of the innocent children of Germany, Wilson continued. "I am thinking of the children of France, of England, of Italy, of Belgium, of my own United States, of the whole world. I see their little faces turn toward us in unconscious pleading that we shall save them from annihila-tion. I am not asking for a soft peace but a righteous peace." Lloyd George nodded. Orlando, as was his wont, sobbed quietly as he stood by the window.

Saturday, March 29. Another discussion about the Saar. A British expert who had been called to provide advice spent two and a half hours waiting to be questioned by the Four, but never made it into the Council meeting room. ("However, it was interesting going to the place and we had a very comfortable room to sit in where there was a nice collection of beautifully bound books.") Copies of a draft treaty were sent in to the Four, but after five minutes they decided it was all too complex for any decision that day, and they all came out. "Lloyd George and Orlando seemed very vigorous and were talking and chaffing one another. I thought Clemenceau, whom I had never seen before, looked very old and worn; his face is quite yellow, and he gave one the impression that he was rather worn out. I noticed a curious little scene; he went up to Lloyd George, apparently to press some point upon him; I thought Lloyd George's whole attitude and manner of answering him was brutal." A delegation of Polish peasants, clad in thick white wool suits with red embroidery and wearing high cossack caps of shaggy black fur, arrived at the Hôtel Crillon seeking an audience with President Wilson. "We go on feet two days," announced one member of the party, "then two weeks train to see your President. Tell him I got boy thirty years old United States. I like America. I think she help us if she only know." They never had a chance to plead their case. Wilson was named best-dressed of all the leading delegates in Paris.

Sunday, March 30. Lloyd George and Frances Stevenson went for a picnic in the St.-Germain woods. "D[avid] had a complete day of rest, & badly needed it."

Monday, March 31. Emerging from a Council of Four meeting, Foch and Wilson stood together, telling each other jokes. Clemenceau repeated that he could not face his people if he did not get what he wanted, and would resign and leave the others to deal with blockheads like Poincaré.

Tuesday, April 1. Lloyd George went to a dinner without Frances; "D. thinks it better that I should not be seen dining with him in public. I think he is right. . . . The Conferences proceed morning & afternoon & evening, & D. very busy and preoccupied." The decision to raise the blockade against Poland, Austria, Bulgaria, Czechoslovakia, and Rumania was announced. The colonial ministers of the British Empire were becoming quite bitter about not being consulted more often. King Albert of Belgium arrived suddenly in Paris by air. Paderewski, angered that the Four had decided not to give Danzig to Poland but to make it a "free" city, was on his way to protest in person: "If Poland does not receive Danzig the war is lost." For his part, Lloyd George declared that he was thoroughly disgusted with the Poles' incessant and shameless land-grabbing tactics; insofar as they had fought at all in the war, he charged, they had fought on the side of the Germans. Wilson told Ray Baker that he was at the end of his rope, and that if some positive decision were not reached within the next few days, he might have to make a break.

Wednesday, April 2. By their own admission, the four most powerful men in Paris accomplished nothing this day. A British correspondent who interviewed Clemenceau saw that "his face wore an expression of sadness such as I have never noticed before."

Thursday, April 3. The Four met again at Wilson's residence. No signs of progress were readily apparent. "What everybody in Paris is interested in," wrote Oswald Garrison Villard, "is whether the Peace Conference is going to explode or not. In comparison with that everything else has lost color and interest." Lloyd George told Lord Riddell that the chief difference between the ordinary and the extraordinary man was that when the extraordinary fellow was faced with a new and difficult situation, he solved it by devising a daring and unexpected plan. That, the Prime Minister concluded, was the mark of genius in a man of action (such as himself, presumably). *The Times* of London warned: "At a moment when clear-sighted resolution is above all necessary the Conference leaders are showing neither vision nor courage. They appear to mistake interested sentimentality for foresight and obstinacy for courage." During their afternoon meeting, the other members of the Four noticed that Wilson was growing hoarse. At 6:00 P.M., Wilson was seized by violent paroxysms of coughing so severe, reported Grayson, "that it interfered with his breathing." Suspecting that Wilson had been poisoned, Grayson ordered the President to bed. His temperature reached 103. The coughing led to vomiting. He slept very little.

Friday, April 4. Grayson decided Wilson had contracted influenza, although he publicly insisted it was nothing more than a severe cold. Mrs. Wilson remained close by her husband at all times. Too ill to read, the President suffered through the day in restless sleep. On the same floor of his residence, less than twenty yards away, the Four held their daily meeting (with Colonel House substituting for the President), but made no attempt to communicate with Wilson.

Saturday, April 5. An official cable read, "President is better this morning, but confined to bed. No cause for worry." Wilson was well enough to sit up for a brief time. Despite the President's absence and Lloyd George's minor indisposition, the Council of Four met again, with House once more in Wilson's seat. Clemenceau could not hide his joy at Wilson's plight: "He is *worse* today," he told Lloyd George, doubling up with laughter. "Do you know his doctor? Couldn't you get round him and bribe him?" By the end of the day the Council had reached a tentative agreement on the reparations issue. House visited Wilson late in the afternoon and reported on the Council's deliberations; Grayson barred the door to all other callers. The President read a little and chatted with his wife.

Sunday, April 6. A warm spring day. Lloyd George stayed in bed all day with a cold and slight fever. Still weak, sitting with an old sweater about his shoulders, Wilson received the other four American peace commissioners in his bedroom at four o'clock in the afternoon. He had had enough, Wilson told them; it would be beneath their dignity as representatives of the United States to continue to be subjected to the lack of consideration that the Allies had heretofore displayed toward America's disinterested efforts to establish a lasting peace. The French and British methods of negotiation were no better than the petty and demeaning wheedling and bargaining seen every day in the shops of Paris. The President would have a peace based on his Fourteen Points or none at all. He had decided to force Clemenceau's hand by calling for the *George Washington* (now back in

Hoboken, being repainted once more) to return to France to take him back to the United States. Admiral Benson, the special naval adviser to the American peace delegation, ordered the appropriate encoded instructions to be sent to the U.S. naval commander in London to be passed on to Washington. Mysteriously, someone in Paris with considerable authority (possibly House or Lansing) telephoned London with orders not to relay the recall order to the *George Washington*. This, however, caused only a brief delay—and considerable confusion among navy officials in Washington who first learned of the recall orders from reporters—and on April 11 the President's ship sailed for Brest.

Clemenceau asked Grayson if Wilson were bluffing. "He hasn't a bluffing corpuscle in his body," Grayson replied.

18

"Before me continually

is grief and wounds . . ."

President Friedrich Ebert sat in his presidential office in Weimar, absent-mindedly stroking the presidential goatee, and pondered his presidential position. How had he come to this point? Had he not begun with the best intentions? Had he not been sincere in expressing his dream to create "a State whose principal object will be not to extend its frontiers, but to achieve in its own interior the highest ideals of mankind?" But now intellectual liberals like Harry Kessler turned against him and accused his Cabinet of being "weak-kneed as well as sanguinary." Just the other day Theodor Wolff, the editor of the *Berliner Tageblatt,* had declared that the reason why "the German Republic does not give the impression either at home or abroad of being the flower of a new dawn comes from the fact that it has retained most of the old figures, who seem just as flourishing in the new atmosphere as they did under the Kaiser." But these were the only capable men in Germany; who else could he get to run the country? And the workers in the cities hated his government with a vengeance because it had failed to bring about anything resembling the true socialization of industry, because it tolerated Noske's brutalities, because war millionaires still flaunted their untaxed wealth in the exclusive cafés and gambling dens of Berlin, and above all else because there was no food for the poor. Perhaps he was just a commonplace plodder after all, as even some of his admirers admitted, but the alternatives at the moment—Bolshevism or reaction—were hardly more attractive. If the Allies would hurry the shipments of food from Rotterdam, if they would keep their promises of a peace without revenge and follow Wilson's Fourteen Points . . .

Ebert rubbed his hand over the two sharp creases that forty-eight years of nearsighted squinting had etched in his forehead, shrugged, stood up, jammed the ever-present slouch hat carelessly onto his head, and marched out to see what new outrages had been perpetrated today against his government.

All about him, Germany seemed to be at war with itself. Rioting in Frankfurt, strikes in Westphalia and at Essen; the total number of men on strike in the Ruhr basin at the end of March was estimated at 150,000. Noske's White Guards, 60,000 strong, were constantly shifted about to each new center of disorder, always leaving a presence in Berlin to maintain a healthy sense of fear among the populace.

Emboldened by the example of Budapest, and tired of eating goat liver (or worse, horse liver), German workers could not see how a Bolshevist regime could be any more oppressive; "it would," they felt, "at any rate, open the prospect of better things for our children."

A mob in Frankfurt, starving and furious at the remaining vestiges of the *ancien regime* of privilege and rank, stormed a warehouse full of food and stuffed its contents into sacks and baskets; then the mob attacked the police station, liberated dozens of prisoners, and dragged out huge piles of legal papers and archives and set fire to them and the police building. Another band of enraged citizens unearthed secret caches of meat, eggs, and flour in the house of the burgomaster. About $50,000 worth of damage was done to some of the town's larger wine vaults by otherwise responsible men and women. After the soldiers arrived, at least sixteen civilians, including four women, were killed. Stuttgart, famous heretofore primarily for its music, was under a state of siege. More than twenty civilians lay dead and fifty more wounded; a general strike had brought business to a complete standstill before the strike leaders were arrested; crowds in the street stormed army food wagons; government troops fired round after round from the machine guns they had stationed in windows and mounted upon armored cars; meetings were forbidden and an 8:00 P.M. curfew imposed; batteries of tanks scattered pedestrians; strikers set up their own machine guns in trenches, but were shelled by government artillery.

In Essen, workers demanding higher wages occupied the Krupp munitions plant. Noske's troops marched in, threw hand grenades into the midst of a crowd plundering an army baggage van, and posted machine guns and artillery at the entrances to the plant. Within a few hours, two-thirds of the workers were back on the job. Union leaders in Düsseldorf called a general strike and demanded the immediate release of political prisoners, an alliance with Soviet Russia, demobilization of the army, and the elimination of "class justice." Noske dispatched more men to Düsseldorf. The war minister of Saxony was murdered at Dresden by disgruntled soldiers who believed he was preparing to reduce the pensions of wounded veterans. They dragged him from his hiding place in the war ministry, threw him into the river Elbe, and shot him as he tried to swim back to land. Noske sent more troops to Dresden. The black market, fed largely by goods stolen from army depots, was thriving throughout Germany. Crime was rampant, thieves—official or otherwise—went unpunished, police forces were corrupted and unreliable. "The atmosphere is fraught with murder and destruction," reported *The New York Times.*

At a banquet given for Prince Eitel Friedrich Hohenzollern by the Officers' Volunteer Corps, the Kaiser's health was drunk repeatedly. Right-wing rallies through the streets of Berlin no longer brought hoots of derision from every onlooker. General Ludendorff urged resistance to the schemes of the men in Paris: "Do not submit to the will of your enemies. Do not accept peace of annihilation." The Minister of Education appealed to high school and university students to join the growing volunteer corps that were being financed by wealthy Berlin industrialists and bankers. "For of what use," he asked, "would be their years of study and the examinations they have passed if the country perished in anarchy?" Accordingly, Generals Hoffmann and Lettow-Vorbeck announced the formation of a new company of volunteer guards "to preserve order at home and to protect the frontiers of the Empire." The National Union of German Officers, parading with the Imperial colors of red, white, and black at their head and the band of officers playing "Deutschland Über Alles," stood outside the Chancellor's palace and pledged to defend the imperial boundaries. Noske urged schools to provide the coming generation with more open-air exercises and sports to prepare them for the rigors of the martial life.

When the Workers' Councils of Berlin issued a call for a general strike, Freikorps units poured into the city in a massive display of armed might. "Noske guards everywhere," recorded Kessler, "steel-helmeted and loaded with hand grenades." Thirty thousand troops stood at the gates of the city. Cordons of soldiers with bomb-throwers and flamethrowers surrounded Berlin's official district; tramway traffic was suspended and machine guns planted to sweep all lines of approach to the center of the city. The Wilhelmstrasse was once again jammed with artillery. It was an impressive display designed to simulate an armed camp and to intimidate the public, and it worked. Under a dark-gray deluge of rain, the date for the strike came and went. Only Berlin's bank workers walked off their jobs, demanding higher pay. One large bank (the Deutsche Bank) remained open, and when strikers forced their way into the vestibule to try to induce the bank's employees to join the walkout, they were sprayed with a fire hose. When a band of striking female clerks arrived to help, they, too, were hosed down until they gained control of the offending weapon and turned it against the bank's loyal employees. Retreating to the second floor, the employees dropped inkpots on the girls below until troops arrived to restore order. The next day the Deutsche Bank, too, closed its doors. Five leading Berlin industrialists met and decided that Bolshevism was "no longer a menace. It is here."

Ben Hecht reported that an artists' brigade of one thousand cubist, futurist, and expressionist painters and poets had joined the Spartacist ranks; the Revolutionary Artists' Council united with the Soldiers' and Workers' Councils. Eerie figures adorned placards on the streets of Berlin and Munich that threatened to burn all the bad paintings and insipid books now residing in galleries and libraries. Half the paintings in the Royal Art Gallery were on the blacklist. "As for the horrible absurdities shamelessly exposed in the boulevard art shop windows," warned one member of the avant-garde Red guard, "no mercy will be shown them." The revolutionary artists claimed that the Kaiser's regime, with its candy-box art and schoolgirl poetry, had crushed modernism: "Wilhelm was the arch imbecile of the age in matters of art. . . . [Now] classicism must go." Locked in a dispute over whether Goethe's works could stay or go, the artists' council compromised by voting to do away with Lessing instead.

And all the while the cabarets were filled to overflowing every night, and lines of cars and droshkies discharged parties of elegantly dressed men and women in front of theater entrances. Champagne corks popped as Berliners sang their latest song to a rollicking tune that for an hour or two put swagger in their hearts and laughter on their lips:

> Dance, my little girl, dance,
> We have yet a few hours to sing;
> So dance, my little one, dance,
> Who knows what the morrow will bring?

Harry Kessler attended a meeting of the Berlin "Democratic Club" and called it a "sheer waste of time. With few exceptions, the most appalling collection of philistines. A mixture of corpulence and moneybags that can only arouse disgust. What is supposed to be democratic about them, other than their middle-class manners, is inconceivable. In France the same species at least keeps little girls; in Britain, Bible classes. Here this fauna, thanks to the revolution, crawls out of its cocoon as republican. . . . These are the creatures now being preserved at the cost of bloodshed."

A poster on the Berlin streets showed maniacal skeletons setting fire to orphans' homes and dismembering women, above the caption HERE IS WHAT BOLSHEVISM MEANS. In a small shop, a shoemaker repaired another pair of shoes. "It makes no difference to me who is ruler of Germany. I shall always be a shoemaker. Yes, the war was a mistake, and killing Liebknecht was a mistake, and maybe Ebert is a mistake. The only thing is not to make any mistakes fixing shoes. I never bother my head about anything else. Why should I? The world will never change for me. . . ." Behind the counter, the shoemaker wore no shoes himself. Both his legs had been cut off at the knee; he had received a Black Iron Cross at Verdun, where his legs lay still.

"Nothing in Germany now is certain except the uncertainty of the morrow," wrote Count Johann von Bernstorff, the former German ambassador to the United States, but he was mistaken. One other certainty was the nearly unanimous resistance of the German people to the peace treaty being prepared at Paris. The loss of Danzig was precisely the sort of blow to national pride that rallied the nation behind Ebert when he warned that "if the peace terms mean suicide, they will not be signed. Rather than political and economical death, Germany will choose political and economical madness." The labor unrest in Britain and France, and the growing urge to demobilize the Allied armies immediately, combined with the disagreements at Paris to encourage Ebert and Scheidemann and their colleagues to threaten passive resistance to any harsh peace terms. Foreign Minister Ulrich von Brockdorff-Rantzau told a group of former Imperial officials that "it is a question whether we have not everything to gain and nothing to lose by passive resistance. Neither the Peace Conference nor the Entente would long survive a refusal to sign." If all else failed, Germany could turn to Lenin's Russia for support. Others warned that even if the Allies coerced Germany into accepting a punitive treaty now, they would merely be storing up trouble for the future. An association of German religious and philosophical societies addressed an appeal to Wilson: "Only one thing could again weld the Germans of every State into a warlike power—the continuation of the policy of hate and annihilation that has been pursued by the Allies."

Winston Churchill agreed. "With Russia on our hands in a state of utter ruin, with a greater part of Europe on the brink of famine, with bankruptcy, anarchy, and revolution threatening the victorious as well as the vanquished," Churchill told a London gathering on April 11, "I do not think we can afford to carry on this quarrel, with all its apparatus of hatred, indefinitely. I do not think the structure of the civilized world is strong enough to stand the strain."

For the moment, Ebert, Scheidemann, and Noske remained in power primarily because there was no appealing alternative. Although there were more demonstrations of affection for the Kaiser, they represented rather the power of nostalgia and a longing for the old order and discipline; the masses would never accept William Hohenzollern again. Still pacing up and down in the garden in his long gray cloak worn over an old field uniform, wearing a soft, feathered hat drawn down low over his face, William had only four attendants left of the entourage that had followed him across the border in November. He had just received unofficial word that the Allies had decided not to put him on trial for his life. And so he continued to practice his hobby, sawing wood for three hours every day while his wife sat and read a newspaper nearby. On March 15 he sawed through his thousandth tree since settling at Amerongen; a snapshot was taken, and a few of the logs were converted into souvenirs and marked in red ink with the inscription "W2" and presented to his servants and members of the Bentinck family. (Expert sawyers in the neighborhood estimated that if William had been paid at the trade union rate for sawing wood, he would have made $30 thus far, or fifty cents per working day.)

No, the discredited Hohenzollerns were no longer a viable alternative to the weak-kneed Socialist Republic. But if another force appeared that was neither Bolshevist nor a reincarnation of the detested elitist imperial faction . . .

Still inspecting old gas masks in the garrison barracks at Munich, Adolf Hitler watched as Bavaria suffered through a bizarre series of convulsive shocks following the murder of Kurt Eisner. "Munich is hungry; Munich is cold; Munich has no coal, no gas, no electric light; Munich is full of war misery," reported the *Manchester Guardian*. Out of the confusion of armed bands roaming the streets and the welter of rival claimants for authority, the Landtag chose a relatively innocuous Socialist named Adolf Hoffmann, formerly Minister of Worship in Eisner's Cabinet, to head the new government. His position was hardly secure; when the Assembly finally reconvened in mid-March, there were machine guns posted on the roof and guards at every entrance to search deputies and journalists for weapons. The swirling mixture of leftist factions in Bavaria prevented Hoffmann from establishing any sort of authoritative control. To make matters worse, Hoffmann had no reliable military force to bring order out of the chaos. Distrusting the resurgent militarist sentiment in Berlin, his government had forbidden the establishment of recruiting stations for Noske's volunteers corps, or even the publication of posters or advertisements encouraging enlistment.

On April 1, the Krupp munitions works in Munich ceased operation, throwing four thousand more families onto the unemployment rolls.

Events then followed one upon the other with dizzying rapidity, and even those in the midst of the confusion could hardly keep track of who—if anyone—was in charge. Delegates from the Workers' and Soldiers' Councils met and decided to dump Hoffmann and establish a soviet republic in alliance with Hungary and Russia. Hoffmann was in Berlin at the time, discussing the secession of Bavaria from the German empire; the remaining members of his government fled Munich and set up a rival center of power in Bamberg, vowing to fight the soviets from the countryside.

The republic was to be born officially on April 7. The intrepid and peripatetic Ben Hecht arrived in Munich on the sixth, expecting to see Red Guards and reactionaries and Socialists battling each other in the streets when he alighted from the train. Instead, he stood blinking his eyes at a sunny avenue filled with crowds of amiable Sunday strollers carrying alpenstocks and wearing Tyrolean feathers in their green hats, and processions of small children carrying decorated candles on their way to Mass. In the distance he heard the strains of Handel's *Largo* from an open-air concert. "The quietest and most orderly spot in Germany today," Hecht reported, "is Munich." So far as he could see, the feared Red Terror had been virtually nonexistent, and Hecht concluded that "a Baltimore policeman would fall asleep were he patrolling in the heart of the world-shaking communist uprising in Munich."

It was the calm before the storm. The next morning at six o'clock, Hecht awoke to the roar of shuffling feet in the street below. Newspapers had published at dawn the proclamation of the Bavarian Soviet Republic, a "Republic of Councils" whose outlines had been drawn up only minutes before midnight by four dozen members of the Assembly, meeting in the throne room of King Ludwig's former palace. The new regime's platform called for independence from Prussia, alliance with Russia and Hungary, the confiscation of all private estates, and the socialization of industry. Workingmen stared proudly at the proclamations posted on every public building in Munich; they dragged their complaining children about the streets to see what the birth of a workers' republic looked like. Every now and then a woman's voice rose above the noise of thousands of citizens walking through the city: "Comrades! Long live the world revolution!" Hecht heard some in the crowd humming or whistling the tune that he described as "the theme song of the revolution"; its chorus ran:

> I know in the willows a little hotel,
> In a forgotten little street,
> Where the night is too short,

And the dawn comes too soon—
Come with me, my little Countess,
Why worry what tomorrow will bring?
The world holds but sunshine and song,
And once you have spent the night kissing
You'll never do anything else.

No one could say the revolution had improved Bavarians' taste in song lyrics.

The new regime immediately threw a blanket of censorship over all of Munich's newspapers and appropriated the largest houses in the city to provide shelter for the families of unemployed workers. The Landtag was dissolved, factories were turned over to worker-management councils, and students at the university declared the faculty senate deposed and adminis- trative powers transferred to a Council of Students and Professors. Some of the soviet's less conventional actions, however, inspired considerable wonder and amazement among the populace. The Commissar of Housing, out of some bizarre sense of architectural propriety, decreed that hence- forth every house could contain no more than three rooms, with the living room located directly above the kitchen and bedroom. The Commissar for Foreign Affairs, Franz Lippe (who looked, said Hecht, "like a traveling hypnotist," and who had recently been a patient in a mental institution), sent a vitriolic message to Moscow complaining that some wayward com- rade had stolen the keys to the ministry toilet. Lippe promptly declared war on Würtemberg and Switzerland, "because these dogs have not at once loaned me sixty locomotives. I am certain that we will be victorious. Furthermore, I will ask the Pope, with whom I am well acquainted, to grant his blessing for this victory." Lippe then proceeded to tear out almost all the telephones in his office, apparently because the sound of ringing bells threw him into a sort of epileptic fit. He let one bell-less phone remain, and spent much of his time trying to call Clemenceau to arrange a separate peace for Bavaria. To no one's surprise (except perhaps his own), he never got through.

Most of the leaders of the Soviet Republic of Bavaria were denizens of Munich's bohemian culture: failed poets and third-rate drama critics who wasted their time and energy quibbling over minor points of cultural and political philosophy. The dark-eyed and gentle-mannered playwright Ernst Toller, still in his twenties, was perhaps the most talented artist among the group, but having left his studies at the university only a few months earlier, he was obviously unequal to the responsibilities thrust upon him as President of the Central Council. Nevertheless, he sat amid the clutter in his "office"—a converted bathroom within Ludwig's palace—and patiently listened to the complaints and recommendations of hard-faced workingmen. Erich Mühsam, the Republic's ambassador to Moscow, impressed Ben Hecht as "a frightened middle-aged man . . . dressed in a shabby frock coat, a pair of baggy trousers, a flowing black tie and a rakishly tilted black velvet fedora," and the proud owner of "a grotesquely trimmed red beard." Mühsam, however, refused to leave Munich to take up his post at Moscow. He had written a revolutionary poem, "The Sun of Liberty," and now he began touring the city in an open truck; whenever he came upon a group of people in the streets, he launched into an impassioned recitation of his magnum opus. The people quickly tired of his declamations and took to chasing him whenever he appeared, waving their guns at him and threatening him with all sorts of dire consequences if he started in on his poem again. The Minister of Public Instruction, Gustav Landauer, stood nearly seven feet tall, but hardly anyone knew what he looked like—his face was hidden behind a massive, bristling growth of beard.

These men were amateur politicians. The professional Communist activists remained aloof from the Toller government, believing that the poets had stolen the soviet revolution. Led by Max Levien and Eugene Leviné (rumor had it that both had been named Levien, and that Leviné had changed his name to avoid confusion), the hard-core Red element gathered in the back room of a weatherbeaten subterranean café to plan their next move. Levien, a thirty-four-year-old doctor of zoology at the University of Munich, charged that the soviet government did not adequately represent the interests of the proletariat, and vowed to continue the fight for a pure Bolshevist state exactly along the lines of Lenin's Russia, saying, "I will not enter into such a masquerade as this." Like Lenin, Levien would not hesitate to employ terror to advance the cause.

Threatened from the Left within the city, Toller's government also faced opposition from the Right, from the rural areas surrounding Munich. Exasperated by repeated visitations from Red Guards appropriating farmers' food supplies, and justifiably suspicious of the new paper money issuing from the government's printing presses, the Peasants' League of Southern Bavaria refused to send any more provisions to Munich until the soviet regime was overthrown. Those few farmers who did still bring food into the city insisted on bartering for tangible goods: one dead pig for a sofa. Troops loyal to Hoffman (who was now hiding in Bamberg) assembled in Nuremburg for a counterrevolutionary thrust. And of course in

Berlin there was Noske. "Munich will be compelled by arms to return to order," the Bloodhound vowed. "We must hit with all our energy rather than allow the country to be precipitated into an abyss. If blood is spilled it will be on the heads of the Communist maniacs."

By the evening of April 9, Munich was completely cut off from the rest of Bavaria. No food or milk reached the city except the little that could be scavenged from the immediate suburbs. The government instituted house-to-house searches to confiscate food and weapons. Railroad, telegraph, and telephone service were suspended. When it became known that many of the soviet leaders were Jews, incendiary anti-Semitic pamphlets began to circulate throughout the city, and demonstrations called for the ouster of all Jews from the government. Most of the Munich garrison—apparently including Hitler, despite his later claims that he had helped lead the counterrevolution—remained neutral. But in the Hotel Vierjahreszeiten, a clandestine political organization known as the Thule Society, elitist and anti-Semitic and dedicated to a romantic ideal of pure Nordic culture, plotted to overthrow the Bolshevisks with the aid of a considerable war chest donated by wealthy Bavarians. The Thule Society also maintained close ties with various Freikorps units. Its insignia was a swastika with a dagger enveloped in laurel leaves.

On the morning of April 13, Palm Sunday, Hoffmann's forces within Munich essayed a coup; it failed miserably, but the attempt induced Levien and Leviné to seize control from Toller's gang of café artistes. With twenty thousand Red Guards at his disposal, Leviné promptly dispatched eight thousand men under the command of Toller (who had been imprisoned briefly and then released) to confront the approaching right-wing militia at a small town known as Dachau.

19

"I am black;

astonishment

hath taken hold on me . . ."

RATS, RATS, AND MORE RATS; a situation reminiscent of a previous invasion immortalized by Browning:

> Great rats, small rats, lean rats, brawny rats,
> Brown rats, black rats, gray rats, tawny rats,
> Grave old plodders, gay young friskers,
> Fathers, mothers, uncles, cousins,
> Cocking tails and pricking whiskers,
> Families by ten and dozens,
> Brothers, sisters, husbands and wives . . .
> Made nests inside men's Sunday hats,
> And even spoiled the women's chats,
> By drowning their speaking
> With shrieking and squeaking
> In fifty different sharps and flats.

Although a number of county councils throughout England had instituted action against the burgeoning rat menace, their reprisals were neither as vigorous nor as widespread as necessary for total victory. Some counties, such as Cornwall, employed professional poisoners, while others relied upon the payment of bounties to stimulate the slaughter of rodents. Worcestershire, for instance, paid two shillings per dozen rats' tails. In Leicestershire, where representatives to receive dead rats had been appointed in every parish, the government paid thruppence for each corpse; in an eight-week period, 29,378 rats had perished in the holocaust in that county.

* * *

General Smuts's instructions for his mission to Budapest were kept deliberately vague. In broad terms, he was to try to persuade the Hungarians to withdraw behind the new armistice line set by the Peace Conference, to ascertain the strength of Béla Kun's government, and to test Kun's willingness to reach an agreement with the Allies. Unofficially, Smuts also was to determine whether Kun was worth using as a conduit to Moscow.

The mission left Paris at 7:15 on the evening of April 1. On the morning of April 3, Harold Nicolson awoke in Austria. He was immediately struck by the dilapidated condition of everything and everyone. "The suburban trains are packed with people and nearly all the windows are broken. They only run about four a day owing to fuel shortage. Everybody looks very pinched and yellow: no fats for four years. The other side of the blockade." Upon arriving in Vienna, Nicolson noticed the city's unkempt appearance, with "paper lying about: the grass plots round the statues . . . strewn with litter: many windows broken and repaired by boards nailed up. The people in the streets are dejected and ill-dressed: they stare at us in astonishment. . . . I feel that my plump pink face is an insult to these wretched people.

Hungarian aviators flew over the city and dropped propaganda pamphlets. Nothing else was moving. Two of Smuts's soldiers were accosted by a child begging for food. When one of the men gave him a biscuit, they were immediately set upon by a ragged swarm of children who nearly tore off all the pockets on their uniforms, searching for any more food anywhere. (Austrian parents had begun to send their starving children into Switzerland to be fed, but many arrived in such pitiable condition that they were unable to digest even diluted milk.)

Receiving a safe-conduct pass from the Bolshevik representative in Vienna, the train proceeded to Budapest, arriving during the night. At the station and in the streets of the city, Béla Kun's Red Guards seemed to be everywhere; they were perhaps the least popular and most visible—and most dangerous—symbol of the Soviet regime in Hungary. They had the disquieting habit of invading any shop that was open and appropriating "presents" for themselves, which they ostentatiously carried around the streets displayed on a hat stand, itself stolen from a restaurant. An American observer stationed in Budapest told Nicolson that fifteen hundred "wild men" from Vienna had arrived the night before to join the Guard.

Smuts and his colleagues remained on the train while Kun came to them. Nicolson was the first to greet Kun: "A little man of about thirty: puffy white face and loose wet lips: shaven head: impression of red hair: shifty suspicious eyes: he has the face of a sulky and uncertain criminal." Kun informed Smuts that he would very much like to arrive at a settlement with the Allies, but that he had been swept into office on a wave of nationalism; he could not now accept the boundary proposals that had forced Karolyi to resign. Smuts assured him the proposals were merely a temporary armistice arrangement and not a permanent boundary settlement. The discussions continued off and on throughout the day. Nicolson found it somewhat disconcerting to hold a diplomatic conference in a train carriage. "One has to turn sideways all the time, which gives one a funny feeling and a stiff neck." Smuts gave Kun a set of proposals to consider, which Kun then took away to his Cabinet.

While they awaited Kun's reply, Nicolson and several others toured the city. They found most of the shops shut; "it seems even sadder and more unkempt than Vienna. Everything bedraggled. Rain pouring on yellow faces and clothes in rags." Oddly, there were enormous bags of popcorn available for the populace on nearly every street corner. But save for the Red Guard and the red flags flying from every building, there was no other sign of a Bolshevist revolution "except a universal sadness and shabbiness."

Kun returned to the train shortly after six that evening. They all sat in the carriage as the rain beat a soft rhythm on the roof and glistened in the candlelight, "golden drops upon the pane. How sad it all is." Béla Kun, thought Nicolson, "does not strike me as a man who enjoys the fruits of office. He sat there hunched, sulky, suspicious, and frightened." Kun explained to Smuts that if his government ordered a withdrawal of Hungarian forces, it would not be obeyed; and if the Soviet Cabinet resigned, which it would do if the withdrawal were insisted upon, there was no other party capable of assuming power, and Hungary would be plunged into chaos. If the Allies continued their present pro-Rumanian policy, therefore, they must be prepared to run Hungary on their own responsibility and to occupy the entire country.

The next day, Smuts gave Kun a draft agreement providing for Allied occupation of a neutral zone between Hungary and Rumania. If Hungary accepted, the blockade would be lifted. Obviously eager to accept, Kun first had to obtain approval from Moscow. At seven o'clock that night, Kun returned with a note accepting the agreement but adding a condition requiring Rumanian withdrawal behind a new boundary line. Smuts told Kun he could accept no reservations; either Hungary accepted the Allied terms *in toto* or there was no deal. Still Kun and his colleagues held out, apparently expecting Smuts to propose a compromise. (Although they did not know it, Smuts already had decided that Kun's government was not to be taken seriously and could not enforce any treaty it signed, and hence he was determined to break off negotiations right then and there.)

Suddenly Smuts stood up and bade the Hungarians goodbye: "He conducts them with exquisite courtesy on to the platform. He shakes hands with them. He then stands on the step of the train and nods to his A.D.C. They stand in a row upon the platform, expecting him to fix the time for the next meeting. And as they stand the train gradually begins to move. Smuts brings his hand to the salute. We glide out into the night, retaining on the retinas of our eyes the picture of four bewildered faces looking up in blank amazement."

Returning to Paris on the morning of April 9, Nicolson immediately went to his hotel room and took a bath.

Smuts reported to Lloyd George at breakfast the next day. He informed the Prime Minister that while he did not believe Béla Kun represented a serious threat to British interests in Eastern Europe, the division of Austria-Hungary into a welter of five competing states was having a most damaging effect upon the region's economic life. One place had no food; another had no coal. "It was a world that we cannot imagine," Smuts said, "a world completely gone to pieces."

Wilson had summoned the *George Washington*; whether he meant it as a bluff or not, the shock sobered everyone into an understanding of the devastating price of a failure at Paris.

Monday, April 7. "The Big Four are rushing things fast," reported Charles Seymour, "and some of the difficulties which seemed so serious a week ago are apparently disappearing. . . . They are apparently going in for settlements on large general lines, and some of the labored hours we have spent in working out details may go for nothing. But we don't object strongly so long as they realize the necessity for speed. Everything is now in the hands of the Four. . . ." Paderewski arrived in Paris to try to change the Council's decision regarding Danzig, and was greeted by a cheering throng of admirers who threw flowers in his path. Paderewski was easily the most popular of all foreign dignitaries in the city, his hotel room filled to overflowing with bouquets from his fans. He wasted no time in paying an official visit to Clemenceau, who received the Polish pianist warmly. "And who do I see here but the great Paderewski!" the Tiger exclaimed. "I can hardly believe it is the great pianist before me, the great Paderewski! And now you are the Premier of Poland." Paderewski nodded proudly. Clemenceau slowly shook his head: "What a comedown. . . ."

Ray Stannard Baker told reporters once again that Wilson would brook no further compromise of his Fourteen Points. The President was still confined to his rooms; Baker walked into his study and found Wilson "looking thin and pale. A slight hollowness of the eyes emphasized a characteristic I had often noted before—the size and luminosity of his eyes . . . and he looked at one with a piercing intentness." Wilson reaffirmed his intention not to compromise his principles past the breaking point. "Then Italy will not get Fiume?" Baker asked.

"Absolutely not—so long as I am here."

"Nor France the Saar?"

"No."

Tuesday, April 8. The day's French newspapers were heavily censored to prevent any leakage of information about the decisions being taken by the Council of Four. The Paris editions of the *Chicago Tribune* and *New York Herald* carried blanks in their headlines and large white spaces in their accounts of the conferences. In their morning session, the Four (with House sitting in for Wilson again) discussed Lloyd George's proposed solution for the Saar Valley, which would split the region off from Germany for a time and give France administrative control (and the rights to the coal mines) under a League of Nations mandate. That afternoon, Wilson put in his first appearance since his illness began, and agreed that France might be given control over the Saar's subsoil while Germany retained control of the surface. Off went a commission of experts to draw up the appropriate language.

But a final compromise on the reparations imbroglio, which had earlier appeared imminent, now seemed to be in jeopardy. Wilson insisted that the total bill be no more than Germany could pay within thirty years. Clemenceau wanted Germany to pay everything she owed, no matter how long it took. Pressured by a telegram from two hundred MPs reminding Lloyd George none too gently of his campaign promises, the Wizard of Wales nimbly backtracked into a more intransigent attitude of making Germany pay "to the utmost farthing."

At Clemenceau's request, President Poincaré commuted Emil Cottin's sentence of death to ten years' imprisonment.

Wednesday, April 9. Nicolson found upon his return that "everything is being rushed at a feverish pace. The Sarre, reparations, everything is boiling over at the same time." And no one but the Four knew what—if anything—had been decided. "The doings of the Council of Four," wrote Lord Riddell in his diary, "have been shrouded in mystery." Riddell believed that "no four kings or emperors could have conducted the Conference on more autocratic lines."

Wilson took a limousine ride around Paris with Admiral Grayson. It was the first time the President had been out of his residence since his illness.

Thursday, April 10. "It is extraordinary how little has been agreed to since we left," wrote Nicolson in his diary. "In fact I see no progress at all, only further oceans of disagreement—and the general depression is terrible. We are getting weaker every day and our enemies know it. 'Peak upon peak, and Alp on Alp arise.' . . . The whole situation, in fact, is full of menace, uncertainty, tension, sorrow and discontent."

Wilson went to call upon Baron Makino, head of the Japanese delegation, at his hotel. On the way up to the baron's room, the elevator car stuck midway between floors. It simply would not go any higher, and so the balky car was lowered to the lobby and Wilson made his way up the stairs through a crowd of curious onlookers to Makino's apartment. Paderewski lunched with Lloyd George and Frances Stevenson and regaled them with tales of Poland's glorious history. The evocation of events long, long past put Lloyd George in a pensive mood. "It just shows you," he sighed, "how difficult is our present task. We are digging up the foundations of a very old world."

To Ray Baker, Wilson looked "old and worn. Things are not going well. . . . I saw him standing with Grayson [in his study] close to the window. The sash had been thrown up and Grayson was exercising the President by standing with him foot to foot, and with clasped hands pulling him vigorously back and forth. The President turned to me with the remark, 'Indoor golf.' " That evening the League of Nations Commission wrapped up its work on the revised Covenant, incorporating an amendment reportedly written by Colonel House specifically excluding the Monroe Doctrine from the League's jurisdiction. Wilson spoke for five or six minutes around midnight, passionately urging immediate acceptance of the Covenant with no further changes; reporters noticed that he looked quite pale.

Friday, April 11. House had talked himself hoarse.

In a private moment of candor, Lloyd George admitted to Bonar Law and Riddell that he thought Wilson "more sincere than he had done at first. [Wilson] talks a lot of sentimental platitudes, but believes them. He is not a hypocrite nor a humbug. He is sincere. The difference between his point and that of old Clemenceau is marked. The old boy believes in none of Wilson's gods and does not understand them." Then the Prime Minister added, "I am sorry Clemenceau is failing. It is very marked. Now he so often asks for twenty-four hours in which to make up his mind. Before, he made it up in twenty-four seconds. A truly wonderful person."

Saturday, April 12. A rainy, dismal day in Paris. Their maps drawn and their reports written, the American experts began to pack their bags for the return trip to the United States.

For the next three days, Colonel House carried messages back and forth between Wilson and Clemenceau; by April 15 the Saar, Rhineland, and League of Nations quarrels had been resolved. House reported that the President made "a wry face" over some parts of the compromise, but in the end he swallowed the whole package. France received the Saar coal mines for fifteen years while the League of Nations would administer the territory; at the end of that time the Saar's residents would be allowed to decide their own future via plebiscite—to stay with France or rejoin Germany. Wilson agreed to permit an Allied—mostly French, of course—military force to occupy the Rhineland for fifteen years ("until the League is seasoned—until it has proved its mettle," explained Clemenceau), which period could be extended if Germany did not respect the terms of the peace treaty (including payment of the reparations bill in full and on time). All military fortifications on the left bank of the Rhine and within a fifty-kilometer strip on the right bank were to be permanently destroyed, thereby depriving Germany of one staging area for another invasion of France. America and Britain renewed their pledge of a defensive treaty, conditional upon legislative approval: both Parliament and Congress had to approve the treaty before it would become effective. If the United States Senate rejected the treaty (as it surely would), Britain was also released from its commitment. In return, France agreed to accept the League Covenant with the Monroe Doctrine expressly included.

Clemenceau believed he had won nearly everything he wanted. Wilson had his League and Germany had not been permanently dismembered. Lloyd George had already won most of his objectives, save for a final decision on the reparations split, and had departed—quite satisfied—for London late on the afternoon of April 14. Fed up with newspaper baron Lord Northcliffe's public attacks upon him, and angered by the continuing revolt of the "indemnity cave" of Conservative MPs (Lloyd George had threatened to hold another snap general election if they didn't stop whining), the Prime Minister was preparing a full-scale counterattack in the House of Commons for April 16.

As Lloyd George suffered through a rough Channel crossing, President Wilson announced in Paris that sufficient progress had been made to invite the German peace delegation to receive the treaty from the Allies on April 25. They would have to stay in Versailles, though; Clemenceau did not want them in his capital, and the French government claimed that it would not guarantee the Germans' safety if they entered Paris. Besides, it was in Versailles forty-eight years ago that France had signed the final treaty of surrender to the Second Reich of Chancellor Bismarck. Green leaves began to appear on the chestnut trees along the Champs Elysées, and the magnolias were in bloom.

The Cabinet of Dr. Caligari, Part Four. As it gradually dawns upon Francis and the doctors at the asylum that the director has assumed the twisted personality and the misbegotten mission of the mad monk Caligari, they decide to confront the miscreant in his quarters. To achieve the maximum shock effect, they bring with them the lifeless body of Cesare. Once inside the director's room, Francis bravely strides up to his antagonist and declares, "The circle is closing in—Dr. Caligari!"

When the director sees Cesare's stiff form lying before him, he breaks down and weeps over the body. All his dreams—gone forever. Then, realizing the game is up at last, he tries to flee, but is surrounded and subdued by doctors and attendants, and restrained in a straitjacket.

This was the end of the film as originally written. But the producer feared that its theme was too blatantly antiauthoritarian for the Germany of 1919—the director of the asylum being more dangerously insane than the inmates, the director hypnotizing and training the common man (Cesare) to do his killing for him—and so he inserted the opening scene (Francis telling his story to a friend on a park bench) and a closing sequence. Thus we now cut to Francis sitting on the bench, his story concluded as he tells his companion that today Caligari is "a raving madman chained to his cell."

And suddenly it becomes apparent that the bench is not in a park, but in the courtyard of the asylum; and Francis is just another patient, wandering among assorted kindred lunatic spirits. Suddenly he spots the man he believes to be Cesare, tenderly caressing a flower as he stares vacantly into the distance. Francis raises the alarm: Do not let Cesare prophesy for you, or you will die. Francis's face begins to take on the simpering expression of a man about one brick shy of a full load. He sees his beloved, Jane, and asks her when she will marry him. Jane, who is obviously completely insane, gazes soulfully at the sky and answers, "We who are of royal blood may not follow the wishes of our heart."

Then, strolling amiably down the steps comes the director, immaculately dressed, no longer wearing an outrageous hat, his white hair neatly combed. "You fools!" Francis shouts to his fellow inmates. "This man is plotting our doom! We die at dawn!" He rushes upon the director. "He is Caligari!" This time it is Francis who is subdued by the attendants and carried off to be placed in a straitjacket.

Coolly, rationally, the director examines Francis and makes his diagnosis. Turning to face the camera, he speaks reassuringly: "At last I recognize his mania. He believes me to be the mythical Caligari. Astonishing! But I think I know how to cure him now." The rest of the picture fades and we are left only with the image of the director's face—calm, dispassionate, and determined to cure his poor deluded patient.

At brigade headquarters in Jullundur on April 10, Brigadier General Reginald E. H. Dyer could see his duty quite clearly. He knew how to cure the delusions then raging throughout the land. Born in India of Irish parents, Dyer had been educated in Ireland and then returned to India to commence a distinguished military career in the service of the Raj. Fifty-five years old and still ruggedly handsome (though notoriously short-tempered and suffering from arteriosclerosis and a number of service-related injuries), he was not a particularly imaginative man, being possessed of certain fixed ideas that governed his reactions to whatever situation presented itself—for instance, that Indians were socially inferior to Europeans and had to be kept in their place. But since the most visible and vital symbol of British authority in India—the army—was always vastly outnumbered by the natives, the mass of Indians had therefore to be kept perpetually overawed by the threat of dire retaliation by the military forces. The natives had to know, in other words, that if they ever stepped out of line they would pay dearly.

The present disorders were worse than anything Dyer had yet encountered, but he was certain he could end them most efficiently. They had been set off by that little fakir Gandhi and his campaign of civil disobedience to the Rowlatt laws. Right now, in the territory served by Dyer's 45th Brigade, the worst trouble appeared to be in Amritsar, about fifty miles northwest of Jullundur and one of the wealthiest and most populous cities in the heart of the Punjab. It was also the sacred city of the Sikhs, the site of their Golden Temple.

Earlier on the same day, in hopes of preventing further disorders, the local magistrates had deported two of the most prominent nationalist agitators from Amritsar. Instead of calming the populace, however, this misguided action only fanned the flames further. When the people of the city learned of the government's action, they went on a rampage. The Amritsar telegraph office was destroyed and its instruments smashed. The railway station was attacked, and stones were thrown at one of the magistrates. Then the mob gathered at the National Bank. The bank manager, A. J. L. Stewart, and the accountant, G. C. Scott, were murdered, their bodies soaked with kerosene and burned. Later the main building was also set afire. Another bank was attacked, the manager killed, and his body thrown into the street. The town hall was burned down. The Zenana Hospital was also threatened, and just outside of its walls a woman missionary doctor, Miss Marcia Sherwood, who had been riding her bicycle down the street, was savagely beaten with shoes and sticks by a gang of young Indian toughs and left for dead. Discovering that communications with the rest of India were completely cut off, the Deputy Commissioner had sent a light engine along the railway to connect the telegraph wires outside of town and send a message through to the 16th Indian Division at Lahore. Lahore then telegraphed Dyer, and Dyer dispatched three hundred men as reinforcements to Amritsar.

Determined to restore order no matter the cost, Dyer extinguished his cigarette and prepared to go to Amritsar himself.

The notion had come to Gandhi as if in a dream one morning as he lay in the twilight state between sleep and consciousness: he would call for a *hartal*, a day of self-purification, when all business would be suspended in every corner of India, when people would desist from riding and driving and would walk barefoot, when black flags would wave in front of houses and be carried in processions, and when the land would spend the day in fasting and prayer. This was the means Gandhi chose to dramatize and galvanize the opposition to the hated Rowlatt legislation. The date was first set for March 30, then changed to April 6. Word of the delay did not reach Delhi in time, however, and so that city observed the hartal on the original date. At the start, Gandhi deemed the hartal "a most wonderful spectacle," but as the movement gathered strength across India, it begat violence; the famine, the sickness, the high prices, the lingering resentment against the British for attempting to shanghai natives into military service during wartime, all the frustrations of the people burst through the bonds of nonviolence within which Gandhi had sought to conduct the protest. Alarmed, Gandhi issued a manifesto from Bombay instructing his followers to conduct all future demonstrations in silence and in accordance with police regulations. The satyagraha pledge, he reminded India, "is no small thing. It means a change of heart. It is an attempt to introduce the religious spirit into politics. We may no longer believe in the doctrine of 'tit for tat'; we may not meet hatred with hatred, violence with violence, evil with evil; but we have to make a continuous and persistent effort to return good for evil. . . . Nothing is impossible."

Unfortunately, no one but Gandhi seemed to be able to exert a restraining influence on the growing element of violence in the movement, and so the call went out for Gandhi to come to the Punjab to calm the disorders there. But the government had invoked the Defence of India Act and forbidden Gandhi to enter the Punjab, believing in an understandable if unimaginative way that the presence of a man publicly sworn to disobey the law would only further incite the mobs. So when Gandhi arrived at a railway station outside Delhi, he was arrested and returned to Bombay Presidency on the next train as an ordinary first-class passenger. Upon his arrival in Bombay shortly after noon, he was released and allowed to return to his home. If he could not appear in person in the Punjab, at least he could make his position emphatically clear. At a mass meeting on the evening of April 11, Gandhi issued the following message: "I have received what I was seeking—either the withdrawal of the Rowlatt legislation or imprisonment. Departure from truth by a hair's breadth or violence committed against anybody, whether Englishman or Indian, will surely damn the great cause which the Satyagrahis are handling." Of course, word of Gandhi's arrest simply inflamed the people even more against the British government of India.

Sir Michael F. O'Dwyer, the departing Lieutenant-Governor of the Punjab and one of the men responsible for banning Gandhi from the territory (O'Dwyer's original intention had been to deport him to Burma), shared Dyer's faith in the efficacy of overwhelming force as a deterrent. "The situation was, for the moment, critical," O'Dwyer warned at a farewell dinner on April 11. "The Government would do its duty without hesitation." And he shouted with raised fist at an Indian attorney, "Remember, there is another force greater than Gandhi's soul-force."

General Dyer arrived in Amritsar at 9:30 P.M. on April 11. He immediately assumed command of the situation at the request of the Deputy Commissioner, despite the fact that martial law had not yet been formally proclaimed. On the following morning, Dyer marched a small column of troops through the city, bringing forth shouts of derision from the people in the streets. A proclamation was issued warning the people against assembling together on pain of being dispersed by force of arms. Dyer himself spent several hours on the morning of April 13 making the proclamation known throughout the city. The message was read in the vernacular at eighteen different points throughout Amritsar, accompanied by the beating of drums. It was, Dyer believed, fair warning to everyone.

On April 12, another message from Gandhi was read to the crowd at Bombay. Much of it was inaudible beyond a few yards from the speaker, owing to the constant chants of *"Jai! Jai!"* ("Victory! Victory!") According to *The Times* of London, Gandhi told his children that he understood that "much excitement and disturbance had followed his detention. This was not satyagraha. . . . If the movement could not be conducted without the slightest disturbance from their side it might have to be abandoned or be given a different form in a still more restricted shape. . . . If Englishmen had been injured and died, it would be a great blot on satyagraha, for to him Englishmen, too, were their brethren."

On Sunday, April 13, processions of about ten thousand people crowded through Calcutta, but there were few disturbances. The rest of Bengal remained quiet. In the United Provinces, shops closed and meetings were held in the larger towns, but again there was no violence. Delhi was quiet, with shops closed and three mass meetings.

In Bombay, Gandhi led his followers in a ritual bathing in the sea in the morning and addressed a meeting later in the day, again exhorting India to forswear bloodshed. In Amritsar, thousands of pilgrims poured into the city to celebrate Baisakhi Day, one of the most important Sikh festivals.

The real danger, Dyer believed, lay not in the city itself but in the villages outside Amritsar. If those areas rose in rebellion, there would be a situation parallel to the fearsome Mutiny of 1857.

At 12:40 in the afternoon of April 13 Dyer learned that a meeting was to be held in the evening at a place just outside the city called Jallianwala Bagh; at first Dyer did not believe the crowd would actually gather in defiance of his warnings, but around four o'clock he received definite confirmation that the meeting had assembled. Dyer immediately marched off for Jallianwala Bagh with a force of twenty-five British rifles, twenty-five Indian rifles, forty Gurkhas, and two armored cars equipped with machine guns. It was very hot, and so the column traveled at an ordinary walking pace. Dyer reached his destination sometime between 5:00 and 5:15 P.M.

Jallianwalla Bagh was a piece of low-lying wasteland, about the size of Trafalgar Square, enclosed by high walls. Formerly a garden, it had long been a popular site for large gatherings. There was only one entrance of any appreciable size to an alleyway outside. The armored cars would not fit through the entrance, so Dyer was forced to leave them outside. He deployed his men on a piece of raised ground at the northern end of the Bagh; at the southern end there was a peaceful meeting of more than six thousand unarmed men, women, and children listening to an orator whom Dyer thought he recognized as a prominent participant in the recent political agitation. They were meeting in defiance of his proclamation; it did not occur to Dyer that many in the crowd may have just arrived in Amritsar from the countryside and had never heard of his proclamation. In Dyer's eyes, these were people who believed in their hearts that the British Raj had come to an end; they were not innocent, they were flouting his orders, and he considered it his duty to disperse the gathering. He did not now, however, tell them to break up the meeting or give them a chance to go home before they faced his guns. "I think it is quite possible I could have dispersed the crowd without firing," the general testified later to a commission of inquiry, "but they would have come back again and laughed, and I should have made what I consider to be a fool of myself. . . . I considered it was my duty to fire, and fire well." He would punish those who had disobeyed him and send a message throughout the Punjab.

Within thirty seconds of his arrival, Dyer ordered his troops to open fire. A huge roar of pain arose from the crowd. Dyer continued firing even after people tried to run away; with the narrow exit blocked, there was no escape possible. Dyer told his men not to fire in volleys, but to take their time. Some women dove into a well, the only refuge; children ran terrified across the courtyard. Dyer thought a little firing would not be sufficient. Minutes passed—no one could tell for certain how many—and the firing continued. Not until his troops ran short of ammunition did Dyer give the command to stop firing. Altogether, 1,650 rounds had been fired. At close range into a dense crowd in a confined space, nearly every bullet from expert marksmen found a mark. Dyer: "It was a horrible duty I had to perform. I think it was a merciful thing. I thought I should shoot well and strong, so that I or anybody else should not have to shoot again. If I had the right to fire one shot, I had the right to fire a lot of rounds. I arrived at the logical conclusion that I must disperse the crowd, who had defied the arm of the law. There was no medium course. The one thing was force."

The dead numbered at least four to five hundred, the wounded three times as many. Dyer did not attempt to attend to the wounded: "No, certainly not. It was not my job. Hospitals were open, and they could have gone there." The Deputy Commissioner also took no measures to remove the dead or wounded, claiming that he had received no orders on that point. Dyer was in charge, and the Deputy Commissioner said he was neither asked to do anything nor did he initiate any action himself. That night Dyer went into the streets of the city and found everything quiet. Jackals and wild dogs tore at the corpses in Jallianwala Bagh; vultures joined the feast. One women spent the night with the dead body of her husband amid the lifeless forms with upturned faces staring at the starry sky: "I shall never forget the sight. I was alone all night in that horrible jungle. Nothing but the barking of dogs and braying of donkeys was audible. Amongst hundreds of corpses I spent my night crying and watching." The next day, Dyer issued orders permitting the dead to be buried or burned. O'Dwyer sent him a telegram approving of his action. The report to the India Office read, "At Amritsar, on April 13, the mob defied the proclamation forbidding public meetings. Firing ensued, and 200 casualties occurred."

On April 14, the day after the massacre at Amritsar, Lord Chelmsford, Governor General of India, issued a declaration charging Gandhi's passive-resistance campaign with indirectly promoting "a sense of unrest and excitement which was bound to react, and has reacted, on the more ignorant and inflammable sections of the population." Deploring the attacks upon European civilians at Amritsar, the statement continued: "It remains for the Governor-General to assert in the clearest manner the intention of the Government to prevent by all means, however drastic, any recurrence of these excesses. He will not hesitate to employ the ample military resources at his disposal. . . ."

The name Amritsar means "pool of nectar."

FIVE

THE DAYS
OF
WRATH

"Is counsel perished

from the prudent?

Is their wisdom vanished?"

20

"Weep sore for him

that goeth away;

for he shall return no more,

nor see his native country. "

A tall, solemn figure clad in black strode across the stage and took his place before the keyboard. His head bowed over his instrument, his long gaunt face and deepset eyes a mask of human sadness, his close-cropped hair and high, broad forehead a mark of his Russian heritage, Sergei Rachmaninoff began to play. He played and his audience melted away and he was left drifting in the music—but no, not drifting: marching passionate through the white crystalline light, the vigorous biting rhythms striking whiplike on iron, the resonant chords calling up cascades of pure and cold colors, the whole a finely chiseled sculpture standing in a rain that might be tears. Chopin, the *Appassionata*, Chopin, Liszt, more Chopin, and inevitably his own Prelude in C-sharp Minor. Then he returned and bowed gravely to acknowledge the cheers of those who heard.

A refugee from his beloved Russia, Rachmaninoff had fled the Bolsheviks, who permitted him to take with him only five hundred rubles for each member of his family. His estate was requisitioned and plundered. After a sojourn in Sweden, Sergei and his family departed for America (where he had toured nine years earlier) on a small Norwegian steamer, arriving in Hoboken on November 10, 1918—one day before the Armistice. (The uninhibited celebrations in New York the following day made him wonder if he had landed in a vast insane asylum.) Rejecting offers to conduct, and unable to support himself solely by composing, Rachmaninoff embarked upon a career as a concert pianist. Boston, New York, alone or with the Russian Symphony or the New York Symphony Society, always with his trademark Steinway, Rachmaninoff was adored by his fans ("I have seldom seen a New York concert audience more moved, excited and wrought up," wrote one fellow composer after a Rachmaninoff performance), but often scorned by critics, who, with a remarkable lack of insight, failed to discern in his music the mark of any significant innovation or personality. "Metaphorically speaking," complained Edward Sackville-West, "Rachmaninoff shut himself up in a dark room, frightened himself to death, and then translated his soul-storm into the language of music."

Rachmaninoff was homesick. Never truly at ease in America—in his lifetime he read only one book in English, Sinclair Lewis's *Main Street*—he once told a friend, "Even the air does not smell here the way it does in Russia." Yet in 1919, when there was no peace in Europe, and even less in Russia, there was no other place for him.

Lloyd George stood and surveyed the Commons. The House was crowded to overflowing early on the afternoon of April 16, the excess of members spilling into the side galleries. A full bench of ministers was present: Churchill and Sir Eric Geddes on the Prime Minister's right, Bonar Law and Austen Chamberlain on his left. There were more Labour members in attendance than anyone had seen for weeks. In the Peers' Gallery, in the seat over the clock—the seat from which the future King Edward VII had so often listened to the debates of those he had called his "faithful Commons"—sat the Prince of Wales on his own first visit to the House. "I saw him as he crossed the lobby," wrote the *Manchester Guardian*'s parliamentary correspondent of the heir to the throne, "very young-looking and also very pleasant to look upon—one would say a very charming, typical English boy." Nearby, in the Diplomatic Gallery, the American ambassador watched the proceedings with considerable interest.

Speaking in his usual easy, unforced tone, Lloyd George wasted no time in getting to the point. Stung by the criticisms of the Northcliffe press and annoyed by the presumptuous demands of the "indemnity cave" led by Messrs. Kennedy Jones and Horace Bottomley, the little Welshman began by explaining the difficulties of solving such matters as reparations, French security, and the League of Nations while the world's nerves were still rubbed raw, and when the negotiations were being held in a place where "stones are rattling on the roof and crashing through the windows, with wild men screaming through the keyhole." When all was said and done, there would be no conflict between his election pledges and the final terms of the peace treaty, Lloyd George promised. Beyond the issues of the German treaty, of course, lay the dilemma of Russia; and while the Prime Minister had never even discussed official recognition of Lenin's regime (there were cheers from the Conservative benches for this lie), he had come to believe that the Allies must allow Russia to work out its own destiny. Certainly his government had no intention of sending great numbers of troops (and no conscripts at all) or pouring vast sums of gold into the Russian morass: "better that Russia should be Bolshevik than Britain bankrupt." But on the other hand, neither would Britain turn its back on the anti-Bolshevik forces it was currently aiding. In other words, the present *cordon sanitaire* would be maintained.

Then Lloyd George turned his attention to Lord Northcliffe, owner of *The Times* and the sensationalist *Daily Mail*, the man who had helped topple Asquith in 1916, and who had wholeheartedly supported Lloyd George for the duration of the war. Allegedly disgruntled when he was not given the honor of representing his country as a member of the British delegation to the Peace Conference, Northcliffe had retired in ill health to his estate at Fontainebleau, whence he began a concerted attack on the Prime Minister's endeavors in Paris. Lloyd George was being too soft on the Germans, Northcliffe argued ("They will cheat you yet, those Junkers!" screamed the *Daily Mail's* headlines); the little Welshman had fallen under the spell of Wilson, and was selling out British interests for his own personal glory. (Northcliffe was also wary of "the pressure of the international Jew" at the Peace Conference.)

Now, against the venom of the Northcliffe press—the "grasshopper press" ("here today, jumping there to-morrow, somewhere else the next day")—which had called for "hanging everybody all round, including the Government, I suppose," Lloyd George replied with mock sympathy and biting sarcasm:

I AM PREPARED TO MAKE SOME ALLOWANCES FOR EVEN A GREAT NEWSPAPER PROPRIETOR. AND WHEN A MAN IS SUFFERING UNDER A KEEN SENSE OF DISAPPOINTMENT, HOWEVER UNJUSTIFIED, OR HOWEVER RIDICULOUS HIS EXPECTATIONS MAY BE, A MAN UNDER THOSE CIRCUMSTANCES IS ALWAYS APT TO THINK THAT THE WORLD IS BADLY RUN. WHEN A MAN HAS DELUDED HIMSELF, AND ALL THE PEOPLE WHO COME NEAR HIM, INTO THE BELIEF THAT HE IS THE ONLY MAN WHO CAN DO ALL THINGS, AND IS WAITING FOR THE CLAMOR OF THE MULTITUDE THAT IS GOING TO DEMAND HIS PRESENCE THERE TO DIRECT THEIR DESTINIES, BUT THERE IS NO CLAMOR, NOT A SOUND, IT IS RATHER DISAPPOINTING. IT IS UNNERVING AND UPSETTING.

Nevertheless, it was the Prime Minister's duty to warn Britain's allies not to take Northcliffe's pronouncements too seriously; after all, even the venerable *Times* under his leadership had become nothing more than "the threepenny edition of the 'Daily Mail.' " (This was, of course, exaggeration for the sake of ridicule.)

Once Lloyd George had hit his stride, there were virtually no interruptions from the House to his monologue, save for frequent laughter at Northcliffe's expense. It was a virtuoso performance. All except the extreme reactionaries went home satisfied and reassured. In fact, the wizard had once again spun his magic, for he had calmed the fears of his supporters with little but wit and soothing promises. "He did splendidly," remarked an admirer. "He told them nothing at all."

Lloyd George himself went off after the speech to luncheon in the ministers' dining room with the Prince of Wales and the parliamentary leaders of both the Liberal and Conservative parties; the prince confessed that although he had been very interested in the beginning, before the speech was quite over he had got altogether too hungry to keep his mind on it. (And since it was half-past two by the time it was all done, who could blame him?)

Then Lloyd George prepared to return to Paris. He was leaving behind him a labor situation that, for the time being, appeared to be relatively peaceful, even though over a million Britons were receiving unemployment donations. Approximately half of these were women, who were rapidly being forced back into such low-paying and low-prestige occupations as domestic service. The much-heralded National Industrial Conference had achieved little of substance. It did give labor the opportunity to meet with capital on an equal footing under government auspices, and the conference issued a report on April 4 recommending a maximum work week of forty-eight hours, more generous unemployment benefits and old-age pensions, improved housing programs, and expanded government development projects (especially in times of high unemployment). The NIC also proposed that a permanent conference be established to discuss industrial relations in an atmosphere of peace and cooperation, and this was done; but the government simply had no intention of pressing ahead with any ambitious labor programs for the time being.

The Sankey Commission, on the other hand, at least managed to use the relentless glare of publicity to penetrate the sordid recesses of life in the coal regions and to expose the reprehensible conditions in the mining industry. Created by act of Parliament, the Sankey Commission enjoyed the power to compel witnesses to attend and testify, and to produce documents requested by any of the commission's members. Sitting amid "the gold, blue and red glories of the King's Robing Room in the House of Lords," the miners' representatives turned the Commission's hearings into a grand jury, "investigating the industry, cross-examining the royalty owners and questioning their contribution to society, and in general building up the case for nationalisation." The star of the show was Robert "Bob" Smilie, president of the Miners' Federation, a man of solid character and physique, dressed in an old but respectable gray suit, pulling on an old pipe, nearly seventy years old and still quick, alert and vigorous, determinedly asking one question after another in his soft Scots accent, quoting with equal facility from the Scriptures and socialist philosophical tracts. "There is a very old book," Smilie reminded one witness, "which says, 'the earth is the Lord's and the fullness thereof,'" and if one accepted the Gospel as truth, then the earth's bounty could not be the property of individuals— specifically, individuals such as the coal mine owners.

Forced for the first time to divulge their earnings, the coal barons admitted that even after the excess-profits tax and other wartime levies, they still had made an average profit of over 25 percent in the past four years. Wartime charges of profiteering had not been unfounded, and these revelations aroused public indignation anew. The miners had not fared as well as their employers. Statistics revealed that mining was as deadly as war: from 1907 to 1916, over twelve thousand miners had been killed outright by accidents, and more by disease; over the past twenty years there had not been fewer than an average of 160,000 miners injured every year. "There is blood on all the coal we burn," charged one angry newspaper. Sir Richard Redmayne, the Chief Inspector of Mines, testified that the present system of individual ownership of the mines was wasteful and extravagant in terms of supplying the nation with an essential product. But the most regrettable waste lay in the dehumanizing conditions of life in the colliery towns. The death rate among children under twelve months of age in the mining districts was a staggering 16 percent. The houses of coal workers were acknowledged to be "a disgrace to any country." Traveling through "the mean, unpaved streets of the Scottish mining towns," one witness found thousands of people

HERDED INTO ROOMS WHICH POSSESS NONE OF THE AMENITIES OF DECENT LIFE, WHICH HAVE NO INSIDE WATER SUPPLY, NO SINK, NO PANTRY, NO SCULLERY, NO CUPBOARD OR WARDROBE, NO INSIDE WASHHOUSE. SANITARY ACCOMMODATION IS SOMETIMES NONEXISTENT, AND IS SOMETIMES SHARED WITH FOUR OR SIX HOUSEHOLDS, AND IS OFTEN OF AN UNTHINKABLY PRIMITIVE TYPE. . . . AS MEN AND WOMEN MARRY THEY ARE CONDEMNED TO ATTACH THEMSELVES TO SOME ALREADY OVER-CROWDED FAMILY PACKED IN TWO OR THREE ROOMS. . . . PEOPLE SPEAK OF WEST SCOTLAND AS A SEED-PLOT OF REVOLUTIONARY THOUGHT. BUT WHEN THE

WORKER REFLECTS THAT THE WORST AND MOST INSANITARY OF THE
HOUSES TO WHICH HE IS TIED ARE THE PROPERTY OF WEALTHY COLLIERY
FIRMS, IT IS NOT TO BE WONDERED THAT HIS FAITH IN A PROVIDENTIAL
DISPENSATION OF WORLDLY GOODS IS RATHER SHAKEN.

Mr. Justice Sankey's interim report, issued on March 20, recommended
a wage increase of two shillings per day for adult workers, a seven-hour
day (and possibly a six-hour day by 1921 if economic conditions permitted), and a levy on each ton of coal to improve the housing and amenities
of the mining districts, which were formally recognized as "a reproach to
our civilisation" for which "no judicial language is sufficiently strong or
sufficiently severe to apply to their condemnation." The crux of the matter,
though, remained the question of nationalization. Here the miners' representatives and the coal interests took widely divergent positions, between which Sankey steered a middle course: "The present system of
ownership and working in the coal industry stands condemned," he concluded, "and some other system must be substituted for it, either nationalisation or a method of unification by national purchase and/or joint
control." At any rate, Sankey strongly urged that miners be given "an
effective voice" in the direction of the mines right away. "For a generation
the colliery worker has been educated socially and technically. The result
is a national asset. Why not use it?"

The government accepted most of Sankey's recommendations and carried over the question of nationalization for further inquiry. (Unlike his
Conservative allies, the idea of nationalization posed no horrors for Lloyd
George; when a panicky Bonar Law told him that the mine owners'
intransigence might force the government into nationalization "before we
are ready," the Prime Minister replied, "Well, if it does, that will not be
very serious. It has to come. The State will have to shoulder the burden
sooner or later.") Lloyd George breezily insisted that the miners would
never reject the Sankey package even without nationalization, and after
several brief wildcat strikes in the Rhondda Valley and Nottinghamshire,
and a flurry of acrimonious public exchanges between Bonar Law and
Smilie, the miners voted overwhelmingly to accept the gains embodied in
the report and called off their proposed strike. They would, however,
continue to watch as the commission resumed its deliberations regarding
the nationalization of the nation's mines. Meanwhile, the railway workers—another branch of the Triple Alliance—who had been threatening
their own strike, also postponed any job action in return for vague government promises to "standardize" wages.

With the laughter and applause of the Commons still ringing in his ears, it was no wonder that a buoyant Lloyd George returned to Paris on April 17 quite enchanted with himself and the way things were going on the home front. "You are a great little man—always full of courage," Riddell told him. "Well," Lloyd George replied, "it never does to let your heart slip down." At the time, the Prime Minister was completely unaware of the disaster at Amritsar.

Neither Lloyd George nor anyone else outside the Punjab was yet aware of the extent of the Amritsar massacre, primarily because Lieutenant-Governor O'Dwyer had immediately clamped a tight lid of censorship on news from the Punjab to the outside world. Word had spread throughout the towns and villages in the surrounding area, though, and it seemed that General Dyer had achieved his objective. There were no more riots.

Dyer's action was the most extreme example of armed repression in India since the Mutiny of 1857–58, but British military authorities in other sectors adopted only slightly less radical measures to put down the disturbances touched off by the Rowlatt agitation. At Gujranwala, airplanes dropped bombs on a crowd of demonstrators and then proceeded to strafe the survivors with machine-gun fire. At Kasur, a half-dozen schoolboys were chosen to be flogged not because they had participated in the disorders, but because they were the biggest boys; if they were innocent, the local commander explained, that was simply their misfortune. The entire male population of Kasur was then assembled for an "identification parade" lasting six hours, and those suspected of participation in the riots were placed—150 at a time—in a cage erected outside the railroad station. At Lahore, sixty-six Indians were sentenced to whippings. The military district commander later told an investigative commission that though he was not a doctor, "he could not imagine that this punishment could have had any serious effect on the health of the whipped." A martial law notice at a college outside of Lahore was found torn, and the students there were consequently forced to march sixteen miles a day to and from the nearest fort for three weeks. A priest and some others in a wedding party were arrested and flogged because they had violated a ban on processions of more than ten people.

Although Gandhi did not learn of the Amritsar massacre until June, the huge crowd that gathered at Gandhi's ashram at Sabarmati on April 14 heard the Mahatma declare that he and they must all do penance for the destruction of human life and property during the recent campaign of protest. He asked the people to fast for twenty-four hours; Gandhi himself would fast for three days. By April 18 he had decided to suspend the satyagraha for the time being, although he remained steadfastly opposed to the government's course. "I am sorry," Gandhi said, "that when I embarked upon a mass movement I underrated the forces of evil, and I must now pause and consider how best to meet the situation." He admitted that he had been guilty of "a Himalayan miscalculation" in launching the satyagraha before the people were ready to walk with him along the narrow path of truth. Satyagraha would triumph, but first he must teach his children how to follow without disobedience.

Dyer, however, was not yet done. On April 19, he visited Miss Sherwood—still on the critical list—in the hospital, and emerged determined to ensure that no British woman would ever again be thus abused in the Punjab. "We look upon women as sacred," Dyer later explained. "I searched in my mind for a form of punishment that would meet the assault. I did not know how to meet it." He met it by declaring that the street where Sherwood had been beaten, the Kucha Kaurhianwala, should also be looked upon as sacred. Between the hours of six o'clock in the morning and eight o'clock in the evening, any Indian who wished to go down the street would have to do so crawling on all fours.

Dyer claimed that "it never entered my mind that any man in his senses would voluntarily go through that street." What about the people who lived there? Certainly, Dyer reasoned, some of the houses had back entrances the residents could use instead; for those that didn't, well, they could wait and go out after 8:00 P.M., or else walk along the flat roofs instead to get to another street. To emphasize the point further, six youths suspected of beating Sherwood were publicly lashed in the same street—without the benefit of trial, of course. Dyer believed the floggings would be productive of a good impression.

The crawling order was at least as much of a Himalayan miscalculation as Gandhi's satyagraha campaign. It was revoked by order of Dyer's superiors on April 21. (Dyer said several months later that he would have revoked it himself on April 20, but he had other things on his mind at the time.) Still, the damage had been done. Dyer had inflicted a wound upon Indian pride that the British could never heal. Incensed, the Indian author and educator Rabindranath Tagore resigned the knighthood recently bestowed upon him by the King, and wrote in a cold fury:

THE ENORMITY OF THE MEASURES TAKEN BY THE GOVERNMENT IN THE PUNJAB FOR QUELLING SOME LOCAL DISTURBANCES HAS, WITH A RUDE SHOCK, REVEALED TO OUR MINDS THE HELPLESSNESS OF OUR POSITION AS

BRITISH SUBJECTS IN INDIA. THE DISPROPORTIONATE SEVERITY OF THE PUNISHMENTS INFLICTED UPON THE UNFORTUNATE PEOPLE AND THE METHODS OF CARRYING THEM OUT, WE ARE CONVINCED, ARE WITHOUT PARALLEL IN THE HISTORY OF CIVILISED GOVERNMENTS, BARRING SOME CONSPICUOUS EXCEPTIONS, RECENT AND REMOTE. CONSIDERING THAT SUCH TREATMENT HAS BEEN METED OUT TO A POPULATION DISARMED AND RESOURCELESS, BY A POWER WHICH HAS THE MOST TERRIBLY EFFICIENT ORGANISATION FOR DESTRUCTION OF HUMAN LIVES, WE MUST STRONGLY ASSERT THAT IT CAN CLAIM NO POLITICAL EXPEDIENCY, FAR LESS MORAL JUSTIFICATION. . . . THE TIME HAS COME WHEN BADGES OF HONOUR MAKE OUR SHAME GLARING IN THEIR INCONGRUOUS CONTEXT OF HUMILIATION, AND I FOR MY PART WISH TO STAND, SHORN OF ALL SPECIAL DISTINCTIONS, BY THE SIDE OF THOSE OF MY COUNTRYMEN WHO, FOR THEIR SO-CALLED INSIGNIFICANCE, ARE LIABLE TO SUFFER A DEGRADATION NOT FIT FOR HUMAN BEINGS.

Upon learning of the crawling order, Gandhi was appalled to the depths of his great soul. From this moment forward, he proclaimed, "co-operation in any shape or form with this satanic government is sinful."

Whatever claims to moral supremacy the British Raj had previously enjoyed now had disappeared in the blood and humiliation of the Punjab. India—and Gandhi—would never rest content under the domination of a government that had turned loose to wreak havoc such a man as Brigadier General Reginald Dyer.

"The only exciting thing about this fight between Jess Willard and Jack Dempsey is the fact that Willard is liable to be arrested for manslaughter. It's no contest at all." So spoke veteran heavyweight Jim Flynn, reportedly the only man ever to knock out Dempsey (it happened very early in Dempsey's career). As the date for the bout drew nigh, both champion and challenger spared no hardship to hone their pugilistic skills to the highest pitch. Dempsey continued to tour the vaudeville circuit with the Seashore Flirts, while Willard interrupted his rigorous training routine at his farm in Lawrence, Kansas (he was down to 270 pounds by late April; Dempsey weighed 197) to travel to Los Angeles to make a movie feature, *The Challenge of Chance* (co-starring Arline Pretty), at the Brunton Studios on Melrose Avenue. The studio planned to film part of Willard's actual training regimen, then stage a fake fight wherein Willard routed a band of Pancho Villa's *bandidos* with nothing but his fists; then the giant Kansan would drive a herd of horses across a river, and wrap it all up by rescuing

Miss Pretty from dire peril. For this the champion would earn nearly $100,000.

From Chicago came a rumor that the fight with Dempsey would be nothing more than a motion-picture stunt, with Douglas Fairbanks serving as referee. Jack Kearns, Dempsey's trainer, angrily squelched the story: "I do not even know Douglas Fairbanks. . . . If any move were on foot to turn the fight into a motion picture production I certainly would know of it." But amid published reports that Willard was starting to round into excellent condition, Kearns and Dempsey hurriedly put out a call for new sparring partners—*big* ones.

Tex Rickard, meanwhile, had finally found a site for the July 4 title bout: Toledo, Ohio. The other leading contenders had been Paris (still stuffed with Anglo-American visitors with extra cash in their pockets), Pocatello, Idaho, and Cumberland, Maryland. According to Dempsey, Toledo "was in those days a haven for prominent gamblers and hustlers who were on the lam." Although Ohio law prohibited fighting for a purse, Governor James M. Cox allowed Mayor Schreiber of Toledo (who also served as head of the local boxing commission) to exercise his own judgment in interpreting the relevant statutes; so Willard and Dempsey would officially stage an "exhibition" and receive "salaries" for their efforts. Unofficially, of course, everyone knew it remained a championship prizefight, and Cox's decision brought a unanimous protest from the members of the Ministers' Union of Cleveland, who condemned the fight as a menace to public morals. Undaunted, Rickard announced that he was building a special octagon-shaped arena for the occasion, at a site known as Bay View Park, to accommodate between fifty and sixty thousand spectators, who would each be charged from ten dollars (for a seat 260 feet away from the ring) to sixty dollars (ringside) for the privilege of viewing the bout. And to ensure that both fighters were in peak physical condition, both Willard and Dempsey would be required to spend the last five weeks before the match training at the site.

In Rome, the shrill, earsplitting screech of the trams cut through the green and golden euphoria of springtime. The trees were tipped with new leaves, and the early creepers put forth fresh growth along the roof-top gardens and terraces—but Italy was in an ugly mood. The men in Paris still had not rendered their decision on Fiume, and daily the demonstrations in Rome swelled in intensity.

Beyond the irredentist agitation lay the growing belligerence of both the militant Socialists and the rapidly spreading Fascist movement. By the middle of April, Fasci had been organized in Rome, Genoa,

Verona, Parma, Naples, Turin, Padua, Trieste, Venice, and Bologna; a twenty-thousand-member national association of arditi also had decided to enter into a formal alliance with Mussolini's *sansepolcristi*. It did not take long for these new disciples—the Italian counterparts of Germany's Freikorps recruits—to display their eagerness to bash radical heads in the streets.

The Italian Socialist Party had planned a mass meeting for April 10 at the Piazza Venezia in Rome, to be followed by a "proletariat procession" to the Piazza del Popolo as a demonstration of labor solidarity and a commemoration of Lenin's birthday and the murder of Liebknecht and Luxemburg. The city government refused to allow any of it. Thereupon the Socialists announced that they would not only go ahead and hold the procession anyway, but would also institute a one-day general strike to protest the government's attitude. When the strike date came, the streets of Rome were lined with cavalry and *carabinieri* in anticipation of trouble. Most of the 100,000 workers in the procession maintained their composure and everything went off smoothly, save for a brief altercation when a counterdemonstration of arditi crossed the Socialists' path. Several days later, however, a participant in another Socialist rally, this time in Milan, was killed in a clash with police and stone-throwing rightist vigilantes in the Via Borsieri. As usual, the Socialist Party retaliated by calling a general strike in the northern city.

All was calm in Milan when the strike began on the morning of April 15, and a huge workers' meeting in the afternoon passed peacefully until a squad of radical leftists carrying a red flag and chanting revolutionary slogans tried to march into the center of the city. They were met at the Piazza del Duomo by a fun-seeking band of arditi and Fascists who set upon them with considerable brio. The ensuing collision produced numerous injuries (especially among the Socialists) and revolver shots from both sides. The leftists retreated up the Via Dante. Having tasted blood, the Fascists—led by two of Mussolini's sansepolcristi—swarmed up the Via San Damiano to the offices of the major Socialist newspaper, *Avanti!* Understandably alarmed at the approach of such an unsavory aggregation, the besieged occupants panicked and began firing, none too accurately; an army private guarding the building was fatally wounded. That set the arditi off on a rampage. Forcing their way past the military guard, they smashed the newspaper's printing machinery, destroyed its list of subscribers, and, just for good measure, set fire to the furniture. Four civilians were shot dead, at least thirty wounded, and over fifty arrested when police reinforcements finally arrived.

Mussolini, who had not believed his forces were yet ready for a full-scale street battle, watched from a safe place and decided that this sordid fracas represented "the first episode of the civil war" and the initial fruits of the Fascist revolution. According to one of Benito's biographers, the incident also taught Mussolini "that when the victims of street violence were on the extreme left the police would intervene very little if at all; also that the socialists, for all their talk of revolution, were essentially pacifists who could be easily overcome by a tiny group of men prepared to shoot and be shot." Gathering a personal army of arditi around him—for he feared reprisals—and fortifying the offices of his own newspaper with a small-scale arsenal, Mussolini waited to hear the news from Paris that would give him even more ammunition for his crusade against the decadent and dis-credited old order. And in Milan, the choirs of the cathedral and the smaller churches went on strike for higher wages. There would be no music for Holy Week services in the city.

When the Adamses awoke in Quincy on the chilly Massachusetts spring morning of April 15, they could not pick up the telephone to discuss the latest news from Back Bay with the Lodges as they might have done on other days, nor could the Lodges pick up the phone and speak to the Cabots, although presumably the Cabots could still talk to God as they reputedly did almost every day. At 7:00 A.M., eight thousand telephone operators, all of them employees of the New England Telephone and Telegraph Company, had walked off their jobs with a demand for higher wages, thereby paralyzing communications from Connecticut to Maine. The operators were asking for starting pay of ten dollars a week and a maximum salary of twenty-two dollars per week after four years' service; the current wage scale went from six dollars a week for novice operators to sixteen dollars after seven years. But the strike was also a warning to the government and the rest of the nation that organized labor still had the power to shut down the daily routine of life in twentieth-century America. The federal government—specifically Postmaster General Albert Burle-son—had taken control of the nation's telephones for the duration of the war (remember that the nation was still officially at war), and Burleson had antagonized the unions by consistently refusing to recognize the right of even temporary government employees to organize. (Postmaster General Burleson was not particularly receptive to newfangled ideas. He was so adamantly opposed to the change to daylight savings time, now in its second year, that he refused to advance the clocks in his home one hour in the spring, and went about his duties in Washington on standard time throughout the summer, thereby creating considerable havoc with his schedule of personal appointments.)

Thus American labor officials chose to make the telephone operators' strike a test case, and they chose their ground wisely. Mayor Andrew J. Peters and the Boston Chamber of Commerce tried to negotiate a last-minute settlement, to no avail. Governor Coolidge asked Burleson to intervene; Burleson refused. So out walked the women, setting up lines of pickets who paraded up and down the sidewalks in their Sunday best, complete with Easter bonnets. Chaos ensued. Business transactions were nearly impossible without telephone connections; newspapers could not even gather reports of the strike's effect. By April 18, nearly twenty thousand telephone workers were on strike in five states, putting more than 630,000 phones out of commission. Despite the inconvenience, the public appeared to sympathize with the strikers. Their demands appeared quite reasonable; in fact, when people learned of the operators' proposed wage scale, the response was often amazement at their present low pay.

Most of the operators had at least a high school education, and, of course, additional training at the "A" and "B" switchboards. It was not a job for women of faint heart. When a customer picked up the receiver on his or her phone, a signal lamp flashed on the "A" switchboard. Each "A" operator was responsible for about sixty lines on her board. Local calls could be put through directly (except in Boston); others were "trunked" (passed to another exchange). In the latter case, an "A" operator would press a button to connect her with a circuit on a "B" board, whereupon the "B" operator would complete the call to the desired number. In a busy hour, an operator might have as many as twenty or more connections on line at the same time. A "B" operator also was responsible for several different exchanges, and had to serve an uninterrupted flow of calls from impatient "A" operators, each of whom wanted her line put through first. To make matters more complicated, an operator was required to keep a careful record of each call and its length if the customer was paying on a "measured service" basis, as most people were in New England in 1919. Supervisors and the chief operator were available to help in times of overflow, but normally they spent their days pacing up and down behind the operators, selecting random calls for a stopwatch check to ensure accurate reports. Not surprisingly, it was quite common for an operator to faint at her switchboard and be trundled off to the restroom to be revived.

Management tried several expedients to muddle through the strike. It hired students from the Massachusetts Institute of Technology to man the main exchange in Boston, but when the replacements left company headquarters at the end of the day they were set upon by angry strikers who pummeled them until the students reached the sanctuary of a nearby hotel. Twenty Harvard students who decided to take up positions at the switchboard for "a little excitement" found themselves facing fifty operators and more than one hundred male strike sympathizers on the sidewalk outside the exchange in Cambridge; they were returned to the university in police wagons for their own protection. In Providence, Newport society matrons (including the daughter of the late Julia Ward Howe) and their maids volunteered their services as operators. Hissed and jeered by the pickets, they ordered taxicabs to take them home after an exhausting three-hour stint at the switchboards, but the cabdrivers, who sided with the strikers, refused to pick them up.

Increasingly alarmed at the image of the administration picking on women who were underpaid to start with, Democratic Party officials in Massachusetts wired to Paris for Wilson: "Burleson wrecking the party. Remove him and settle this strike." Wilson refused to intervene, claiming that he felt he could not act intelligently at such a distance. Congressman James A. Gallivan told a meeting of strikers at the Grand Opera House that "this town and state are with you. . . . If Congress were in session, Burleson wouldn't dare do this. He thought you'd quit, but don't you do it." Another labor official told the operators that they were "in the trenches today fighting a Prussian."

As the public clamor for action grew too loud to ignore, Governor Calvin Coolidge prepared to take over the phone lines in Massachusetts and run them under state authority. Finally Burleson gave in and sent his deputy to negotiate with the women. On April 20 a tentative agreement was reached, granting the operators most of their demands, and everyone went back to work. The Adamses could call the Lodges once again, and they could chat to their hearts' content about the scandalous way Wilson and the Democrats were ruining the country.

The Adamses could also discuss the dismal performance of the Boston Braves on Opening Day, if either they or the Lodges took notice of such brutish pastimes. (Baseball was especially brutish in Boston, where one could not help but cringe as the Braves were pummeled and pounded day after day.) On April 19, which also happened to be Patriots' Day, the Braves hosted the Brooklyn Dodgers in a doubleheader; five thousand soldiers of the 26th Division attended as the Braves' special guests for the day, and a military band provided musical fireworks. Boston fans gave an especially warm welcome to the hometown club's brilliant shortstop, Walter James Vincent "Rabbit" Maranville. Recently discharged from the navy, the diminutive (five-foot-five) Rabbit received a lovely floral tribute before the game. He then proceeded to make several costly errors, as the

Braves dropped both ends of the doubleheader (5–2, 3–2) to the Bums.

Beantown spirits were restored four days later when the Red Sox debuted against the Yankees in New York. In the very first inning, in his first plate appearance of the 1919 regular season, Babe Ruth stroked a two-run homer, starting the Red Sox off to a 10–0 victory. In St. Louis, Kid Gleason's White Sox pounded out twenty-one hits and scored a 13–4 triumph over the hapless Browns. Shoeless Joe went three for four (including a double), Eddie Collins clouted a homer, and Lefty Williams went the distance, striking out six. The next day Jackson gathered three more hits as Chicago won again, 5–2, behind Eddie Cicotte's sparkling complete game effort.

To a casual outside observer, the saga of revolution in Bavaria may have resembled nothing so much as a game of political Ping-Pong. Nearly every prominent citizen in Munich had been arrested by one faction or another in the past month. Trying to follow the course of Bavarian affairs from Moscow, Lenin became completely confused about who was in power on any given day, and who the current regime represented (if anyone), and so he simply gave up sending congratulatory telegrams, sat back, and awaited news of further developments.

After the abortive Hoffmann putsch of April 13, the Communists under Levien and Leviné had assumed control from the coffeehouse soviets. They immediately proceeded to recruit thousands of men into the Red army, promising extraordinarily high pay and free food, liquor, and women. More than ten thousand men enlisted with alacrity, although their discipline and devotion to duty were more than slightly suspect. Still, the Communists were far more effective (i.e., ruthless) than their predecessors. "Revolution cannot be made with soft, compassionate hearts," Leviné told an assembly of the Workers' Councils. "It demands a stern, relentless will." As he and his comrades desperately struggled to develop some sort of reliable party machinery, they banned all opposition newspapers and proceeded to throw noble and bourgeois hostages into prison. Soon people were afraid to venture out of doors. The city streets were often nearly empty during the daylight hours, and completely desolate after the seven-o'clock curfew: "The dark city became hollow and silent," reported Ben Hecht from the scene. "As a matter of fact," declared one conservative leader in Munich in mid-April, "the communists led by Levien are the only intelligent elements in the situation. They know that a dictatorship cannot be imposed on the nation by namby-pamby tactics." Workers congratulated themselves on the new regime's determination, laughing and vowing that "now we can get down to real business." Perhaps; but the gentler soul of Ernst Toller—arrested, released, and then assigned to command the Red Guard forces at Dachau against Hoffmann's forces advancing from Bamberg—accepted the new regime without enthusiasm: "We were not ready for socialism yet, but this collapse, I fear, is only the beginning."

At Dachau, about twenty-five miles north of Munich, the Red forces (aided by townspeople throwing stones) routed Hoffmann's outnumbered and panic-stricken troops on April 20. Toller received orders from Munich to execute the forty-one prisoners he had captured during the brief battle; the poet refused. The lingering danger of invasion forced the government to maintain its defenses—the Krupp munitions plant in the north end of the city was transformed into a fortress, rail lines were torn up to keep out opposition troops (the peasants in the surrounding countryside tore up more rail lines to keep food from going into the city), and all the main roads leading into Munich were slashed with trenches and covered with field artillery and machine guns and barbed-wire entanglements—but for a brief breathing spell the radicals could concentrate their attention on social reforms. There was certainly no dearth of suggestions from the community of cranks inhabiting the Bavarian capital. Cubist paintings were reproduced in the newspapers as the true "people's art"; the "art dictator," Herr Tautz, vowed to purge the galleries of *Kitsch* and decreed that "no slop, no best-sellers and no sentimental gush for schoolgirls" would ever again see the light of day; and Leviné's wife saw the Wittelsbach Palace flooded with people from dawn to dusk:

INVENTORS APPEARED WITH WORLD-SHATTERING SCHEMES WHICH, PUT INTO EFFECT, WOULD GUARANTEE WEALTH, PEACE AND OTHER DAZZLING PROSPECTS; AUTHORS OF NEW EDUCATIONAL REFORMS; PROTAGONISTS OF MARRIAGE REFORM, WHICH WAS REGARDED AS THE 'FIRST AND FOREMOST TASK OF A SOVIET REPUBLIC.' . . . ASTROLOGERS ALSO BESIEGED THE GOVERNMENT OFFICES. THEY PROPOSED TO ASK PROVIDENCE ABOUT THE DESTINY OF THE FOUNDERS OF THE SOVIET REPUBLIC AND WERE SEEKING INFORMATION ABOUT DATES OF BIRTH AND OTHER WEIGHTY ASPECTS FROM THEIR RELATIVES AND FRIENDS. THE STARS WERE SO FAR BENEVOLENT, THE SOVIET REPUBLIC WAS TO WIN THROUGH.

But the astrologers failed to take account of the Bloodhound. Following the rout at Dachau, Adolf Hoffmann had no choice but to ask the central government in Berlin to intervene to restore the Majority Socialists to power in Bavaria. And that meant Noske and his Freikorps columns, who relished the challenge. As April began to fade, Noske took supreme command of all troops in opposition to the Communist government of Munich, and a force of over thirty thousand of the most hardened and sadistic men under his nominal (*very* nominal) control advanced inexorably toward the Bavarian capital.

21

"If heaven above can be measured,

and the foundations of the earth

searched out beneath . . ."

"Have you been up?"

In Britain, the Air Ministry decided to suspend its wartime prohibition on civilian flying for six days, from April 17 to 22—just in time for the Easter holidays. It was the first time in four years that ordinary citizens would be able to share the adventure of flight, and the queues formed early every morning at aerodomes across England. Airplane companies charged two guineas per person and provided each passenger with a topcoat and helmet. There was an extra charge for insurance, for which there was a brisk demand. Surprisingly, the short flights (known as "flips") proved especially popular among the elderly, and among women and children. Less adventurous souls stood and watched the giant planes—still adorned with most of their combat modifications—depart and return: "Nobody can watch an aeroplane ascend or descend and not feel a thrill. Perhaps nobody ever quite outlives the feeling of surprise he felt when he first saw a flying machine leave the ground."

A flip around London: At Cricklewood Aerodome, you sit with nine other passengers and a pilot in a Handley-Page bomber just like the one that took General McEwen to India. The plane, twenty feet high and sixty-five feet long, with a six-hour supply of petrol, a full load of luggage (mostly mechanics' tools in case of emergency), two 350-horsepower Rolls-Royce engines, and its human cargo, weighs nearly seven tons. There is a stiff thirty-mile-an-hour wind blowing head on. The pilot, Lieutenant Colonel Douglas, has received the usual warnings from the Air Ministry: no flying low or stunting over towns or seashore resorts or over any houses or tall buildings; no flying low in the vicinity of ammunition depots (an unnecessary warning for your pilot, you hope) or over telephone and telegraph wires, and no "buzzing" of grazing animals or roads frequented by horses or traffic.

You crawl under the machine—the propellers are already whirling—and clamber up into the body into your natty but comfortable little seat. A Boy Scout brings you a cap and goggles, and the plane starts to waddle ungracefully across the ground. It turns, seemingly headed back to the hangars to waddle some more, but instead there comes an unexpected feeling of buoyancy and the earth drops away slowly. You skim just over the tops of the trees in the nearby park and now the earth is falling away more quickly, and suddenly the city below looks like an artist's rendition of a model town with severe, straight highways and silver ribbons of river and intricate patterns of red suburban houses. With the vast blue of the distance and the white veil of clouds above, what you notice most is that there is none of the usual uproar from the city up here; on the other hand, the noise of the propellers precludes any witty or profound observations between passengers. The gusts of wind are like a gentle electric shock against your body.

Without warning the plane banks and the city below is perched on the edge of a chasm and the river is running from top to bottom and you wonder if London will fall off the precipice and sink into the sea forever. It is an extraordinarily disorienting sensation. Then the pilot rights the plane and you ascend to two thousand feet, and with the exultation you understand why men and women risk their lives in such a venture. You recall that a government spokesman recently confirmed that, statistically speaking, one would have to fly about 180,000 miles on short flights such as this before one would meet with an accident, but it was just two days ago that three fliers went down in the Channel off the coast by Dungeness when their engines failed and they were forced to make a landing in the sea; they stayed alive for hours, but no one knew where they were and so they drowned and their bodies floated toward shore near Littlestone. The Hythe fishermen would not fetch them out of the water because their superstitions forbade any contact with dead bodies in the sea. Now the green geometric designs on the ground are growing larger and larger; only a small bump, and an easy landing. The plane lumbers toward the hanger.

Jules Vedrines was going down.

Easter Monday, April 21. Wearing his French lieutenant's uniform, for he was on an official mission, Vedrines had left the military airport at Villacoublay, just outside Paris, at 6:20 that morning in the same big bombing plane he had planned to fly on a raid over Berlin just before the Armistice came. Now he was carrying a government mail packet and a passenger—a mechanic—and was bound for Rome on the nonstop flight he had spoken of with such enthusiasm on the day he landed on the roof of the Galeries Lafayette.

At 10:30, one of his engines stopped. He was over Saint Rambert d'Albon, about fifty miles south of Lyon, over the orchards and opulent farmlands along the banks of the Rhône River. Once before—in 1912—Vedrines had suffered a crash, while on a flight from Douai to Madrid, and had survived a fractured skull. Now he sought a safe place for an emergency landing. He saw a large clover field below and to the left. Vedrines guided the plane as it dropped faster and faster like a stone.

Two farmers had noticed something odd about the plane flying overhead; one of its propellers was standing still, clearly visible even to their untrained eyes from the ground. They ran to where the plane came down and found the wreckage of the machine and the bodies of two men tangled among a mass of vines. Death had come instantly. The farmers saw the mail packet in the debris. The bodies were taken to a hangar.

Easter Monday, Camp Mills, New York.

ARRIVED IN CAMP MILLS EASTER AFTERNOON. HAVE BEEN EATING PIE AND ICE CREAM EVER SINCE. WIRE ME HERE USUAL ADDRESS. HOPE TO BE IN FUNSTON SOON. NEW YORK GAVE US A GRAND WELCOME. GOD'S COUNTRY SURE LOOKS GOOD. HARRY.

Captain Harry S Truman was home. It had been a rough crossing, he later told Bess, in fact the most miserable ten days he had spent during the whole war. "We had a fine boat, brand new and never used before, but she was empty except for our baggage and ourselves and she did some rolling. I am not a good sailor and you can guess the harrowing details. Of course I could get no sympathy." Even his own men laughed at him, Truman said. He claimed he had lost about twenty pounds ("and I can afford to lose it"), but promptly gained much of it back by spending his first four days in New York eating real honest-to-goodness American chow.

The city had given them a marvelous reception: the mayor's boat welcomed them, the YMCA provided chocolate, the Knights of Columbus gave out cigarettes, the Red Cross distributed homemade cakes, and the Salvation Army passed around chocolate Easter eggs and offered to send free telegrams to loved ones and/or relatives. After disembarking at Pier One in Hoboken, the doughboys were taken to Camp Mills and given baths and plenty of new clothes; then they made the rounds of the canteens and free shows. "I'll bet ten barrels wouldn't hold the ice cream consumed that first evening," Truman bragged. Several days later, Captain Truman wrote, "my Dago barber gave me an Italian dinner at his sister's house

... yards and yards of spaghetti, chicken and dumplings, rabbit and peas and all the trimmings. I nearly foundered myself. Hope to see you soon and make up for lost time. Sincerely, I love you. . . ."

Harry left Camp Mills on April 30 and arrived home on June 1.

In Ireland, the bloody cycle of rebel attacks and government reprisals started to spin out of control. Even such a routine act as setting the hands of a clock could cost a man his life. At 11:00 P.M. on March 29, J. C. Milling, the resident magistrate at Westport, County Mayo, stood up and, taking a light with him, went from the drawing room of his home into the dining room to advance the clock there to daylight savings time. The blinds had been drawn in the room he left; they were not drawn in the room he entered. Four shots shattered the window. Milling dropped the light and sank to the floor. He struggled back to the drawing room and collapsed as his wife ran in. The next day he died of a bullet wound in the abdomen. The coroner's jury declared in its verdict that Milling had been "foully murdered by bullets fired at him by some person or persons unknown." The government promptly declared the district of Westport a military area; less than a week later, a young man was arrested when British soldiers found a rifle buried at the back of his house just outside of town.

Visiting hours at the Limerick workhouse hospital ran from one to three o'clock on Sunday afternoons. One of the prisoner-patients kept there was Robert J. Byrne, a Sinn Feiner who had gone on a hunger strike after receiving a sentence of twelve months' imprisonment with hard labor. At two-thirty on the afternoon of April 6, twenty to thirty men rushed into the hospital during visiting time, shot and killed one constable, shot another in the spine, tied up the warder and several policemen and dragged them into the operating theater, and fled with Byrne in a donkey cart. In the melee, however, Byrne had been shot twice—once in the back and once in the neck. He died later that evening. Police arrested the men and women in the house where Byrne's body was found. Following a meeting at the Viceregal Lodge in Dublin, Lieutenant-General Sir Frederick Shaw, commander-in-chief of British forces in Ireland, proclaimed Limerick a special military area.

By April 12, County Mayo and the cities and counties of Cork, Kerry, Roscommon, and Tipperary had all been proclaimed in a state of disturbance, requiring additional police protection. The residents of Limerick promptly declared a general strike in protest of the harsh military rule imposed upon them. The city was in a virtual state of siege, under martial law, with British troops in full battle dress in the streets, and barbed-wire entanglements at every bridge (no civilians could cross without a special permit from the military authorities). Machine guns were stationed at strategic points, and armored cars patrolled every part of the city.

In Dublin, the Dail Eireann recently had held another public session and formally elected Eamon De Valera as the new president of the Irish Republic. The number of deputies in attendance had increased since the January meetings, owing to the escape of another twenty prisoners from Mountjoy Prison (one of the Irish MPs who escaped left a gently mocking note saying that he had found the prison a wee bit too uncomfortable and hence had been compelled to take his leave before his time was up), and the subsequent face-saving decision by the British government to release all the rest of the Sinn Fein political prisoners before it was embarrassed by more jailbreaks.

The Dail proceeded as if the Irish Republican government were a living political organization ready to take over the administration of the country. "We shall conduct ourselves towards them [the British] in such a way as will make it clear to the world that we acknowledge no right of theirs," De Valera proclaimed. (In a more philosophical moment, he added that "A Chinn Chomhairle agus a lucht na Dala, an chead rud ata orm a dheanamh na cursai na hAireachta do chur os bhur gcomhair," and who was there to argue with him?)

Father O'Flanagan, perhaps the most famous Sinn Fein priest, urged the Dail to move forward from its propaganda efforts to the more difficult task of organizing the national strength of Ireland, concentrating always on the one overriding objective of expelling the enemy's forces from the island. Michael Collins, the newly elected Minister of Finance and, more important, the Director of Intelligence and guiding genius behind the rapid growth of the rebel commando movement, wrote to his sister (a nun in an English convent) on April 13: "The week which has passed has been a busy one for us—perhaps it has been an historical one for very often we are actors in events that have very much more meaning and consequence than we realise. At any rate—permanent or not, consequence-full or not—last week did, I feel, mark the inception of something new. The elected representatives of the people have definitely turned their backs on the old order and the developments are sure to be interesting. . . . At home we go from success to success in our own guerrilla way. . . ."

Lloyd George's government was not sure what to do except pour in more troops. By the end of April there were some 44,000 British soldiers preserving the King's rule in Ireland. In the sarcastic view of one of the few Irish nationalists who still chose to sit in the House of Commons, the

Cabinet's policy reflected nothing more than the "traditional English hatred of imagination and utter lack of vision of British politicians." Lloyd George himself seemed to notice no discrepancy between his government's actions in Ireland and his personal (and no doubt sincere) elation at the newly won independence of small nations in Central and Eastern Europe. The most remarkable spectacle of the Peace Conference, he told a kindred audience of Welshmen in March, "is the sight of little nations that have been buried for centuries, that have been hidden under the *debris* of tyranny, out of sight, and everybody thought they had been done for ever. But there has been a resurrection. One after the other appeared before the judgment seat of the nations, to give an account of the wrongs from which they have suffered in the past, to ask for redress. It is a wonderful sight."

A less wonderful sight for British eyes was the Irish-American delegation making the rounds of the hotels in Paris, in search of official support for its mission. Appointed by the Irish Race Convention that had met in Philadelphia earlier in the year, the delegation consisted of Frank P. Walsh, former co-chairman (along with ex-President William Howard Taft) of the United States National War Labor Board, Michael J. Ryan, a prominent Philadelphia attorney, and Edward F. Dunne, former governor of Illinois. All of these men also had participated in the meeting with Wilson in New York just before the President returned to Paris, and now they were embarked on what Walsh grandiloquently described as "the most unique and beautiful adventure that men were ever privileged to undertake"—namely, a mission to the Peace Conference to ask that Ireland be granted the right of self-determination.

When they arrived in Paris on April 11, the delegates were met first by the Irish Republic's representative to the conference, one John O'Kelly (who bravely proclaimed from his hotel room that "the war will be carried into the enemy's camp and England will have brought home to her own doors in most unwelcome form vivid evidence of Irish antipathy to English rule"). O'Kelly warned Walsh that they would receive no more attention from the great powers in Paris than he had received already, but the Americans proceeded undaunted. Walsh did manage to see Wilson for a brief moment on April 18, and secured an interview the following day with Colonel House. (Wilson could not simply ignore Walsh. The administration had recently received a fresh reminder of the widespread support that the movement for Irish independence enjoyed in the United States: just before the Forty-third Congress ended, the House of Representatives had passed by a margin of 216 votes to 41 a resolution in favor of self-determination for Ireland.)

Wilson and House persuaded Lloyd George to grant passports to Walsh, Ryan, and Dunne to visit Ireland on a "non-political" mission. Apparently the Prime Minister permitted the tour in the belief that it would provide an opportunity to put the British case more favorably before the Irish-American community. In any event, the trip was a fiasco for both sides. The delegates, arriving in cars bedecked with flags of the United States and the Irish Republic, were welcomed in Dublin on the evening of May 3 by De Valera, Father O'Flanagan, and numerous members of the Dail. They attended Mass and did a bit of sightseeing. Then the British suffered another attack of the muddleheadedness that chronically afflicted them in the moist Irish climate.

The Lord Mayor of Dublin had planned a gala reception for Walsh and his fellow Irish-Americans at the Mansion House on the evening of Friday, May 9. At 5:25 that afternoon, an armored car and three trucks filled with British soldiers armed with machine guns and rifles with fixed bayonets arrived in Dawson Street. A large body of police joined them several minutes later, and the entire gang cordoned off all the streets in the area. They had received a tip that some of the Sinn Fein deputies who had recently taken their departure from British hospitality prematurely by climbing the walls of Mountjoy Prison would be present at the gathering, and so scores of soldiers poured into the Mansion House to search for the renegades. The deputies, of course, were nowhere to be found, having fled by a prearranged escape route. After a brief conference with Walsh and the outraged Lord Mayor, the British commander called off his troops. It was, incidentally, the last public meeting the Dail would dare to hold for several years.

Following close upon the heels of this inspired British version of a Keystone Kops routine, Walsh and company decided to visit Westport. As they approached the district, accompanied by Father O'Flanagan and other prominent Sinn Feiners, they encountered a barricade set up by British troops, complete with armored cars drawn across the road, and a large force of police armed with carbines. Walsh asked why they could not proceed into Westport. The military officer in charge replied that he had received orders to keep them out. But the Prime Minister had told them they could visit every part of Ireland, Walsh insisted, and they all possessed valid passports; besides, he said, his family came from Westport and he wished to visit the ancestral home. The British commander remained unmoved. Meanwhile, a crowd had gathered, urging the Americans on; in reply, a short-tempered English Tommy ripped an American flag with his bayonet. The delegates returned to Castlebar.

When they got back to Paris, Walsh and his friends found that because of their flagrant association with revolutionary elements in Ireland, Lloyd George had decided not to grant them an interview after all. The entire incident had further strained Anglo-American relations on the one issue that had the greatest potential to create a serious rift between the two nations. The *Manchester Guardian* decided that the British military's actions in Dublin and at Westport had been "silly and undignified." "Perhaps, however," the *Guardian* concluded, "it was felt that the experience of our American visitors would be incomplete unless they were permitted to see the futile and ridiculous as well as the unconstitutional aspect of Irish government. In that case it was really very considerate of the military authorities to arrange in swift succession two such typical displays."

And the violence continued. At Collinstown Aerodome, four miles outside of Dublin, fifty masked men carried out an early-morning raid for weapons and made off with over seventy-five rifles and 1,800 rounds of ammunition. The British responded by promptly firing without warning several hundred Irishmen who had been working at the aerodome. At the Knocklong railway station in County Limerick, a half-dozen armed men rushed a train compartment and rescued a Sinn Fein prisoner, killing two constables in the process. Police conducted an exhaustive search for the culprits throughout the Glen of Aberlow, using airplanes, military cars, and motorcycles to cover virtually every inch of ground and search every house in the district. The son of a Sinn Fein MP was arrested, and the shops of several other Dublin Sinn Feiners were sacked, but that was all. At the inquest, the jury declared that the constables' deaths had been caused by bullets fired by persons unknown, and impudently took the occasion to blame the British government for the crime, calling upon Whitehall to cease arresting respectable people, and urging it to put into effect President Wilson's point on self-determination for all small countries such as Ireland.

After returning to Paris, the Walsh delegation received a bizarre communication from a slightly unconventional—even for Ireland—Irish writer temporarily residing in Zurich, Switzerland. For some months past, James Joyce had been pursuing a libel suit that he had recently dropped, but for which he was now being charged court costs and damages totaling 179 francs. Convinced that the judge's verdict against him represented an attack upon the virtue of true art by the philistine forces of organized civic iniquity, Joyce wrote to nearly everyone he could think of who might be willing to rescue a persecuted expatriate Irishman in distress.

As he awaited some response to his plaintive inquiries, Joyce betook himself to Locarno for a holiday, where he heard the story of a Baroness St. Leger, a maker of dolls, who lived out on the Isola da Brissago. The baroness had a reputation for giving outlandish entertainments and had—so the legend went—buried seven husbands (more or less), thereby earning the sobriquet of Circe, or "the Siren." She also had hung paintings of scenes from the *Odyssey* on the walls of her house. Since he was at that time struggling to complete *Ulysses* ("It is as difficult for me to write it as for my readers to read it"), Joyce asked if he could make Circe's acquaintance and view the pictures himself. The baroness agreed. It turned out to be a wasted trip; Joyce found the paintings disappointing and uninspired. He listened politely as the baroness recounted for him the erotic story of a life of considerable dissipation, but Joyce found it all too outlandish for his purposes. "A writer," he later told a friend, "should never write about the extraordinary. That is for the journalist." (Unfortunately, Joyce gave no guidelines to historians on such matters.)

The Siren had nothing on Henri Landru. According to police information, ten women and one boy had visited this modern Bluebeard at his villa at Gambais on the borders of the Rambouillet Forest just south of Paris; none had ever been seen again.

All the missing women were between forty and fifty years of age, most of them widows, all with excellent reputations. Apparently they had met Landru (a swindler and confidence man with seven convictions in the past fifteen years) at various times over the past five years through matrimonial advertisements. After accepting his hospitality and living with him for some time, they had permitted him to take over their savings accounts and either sell their household goods or else move everything to his villa, since Paris, as Landru earnestly assured them, was not a safe place for valuables during the air raids. (One of Landru's sons had helped him move the furniture; apparently unaware of what was going on, he later claimed that he thought his father was in the antique business.) A number of the women had gone—one at a time—to live with Landru at his Gambais residence, which he had rented in 1912 under the name of Georges Dupont; the one-story villa, which also had two sheds and a large garden on the grounds, was almost entirely surrounded by walls. The nearest house was over five hundred yards away. The village cemetery was only a little farther down the road.

Landru seemed to be just the sort of man to attract lonely middle-aged women. A short, serious, dark-bearded, slightly awkward middle-aged man, his gentle manners and almost pathetically chivalrous demeanor—he loved to dress up like an eighteenth-century nobleman and give flowers to his mistresses—apparently aroused sympathy and affection in women who had not had their fair share of romance themselves. One of Landru's neighbors described him as "a very nice gentleman, but rather shabby." He also displayed some talent as a contortionist.

Official suspicions of Landru's activities were first aroused when a rural policeman noticed thick smoke and sparks coming from the chimney of Landru's villa for several consecutive nights during a stretch of warm spring weather. Checking with a number of Gambais residents, the police found that they, too, had on several occasions noticed a heavy, ghastly smelling smoke coming from the house. In fact, they believed that the appearance of the smoke coincided with the disappearance of each of the ladies who had visited Monsieur Landru. Investigators found eleven numbered dossiers in Landru's garage, each relating to a prospective bride (one of whom had a fifteen-year old son who also had vanished). In his pocket diaries Henri had written the name of each woman and some cryptic notes apparently referring to the purchase of train tickets; but where his entries showed that he had bought two tickets to stations near Gambais, time and again he had paid for only one return to Paris.

Facing a procession of indefatigable but frustrated investigators, Landru refused to answer any questions, replying simply, "I know nothing. Look." Gendarmes scoured the villa and grounds, but their first searches turned up only the dead bodies of three dogs and one cat (possibly the pets of two of the alleged victims) buried under a heap of leaves. The animals had been strangled with a cord. Landru retained the noted attorney Maître Moro-Giafferi to undertake his defense. Searching for more concrete evidence, the Paris police began studying the descriptions of all unidentified female corpses recovered from the Seine since 1914.

"Nobody is going to get all he wants." A prescient warning from Winston Churchill. "It is not a game of grab that we are playing, but a question of a peace that shall be a just peace, and a lasting peace. If this is achieved, individual disappointment will be forgotten in the general joy. If it is not achieved, a paper triumph for any country for the time being would be of no use at all." Easy for an Englishman to say.

Wednesday, April 16. Fiume: "a miserable Dalmatian fishing village," grumbled André Tardieu. A group of a half-dozen American experts sent a personal letter to Wilson urging him to reject Italy's claim to the coastal city. The Italians had no valid right to Fiume, the experts argued, and had only put forward their claim in a shameless effort to garner as much loot as possible to please their constituents at home. "If Italy gets Fiume as the price of supporting the League," wrote Charles Seymour, "she will have brought the League down to her level. . . . Better a League without Italy than a League based on Italian participation bought at a price." Here at last was a clear-cut case for the application of Wilsonian principles: "I think that the President never had such an opportunity in his career for striking a death blow to the discredited methods of Old World diplomacy."

Paderewski, still seeking Danzig, visited the Opéra and received a standing ovation from the audience. Harold Nicolson stood up grudgingly and noticed that the Premier's wife "looks like hell in orchids." (Mrs. Paderewski's hobby was raising chickens. At her Swiss chalet, where Paderewski used to relax between lengthy concert tours before the war, she maintained an extensive poultry farm.) Meanwhile, Mrs. Wilson was seen making numerous trips to the dressmakers of Paris for new spring and summer gowns. All fashion-conscious Americans were eagerly waiting to see what fresh styles she would bring home.

Thursday, April 17. Lloyd George returned to Paris and remarked that "England is much saner than this place. It is far too excited." The Prime Minister, observed one British reporter, dressed much better than he used to ("and is in point of fact immaculate"), but "still wears his hat over the bridge of his nose, carries his left shoulder rather lower than the right, and remembers everybody he ever knew." The Ham Fair, which formerly was known as the Old Iron Fair, opened in the French capital to the cries of vendors ready to sell their knickknacks and antiques at exorbitant prices to unwary foreigners ("*Fouillez, mes braves gens, fouillez*"). There were a million more people in Paris than in the years before the war, and hence a continuing shortage of housing and domestic servants.

Wartime regulations, still in force, required restaurants to close promptly at 9:30 P.M., earning Paris an unwanted reputation as "the only town where people go to bed early." One party at a cozy café was interrupted at 9:35 by the owner of the establishment, crying that the police were at the door. "We were assisted into our overcoats by shaking hands and gently shoved into the muddy street," complained one member of the evicted party. "A persistent, cold rain was falling. . . . The silence was interrupted only by the metallic sounds of shop fronts being pulled down. (Paris at night is a city of steel fire shutters.) The footpaths reflected the glimmer from the streetlamps, which blinked like eyes moistened with tears. Where to go? That was the question."

April 18. Good Friday. Wilson, Lloyd George, and Clemenceau met at the Ministry of War from 5:00 P.M. until 8:00 P.M. The Drafting Committee was hard at work drawing up a formal version of the peace treaty, even though a number of issues remained unresolved. Marshal Foch was asked to formulate plans detailing the military measures to be taken should the Germans refuse to sign the treaty. The other three American peace commissioners, Secretary of State Lansing, General Bliss, and Henry White sent Wilson a memorandum strongly opposing any grant of Italian sovereignty over Fiume. A depressed American correspondent admitted: "With every illusion of Paris shattered, I was never as unhappy but once, and that was when I was waiting to be operated on in Baltimore."

Saturday, April 19. The Council of Four gathered at Wilson's house at eleven o'clock in the morning. Orlando ("the smooth and silky Sicilian") put forth Italy's claims, first to Fiume (on the basis of self-determination, for everyone knew the city's population was overwhelmingly Italian; a recent census counted 19,684 Italians among a total population of 31,094), and then to Dalmatia and the islands off the coast (on the basis of Italy's need for strategically defensible frontiers). Wilson objected strongly to both demands. "The whole question," the President argued, "resolved itself into this: we were trying to make peace on an entirely new basis and to establish a new order of international relations. At every point the question had to be asked whether the lines of the settlement would square with the new order." The American people, he said—indeed, the people of the whole world—were disgusted with the old order, and would not put up any longer with governments that supported it. Wilson turned to indicate his colleagues. "We sometimes spoke in these conversations as though we were masters of Europe. We were not so in reality. If the new order of ideas was not correctly interpreted a most tragical disservice would be done to the world." No, Italy could not have Fiume.

Clemenceau conceded that France and Britain had signed the secret Treaty of London with Italy in 1915—to induce Italy to join the Allies— and that the terms of that treaty clearly promised Dalmatia to Italy, but just as clearly gave Fiume to the new state of Croatia (Yugoslavia). Italy could either abide by the treaty or not, but it could not accept one clause and reject another within the same treaty. Clemenceau shook his heavy head and said it would be deplorable if his Italian friends should break away from their allies on such a pretext: "He believed they were making a great mistake. It would serve neither their own use nor the cause of civilisation. . . . Later on the cold and inevitable results would appear when Italy was alienated from her friends. He could not speak of such a matter without the gravest emotion." In an aside, the Tiger then warned Orlando that he,

Clemenceau, was not to be confused with the saintly King Stanislas of Poland "who, when he was bitten by a dog, not only pardoned the animal but gave him a chunk of cheese in addition." France would live up to its treaty pledge if Italy insisted, but at the same time Clemenceau would convey "a frank expression of my profound contempt" for Italy's request. And that was all the Tiger would give Orlando and Sonnino.

Lloyd George, heretofore silent, brandished a map that allotted the territories of the former Austro-Hungarian Empire according to the terms of the Treaty of London. Fiume was definitely supposed to be in Croatia. Even if one disregarded the treaty, the Peace Conference could hardly distort the principle of self-determination so grotesquely by applying it to an island of Italians in a small city encircled by a sea of Yugoslavs in the suburbs and surrounding countryside.

Orlando replied that perhaps he would accept Dalmatia on the basis of the Treaty of London and then discuss Fiume later. Wilson, one of whose Fourteen Points strongly condemned precisely the sort of secret and cynical bartering of peoples that the Treaty of London represented, refused to have anything to do with such a bargain, and made perfectly clear his willingness to go public with his opposition. The Italians in turn repeated their thinly veiled threats to withdraw from the conference if they did not get what they wanted. Lloyd George warned them that if they were not in Paris when the peace treaty was presented to the Germans (the ceremony was scheduled for Friday, April 25), Italy might forfeit all claims to compensation. After four hours of discussion (an unusually long session for these elderly gentlemen), the Council was adjourned until the following day. Wilson had a long conference with Clemenceau at the War Office later in the afternoon; then Clemenceau met with Marshal Foch immediately afterward.

The unexpectedly lengthy meeting had forced Lloyd George to cancel his plans to spend the afternoon touring the devastated areas with Frances Stevenson; they were to have stayed the night in Amiens, returning to Paris on Easter Sunday evening. "D. very tired after a heavy day," Frances told her diary, "& we dined very quietly & went to bed early. The Italian claims are giving a certain amount of trouble.... D. says they [the Italians] are making a mistake."

Meanwhile, Foch stirred up a hornet's nest for Clemenceau by informing a British reporter that "our peace must be a peace by victors, not of the vanquished." In other words, the venerable Marshal wished to cut Germany off at the Rhine. (This less than a week after Clemenceau and Wilson had finally reached an accord on the divisive and emotion-laden

Rhineland issue.) "Having reached the Rhine, we must stay there," Foch cried. "We must have a barrier. We must double-lock the door"—lock and bar it against the 70 million Germans who, Foch believed, had not yet abandoned their aggressive national proclivities.

Easter Sunday, April 20. A warm, nearly perfect Paris spring day. Lloyd George arranged for the meeting of the Four at Wilson's house to start at 10:00 A.M., so that he and Frances and several friends could have time for a drive before lunch and a picnic out of doors. Vast crowds thronged the cathedrals and boulevards. Charles Seymour went to the Madeleine to hear High Mass, including a Mozart kyrie and Sanctus. Spring winds frolicked with the skirts (slit up both sides) of girls on the streets of Paris. The *George Washington* arrived at Brest. Nicolson was in Britain on holiday.

Orlando began the Council meeting by reading a prepared statement in which he reaffirmed his position regarding Fiume. "I affirm here that if Fiume is not granted to Italy there will be among the Italian people a reaction of protest and of hatred so violent that it will give rise to the explosion of violent contrasts within a period that is more or less close." Nevertheless, to save the alliance, Orlando would refrain from an open break with his allies if the conference formally agreed to guarantee Italy everything she was to receive by the Treaty of London.

At first, no one spoke. The others waited for Wilson. Wilson sighed. (How could he make them understand?) Then the President, slowly, in his Southern drawl, announced that he found it incredible that Italy would take such a position. Without the United States' help, the Allies never would have won the war. (Clemenceau and Lloyd George nodded their assent.) America rejected secret treaties on principle and had no intention of endorsing this one, Wilson continued. Would Italy dare break the alliance over this issue and chance a resumption of war, now or in the near future? Orlando confessed that his heart was torn between the rights of Italy and the friendship of the Allies, but in the end he felt he must stand fast for his country's honor.

Lloyd George broke in and admitted that for once he could not see a path to a compromise solution. So, choosing the path of least resistance, he reaffirmed Britain's willingness to stand by its treaty obligations to Italy, the commitment already "honoured by Italy in blood, treasure, and sacrifice." Britain, he said, would support (albeit reluctantly) Italy's demands for the territories promised by the Treaty of London.

This display, however halfhearted, of British affection for Italy gave every appearance of overwhelming the sensitive soul of Signore Orlando. He began to gulp as if he were a child about to cry, then stood up and went to the window, leaned on the bar that ran across it, and put his head in his hands, weeping. He took out his handkerchief and wiped his eyes and tear-stained cheeks. (He was plainly visible to people standing in the road below, who thought wrongly that the other three were bullying him again.) Wilson got up and took Orlando's hand. The discussion moved on to the impending arrival of the German peace delegates. The weather turned cold in the afternoon.

Afterwards the British party went for a drive, lunched in the woods (Lloyd George spent the time expounding upon the virtues of taking one's meals in the open air), and went on to inspect a few deserted battlefields. "D. so sweet and in such good spirits," confided Frances Stevenson to her diary. The Prime Minister waited until the day was nearly over before telling his colleagues that the German government had sent a telegram announcing that their delegates would come to Paris only to receive the treaty and then take it back to Weimar for official discussion. The Council of Four had replied that they would not deal with mere messengers; the Germans must send plenipotentiaries empowered to sign the treaty on their own.

The Louvre finally had reopened and brought out some of the old masters—Raphael, Leonardo, Titian, Rubens—three or four paintings by each. The Venus de Milo was on display again. Picture postcards of French generals and famous personalities of the Peace Conference were on sale at kiosks along the Left Bank. Wilson spent the afternoon driving about Paris with his wife, interrupting his pleasure once for a brief conference with Clemenceau.

Monday, April 21. Lloyd George and Frances Stevenson began the day with a stroll to the Arc de Triomphe. The heavy iron chains and solid iron posts that had prevented traffic from going through the monument for so many years were due to be removed soon in preparation for the grand victory fête. "There is nothing to compare with these little walks with D.," wrote Frances, "when we unburden our hearts to each other and feel that we are about 10 years old." The German government agreed to send six plenipotentiary delegates, headed by Foreign Minister Count Brockdorff-Rantzau, to Paris, but they would not arrive until Tuesday, April 28. Wilson did not attend the Council meeting in the morning, but met instead with his experts for an hour at the Hôtel Crillon at noon, soliciting their opinions on a public statement he planned to make regarding Fiume.

The Council of Four—or rather Three, since Orlando did not appear this time—met in the afternoon at Wilson's residence ("The Little White House"). In the course of a rather rambling discussion, Clemenceau told

Lloyd George that he had never lost sleep over the abusive criticism of his foes, but that he had a great fear of making a fool of himself. Wilson said he felt the same way. "It is the same with me," Lloyd George admitted. "I never mind being abused, but if I feel that I have made a fool of myself I could kick myself out of bed." That evening, President and Mrs. Wilson, Balfour, and Lord and Lady Derby attended the opening of Sir Alfred Butt's new Palace Theatre in the Rue Mogador. After the playing of national anthems and much cheering, everyone settled down to enjoy the popular variety review *Hullo, Paris!*

Tuesday, April 22. There was a contest among the American soldiers and civilians at the Crillon to see who had the most useless job. One finalist was a doughboy who had been detailed to guard the hotel roof. Back and forth he strode between the chimneys, his fixed bayonet at the ready, watching to prevent the phone lines from being tapped or spies from being dropped from airplanes or balloons. Another who made the final cut was the expert on a certain European country; the expert had never been invited to attend a single Council meeting, not even to listen. But the winner was the Iowa private (an electrician before the war) whose job it was to stand at the hotel entrance and whirl the revolving door. Watching a bulky Secret Service agent try to time his leap into the doorway so as to avoid serious bodily harm, the private simply shook his head: "It would have been easier for that fellow to push the door himself than it was for him to figger out how fast I was going to swing it."

Clemenceau told an old American friend that he was getting sick and tired of the greedy jackals at the Peace Conference. "How I would like to retire into the Vendée and write a sequel to my philosophy of history. . . . But just because 'je faisais la guerre,' they tell me I must make the peace. I hope we shall be successful, but it is going to be difficult, most difficult."

Wednesday, April 23. A leisurely breakfast in bed was out of fashion; ever since Lloyd George began inviting friends in for informal business meetings during his morning repast, more and more British and American delegates had taken up the custom of working breakfasts. The usual fare included bacon, eggs, kippers, toast, and coffee.

The Three (no Orlando again) met at Wilson's house at 11:00 A.M. Orlando had sent Lloyd George a memorandum with the latest Italian proposal for Fiume. It offered no basis for further negotiations. The Three decided to ask the Italians if they intended to meet Brockdorff-Rantzau and his entourage when the Germans arrived at Versailles on Tuesday next.

Then Wilson made what some critics consider his biggest mistake of the conference. He issued a public message, typed on his own battered old typewriter, explaining his reasons for opposing the cession of Fiume and Dalmatia to Italy. (Later, when the storm broke over his head, Wilson would maintain steadfastly that his statement had been intended primarily for consumption in the United States, to let American voters—especially the Italian-American community—know why he would not accede to Italy's demands.) Perhaps the cheers of his triumphal January procession were still cascading through his memory; perhaps the faces of the people who had looked at him imploringly as he rode through the streets of Rome, Milan, Genoa, and Turin still obsessed his exhausted mind.

At any rate, it was the sort of principled statement many of his supporters had been urging him to make for months against the alleged rapaciousness of Britain and France. Having lost those opportunities, he now struck the blow against Italy. Fiume, the President said, was a vital outlet to the sea for the brave but struggling new Slavic states formed from the moribund remains of the Austro-Hungarian Empire. Certainly Italy need fear no aggression from this quarter, for each of the new Balkan states would accept a limitation of armaments under the supervision of the League, which would make offensive military operations on their part impossible. Besides, the Four had already given Italy the Brenner Pass, the German-speaking Tyrol, and Trieste. The conference had to settle *this* question in accordance with the new spirit abroad throughout the world: "To assign Fiume to Italy would be to create the feeling that we had deliberately put the port upon which all these Slav countries chiefly depend for their access to the Mediterranean in the hands of a Power of which it did not form an integral part, and whose sovereignty, if set up there, must inevitably seem foreign, not domestic, or identified with the commercial and industrial life of the regions which the port must serve."

He may have made a logical case, but by issuing the statement at this time and in this manner, Wilson created the widespread and not entirely incorrect impression that he was going over Orlando's head and appealing directly to the Italian people to repudiate their government's claims. The Italian delegation immediately announced that "as a result of the declaration by President Wilson on the Adriatic question the Italian delegates have decided to leave Paris to-morrow." From Rome, 208 senators and 322 deputies of the Italian Parliament sent a telegram to Orlando assuring him of the full support of the nation. Italian authorities advised the thousands of American soldiers on leave in Rome not to wear their uniforms in public. The free trips to the Adriatic for American reporters, arranged by the Italian government, were canceled.

Lloyd George returned to his flat around seven o'clock that evening, and announced, "Well, the fat is in the fire at last!" He said it was too bad Wilson had not given him more time to try to arrange a compromise. "The President read the statement again to-night," Lloyd George told Riddell. "He is very pleased with it. Old Clemenceau said it was very good. He is an old dog. He had heard it all before and so had I. The position is very serious." At dinner, the discussion turned to Wilson. "I am one of the few people who think him honest," Lloyd George said. "I think he has a genuine love of liberty and is genuinely anxious to improve the position of the under-dog. He is against the domination of the rich. Occassionally he has to deviate for political reasons, but every politician has to do that." At ten, a telegram arrived from Orlando announcing his imminent departure. "Good riddance," Nicolson decided. Lloyd George sent back an invitation to breakfast; Orlando declined.

Thursday, April 24. American army authorities decided that every man should be given three days' leave in Paris before sailing for home. An estimated two thousand doughboys a day were on sightseeing tours in the city.

Lloyd George, agitated and pale, went to see Orlando to try to persuade him to stay. "I am taking this unusual step," the Welshman confided, "because I wish to call your attention to the fact that the situation with which we are confronted is grave, very grave. It is not only critical for Italy, it is critical for all of us. All Europe needs America. Without America Europe cannot continue to live. I have come to tell you that Wilson, as always obstinate, is greatly irritated now." Orlando remained unmoved. The Three met later that morning. Orlando joined them for the afternoon session at Lloyd George's flat (automobiles surrounding the house, Wilson's Secret Service agents in the hallway), and bade them farewell. He would return, he said, after having consulted with his Parliament on this most distressing matter: "The people must decide when he explained the situation to them." Lloyd George came out of the meeting to look for some ice cream; he settled for tea. Before Orlando left, Lloyd George handed him a letter from Clemenceau and himself, asking Italy to reconsider its policy, if for no other reason than to maintain a united Allied front in the face of the German delegates who would be arriving shortly. Wilson, Lloyd George, and Clemenceau all assured Orlando of their fondness for him. "You may be still fonder of me next week," the Sicilian replied, "when you may well be confronted with D'Annunzio in my place." From London, a group of British labor leaders, including Bob Smilie, the charismatic Miners' Federation president, sent Wilson a telegram congratulating him "on your magnificent declaration for peace based on the fourteen points. We are certain that the Italian workers will associate themselves with the international workers in supporting you."

The Italian delegation left its rooms at the Hôtel Edouard VII at 7:45 that evening, Orlando vowing as he got into his car that even if the Peace Conference gave Italy everything it wanted, "we would go just the same. President Wilson said that our Government did not represent Italy. I must go and face Parliament, to see if he is right or if he makes a big mistake." It required eighteen cars to take everyone and all the baggage to the train station. Hundreds of Italians shouted encouraging cheers to the departing delegates and cried out, "*Abasso Veelson.*" The train left for Rome, where Prince Faisal was at that moment being entertained by King Victor Emmanuel and the Pope.

Wilson issued a statement in the United States denying that he had promised a defensive treaty or alliance to France.

Lloyd George took off for a vacation in the French countryside. Balfour lounged in the lobby of the Hôtel Majestic, wearing a flannel shirt, a frock coat, gray flannel trousers, and brown tennis shoes: a compromise between tennis and the Council of Ten.

French authorities stepped up their preparations for the German peace delegates. They were building a six-foot-high barrier extending from the Hôtel des Reservoirs, where the Germans would be housed, to the Trianon Palace, where the preliminary ceremonies would be held. A guard of soldiers would patrol the nearby park, from which the public would be excluded. The Hall of Mirrors at Versailles was being refurbished by an army of marble polishers, upholsterers, and cabinetmakers. Carpets worth one million dollars were being installed, and tapestries and furniture from the reign of Louis XIV had just arrived from government storehouses. The table upon which the final treaty would be signed was already finished: eighty-one feet long, fashioned of oak and pine, with a green cloth top.

American audiences would not be able to see Mlle. Alice Dolysia in *Friendly Enemies* after all. The popular French musical comedy star had her pen poised, ready to sign the contract, when someone mentioned the impending start of prohibition in the land of the free. "What?" she shouted in disbelief. "Do you mean that I can't drink a glass of wine with my dinner as I have been doing all my life?" The producer reluctantly admitted that such was indeed the case. "Then you may tear up the contract," Dolysia said. And so they did.

22

"He shall mightily roar

upon his habitation;

he shall give a shout,

as they that tread the grapes . . ."

Ernest Hemingway, erstwhile American canteen officer in Italy, had far less use than Harry Truman for the sacred soil of the good old U.S.A. From his home in Oak Park, Illinois, Hemingway advised a former comrade-in-arms who was now ensconced in Sicily to avoid coming to America "as long as you can help it. That is from one who knoweth. I'm patriotic and willing to die for this great and glorious nation. But I hate like the deuce to live in it." He had begun to send stories off to *The Saturday Evening Post*, but as yet he had received no answers. He was also trying to save money for the woman of his dreams. Or so he said. His parents wanted him to go the University of Wisconsin, where, he admitted, there lived "some very priceless femmes."

Hemingway was obsessed by his memories of Italy. Terribly homesick, he could hardly bring himself to write about it:

WHEN I THINK OF OLD TAORMINA BY MOONLIGHT AND YOU AND ME, A LITTLE ILLUMINATED SOME TIMES, BUT ALWAYS JUST PLEASANTLY SO, STROLLING THROUGH THAT GREAT OLD PLACE AND THE MOON PATH ON THE SEA AND AETNA FUMING AWAY AND THE BLACK SHADOWS AND THE MOONLIGHT CUTTING DOWN THE STAIRWAY BACK OF THE VILLA. OH JIM IT MAKES ME SO DAMN SICK TO BE THERE, I GO OVER TO THE CAMOUFLAGED BOOK CASE IN MY ROOM AND POUR OUT A VERY STIFF TALL ONE AND ADD THE CONVENTIONAL AMOUNT OF AQUA AND SET IT BY MY TYPEWRITER, SLANG FOR MILL, BATTERED KEY BOARD, ETC. . . . I DRINK TO YOU.

Italy had been cold in April. Cynics claimed that Orlando and Sonnino were making all the fuss about Fiume just to give people something to think of besides the strikes and the weather. Right now the tram operators in Rome were doing their part by striking, but, perversely, only on Sundays, to cause the maximum inconvenience to their fellow countrymen, who were in the habit of taking long excursions into the country on weekends. Still, one could travel by train as far as the delightful and sparkling Monte Gennaro, where the ground was covered with blue and yellow anemones, brilliant cyclamens, and, if one went higher up, yellow orchids and tiny pansies.

As Orlando's train rolled through Italy in an impressive albeit slightly hysterical reprise of Wilson's January progress, every stop, every speech sealed Orlando's political fate. The people wanted to hear the Prime Minister defy the pusillanimous Allies who would steal Italy's victory from her; and so he did. At Genoa, where the train stopped at fifteen minutes before midnight on April 26, Orlando stood at a window and promised the immense crowd surrounding the station that "Italy, great and victorious, will not renounce her claims." Imposing outbursts of patriotic fervor already had shaken Rome: processions carrying the flags of Italy, Fiume, and Dalmatia made their way from the Piazza Colonna to the Piazza del Capitolio, the marchers showered with cheers of support from balconies, windows, and pavements. The proprietor of the Wilson Caffe in Rome had to cover the "Wilson" on his sign with a tarpaulin. Peasants who had hung Wilson's picture on their walls next to the Virgin Mary tore down the blasphemous image of the apostate American. Prince Colonna, the mayor of Rome, urged the city to revoke the honorary citizenship bestowed in January upon "that false prophet Wilson." Every government office closed; two thousand municipalities wired Sonnino demanding that he stand firm; D'Annunzio insisted that "I was never prouder of being Italian. Of all my splendid hours this surely is the most solemn. There is nothing greater in the world than this. Italy remaining fearlessly alone against everybody, with her strength increased by sacrifice. Italy is great and pure, and I say to her, 'don't surrender an inch.' . . . The Allies are iniquitous, ungrateful, and forgetful." Fiume was full of posters showing Wilson wearing an iron-spiked German helmet; the residents vowed to blow up their beloved town rather than have it "fall into the hands of their hereditary enemies and implacable persecutors."

All of this did Orlando absolutely no good at all. He and Sonnino had helped whip Italy into a frenzy over Fiume, but what were they going to do if—or, more likely, when—the Allies refused to give them the city? Orlando had never deemed Fiume a vital Italian economic or strategic interest. Its only value to his country, he had admitted to Colonel House,

was as a symbol to flag-wavers such as D'Annunzio, to prove that Italy had not fought the war in vain. ("We did not go into this war for ideals," one candid Italian official confirmed. "We joined the Allies in order to get control of the Adriatic.") Without Fiume, Orlando could not maintain himself in office against the nationalist reaction. And so he sought any means at hand to obtain it. But Wilson refused to budge, and, the Italians having left Paris, there was no other pressure Orlando could bring to bear upon the President.

So, while the frenzied celebration that greeted his arrival in Rome may have gratified Orlando's ego, it must have seemed a bittersweet triumph. At the train station, he asked the multitude who met him "whether the Government and the Italian delegation have faithfully interpreted the thought and will of the Italian people." A unanimous shout of "*Si!*" Then a brief and defiant speech as Orlando proclaimed, "I am with you, a brother amongst brothers, and also a chief who asks to obey and follow the will of the people. It may be that we will find ourselves alone, but Italy must be united and have a single will. Italy will not perish." "Down with President Wilson!" roared the mob; then, to make it clear that this was only a personal vendetta, it chanted, "Up with the United States!" Orlando's driver then tried to start the car that would take the Prime Minister to the Quirinal Palace just a short distance away, but within several minutes the crowd had packed so tightly around the vehicle that it was unable to move. The engine stalled. For over an hour Orlando stood in the open-topped car in the Strada Nazionale as flowers rained upon his head and the men around him vied for the honor of dragging the car forward. Meanwhile, the rest of the procession had already reached the Quirinal without him, and so the King and Queen and the Crown Prince and the Duke of Genoa all came out on the balcony to acknowledge the people's applause. When Orlando finally arrived at the palace (two hours after he had started out), the royal family all came out again to appear beside him.

Several days later, thousands stormed the Parliament building to hear Orlando's speech; by 9:00 A.M. the chamber was already full and the doors closed, leaving a crowd outside cheering and singing in the rain. Aged senators who had not attended a session in years came to see the show. At two o'clock, Orlando stood and began his speech amid a thunderous standing ovation and shouts of "Viva Fiume! Annexation! Annexation!" After all the rhetoric was over, the legislature voted 382 to 40 to stand solidly behind the government's policy. Orlando had his mandate, and more. On May 4, D'Annunzio stood in the Augusteum—every seat taken, every spot of standing room filled with women in mourning black or bright colors and men in khaki with honor ribbons over the heart, the flags of Italy and Fiume and Trieste draped everywhere—and hypnotized an audience of thousands. The poet stood on the stage in a simple soldier's uniform, extolling the spirit of the patriot Cavour, spitting on the foreign financiers, reverently calling back the men who had died for Italy. And there with the dead he paused, black eyes in a chalk-white face, waiting in the total quiet. Then, arms raised to heaven: "Do you not hear? Listen! Do you not hear the tramp of an army on the march? The dead are coming more swiftly than the living! And all along their route they find the footprints of those who went before them!" He paused, motionless. And the weight of the men coming from beyond descended over the audience and the spell was complete. A minute passed, and the people suddenly leaped to their feet as one and vowed to follow wherever the poet led. Later that day, D'Annunzio was taken ill with fever.

News reports from Rome had stated that Orlando and Sonnino would never return to Paris until the Allies were "officially disposed to confer with Italy on a new basis." On May 6, the Prime Minister and the Foreign Minister boarded a train for France. Mussolini laughed derisively at the powerless and humiliated old men.

At Burlington House in Piccadilly, Professor Young of the Royal Military Academy gave a lecture on modern explosives to the Society of Engineers. The accompanying demonstration, an intrepid observer testified, "kept his listeners in a constant state of apprehension." Young stood surrounded by coils of instantaneous fuse, specimens of high explosives of varying destructive power, and assorted detonators of tremendous disruptive force. First he touched off guncotton and dynamite; then, with the aid of a hammer and anvil, he conducted in a distressingly casual manner an experiment with blasting gelatin (which he said was at the head of the class, explosively speaking), until the building was filled with the echoes of a series of deafening roars. The last word in modern detonators, Young concluded, was fulminate of mercury: "it is very dangerous to handle." He thereupon promptly proceeded to hammer some of it on the anvil. The uproar was, well, the last word for the evening.

Walter Lippmann, a regular contributor to *The New Republic*, wrote to Bernard Berenson at the latter's villa outside of Florence. President Wilson's recent visit to the United States, Lippmann had decided, "did not help him much, and he left a lot of carefully minded people with the impression that he was not quite sure what his own product meant.

Frankly, people are very much annoyed at being neglected. . . . The main interest here, however, is not what's going on in Paris at all,—the people are shivering in their boots over Bolshevism, and they are far more scared of Lenin than they ever were of the Kaiser. We seem to be the most frightened lot of victors that the world ever saw. . . ."

On Monday, April 28, a small package bearing the inscription NOVELTY, SAMPLE, GIMBEL BROS., NEW YORK arrived at the office of Bolshevik-bashing Mayor Ole Hanson of Seattle. The mayor was out of town, so one of Hanson's clerks decided to open the package. Luckily for him, he opened it upside down. Nothing happened.

On April 29 a similar package arrived at 789 Peachtree Street, the residence of former United States Senator Thomas W. Hardwick of Georgia. It had been mailed from New York to Hardwick's home in Sandersville and forwarded to his Atlanta address. Ethel Williams, the senator's Negro maid, opened the package. It blew off both her hands. Standing nearby, the senator's wife was cut by flying bits of glass from a broken window.

On April 30 a package addressed to "Mr. K. M. Landis" was delivered to the chambers of Federal Judge Kenesaw Mountain Landis in Chicago. Landis was hearing cases in Rockford, Illinois, that day and the package lay on his desk for hours, undisturbed.

The same day a package arrived at the home of Representative John L. Burnett in Gadsden, Alabama. Burnett tried to open it, but the lid stuck.

At 2:00 A.M. on May 1, worn out from his evening's work at the United States Post Office at 765 East 183rd Street in the Bronx, Charles Kaplan bought an early edition of a morning newspaper and fell asleep shortly after boarding a Third Avenue subway train at the 34th Street station. At 59th Street he woke up and began to scan the paper indifferently. Kaplan was still half asleep as he read of the explosion at Senator Hardwick's home. By the time he finished the article, all the cobwebs were gone. At 99th Street he jumped out of the train and ran downstairs and then up to the opposite platform just in time to grab an approaching train heading south. Kaplan paced the car nervously until he reached 34th Street once again. He leaped out and ran up to the street and caught a passing crosstown trolley car and ran into the post office building and into the office of his night supervisor, Henry Meier. "For the love of Mike," Kaplan gasped, waving the newspaper spasmodically in the air. "See, see, see!" He shoved the paper at Meier. "Hardwick—bomb—explosion—packages." Meier told Kaplan to calm down and explain himself. So Kaplan dragged him to another part of the main floor and showed him the sixteen packages he had put aside earlier that day for lack of sufficient postage. All bore the same markings as the bombs already delivered.

Investigators later determined that all the packages had been mailed from postal boxes on the West Side of New York City between 20th and 36th streets. They had been sent at different times—those bound for distant cities mailed earliest—apparently all timed to arrive on the socialist holiday of May 1; obviously the sender underestimated the efficiency of the postal service in getting some of the bombs to their destinations ahead of schedule. The packages were eight inches long, two inches wide, and two inches deep (about the size of a biscuit package, someone said), covered in a light manila-colored wrapper. (A Gimbel's representative said that the wrappers were obviously counterfeit; the store didn't use such high-quality paper to mail its merchandise.) On one side there was the return address:

GIMBEL BROS.

32nd St.   Broadway   33rd Street
                 New York City

On another side was printed the word NOVELTY in a box, and below that was a printed drawing of a man with an alpenstock in his hand and a pack on his back. To the right was the typed address of the recipient. On a third side, red letters an inch high read SAMPLE, apparently to arouse curiosity and guarantee that the packages would be opened with alacrity. It took bomb-disposal experts six and a half hours to dismantle one of the insidious devices. Inside was a tapered glass bottle designed to break when the package was opened, allowing a powerful acid to trickle through cotton wadding into three tiny fulminating caps, thereby setting off the three sticks of dynamite firmly wedged into place underneath.

The sixteen packages Kaplan had set aside all bore sufficient stamps for parcel-post delivery, but someone had made the mistake of putting red paper seals on the ends to secure the wrappers before mailing them. That made them first-class mail, and that meant they needed additional postage. The men who would have received these bombs but for this simple twist of fate included Supreme Court Justice Oliver Wendell Holmes, Attorney General A. Mitchell Palmer, Mayor John Hylan of New York, John D. Rockefeller, J. P. Morgan, Secretary of Labor William B. Wilson, and Commissioner of Immigration Anthony Caminetti. One more bomb was found before the day was over. Realizing that Senator Lee Overman (chairman of the Senate committee investigating radical activities in America) might be a potential target, postal workers in Salisbury, North Carolina, decided to search the pile of wedding presents waiting to be delivered to Overman's two daughters, who had been married in a joint ceremony at the senator's home on the night of April 30. And sure enough, there lay a small package bearing the notorious Gimbel Brothers label.

All of the potential targets had played prominent roles in recent months in suppressing radical dissent, deporting aliens, or introducing legislation to restrict immigration (except Rockefeller and Morgan, who apparently had found a place on the list solely because of their stature as representatives of the capitalist plutocracy). Detectives thus focused their search upon foreign-born radicals, but after a week of intensive investigation their only clue was that the typewriter used by the perpetrator(s) had a defective *k* and a *w* out of alignment. No one could be sure whether more bombs were already out there somewhere, making their way through the postal system, and so for a while every package (candy, Kodak film, legislative manuals) addressed to anyone of prominence was scrutinized with rigorous care. Eventually seventeen more bombs were found, but never the bomber (or bombers). Meanwhile, the incident gave men like Hanson—who was out touring America, capitalizing on his new-found fame and drumming up grassroots support for a presidential bid in 1920—more ammunition for their anti-Red crusade. "I trust Washington will buck up and clean up and either hang or incarcerate for life all the anarchists in the country," Ole defiantly declared to a cheering Topeka audience. "If the Government doesn't clean them up I will. I'll give up my mayorship and start through the country. We will hold meetings and have hanging places."

23

"And seek the

peace of the city . . ."

"Any spring is a time of overturn," wrote John Dos Passos long afterward,

BUT THEN LENIN WAS ALIVE, THE SEATTLE GENERAL STRIKE HAD SEEMED
THE BEGINNING OF THE FLOOD INSTEAD OF THE BEGINNING OF THE EBB,
AMERICANS IN PARIS WERE GROGGY WITH THEATRE AND PAINTING AND
MUSIC; PICASSO WAS TO REBUILD THE EYE, STRAVINSKI WAS CRAMMING
THE RUSSIAN STEPPES INTO OUR EARS, CURRENTS OF ENERGY SEEMED
BREAKING OUT EVERYWHERE AS YOUNG GUYS CLIMBED OUT OF THEIR
UNIFORMS, IMPERIAL AMERICA WAS ALL SHINY WITH THE NEW IDEA OF
THE RITZ, IN EVERY DIRECTION THE COUNTRIES OF THE WORLD STRETCHED
OUT STARVING AND ANGRY, READY FOR ANYTHING TURBULENT AND NEW,
WHENEVER YOU WENT TO THE MOVIES YOU SAW CHARLIE CHAPLIN.

New York in the spring of 1919 "had all the iridescence of the beginning
of the world. The returning troops marched up Fifth Avenue and girls
were instinctively drawn East and North toward them—this was the greatest nation and there was gala in the air." So F. Scott Fitzgerald would
remember his beloved "lost city" thirteen years later. These spring days of
1919 were, he came to believe, "the four most impressionable months of
my life," though not all the impressions were joyous. His writing career
apparently going nowhere, his long-distance love affair with Zelda perhaps
slipping away, Fitzgerald once climbed out on a window ledge of the
Yale-Princeton Club on Vanderbilt Avenue and threatened to jump off.
Accustomed to such melodramatic posturing, none of his friends bothered
to ask him to come back in.

   The days passed in a sort of alcoholic daze; a Sunday morning might find
Scott with a friend staggering home, rolling empty champagne bottles
down Fifth Avenue.

As I hovered ghost-like in the Plaza Red Room of a Saturday afternoon, or went to lush and liquid garden parties in the East Sixties or tippled with Princetonians in the Biltmore Bar I was haunted always by my other life—my drab room in the Bronx, my square foot of the subway, my fixation upon the day's letter from Alabama—would it come and what would it say?—my shabby suits, my poverty, and love. While my friends were launching decently into life I had muscled my inadequate bark into midstream. The gilded youth circling around young Constance Bennett in the Club de Vingt, the classmates in the Yale-Princeton club whooping up our first after-the-war reunion, the atmosphere of the millionaire's houses that I sometimes frequented—these things were empty for me. . . . I had a girl. I wandered through the town of 127th Street, resenting its vibrant life; or else I bought cheap theatre seats at Gray's drugstore and tried to lose myself for a few hours in my old passion for Broadway. I was a failure—mediocre at advertising work and unable to get started as a writer. Hating the city, I got roaring, weeping drunk on my last penny and went home. . . .

New York: Brigadier General Douglas MacArthur, wearing a raccoon coat and a hand-knitted scarf, was the first man down the gangplank when the troopship *Leviathan* docked in New York harbor on April 25. His men, the much-decorated veterans of the famous Rainbow Division, had decided to forgo the honor of a parade down Fifth Avenue, but still the great man took umbrage at the lack of public reception upon his arrival: "Amid a silence that hurt—with no one, not even the children, to see us—we marched off the dock, to be scattered to the four winds—a sad, gloomy end to the Rainbow. There was no welcome for fighting men . . . no one even seemed to have heard of the war." There was, however, a ball in his honor at the Waldorf-Astoria; MacArthur wore full dress uniform—including spurs—to the celebration that evening. "I was dancing," MacArthur recalled later, "and the maitre d'hotel came over to me. He said it was against the rules to wear spurs on the dance floor. I said, 'Do you know who I am?' He said, 'Yes, General.' And I took my lady and we walked off the dance floor, and I never set foot in that place again." (Nevertheless, MacArthur did eventually return to the Waldorf, taking up more or less permanent residence in the hotel after President and ex-doughboy Harry Truman removed him from command in Korea.) On June 12, MacArthur became the youngest man ever to serve as superintendent of the United States

Military Academy at West Point. He was living with his mother at the time.

New York: Anais Nin had just celebrated her sixteenth birthday. Strolling down Broadway early on a chilly evening, the perceptive young writer saw, much to her amusement,

ALL THOSE LADIES WALKING WITH LITTLE TINY STEPS. THEY ALMOST ALL LOOKED LIKE PAINTED DOLLS. EACH WAS SURROUNDED BY SEVERAL MEN AND THEY LOOKED TERRIBLY ARTIFICIAL. THE MORE EXTRAVAGANTLY THEY WERE DRESSED, THE MORE ATTENTION THEY GOT FROM THE OPPOSITE SEX, WHICH WOULD STOP WALKING TO ADMIRE THEM. SOME OF THE MEN STROLL AROUND ON THE STREET CORNERS AND STAND THERE TO WATCH THE PEOPLE GO BY. THEN WHEN A "LADY" COMES ALONG, THEY FOLLOW HER. IT WAS ALL VERY FUNNY AND VERY DUMB AT THE SAME TIME . . . EACH ONE PLAYING HIS ROLE ON BROADWAY AND WALKING THE WAY PEOPLE WALK IN A BIG CITY LIKE NEW YORK, AIMLESSLY AND GOING NOWHERE, MADE UP FOR THE PLAY AND DISGUISED FOR THE ETERNAL MASQUERADE.

New York: At the Chu Chin Chow Ball, held at the Hotel des Artistes, five hundred women—actresses, models, society belles—vied for the title of "The Girl of the Golden Apple," the most beautiful woman in America. A panel of noted artists, including Charles Dana Gibson and Chandler Christy, judged the contestants as they slinked coyly past the reviewing stand. Unanimously the judges selected Mrs. Edith Hyde Robbins, daughter of the famous painter Raymond Hyde; this evening she was wearing a Persian costume with a silver silk bodice and pantaloons adorned with ropes of pearls. As Christy knelt to present her with a golden apple on a jeweled silver server, all Mrs. Robbins could say was, "I don't deserve it. There are lots of girls here prettier than I am." Nevertheless, she began to write a newspaper advice column for aspiring beauties, providing them with words of wisdom such as, "Develop the decorative sense. By this, I don't mean wear things and do things just because they are beautiful in themselves, but because they are becoming to you."

To the Irish novelist Shaw Desmond, the city was "like a giant grapefruit. It is segregated into water-tight compartments. It is not a city—but a city of cities. The men and women I meet each day know nothing of their fellows. My waiter, Alphonse, doesn't know that a few hundred yards away there is a block of streets around Sixty-first where only black men live. The Irishman I met yesterday in the subway had never been in Wall Street. Chinatown is only a name to the information bureau. And I am told that only 65 per cent of New Yorkers speak American."

* * *

Paris in the spring of 1919: black American soldiers strutted about Paris with their wives or girlfriends, the women dressed in smart spring frocks, their heads tied up in brilliant bandannas. Jazz bands flourished; "to see a jazz band in all its glory," said the *Manchester Guardian*, "you must go to Paris. . . . They play with the sustained vigour possible only to darkies, and if you give them plenty of champagne, as you are expected to do, they begin to sing as well as play, then to shout, and then to yell. They are immensely popular with Parisians, who, say the resident Americans, spoil them completely and have raised their taste in cigars to preposterous standards."

Paris was a city "already in the disintegration of victory." Having accumulated a well-meaning if rather undistinguished record of military service, John Dos Passos was granted permission by the army to continue his studies (ostensibly in anthropology) at the Sorbonne. In fact he spent most of his time reworking the manuscript for "Seven Times Round the Walls of Jericho," but also found time to hear and see and begin to understand the startling wave of artistic revolution coursing through the city: the tubercular and drug-addicted Amedeo Modigliani, whose sculptures and paintings were heavily influenced by primitive African masks, and who had only one more year to live; Pablo Picasso, preparing to embark upon the tempestuous artistic voyage that would take him to *Guernica* nearly two decades hence. "This, too," wrote Dos Passos, "was the Paris of new schools of music. Satie presided over Les Six. There was Poulenc, and Milhaud. Stravinsky was beginning to be heard. The Diaghilev ballet was promoting a synthesis of all the arts." But life in the Paris of the Peace Conference also had made Dos Passos a cynical young man, just as events in Berlin had chilled the naïve American enthusiasm of Ben Hecht. Watching the Big Three or Four and their deputies wrangling over territories day after day and sending their armies north and south and east to make the world safe for capitalism while the world seemed to be going to hell convinced Dos Passos that "life in the militarized industrialized nations had become a chamber of horrors and we believed that plain men, the underdogs we rubbed shoulders with, were not such a bad lot as they might be."

"But Winter lingering chills the lap of May": the words of Oliver Goldsmith a century and a half before found a new resting place in 1919.

May Day: Thursday, May 1. In Paris, a cold, heavy drizzle chilled the entire day. Everyone—except the undertakers (*les croquemorts*, in Parisian slang)—had gone on strike for at least part of the day, and so the city appeared deserted in the early morning—"like Edinburgh on Sunday," Nicolson grumbled. Americans in the Hôtel Crillon used candles to light their rooms and did without hot water or elevators; they had been ordered to keep their cars off the streets, but a few could not pass up a once-in-a-lifetime opportunity, and soon a pair of long gray official peace delegation cars went roaring down the Rue Lafayette at full speed. The street vendors had deserted their stations, save for the women with baskets full of lilies of the valley (and red rosettes as a sideline).

Paris was flooded with placards announcing the reasons for the one-day general strike: "I strike to demand, first, the eight-hour day; second, total amnesty; third, rapid demobilization; and fourth, a just peace and disarmament. I strike to protest against, first, intervention in Russia; second, income taxes on wages; third, martial law; and fourth, the censorship." Paris still suffered from a far higher cost of living than either London or New York, and French industry had not yet begun to recover from the dislocations caused by the war. The sight of the Peace Conference, of which so much had been expected, seemingly slipping back into nothing more than a cynical effort to restore the discredited old order of economic privilege convinced the French working class that its sacrifices in the war had, in the end, brought no gains. Clemenceau, the father of victory, was the man who presided over the reactionary swing back to 1914, and so the bitter and disillusioned crowds that gathered in the streets this day mercilessly hooted the Premier, who, many remembered, had himself been arrested and convicted for radical activities on a similar occasion in 1870.

Labor officials had planned a massive peaceful demonstration for the Place de la Concorde. Fearing that the radical element among the workers would seek to turn the proceedings into the opening volley of a small-scale revolution, Clemenceau's government forbade the demonstration. The Socialist and trade union leaders decided to go ahead with their plans anyway. Nothing much happened until after two o'clock in the afternoon (Parisians would not lightly forgo the pleasures of their customary *dejeuner à la fourchette*), when a crowd of nearly twenty thousand working men and women and boys (including a curious Dos Passos), wearing cloth caps and little rosettes of red ribbon in their buttonholes, began to assemble outside the columns of the Madeleine. Meanwhile the rain fell more steadily. About an hour later, the demonstrators set off down the Rue Royale, singing the "Internationale." As they passed by the Hôtel Crillon they shouted, *"Vive Wilson!"* although hardly anyone bothered to go to Wilson's residence to express such sentiments in person. All the approaches to the Place de la

Concorde had been sealed off by the government. Provincial troops were stationed around the outside of the cordon, and cavalry and police on the inside. As the crowd pressed against the steel-helmeted soldiers who were still wearing their weather-worn wartime uniforms (*"Vive le poilu!"* the people cried), they were permitted to pass through without incident.

But the cavalry was less forbearing. Although no shots were fired, the troops on horseback set out to disperse the procession with the flat sides of their sabers; men, women, and children dropped to the ground bleeding. Charles Seymour, watching the procession, found it an impressive and frightening spectacle: "I shall never forget the sight of that black crowd coming down the street waving its red flags at the moment it ran into the troops. It might have been Petrograd, or the Revolution of 1848, which started close to here and in very much the same manner." The police displayed even less sympathy than the dragoons, clubbing with rifle butts or hammering with their fists and then kicking anyone who came within reach. Another member of the American peace delegation, James T. Shotwell, a Columbia University history professor serving as one of Wilson's expert advisers, stepped out of the Crillon and saw "a man with a bad cut down the back of his head and across his neck. He was having his hand bandaged as well, having had two fingers cut off.... This cutting had been done not by the soldiers but by the police, who are skilled in breaking up crowds but who individually strike one as cowardly and provocative. They lose their nerve and kick men when they are down and in general act as though they were afraid of the crowd." A red flag was torn from a demonstrator. A fire brigade appeared and sent a foul-smelling chemical spray into the melee. Horses trampled those who fell. Dos Passos and a friend ducked into a café just as the owner was barring the door. The workers struck back with stones and pieces of cast iron and an occasional revolver shot. For the rest of the afternoon the Americans who ventured out of the Crillon saw the city's streets become a scene of complete chaos. American Red Cross ambulances sped from one avenue to another, picking up hundreds of wounded, both police and strikers. A blind veteran stood in an abandoned car and pleaded for peace. Umbrellas, hats, coats, and broken clubs littered the streets along with the wounded and an occasional dark bloodstain. Several Socialist deputies were injured. One worker was killed near the Opéra, another fatally wounded while on his way home, shot by a demonstrator's gun. The police reported 428 wounded, a dozen seriously.

At the end of the day, James Shotwell walked over to the Pont Alexandre III: "There was an army kitchen serving out coffee to the troops there, and one of the soldiers with whom I had a little chat told me that they had been ordered out from Versailles at two in the morning. He didn't mind it for himself, but his horse had had nothing to eat all day. He told me that the cavalry was drawn from central France. He was from Lyons and it didn't take much questioning to see that he had little sympathy with the police."

Undoubtedly it would all have been much worse if the weather had not been so bad; as one perceptive observer noted, "only a duck can demonstrate successfully in a deluge of rain." The Socialists blamed the government for turning a perfectly peaceful demonstration into a contest of strength with the police; the government replied that it had nipped an incipient revolution in the bud. And in the end, nothing had been gained by anyone. "The trade unionists, who wanted the demonstration, half succeeded. M. Clemenceau, who did not want it, also half succeeded, and more than a little hate has been engendered." Around midnight, Shotwell looked out over the roof of the Crillon and "saw against the sky the dark figure of the sentry posted there, walking up and down with his gun on his shoulder, and it gave a queer sense of a beleaguered city, in the midst of the unsettled social forces of Europe today."

On the morning of May 2, Mrs. Wilson went for a walk through the streets, accompanied only by her secretary. The pavements had been scrubbed and swept clean of debris and blood. She walked down the Place de la Concorde and crossed the Rue Royale. No sign of the skirmishes remained.

One day later, a nineteen-year-old boy named Raymond Cornillon was arrested for loitering outside Clemenceau's house. Police searched his pockets and found a stiletto, a series of anarchist pamphlets, and a rolled-up black flag bearing the inscription COMMUNIST AND ANARCHIST FEDERATION OF THE SEINE. Cornillon acknowledged that he was an acquaintance of Emil Cottin and that he, too, had intended to attack Clemenceau. But, he added, "I did not wish to kill him, for I am not a murderer. I wished only to attract attention."

May Day in the United States. In Cleveland, a socialist procession was disrupted by soldiers who tore down a red flag and demanded that several veterans marching with the socialists remove either their army uniforms or the red bands they wore over their chests. The veterans refused, and a full-scale battle ensued between the marchers and the troops. Mounted police, aided by army tanks and trucks, tried to restore order by running down the socialists. Patrolmen pursued demonstrators into hotel lobbies to bludgeon them. One man was killed when a detective fired blindly into the melee. Several hundred people—including clergymen attending an ecumenical convention—were clubbed by police or trampled in the chaos.

In New York, soldiers and sailors stormed the newly opened offices of the Socialist newspaper *The Call*, smashed the equipment and furniture, and threw the employees out of windows and doorways into the street and then beat them while police stood and watched. (The attack was eerily reminiscent of the arditi assault upon the offices of *Avanti!* in Milan, proving that the war had accomplished—if nothing else—the brutalization of so many of the survivors from every nation's army.) In Boston, a clash between police and demonstrators produced scores of injuries and more arrests.

May Day, Manchester, England. The annual parade of donkeys, first sponsored in 1881 by the Band of Kindness, was held in the yard of the Albert Street police station. Prizes totaling fifteen pounds were awarded by the Lady Mayoress to the owners whose donkeys bore evidence of the greatest care and humane treatment. There were thirty-eight entries this year, all gaily decorated with flowers and ribbons. The animal who won first prize was generally considered to be an outstanding representative of his kind.

May Day, Berlin. The early-morning streets lay dreary and deserted. In the days of the Kaiser, the workers had turned this day into a demonstration of millions of men and women marching behind enthusiastic bands, chanting slogans of the millennium to come when the people finally ruled. A smug businessman looked out over the capital of a nation ruled by the Majority Socialists in 1919 and gave a mocking laugh: "Now that time has come and the masses rule. And see: There are no parades, no bands and no singing. The dream is gone and the reality is here. Workingmen shoot down workingmen. The armies under Herr Noske, the people's general, attack armies under Max Levien, another people's general." Besides, Noske had forbidden any demonstrations this day, and no one challenged Noske any longer. Silence also reigned because the city was awaiting the final verdict from Paris: "One does not celebrate the crack of doom," spat a bitter radical Socialist leader. In the evening, people wandered aimlessly through the streets to the music of barrel organs because there was nothing else to do.

May Day, Budapest. Determined that the people should at least remember what had been tried, Béla Kun decreed that this would be a red-letter day in the history of the Soviet Republic of Hungary. Thousands of Red Army soldiers marched to patriotic and socialistic tunes through the streets; men, women, and girls stood on the sidewalks waving red banners. Street cars were painted red, autombiles were red, the railway stations, even the lampposts were splashed with red paint. Twenty-foot-high plaster casts of Lenin and Karl Marx towered over the parade. After dark, hundreds of crimson electric lights shone down on the continuing revels. "The most remarkable feature of the situation now prevailing," reported an Associated Press correspondent, "is the fact that there is absolutely no disorder. There have been relatively few executions, although the jails are almost bursting with prisoners."

May Day, Munich. Noske's troops surrounded the city. Within, the Red Army had dissolved in a mad panic of fear, thousands of soldiers throwing away their weapons and red armbands. The Communist government was rapidly disintegrating in an endless round of acrimonious disputes. Levien had fled. Toller had gone into hiding. Outside the city, the Freikorps commanders agreed to delay their triumphal entrance for twenty-four hours to allow the radicals their final little May Day celebrations.

That plan changed when word arrived that the Communists in the city had massacred ten hostages—eight members of the reactionary, anti-Semitic Thule Society and two captured officers of the German army—in the Luitpold Gymnasium. The bodies reportedly had been mutilated and castrated. Enraged, the Freikorps sadists were turned loose to exact vengeance, and vengeance they gladly took. They encountered virtually no resistance, but that mattered little to them. Some soldiers enjoyed themselves in devising more sophisticated and satisfying means for torturing "Spartacist whores"; others were content to rape any girl suspected of Communist sympathies. The workingmen of Munich, of course, were beaten and shot merely for looking like a Spartacist or a Jew. Better to kill the innocent, the orders read, than let the guilty go free. Leviné was nowhere to be found as yet, and so the conquerors amused themselves with lesser prey like Gustav Landauer, Minister of Education. Landauer was beaten in the face with rifle butts and shot in the head and then shot in the stomach, and when he still lived he was kicked to death and his body left to rot in a courtyard.

For nearly a week the city bled. At first the gravediggers could not keep up with the pace, and so more than 250 bodies were stored temporarily in the Medical Institute until the city's cemeteries were ready to receive them. Finally the Freikorps boys, caught up in a wave of playful savagery, went a little too far. They blasted their way into a peaceful meeting of a small

Catholic society, mistaking it for a gathering of revolutionaries, and murdered twenty-one innocent civilians. Orders were issued not to do this sort of thing again, and by May 14 the troops were marching out of the city and back to Prussia. The Socialist government of Adolf Hoffmann returned and took up again the twisted reins of power.

The army left behind a city encased in morbid fears and haunted by grotesque nightmares and psychotic voices. It also left behind an informer plucked from the local garrison, a former painter, who seemed to his army superiors to be more high-strung and nervous than normal, but who was told to remain in Munich to undergo further political indoctrination so as to improve his usefulness for the future.

Amid all the sadness and savagery of the spring, there came an occasional reminder of the joyous and indomitable spirit that still flourished in spite of everything. At a hospital for blinded American soldiers, Helen Keller appeared and told the men of the struggle that lay before them: "The hardest part is the loss of one's personal liberty. I know I will appreciate in the next life the eyesight I never had in this. It is a difficult task, being blind, a violent shock which throws you from solid earth down the dark waters of the years." Yet she knew they could win, for she had won despite being deaf as well. "You must remember that being blind is just another handicap to overcome, just as you took another few yards of ground, another trench in your struggle over there."

Then she danced with the men, danced with an easy, lovely grace, the light shining in her blue eyes; she danced waltzes and fox-trots and two-steps, pulling each man along with her in turn and ignoring the frequent collisions, because nothing could spoil the joy of the dance. One soldier who had lost both his sight and an arm knew the best time since he had returned home: "Miss Keller was so sparkling and full of wit you just felt what a fool you'd been to think there was anything wrong with you. She's so at ease and so sure of herself that she makes you sure."

24

"Ye shall not be unpunished . . ."

There was, unhappily, one more opportunity for the sword to fulfill its assigned task that spring. Halfway around the world from Munich, Japanese police and soldiers were slaughtering thousands of Koreans who dared to demand independence for their land. Japan had been exploiting the Korean peninsula unofficially since 1875; in 1905 the Korean Imperial Government had been dissolved, and under the terms of a treaty signed (under duress) on August 23, 1910, Korea agreed formally to join the Empire of Japan. The Korean Emperor was deprived of all temporal power, and the office of Japanese Governor-General was established as supreme authority in the land.

Admittedly, Japanese rule provided Korea with certain material benefits: new railways, roads, and ports, modernized agriculture, industrial development, and towns transformed into twentieth-century cities. At the same time, however, Japan installed an extraordinarily autocratic political system, dominated by the Governor-General, from whom there was no appeal; and the ancient Korean culture was almost totally suppressed. Korean literature was burned, the study of Korean history banned, newspapers suppressed, and teachers forced to conduct their classes only in Japanese. Such foreign domination was intolerable to an ancient and proud people, and in early 1919 Korean refugees in Asia and the United States formed several republican governments-in-exile and appointed delegates to the Peace Conference to see if self-determination did not apply also to the Orient.

To attract worldwide attention to their demands, Korean patriots launched the March 1 Movement, a series of declarations and popular demonstrations in which hundreds of thousands of Koreans marched and shouted *"Tongnip manse!"* "Long live Korean independence!" It caught the Japanese government completely by surprise. The widespread uprising lasted nearly three months, and was not suppressed until six infantry battalions and thirteen thousand police were turned loose to quell the disorders. And quell them they did. American observers, including missionary teachers—a number of whom were arrested for encouraging such notions as human dignity and independence in their Korean pupils—told of young men being dragged away and flogged, schoolgirls tied by their hair to telegraph poles and beaten horribly and then thrown into jail, Korean Christians tied to crosses and tortured. One missionary reported that "old men and women and children have been indiscriminately abused, beaten, cut down with swords, struck by firemen with pikes, officially flogged at the police station, pierced by bayonets. . . ." A story that may not have been apocryphal told of a young woman who defiantly held the Korean manifesto of independence high in the air, until a Japanese soldier swung his sword and cut off her hand; she picked up the document and held it high with her other hand, and so he cut that one off, too. The Japanese government admitted that an overzealous commander had herded twenty-nine Koreans into a church, sealed the doors and windows, and then set the building afire. Official reports confirmed 7,509 Koreans killed, 15,961 injured, and 46,948 arrested, although the true figures were almost certainly much higher.

Japanese officials shook their heads and said that their Korean subjects somehow appeared to have confused "self-determination" with "independence." "Japan's position," announced a government spokesman, "is that of any well-meaning householder deeply interested in keeping quiet, clean immediate surroundings, and who is unfortunately disturbed by family brawls and incompetent sanitation of disorderly neighbors." But in the United States, Syngman Rhee, secretary of state of one of the provisional governments of Korea, insisted that his people were perfectly capable of ruling themselves as they had done throughout the many, many centuries. Japan, he vowed, could never win: "With all of her mighty army, she can never reduce the 20 million Koreans to a permanent serfdom. Our fair warning to her is that she give up the dangerous policy of Prussian militarism and adopt the modern principle of American democracy, which has almost encircled the entire earth."

Alas for Rhee and his compatriots, the Koreans received no satisfaction from the men at Paris. The U.S. State Department officially declared the revolt an internal matter for Japan to handle. Still, the orgy of violence created widespread revulsion in America. Joined with the reports of clashes between Japanese and American troops guarding the Trans-Siberian Railway in easternmost Russia, and the anti-American riots in Tokyo (fomented in part by Japanese militarists who feared an expanded American presence in the Far East—first the Yankees had interfered in China by issuing the Open Door notes, then they had conquered the Philippines and assimilated Hawaii, and now they had encouraged Korea to revolt), the Korean massacres further strained the already fragile relations between Washington and Tokyo.

As the Peace Conference entered the final stage of its labors and prepared to bring forth the long-awaited treaty (six months after the Armistice), the weather once again cast a miserable, chilling pall over everyone and everything in Paris. By this time it had become obvious that the crushing complexity of the world's problems had once again evaded any attempt to find a definitive solution. There would be no millennium, no Promised Land or earthly paradise—only more gray skies and a few dimly recognized landmarks to guide the way through the mists. The cold rain returned, calling forth a sea of black umbrellas. Still preoccupied with the threat to an exhausted world from Soviet Russia, Winston Churchill walked with the American economic expert Bernard Baruch through the Bois de Boulogne on a dark Paris day with a blustery wind rising. Suddenly Churchill stopped and raised his walking stick; pointing to the ominous clouds rolling in low over the eastern horizon, his sharp voice rumbled, "Russia! Russia! That's where the weather is coming from!"

After the Italians left, the Japanese decided the time was right to press their claims to the German economic concessions in Shantung Province and Kiaochow Bay in northern China. Japan had insisted upon nothing else during the entire conference; now Baron Makino and his colleagues threatened to withdraw (and they were perfectly serious about it) unless they were accorded the rights and holdings—primarily railroad and mining properties—to which they were entitled by treaties with China, Britain, and France, and that their armies had captured and still held. With Italy gone and the German delegates on their way to receive the treaty, Wilson, Lloyd George, and Clemenceau could not afford to have another major power depart and make a shambles of whatever remained of Allied unity. And so they gave Japan what it wanted.

In early May, the conference formally approved the amended League of Nations Covenant, complete with the notorious Monroe Doctrine reservation. The question of indemnities was fudged and handed over to an inter-Allied commission for further study when emotions were cooler; but an ill-advised "war guilt" clause was inserted as a preamble to the reparations section of the treaty, asserting that Germany and her allies were responsible for causing all the losses of the war. William Bullitt went around Paris grousing about the failure to make peace with Lenin. The Kaiser was ordered to stand trial for his war crimes, but no one cared to make a formal request to Holland for extradition, so William stayed behind the walls of Amerongen Castle. At a dinner given in his honor at the Crillon, Premier Paderewski confided that he had not even touched a piano since 1916; entranced with the Polish pianist, Charles Seymour was surprised to notice "the benevolence of his eyes, not expecting that in a temperamental genius. I was also surprised to see that his hands are large, not tapering, the fingers not very long and very thick. They are obviously very muscular."

Orlando was on his way back to Paris (Lloyd George and Clemenceau had threatened to scrap the Treaty of London altogether if Italy failed to return to the conference immediately), but Italian troops were landing along the Dalmatian coast and at strategic points in Asia Minor, a development looked upon with considerable suspicion by both Wilson and Lloyd George. James Shotwell attended a birthday party complete with cake and candles for the eleven-year-old daughter of one of his colleagues: "From where I could see her, the child's face in the Crillon gave me a full realization of how dull and dried up a lot of old fogies we have been sitting around here without a chance to have so much as a look into a child's face." Wilson, his wife, and Admiral Grayson went for an automobile ride in the Fontainebleau forest, stopping to admire the Hôtel Barbizon. Britain prepared to receive a mandate to govern Palestine, and an inter-Allied commission was assigned to study the question of boundaries for Syria.

"I have done my best," Clemenceau told a French journalist. "I think it is a good peace."

On May 6, the conference held one of its rare plenary sessions—this one in secret—to hear a summary of the terms of the treaty (the complete text was not yet ready) that would be presented to Germany the next day. André Tardieu read the summary; China protested the Shantung decision; an Italian representative made a reservation over any terms not acceptable to his government (i.e., Fiume, which in fact was not officially assigned to anyone in the treaty); and Marshal Foch stood up and protested that the fifteen-year occupation of the Rhine bridgeheads was insufficient for French security. None of that made any difference, but after it was all over, Clemenceau rolled up to Foch in a rage. "And why, Monsieur le Marechal," the Tiger demanded, "did you choose to make such a scene in public?" Foch threw out his chest and twirled his moustaches. "*C'est pour faire aise à ma conscience.*"

On the same day, Lloyd George and Wilson sent official notes to Clemenceau pledging immediate aid in the event of an unprovoked German attack upon France.

When T. E. Lawrence heard the peace terms, his mind flew back to the exultation he and his Arab brothers-in-arms had felt during the last days of the war, when they all believed they were fighting for a sublime if indefinable ideal. It was a deep, all-engulfing feeling shared by hundreds of thousands of men in other lands who had dared to dream, and who now shared Lawrence's anguish:

> WE WERE FOND TOGETHER BECAUSE OF THE SWEEP OF THE OPEN PLACES, THE TASTE OF WIDE WINDS, THE SUNLIGHT, AND THE HOPES IN WHICH WE WORKED. THE MORNING FRESHNESS OF THE WORLD-TO-BE INTOXICATED US. WE WERE WROUGHT UP WITH IDEAS INEXPRESSIBLE AND VAPOROUS, BUT TO BE FOUGHT FOR. WE LIVED MANY LIVES IN THOSE SWIRLING CAMPAIGNS, NEVER SPARING OURSELVES: YET WHEN WE ACHIEVED AND THE NEW WORLD DAWNED, THE OLD MEN CAME OUT AGAIN AND TOOK OUR VICTORY TO REMAKE IN THE LIKENESS OF THE FORMER WORLD THEY KNEW. YOUTH WOULD WIN, BUT HAD NOT YET LEARNED TO KEEP: AND WAS PITIABLY WEAK AGAINST AGE. WE STAMMERED THAT WE HAD WORKED FOR A NEW HEAVEN AND A NEW EARTH, AND THEY THANKED US KINDLY AND MADE THEIR PEACE.

The German delegation (six plenipotentiaries and a staff of approximately 150 aides) left Berlin on the afternoon of April 28. No cheering crowds marked their departure from the siding of a Potsdam station, no military bands played patriotic airs, no children offered flowers, no Ebert and no Scheidemann (and certainly no Noske) showed up, although there were a few movie cameras to record the lugubrious scene for posterity. The luggage van was locked and sealed. When the train passed Essen it became the responsibility of the French government, which took care to slow its progress so the passengers could get a long, close look at the devastated French countryside; the most audible expressions of grief from inside the train, however, came when the cars passed a group of German prisoners-of-war in their gray uniforms working in the fields.

At twilight that evening the train (its olive-green coaches still wearing the spread-eagle symbol of Prussian militarism) arrived at the little country station of Vaucresson, an out-of-the-way place on a little-used railway line in the woods outside of Versailles. A cold, hard rain fell. A few gas lamps burned cheerlessly on the single illuminated platform. The only witnesses were a few minor French officials, some detectives, and several dozen journalists and photographers. An incredulous voice came from a window of one of the coaches: "Can this be Versailles?" A tall, rigid, distinguished figure in a gray coat—the forty-nine-year-old German Foreign Minister, Count Ulrich von Brockdorff-Rantzau—descended, and the rest of the delegation followed him onto the platform. The prefect of the department of Seine-et-Oise gave a dignified bow and officially acknowledged the Germans' presence in France; the three-sentence speech had been carefully designed to strike just "the right touch of iciness in courtesy without overdoing it." Brockdorff-Rantzau, who recently had been ill and looked it, uttered a few diplomatic words in reply, and off the Germans walked, most of them forced to carry their own luggage, through the drizzle and a merciless bombardment of magnesium flares from the photographers, to the cars that would take them on the three-mile trip through the mud and darkness to their quarters in Versailles. They arrived at the huge, ugly Hôtel des Reservoirs (where Bismarck and his staff once lived) at 9:00 P.M. A blue-uniformed French soldier stood guard at the gateway.

The Germans had been under the impression that they would be presented with the treaty almost immediately upon their arrival, but on one pretext or another the Allies kept postponing the ceremony for over a week. This struck Brockdorff-Rantzau as a calculated insult (which it was in part, although inefficiency and last-minute squabbling among the hosts also played a role), and there was muttered talk about returning to Berlin. In the meantime the French authorities erected barricade fences of wood and wire around "the German quarter" in Versailles, enclosing the hotel, part of the nearby park, and the road to the Trianon Palace Hotel, where the ceremonies would be held. The official explanation was that the fence was needed to keep the Germans safe from attacks by war-crazed Frenchmen thirsting for revenge, but it also kept the German delegates from sneaking into the city and, not incidentally, made them feel like caged animals. "We have a feeling of imprisonment," wrote a German journalist accompanying the delegation, "particularly when the curious French people look through the park fence. The feeling of being in a concentration camp increases the picture." There was constantly a crowd lined up along the fence, watching the comings and goings of the people in and out of the stucco-fronted hotel, and the spectators wagered on which were German delegates and which were Allied visitors. ("He must be a German," sniffed one elderly Frenchwoman in settling an argument. "We don't have boots like that.")

Inside the hotel, which had once belonged to Madame de Pompadour, the Germans whiled away the hours playing billiards or card games under a portrait of Madame de Maintenon looking down from the wall with a cynical smile. Some of the delegates had brought their golf clubs, but French authorities refused to let them tee off. Time weighed heavily on everyone's hands, and there were occasional misunderstandings; one German secretary nearly caused a diplomatic incident when she ventured into a drugstore to buy tooth powder and was unceremoniously ejected; a pack of schoolboys stood outside the hotel chanting *"Vive Clemenceau!"*; and the Germans kept complaining that both the telephone connections and the direct telegraph lines from the Eiffel Tower to Berlin broke down far too frequently. (This was not, however, done deliberately to inconvenience the Germans; French telephone and telegraph service was notoriously bad, by far the worst in Western Europe.) Groups of Germans walked about aimlessly in the park, or sat under the Fountain of Neptune and spoke of politics. "Nobody knows what is doing," reported an American correspondent, "and one notes only the increasing nervousness of the French."

May 7. The fourth anniversary of the sinking of the *Lusitania,* and the day when the treaty would at last be presented to Germany. Lord Riddell wrote in his diary that "when I got up, I said to myself, 'This is going to be one of the most interesting days of my life.' And it was."

It was a marvelous day, the sort of gorgeous spring weather that seemed to have been made expressly to show off the splendors of the French countryside. At two o'clock in the afternoon, Riddell started for Versailles, driving through the Bois de Boulogne, past the golf course at St-Cloud where Wilson had spent New Year's morning, and on through the woods of Versailles: "There was nothing to show that this was a momentous day in the world's history. Then suddenly I heard behind me the insistent and prolonged note of a motor-horn. It was Clemenceau in his Rolls-Royce, driving to Versailles at fifty miles an hour, one gloved hand on each knee and 'a smile on the face of the Tiger' that made one feel that the drama was really beginning. He was gone in a flash."

At Versailles, too, it appeared to be just another day, except for the area around the vast Trianon. (The hotel was no stranger to distinguished visitors, having hosted meetings of the Allied Supreme Military Command during the war. Before 1914 it had been a fashionable holiday spot.) There the bustle of soldiers and spectators had begun, with cinema cameras whirring—Clemenceau had already arrived by the time Riddell got there, of course—and reporters taking up their stations in the cramped tents erected amid the shrubbery on the hotel grounds. (Clemenceau and Lloyd George had wanted to exclude journalists from the ceremony altogether, but Wilson insisted that a select group be admitted, and a threatened mass revolt by the correspondents at the conference finally persuaded Clemenceau to allow forty reporters inside.) Riddell needed three separate passes to get through the guard of sixty soldiers stationed outside the Trianon's doors, and then he walked down a long, cool corridor, through folding glass doors, and into the conference hall (actually the hotel restaurant on other, less ceremonious, occasions). Riddell saw the hall as "a coffee-room of a very, very high-class hotel, decorated in white throughout, with great windows opening on to beautiful gardens in which the trees stood dressed in their fresh Spring green." He stepped off the dimensions of the room while no one was watching, and found it to be about seventy-five feet square. There were four long, green baize-covered tables set up to form a rectangle, and in the area inside the quandrangle, surrounded, sat another smaller table reserved for the Germans. (It was deliberately set up to make the Germans feel like prisoners receiving sentence from a court of justice.) Around the walls ran an outer fringe of tables laid with red cloths for secretaries and minor officials. Sunshine poured in through the high windows that covered two walls; a third wall was covered with mirrors, and the fourth was painted white. The ceiling, too, was white. The reflected glare was dazzling and dizzying. The trees in the park outside swayed in the breeze.

At 2:20, servants laden with huge stacks of the printed terms of peace entered the room and distributed them around the tables, one copy to each delegation except the Germans; they would get theirs later. Five minutes later, Clemenceau and Pichon looked in to make sure everything was as it should be, and then retired to await Wilson's arrival. At 2:30 Lansing stuck his head in for a moment. Reporters found their assigned chairs, gilded and covered with red satin. The five German journalists allowed to view the proceedings looked around uneasily and began taking copious notes of the setting. Outside, Lloyd George and Balfour, Wilson (alone), and Premier Venizelos of Greece (whom everyone but the Italians agreed was one of the most capable men in Paris that spring) emerged from their cars in quick succession. Foch came at 2:40 and inspected the honor guard, drawn from the Chasseurs Alpins. The Germans arrived at virtually the same time as Foch, but entered by a side door, to avoid an embarrassing scene.

By 2:50, nearly all the representatives of the smaller nations had taken their places around the hollow rectangle. Nervous laughter echoed around the room as the tension sometimes broke through; the Japanese sat impassively as always. At 2:55, Clemenceau, Lloyd George, Wilson, and the

American delegation walked into the room together and moved informally across the brown carpet to their seats: oak chairs with cane seats and backs. There had been rumors that the Allied delegates would be in evening dress, but the traditional British dislike for evening wear during daylight hours and Clemenceau's personal hostility toward formal wear quashed that notion. Everyone seemed to have dressed as they liked: Clemenceau was arrayed in an ordinary morning coat; Wilson wore a dark suit with a gray tie, a white handkerchief spilling carelessly out of the breast pocket of his coat, and was one of the few to have brought a silk top hat (he never wore a bowler) to the proceedings; he had, of course, deposited his hat in the anteroom, where the Germans were now checking their hats and coats. Foch was virtually the only man in uniform. At 2:57, Orlando and Sonnino came in and walked over to shake hands with Wilson and Clemenceau before going to their places (somewhat off to the side). Clemenceau sat in the center of the head table, flanked on his right by Wilson, with whom he chatted casually, and on his left by Lloyd George, who whispered something to Balfour. Among the 205 people in the room, there was only one woman, a British War Office shorthand writer with an expert knowledge of German; she sat in one of the window recesses. Paderewski made a belated appearance ("looking very much like the representations one sees of the British Lion"), gave a small concert bow out of habit, and hurried off to his chair.

At several minutes past three, the folding glass doors were suddenly thrown back, and the chief attendant, dressed in a dark blue suit (some said it was black), wearing an immense, glittering silver ceremonial chain of office, entered and announced in a stentorian voice, *"Messieurs les plenipotentiaries allemands."* Most of the assemblage stood up. Brockdorff-Rantzau, hands clasped in front of him and holding his gloves, his face sallow and black rings under his deepset dark eyes ("like a death's head," thought Riddell), made a slow, uncomfortable bow of his head and, walking with a slight limp, led the other five German delegates, their secretaries and interpreters to their seats. Riddell noticed that Brockdorff-Rantzau's face was covered with perspiration, and that he seemed "a stiff, precise, industrious, mechanical, tactless sort of man." Another observer thought the German Foreign Minister gave off an impression of controlled agitation and emotional stress. In any case, Brockdorff-Rantzau did not look well. He bowed stiffly again to Clemenceau before sitting down.

Clemenceau stood up and rapped on the table with his ivory paper knife. Completely in control of the ceremony and his emotions, he intended to keep this short and simple; everyone had been told that the proceedings would last only about fifteen minutes. Clemenceau declared the session opened. (His words were translated into English by Mantoux and into German by someone else; the German translation was poor and halting.) "Gentlemen, Plenipotentiaries of the German Empire: It is neither the time nor the place for superfluous words. You have before you the accredited plenipotentiaries of all the small and Great Powers united to fight together in the war that was so cruelly imposed upon them. The time has come when we must settle our accounts. You have asked for peace. We are ready to give you peace. We shall present to you now a book which contains our conditions."

It was 3:17 when Clemenceau's speech was translated, and the Chief Secretary of the conference, Paul Dutasta, thickset and balding, crossed the room almost unnoticed and entered the hollow rectangle and laid a copy of the treaty in a white paper cover before Brockdorff-Rantzau. The German bowed as he took it, looked at it quizzically for a moment, then laid it aside.

Clemenceau told the Germans there would be no oral discussions over the treaty terms; if they had any "observations" they must submit them in writing within fifteen days (really two weeks, but he used the French idiom). Brockdorff-Rantzau nervously pushed his tortoiseshell glasses up and down on his forehead. The other German delegates sat motionless. Foch sat with his chin in his hand, apparently paying little attention to the proceedings, never looking at the German delegates, gazing wistfully out the windows to the lovely French countryside beyond.

Following the translation, Clemenceau asked if anyone wished to speak. Brockdorff-Rantzau raised his hand ("after the manner of a school-boy," Riddell thought). The Three had not expected this. Momentarily startled, Clemenceau gave a questioning look, then frowned and nodded.

Brockdorff-Rantzau adjusted his glasses again and began to read his speech in a guttural German baritone—but he was still sitting down! There was an almost audible gasp from the rest of the room. Since Clemenceau had stood up to speak, everyone considered Brockdorff-Rantzau's refusal to return the courtesy an astounding, if typically Prussian, insult to the Allies. (In fact, those who could see Brockdorff-Rantzau's legs realized they were shaking so badly that they could not possibly have supported him. Besides, many of the speeches at the infrequent formal conference sessions had been delivered sitting down. But the tension in the room magnified such trifles into a major controversy.) A stunned silence fell upon the room; everyone strained to hear each word of the German speech. Clemenceau, in fact, could not hear the two translators who stood, perspiring nervously and stammering a bit, beside the German table. He testily asked them to come closer. ("Louder!" called someone in French.) The interpreters approached the head table, but Clemenceau still could not hear properly, and finally they came and stood almost directly in front of the Three. The interpreter translating the German speech into English had a Midwestern American accent.

Everyone watched Clemenceau's reaction to Brockdorff-Rantzau's words. "We know," the count began, "that the power of German arms is broken. . . . It is demanded of us that we shall confess ourselves to be the only ones guilty of the war. Such a confession in my mouth would be a lie. . . ."

Clemenceau stiffened and started to interrupt, then turned to whisper something to Wilson; Lloyd George, who often showed displeasure by stirring uneasily in his seat as if he were about to get up and punch someone, began to shift himself about.

"A wrong has been done to Belgium," the German continued, "and we are willing to repair it. But in the manner of making war also Germany is not the only guilty one. Every nation knows of deeds of people which the best nationals only remember with regret. . . ."

Clemenceau tapped his paper knife slowly on the table and adopted a half-attentive, half-bored posture; Wilson, as he usually did when concentrating completely on someone's words, played absentmindedly with a pencil. Outside, clouds came over the sky and blocked out the sun.

"The hundreds of thousands of noncombatants who have perished since the eleventh of November by reason of the blockade were killed with cold deliberation after our adversaries had conquered and victory had been assured to them. Think of that when you speak of guilt and of punishment. . . ."

Lloyd George snapped his ivory paper knife in pieces; Wilson leaned back in his chair with his hands in his pockets.

"Gentlemen," concluded Brockdorff-Rantzau, "the sublime thought to be derived from the most terrible disaster in the history of mankind is the League of Nations; the greatest progress in the development of mankind has been pronounced, and will make its way. Only if the gates of the League of Nations are thrown open to all who are of goodwill can the aim be attained, and only then the dead of this war will not have died in vain."

Brockdorff-Rantzau replaced his glasses in their case, spread his hands upon the table, and waited.

Clemenceau rose and with a few sharp sentences declared the session closed. Some of the other delegates began to leave, but sat down again when Clemenceau barked, *"Restons à nos places,"* forcing the Germans to depart alone. Brockdorff-Rantzau walked to the anteroom and handed in his hat check, waited three minutes while the attendants gathered his belongings, and then went out to the cars that had been drawn up outside a few moments earlier. The French soldiers of the honor guard turned their backs on him. He slowly took a cigarette out of his case, accepted a light, stepped into the car, and was gone. It was nearly four o'clock. The sun had come out again.

After the Germans had departed, Lansing and House emerged into the sunshine, then Pichon, Foch (smoking a cigar and smiling an I-told-you-they-were-swine smile), Venizelos, and Bonar Law (also smoking a cigar). Paderewski appeared at four-thirty, with Tardieu and General Smuts. The crowd was beginning to grow uneasy at the delayed appearance of the Big Four, but the chiefs had only adjourned to hold a brief meeting to consider their next move, and several minutes later Wilson came out, looking serious, but flashing a slight smile and giving the usual wave of his top hat to the people. Then came Clemenceau, getting the first real cheer of the afternoon, then Orlando, and finally Lloyd George, whose reception was nearly as warm as Clemenceau's.

On the way out, Wilson told Riddell, "The Germans are really a stupid people. They always do the wrong things. They always did the wrong thing during the war. That is why I am here. They don't understand human nature. This is the most tactless speech I have ever heard. It will set the whole world against them." Indeed, it appeared that Brockdorff-Rantzau had succeeded in temporarily smoothing over the divisions in the Allied ranks.

"This is a great day for you," Lloyd George told Clemenceau. "I don't mind telling you that it is," the Premier replied. Lloyd George nearly added, "What a splendid ending for you," but stopped himself just in time. Of course, the little Welshman knew, it really *was* the beginning of the end for the grand old man who had watched from the heights of Montmartre fifty years before as the Germans needlessly and maliciously burned the castle of St-Cloud.

While driving back to Paris, Riddell gave a ride to a stranger, and the conversation turned to the remarkable careers of men such as Lloyd George, Wilson, and Clemenceau. Yes, said the stranger, but you must also remember that Charlie Chaplin used to tend bar and had, in fact, personally served him (the stranger) with many drinks in those days. Then Chaplin had joined a well-known British traveling troupe and had eventually been discovered by some perceptive filmmaker. "I think that beats Clemenceau,

Lloyd George & Co. hollow," the stranger laughed. Riddell spent the rest of the trip "wondering whether it is better to be born with a high-class brain or funny feet."

When Lloyd George got home to Frances Stevenson, she saw that he was "quite exhausted with emotion—ill, in fact, & it was some time before he became himself again." Lloyd George told her that he could have gotten up and punched Brockdorff-Rantzau, and honestly had the greatest difficulty in restraining himself. "He says," wrote Frances in her diary, "it has made him more angry than any incident of the war, & if the Germans do not sign, he will have no mercy on them. He says for the first time he has felt the same hatred for them that the French feel. I am rather glad that they have stirred him up, so that he may keep stern with them to the very end. If they had been submissive and cowed he might have been sorry for them." The Brockdorff-Rantzau incident, Lloyd George admitted to Riddell, had made him angrier than he had been for a long, long time; in fact, he had noticed that the British and American delegates seemed more upset with Brockdorff-Rantzau's conduct than did the French. He had asked Clemenceau why this was so. "Because," replied the Tiger, "we are accustomed to their insolence. We have had to bear it for fifty years. It is new to you and therefore it makes you angry."

That evening the German delegates conferred among themselves until midnight.

SIX

THE DAYS
OF THE
WHIRLWIND

---

*"Who is the wise man,
that may understand this?"*

25

"I have put a yoke of iron

upon the neck of all these nations . . .

and I have given him

the beasts of the field also . . ."

Who could tell what nastiness lurked in a gallon of the finest milk an English cow could give? In the spring of 1919, someone sent to the Ministry of Food a once-white cloth through which 22.5 gallons of milk (the sort that might be purchased by an average London consumer) had been strained. The disgusting result was a cloth caked with a mass of dark brown foreign matter—most of which appeared to be cow manure. Good fertilizer perhaps, but hardly part of anyone's minimum daily nutritional requirements. In an effort to promote an awareness among milk producers (the farmers, not the cows) of the importance of cleanliness, and to ensure purer dairy supplies for unsuspecting British city dwellers, the National Clean Milk Society offered to send its experts to any farm in the country to demonstrate modern sanitary procedures, free of charge.

This was the treaty brought forth by the men at Paris after nearly four months' labor: A League of Nations—excluding, for the time being, Germany and Russia—was to be formed to investigate, discuss, and perhaps settle international disputes before the world again slid dazedly into war; Germany was required to admit its guilt for causing all the war losses and damages suffered by the Allies, and to pay a yet unspecified sum in reparations (including even the cost of pensions to be paid to Allied veterans) over a thirty-year period, the precise figure to be determined by an inter-Allied Reparation Commission that would render its definitive decision by May 1921; in the meantime, Germany would pay one billion pounds sterling (25 billion francs) or approximately five billion dollars in goods or gold by May 1921 as a first installment. As part of the territorial settlement,

Germany would return Alsace-Lorraine to France, cede coal-rich Upper Silesia to Poland, and grant certain small areas of disputed territory to Belgium; France would also receive ownership of the Saar Valley coal mines for fifteen years. All of the Second Reich's overseas colonies, rights, and properties, were to be handed over to the Allies or the League of Nations. Danzig would become a free city and Poland would receive right-of-way through a corridor to the port. The Allies appropriated all German merchant ships over 1,600 tons and half of those between 1,000 and 1,600 tons; in addition, Germany pledged to build merchant ships totaling 200,000 tons annually for the Allies for five years. All fortifications for fifty miles east of the Rhine were slated for destruction. The once-fearsome German military machine was completely dismantled: conscription was forbidden, the army was limited to 100,000 men (only slightly greater than the tiny American prewar army), the German military air force was abolished, and the navy reduced to six battleships, six light cruisers, twelve torpedo boats, and *no* submarines. For good measure, the Allies prohibited the manufacture of nearly all arms and ammunition within the German Republic. Allied forces were given the right to occupy German territory west of the Rhine, including the bridgeheads, for a period of up to fifteen years, the term of occupation to be extended if Germany failed to observe her treaty obligations. The Allies reserved the right to ask the Dutch government to surrender the Kaiser for trial. Germany was required to recognize the independence of Czechoslovakia, Austria, and Poland. And, finally, France, Britain, and the United States pledged to assist one another in the event of enemy attack. Violations of the treaty by Germany would be treated as an act of war.

The German government had fostered the impression—not entirely correct—among the folks at home that it had surrendered on the assumption that the terms of peace would be based exclusively on Wilson's Fourteen Points. In fact, Germany had officially accepted the Fourteen Points and all of Wilson's elaborations thereof when it signed the Armistice agreement; unfortunately for the sake of diplomatic precision, some of the President's additional statements contradicted one another or the original Points, and many were certainly vague enough to permit a variety of interpretations. But clearly, the Germans now argued, a horrible mistake had been made by someone, somewhere along the line.

In the rush of last-minute compromises and with the plethora of expert committees all working independently and each contributing its own individual section of the treaty, virtually no one—and certainly none of the Big Three—had had an opportunity to read the peace terms in their entirety (440 articles, 75,000 words, about 200 pages) before they had been presented to the Germans. So May 7 was the first time that anyone, except perhaps the printer, had been able to see how all the terms fit together to form a peace settlement for the world.

And was it a just treaty, a wise treaty?

The New York Times:

IT IS A TERRIBLE PUNISHMENT THE GERMAN PEOPLE AND THEIR MAD RULERS HAVE BROUGHT UPON THEMSELVES. NOT ONLY IS THEIR MILITARY POWER TO BE DESTROYED, BUT THE MILITARY SPIRIT WILL BE CRUSHED OUT OF THEM BY THE STERN BUT NECESSARY CONDITIONS THE NATIONS IMPOSE. . . . CAN GERMANY LIVE UNDER THESE CONDITIONS? ALL THE WORLD CAN SEE THAT THEY ARE TERRIBLY SEVERE. BUT THE WORLD KNOWS, TOO, THAT THEY ARE JUST. . . . THE PUNISHMENT GERMANY MUST ENDURE FOR CENTURIES WILL BE ONE OF THE GREATEST DETERRENTS TO THE WAR SPIRIT.

General Ludendorff: "If these are President Wilson's fourteen points, then America can go to hell."

Francis Stevenson: "Everyone seems delighted with the peace terms, & there is no fault to find with them on the ground that they are not severe enough. Someone described it as 'a peace with a vengeance.'"

General Jan Smuts: "I am much troubled over our peace terms. I consider them bad. And wrong. And they may not be accepted. The world may lapse into complete chaos. And what will emerge? I don't know what to do."

The *Philadelphia North American:* "The Germans don't like the peace terms, but they ought to remember that if they did nobody else would."

Herbert Hoover:

I WAS AWAKENED AT FOUR O'CLOCK ON THE MORNING OF THE SEVENTH OF MAY, 1919, BY A TROUBLED SERVANT WHO EXPLAINED THAT THERE WAS A MESSENGER WAITING WITH A VERY IMPORTANT DOCUMENT WHICH HE WOULD GIVE TO NO ONE ELSE THAN MYSELF. IT WAS THE PRINTED DRAFT OF THE PEACE TREATY WHICH WAS TO BE HANDED TO THE GERMANS THAT DAY. I AT ONCE READ IT. WHILE I HAD KNOWN MANY OF THE IDEAS, AGREED UPON BY COMMITTEES, I HAD NOT BEFORE ENVISAGED IT AS A WHOLE. I WAS GREATLY DISTURBED. IN IT HATE AND REVENGE RAN THROUGH THE POLITICAL AND ECONOMIC PASSAGES. MANY PROVISIONS HAD BEEN SETTLED WITHOUT CONSIDERATION OF HOW THEY AFFECTED OTHER PARTS. CONDITIONS WERE SET UP UPON WHICH EUROPE COULD NEVER BE REBUILT OR PEACE COME TO MANKIND. IT SEEMED TO ME THE ECONOMIC

CONSEQUENCES ALONE WOULD PULL DOWN ALL EUROPE AND THUS INJURE
THE UNITED STATES. I AROSE AND WENT FOR A WALK IN THE DESERTED
STREETS. . . .

The *Chicago Daily News:* "What did Germania think—that the nations
were going to make her Queen of the May?"

Count von Bernstorff: "It is an imperialistic peace. It is the worst in
history. It is the maximum. We cannot sign."

J. L. Garvin, editor of *The Observer:* "It is founded on a balance of
unequal forces, and, as they will not endure, it must be amended by the
work of the future to produce equilibrium. . . . There will be quarrels,
conspiracies, agitations, assassinations, revolutions and collapses. The motley patchwork, which has been stitched together, will have to be picked
up throughout, thread by thread."

In Peking, students rioted against the Peace Conference's refusal to
restore Chinese sovereignty over Shantung Province.

Secretary of State Lansing: "For the first time in these days of feverish
rush of preparation there is time to consider the treaty as a complete
document. . . . The impression made by it is one of disappointment, of
regret, and of depression."

The *Manchester Guardian:*

WOULD IT NOT BE BETTER TO FIX A SUM WHICH GERMANY MAY FAIRLY
HOPE TO PAY WITHIN A SHORTER PERIOD, AND THUS TO DO WHAT WE CAN
TO HELP HER PAY IT? AT PRESENT HER INDUSTRIES ARE RUINED, HER
PEOPLE ENFEEBLED, HER GOVERNMENT IN TOTAL DISORDER. SHE IS NOT IN
A POSITION TO RESIST ANY TERMS WE MAY CHOOSE TO IMPOSE. BUT A WISE
POLICY WILL TREAT HER NO LONGER AS AN ENEMY TO BE FEARED AND
DESTROYED, BUT AS PART OF THE EUROPE OF WHICH WE OURSELVES FORM
AN INTEGRAL PART, AND WHICH FOR MANY A LONG YEAR WILL NEED ALL
OUR HELP AND ALL OUR CARE TO SAVE IT FROM RUIN.

Henry White: "We had such high hopes of this adventure; we believed
God called us, and now at the end we are put to doing hell's dirtiest work,
starving people, grabbing territory—or helping to grab it for our friends;
standing by while the grand gesture of revenge and humiliation links this
war up with the interminable chain of wars that runs back to Cain. It was
not for this that our Americans died—clean beautiful great visioned men
who came seeking the Grail."

Premier Hirsch of Prussia: "These conditions represent purely a 'mailed
fist' peace which, if it were to come to pass, would mean slavery for the

Fatherland and fresh unrest and fresh bloodshed for the whole of Europe."

Walter Lippmann: "The situation created by the treaty is . . . profoundly discouraging to those who cared most for what the President has been talking about. For the life of me I can't see peace in this document, and as the President has so frequently said, statesmen who cannot hear the voice of mankind are sure to be broken."

The Dutch press generally considered the terms "a mockery of the principles of President Wilson," but Swiss newspapers were more lenient: "On the whole the treaty is just." Czechoslovakia, Poland, and Belgium were satisfied, with only minor reservations.

Chancellor Philipp Scheidemann: "These conditions are nothing else than the sentence of death for Germany."

The *Cleveland Press:* "It's a hard bed, Heinie, but who made it?"

Will Rogers: "I thought the Armistice terms read like a second Mortgage, But this reads like a FORECLOSURE. If Germany ever wants to go to war again she will have to fight with BEER STEINS."

Senator Warren G. Harding: "The big issue is that raised by the League of Nations which is to carry out many of the treaty provisions. I doubt whether the Senate will consent to this country entering upon responsibilities and limitations of which we do not know."

The *Daily Telegraph* (London):

THE ACCEPTANCE OF THESE TERMS WILL LEAVE GERMANY AN UNRECOGNIZABLE GHOST OF THE EMPIRE OF FIVE YEARS AGO, BLOATED AS IT WAS WITH CRIMINAL ANNEXATIONS, ARROGANT WITH WEALTH, AND CRAZED WITH THE CONSCIOUSNESS OF UNPARALLELED MILITARY POWER. THIS IS EVIDENT, AND THERE IS ANOTHER THING NOT LESS EVIDENT ON ANY HONEST CONSIDERATION OF THE FACTS. THE PEACE IS RIGIDLY A PEACE OF JUSTICE. NOT ONE EXTREMIST DEMAND HAS SURVIVED THE ORDEAL OF THE CONFERENCE. . . . THIS TREATY ENDS THE STRUGGLE WITH GERMANY RIGHT WELL.

President Ebert: "It is unbearable for the German people, and, even if we put forth all our powers, impracticable. Violence without measure or limit is to be done to the German people. From such an imposed peace fresh hatred would be bound to arise between the nations, and in the course of history fresh killing."

The *New York Call:* "Accept it, children, with faith and resignation— and prepare for the next Armageddon."

John Maynard Keynes:

THE POLICY OF REDUCING GERMANY TO SERVITUDE FOR A GENERATION, OF DEGRADING THE LIVES OF MILLIONS OF HUMAN BEINGS, AND OF DEPRIVING A WHOLE NATION OF HAPPINESS SHOULD BE ABHORRENT AND DETESTABLE,—ABHORRENT AND DETESTABLE, EVEN IF IT WERE POSSIBLE, EVEN IF IT ENRICHED OURSELVES, EVEN IF IT DID NOT SOW THE DECAY OF THE WHOLE CIVILIZED LIFE OF EUROPE. SOME PREACH IT IN THE NAME OF JUSTICE. IN THE GREAT EVENTS OF MAN'S HISTORY, IN THE UNWINDING OF THE COMPLEX FATES OF NATIONS JUSTICE IS NOT SO SIMPLE. AND IF IT WERE, NATIONS ARE NOT AUTHORIZED, BY RELIGION OR BY NATURAL MORALS, TO VISIT ON THE CHILDREN OF THEIR ENEMIES THE MISDOINGS OF PARENTS OR OF RULERS.

England's racing season of 1919 had already opened with the Grand National at Aintree, several miles outside of Liverpool. Poethlyn, the nine-year-old brown gelding by Rydal Head out of Fine Champagne, with the veteran rider Piggott up, established himself early on in the betting ring as the favorite, the odds varying slightly from seven to two to three to one. "What is Poethlyn?" asked a nervous-looking young man. "Three to one, sir," replied a bookmaker, holding out his hand expectantly. "But it's such a rotten price," muttered the prospective bettor uncertainly, fingering his roll of banknotes in obvious reluctance to part with them. "Very nice price if you win," said the bookie. "If you don't win"—he threw open his arms and grinned—"price don't matter."

Shortly before the scheduled start of the day's card, out of the blue sky and wispy clouds fell tiny balls of hail, at first unconvincingly, and then more steadily until the hats and coats of the pallid-faced townspeople were covered with gleaming white crumbs. Then, after spring reappeared for two races, the sky grew overcast and for a brief moment winter returned in the form of a heavy snowstorm that sent the horses back to their paddocks. Five minutes later the weather had cleared, and the race was on. Twenty-two horses ran as the flag fell; Ballyboggan, the pride of Ireland, left the gate as the second choice; Svetoi ran at 50 to 1, All White and Picture Saint at 100 to 1. Four and a half miles and thirty fences to go.

Carrying the extremely heavy burden of twelve stone, seven pounds (175 pounds), Poethlyn allowed his stablemate Pollen to set the pace, remaining comfortably several lengths behind. Ballyboggan made his move, and the water flew beneath pounding hooves. On the second time around the course, as the leaders again passed Valentine's Brook, Piggott urged Poethlyn on, moving in front, leaving the others behind. By the time they approached the last two fences—the only swampy and treacherous part of the course—it was obvious that nothing short of a disaster would keep the favorite from winning. And win he did, convincingly, by eight lengths, Ballyboggan finishing second, and Pollen third. In all, eleven horses finished the course—rather a good showing. An English crowd knew how to appreciate a fine horse, no matter whether they had laid their bets on him or another, and amid the loud and long cheers as the trophy cups were presented to the owner, trainer, and rider, there was talk that Mrs. Hugh Peel's gelding deserved to be mentioned in the same breath with the other great steeplechasers of recent years: Jerry M., Cloister, and Manifesto.

On the day the terms of peace were published in Berlin, the racetrack at Karlhorst took in more than 130,000 marks in gate receipts, and the betting sheds distributed 3,500,000 marks to the lucky winners. In Berlin the ice palaces and the Palais de Danse were spectacular and gorgeous and expensive. Flower girls pestered customers as usual at the better restaurants. There was another wave in the orgy of spending out of fear that the government would impose confiscatory taxes to pay the heavy indemnities demanded by the Allies. Hoards of German gold fled across the frontiers into Denmark and Holland for safekeeping.

Believing the German people to be "in deep distress and weighed down by cares" because of the calamitous peace terms, President Ebert proclaimed a week of mourning for the nation, suspending dancing, gambling, cabarets, horseracing, first-class theaters, and all other frivolous public amusements; only such theatrical productions "as correspond with the seriousness of these grievous days" would be permitted. Meeting temporarily in the assembly hall of the University of Berlin on the Unter den Linden (the Reichstag building had been overrun by vermin and was being fumigated at the moment), every party in the German political spectrum save for the left-wing Independent Socialists rose in the National Assembly and expressed righteous indignation at the terms from Paris. "Away with this murderous scheme," shouted Scheidemann. Another deputy promised, "If this treaty comes to pass I will bring up my children in hatred." Public demonstrations in Upper Silesia protested the award of that territory to Poland against its will; the crowds there sang "Deutschland Über Alles" and people waved the old imperial flag of white, black, and red. An American observer believed that the wave of revulsion was giving Prussian militarism fresh hope, "and reaction is restlessly stirring in chrysalis. . . . Everything is possible in Germany before the expiration of the time limit for signing the peace." Placards distributed in Berlin called upon loyal citizens to massacre the Jews who had allegedly killed two hundred good German children at Eastertime; there were reports from Vilna of scores of Jews murdered, and leaders of the Jewish community in Berlin quietly visited the American commission in the Hotel Adlon to ask for protection.

Matthias Erzberger, the leader of the Catholic Centrist party, the man who had signed the Armistice—it seemed a lifetime ago—in November in a railroad car in the forest of Compiègne, told Ben Hecht that "we are not a defeated people, we Germans. We are a starved people. Marshal Foch won all his victories after and not before the armistice." The truth was that Germany was both defeated and starved. The truth was that the German people were simply far too exhausted from war and revolution and reaction and starvation to do much more than shake their heads in sadness when they heard of the peace treaty. Halfhearted rallies in the Koenigsplatz, with the statue of Bismarck nearby, heard speakers railing against the "brutal dictated peace" and the "betrayal by Wilson" and der gewalt Friedens— "the peace by force"; but the listeners displayed little emotion of their own. Ebert increased the Berlin garrison in anticipation of violent demonstrations against the peace terms, but there was really no need. A general feeling of anger and despair there was, yes, but also listlessness, feebleness, broken spirits—and no one knew what to do that would make any difference. A group of scarred German veterans sat talking in a dilapidated café: "Whatever comes now, we will not fight again. They have killed the Fatherland, but we will not go to the trenches again." "Cowards!" shouted another.

"Perhaps we will sign and perhaps not," murmured one old Junker. "What difference does it make? . . . If you ask Downing Street, London, Downing Street would tell you that it is all immaterial—Germany is crushed, Russia is crushed, and England has added another noble slice of Africa to her possessions and so England is content and even magnanimous."

Hecht attended an exhibition of Dadaism at a gallery in Berlin, where a thousand well-dressed, wealthy women and men of distinction crowded into a chamber to see paintings that were vague smears of color on the wall, to hear absurd, nonsensical poems read by ragged poets, to listen to music that was "a smear of sound" and that gave Hecht a splitting headache. "It is wonderful," sighed a dignified, middle-aged woman. "It is a new art which teaches us to laugh at ourselves and appreciate the imbecility of the universe." (Then she downed another half-liter of wine.) The leader of the revels, one of Berlin's foremost architects, assured everyone that Dadaism "is the thunderbolt of laughter. It is the quintessence of caricature. It is the saturnalian slapstick for reason." And so it suited life in Berlin in May of 1919.

Rosa Luxemburg's body, swollen and almost unrecognizable, floated up against one of the locks of the Landwehr Canal. Divers had to pry it loose from the dike. Wary of fresh Spartacist uprisings in Luxemburg's memory, Noske ordered her body taken to Zossen, twenty miles south of Berlin. Private Otto Runge, who had clubbed Rosa and Liebknecht with his rifle butt, was tried and sentenced to two years' imprisonment and two weeks of solitary confinement, and the loss of his civil rights for four years. He served only a few months of the sentence. Lieutenant Vogel, who had shot Luxemburg, was sentenced to two years in prison for illegally disposing of a corpse. He escaped with a forged release order supplied by his friends in the army and fled to Holland; he was eventually granted amnesty. One other soldier involved in the incident received a sentence of six weeks in solitary confinement; he, too, escaped to Holland. The rest of the accused were acquitted.

Mob violence and the lawless lynching of Negroes, declared Charles Evans Hughes, was a pernicious manifestation of the Hun spirit that must be exorcised forever from America. Speaking to the National Conference on Lynching, which was meeting in Carnegie Hall on the evening of May 5, Hughes—the former Republican presidential candidate who had been defeated by Wilson in 1916—condemned lynching as murder of the foulest sort. He told the 2,500 blacks and whites in the audience that justice in America and equal protection of the laws was every man's birthright and need not be earned: "It is not necessary that any one should give his blood, either directly or vicariously, to obtain justice in this country. But to the black man, who in this crisis has proved his bravery, his honor and his loyalty to our institutions, we certainly owe the performance of this duty, and we should let it be known from this time on, in recognition of that supreme service, that the black man shall have the rights guaranteed to him by the Constitution of the United States."

Hughes's noble sentiments notwithstanding, racial tensions began to increase steadily in the United States in the spring and summer of 1919. Hundreds of thousands of blacks had moved northward to take over good-paying industrial jobs as white workers were drafted into the army; thousands more had joined the American Expeditionary Force and fought on the Western Front in all-black fighting units (commanded by white officers, of course). In the cities of the North they now moved into neighborhoods where no blacks had gone before. They walked along crowded sidewalks, they sat at restaurant tables, they went to movies along with whites. And those who had served their country in the war were not about to sit back and let the white establishment deny them precisely the rights for which they had supposedly fought abroad.

But the same syndrome of wartime emotionalism, violent hatreds, and one-hundred-percent Americanism that had already produced irrational fears among native-born Americans of the recent waves of immigrants from Eastern and Southern Europe also served to heighten anxieties over presumptuous ("uppity" was the word used) blacks who no longer knew their place and who threatened to overturn the established, comfortable social order. Racial incidents began to multiply across the nation. In Harlem, a streetcar conductor hit a black youth over the head with his stick and threw him off the car; half an hour later a dozen blacks—several in soldiers' uniforms—jumped aboard the same car and assaulted the conductor (actually, it was a different conductor, one who had just come on duty, but nobody seemed to notice), and chased him into the public library near Lenox Avenue. The riot grew quickly, and soon there were three thousand whites and blacks gathered in front of the library, throwing stones, bricks, furniture (commandeered from the library), and beer bottles at one another.

In Jenkins County, Georgia, a gun battle broke out between police and a carload of blacks bringing in a preacher from another part of the state. When it was over, six men were dead: four blacks, one marshal, and a county policeman. Another black man was arrested and then taken from the jail and lynched. Several churches and lodge buildings in the black district were burned. Near Warrenton, Georgia, a posse chased a black farmer who had allegedly shot his divorced wife and wounded her sister and four white men. Following an exchange of shots, he fled into a swamp. The posse poured gasoline on the shallow water and set the swamp afire to drive their quarry out into the open. When they captured him, they hanged him and riddled his body with bullets and then brought his body into town and burned it in front of three hundred curious onlookers. Apparently no peace officers were anywhere to be found when the black man was captured, or when he was hanged, or shot, or burned.

A race riot broke out in Charleston, South Carolina, on the evening of May 8 after an altercation in a pool hall between local blacks and sailors from a nearby naval training station. For several hours an angry mob of white civilians and sailors held control of the city streets, stopping trolley cars and pulling off black passengers. One black man was shot down as patrons of an outdoor café looked on. After two blacks were killed and at least seventeen people injured, marines with riot rifles reestablished order.

The National Association for the Advancement of Colored People (of which Oswald Garrison Villard was a leading member) sent a telegram to Governor Bilbo of Mississippi, inquiring into the fate of a black named Eugene Green who had been seized by a mob. The Jackson *Daily News* printed its reply: the NAACP "need not remain in the dark concerning the fate of Green. He was 'advanced' all right from the end of a rope, and in order to save burial expenses his body was thrown into the Yazoo River." On May 13 the NAACP announced the start of a nationwide campaign "to defend the constitutional and legal rights now denied more than four-fifths of the Negro race in America" (the right to vote, the right to a fair trial, a decent education, and equal use of public services and public transportation)—in short, "to make America safe for Americans."

Spreading out from the South, where it had been founded on Thanksgiving night, 1915, on Stone Mountain, Georgia, by a half-crazed, hungry Methodist preacher named William Simmons, the revived Ku Klux Klan still had fewer than five thousand members. But it fed on the same fears that spawned the Red Scare, and its targets were as much Catholics, Jews, foreigners, and "immoral" white trash as blacks. As W. J. Cash has pointed out, the Klan was as authentic a folk movement as the Nazi phenomenon in Germany, "to which it was not without kinship." One can almost hear the boots of Noske's Freikorps troops marching into Munich to purge the city of its sickness—or the Fascists of Milan assaulting the enemies of the homeland as Mussolini looked on lovingly—in Cash's account of the Klan's pursuit of pure American virtue:

HERE IN GHOSTLY RIDES THROUGH THE MOONLIT, AROMATIC EVENING TO WHIP A NEGRO OR A PROSTITUTE OR SOME POOR WHITE GIVEN TO VIOLATING THE SEVENTH COMMANDMENT OR DRINKING UP HIS SCANT EARNINGS INSTEAD OF CLOTHING HIS CHILDREN, OR MERELY GIVEN TO STAYING AWAY FROM CHURCH; TO TAR AND FEATHER A LABOR ORGANIZER OR A SCHOOLMASTER WHO HAD TALKED HIS NEW IDEAS TOO MUCH—IN SLOW, SWAYING NOON-DAY PARADES THROUGH THE BURNING SILENCE OF TOWNS WHERE EVERY NEGRO WAS GONE FROM THE STREETS, AND THE JEWS AND THE CATHOLICS AND THE ALIENS HAD THEIR HOUSES AND SHOPS SHUTTERED— HERE WAS SURCEASE FOR THE PERSONAL FRUSTRATIONS AND ITCHES OF THE KLANSMAN, OF COURSE. BUT ALSO THE OLD COVETED, SPLENDID SENSE OF BEING A HEROIC BLADE, A CRUSADER SWEEPING UP MYSTICAL SLOPES FOR WHITE SUPREMACY, RELIGION, MORALITY, AND ALL THAT HAD MADE UP THE FAITH OF THE FATHERS: OF BEING THE DIRECT HEIR IN CONTINUOUS

LINE OF THE CONFEDERATE SOLDIERS AT GETTYSBURG AND OF THOSE OLD
KLANSMEN WHO HAD ONCE DRIVEN OUT THE CARPETBAGGER AND THE
SCALAWAG; OF PARTICIPATING IN RITUALISTIC ASSERTION OF THE SOUTH'S
CONTINUING IDENTITY, ITS WILL TO REMAIN UNCHANGED AND DEFY THE
WAYS OF THE YANKEE AND THE WORLD IN FAVOR OF THAT ONE WHICH HAD
SO LONG BEEN ITS OWN.

Zelda to Scott, after one of his several visits to Montgomery in the late
spring of 1919:

"Scott, my darling lover—everything seems so smooth and restful, like
this yellow dusk. Knowing that I'll always be yours—that you really own
me—that nothing can keep us apart—is such a relief after the strain and
nervous excitement of the last month. I'm so glad you came—like Summer,
just when I needed you most. . . ."

Scott was preparing to pack up and leave New York, to return to St.
Paul, Minnesota, and try to persuade a publisher to accept the novel he had
tentatively titled *The Romantic Egoist* but that was now undergoing extensive revision. Meanwhile, Zelda had spent a day in an Alabama graveyard,
struggling to unlock a rusty iron vault in the side of a hill in which a body
lay buried. The vault was "all washed and covered with weepy, watery
blue flowers that might have grown from dead eyes," she tried to explain
to her lover, "sticky to touch with a sickening odor—The boys wanted to
get in to test my nerve—to-night—I wanted to *feel* 'William Wreford,
1864.' Why should graves make people feel in vain? . . . Isn't it funny how,
out of a row of Confederate soldiers, two or three will make you think of
dead lovers and dead loves—when they're exactly like the others, even to
the yellowish moss? Old death is so beautiful—so very beautiful—We will
die together—I know. . . ."

26

"We have heard a voice of trembling,

of fear, and not of peace . . ."

It had rained on Friday and so the track was still muddy. At the forty-fifth running of the Kentucky Derby, a record crowd of fifty thousand spectators gathered, the grandstand full of governors and senators and enough millionaires to make Churchill Downs look like Newport in August. The purse this year was the largest ever—$20,825—and the popular favorites appeared to be Billy Kelly, the speed merchant who had dominated the two-year-old field in 1918, and Eternal, the choice of the West. Rated slightly lower were Be Frank, from the Calumet Stable entourage owned by Cornelius M. Garrison, and Harry Payne Whitney's temperamental Vindex. And then there was Billy Kelly's stablemate Sir Barton, born in Kentucky and trained in Maryland, a chestnut son of Star Shoot out of Lady Sterling (a daughter of the legendary Hanover), owned by a Canadian millionaire, Commander J. K. L. Ross. The even-tempered Sir Barton had lately shown considerable promise for trainer Guy Bedwell, but nonetheless had failed to win any of the six races in which he had run.

Sir Barton, carrying just 112 pounds, immediately broke in front as the twelve horses left the gate. They swept by the grandstand, Sir Barton with his long, raking stride still leading Eternal, with Billy Kelly four lengths back; at the half-mile mark Sir Barton led by two lengths; at the three-quarter pole the margin had been cut to half a length, with Billy Kelly, Vulcanite, and Under Fire close behind. Then Sir Barton's jockey, Johnny Loftus, turned him loose and breezed through the stretch. He won going away, five lengths ahead of Billy Kelly. Sir Barton ($7.20 to win, $6.70 to place, and $6.00 to show) was the first maiden ever to win the Kentucky Derby, and Ross the first Canadian to own a Derby winner. It was Loftus's second Derby victory in four years. Eternal, clearly bothered by the mud, finished tenth, and Vindex struggled home last.

Just four days later, on Wednesday, May 14, Sir Barton, Eternal, and Billy Kelly met again in the Preakness at Pimlico, before the largest crowd in Maryland racing history. This time Sir Barton received no maiden weight allowance and carried the standard 126 pounds. The track at Pimlico was as fast as a speed horse like Billy Kelly could want, and the Western colt jumped out after Sir Barton right from the start (which had been delayed for five minutes due to the fractiousness of the horses in the gate). Nevertheless, the result was the same: "Sir Barton at the quarter, Sir Barton at the half, Sir Barton at every post—Sir Barton all the way—and he won as he pleased." Loftus never had to use the whip, even easing up through the stretch run, as his horse was never pressed or extended. The winning time was 1:53, far off the track record, but then Sir Barton was practically cantering at the finish. This time Eternal finished second, four lengths back. Again a cherished American racing trophy—in this case the Woodlawn Vase, made in 1860 and buried in the Kentucky ground during the Civil War to keep it out of Yankee hands—went north of the border to Commander Ross, along with $24,000 in prize money.

In June, Sir Barton completed his sweep by winning the Belmont Stakes in equally convincing fashion. Never before had one horse won all three of the most prestigious races in America for three-year-olds; not until 1930 would another horse win the Triple Crown.

On the brilliant, clear afternoon following the presentation of the treaty to the Germans, Wilson, his wife, and Admiral Grayson rode out to the track at Longchamps to spend a day at the races. (Lloyd George was playing golf in the country, Clemenceau taking a long, relaxing automobile ride.) It was the grand reopening of the track where placid French cows had been pastured since the last Grand Prix was run in 1914; remarkably, the course showed only a few minor scars from its wartime experience.

It was a spectacularly popular event, as Parisians and English and American officials and soldiers flocked to the track, setting new records for admission fees (the total take was more than twice as much as before the war) and parimutuel wagers (3,500,000 francs in one day). The first two races that day were won by American-owned horses, one of which was W. K. Vanderbilt's renowned McKinley, who may well have had more spirit and certainly showed more speed than his presidential namesake. All the excitement did not come from the horses, however. The doyens of Paris *haute couture* sent their models and actresses to Longchamps to show off the latest fashions, and when the young ladies paraded inside the grandstand—right in front of Wilson—the President could see that they were wearing high-heeled pumps but no stockings. None at all. It was the second attempt since the Armistice to launch the brazen bare-legged style; nor were legs the only things that were bared. Low-necked, sleeveless dresses, slightly shorter than last season's, also greeted the President's eye. The *femmes* of France doubtless were tired of paying ten dollars for a pair of diaphanous hose that ran the first time they were worn, but across the Atlantic, the self-appointed guardians of conventional American fashion had no intention of adopting the scandalous new style. "American women will go without other things before they give up their stockings," sniffed Chicago society matron Mrs. Samuel T. Chase. "Personally, I would rather give up hats. The fashion is absurd."

"*Les notes! Encore les notes! Toujours les notes! Et Allemagne est sauvée!*" The Allied delegations at Paris might have been allowed a parody of Danton's lament as they suffered through an onslaught of protests and complaints from Germany on nearly every section of the peace treaty. Brockdorff-Rantzau led off with an assertion that "on essential points the basis of the peace of right agreed upon between the belligerents has been abandoned. . . . The draft of the treaty contains demands which no nation could endure." Clemenceau, as president of the conference, replied that the Allies had kept the Armistice principles clearly in mind throughout their deliberations, and besides, the Germans had been invited to make specific practical suggestions about the treaty and not to argue about its philosophical foundations. (In large part the disagreement was a matter of viewpoint: the Germans spoke of justice and thought of mercy; the Allies equated justice with fair—and accordingly severe—punishment for Germany's war crimes. In fact, even Lloyd George agreed that if the Allies exacted truly "just" compensation in treating with Germany, the Huns would be completely obliterated.) Brockdorff-Rantzau then announced in another note that Germany had some recommendations to improve the League of Nations Covenant—a tactless move that was certain to irritate Wilson; did these Germans dare suggest that they could improve upon the crowning glory of his life's work?—and then the count complained about the conference's decision to keep Germany out of the League until it proved itself reformed and worthy of membership. Clemenceau icily assured Brockdorff-Rantzau that his suggestions had been passed along to the proper committees.

Then Brockdorff-Rantzau got down to the crucial points of the economic and political clauses. "In the course of the past two generations," he explained to Clemenceau—as if he were an instructor lecturing an especially obtuse student—"Germany has passed from an agrarian State to an industrial State. As an agrarian State Germany could feed forty million people. As an industrial State she was in a position to provide food for a population of sixty-seven millions." This had been achieved, of course, by exporting industrial products to pay for the necessary imports of food-stuffs: Germany had been forced to import 12 million tons of food in 1913 alone. In addition, about 15 million Germans had relied either directly or indirectly on foreign trade for their livelihoods before the war. By the terms of the treaty, however, Germany would forfeit virtually its entire merchant fleet, its colonies (and the raw materials and foodstuffs they provided), and some of its most productive agricultural regions (including about 21 percent of the nation's corn and potato crops). Thus more food must be imported; but it could never be paid for, since by the same treaty Germany was compelled to suffer the loss of one-third of its coal produc-tion and three-fourths of its iron ore production, thereby severely cur-tailing the nation's industrial activities and producing widespread unemployment. Unable to raise enough food to feed itself, with its indus-trial machine shattered, and almost totally bereft of shipping, Germany would die. The German note concluded:

> IF THE PEACE STIPULATIONS ARE CARRIED OUT, THIS SIMPLY MEANS THAT MANY MILLIONS OF PEOPLE IN GERMANY WOULD PERISH. THIS PROCESS WOULD DEVELOP RAPIDLY, AS OWING TO THE BLOCKADE DURING THE WAR AND ITS SHARPENING DURING THE ARMISTICE THE NATION'S HEALTH IS BROKEN. NO RELIEF WORK, OF HOWEVER GREAT A SCOPE AND DURATION, COULD STOP THIS DYING *EN MASSE*. THE PEACE WOULD DEMAND OF GER-MANY SEVERAL TIMES AS MANY HUMAN LIVES AS FOUR AND A HALF YEARS OF WAR SWALLOWED UP. . . . IF THIS PEACE TREATY IS SIGNED, A DEATH SENTENCE IS THEREBY PASSED ON MANY MILLIONS OF GERMAN MEN, WOMEN, AND CHILDREN.

This protest struck a responsive chord in a number of British and Ameri-can economic experts, including Keynes and Hoover. Lloyd George, too, began to squirm uneasily, as it gradually began to dawn on him that perhaps the treaty was a bit too harsh on the Huns after all, and that maybe they wouldn't sign and then some other family would soon be receiving its mail at Number 10 Downing Street—although the Prime Minister was never so alarmed that he volunteered to surrender any British gains from the conference; any concessions at this stage of the game would have to come from France. But throughout the furor Wilson remained unmoved, a veritable Rock of Gibraltar—or was it the Rock of Ages? In fact, Ray Stannard Baker noted that his boss was "in the best spirits in weeks," with the burden of writing a treaty for the peace of the world finally off his shoulders: "For better or worse something has been done." In the course of the last several months, Clemenceau and Lloyd George had convinced Wilson that the application of his principles to the real world of 1919 required certain modifications, and he had grudgingly made such adjustments; but he would not now go back and reopen those questions just because Lloyd George had suddenly gotten cold feet (Wilson described the Welshman as being in a "perfect funk"). The President added that such last-minute, panic-stricken cries for changes in a treaty in which he had already invested so much effort and emotional energy made him "very sick" and "tired." Besides, this was precisely the sort of situation for which the League had been so carefully designed: to remedy any inequities in the treaty once emotions had cooled, and to adjust the peace terms to constantly changing circumstances. As Colonel House explained to a friend, "I see some defects, too, and I am aware that in some respects we have not lived up to our ideals, but we have been dealing with men and not with angels. As the treaty carries with it the machinery for its correction, before it is ratified and before the Covenant is generally recognized as the hope of our civilization, I think it unwise to point out and dwell upon the defects and the shortcomings of our work, although I am aware at least of some of them."

And it was here that the open resurgence of militarism within Germany since the days of the Armistice came back to plague the Ebert-Scheidemann-Noske regime. Back in February, at the beginning of the conference, Clemenceau had voiced his conviction that Germany had not undergone a change of heart, that the new Majority Socialist regime was merely a reincarnation of the Second Reich in a slightly altered guise. "The Germans had succeeded in forming a Government," Clemenceau reminded Wilson and Lloyd George, "and the first words spoken in the National Assembly had been: 'Deutschland über Alles.' The second thing done had been to place all power in the hands of the accomplices of William II." Within Germany, the Independent Socialists recognized how the Freikorps rampages throughout Germany over the past four months, the rallies for Hindenburg and the Kaiser, and the rape of Munich all kept the memories of the infamous Hun atrocities in Belgium and northern France alive in the Allies' memories: "By reestablishing militarism the present Government has strengthened the mistrust of Germany. We have no hope that the Entente Imperialists will substantially alleviate the conditions."

Still the notes continued to flutter out of the Hôtel des Reservoirs. By May 21 eleven messages had been relayed to Clemenceau, and six more were on the way. By then the sheer volume of protests had begun to wear upon everyone's nerves (Nicolson spent a dispiriting day translating one of the notes, "which," he complained, "descend upon us like leaves in Vallombrosa"), and the force of the German arguments was lost in the avalanche of verbiage (the longest German note weighed in at 65,000 words). The whole process of protest and rebuttal soon turned into an undignified squabble over minor details and real or imagined insults and old, old grudges. A wily diplomat like Talleyrand might have turned the divisions and uncertainties in the Allied delegations to advantage, but Germany had no Talleyrand—only the supercilious and heavy-handed Brockdorff-Rantzau and his notes and more notes.

On 44th Street in New York City, not far from the old Hippodrome Theater, there once stood the offices of a magazine called *Vanity Fair*. It was what was known in those days as a magazine of "taste"—or, in the words of a disgruntled former employee, a "whited sepulchre." *Vanity Fair* generally parroted the party line of the Continental cultural establishment, and put a premium on the sort of cautious, haughty wit that never really punctured but rather reinforced the conventions and pompous pretensions of the smart set. Its motto might have been: Satire is good for circulation, but never antagonize an advertiser.

In May 1919 a new managing editor joined *Vanity Fair* at a salary of one hundred dollars a week: twenty-nine-year-old Robert Benchley, a former editor of the *Harvard Lampoon*. Although Benchley was constantly and unabashedly bewildered by the never-ending tribulations of fate, he remained unfailingly polite through it all, a man of gentle good humor whom nearly everyone cherished as one of the true human treasures of the world. His first article for *Vanity Fair* was entitled "No Matter from What Angle You Looked at It, Alice Brookhansen Was a Girl Whom You Would Hesitate to Invite into Your Own Home." Benchley soon made the acquaintance of the magazine's drama critic, Mrs. Dorothy Parker, a seemingly innocent but entirely capable young woman given to wearing an unwieldy and bedraggled feather boa; her husband, Eddie "Spook" Parker, still had not come home from the war and had, in fact, recently been assigned to the American army of occupation in the Rhineland. Just a few days after they met, Benchley and Parker were joined by Robert Sherwood, a six-foot-seven veteran of Harvard and the Canadian Black Watch who *Vanity Fair*'s editor, Frank Crowninshield, had just hired on a three-month trial basis.

Life in the magazine's offices could be more than a little stuffy with Crowninshield in charge, but Parker, Benchley, and Sherwood usually found ways to lighten the atmosphere. Employees were forbidden to discuss their salaries, so Parker, Benchley, and Sherwood wrote their salaries on placards that they wore around the office, pretending nothing was amiss. Employees were told not to call each other by their first names, so Dorothy began to refer to Benchley as "Fred." (It seemed funny at the time. Probably you had to have been there.) Employees arriving after the assigned morning hour were instructed to fill out tardy slips explaining why they were late; arriving eleven minutes late one morning, Benchley grimly explained that the Hippodrome's performing elephants had escaped just as he was getting to the office. Trying to be a Good Samaritan, he had trailed the renegade pachyderms into and out of the Plaza Hotel and then skillfully rounded them up along the Hudson docks before they could board a steamer for Boston.

This whimsical trio—all, incidentally, conspicuously lacking any particular qualifications for the positions they held at *Vanity Fair*—began to lunch together just down the block from their offices at the comfortably informal (but not inexpensive) Algonquin Hotel, also a favorite of actors and actresses from the neighboring theater district. Actually, the lunches started as the result of an escort service that Benchley and Parker provided for Sherwood. It seems that every time Sherwood set foot outside the magazine's offices, he was accosted by a band of midgets performing at the Hippodrome. They would scamper about him, grabbing his knees, jeering at the unnatural height of the giant, and generally making his life miserable. "They were always sneaking up behind him and asking him how the weather was up there," Parker recalled. " 'Walk down the street with me,' he'd asked, and Mr. Benchley and I would leave our jobs and guide him down the street."

There, in the Algonquin in May, Benchley rekindled his acquaintance with three men who had just returned from France, where they had served on the staff of *Stars and Stripes*: Franklin Pierce Adams ("an erudite and witty man who greatly resembled a narrow-shouldered moose" and who was known to readers of his famous *New York Tribune* column, "The Conning Tower," simply as F.P.A.), Alexander Woollcott (*The New York Times*'s acerbic drama critic), and Harold Ross, a wandering editor in search of a magazine. Benchley introduced them to his new friends from *Vanity Fair*, and soon a series of bright insults, inside jokes, and witty ripostes began to fly back and forth across the Algonquin Round Table.

* * *

Waiting was the hardest part. For six weeks, Harry G. Hawker waited in the little city of St. John's in Newfoundland. Six weeks of miserable weather: it was either bad at this end, stormy in the middle of the Atlantic, or threatening on the other end, off the Irish coast. Snow, dense fog, gales, rain, heavy winds, high seas—always lousy weather, bloody depressing, and no takeoff.

Harry G. Hawker, a twenty-seven-year-old Australian test pilot, had come to England to learn to fly, working his way up from a job as a mechanic with the Sopwith Company. Hawker already had won the prestigious British Michelin trophy in 1912 for his endurance flight of eight hours and twenty-three minutes, and was the former holder of the British altitude record. During the war, he had worked with Sopwith's engineers to test the performance of experimental planes, and now he was about to start the most demanding flight of his illustrious career.

In the late winter of 1919, the *Daily Mail* (Lord Northcliffe's sensationalist newspaper so scathingly scorned by Lloyd George) announced that it would pay a prize of ten thousand pounds (about $50,000) to the crew of the first airplane to cross the Atlantic. The offer immediately drew three serious entries: Hawker and his navigator, Lieutenant Commander MacKenzie Grieve of the Royal Navy, with their single-engine Sopwith; Captain Frederick P. Raynham and Major C. W. H. Morgan in a Martinsyde triplane; and Major J. C. P. Wood and navigator Captain C. C. Wylie, in a Short Brothers biplane called the *Shamrock*. Wood planned to fly from Ireland to North America, while Hawker and Raynham were going to head east from Newfoundland.

Under a heavy cloak of secrecy, four aviation crews from the United States Navy also were preparing to fly across the Atlantic. There were important distinctions between the American and the British ventures: the American navy pilots were not, of course, entered in the *Daily Mail* competition; the Americans would be flying Curtiss seaplanes rather than the land-based airplanes the British pilots would be using (a seaplane's ability to float on the water being a not inconsiderable advantage when one was flying across nearly two thousand miles of ocean); the Americans would try to fly together and render assistance to one another if necessary; and— very important—the Americans were heading for the Azores, which was "only" a 1,300-mile nonstop flight, approximately six hundred miles less than the distance from Newfoundland to Ireland. After refueling, the navy planes would continue on to mainland Portugal. As a further precaution, navy officials had stationed destroyers and battleships in a line along the seaplanes' flight path, to monitor their progress and report any difficulties.

December 31, 1918: President Woodrow Wilson and King George V on the way to the railway station in London, at the conclusion of Wilson's official visit to England. *Library of Congress*

Street fighting in Berlin during the Spartacist uprising in January 1919. *UPI/Bettmann Newsphotos*

Government troops awaiting a Spartacist attack in the Unter den Linden, Berlin. *UPI/Bettmann Newsphotos*

The Big Four—(from left) Lloyd George, Orlando, Clemenceau, and Wilson—outside the Quai d'Orsay, Paris. *Library of Congress*

Prime Minister David Lloyd George of Great Britain, "the Welsh Wizard." *National Archives*

Premier Georges Clemenceau of France, "the Tiger." *National Archives*

Prime Minister Vittorio Orlando of Italy. *National Archives*

Prime Minister Ignacy Jan Paderewski of Poland. *National Archives*

Wilson and Admiral Grayson playing shuffleboard on the deck of the *George Washington* on the way home from Paris in February. *National Archives*

Vladimir Ilyich Lenin (center), flanked by two of his comrades, Joseph Stalin (left) and Mikhail Kalinin. *UPI/Bettmann Newsphotos*

An American military encampment in the frozen wasteland of northern Russia, outside Archangel. *National Archives*

General Reginald E. H. Dyer, the British commander who ordered the massacre at Amritsar. *UPI/Bettmann Newsphotos*

Two men who began their rise to power in 1919:

Ex-corporal Benito Mussolini.
UPI/Bettmann Newsphotos

Corporal Adolf Hitler (seated at left). *UPI/Bettmann Newsphotos*

Two of the greatest hitters who ever lived:

"Shoeless Joe" Jackson, Chicago White Sox slugger. *National Baseball Library, Cooperstown, New York*

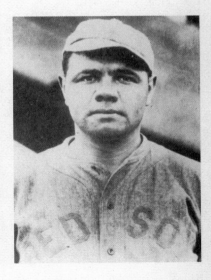

Babe Ruth, star outfielder and pitcher for the Boston Red Sox. *Babe Ruth Birthplace Foundation Inc.*

The Great Soul: Mohandas K.
Gandhi and his wife.
UPI/Bettmann Newsphotos

Béla Kun (seated), leader of the short-lived Hungarian Soviet Republic.
UPI/Bettmann Newsphotos

Dr. Albert Einstein.
UPI/Bettmann Newsphotos

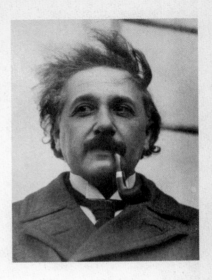

The German delegation to the Paris Peace Conference, standing outside the Hôtel des Reservoirs. Count Ulrich von Brockdorff-Rantzau, head of the delegation, is standing (and scowling) fourth from the left. *National Archives*

Presentation of the peace treaty to the Germans on May 7 in the conference room of the Trianon Place Hôtel at Versailles. Clemenceau is standing at the extreme right; Brockdorff-Rantzau is seated facing him at the extreme left. *National Archives*

President Friedrich Ebert of Germany (second from right, holding his top hat in front) reviewing the troops of the Weimar Republic. *UPI/Bettmann Newsphotos*

Harry Hawker (right) and
MacKenzie Grieve, the aviators
who tried—and failed—to cross
the Atlantic nonstop in May of
1919.

The funniest man in the world,
Charlie Chaplin, with his newest
discovery—Jackie Coogan, during
the filming of *The Kid. Library of
Congress*

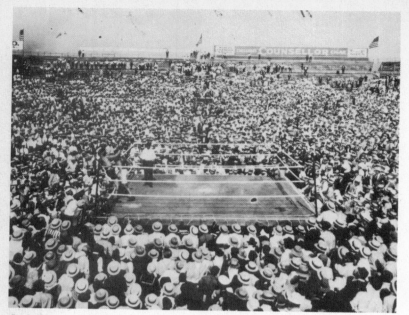

Jack Dempsey (in the light trunks) demolishing Jess Willard in the
heavyweight title fight in Toledo, Ohio, on July 4. *Library of Congress*

Woodrow Wilson in an automobile procession through Sioux City,
Iowa, during his September tour to drum up public support for the
League of Nations. *UPI/Bettmann Newsphotos*

Wilson speaking to the crowd in San Diego on September 19; Mrs.
Wilson is at the extreme right. *UPI/Bettmann Newsphotos*

William "Kid" Gleason, manager of the ill-fated Chicago White Sox. *National Baseball Library, Cooperstown, New York*

Eddie "Cocky" Collins, star White Sox second baseman, who was not a part of the World Series fix. *National Baseball Library, Cooperstown, New York*

The infamous Chicago Black Sox, the men who threw the World Series in return for payoffs from gamblers.

Chick Gandil, ringleader of the conspiracy. *National Baseball Library, Cooperstown, New York*

Star pitchers Claud "Lefty" Williams and Eddie Cicotte. *National Baseball Library, Cooperstown, New York*

Joe Jackson, who later retracted his confession and maintained his innocence of any wrongdoing. *National Baseball Library, Cooperstown, New York*

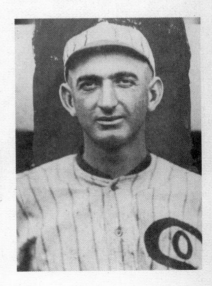

Woodrow Wilson, shortly before his death in 1924. *Library of Congress*

All of these distinctions made the American effort look more like a major military operation, planned down to the last detail, than a test of individual flying skill. Still, the British pilots knew that history would remember only the final result if the Americans succeeded in crossing the Atlantic first. So Hawker and Raynham waited impatiently for the weather to clear while the American Curtiss seaplanes (known, with the flamboyance and creativity typical of American military nomenclature, as NC-1, NC-2, NC-3, and NC-4) completed their test flights—once taking Acting Secretary of the Navy Roosevelt up for a ride—and made their way from Rockaway Bay to Halifax to begin their journey across the bounding main.

Major Wood was the first to take off, leaving Eastchurch, England, on April 18 for the Curragh (just outside Dublin), whence he would proceed across the Atlantic. Unfortunately, engine trouble from an air lock in the fuel system caused the biplane to fall into the sea several miles off the Irish coast near Holyhead. For thirty minutes Wood and his navigator clung to the overturned body of the plane, until a rowboat dispatched from shore rescued them.

Four weeks later, shortly after seven-thirty on the evening of May 16, three of the American seaplanes finally left Trepassey harbor in Newfoundland, bound for the Azores. The giant planes each had a wingspan of 126 feet, and each was equipped with four Liberty motors (four hundred horsepower each) as well as a four-leaf clover. Within a few minutes they had flown out of sight beyond the eastern horizon.

Unwilling to wait any longer (Hawker had publicly vowed to "beat the Yankees across"), Hawker and Grieve completed their preparations and made ready to leave. Their Sopwith was far smaller (with a wingspan of forty-six feet) and less powerful than the American seaplanes, and carried only one 350 horsepower, twelve-cylinder Rolls-Royce Eagle Monk III engine and enough fuel for twenty-four hours. They were going to try to make the flight in twenty hours, which meant that the engines would be going on full power the whole time—1,800 revolutions per minute for 1,200 minutes. There were no pontoons or "box-floats" to keep the plane afloat in the event of a forced landing in the water. To lighten the plane and conserve precious fuel, Hawker planned to release the undercarriage as soon as the Sopwith took off, which meant that he would have to make a crash landing under even the best conditions, no matter whether he came down on land or water. Although as a rule Hawker scorned protective clothing (he also disdained the use of oxygen on his high-altitude flights) he and Grieve did wear full-length, inflatable suits that would help them keep afloat for a while; but if the plane went down in mid-ocean their chances of survival were virtually nil, especially since Hawker had decided to take the shortest route possible, which lay far outside the major shipping lanes. Any mechanical malfunction, any navigational error, and Hawker and Grieve were as good as dead.

On the afternoon of May 18, thousands of spectators gathered to watch the departures of both Hawker and Raynham. It was a cold, clear, sunny day in Newfoundland, although the latest weather reports called for heavy storms far across the water to the east. But with the Americans already on their way, the British pilots would wait no longer. ("Hang the weather!" shouted Hawker to the weather bureau. "I go this afternoon though it leads me to the Pacific.") Raynham, using the field at nearby Quidi Vidi, drew the larger crowd of admirers, but as the huge Martinsyde triplane taxied along the bumpy ground, an axle buckled from the weight of the fuel; the plane's nose suddenly toppled forward and the machine fell heavily back to earth. Raynham and Morgan were bruised and cut, but not seriously injured. The damage to the Martinsyde was irreparable.

Meanwhile, Hawker and Grieve made a final inspection of their Sopwith, and then climbed calmly into the cockpit. At 3:21 they turned diagonally across the uneven field and, after a brief three-hundred-yard run, took off from St. John's into a light northeasterly breeze. They flew over Quidi Vidi and signaled farewell to their disappointed rivals. Spectators heard the roar of the Sopwith as it grew smaller and smaller in the brilliant cloudless sky, saw the propeller sparkling like a signal lamp, murmured to themselves "Godspeed," but shook their heads in doubt. It was, wrote *The New York Times*'s observer, the start of "the most perilous airplane flight in history." (At the Royal Aero Club in London, the club's secretary maintained a proper, stiff-upper-lip lack of concern: "People have flown for twenty-four hours without coming down lots of times. The only reason it hasn't been done oftener is because it's so boring. There is no reason why one shouldn't keep up as well over the sea as over the land.") Hawker pulled a lever and the Sopwith's undercarriage dropped away and the plane rose faster, disappearing from view at 3:37, at about five thousand feet. They ran into thick fog off the Newfoundland banks, rose above it, and lost sight of the sea.

The last wireless message Hawker received advised him of a deep and dangerous new depression developing over the eastern Atlantic.

Béla Kun had moved out of his office in the old palace of Emperor Francis Joseph and taken up residence in the less pretentious Hungaria Hotel (now rechristened the Soviet House). Machine guns guarded the hotel entrance, and Red Guards wearing leather uniforms with the insignia of their special battalion stood outside Kun's door. Kun greeted an American correspondent with an affable grin: See, he said, I am still alive, even though the newspapers in Vienna have reported my death on ten separate occasions. Kun was indeed still alive and, much to the dismay of the reactionaries of the Allied nations, still in control of Hungary. He stoutly defended his government's recent seizure of gold, jewelry, and diamonds from the wealthy citizens of Budapest. Those trinkets, Kun said, were taken from war profiteers who had bought them with the blood of Hungarian soldiers. (In the streets of the city the government had plastered placards with the Ten Commandments of the proletariat, one of which admonished workers: "Do not take property, jewels or money from the bourgeois. We will take them.")

Thus far it had been a surprisingly mild revolution. "There will be no Red terror if there is no White terror," Kun promised his American visitor. Production had been centralized—not a bad idea when raw materials were in short supply, as the Allies had discovered during the war—and power vested in the Workers' Councils; all cultural and educational activities were free to everyone; hospitals were opened to the public; courses in ethics replaced religious instruction in the schools. The imperial judicial system had been overhauled and workers became judges (including a woman, one of the first female judges in Europe). Most cases on the court's docket seemed to involve petty larceny, alcoholism, or the hoarding of jewelry. A soldier who had gotten drunk and walked down the street punching everyone he met was slapped with a two-year prison sentence; the man who had sold him the liquor was sentenced to one year. But a woman accused of stealing a small sum of money was acquitted because the judges knew she was not quite right in the head.

Kun had managed to retain supreme authority in his own hands, and it was his continuing popularity among the common workers of Budapest that allowed him to ignore the demands of his extremist colleagues for stiffer communistic measures. The man at whom Nicolson and Smuts had sneered now proved to be quite an effective leader after all. He played upon the emotions of the crowd like a revivalist preacher. Philip Marshall Brown, the deputy head of the American mission in Budapest, met with Kun shortly after Smuts had left the city. "I was greatly impressed by his immense vitality and shrewdness," Brown reported. "Not impressive in personality, he is nevertheless a force to be reckoned with. He knows what he is after, is a sincere Socialist, and evidently most resourceful. His whole policy seems how to avoid, if possible, the regrettable excesses of the Russian Socialists, which have given the name Bolshevist so sinister a significance."

"We are not at war with the Entente," Kun insisted, although shortly after the departure of the Smuts mission, orders had gone out from Paris— from the French government, not the Peace Conference—to the Rumanians to continue their advance into Hungarian territory. The resumption of the Rumanian invasion apparently caught Kun by surprise. He still had entertained a hope that Smuts would persuade the Allies to reopen negotiations with the Soviet Republic of Hungary, but actually Smuts was working toward quite the opposite end. In the Council of Four, Wilson continued to oppose military action against the Kun regime, and was in fact considerably disturbed by the continued Rumanian offensive against Hungary; caught up in the rush of more important events in early May, however, Wilson did not press the point too vigorously. Meanwhile, Hoover and the Allied Supreme Economic Council tried, none too subtly, to use the promise of lifting the blockade as a carrot to encourage forces within Hungary to overthrow Kun and his "Bolshevist-Jewish Mafia."

Once again, Allied strategy misfired. Faced with the unremitting hostility of Paris, and threatened from the east by the continuing Rumanian invasion and at home by several clumsy counterrevolutionary coup attempts, Kun was able to rally his countrymen through an appeal to both national and class spirit. Left-wing extremists used the manifest internal and external dangers as an excuse to whip up hatred of the bourgeoisie; dozens of prominent members of the *ancien regime* were seized as hostages. Realizing at last that "the Allies intend to strangle us," Kun ordered the nation mobilized. Lenin sent encouragement from Moscow: "*Ne vous enervez pas.* The events on the Rumanian front are not as serious as you imagine.... The mobilization of our Internationalists is in process at Kiev. Trust in the development of the world revolution of the proletariat, which is just a matter of time. Until then, fortify the city [Budapest], stock up munitions and food, arm the entire proletariat and have them join in the struggle. Hold until assistance reaches you. . . ."

In the space of little more than three weeks, the bedraggled Hungarian army was transformed into a remarkably effective fighting force through the training of 100,000 workers by officers of the old regime whose patriotism overrode their dislike of Kun's politics. Fortunately, Hungary's southern border remained relatively secure, as the Yugoslavs were preoccupied with their quarrel with Italy; to the north, the Czechs were in even more disarray than the Hungarians. Accordingly, the Red army moved out from Budapest and launched an offensive against Czechoslovakia on May 19. By the end of the month it had achieved a stunning series of successes, and Kun's authority in the capital was stronger than ever.

Meanwhile, throughout all of Eastern Europe the hunger went inexora-bly on. "We are now at the worst phase of the European famine that was inevitable after this world war," said Hoover. A member of the American Relief Committee came to an equally grim conclusion: "If you drew a line from the Baltic to the Black Sea, you would find for a hundred miles or so on either side of that line such a picture of devastation and human suffering as would not be believed by anyone who had not seen it. The state of Germany as compared with that of these regions is one of booming prosperity." The Supreme Economic Council in Paris had accepted the responsibility for the direct care of one million children, and British and American charitable organizations contributed nearly a million dollars for relief, but still the efforts were not enough. One hundred thousand people in eastern Poland suffered from typhus. In a hospital in Poland the diet consisted of water and a few ounces of bread every day. A day nursery in Austria provided the following meals for its children: ersatz black coffee with saccharine and three small pieces of bread for breakfast, soup made of sauerkraut or carrots for lunch, and coffee alone at four o'clock; many of the children's parents could serve them only a tasteless mush for supper. A British doctor visited Vienna and returned shaken by what he had seen: "What impressed me most was the appalling condition of every old person I saw, and of 95 percent of the children. The old people were like walking death's heads. . . . What struck me most when walking about the streets was that there were no toddlers. Children of three and even four were being carried by their mothers. The children did not run about, or shout, or quarrel. It was four days before I saw a child playing."

Vienna's plight was perhaps the most desperate. Not surprisingly, the Big Three in Paris worried that the Red tide would roll into Austria from Hungary. "Austria presents a peculiar spectacle," wrote one observer. "It is like a man whose relatives are all dead and who has been stripped of his most valuable possessions and is without physical resources to recoup his position. He must either attach himself to some benevolent person or die." So the Allies sent twelve trainloads of food into Austria every day, and the authorities in Vienna were told in no uncertain terms that these provisions would be forthcoming only so long as the Bolsheviks were kept at bay.

It was not an easy task. Communist agitators—including agents from Hungary—continually kept alive a spark of agitation among the unem-ployed and the weary disabled soldiers and returned prisoners. At one gathering on the steps of the mock-Gothic city hall, a depressed and sullen group of gray-faced people milled aimlessly about, listening to more of the same words that held out glittering promises but somehow failed to inspire any confidence among the desperate. Then came news of a march through the city to the Reichsrath (parliament) building, a procession of twenty thousand marchers with red banners. As the demonstrators arrived at the Reichsrath, a blue-jacketed sailor climbed a lamppost and shouted "We are hungry!" six times over. Someone raised the red flag on the official flagpole, and someone else tied a red bow around the neck of Apollo's statue. Police began to arrive. Street toughs shattered the windows of the parliament building and broke down the door. Mounted police charged with drawn swords. More police fired their rifles indiscriminately into the crowd. Disabled soldiers among the demonstrators who fell with fresh wounds were tended by the practiced hands of comrades who had survived four years in the trenches. Someone cried out, *"Nicht laufen"*: "Don't run." The mob, angered by the shooting of wounded veterans, shook their fists at the police and yelled, "Murderers!" A coal truck was overturned, and chunks of coal hurled through the windows of the Reichsrath; more was tucked into aprons and taken home for fuel. A passing car was commandeered and its gasoline used to set fire to the building.

"What do we want with a Parliament?" "All power to the Soviets!" "We're all Bolsheviks now." "Four years ago there were no Bolsheviks. It's the war that has done it." The Reichsrath flames were licking against the dessicated vestiges of the old society. A vengeful veteran who had lost both his legs scampered about on his hands, a manic grin on his desperate face, maimed for life but still seeking to repay those who had sent him off to war.

After twenty minutes, officers of the Volkswehr (a sort of socialistic national guard) appeared and began to calm the crowd. They used no force, just firmness and gentle persuasion. "The Volkswehr sympathizes with the just demands of the people. . . . We will keep order." "Comrade, please, a little way back." "Comrade, if you don't mind, will you please step over this railing?" And the people obeyed, while inside the fire was put out for the time being. Soon, flickering green-yellow tongues of flame appeared along the streets as a lamplighter made his rounds. A police horse felled during one of the charges was carved up into steaks, the meat smuggled into dark houses. Only the saddle and the skeleton remained.

"This is how the matter stands," said the officer. "I have been appointed judge in this penal colony. Despite my youth. For I was the former Commandant's assistant in all penal matters and know more about the apparatus than anyone. My guiding principle is this: Guilt is never to be doubted. Other courts cannot follow that principle, for they consist of several opinions and have higher courts to scrutinize them. That is not the case here, or at least, it was not the case in the former Commandant's time."

The explorer to whom this explanation was directed may have looked slightly dubious, for the officer continued to explain. The condemned prisoner who now stood before them, the officer said, had been assigned to sentry duty, and had been ordered to get up every hour on the hour and salute the captain's door. Last night his captain had arisen at two in the morning and found the sentry asleep. The captain had begun to thrash him; but instead of begging his superior's pardon for his sin, the sentry had seized the captain and threatened him. "That's the evidence," said the officer. "The captain came to me an hour ago, I wrote down his statement and appended the sentence to it. Then I had the man put in chains. That was all quite simple. If I had first called the man before me and interrogated him, things would have got into a confused tangle. He would have told lies, and had I exposed these lies he would have backed them up with more lies, and so on and so forth. As it is, I've got him and I won't let him go.—Is that quite clear now?"

The punishment was always to lie strapped to a bed beneath an instrument known as the Harrow, a mechanical device that wrote with tiny needles a sentence upon the prisoner's body: the words of the specific commandment that the prisoner had violated (in this case, "Honor Thy Superiors"). As the words were written, the body was gradually rotated, so that the result was a sentence engraved upon the entire breadth of the body. After six hours, the officer explained, the prisoner always experienced a moment of enlightenment, when he suddenly deciphered— through the writing motion of the Harrow—the precise words of the sentence. Then, when he was quite dead, the machine tossed his pierced body into a pit below.

"*In der Strafkolonie,*" or "In the Penal Colony": the title of a short story by Franz Kafka, published in May 1919. Alive in Prague, Kafka wrote to a friend regarding the tale: "Personal proofs of my human weakness are printed . . . because my friends, with Max Brod at their head, have conceived the idea of making literature out of them, and because I have not the strength to destroy this evidence of solitude. . . ."

On May 12 Eugene Leviné was arrested in Munich, betrayed by a friend. The Communist was tried and sentenced to death. On May 29 he wrote from prison to his wife: "I am very sad, I am filled with such deep sadness. Death itself does not concern me. A few last minutes, the rattle of the guns, perhaps my last salute to the world revolution. Oh, it is not that. Not death, not dying, but parting with life." On June 5, Leviné wrote in his diary, asking his wife to kiss their son for him. As he walked to the place of execution, he told the warder, "I know it is hard on you, an old man, to do this duty." He refused the blindfold and, just before the guns fired, shouted, "Long live the world revolution." The first round hit him directly in the heart.

At the University of Munich, Adolf Hitler sat through indoctrination lectures sponsored by the Reichswehr. He learned of the dangers of the German nation being caught in the golden chains of "interest slavery" (and everyone knew who the moneylenders were); he learned that German history was the story of the Teutonic master race. And occasionally, when there were discussions at the end of a class, Hitler would stand and attack the Jews who were defiling the purity of the German nation. At first an undistinguished speaker, Hitler found that as he rose more and more frequently his rhetoric, uttered with obvious sincerity and passionate conviction, could easily sway an audience.

27

"Their widows are increased

to me above

the sand of the seas."

Silence. No news of Hawker. No ship reported sighting the Sopwith, no one received any wireless message. The weather continued rough in the Atlantic to the west of Ireland, hampering search efforts. Some believed that cold air from the icebergs a hundred miles off the Newfoundland coast had damaged the plane's engine, and that Hawker and Grieve had gone down shortly after leaving St. John's. The Admiralty at Queenstown ordered every available vessel to search for them. The only clue was the sighting of a red flare by a cable ship approximately midway across the ocean.

After two days it was obvious that the plane had long ago exhausted its fuel supply and crashed somewhere in the Atlantic. Hawker's wife and seven-month-old baby daughter, who had gone down to meet him at the Sopwith aerodome at Brooklands, returned to their home in Surbiton. Realizing the situation was hopeless, the Admiralty prepared to call off the search. King George sent his condolences to Mrs. Hawker: "I feel the nation has lost one of its most able and most daring pilots. He sacrificed his life to the honor of British flying."

"It seemed as if there was not a thrill left to the world when the war ended, but everyone—old and young, fresh or jaded—hung breathlessly on the news from the sky," wrote the *New York Tribune* in its eulogy to Hawker and Grieve. "In the deliberate hazarding of all on the chances of great success there has been no venture to equal this. Our hats are off to the sporting courage behind such daring. Our sympathy goes out at his failure by such a slender distance, and our heartiest congratulations follow on the whole splendid deed. By such feats we know what the human race is capable of."

28

"Arise, and let us go by night,

and let us destroy her palaces."

After the tension and difficulties of dealing with the Germans, the arrival of the Austrian delegates at the Peace Conference was a positive relief. True, the Hapsburg empire had warred for four years against the Allies, but no one—except, significantly, the Italians—bore the same hard feelings toward the Austrians as they did toward the Huns. So when the special train from Vienna bearing the Austrian delegation pulled into the Gare de Grande-Ceinture at St-Germain shortly before six o'clock on the warm, sleepy evening of May 14, it was greeted with official joviality and the unalloyed good wishes of a crowd of mildly curious onlookers who wore their Sunday best as they strolled among the blooming lilac bushes and the chestnut trees in full flower. The head of the Austrian delegation, Chancellor Karl Renner (a Socialist and a steadfast and cultured pacifist who had fought against the war ever since it shattered the world of August 1914), descended first, hat in hand, and was immediately greeted by Monsieur Challiel, the prefect of the department. "You will be received here with the traditional courtesy of the French," Challeil graciously assured Renner, as the Italians gnashed their teeth angrily in the background. Renner—a plump, round-faced, balding gentleman wearing gold spectacles and a graying beard, looking "like a typical commercial man of fifty or so . . . a solid and trustworthy appearance"—seemed to be genuinely taken aback and somewhat embarrassed by the warmness of this reception, and at once gallantly apologized (in French) for not being able to speak French very well. Then Renner launched into a voluble explanation in German of something or other, until after a minute or so he realized that he was supposed to be a diplomat and hence constantly on his guard against saying too much, and so he settled down into a pleasant exchange of courtesies: "I hope I may go away with as joyful a heart as I bring." These formalities successfully completed, the Austrians were taken by car through shady avenues to their quarters in the luxurious Reinach villas overlooking the Seine. There were no high fences strung with wire, and no heavily armed sentries pacing the streets.

If the Austrians had expected to receive their version of the treaty soon after they arrived, they were in for a major disappointment. The Council of Four had not yet decided on the final boundaries of Austria and the other successor states of the Hapsburg empire, and so there was now a rush to get the whole business settled. Orlando and Sonnino continued to seek advantages wherever and however they could (Nicolson again found reason to complain of the Italians' "incessant ill temper, untruthfulness, and cheating"); Wilson and most of his experts remained more firmly opposed than ever to the Italian land-grabbing schemes; Clemenceau, while harboring a vague desire for a strong Austria to restrain Italy, generally acted as if he couldn't care less, and in fact he probably couldn't ("More than ever does he look like a gorilla of yellow ivory," thought Nicolson); and Lloyd George fluttered about, trying to carve up Turkey to supply Italy with concessions in Asia Minor in lieu of Fiume.

By virtue of their expertise in Central European affairs, Charles Seymour and Harold Nicolson were both intimately involved in these boundary deliberations. Nicolson kept getting dragged along into meetings of the Council of Five by Balfour; one such conference, held in the Quai d'Orsay, struck Nicolson as particularly absurd:

THERE, (IN THAT HEAVILY TAPESTRIED ROOM, UNDER THE SIMPER OF MARIE DE MÉDICIS, WITH THE WINDOWS OPEN UPON THE GARDEN AND THE SOUND OF WATER SPRINKLING FROM A FOUNTAIN AND FROM A LAWN-HOSE)—THE FATE OF THE AUSTRO-HUNGARIAN EMPIRE IS FINALLY SETTLED. HUNGARY IS PARTITIONED BY THESE FIVE DISTINGUISHED GEN-TLEMEN—INDOLENTLY, IRRESPONSIBLY PARTITIONED—WHILE THE WATER SPRINKLES ON THE LILAC OUTSIDE—WHILE THE EXPERTS WATCH ANXI-OUSLY—WHILE A. J. B. [BALFOUR], IN THE INTERVALS OF DIALECTICS ON SECONDARY POINTS, RELAPSES INTO SOMNOLENCE—WHILE LANSING DRAWS HOBGOBLINS UPON HIS WRITING PAD—WHILE PICHON CROUCHING IN HIS LARGE CHAIR BLINKS OWLISHLY AS DECISION AFTER DECISION IS ACTUALLY RECORDED—WHILE SONNINO, RETURNED TO CANOSSA, IS RUGGEDLY POLITE—WHILE MAKINO, INSCRUTABLE AND INARTICULATE, OBSERVES, OBSERVES, OBSERVES.

Seymour was equally unimpressed by the great men (known irrever-ently as *les grosse légumes*) at work during one of the rare meetings of the Council of Ten. Orlando, he thought, looked "very white and worn and says very little and without much pep"; Clemenceau, more irritable than ever, badgered Sonnino mercilessly ("You must want one thing or the other, M. le Baron Sonnino"); Wilson, who by turns either ignored his experts completely or relied on them wholeheartedly, today was in the mood for advice: "If anyone who knows about this will tell me what to do, I will do it." (Seymour, incidentally, believed Wilson to be "head and shoulders above his colleagues" in his ability to grasp the essentials of any matter at once, although Seymour did concede that Balfour—despite being no longer at the height of his powers—still had the best mind in Paris.)

Several days after Nicolson had sat morosely watching the dismemberment of Hungary, Lloyd George invited Orlando and Sonnino to his flat in the Rue Nitot to try to find a way out of the Adriatic deadlock. Everyone sat in the dining room around a map: a pie about to be sliced and digested. The Italians asked for Scala Nova. "Oh, no," protested Lloyd George, "you can't have that—it's full of Greeks." The Welshman then pointed out other enclaves of Greeks in the region; Nicolson tried to correct him, but Lloyd George remained adamant: "But yes, don't you see it's coloured green." Alas, Lloyd George had mistaken a topographical map for an ethnographic map, confusing the green of the valleys with Greeks and the brown of the mountains with Turks. When someone whispered the truth in his ear, he accepted the correction "with great good humour." After more badinage about coal mines, the Italians were awarded a League of Nations mandate over the Adalia region; someone mentioned that the League Covenant called for the mandatory power (Italy) to take due consideration of "the consent and wishes of the people concerned." The Italians, observed Nicolson, found this phrase very amusing. "How they all laugh! Orlando's white cheeks wobble with laughter and his puffy eyes fill with tears of mirth." Even the urbane Balfour, who had seen everything during four decades of diplomats and politicians, was shocked at this unseemly display of cynicism.

With this preliminary work out of the way, the Council of Four convened and took up the boundary question once again, Lloyd George still trying to conciliate Italy at the expense of the peoples of Asia Minor. "It is appalling," Nicolson wrote to his wife, "that these ignorant and irresponsible men should be cutting Asia Minor to bits as if they were dividing a cake. . . . Isn't it terrible, the happiness of millions being decided in that way, while for the last two months we were praying and begging the Council to give us time to work out a scheme?" Balfour set aside his elegant languor long enough to condemn the Big Three bitterly as "those three all-powerful, all-ignorant men sitting there and carving continents." He issued a written protest to Lloyd George; eventually the Prime Minister abandoned his Adriatic scheme.

Sometimes it seemed as if it really mattered not at all what the men at Paris decided, for events in Southern Europe were moving ahead on their own momentum. The Austrians were harassing the Yugoslavs along the Corinthian border. Yugoslavian infantry had already occupied Marburg. The Italians had landed large military forces at Zara and Sebeico, on the Dalmatian coast between Fiume and Spalato, and were fortifying ridges and mountain passes to the east. The Greeks, in turn, were landing their own forces at Smyrna. Meanwhile, Chancellor Renner and his colleagues were growing quite impatient at the delay in receiving the terms of peace (although at least they were eating well at the French government's expense at St-Germain).

Finally, on May 29, the Four met at Wilson's house and completed their work on the Austrian treaty. Then, having made their decisions, they called the experts (cooling their heels upstairs) into a drawing room to explain what they had done. Clemenceau, wearing his gray gloves as always, eased himself onto a sofa next to Lloyd George; Orlando stood expressionless; Wilson unfolded a map on the carpet in front of a big fireplace and cheerily began to show how the people and the land (today happened to be Yugoslavia's turn) were to be divided up. Everyone except Clemenceau and Lloyd George joined him kneeling on the floor; "It is like hunt the slipper," Nicolson thought. Seymour was in the front row when he felt someone pressing from behind; he "looked around angrily to find that it was Orlando, on *his* hands and knees crawling like a bear toward the map. I gave way and he was soon in the front row." Wilson did such a good job of explaining everything (the professor once more) that everyone except the Italians came away satisfied. Orlando tried one last time to obtain an important railway tunnel, arguing that it would be "inconvenient" to leave one end of the tunnel in one country and the other end in another. Wilson, still kneeling, glanced imploringly to heaven for help and, like Moses descending from Mount Sinai, replied, "Why, I have not come to Purris [sic] to discuss convenience: in my judgment the test is what the people themselves waant [sic]." No doubt, thought Nicolson, Wilson was sincere; "Yet he must know somewhere inside himself that our minds long ago have slid away from all such altitudes."

Thus was the Treaty of St-Germain completed.

One of the American seaplanes, the NC-4, arrived safely at the Azores after a flight of thirteen hours and eighteen minutes (average speed ninety miles an hour). The other three failed to complete the journey, but their crews were rescued. No sign of Hawker. Northcliffe offered to pay the ten thousand pounds in prize money to the families of Hawker and Grieve.

As the Balkans and Asia Minor were divided and subdivided, as the Germans continued to get on everyone's nerves with their notes, the atmosphere at the Peace Conference changed subtly: too many people had nothing to do, too many people were upset at the terms of the German treaty; no one knew whether the Germans would sign or whether they would refuse, bringing on a grotesque reincarnation of the war and still more death and starvation. Marshal Foch had left Paris to inspect the Allied headquarters along the Rhine, to make certain everything was in readiness if the Big Three should decide to invade Germany. The work that had taken so long and had seemed complete was now thrown into question: Would the treaty undergo severe revisions or would it be jettisoned completely? Everything lay in a twilight of uncertainty, awaiting the coming of the night, after which perhaps—perhaps—the dawn would follow.

The weather, though, was marvelous, Paris at its best, the streets full of taxis, French drivers quite reckless ("There is no speed limit," complained Frances Stevenson, "& little regard for human life. I suppose this is the result of the war"), the sidewalks full of gaily dressed citizens. A procession in honor of Joan of Arc took over the boulevards one day, with Sunday-school children marching alongside cassocked priests and Boy Scout bands, all the boys and girls earnestly trying to keep their little feet in time; "but," reported Shotwell with amusement, "it was the most ragged bit of marching I have ever seen." Music wafted from the Ambassadeurs; café patrons sat nearly comatose in the dazzling sunshine, stupidly watching the people walking past; the magnificent fountains at Versailles were turned on—for the first time since the war began—for a test preliminary to the grand display planned for the signing of the treaty.

Winston Churchill appeared again in Paris. He had been flying every day and loving it, and so he naturally brought up the Hawker tragedy when he saw Lloyd George. "The *Daily Mail* are making great copy out of it," Churchill said, "dwelling on the feelings of his wife, 'the poor little woman who is now a widow. ...' " "Yes," snapped Lloyd George angrily, "but who made her a widow?" Frances Stevenson reported that David—Churchill and Frances were almost the only two people who called Lloyd George by his first name—was quite upset about the whole affair, believing it to be a shabby stunt by the newspaper to increase its circulation.

Alexander Kerensky, the liberal who had tried to rule Russia after the

Czar abdicated, arrived in Paris to urge the Allies not to recognize Admiral Kolchak's White government, for Kolchak would simply reinstitute the old reactionary regime and launch a White terror throughout that sad country. Lord George Riddell and Ramsay MacDonald agreed that Lenin would be known to posterity as a great man, although, the socialist Mac-Donald added, "Russian events have shown that drastic changes are impracticable. You can only go step by step. But had it not been for Lenin the steps would have been very slow and halting. He has infused new life into the betterment movement." Lloyd George told Riddell a story of Clemenceau riding through the Bois; when the old man passed some pretty girls, they blew kisses to him. The Tiger returned the gesture and with a touch of sadness said softly, "It is hard, is it not, that one has never made a success until now, when it is too late?" British delegates passed around the latest witty saying: "Bonar Law cares but doesn't know; Balfour knows but doesn't care; Lloyd George neither knows nor cares." Harold Nicolson wrote to his father that "there is not a single person among the younger people here who is not unhappy and disappointed at the terms"—particularly the reparations provisions, which were "immoral and senseless." The only members of the British delegation who approved of the treaty, he added, were "the old fire-eaters." Frances Stevenson wondered whether she should marry a young man named Bertie Stern who had come to visit her in Paris. It was, she admitted, a great temptation; yet "I know I should not be happy now away from D. & no-one else in the world could give me the intense & wonderful love that he showers on me." Eventually Lloyd George told his "darling little girl" that he simply could not let her leave him. "So that is final," she wrote in her diary, "& I am very glad."

In the course of one day (May 19), Wilson suffered through sixteen official appointments, including meetings with Prince Charoon of Siam, a delegation of Carpatho-Russians, the president of the Celtic Circle of Paris, the Archbishop of Trebizond, and the president of the National Union of Railwaymen of France. Colonel Stephen Bonsal, a former international correspondent who was now acting as an adviser to Colonel House, saw Wilson and wrote in his diary that "the President looked wretched and evidently he is very tired, but there is still plenty of fight in him. It is a thousand pities he was not given an opportunity to recuperate from that strange illness that overtook him early in April."

American delegates were warned to beware of packages arriving in the mail bearing a "Gimbel Brothers" label. At the Crillon, a group of about a dozen young American officials—known collectively as the Jeunesse Radicale—who for various reasons opposed the treaty, met in a restaurant to decide upon a course of action. The group included Samuel Eliot Morison, Christian Herter (who would later succeed John Foster Dulles as Secretary of State in the late 1950s), William Bullitt, and Adolf Berle. Lincoln Steffens joined them, and later recalled the occasion:

I WAS THE ONLY OLDER MAN THERE TO SEE THAT SIGNIFICANT SCENE; ALL THOSE CONSCIENTIOUS, HIGH-BRED, MOSTLY RICH YOUNG GENTLEMEN AND THEIR WIVES, WHO WANTED TO DO RIGHT AND HAD TO DECIDE THEN AND THERE WHETHER TO SACRIFICE THEIR CAREERS, AS THEY HONESTLY BELIEVED, BY AN OPEN CHALLENGE TO THE WRONG DONE BY THEIR GOVERNMENT, BY THEIR DEPARTMENT, OR YIELD AND PLAY THE GAME. THEY ASKED MY ADVICE, SURE, I COULD SEE, THAT I WOULD BE FOR THE HEROIC COURSE. AND I WOULD HAVE BEEN IN THE OLD MUCKRAKING DAYS. BUT, AS I SAID, I HAD SEEN THE RUSSIAN REVOLUTION, THE WAR, AND THIS PEACE, AND I WAS SURE THAT IT WAS USELESS—IT WAS ALMOST WRONG —TO FIGHT FOR THE RIGHT UNDER OUR SYSTEM; PETTY REFORMS IN POLITICS, WARS WITHOUT VICTORIES, JUST PEACE, WERE IMPOSSIBLE, UNINTELLIGENT, HEROIC BUT IMMORAL. EITHER THEY AND WE ALL SHOULD LABOR TO CHANGE THE FOUNDATION OF SOCIETY, AS THE RUSSIANS WERE DOING, OR GO ALONG WITH THE RESULTANT CIVILIZATION WE WERE PART OF, TAKING CARE ONLY TO SAVE OUR MINDS BY SEEING IT ALL STRAIGHT AND THINKING ABOUT IT CLEARLY.

Bullitt and eight others, including Morison and Berle, sent letters of resignation to their superiors. Thirteen years later, in the summer of 1932, Berle told a friend that he had no regrets: "Inexperienced as we were, I think we did foresee, accurately, that a treaty based on hatred and irritation, and an endeavor to perpetuate the advantage of war in favor of the Allies under the cover of a so-called peace, would produce nothing but long drawn out misery." Six of the resignations were not accepted, since Berle and several others were still in the army, but Lansing accepted Bullitt's with alacrity. Totally disillusioned by his experiences at the Peace Conference, Bullitt fired a parting salvo at Wilson. "It is my conviction," he wrote with bitterness to the President, "that if you had made your fight in the open, instead of behind closed doors, you would have carried with you the public opinion of the world, which was yours. . . ."

Brockdorff-Rantzau sought a personal interview with Wilson, but was refused. Members of the German delegation reportedly were becoming afflicted with attacks of nervousness and depression; "the food," they complained, "is getting on everyone's nerves." They claimed they felt like geese in a cage waiting to be slaughtered. The Allied Supreme Council formally announced that if the German government accepted the treaty, the blockade would be completely and immediately removed; if Germany refused to sign, it would be reimposed completely and immediately. The Allies had an estimated 13 million men still under arms, Germany and Austria-Hungary fewer than one million. The watch on the Rhine, it was said, was never keener than tonight.

After seven days, Hawker appeared again.

At nine o'clock on the morning of May 25, a coast guard station in the islands off the northwestern coast of Scotland received a visual signal from a Danish steamer, the *Mary:* "Saved hands Sopwith aeroplane."

The station signaled back, "Is it Hawker?"

"Yes."

The *Mary* had left New Orleans on April 28, bound for its home port of Horsens, on the southeast coast of Jutland. In the early hours of the morning of May 19, the day after Hawker and Grieve had left St. John's, the *Mary*'s second mate sighted an airplane in distress, landing roughly in the water about two miles ahead. The seas were extremely high, a heavy gale raging from the northeast and increasing in intensity; it took half an hour for the crew to launch a lifeboat—at considerable risk to themselves—and another hour to reach the airplane. Hawker and Grieve were clinging to the body of the plane, waves constantly crashing over them (and Hawker constantly seasick). It was 8:30 A.M. Several hours later, the storm had become so bad that no rescue attempt would have been possible.

Once on board the steamer, Hawker and Grieve refused food; they were so exhausted that all they wanted to do was sleep. The *Mary* had no wireless, so they were unable to notify their families that they were safe.

What had gone wrong? Hawker later explained that after they had battled a strong northerly wind that had blown them steadily off course for five and a half hours following takeoff, the water filter between the airplane's radiator and the cylinder jackets became clogged with refuse (perhaps bits of solder, Hawker thought) which had been shaken loose by the action of the motor working at high speed for an extended period. The engine temperature rose rapidly; Hawker took his plane down several thousand feet and the temperature returned to normal. Everything went well for another few hours, until the circulation system again became choked. The engine began to boil. At the same time, a heavy rainstorm blew up. Realizing that they were never going to reach land, Hawker and Grieve decided to play it safe. At dawn, twelve and a half hours into the flight—over halfway across the ocean—Hawker changed course and flew diagonally across the main shipping route for about two and a half hours, when, said Hawker, "to our great relief, we sighted the Danish steamer, which proved to be the tramp *Mary*. We at once sent up our Verey light distress signals. These were answered promptly, and then we flew on about two miles and landed in the water."

Mrs. Hawker received the news of her husband's safety as she left her parish church at Hook. An experienced pilot herself, she had never given up hope; Hawker had warned her that if they were forced to land in the water, they might be picked up by a ship without a wireless. Outside her house, her friends now posted a sign: "Mr. Hawker has been found." That evening the vicar turned the regular parish church service, with Mrs. Hawker and her sister in attendance, into a service of thanksgiving for Hawker's safety. For his text he chose Luke 15:24: "For this my son was dead, and is alive again; he was lost, and is found."

When the *Mary* reached Loch Erribol, it was met by the destroyer *Woolston,* and Hawker and Grieve were conveyed to Scapa Flow, where they received a hero's welcome from the men of the Grand Fleet. "I thank you for your kind greeting," Hawker replied. (From their berths, German sailors left behind as caretakers on the captured ships of the Imperial German Navy interned by the British at Scapa Flow could hear the joyous celebration.) On Tuesday, May 27, Hawker and Grieve—both quiet and modest men who were not too keen on public displays—returned from the north of Scotland to London by train. Once arrived in the city, they were nearly devoured by the tens of thousands of Londoners who filled the streets from King's Cross to Tottenham Court Road and along the parade route up to the doors of the Royal Aero Club. "Nothing," wrote the *Manchester Guardian*, "has stirred the imagination of the street for a long time like [Hawker's] amazing story. That may seem strange with the innumerable romances and tragedies of the war so short a way behind us, but it is the fact." A group of overly enthusiastic and none-too-sober Australian soldiers on leave in London disrupted the ceremonies by capturing their celebrated fellow countryman and bearing him triumphantly through the city, first on their shoulders and then in an automobile that they dragged forward with a rope; Hawker escaped their attentions only by grabbing hold of a passing mounted policeman and riding off to a more dignified celebration at the Aero Club.

The next day, Hawker and Grieve were received by King George, Queen Mary, and the student pilot Prince Albert at Buckingham Palace. The airmen told their story once more, and then the King presented them with the Royal Air Force Cross, which previously had been awarded only to war heroes. On the weekend of May 31 and June 1, Hawker again was in the air, flying in an exhibition at the aerodome at Hendon. Someone asked him if he would attempt the Atlantic crossing again. "I want to," Hawker replied. "It all depends on the Sopwith Company. I am not only willing but eager to make another attempt. The Atlantic can and will be flown."

As the press devoted columns upon columns to Hawker's return, tucked far away in the corner of a back page in a few newspapers was a small item describing the development of a new poison gas known as lewisite. The poison was said to be extremely potent even in small doses; authorities claimed that ten airplanes could carry enough lewisite to destroy all vestiges of life in any of the world's greatest cities. One man who found the coincidence of news stories alarming was John Galsworthy, the author of the series of novels known collectively as *The Forsyte Saga*. Mankind, warned Galsworthy, had now reached the point where it was living in a fool's paradise, for "this exploitation of the air is the devil reincarnate." Clearly, a League of Nations meant nothing "when the laboratory and the aeroplane can wipe out civilisation in a week."

Along a wide belt from South America across the Atlantic to Africa, the sun disappeared for a full five minutes on May 29. While Wilson and his associates knelt over a map on the floor of a drawing room in Paris, while Hitler attended indoctrination classes in Munich, and Béla Kun celebrated Hungary's victories over the Czechs, the moon passed between the earth and the sun, producing a total eclipse. Earlier in the spring, two expeditions, one from the British Royal Society and one from the Royal Astronomical Society, had been dispatched to the "track of totality" in the Southern Hemisphere to take photographs of the sky, and particularly of the star-field around the sun, during the eclipse. One scientific party— including Sir Arthur Eddington—was stationed on the island of Príncipe in the Gulf of Guinea, about one hundred miles off the west coast of Africa; the other, led by Dr. A. C. Crommelin of Greenwich Observatory, had set up its cameras on an appropriately elevated location near Sobral, fifty miles inland from the Brazilian coast. Both parties were armed with two telescopes, one with an aperture of thirteen inches, the other with a four-inch opening.

Since a total solar eclipse did not come along every day, the occasion always served as the opportunity for detailed astronomical experiments and observations. This particular eclipse, however, was the subject of even greater interest than usual within the scientific community, because it provided a chance to test the general theory of relativity first propounded by a German physicist named Albert Einstein in 1915. Very simply put, one part of the theory of relativity held that light was subject to gravitational forces, and that rays of light would bend as they passed by a large body such as the sun. The photographs taken of the area around the sun by the two British expeditions would be compared with others taken before and after the eclipse. If they showed that light did not shift, then Einstein's theory would be discredited; if they showed that light shifted less than Einstein predicted, the deflection might easily be explained away by the presence of particles in the air. But if the full Einstein shift occurred, then the fabric of the laws of Newtonian physics would be irreparably rent. More than two hundred years of human certainty about the workings of the universe would be suddenly overthrown.

Einstein himself presumably was busy at this moment in Berlin, preparing for his forthcoming marriage on June 2 to his cousin, Elsa Einstein Lowenthal. It was the forty-year-old Einstein's second marriage, his first having ended in divorce in February 1919. (The divorce decree stipulated that his first wife would receive any money Einstein received from a Nobel Prize award.) Clearly uneasy with close personal relationships, Einstein in these years was, through the eyes of a friend, "still a young man, not very tall, with a wide and long face, and a great mane of crisp, frizzled and very black hair, sprinkled with gray and rising high from a lofty brow. His nose is fleshy and prominent, his mouth small, his lips full, his cheeks plump, his chin rounded. He wears a small cropped mustache. He speaks French rather haltingly, interspersing it with German. He is very much alive and fond of laughter. He cannot help giving an amusing twist to the most serious thoughts."

The happy couple planned to make their home in Elsa's apartment at Haberlandstrasse 5. Elsa was quite the motherly type, which suited her new husband well, for "Albertle," as she called him, needed to be fussed over and taken care of. And like everyone else in Berlin in the early June of 1919, the newlyweds wondered whether their government would in the end submit and sign the treaty of peace in Paris.

Events in Afghanistan were never uncomplicated. Back in February, the reigning Amir, Habibullah Khan, was murdered while sleeping in his tent. No one saw the killer. Habibullah, who had ruled Afghanistan since 1901—if anyone could be said truly to have governed the obstreperous Afghan tribesmen—had tried to maintain amicable relations with British India. He had even visited Calcutta in 1907; while there, he had been introduced to the Duke and Duchess of Manchester (the latter being the former Miss Helen Zimmerman of Cincinnati). Deeply impressed, Habibullah had offered to purchase the Duchess from her husband on the spot, even though the Amir already owned four wives. The Duke diplomatically considered and then rejected the offer.

It was not clear who had shot the Amir—presumably it had not been the Duke of Manchester—but since Habibullah's pronounced unwillingness to disturb the English sahibs across the border in India had earned him the enmity of the more chauvinistic elements in Kabul, who wished to rid Afghanistan of British influence, suspicion centered upon extreme nationalistic elements in the capital. The Crown Prince, Inayatullah Khan, was widely perceived to be far too indolent to become involved in any complicated political schemes, and he made no move to seize the throne after his father's death. So the succession turned upon the struggle for power between a younger son, Amanullah Khan (twenty-seven years old, chubby, an ardent nationalist and modernizer, and quite a good tennis player), and his uncle Nasrullah. To bring the army over to his side, Nasrullah promised to raise the soldiers' pay to sixteen rupees a month. Amanullah, however, went his brother one better and succeeded in buying the military's support by raising his bid to twenty rupees a month. The minister of finance subsequently tried to persuade the Crown Prince to offer the army twenty-four rupees, but Inayatullah simply couldn't be bothered. Amanullah promptly arrested Nasrullah for complicity in the murder of Habibullah (Nasrullah was almost certainly innocent; the evidence indicates that Amanullah himself may well have been guilty of instigating the crime), sentenced him to life imprisonment, and confiscated his property; then Amanullah convicted an army official, Colonel Ali Raza, of the actual murder of the old Amir and ordered him executed. Finally, the new Amir issued a directive canceling all public works projects so that the treasury could pay the new army wages.

But rumors persisted that an innocent man had been executed, and that Amanullah was shielding the real assassin. As disaffection mounted in Kabul, Amanullah decided to divert his subjects' attention elsewhere, specifically to the opportunity for foreign adventure and plunder (which was always a good bet, especially in Afghanistan). He encouraged attacks by the border tribesmen upon India—where, he had heard, great nationalist revolts against the British had weakened the defenses of the Raj in the northwest provinces—and promised the Afghan army that it would find riches beyond compare awaiting it in the golden land beyond the Khyber Pass, the gateway of invasion into India since time immemorial.

These disturbances were not, of course, anything new to the British, who had from time to time, and without marked success, tried to bring the border area under direct British control. As a matter of fact, in most places there was no clearly defined border between India and Afghanistan; between the two nations lay a sort of neutral zone whose unruly inhabitants, driven into the inhospitable region by the Mongols in the thirteenth century, usually refrained from causing too much trouble only in return for substantial British subsidies.

Unfortunately for Amanullah Khan, his informants in Peshawar had grossly overestimated the degree of disaffection in the Punjab. The initially successful Afghan sallies through the neutral zone and into indisputably Indian territory were directed largely against profitable and easy targets such as caravans and bazaars. Although the Afghan army itself was seriously deficient in men and material (being aptly described as "little more than a mob of bandolier-festooned rag-pickers"), when combined with the frontier tribesmen it was quite capable of creating serious difficulties for the British.

Forced to divert scarce manpower to repel the threat on the northwest frontier, the British government in India ordered a counter-invasion of Afghanistan. Bombs were dropped from decrepit British planes upon rebel strongholds (unable to gain enough altitude to fly over the Khyber Pass, the British pilots had to fly through it, enabling the rebel riflemen actually to fire *down* at the planes); and General Reginald Dyer was dispatched from the Punjab to lead a detachment of three thousand reinforcements. No one could gainsay Dyer's competence on the field of battle, and after two days of fighting against his guns, Afghanistan requested an armistice on June 3. The entire war had lasted less than a month, and there had been no decisive battles. But in the ensuing peace treaty, signed on August 8, Afghanistan won a major objective: the right to conduct its own foreign affairs free of British control, a right conceded by the more farsighted British diplomats, who knew that the days of Empire and the high-handed treatment of natives were numbered (although not yet departed by any means). For the moment, Amanullah remained firmly in control at Kabul.

General Dyer still had not filed his official report on the disturbances at Amritsar in April.

In 1829, Sir Robert Peel had founded the London Metropolitan Police Force, whose members were known familiarly and usually with affection as "bobbies," "peelers," and, from the shiny buttons adorning their uniforms, "coppers." Peel's action was quite controversial at the time, as it flew in the face of considerable opposition from those Englishmen who believed that a force of salaried policemen, organized along semi-military lines, was dangerously akin to that *bête noire* of pre-Victorian England, a professional standing army.

Ninety years later, in the early summer of 1919, Peel's handiwork was once more the center of controversy. The previous August, while the war was still grinding mercilessly on, the city of London had witnessed a confrontation between the fifteen thousand policemen of the force and the Home Office authorities who exercised dictatorial control over them. The police, fed up with low pay (constables received between £117 and £133 a year) and some extraordinarily autocratic promotion and grievance procedures, had walked off their beats. Until the last minute, the government had been convinced that the men would never actually strike, and so it was forced to negotiate, belatedly, an uneasy truce. The Prime Minister himself—who, in classic Lloyd George style, had listened sympathetically to the men's complaints, loudly professed indignation at their sorry situation, and impetuously lashed out at his subordinates: "Why did not somebody tell me about this?"—promised the police that he would personally look into their grievances. Since that time the authorities had done virtually nothing except establish "representative boards" that were supposed to investigate grievances, but mostly sat on their collective hands and entangled the men's complaints in red tape.

A bobby's life was not an easy one. A young man or woman (most of the two hundred female members of the force were relegated to office and telephone duty) who wished to join the Metropolitan Police Force had to be between twenty-one and twenty-seven years of age, perfectly sound in mind and body, and "stand a clear five feet nine inches without shoes or stockings." The recruit needed to possess unexceptionable past references and must, according to the conditions of service signed before a witness, give his whole time to his work (his wife could not keep a shop, for instance). He could not withdraw from the force without leave. He was expected to remain free of debt, to live in a respectable locality, and to dress and educate his children decently. An indoctrination program of rigorous physical drills and courses of instruction taught him "the duties of a constable": how to deal with fires, obstructions in the street, dead bodies, suicides, runaway horses, and broken telegraph wires; how to give the proper attention to premises for the prevention of crime; and what to do in case of a collision between a van and a hackney carriage. A constable usually was quite on his own out on the streets, left alone to deal with emergencies or control a crowd bent upon hooliganism. Although he was supervised by a hierarchy of officers—first a sergeant, then an inspector, and on up the ladder to the Home Secretary and, ultimately, Parliament itself—he had to exercise considerable individual discretion and judgment in the performance of his duties. He was *not* intended to be a cipher, or a machine who merely carried out orders.

Nevertheless, one of the constables' constant complaints was that their officers did indeed treat them as ciphers, and afforded them no respect, subjecting them to petty tyrannies that made their lives miserable and permitting personal grudges to influence decisions on discipline and promotion. The men also demanded higher pay and better pensions, of course. But the major sticking point by far, in late May of 1919, was the question of formal government recognition of the National Union of Police and Prison Officers, the union formed by the policemen to advance their interests.

Lloyd George's government absolutely and without exception refused to have any dealings with any policemen's trade union. Its opposition stemmed primarily from a belief that a union would undermine discipline—the men had to obey the commands of a superior officer at all times, and thus could never be allowed to bargain or negotiate with the Home Office as equal to equal. And, given the growing strength of the Labour Party in the past decade, the authorities also feared that a policemen's union might align itself with other trade unions and become a cat's-paw for radical political interests. "Having regard to the extremely difficult and delicate character of the duties of policemen," Home Secretary Shortt explained, "and especially the bearing of those duties on the liberty of the subject, policemen could not be regarded as on a similar footing to other employees." The government's stance was clear: any policeman who went on strike from this moment on would be dismissed from the force forever. Period.

There was no doubt that most of the policemen in Britain were loyal and devoted public servants, and that they threatened to invoke the strike weapon only as a last resort. But there truly seemed to be no other way to get the government's attention, to force it to negotiate in good faith. Said one police official:

WE RECOGNIZE THE NECESSITY OF DISCIPLINE, AND WE DO NOT WANT A STRIKE; BUT WE FEEL THAT NO OTHER COURSE IS OPEN TO US. OUR GRIEVANCES ARE REAL; THEY HAVE BEEN PUT BEFORE THE AUTHORITIES, AND WE CAN GET NO REDRESS. WHEN OUR CASE IS PUT BEFORE THE WATCH COMMITTEE AND THEY TREAT IT WITH WHAT LOOKS TO US LIKE DISDAIN, WE HAVE NO COURT OF APPEAL. WE ARE CALLED "BOLSHEVIKS." NOW, NOTHING IS FURTHER FROM OUR THOUGHTS THAN TO ADOPT BOLSHEVIK METH-

ODS. ALL WE WANT IS FAIR PLAY. CONSIDERING THE HIGH PRICE OF FOOD-
STUFFS AND CLOTHING WE THINK WE ARE ENTITLED TO A LIVING WAGE.
WE WISH ALSO TO BE PUT ABOVE THE REACH OF TEMPTATION TO TAKE
"TIPS." WE WANT TO BE INDEPENDENT AND DO OUR DUTY TO THE PUBLIC.

Yet there was also another reason why the movement to establish a police union gained special impetus in Britain in the spring and summer of 1919. Many of the bobbies had served in the army during four years of a war filled with muddleheaded military decisions and brutally incompetent policies designed by bumbling Whitehall ministers; and like other demobilized British workers, they had returned home, according to the *Manchester Guardian*, "in such a state of scepticism about official politicians as has probably never before possessed any great mass of men in the world." It was not at all a coincidence that the policemen most insistent upon protest and reform were veterans of the Western Front. And these men were also heartily sick of military discipline, which made Lloyd George's choice of Sir Neville Macready, a distinguished but inflexible professional soldier, as First Commissioner of Police a rather debatable selection. (MACREADY, MAKE READY TO GO, trumpeted one banner at a union meeting, a sentiment supported by other banners proclaiming TYRANNY IS NOT DISCIPLINE and KILL PRUSSIANISM.)

A strike ballot at the end of May resulted in a ten-to-one vote in favor of a strike among London policemen; in Liverpool, nearly 95 percent of the police force were fervent union men. Although Lloyd George refused to receive union representatives in Paris, claiming that he was still too busy settling the affairs of the world to intervene in this dispute, he did ask them at least to "let me know before you take any drastic action" and, if possible, to await his return to London following the conclusion of the Peace Conference. In addition, the government, with its back to the wall once again, agreed to increase police wages to a new minimum of three pounds ten shillings per week, and to institute a Commission of Inquiry to investigate the situation thoroughly. Reluctantly the Union Executive agreed on June 1 to postpone any strike action until twenty-one days after the peace treaty was signed. (Some skeptics, with more than a little justification, thought that they would see the crack of doom, or at least the Second Coming, before a finished treaty.) But the union also promised that if no action had been taken by the time the Triple Alliance met at Southport on June 24, then all bets were off, and the threat of a general strike—including most of the nation's urban police force—could become a real possibility.

* * *

BEST-SELLERS OF 1919:

FICTION: *Blood and Sand,* by Vicente Blasco Ibáñez; *Tin Soldier,* by Temple Bailey; *The Four Horsemen of the Apocalypse,* also by Blasco Ibáñez; Joseph Conrad's latest novel, *Arrow of Gold;* and *Dawn,* by Eleanor H. Porter.

NON-FICTION: *Years Between,* by the venerable Rudyard Kipling; *Raymond,* by Sir Oliver Lodge; Brigadier General A. W. Catlin's *With the Help of God and a Few Marines; Echoes of the War,* by the creator of Peter Pan, J.M. Barrie; and Henry Van Dyke's *The Valley of Vision.*

A few minutes after eleven o'clock on the evening of June 2, Attorney General A. Mitchell Palmer, dressed in his pajamas, sat reading in the front room on the second story of his house, at 2132 R Street, N.W., in Washington. His wife was already asleep in the rear bedroom. At 11:15, Palmer stood up, turned off the light, and had started for the bedroom when he heard something falling on the lawn below. Seconds later he was showered with broken glass from a tremendous explosion. An elk's head was thrown, twisted, from a wall onto the floor.

The bomb tore out the façade of the house; for a hundred yards throughout the fashionable neighborhood, the force of the blast ripped doors off their hinges and shattered windows. (Franklin D. Roosevelt lived across the street at number 2131. "I had just placed my automobile in the garage and walked home when the explosion took place," Roosevelt recalled. "It happened about three minutes after I had entered my house.") The pungent, acrid fumes from the explosive mixed with the smell of burning leaves and lingered in the air for hours. Palmer was not injured. He walked, shaken and momentarily speechless, down the steps—still in his pajamas—through the litter of glass, wood, and plaster, and out into the street, followed a few minutes later by Mrs. Palmer.

Outside lay the scattered remains of the man who had planted the bomb. Detectives theorized that he had placed the device—packed with nitroglycerine, they suspected—on the middle one of the three heavy slabs of stone that made up the Palmer doorsteps, lit a short fuse, and then fled. Apparently the fuse burned more quickly than expected, and in his panic the bomber—who was wearing sandals with rubber heels—tripped over one of the stones and fell, catching the full force of the blast. Fifty feet from Palmer's front steps lay the lower part of a leg; another leg was found nearby; additional "ghastly relics" had been hurled into the next block and onto S street, which meant that they must have risen sixty feet in the air and traveled at least seventy-five yards (one grisly mass flew through a window and landed in a second-floor room of a Norwegian diplomat's house). Hundreds of minute particles of flesh covered the pavement and trees and the fronts of houses. Authorities collected as much as they could and took everything to the District morgue, where the coroner tried to put it all together to establish the bomber's identity.

From beneath a pile of leaves and torn branches showered down by the blast, police raked several pieces of a satchel and a pamphlet printed on pink paper, with the title *Plain Words*. Its message was a declaration of war:

THE POWERS THAT BE MADE NO SECRET OF THEIR WILL TO STOP, HERE IN AMERICA, THE WORLD-WIDE SPREAD OF REVOLUTION. THE POWERS THAT MUST BE RECKON THAT THEY WILL HAVE TO ACCEPT THE FIGHT THEY HAVE PROVOKED. . . . WE HAVE BEEN DREAMING OF FREEDOM, WE HAVE TALKED OF LIBERTY, WE HAVE ASPIRED TO A BETTER WORLD, AND YOU JAILED US, YOU CLUBBED US, YOU DEPORTED US, YOU MURDERED US WHENEVER YOU COULD. NOW THAT THE GREAT WAR, WAGED TO REPLENISH YOUR PURSES AND BUILD A PEDESTAL TO YOUR SAINTS, IS OVER NOTHING BETTER CAN YOU DO TO PROTECT YOUR STOLEN MILLIONS, AND YOUR USURPED FAME, THAN TO DIRECT ALL THE POWER OF THE MURDEROUS INSTITUTIONS YOU CREATED FOR YOUR EXCLUSIVE DEFENSE, AGAINST THE WORKING MULTI-TUDES RISING TO A MORE HUMAN CONCEPTION OF LIFE. . . . DO NOT EXPECT US TO SIT DOWN AND PRAY AND CRY. WE ACCEPT YOUR CHALLENGE AND MEAN TO STICK TO OUR WAR DUTIES. . . .

It was signed, "The Anarchist Fighter."

A miraculously undamaged black felt hat lying in the gutter near Palmer's house contained a red railroad coach receipt that had been punched at Philadelphia at six o'clock that evening, leading detectives to believe the bomber had come from that city on the Baltimore & Ohio express that had arrived in Washington at 9:15. They immediately thought back to the bombings in Philadelphia five months earlier. From the remnants of an Italian-English dictionary at the scene, the authorities deduced that the bomber probably had been an Italian immigrant. They also concluded that he had been "a swarthy man with dark hair and of slender build," who wore "a collar of a well-known make with a Chinese laundry mark," a black (as near as they could tell) suit with green stripes, tan lisle socks (Roosevelt concluded from this hosiery that the man had been poorly dressed), winter underwear, and a cheap white shirt with green and yellow stripes. The sweatband of the hat carried the name of its maker: De Luca Brothers, of 919 South Eighth Street, Philadelphia. In a torn wallet found near Palmer's lawn was a picture of a young boy and a number of canceled United States postage stamps, apparently intended to be new additions to the child's collection.

Just as the May Day bombs had been mailed to victims throughout the country (and the newspapers never tired of pointing out that no arrests had ever been made in that case), so the attack on Palmer's house was only the most spectacular of a series of bombings on the night of June 2, in which ten bombs exploded in eight cities. In nearly every case, the bombs had been planted near private homes, including those of a New York judge, the mayor of Cleveland, a Massachusetts state legislator, a Boston magistrate, a silk manufacturer in Paterson, New Jersey, and an immigration official in Pittsburgh. A Catholic church in Philadelphia (Our Lady of Victory) also was bombed. None of the intended victims was seriously injured, although one innocent elderly woman, a caretaker in the basement of New York Justice Gott's house, was killed.

At once there came cries for drastic action to wipe out the Red peril. "The outrages of last night indicate nothing but the lawless attempt of an anarchistic element in the population to terrorize the country and thus stay the hand of the government," declared Palmer. "This they have utterly failed to do. The purposes of the Department of Justice are the same today as yesterday. These attacks by bomb throwers will only increase and extend the activities of our crime-detecting forces." To give force to this threat, Palmer carried through a reorganization of the detective branch of the Department of Justice, appointing William J. Flynn, formerly head of the Secret Service, as chief of the new bureau of investigation, and Francis P. Garvan of New York as Assistant Attorney General with general responsibility for all the department's investigative work and special crimes prosecution. Sixty-one arrests were made across the country in connection with the bombings (forty-five in Cleveland alone, including the entire student body of an automobile repair class), but all of the accused eventually were released. Cabinet members, congressmen, and judges in every major city were placed under increased guard, and police stepped up their surveillance on friends and associates of such radicals as Emma Goldman and Alexander Berkman. From Congress once more there arose calls to restrict immigration, deport aliens (only a dozen of the radicals brought from the West Coast to Ellis Island had been sent back to Europe so far), and outlaw meetings of anarchist organizations. The June 2 bombings were almost certainly the work of a few psychotic anarchists acting on their own, but in the overcharged atmosphere of the time, the incidents gave the forces of Americanism still more credibility and a great deal of ammunition for their crusade.

* * *

"It doesn't matter whether you believe in it or not. The day of argument on it is past. The whole nation demands it." So spoke Mrs. Abby Scott Baker, former traveler on the Prison Special, the suffragette express whose passengers wore costumes that duplicated the garb worn by their sisters while incarcerated in the Occoquan Jail, just outside Washington ("shapeless blue calico wrappers, with washrags pinned at the belt").

Alice Paul and the National Woman's Party had not been idle since the defeat of the suffrage amendment (a.k.a. the "Savage Susie" amendment) by the Senate in March. The NWP had created one of the most sophisticated lobbying machines yet visited upon the Capitol; its foundation was an elaborate index-card system, completely cross-referenced, that kept tabs on each congressman's background (ancestry, education from prep school to college, previous jobs, church affiliation); family (number of children, father's birthplace, mother's education, brother's occupation); military record (including any battlefield action); literary work (if any) and lecture topics; favorite newspapers; recreations, hobbies; and lodges or clubs to which he belonged; personal habits; state of health; and, finally, his voting record on suffrage measures. Every piece of information that could be brought to bear upon a congressman to swing his vote in favor of women's suffrage was included. "There is a definite purpose in every card," explained Miss Maud Younger, who, as chairman of the NWP Lobby Committee, served as guardian of the index. For instance, Miss Younger continued, "it is important to know all about the mother, and that explains why a whole card is devoted to her. Mothers continue to have a strong influence over their sons. Some married men listen to their mothers more than to their wives. You will hear a man telling his wife how his mother used to do it, and then we know from his frequent reference to his mother that if we can make of her a strong advocate for suffrage we have the best of chances of winning the son."

Of course, some senators were incorrigible. Henry Cabot Lodge had long ago decided that he would oppose women's suffrage because "I would not want women to descend to the level of man." The irascible Senator James A. Reed of Missouri once told a lobbyist, "Women know nothing about politics. Did you ever hear a bunch of women talk? It may be about literature (Reed pronounced it "literatoor"), church, fashions, children, or the theatre." In a shot aimed directly at the peripatetic militants of the NWP, Reed added that "I think 999 out of every thousand women do respect the law and the Constitution, but most of them are at home—a mighty good place for a woman to be."

While the militants were ranging about the country in the Prison Special or lobbying recalcitrant senators in Washington, the National Women's Suffrage Association—the less radical wing of the suffragette movement—gathered in St. Louis to hold its jubilee convention and to establish a nonpartisan, nonmilitant, and nonsectarian national organization that would carry the fight for women's rights into every town and county in America. The association's president, Carrie Chapman Catt, stated that its purpose would be "to sweep out of the way certain relics of antiquity, neglected details in the laws which while they do not oppress women as a whole do injustice to a minority unable to defend themselves." There certainly were antiquated laws that needed to be changed: in Florida, the legal age of consent for a girl for sexual relations was ten years; in Louisiana, a mother had no legal standing as guardian of her children. While the convention succeeded in organizing its new association—which would be known as the League of Women Voters—it decided that the League would not formally be born until the association met in February 1920 for the centennial celebration of Susan B. Anthony's birthday. *The New York Times*, incidentally, looked upon the League of Women Voters with considerable apprehension. Fearing that the formation of this new "special interest" organization portended an escalation of the political war between the sexes, the *Times* predicted that the League would never amount to much because "the great majority of women are well aware, either from conscious reflection or intuitively, that women have no 'special interests' in any proper sense of that term, and that their political efficiency depends on their assimilation as soon as possible with the general voting body."

On May 21 the House of Representatives, which had narrowly approved the suffrage amendment in the last session, brought it to the floor again and, with a minimum of discussion, passed it again, this time by an overwhelming margin of 304 to 89. Now it went back once more to the Senate, the graveyard of feminist hopes for four decades. This time, however, the climate in the upper chamber proved more favorable; one or two incumbents said that they had changed their views, and the addition of several new pro-suffrage senators finally put the amendment over the top. Late on the afternoon of June 4, following two days of debate (during which Senator Reed again denounced the amendment as "an outrage upon our form of government" and suggested that "suffrage enthusiasts who glorified in jail sentences [lived] in the same mental atmosphere as the gentlemen who put the bomb on the steps of the Attorney General's house last night"), the vote was taken: 56 for, 25 against. Thunderous applause from the galleries swept through the chamber; the presiding officer did not even try to stop it. The amendment was promptly sent to the State Department, where it would be certified to the states. Once three-fourths of the state legislatures had ratified it, women's suffrage would be a constitutional reality in the United States.

Most of the diehard opposition to the amendment had come from Southern Democrats and conservative New England Republicans. Included among the latter were Senators Lodge, Knox, and Brandegee—the leaders of the Old Guard—all of whom, along with Reed, were coincidentally preparing for an even more stubborn and acrimonious battle against President Wilson's League of Nations.

29

"I am weary with repenting . . ."

Sergeant Alvin Cullom York was home, back in the mountains just down the track a ways from Pall Mall, Tennessee. The brawny, red-haired, bashful mountaineer and former pacifist had astounded the world, and especially the enemy, in the Argonne Forest on October 8 by singlehandedly destroying a German machine-gun battalion, killing at least twenty-five Huns with his deadly sharpshooting and capturing 135 more, and reportedly putting thirty-five machine-gun nests out of commission, thereby earning the Congressional Medal of Honor, the Distinguished Conduct Medal, and the Croix de Guerre. "What you did," declared Marshal Foch in presenting the prestigious French military honor, "was the greatest thing ever accomplished by any soldier of any of the armies in Europe." Shucks, York replied modestly, "I couldn't hardly miss 'em, yuh know, they were so close." Now the hero returned to his cabin in Wolf Valley, to his elderly mother, his sisters, and his younger brothers. "What ah like best of all is just to get back," York said in his slow mountain drawl. "It's where ah've been all my life, an' ah reckon it's the best place for me, yes. Ah reckon ah have had chances to leave, but ah ain't specially got a hankerin' for it."

Glad to escape from the attention lavished upon him in New York City (the Stock Exchange suspended business in his honor, and members carried him around the trading floor on their shoulders), whence he had been "rescued" by veteran Tennessee congressman Cordell Hull, who then took him down to Washington for another round of adoration; glad to be just good old "Al" York again, glad to get back to being the second elder of the Church of Christ and Christian Union, the little church that sat along the red clay road that led through town. "Hello, Al. How are ya, Al?" "Oh, fair to middlin'. How's the home and the crops?" After the hoopla of his return died down, York headed straight for Parson R. C. Pile's house to talk over what had happened. It was Pile who had converted Alvin York to God and away from a young life of hell-raising, moonshine, and fighting—his mother had begged him to stop before he killed somebody with his fists in a drunken rage—and it was Pile who had fervently urged York to resist the draft as a conscientious objector. But on this day the parson said that no one, least of all he, bore any grudges against the most famous member of his flock for what he had done in the trenches: "It's all in a man's own conscience what is right or wrong. The hand of God was on Alvah."

Waiting patiently for her sweetheart was eighteen-year-old Grace Williams, the blue-eyed girl with long blond hair who had joined the parson and York's mother in bringing Alvin to a life with God. Before he went away to war, York had asked Grace to marry him; she had promised him an answer when he returned. "Al," his friends ribbed him, "are you going to get married anytime soon?" "Well, ah reckon ah might get married sometime. Anybody's likely to do that, you know." Sure enough, on Saturday, June 7 (five days after Albert Einstein's wedding in Germany), Al and Grace tied the knot, with Governor A. H. Roberts officiating at the ceremony. York laughingly rejected a $100,000 offer to go on the vaudeville circuit ("Wouldn't I look pretty in tights?" he joked); instead, he planned to settle down on the farm the state of Tennessee was buying for him in gratitude for his services to America.

The Chicago White Sox were cruising along in first place in the American League with a 24–8 record. Their fighting spirit—crushed after their 1918 tailspin—had been revived by Kid Gleason, the battling manager who stalked "like a ghost from the ancient days—one of the oldtimers who knew the seamy side of the game twenty-five to thirty years ago." Grantland Rice walked along with Gleason in the gallery as they watched the final round of the U.S. Open golf tournament, and the sportswriter came away impressed. The White Sox "may be beaten," Rice wrote the next day, "but [they] will never quit, for Gleason has set them in this frame of mind."

"There are days when we can't hit much," Gleason admitted, "and there are days when our pitchers go bad. There are days when the breaks are all against us, too, but there are no days when we are not out there hustling and fighting and giving the best we have. And it will be just this way to the end of the race. . . . I believe that every man ought to feel as long as he is willing to fight for it he has got his chance to win."

Fans across the country seemed to have finally forgiven Shoeless Joe

Jackson and the other ballplayers who had chosen to work in the relative safety of the East Coast shipyards instead of serving in the army during the war. In New York, meanwhile, the Giants celebrated after winning the bidding war for the services of the much-sought-after "Fordham Flash," Frankie Frisch, who had just ended a spectacular amateur baseball career by agreeing to a two-year contract with John McGraw's club. (Frisch rejected offers from the Yankees, Tigers, and Red Sox.) The Giants were going to need all the help they could get, because Cincinnati, under the firm guidance of manager Pat Moran, finally had pulled itself together and was surprising everyone by hanging right in there with the leaders on the senior circuit well into May and June. (Moran graciously attributed much of the team's success to his choice of rubdown ointment. "When my players get sore," Moran admitted in a newspaper advertisement, "I don't rub them the wrong way; I use Sloan's Liniment—it penetrates.")

A question from the *Los Angeles Times:* "Are traffic conditions in Los Angeles unavoidably worse than in any other city of its size in America?"

Perhaps, but not because the city and its environs were trapped in a maze of freeways clogged by frustrated motorists. No, the problem in the summer of 1919 was that Los Angeles drivers were simply too somnolent; they cruised through the downtown streets as if they were out for a Sunday drive in the country, they did their window shopping from their cars, and they simply stopped in the line of traffic to wait for a friend to run into and out of a shop. "At six o'clock at night," complained a visitor from the Midwest, "the situation in Los Angeles becomes intolerable. Apparently every automobile owner in the city suddenly decides to motor through the business section at that time to see if there are any new window displays. Broadway, Spring and Hill streets, if that is what you call them, take on the aspect of a Glidden sight-seeing tour."

Recommended solutions included the hiring of additional traffic policemen and the stricter enforcement of jaywalking regulations against pedestrians who crossed the street "at any and every moment." Someone had also suggested, reported the president of the Southern California Automobile Club, "that two lines of traffic should move both north and south on the main thoroughfares, instead of one as at present." Ah, yes . . . those were the days.

A blistering sun baked down upon more than a hundred thousand people sitting in the grandstands around the blazing brick oval speedway at Indianapolis, watching with rapt fascination the seventh annual five-hundred-mile automobile race. For $50,000 in prize money, thirty-three drivers were hurtling along the track at record speeds, then even faster, and occasionally too fast: on the forty-fourth lap, on the back stretch coming out of the north turn, the car of Arthur Thurman, a young driver from Washington, D.C., overturned, killing him immediately. On the ninety-sixth lap, the Roamer Special of Louis Le Cocq spun out of control as the Frenchman tried to take the southwest curve without cutting his speed; the Roamer turned over, the gasoline tank exploded, and both Le Cocq and his mechanic were burned to death. A number of other cars drove straight on through the thick black smoke as a band played a lively tune to distract the spectators' attention, but observers noted that the drivers slowed down slightly after the second crash. Later, Ralph de Palma, the American favorite who had set the track speed record of 89.94 miles per hour in winning the 500 in 1914 (and whose car had collapsed after leading with just one lap to go in 1912), was forced to drop out of contention when a front wheel bearing on his Packard gave out.

After five hundred miles and five hours, forty-four minutes, and twenty-one seconds, the winner was an Indianapolis native, Howard "Howdy" Wilcox, driving a locally owned blue Peugeot racer. Wilcox's average speed was 87.12 miles per hour. Eddie Hearne finished second in a Durant Special, a little less than two minutes behind Wilcox, and the Frenchman Jules Goux came in third. The much-ballyhooed French Ballot racers failed to live up to their advance publicity; only one of three finished the race, and it ended up back in fourth place.

In the elegantly ugly fifteenth-century chateau of St-Germain, where French kings of the Renaissance and the glorious Age of Enlightenment had been born and wed and died, the Hapsburg empire at last came to an end.

On the morning of June 2, small groups of delegates made their way through the tiny courtyard and past the honor guard of dismounted dragoons, and into the chateau that now served—in a marvelously appropriate way—as a national museum of ancient history. First came the Japanese and the Chinese (punctual as always), then Clemenceau, Venizelos of Greece, the urbane Balfour, and most of the rest of the American and British delegations. There was really almost no drama, no tension in the air as there had been four weeks earlier for the confrontation with the Germans at the Trianon in Versailles. Instead, the great men wandered aimlessly in and out of the "Stone Age" room (where the treaty would be presented to the Austrians), chatting among themselves until the clock struck noon.

Suddenly Lloyd George rushed in, wearing a stylish if slightly unconventional light summer suit. But still Wilson's chair remained empty. A messenger was sent to telephone to Paris. Five minutes passed, then ten. Finally Wilson appeared at 12:12 and took his place next to Clemenceau. Orlando was relegated to a seat among the lesser nations, far from the table of the Big Three. Then there was another ten minutes' wait for the Austrians, who had, after all, been waiting themselves for the treaty for nearly a month and were certainly entitled to this small measure of retribution. *"Monsieurs les Délégués Austrichiens"* were announced, and in they marched in morning dress, led by Dr. Renner: the survivors upon whose shoulders rested the legacy of the war and the centuries of empire. Stuffed reproductions of woolly mammoths and pictures of cavemen stared from the walls. Everyone stood up courteously; Renner and Clemenceau exchanged polite bows from across the room; at 12:29, Clemenceau explained the procedure in a straightforward conversational tone (it was 12:29), and his speech was translated into German, English, and Italian; Dutasta laid a copy of the treaty in Renner's hands at 12:39; and then Renner stood up. His speech was not at all antagonistic. The pacifist spoke of the "terrible crime of 1914," and acknowledged gratefully the humanitarian assistance of Hoover and his mission. But, Renner reminded the Allies, Austria was only one of a half-dozen states created from the shattered Hapsburg empire, and it should not be made to bear the cost of the war alone. (Here the proceedings were interrupted by an overzealous photographer who fell into a huge museum display case upon which he had been crouching, splintering wood and glass across the back of the room, spilling out onto the floor mementoes of ancient peoples and states that had vanished long ago. When everyone heard the crash, their initial alarmed reaction was that a bomb had been thrown.) And, continued Renner with dignity, "our revolution was pacific and without military action." Since the old absolutist regime had been overthrown in Vienna, a just peace—not a vengeful one—could best assist his government's efforts to make Austria a democratic bulwark in a chaotic Europe that needed every source of stability it could find. "We trust to your sense of justice and practical spirit not to demand that we be crushed."

Everyone listened sympathetically to Renner's plea, except perhaps the Italians and the Yugoslavs. Then Clemenceau asked if anyone had anything else to say, and since no one had, he gaveled the meeting to a close. The Austrians left first, then everyone else rushed out. It was 1:14 and, after all, time for lunch.

Considering that Austria posed little threat to anyone following the dismemberment of the empire, the peace terms were strikingly harsh.

Much of the language had been lifted directly from the German treaty. The Austrians were forced to demobilize their naval and air forces, and to renounce all extra-European rights. Owing to continuing disagreements among the Allies, some of the precise boundaries and financial terms still were not ready in their final form, but the ones that were included were bad enough. The Hapsburgs had governed a population of over fifty million people; now Austria was left with a territory of less than six thousand square miles and between six and seven million people. Areas of undisputed German-Austrian nationality in Silesia, in the South Tyrol, in Bohemia and Moravia were handed over to other states. For a terribly disheartened Chancellor Renner, what remained was "the tragic remnant of one of Europe's capitals, surrounded by a barren, mountainous country, unable to sustain life and not allowed to die quickly." Austria was, of course, forbidden to join with Berlin in a pan-German confederation.

Vienna was shocked and outraged. The territorial losses, especially, provoked an uproar. "What a terrible disappointment America is for me," mourned President Seitz following an all-night Cabinet session called to discuss the terms of the treaty. "This is driving me to despair. I have no power to enforce such terms upon the population of German Austria, and it will be dangerous for the man who signs them." "All has been taken from us without respect to President Wilson's fourteen points, which is cruel and provoking," wrote one newspaper. Another journal claimed that "the conditions could not have been worse." Combined with news of the discouraging Austrian defeats in clashes with the Yugoslavs on the Corinthian border, with the government's ill-advised decision to try to disband a large part of the Volkswehr militia (which it had really never trusted), and the cumulative effect of Hungarian propaganda, the depressing severity of the peace treaty once again raised the specter of a Bolshevist revolt in Vienna. And within the territories where a German population had been handed over to the Czechs, discontent began to grow at once.

So now the Austrians, like the Germans, began to issue a series of protests against the treaty. Renner asked the Allies why Austria—the new Republic of Austria, that is—had been singled out to bear the burden of the iniquities of the Hapsburg monarchy. "German Austria," complained one Austrian note to Clemenceau, "is in no wise the sole inheritor of the Austro-Hungarian Monarchy's possessions, and cannot be regarded as its sole successor regarding its debts and obligations. In population and territory German Austria is the least important of them all." The note went on to wonder why "the smallest and poorest and most peace-loving of the States which arose out of the former Monarchy should be made the sole inheritor of its guilt, and be expected to bear alone the consequences of the mistakes made by Hungarian, Polish, and Slovene statesmen."

There was considerable sympathy among the expert advisers in the American and British delegations (and the French, to a slightly lesser degree) for Austria's plight. Once again the sum of a treaty's parts had proved far harsher than anyone had imagined. Seymour and his colleagues set to work to try to alleviate some of the worst features of a document that, Seymour believed, "when taken in all its provisions seems to us impossible. It attempts to treat German Austria, which is now a tiny state, with the same degree of severity as Germany. The Austrians say, and it is probably true, that if the proposed conditions are put into the treaty they will either be thrown into the arms of Hungary or of Germany."

As far as the German treaty was concerned, the British delegation (and particularly John Maynard Keynes and General Smuts) still led the fight for substantive concessions. The major changes urged by the British centered upon the issues of reparations, the Polish-German frontier, the admission of Germany to the League of Nations, and the duration of the Rhineland occupation. For Seymour, "the curious, the humorous, and the discouraging aspect of all this is that what they propose now we ourselves advocated at the beginning of the negotiations." Nevertheless, Wilson agreed to hold a plenary meeting of all the American delegates on the morning of June 3 and, after genially greeting each man personally, the President asked for his experts' advice on making concessions in each of these areas. They told their chief that they had concluded that the total reparations bill should be fixed at a specific sum, just as the United States had been arguing all along; that the Polish border settlement should not be disturbed; and that while the fifteen-year occupation of the Rhineland was practically "useless from the military point of view" (General Bliss believed it was designed primarily to give France economic control of the region), it clearly was the least severe arrangement the French would ever accept.

Wilson listened carefully, and then explained his own opinions. First of all, he said, he was still not convinced that Germany's change of heart from imperialism and militarism to peaceful social democracy was "definite and sincere," and hence he, at least, was not prepared to admit Germany into the League of Nations right away. Furthermore, Wilson wholeheartedly opposed any effort to make concessions to Berlin to make it easier for the German government to sign the treaty: "We ought not to be sentimental. Personally I do not want to soften the terms for Germany. I think that it is a good thing for the world and Germany that the terms should be so hard, so that Germany may know what an unjust war means. My concern is only to eliminate anything that is really unjust. I do not want to do anything simply to persuade Germany to sign. We did not write this treaty simply in order to have it signed. We must not give up the things we fought for now, even if we have to fight again." The time for compromise had passed; it would come again when the League began its work; but it was definitely not now. "What is necessary," Wilson concluded, "is to get out of this atmosphere. If the Germans won't sign the treaty as we have written it then we must renew the war; at all events we must not allow ourselves to flop and wobble trying to find something they will sign."

To help rally Allied opinion against Lloyd George's eleventh-hour loss of nerve, Wilson issued a public statement saying that after he had examined the German counterproposals in detail, he (Wilson) had decided that "our treaty violates none of my principles. If I thought otherwise I should not hesitate to confess it, and should try to retrieve this error. But the treaty which we have drawn up is entirely in accordance with my fourteen points."

Keynes disagreed vehemently, and on June 5 he submitted his resignation as Treasury adviser to the Prime Minister. "I ought to tell you," he explained to Lloyd George, "that on Saturday I am slipping away from this scene of nightmare. I can do no more good here. I've gone on hoping even through these last dreadful weeks that you'd find some way to make of the Treaty a just and expedient document. But now it's apparently too late. The battle is lost." Keynes went home and promptly began to write *The Economic Consequences of the Peace*, one of the most devastating critiques of the Peace Conference ever published.

Lloyd George intuitively had come to realize that the world would not long put up with the settlement written at Paris—if he always knew anything, it was which way the cat would jump—but the recognition came too late. Haunted by his election campaign pledges to make the Huns pay to the utmost farthing, trapped between the Conservative hard-liners in Parliament and the Liberal-Labour revulsion at the severity of the peace terms, Lloyd George's nerves began to break. He nearly came to blows with Clemenceau in a meeting of the Three; on June 14 he flew into a rage at Wilson's refusal to give Upper Silesia back to Germany. Doubtless Wilson's refusal to join his crusade to soften the peace terms frustrated the Prime Minister no end. "I cannot quite understand him," Lloyd George told a friend in discussing Wilson's character. "I am not quite sure whether he is always what he appears to be in private. He always seems to keep on the mask."

As the endless pattern of delays and protests and rebuttals continued, the confident spirits in Paris became more and more doubtful that the German government would sign after all. Popular demonstrations raged against the perfidious Allies (and especially Wilson) in Berlin and throughout every major city in Germany and out into the countryside. Orators harangued passersby, exhorting the people to resist a treaty that would enslave their children for generations; poster maps printed in bright colors illustrated the mutilation of the German nation by Allied annexation and occupation, millions of Germans torn from the Fatherland and condemned to a life of subjugation to hostile foreign regimes; a patchwork of placards on the walls of every available building along city streets depicted the startling contrast between Wilson's Fourteen Points and the actual peace terms. Field Marshal Hindenburg, at his headquarters at Kolberg on the troubled eastern frontier, was deluged with requests to oppose Clemenceau's "murderous peace." (Hindenburg, however, refused to take a stand one way or another. The field marshal had just never been quite the same since his beloved army had broken apart in October 1918 and his master the Kaiser had been forced to flee.) Yet at the same time, other popular demonstrations made it quite clear that the German people would not return to the trenches, no matter what. One hundred thousand workers carrying red flags demonstrated in the Lustgarten in favor of peace; their banners read, WE WANT ONLY PEACE, BREAD AND WORK.

"We've had enough of fighting," shouted one soldier at a protest meeting. "You people that are so strong against signing the peace terms, you get out and fight."

"Our sailors were traitors," another veteran cried. "They started the revolution."

"You're a liar," yelled a sailor. "The Kaiser wanted to save his hide and ran away."

"No, no, no." said someone else. "The Jews run things in America; they made Wilson go to war."

Total bedlam broke loose. And the government in Berlin simply did not know what to do. It did not encourage the protests, but neither did it dare to stop them. It was a government that, in the view of one British visitor, had made nearly every mistake that it could have made, but they had been mainly mistakes of stupidity: "To suspect it of intrigue or any deep plans is sheer nonsense." From the start, the specter of Spartacism and social revolution had haunted the minds of the Majority Socialists more than anything else. Once they were in office, their programs to advance social justice had vanished, as they chose to devote their energies instead to the maintenance of order and stability. Only the tarnished promises of radical reforms were left, floating aimlessly in the air like the grin of the Cheshire Cat, a haunting reminder of what might have been. One American critic, disgusted with the Ebert-Scheidemann legacy, claimed that the government had "never uttered a revolutionary phrase or attempted a revolutionary deed." Instead, it had "occupied itself almost exclusively with organizing the military power which would enable it to remain in possession of its job regardless of what it did." Machine guns had replaced the visions of social progress. And so, even now, the nightmare of revolution remained uppermost in the government's thoughts as panic set in. If it signed the treaty, the army might rebel and refuse to support the republic any longer, and without their military bulwark, Ebert and Scheidemann would likely fall and the radicals would bring in the revolution; but if the government refused to sign the treaty and the war resumed, the republic would just as surely fall in the ensuing chaos and famine, and revolution would be equally certain.

Ebert and his colleagues had lost control of the country; they no longer ruled Germany, and it was not certain that they ever really had. No more did the National Assembly at Weimar rule the country. The real power in Germany lay with two deeply antagonistic groups: the Freikorps mercenaries officered by the old Junker military caste, who were about to be absorbed into the Reichswehr, the reorganized German army; and the Workers' Councils, which, despite all the setbacks since November, still represented the mass of working-class opinion. And by the middle of June the resentment of the working classes toward the government appeared to be reaching fever pitch. Noske's most recent atrocities in Leipzig, the escape of Rosa Luxemburg's murderer, Lieutenant Vogel, from jail with the active connivance of the army, and the execution of Leviné in Munich—all these things convinced the German workers that Ebert and Scheidemann had lost control of the forces of reaction and militarism they had encouraged so naïvely just six months ago. The revolution of November 1918 had been betrayed, and for many the sight of this deliberate, orchestrated resurrection of the evils of the old order weighed far more heavily in their condemnatory judgment of the Weimar regime than any decision to sign or not to sign the peace treaty.

On June 13 the funeral procession for Rosa Luxemburg walked slowly and sullenly through the streets of Berlin. In the vanguard was a delegation of men, women, and children bearing banners that said simply UNEMPLOYED. Then came workers dressed in their best clothes, wearing red carnations in their buttonholes, carrying placards of tribute: OUR ROSA— SHE WAS, SHE IS, SHE WILL BE AGAIN. They were followed by women wrapped in carefully mended shawls, rebellious marines, idealistic students, all hungry and bitter but orderly, scowling at the rows of Noske's steel-helmeted troops who lined the way to watch and keep order; Noske's men scowled back. "*Es Lebe die Welt Revolution!*" ("Long live the world revolution!") Two hundred thousand mourners saw the coffin containing Rosa's broken body laid in a grave next to Liebknecht's, in the cemetery just outside the city. Over the lame little revolutionary they placed wreaths of roses and carnations.

Meanwhile, the representatives of all the various German defense forces convened to decide upon an official army position on the terms of the peace treaty. In Paris, the Council of Four asked Marshal Foch what he would recommend as the most effective military action in case the German government refused to sign. Foch suggested a march on Berlin; the sight of Allied troops marching down Unter den Linden would discredit the Junkers more than anything else ever could. Clemenceau, Wilson, Lloyd George, and Sonnino all agreed. The Allies had thirty-nine divisions ready for offensive operations, with virtually no organized German forces capable of resistance. Final preparations began at once for the advance. Three hundred miles to Berlin.

At its meeting in Zurich, the International Congress of Women passed a resolution expressing "its deep regret that the terms of peace proposed at Versailles should so seriously violate the principles upon which alone a just and lasting peace can be secured, and which the democracies of the world had come to accept." The Congress believed that unless the treaty was revised to bring the peace into harmony with the principles so magnificently expressed by President Wilson, "a hundred million people of this generation in the heart of Europe are condemned to poverty, disease, and despair, which must result in the spread of hatred and anarchy within each nation." And looking beyond the flawed treaty, the women condemned "the unemployment, famine, and pestilence extending throughout the great tracts of Central and Eastern Europe, and parts of Asia," all of which represented, in their words, "a profound disgrace to civilisation."

"It's a very dark moment," agreed Walter Lippmann, "and the prospect of war and revolution throughout Europe is appalling."

Jess Willard looked to be in great shape. But, as Grantland Rice astutely pointed out, "They all look good until they have their blocks knocked off."

Willard at last arrived in Toledo on the evening of June 1 and set up shop at the Casino, a clubhouse on the shores of Maumee Bay. He decided not to start working out right away, though; the oppressive heat was bothering him, he said, and he needed a rest after the long drive from Los

Angeles. Besides, he had to go shopping and lay in a supply of rubdown lotions, tapes, and a few downy quilts to stuff under the training ring. The champion rented an elegant house on one of the best streets in Toledo, with a wide green lawn, shrubs, flowers, trees, and a big front porch with willow easy chairs. Meanwhile, in a canvas-enclosed arena at the Overland Club, three-quarters of a mile away, Dempsey sparred five rounds with Bill Tate, four rounds with the Jamaica Kid—who opened a gash over Dempsey's right eye—and three rounds with Terry Kellar. (Tate and the Jamaica Kid were black; Willard refused to spar with black partners.) The challenger also ran seven miles in the morning, rowed three miles around the bay in the afternoon, and then went swimming.

One of Dempsey's favorite companions in camp was Damon Runyon. "I felt that if I ever fell down, I could safely land on either Damon or Gene Fowler," Dempsey later recalled. "Damon would sit and talk with me for hours, listening to my ideas, my plans. . . . He was the most patient man I knew." One week Dempsey would work out with incredible intensity; then for seven days he would rest, to avoid getting stale from overtraining. During the off-weeks, local kids would take turns sitting at Jack's feet or on his lap while he told them tales of the wilderness and wildlife of Colorado. Dempsey, too, felt the heat: "That June was the hottest and most uncomfortable I can remember. Sweat flowed like water from a broken tap. Even the lakeward breeze didn't seem to affect the temperature, which hovered around 104 degrees." A friend gave Dempsey a bulldog that Jack kept chained up for safety's sake; the dog terrorized the camp, snapping at everyone except his beloved master.

By June 6, Willard had begun sparring. When the champion admitted to sportswriters—a species of human being of whom he was not overly fond—that Jack Johnson had indeed broken his jaw and three ribs in their 1915 battle in Havana, Dempsey knew that Willard could be hurt (though Willard scoffed at suggestions that Dempsey ever could hit as hard as Johnson). But the champion promised he would be ready by July 4; the Dempsey fight, Willard said, was "the one I want to be remembered by when I quit the ring." Public interest in the bout grew at an astonishing rate; six hundred fans came just to watch Willard work out, and the advance sale of tickets reportedly had already passed the $300,000 mark. Unknown to Dempsey, Doc Kearns and Damon Runyon had just laid a $10,000 bet at ten-to-one odds that the challenger would knock out Willard in the first round.

"June, 1919," Dempsey remembered. "That month dragged. . . . I couldn't sleep. . . ."

* * *

Paris, too, suffered under a terrible sun in June. Tempers flared, and a rash of strikes broke out throughout the city. Just as one labor dispute was settled, another erupted elsewhere. The Métro workers walked out, joined in a sympathetic strike by bus conductors and chauffeurs, and Paris had to walk through the heat. Strikes by house painters, metalworkers, dressmakers, sugar refinery employees, carriage builders, laundry workers—until there were 500,000 Frenchmen on strike, including nearly 200,000 coal miners in the north.

Just outside the city, detectives continued their search for evidence to link Henri Landru with the murders of his lovers; the list of his alleged victims had now reached twenty. (Eventually, Landru would be accused of the murder of virtually every runaway wife and missing girl in France since 1914.) In the charred debris left in the stove of Landru's villa, police found fragments identified as part of the bone structure surrounding a human eye. Apparently the bone had been cut with a fine saw. An army surgeon came forward and testified that he had been passing by the villa one evening several months before, when he saw smoke rolling from the chimney and smelled the strong odor of burning meat. Then he had seen a bearded man come out of the villa and throw a package in a nearby pond. Another helpful citizen said that he had been fishing for pike in that same pond and had brought up a large chunk of decomposed flesh; thinking it had been placed there for bait, he threw it back. Police dragged the pond and found a piece of blackened bone, a woman's stocking, and smoke-blackened stones just like those that had been found in Landru's garden. They also found three pieces of skull and part of a human shinbone buried under a garden wall which adjoined the village cemetery.

It was extraordinary, remarked a British observer, how easily a stranger of no more than average handsomeness could persuade dozens of otherwise sensible Frenchwomen that he had fallen in love with them at first sight. Twenty-year-old Annette Fauchet told Chief of Detectives Tanguy and his assistants that she had met Landru through her aunt, who had been infatuated with the flim-flam man. "He made me sit in a chair," Annette testified, "and uncoiled my hair. He went down on his knees, took my hands, fixed me with his eyes, and said, 'Annette, I am your master; you belong to me.' I suddenly felt queer. I saw a diabolical glint in his eyes and must have become unconscious, because I remember nothing more. I don't want to see him again—he terrifies me; he must be the devil." When they searched the inside of the villa again, police found a book on celebrated poisoners, a cache of letters from Landru's alleged victims, and linen marked with the names of some of the women. As they put Landru in the car and began to drive back to the station, a crowd of angry onlookers rushed forward, shouting, "Kill him!" Several women pounded furiously with their fists on the doors and windows of the closed car.

In a half-serious spirit, the socialist press in France suggested that Clemenceau's government had concocted much of the gruesome Landru story to divert public attention from more troubling matters of national concern.

30

"Thou hast heard, O my soul,

the sound of the trumpet,

the alarm of war . . ."

Monday, June 16. An exhibit of bronze busts of the peacemakers, as seen through the eyes of the noted sculptor Jo Davidson, opened in the afternoon at a gallery on the Rue Caumartin. The bust of President Wilson showed an extraordinarily firm countenance without a hint of sourness; the head of Marshal Foch was scowling; General Tasker Bliss appeared with a whimsical smile on his face. Visitors also were subjected to stares from the likenesses of Marshal Joffre, André Tardieu, Bernard Baruch, and Secretary Lansing, the last being still in the plaster stage, the only bust not yet set in bronze. In the cafés outside, Parisians were still buzzing about the victory of an American horse, William K. Vanderbilt's Tchad, in the French Derby before an immense crowd at Longchamps the day before. Clemenceau settled the transport workers' strike by promising substantial raises in pay; when told the maximum salary of the Paris tramway workers was only 315 francs per month for women and 400 francs for men, Clemenceau turned to his Minister of Transports and Public Works and said, "You see it isn't much, 315 and 400."

At 6:20 P.M., the secretary of the Peace Conference, Paul Dutasta, arrived in Versailles by car from Paris with two parcels wrapped in plain brown paper. He was escorted to the reading room of the Hôtel des Reservoirs, where, at 6:49, he handed a copy of the revised treaty and a covering note from Clemenceau (actually written by Philip Kerr, Lloyd George's private secretary, later raised to the peerage as Lord Lothian) to Herr von Simons, the secretary of the German peace delegation. Simons handed the treaty to his superior, Baron von Lersner. Dutasta spoke in French; Simons spoke in German; neither seemed to understand precisely what the other said, but it was clear that the Allies had imposed a time limit upon Germany. If the treaty was not signed in five days from the moment Dutasta delivered it, the Armistice would end and the Allied armies would resume their advance through Germany. Dutasta asked for a receipt. Simons wrote one in long-hand and dated it "about seven o'clock."

There had been no time to reprint the entire treaty, so the few changes that had been made were written in red ink over the original text. The changes included a plebiscite to allow Upper Silesia to decide its own fate, minor frontier changes in West Prussia, a temporary increase in the size of the German army, and an assurance to Germany of membership in the League of Nations in the near future, *if* Germany fulfilled its treaty obligations. Brockdorff-Rantzau's voluminous notes of protest clearly had been in vain. Clemenceau's note left the Germans under no illusions as to their present situation:

THE [GERMAN] REPLY PROTESTS AGAINST THE PEACE ON THE GROUNDS THAT IT CONFLICTS WITH THE TERMS UPON WHICH THE ARMISTICE OF THE ELEVENTH OF NOVEMBER, 1918, WAS SIGNED, AND THAT IT IS A PEACE OF VIOLENCE AND NOT OF JUSTICE. THE PROTEST OF THE GERMAN DEL-EGATION SHOWS THAT THEY FAIL TO UNDERSTAND THE POSITION IN WHICH GERMANY STANDS TODAY. THEY SEEM TO THINK THAT GER-MANY HAS ONLY TO 'MAKE SACRIFICES IN ORDER TO OBTAIN PEACE,' AS IF THIS WERE BUT THE END OF SOME MERE STRUGGLE FOR TERRITORY AND POWER. . . .

IN THE VIEW OF THE ALLIED AND ASSOCIATED POWERS THE WAR WHICH BEGAN ON THE FIRST OF AUGUST, 1914, WAS THE GREATEST CRIME AGAINST HUMANITY AND THE FREEDOM OF THE PEOPLES THAT ANY NATION CALLING ITSELF CIVILIZED HAS EVER CONSCIOUSLY COMMITTED. . . . GER-MANY'S RESPONSIBILITY, HOWEVER, IS NOT CONFINED TO HAVING PLANNED AND STARTED THE WAR. SHE IS NO LESS RESPONSIBLE FOR THE SAVAGE AND INHUMAN MANNER IN WHICH IT WAS CONDUCTED.

Clemenceau listed the crimes: Germany had raped Belgium; initiated the use of poison gas; begun the bombing and long-distance shelling of towns for the express purpose of terrorizing innocent civilians; commenced sub-marine warfare; practiced barbarities against prisoners of war; and carried thousands of people from conquered lands into slavery in German territo-ries.

THE CONDUCT OF GERMANY IS ALMOST UNEXAMPLED IN HUMAN HISTORY. THE TERRIBLE RESPONSIBILITY WHICH LIES AT HER DOORS CAN BE SEEN IN THE FACT THAT NOT LESS THAN SEVEN MILLION DEAD LIE BURIED IN EUROPE, WHILE MORE THAN TWENTY MILLION OTHERS CARRY UPON THEM THE EVIDENCE OF WOUNDS AND SUFFERING, BECAUSE GERMANY SAW FIT

TO GRATIFY HER LUST FOR TYRANNY BY A RESORT TO WAR.

THE ALLIED AND ASSOCIATED POWERS BELIEVE THAT THEY WILL BE FALSE TO THOSE WHO HAVE GIVEN THEIR ALL TO SAVE THE FREEDOM OF THE WORLD IF THEY CONSENT TO TREAT THE WAR ON ANY OTHER BASIS THAN AS A CRIME AGAINST HUMANITY AND RIGHT. . . .

A peace of justice this treaty certainly was, concluded Clemenceau, but a peace of justice for all: "There must be justice for the dead and wounded, and for those who have been orphaned and bereaved, that Europe might be free from Prussian despotism. . . . There must be justice for those millions whose homes and lands and property German savagery has spoliated and destroyed."

The treaty was final. There would be no further changes.

Stunned by the Allies' refusal to mitigate the severity of the peace terms, Brockdorff-Rantzau and his colleagues left the hotel under French escort—a weakened escort, since there was a partial police strike, too, in progress—to board a train for Weimar, where President Ebert and his ministers would consider the "revised" treaty. On the way to the station, several female typists on the German staff allegedly taunted and made faces at the inevitable rows of French spectators. The crowd responded by hurling bricks, sticks, and stones (which had already been piled up at several points along the route expressly for this purpose) at the Germans and their cars; several members of the delegation were slightly injured, but two French military chauffeurs driving the delegates to the station were badly cut by flying glass. The incident enraged the departing delegates and aroused further hostility among the German public, despite Clemenceau's apology for his countrymen's "reprehensible act."

In Vienna, seven people were killed and more than sixty seriously injured when a procession of six thousand Communist supporters—mostly young people—clashed with police. Austrian authorities blamed Hungarian propaganda for inciting the riot. ("Proletarians and soldiers: Look to the East," read a propaganda pamphlet. "The Hungarian proletariat has overthrown its exploiters and scattered its rapacious enemies.") At the Hungaria Hotel in Budapest, Béla Kun said it made no difference to him whether the German government signed the peace treaty or not, because "another revolution, this time of the proletariat, is certain to come. Germany is destroying the existing harmony between the Socialists and the bourgeois and as a capitalist nation is dead. Communism, Bolshevism, or whatever you call it is bound to go ahead throughout the world, though it may take different forms in the different countries."

At Kolberg, sleep would not come to Field Marshal Paul von Hindenburg—it was, many said later, the only night in his life that Hindenburg could not sleep. After his tortured night of doubt, Hindenburg decided that he would once again simply refuse to commit himself; he knew Germany could not resist an Allied invasion, but the venerable Supreme Commander of the German Imperial military forces could not betray his honor or his lifelong ideals. He would not recommend that the civilian government sign the treaty.

Tuesday, June 17. Weimar was quiet and serene, with flowers in bloom, and moss in various shades of green and brown among the gardens. Here, one was back in the time of Goethe, Schiller, and Liszt. Here a visitor could imagine that war and revolution had never been.

In the vast circle of palaces that Duke Karl August had fashioned over one hundred years before, Ebert, Scheidemann, and Noske met in yet another Cabinet session to decide what to do. Several weeks earlier, the Cabinet had seemed united in opposition to the treaty. Now, after pondering the consequences of a refusal to sign, the government found itself thoroughly divided. Matthias Erzberger, the brilliant, nakedly ambitious—and therefore despised—leader of the Centrist party, the party that controlled the second largest body of votes in the National Assembly, had met unofficially in late May with several American military officials and had come away convinced that the Allies would never grant substantial concessions to the original treaty draft. And the more Erzberger thought about the consequences if Germany rejected the treaty, the more he drew back from the maelstrom he saw swirling beyond the edge:

PLUNDERING, DEATH, AND MURDER WOULD BE THE RULE OF THE DAY. IN THE GENERAL CONFUSION, THERE WILL NO LONGER BE A COMMUNICATIONS SYSTEM. THE BREAKUP OF GERMANY WILL FOLLOW. . . . THE INDIVIDUAL FREE CITIES WILL NOT BE ABLE TO RESIST THE PRESSURE OF THE ALLIED OFFERS TO AGREE TO PEACE TERMS WITH THEM. . . . SMALL GERMAN STATES TOO WOULD DECLARE THEMSELVES INDEPENDENT AND SEEK TO ESTABLISH RELATIONS WITH OUR OPPONENTS. THE MAP OF THE GERMAN REICH WOULD THEN DISAPPEAR, AND IN ITS PLACE A CHECKERED COLLECTION OF LITTLE STATES WOULD APPEAR, AS HAS ALWAYS BEEN THE DREAM OF FRANCE.

Four thousand miles away, Philander C. Knox, former United States Secretary of State and now a Republican senator from Pennsylvania, stood in the Senate and urged his colleagues not to accept the League of Nations Covenant: "It is hard to conceive of any man traditional in Americanism lending his support to such a monstrosity." Knox claimed that the Covenant would create a "supergovernment" empowered to interfere in the domestic affairs of the League's member nations, and that it would destroy the long-cherished Monroe Doctrine. Discard the League, urged Knox, and let us conclude peace immediately with Germany: "Six long, weary months have been consumed by the peace conference at Paris. . . . There have been times when it seemed that we nations who entered the conference sworn friends would leave it bitter enemies, and this unhappy contingency is not yet put from us. And still we wait. Meanwhile, Europe is in turmoil, to the point of anarchy and chaos."

In Berlin, where a strike of newspaper printers had left the people at the mercy of rumors for three days—would there be a coup by the military, or by the Workers' Councils?—the journals prepared their editions for tomorrow, their rhetorical battles reflecting the deep divisions within the city. Prince Max of Baden, who had persuaded—forced, in fact—the Kaiser to abdicate in November, urged resistance to the Allies. "It would be best," Prince Max wrote in the *Berliner Tageblatt*, "to place the enemy in a position where he must use inhuman means against us. We must not save him the odious task of setting his troops in motion not for a Wilson peace, but for a peace of revenge to be visited upon an unresisting people. That would be the worst moral defeat in history." But a less exalted writer in a more modest journal had his own succinct advice for Ebert: "Rather the end (and peace) with terror than terror without end." Fly sheets appeared in the streets of Berlin denouncing Erzberger as a man who would betray his country. The *Neue Berliner*, a radical paper, appeared with an enormous headline announcing its account of the Paris stone-throwing incident: ATTEMPTED MURDER OF THE GERMAN PEACE DELEGATION. "It was like 1914," wrote Harry Kessler in his diary. "And just as stiflingly sultry and sunny as it was then at the end of July."

Orders were given to all Allied forces in the Rhine bridgehead areas to have their troop concentrations completed by Friday, June 20, in preparation for an advance. General Pershing announced that the Fourth and Fifth Divisions of American regulars had been taken off the list of units scheduled to return to the United States in the near future. Back in Paris, Harold Nicolson complained: "Desultory work all day. It is maddening having nothing to do, with so much to be done."

Shortly before midnight, a gang of fifty Spartacist prisoners escaped from the prison at Weimar and attacked the castle where the Cabinet was meeting. They were repulsed by guards with machine guns.

* * *

Wednesday, June 18. Fearing a leftist coup, reinforcements of government troops had poured into Weimar during the night. So had the premiers of Bavaria (Hoffmann again), Würtemberg, Baden, and Saxony; they now joined the Cabinet discussions. The train bearing Brockdorff-Rantzau and the German peace delegation arrived in the capital early in the morning. Haggard from lack of sleep, the Foreign Minister and two colleagues took breakfast and then proceeded directly to the Cabinet meeting. There Brockdorff-Rantzau announced the delegation's unanimous recommendation that the government refuse to sign the treaty. He personally believed that divisions among the Allies would soon widen into a deep fissure and enable Germany to obtain more favorable terms in the very near future. His message delivered and his duty done, Brockdorff-Rantzau turned his back on the whole mess and left the meeting and went for a walk in the park.

President Wilson and his entourage arrived in Belgium at 8:45 in the morning. He was received at the border by King Albert and Queen Elizabeth and flocks of wide-eyed schoolchildren. The royal and presidential parties immediately set off on an automobile tour of the battlefields of Flanders. Wilson passed a sign overlooking the graves at Ypres, where vandals had looted the swampy field for relics: "This is Holy Ground. No stone of this fabric may be taken away. It is a heritage for all civilized peoples. By order, Town Mayor, Ypres."

British naval authorities ordered all Allied ships unloading food in German ports to cease discharging their cargoes; Wilson quickly issued a countermanding order to American ships, telling them to disregard the British commands. But the Admiralty did detain a number of large American steamers that were still in British ports, being loaded with foodstuffs bound for Germany. The Royal Navy moved toward a state of war. All leave was canceled. Twelve British cruisers and a number of destroyers arrived at Copenhagen.

For the first wave of an invasion, Allied plans called for the occupation of Essen, Frankfurt, and Mannheim. The Peace Conference gave Germany two more days—until 7:00 p.m., June 23, to sign the treaty. Margaret Wilson arrived in Paris after a seven-month tour of France, during which she had entertained (with her singing) Allied soldiers. Miss Wilson pooh-poohed rumors of hostility between American doughboys and their French hosts. "My own personal experiences, of course, were invariably delightful," she said.

Municipal elections in Bavaria gave the Catholic Center party majorities everywhere except in Munich, where the left-wing Independent Socialists remained strong. Saxony was wracked by food riots. A railroad strike began to spread across Germany; disturbances appeared in Westphalia and the Ruhr. The atmosphere grew more inflammable with every passing day, as the bourgeoisie hid behind "Noskism" and the workers drifted toward Spartacism again.

Baron Makino, the Japanese Foreign Minister, told a reporter in Paris that he found it incomprehensible that Germany would decide *not* to sign the treaty. Such an act, he said, would widen even further the gulf that separated the German nation from the rest of the world: "She cannot rise until she has purged herself of that love of power and disregard of her neighbor's rights which brought ruin upon her."

The famous, irascible volcano on the island of Stromboli, just off the west coast of Sicily, erupted once again as it had done periodically for the past two thousand years.

Disgusted with the pusillanimous policies of the politicians, Gabriele D'Annunzio had resigned from the Italian army and was planning his own private raid to rescue Fiume from the evil clutches of the Yugoslavs. The National Council of Fiume, meanwhile, voted to establish its own independent army to defend the city's liberty; the council also decreed that justice throughout the territory of Fiume should be administered in the name of King Victor Emmanuel of Italy.

David Lloyd George walked through the stifling heat across the battlefields of Verdun.

Gustav Noske met with General Wilhelm Groener, who had just arrived in Weimar from Hindenburg's headquarters. Of all the members of the German military officer corps, who as a class suffered from wildly deranged notions of martial duty and glory and completely suicidal sentiments of Prussian honor, Groener was perhaps the most realistic. Like Erzberger, he understood that an Allied invasion could easily destroy the precious unified German confederation that had, after all, only been in existence for less than fifty years. Bavaria, the Rhineland, all the great and tiny states would split away, leaving Prussia alone again. After listening to Groener, Noske returned to the Cabinet meeting convinced that resistance to the treaty would be catastrophic.

Wilson and the King of the Belgians arrived in Brussels at 9:15 P.M. and drove to the royal palace amid the cheers of the crowd that had gathered at the Quartier Leopold Station.

At 10:30 P.M., orders were flashed to the American troops across the Rhine to step up their preparations for war. Once again, the men slept in the open, with the flames from kitchen fires flickering through the darkness. The first American objective would be the town of Cassel, thirty-seven miles away.

People gathered in the streets of Weimar to watch the lights burning in the windows of the castle where their government was trying to decide whether to live or die.

Thursday, June 19. In Rome, Orlando's government collapsed—"dropped to the ground," someone said, "like an empty sack." Orlando had failed to stem both the high cost of living and the nearly continuous wave of strikes that had swept over Italy since the winter like a plague of Spanish influenza. The labor situation had reached the point of absurdity: general strikes in Milan, Naples, Verona, Genoa, and Turin; riots, street demonstrations, disorders in nearly every major city; almost all of the elementary school teachers in the country had walked off their jobs on June 11, and even some village priests went out on strike. Most disconcerting to the Italian way of life, however, was the decision by the waiters of all the restaurants in Rome to strike, shutting down every restaurant, inn, and café in the city, leaving patrons to dine on only a chunk of bread and cheese, or a bunch of cherries. And, of course, Orlando and Sonnino had failed to deliver Fiume to Italy. Not lacking for enemies in the fractious world of Italian parliamentary politics, Orlando was soundly defeated in a vote of confidence in the Chamber. Amid the wave of disgust and weariness with "the weeping orator" from Sicily, only seventy-eight out of 340 deputies voted in his favor. Italy was now without a government. "Nobody cares for Orlando," wrote one perceptive observer, "but nobody would like now to accept his legacy of affairs."

The weather at Weimar was blazing hot. Everyone sweated through the days, and the nights brought little relief. After nearly twenty-four hours of continuous debate (meals were brought in from outside), the Cabinet found itself hopelessly divided. All it could agree to do was submit the question of the treaty to the members of the National Assembly for their recommendation. And as each party's officials caucused, a formal council of war called by the Prussian Minister of War, General Reinhardt, met in another part of the city. By this time the memories of November defeat had faded, and the German high command had convinced itself that the army had been betrayed by weak-kneed politicians who had forced the Kaiser to flee and incited the common soldier and sailor to revolt. The legend of the *Dolchstoss*, the "stab in the back," had already been born. Now the commanders were again ready and more than willing to wage a glorious war to defend the Fatherland—to perish, if necessary, in furious battle rather than surrender again. So, realizing that the generals would adopt almost any course short of surrender, Gustav Noske told them that at least half of the Cabinet, and possibly Ebert, too, would soon resign rather than take upon themselves the responsibility for a decision on the treaty. Perhaps Noske would then be asked to form a new government. Delighted with the prospect of the Bloodhound—the man who had turned the soldiers loose again and again, the man who allowed the Freikorps to rampage unrestrained throughout Germany—as dictator of the German nation, the generals changed their reactionary minds and agreed to support the signing of the treaty, as long as the hated articles condemning the Kaiser and confirming Germany's war guilt were removed. Here, they thought, was a clever way out. Yes, they laughed, go ahead and let the cowards sign the treaty. Noske will soon allow us to put things right. The Fatherland will rise again from the ashes.

Wilson spent the day in a Belgium that still bore the marks of its devastation by Germany. He saw the wrecked mines at Charleroi, stood among the ruins of the Louvain Library (destroyed by the Germans in 1914), where a Doctor of Laws degree was conferred upon him, addressed the Belgian Parliament, visited with Cardinal Mercier, and attended a gala dinner given by the King and Queen at the palace.

Foch was directing Allied preparations for war from his headquarters at Coblenz. The marshal was forming one front from the Rhine to the Danube, and another with the Polish and Czech troops who stood poised and ready to strike Germany from the east and south. The giant British dirigible R-34, heavily armed with bombs and machine guns, flew at a low altitude—plainly visible to people on the ground below—along the German Baltic coast.

"God does not desert us," Field Marshal von Hindenburg told an audience in Kolberg. "We must take care that the great work of Wilhelm I and Bismarck is not crumbled to pieces. Germany and Prussia will again arise. That is my firm belief. . . ."

At the seventy-fifth annual meeting of the American Medico-Psychological Association in Philadelphia, President E. S. Southard put forth the proposition that all human beings suffered to some degree from various psychic disorders that could be classified as types of insanity. "High-brows, Cabinet officers, individual citizens, professors, presidents, doctors, workmen, all have their own individual peculiarities," Dr. Southard informed his colleagues, "as much forms of insanity as the disorders which affect inmates of institutions for the dangerously insane."

There was a continuous stream of automobiles running to and from the castle at Amerongen. The Kaiser had just finished sawing his five-thousandth tree, which he cut into one-inch discs and marked with the date and his initial. Dutch gendarmes increased their guard outside the castle. Late in the day at Weimar, a delegation of civilian officials informed the Prussian Minister of War and his fellow generals in no uncertain terms that "the Prussian people had no intention whatever of resuming the war in defense of the officers' honor. . . . [And] if the officers thought the people were prepared to endure any renewed suffering they were living in the past."

James Shotwell took a sightseeing trip through occupied Germany. He wrote in his diary:

BEYOND SOLLINGEN, ON THE WAY TO BURG, WE RAN INTO BRITISH TOM-
MIES MARCHING OUT TO THE FIFTEEN MILE RADIUS FROM THE BRIDGE
HEAD, TO BE READY FOR THE DASH TO BERLIN IF THAT SHOULD BE NECES-
SARY. THERE WERE LONG LINES OF TROOPS, DIRTY AND HOT IN THE LATE
AFTERNOON SUN. SOLDIERS DROPPED OUT, OVERCOME BY THE HEAT IN
THEIR HEAVY UNIFORMS AND THE HEAVY PACKS THEY WERE CARRYING.
HEAVY HOWITZERS WERE ON THE MOVE, DRAGGED BY TRACTORS; THERE
WERE LIGHT HORSE BATTERIES AS WELL. . . . ONE COMPANY HAD A GOAT
AS A MASCOT. KITCHENS WERE DRAGGED ALONG THE ROADS COOKING AS
THEY CAME. LORRIES PICKED THEIR WAY THROUGH THE TROOPS, WITH
ABOUT THIRTY-FIVE MEN CROWDED INTO EACH. . . . ON OUR ROAD BACK
WE PASSED BIG AIRDROMES. GENERAL SALMOND OF THE AIR CORPS, WHO
WAS WITH US, SAID THEY HAD MORE THAN THEY NEEDED. IF THERE WERE
OPPOSITION THE DEFILES WERE NARROW AND THEY WOULD USE THE AIR.

At 6:30 P.M., orders were f ashed to the American forces across the Rhine to concentrate. NCOs route the men out of billets and clubs and prepared them for the march. German civilians looked on in glum curiosity. A trail of dust followed the 17th Field Artillery as it moved out to the concentration zone.

Harold Nicolson attended a dinner party at the Ritz. Nicolson hated dinner parties. Lloyd George, who had become overheated on the Western Front and then caught a chill, returned to Paris with a bad cold and went straight to bed.

Friday, June 20. The German Cabinet, having failed to obtain a decisive parliamentary majority either for or against the treaty, took another vote: seven for (including Erzberger and Noske), and seven against (including Scheidemann). Deadlock. No formula could be found to satisfy everyone.

At one o'clock in the morning, Chancellor Scheidemann resigned, as did Brockdorff-Rantzau. Four more Cabinet members followed suit. The government had fallen.

Wilson returned to Paris at 9:30 A.M. He said he had enjoyed a good night's rest and was not tired. At eleven o'clock he went to the Crillon for a meeting of the entire American peace delegation.

In the camps of the American Expeditionary Force, Signal Corps troops strung new wires along the roads. Observation balloons were brought up to the front. "Forces of darkness are to be loosened at Paris and idealism is being forced into silence," warned Premier Heinrich Lammasch of Austria. "Militarism seems justified. The mailed fist has been raised again, but on the other side." The *Washington Post* counted twenty-three wars currently wracking the world. "The nerves of Europe," said the *Post* in its editorial on this day, "are at the snapping point."

Rain came at last to England. After an almost rainless May and three weeks of burning June sunshine, the land enjoyed a steady and persistent downpour.

The printers in Paris were busy removing the names of Orlando and the other former Italian peace delegates from the official text of the treaty. Nearly everyone else in Paris seemed to be dancing. "Paris is now dancing mad," observed one fashion correspondent, "and from boys and girls of fourteen to men and women of forty and forty-five, they never seem to tire. Between five and seven, and again after dinner, Paris dances. Never has she danced so much, so wildly, or so industriously. Many of the dresses worn for this amusement (or should it be called a sport?) look like gymnasium costumes, they are so plain, so scanty and so loose-fitting. They hardly pass the knee on the way down and on the way up they stop short as soon as possible."

Berlin newspapers carried pages of military advertisements and appeals to patriotic citizens to enroll in the various militias, corps, and protective societies that abounded in Prussia. The German people, Ben Hecht noticed, seemed unaware of why the world hated them so: "The darkness and bewilderment of the child that has been slapped in the face and thrown into a reeking clothes closet are the uppermost emotions of the man in the street today."

The headline in London's *Evening News:* BRITAIN PREPARES FOR WAR.

Unwilling to desert his country in its hour of desperate need, Ebert struggled throughout the day to form a new government. No matter what coalition he might put together, however, he had already determined not to make a decision on the treaty without a definitive statement from the army on its ability to defend Germany: if the generals told him they could repel an invasion, he could refuse to sign; if they told him they could not, he might then sign without fear that the military lords would later accuse him of betraying the Fatherland.

At 3:00 P.M., the Council of Three met to discuss the German situation and the Italian Cabinet crisis. In Geneva, the betting odds suddenly switched during the day to two to one that Germany would sign the treaty.

Shotwell visited the American section of the Rhineland front. He found the men "encamped in little 'pup' tents under the trees along the wayside, all tucked away as unobtrusively as can be, but waiting for the command to march to Berlin if the Germans do not sign the Treaty. . . . We met a detachment about 7,500 strong marching along the Rhine bank with their flags shining in the sunlight."

In search of a Cabinet, King Victor Emmanuel received a steady stream of parliamentary leaders. It soon became apparent that the new government would be dominated by Giovanni Giolitti, a progressive politician with an unsavory reputation for too much cleverness, whose notorious neutralist leanings often appeared to approach pro-Germanism. Now safely out of office, Sonnino permitted his newspaper to publish two severely anti-French articles, one violently attacking Clemenceau, the other praising Prince Lichnowsky, the former German Ambassador to Britain. Mussolini's Fascists, who despised Giolitti and those who had opposed Italy's entry into the war on the Allied side in 1915, marched in the Piazza del Duomo in Milan.

The British naval force at Scapa Flow prepared to put to sea for torpedo-firing practice.

Harold Nicolson went to Geneva to look for a house.

Saturday, June 21. There still was no government in Germany. Ebert turned to the leaders of the Democratic party, the men who had worked so fervently for peace while the war had ground on and on, but they refused to take office. More than any other party in the Reichstag, the Democrats had believed that the Allies would negotiate a Wilsonian peace (that is, a treaty based on the German interpretation of the Fourteen Points); after seeing the actual peace terms, they felt betrayed, and held themselves responsible for the predicament in which Germany now found itself ("I dare not look my constituents in the face," one pacifist Democrat said), and hence they would not betray their country further by signing this treaty.

Admiral von Reuter, the German officer responsible for the remnants of the Imperial fleet interned at the bleak, bitterly cold Scottish harbor of Scapa Flow, looked about him that morning and was startled to find that most of the British battle squadron that for the past six months had been guarding his helpless ships had now suddenly vanished, leaving behind only a drifter patrol of a few trawlers. Reuter believed this meant the Armistice had ended and the war was about to begin again; he feared his ships would shortly be taken over and used by the Allies to shell German cities. Besides, he recalled the order that his Kaiser had given to every admiral in 1914, that no German man-of-war was ever to be surrendered. Shortly before noon, Reuter raised a prearranged signal of two flags—a pennant with a white ball on a blue background above a yellow-and-blue pennant—to all the other ships of the German fleet lashed into a double line at Scapa Flow: ten battleships, five battle cruisers, ten light cruisers, and forty-nine destroyers. The signal read, "Paragraph eleven. Acknowledge." Immediately the German sailors whom the British Admiralty had left behind to maintain the vessels (two hundred men on each battleship, about a dozen apiece on the destroyers) rushed belowdecks and threw open the valves. The water poured in, the crews abandoned ship and floated about in the chilly water in their lifeboats, and slowly but inexorably the Kaiser's grand fleet began to sink.

The first non-German to notice that anything was amiss was Bernard F. Gribble, an English marine artist commissioned by the American government to do a series of paintings of the German fleet. At 11:45, Gribble, who was sitting in a British guard vessel, noticed a number of German sailors on board the *Frederich de Grosse* throwing their baggage into lifeboats that had already been lowered into the water. Gribble asked the British officer in charge, Second Lieutenant C. Leeth, whether he allowed the Germans to go rowing for pleasure. "No," replied Leeth, "but, by Jove, it looks as if they were." The German sailors then began tossing things overboard even more furiously. After a few moments' reflection, it finally dawned on Leeth what was happening. He panicked. Leeth warned his men to stand ready with cutlasses and rifles, and headed for the nearest ship, the *Frankfurt*, where he ordered the German sailors to return to their ships at once. "We can't," they called back, "we have no oars." (They had deliberately thrown their oars overboard in anticipation of such an order.) Extra oars were thrown out to them, and Leeth again commanded them to return to their ships, or else he would open fire on them. They refused, and so Leeth told his men to fire; six German sailors were killed and at least ten others wounded. More may have drowned as they jumped overboard to escape the barrage. The Germans tried to come alongside Leeth's vessel, but a British sailor kept pushing the lifeboats away. Gribble noticed that the German officers were wearing yellow gloves and smoking cigars. "It was most surprising," he thought, "to observe how swiftly the vessels sank. Most of them turned over to the starboard, and then disappeared." The last German ship to sink was the *Derfflinger*, which turned turtle shortly before five o'clock. Only one battleship, three light cruisers, and twenty destroyers lay safely beached. "At sunset there was, apart from a portion of one of the vessels which had not completely sunk, nothing to be seen on the waters, which in the morning had borne the German surrendered fleet." Fourteen hundred German sailors eventually were fished from the icy water and placed under arrest. Actually, the British had wanted to tow the German fleet out to deep water and sink it anyway, and so in a sense "the Great Scuttle" had done no more than accomplish their own purpose for them, albeit in a rather perverse manner. But of course the incident was extremely embarrassing, since it happened right under the Admiralty's nose when the Royal Navy was, after all, supposed to be guarding the German ships. (Gribble claimed to have heard a British admiral speculate several days before the scuttling that the Germans might try something like this.) And the French were furious; because they possessed far fewer ships of their own than did Britain, they had planned to incorporate their share of the German fleet into the French navy. It was, they charged, one more example of German perfidy, and a distressing portent of British folly in believing the Huns could ever be taught to behave like civilized people.

On the Continent, Shotwell drove through the devastated coal mines and steel works of France, then saw the untouched German industrial machinery just across the frontier. "The contrast," he thought, "was simply overpowering."

As the German fleet was sinking into the chilly waters off the northern tip of Scotland, Ebert finally put together a cabinet in Weimar. His new Chancellor was the conservative Socialist Gustav Bauer, forty-nine years old, a member of the Reichstag since 1912, an expert on labor matters, and a capable if uninspiring organizer. To console Matthias Erzberger, who had dreamed that he would become Chancellor, Ebert created the position of Deputy Chancellor, and gave Erzberger the portfolio of Minister of Finance as well. Noske, similarly disappointed at being passed over for the top spot, agreed to remain as Minister of Defense. The new Cabinet at once convened and began to debate its first, and quite possibly its last, action. Erzberger, who was rumored to be in close contact with representatives of Lloyd George, told his colleagues that the Allies probably would agree to delete the war-guilt clause and their demand for the trial of the Kaiser and other "war criminals" in return for an immediate German signature. That arrangement seemed to suit the Cabinet just fine.

Following widespread Spartacist disorders, Westphalia was placed under a state of siege.

Over 500,000 Allied soldiers stationed in occupied Germany stood ready for a further advance two days hence. They had been given orders to distribute to the civilian population a series of military regulations written by Marshal Foch and printed in German, French, and English, advising the German people that any house from which civilians fired upon Allied troops would be burned, and that all persons guilty of any hostile actions against the invading forces would be subject to military reprisals.

At another evening of Dadaism attended by Ben Hecht in Berlin, a dignitary in evening dress leaped upon a stage and started pounding a bass drum. "Here, here is the broken heart of Germany." Hysterical laughter. "And I said to Herr Ebert, announce Herr Butter before it is too late." A barefoot young girl climbed on top of a piano and began playing the keys with her feet. "The Dadaists have overthrown the government at Rome," someone chortled. "Everywhere Dadaismus is triumphant." One hundred women shouted "Mous!" A sewing machine raced against a typewriter. "Courage! Here comes Nesko and the Government guard." Later the festival's leader, the "Baba," explained, "The Entente is fast reducing the world to one last absurdity. In the nonsense of Dadaism lies the only real sanity Germany has ever achieved. . . ."

Sunday, June 22. At noon the National Assembly at Weimar opened its deliberations. The House and the galleries were filled to capacity. Herr Bauer rose and introduced his Cabinet. "It was exceedingly hard for us to take the decision to join the new Government whose most urgent duty it must be to conclude a peace of injustice," Bauer acknowledged:

THE DISTRESS OF THE LAND AND THE PEOPLE HAS BROUGHT US TOGETHER. WE COULD NOT REFUSE OUR COOPERATION UNLESS WE DESIRED TO RUN THE RISK OF LEAVING GERMANY A PREY TO A CHAOTIC STATE WITHOUT A GOVERNMENT, FROM WHICH THERE WOULD HAVE BEEN NO SALVATION. YOU WILL BELIEVE ME WHEN I SAY WE ARE NOT HERE TO STAND FOR THE INTERESTS OF OUR PARTIES, AND STILL LESS TO SATISFY OUR AMBITIONS. WE ARE HERE BECAUSE OF A SENSE OF DUTY, CONSCIOUS THAT IT WAS OUR ACCURSED DUTY TO SAVE WHAT COULD BE SAVED. . . . ON MONDAY THE WAR IS TO BEGIN AFRESH IF WE HAVE NOT GIVEN OUR "YES." AN ADVANCE IS TO BEGIN FOR WHICH EVERY INSTRUMENT OF MURDER IS READY AGAINST

THE DEFENSELESS, UNARMED NATION. . . . AT THIS HOUR OF LIFE AND
DEATH, UNDER THE MENACE OF INVASION, I FOR THE LAST TIME RAISE IN
FREE GERMANY A PROTEST AGAINST THIS TREATY OF VIOLENCE AND DE-
STRUCTION, A PROTEST AGAINST THIS MOCKERY OF THE RIGHT OF SELF-
DETERMINATION, THIS ENSLAVEMENT OF THE GERMAN PEOPLE, THIS NEW
MENACE TO THE PEACE OF THE WORLD UNDER THE MASK OF A PEACE
TREATY. NO SIGNING ENFEEBLES THIS PROTEST.

Shortly after four o'clock in the afternoon, at the end of a stormy session,
the National Assembly voted, 237 to 138, to endorse the government's
position on the signing of the peace treaty—that is, to sign the treaty
provided the several most humiliating clauses were removed. Using the
recently installed direct telephone line between Weimar and Versailles, the
Cabinet instructed the German representative at Versailles, Baron Haniel
von Haimhausen, to inform the Peace Conference that Germany would
sign the treaty with two reservations: she would not recognize that she was
solely responsible for the war, nor would she undertake any obligation to
deliver up anyone accused of war crimes.

At Paris, the opening ceremonies for the inter-Allied Army games presented a spectacular, colorful pageant for the thousands of spectators who
jammed into Pershing Stadium. The scheduled first round of events included qualifying heats for the one-hundred-yard dash and the mile, several
rounds of the "mysterious game" of baseball, and an exhibition of Arabs
racing on horseback.

Clemenceau, Wilson, and Lloyd George met at Lloyd George's flat in
the Rue Nitot at 6:30 that evening. (The meeting was held there because
the Welshman was still suffering from a sore throat and could not go out.)
Lloyd George was openly distressed by the scuttle at Scapa Flow, and
Clemenceau seethed with indignation at what he recognized as only the
most recent example of Hun treachery. The German message from Weimar, offering a conditional signature, arrived at seven o'clock. A translation
was read to the Three. They discussed the situation until eight, adjourned
for dinner (in the interim, Clemenceau heard Lloyd George's daughter
playing the piano and went up and patted her on the shoulder, whispering,
"I thought it was Paderewski"), then reconvened at nine. Wilson had
drafted a brief reply, which the Three issued to Germany at 9:30:

OF THE TIME WITHIN WHICH THE GERMAN GOVERNMENT MUST MAKE
THEIR FINAL DECISION AS TO THE SIGNATURE OF THE TREATY LESS THAN
TWENTY-FOUR HOURS REMAIN. THE ALLIED AND ASSOCIATED GOVERN-

MENTS HAVE GIVEN THE FULLEST CONSIDERATION TO ALL OF THE RE-
PRESENTATIONS HITHERTO MADE BY THE GERMAN GOVERNMENT WITH
REGARD TO THE TREATY, HAVING REPLIED WITH COMPLETE FRANKNESS,
AND HAVE MADE SUCH CONCESSIONS AS THEY THOUGHT IT RIGHT TO MAKE.
. . . THE ALLIED AND ASSOCIATED POWERS THEREFORE FEEL CONSTRAINED
TO SAY THAT THE TIME FOR DISCUSSION HAS PASSED. THEY CAN ACCEPT
OR ACKNOWLEDGE NO QUALIFICATION OR RESERVATIONS. . . .

The treaty stood as written, and Germany could take it all or leave it
all.

At Sutton Camp, in Surrey, where unrest had been building for the past
ten days, British Tommies who had received orders to return to France
finally mutinied, formed a soviet, and refused to salute their officers or obey
any orders they didn't like. The government dispatched two battalions of
troops with machine guns to the camp and arrested four hundred men and
scattered more than a thousand others to other camps.

French military intelligence reported no German military concentrations along the Western Front. For the first hundred kilometers there
would be no resistance. There were food riots in Mannheim, and Spartacists tried unsuccessfully to storm the prison and police station at Cassel.
Premier Hoffmann prepared to resign his position in Bavaria.

"This evening," mourned Harry Kessler, "I have been indescribably
depressed, as though the entire sap of life has dried up inside me." Noske
was on a train for Berlin. En route, the Minister of Defense was handed
a message requesting his immediate return to Weimar for an urgent Cabinet meeting.

Monday, June 23. The invasion of Germany would begin at 7:00 P.M.

Early in the morning, Baron von Haimhausen presented an official note
from the German government asking the Peace Conference for an additional forty-eight hours to consider its decision. Paul Dutasta took the note
to Maurice Hankey, secretary of the British delegation, and together they
went to Lloyd George's flat; owing to the early hour, no one inside heard
them knocking. They then hurried to Wilson's house and persuaded Admiral Grayson to awaken the President. Carefully—very carefully—they
roused the detective, armed with a revolver, who was sleeping on a mat
outside Wilson's bedroom door. Wilson and his wife were still in bed. "It
is cold here," the President said as he threw back the covers. "Come into
my bathroom, which is warmer." So he read the German note while sitting
on the edge of his bathtub. At nine o'clock the Three convened at Lloyd

George's flat and, thirty minutes later, dispatched their reply to the German emissary: they regretted that it was "not possible to extend the time already granted to your Excellency to make known your decision relative to the signature of the treaty without any reservation."

Berlin swirled with rumors of an impending military coup. "The tension is terrific," wrote Kessler. "Very oppressive weather. Counter-revolution, war, insurrection threaten us like a nearing thunderstorm." At Weimar, Noske bypassed the Cabinet meeting for a conference with General Maercker, the man who had recruited and still commanded one of the first Freikorps units in Germany. Maercker desperately urged Noske not to let the government sign the treaty; if it did, he promised that the entire German officer corps—and every Freikorps unit—would immediately resign. Maercker grasped Noske's hand and begged him to allow the army to make Noske Germany's dictator. Noske's mind boggled. These Prussian officers, these noble Junkers whom he worshiped, wanted nothing more than to raise him—the son of a weaver—to supreme power. Tears streaming down his cheeks, Noske leaped up and shouted exultantly, "General, now I too have had enough of this rotten mess!" Noske then handed his resignation to Ebert, hoping that the government would collapse and he would be left to pick up the pieces.

The National Assembly at Weimar was in agony. Rumors abounded that the Allies had a list containing thousands of names of Germans whom they planned to try as war criminals. Perhaps even the sainted Hindenburg would be subjected to such a gross indignity. By noon, the previous day's majority in favor of signing had faded away. Ebert had only one chance to avoid chaos. He telephoned General Wilhelm Groener at Kolberg. Would the Supreme Command tell him that it could defend Germany? If so, he would refuse to sign the treaty. Would the Supreme Command tell him that resistance was useless? If so, he would sign the treaty. But he would do nothing without a definite indication from Hindenburg and Groener. Ebert told Groener he would call back later for his answer.

Francesco Nitti, the new Prime Minister of Italy, presented his new Cabinet to King Victor Emmanuel at the Quirinal Palace in Rome. Veteran diplomat Tommaso Tittoni replaced Sonnino as Foreign Minister. Mussolini and D'Annunzio also were in the capital, to attend the first convocation of the National Veterans' Association in the Augusteum. Violent demonstrations against the Nitti Cabinet erupted at Turin, Milan, and Florence. The Nationalists despised the new government for its alleged cowardice in 1915 ("The Nitti Cabinet has the fundamental defect of consisting almost exclusively of elements which had opposed the war," claimed one disgruntled Italian politician). Writing in Mussolini's *Popolo d'Italia*, D'Annunzio pleaded with all true patriots to join in "thwarting the conspiracy"; Mussolini's Fasci expelled from their ranks all members who accepted places in the new government. There were rumors everywhere of a military coup to save Italy's honor from being bargained away by the weakness of Nitti and Giolitti.

In the interim between calls from President Ebert, Hindenburg told Groener, "You know as well as I that armed resistance is impossible." But shortly before Ebert was due to call back, the field marshal glanced at his watch and strode from the room, with a careless wave back to Groener: "There is no need for me to stay. You can give the answer to the President as well as I."

From 11:00 A.M. to 1:15 P.M., the Council of Three met to consider the final clauses of the Austrian treaty. The Council adjourned until four o'clock, when it would meet again to consider any new messages from Germany.

Rainstorms broke out all across Germany. Ebert telephoned again to Kolberg. He asked Groener for a final answer. Groener told Ebert that the government must sign the treaty. Once the damnable deed was actually done, saner heads probably would prevail and the army would not revolt. Groener hung up the phone and saw Hindenburg walk back into the room and put his aged hand on Groener's shoulder. "You have taken a heavy burden on yourself," was all the field marshal said.

At 2:30, Chancellor Bauer stood before the National Assembly at Weimar—its members had already learned of Groener's final message from Kolberg—and conceded that the government's efforts to obtain last-minute amendments had failed. "As a result of the Entente's answer the situation has undergone a fundamental change, and we are thereby confronted with the tremendous question—rejection or unconditional signing?" A defeated Germany "was being violated body and soul to the horror of the world," Bauer cried. "We are to be spared nothing, absolutely nothing." At long last, all was lost—for the time being. "Let us sign, but it is our hope to the last breath that this attempt against our honor may one day recoil against its authors." No roll was called and no record kept of individual votes on the recommendation to sign the treaty; instead, members silently rose in their places to indicate their votes. A majority stood in favor of the government's decision to sign. The session lasted less than fifteen minutes. The President of the Assembly, Konstantine Fehrenbach, told a hushed chamber, still stunned with what it had done, that "the Allies might enslave Germany, but could not degrade her. Germany was helpless, but not without honour." Then he pronounced the benediction, commending "the unhappy fatherland to a merciful God."

At 4:30 a message came through to Paris saying that the Germans had decided to sign, but the official note still had not yet been received or translated. Food shops in the Moabit quarter of Berlin were stormed and looted.

Shortly after 5:00 P.M., less than two hours before the war would begin again, Baron von Haimhausen formally presented the German note accepting the treaty to Colonel Henri, the French officer assigned as liaison to the German peace delegation. Henri sped from Versailles to Paris and turned the note over to Paul Dutasta at the Quai d'Orsay at 5:25. At 5:30 P.M., Wilson, Clemenceau, and Lloyd George sat waiting in the study of Wilson's house in the Place des Etats-Unis. Outside, Dutasta stepped out of an automobile and walked straight past the guards and into the meeting room and handed the German message to Clemenceau. "We have waited forty-nine years for this moment," murmured the Tiger as he opened the note. There was silence for a minute, then a sigh. Clemenceau tried to affect nonchalance; after all, France in its glorious history had gone through this sort of thing before: "We have done it many times," he said. After a few minutes of remarking upon how hard the Germans had died, the Council of Three parted, according to one witness, "with good feelings and elation at accomplishment." The official transcript of the meeting concluded with the notation that "orders were given for guns to be fired."

Wilson, Clemenceau, and Lloyd George told the people that peace at last had come to the world. Official statistics revealed that a total of 7,450,200 people had died in the war. Russia had suffered approximately 1.7 million deaths; Germany 1.6 million; France 1.385 million; Great Britain 900,000; Austria 800,000; Italy 330,000; and the United States 48,000.

At 6:45 the air-raid sirens of Paris blasted forth with their awful noise. Cannon in the streets and squares of the city fired violent salutes to peace. At seven o'clock all the ministers of the French government went to the Ministry of War to congratulate Clemenceau. As word of the German surrender spread through Paris, thousands of people poured into the streets. The orchestras in the cafés struck up the Allied national anthems. Wilson's chauffeur took the back streets to avoid the crowds. For some unexplained reason, the wireless station at the Eiffel Tower repeatedly broadcast the cryptic message "Fermez les portes" several times at eight o'clock, and every ten minutes thereafter. The celebration went on long past the eleven-thirty closing time for Paris cafés. Men in khaki pulled the huge captured German cannon from the Place de la Concorde, lifted up laughing girls who sat astride the guns, and then dragged the spoils of war triumphantly through the streets. The Boulevard des Italiens, said a member of Wilson's staff, "was one writhing mass of humanity."

Ships of the British fleet in the Firth of Forth sounded their sirens. Throughout England, bells were rung, bonfires lit, and guns fired, but there was no wholehearted outpouring of emotion to match the Armistice celebration. A crowd had gathered outside the Houses of Parliament shortly after eight o'clock, in hopes of hearing reliable news. Suddenly someone pointed to a rainbow forming in the sky, and everyone watched the gradual unfolding of color. Several people called out, "There is the peace in the heavens." At eight-thirty the rainbow disappeared. At a public meeting in Manchester, a resolution was proposed that peace should be celebrated. But a local branch of the National Federation of Discharged and Demobilised Soldiers and Sailors objected; in view of the government's treatment of discharged men and their wives and dependents, and the fact that thousands of demobilized soldiers were still out of work, the veterans asked that any celebrations be postponed until their grievances were remedied. The veterans' request was approved by an overwhelming majority.

At Weimar, a delegation from the Landesjager Corps waited outside the Assembly, threatening to hang Matthias Erzberger. Erzberger fled to Berlin incognito. In every major city in Germany, processions formed and marched through the streets, singing war songs and cheering the generals of the old empire. A dozen members of the Guards Cavalry Corps walked into the Berlin Arsenal, removed several French battle flags that had been captured in 1870 and 1871 and were now promised to be returned to France, took them to the base of a monument to Frederick the Great, soaked the flags in gasoline, and set them ablaze while soldiers and civilians together sang "Deutschland Über Alles." Afterwards, students at the University of Berlin assembled for patriotic demonstrations. That night, armed mobs spread throughout Berlin, attacking shops, robbing passersby, and firing from rooftops upon isolated bands of soldiers. Streetcars were held up while marauders searched the passengers' pockets and stole women's rings. An uneasy order returned after daybreak. In Hamburg, hungry citizens stormed the city hall and overcame a guard of government troops, seizing a considerable quantity of arms and ammunition; bloody clothing and debris littered the streets. Noske sent more troops to Hamburg and arrested the radical leaders of the Greater Berlin councils for planning a nationwide insurrection. But these riots were not political; they were the spontaneous response of hungry and desperate men and women.

Hindenburg resigned his position as Supreme Commander. He was replaced temporarily by General Groener. Several rifle shots were fired at Erzberger's Berlin residence.

At a dinner given in honor of all the Peace Conference delegates by President Poincaré several days later, Wilson acknowledged that while he had come to love France, he longed to go home. Still, he knew that the past six months had witnessed the fulfillment of a magnificent dream: "As I go away from these scenes, I think I shall realize that I have been present at one of the most vital things that has happened in the history of nations." At another dinner, Clemenceau raised a toast to the League of Nations: "Toward this magnificent and impressive innovation, I ask you to direct all your thoughts and to uplift your hearts in this great act of faith, hope and love." At the same time, Clemenceau urged his comrades to "be careful; keep your powder dry. Be careful. Remind the world that it is living on a barrel of that powder."

On June 27, Wilson held a mass interview with two hundred American and European correspondents at the Hôtel Crillon. Lincoln Steffens asked the President whether he was satisfied with the peace he had made. "Yes," Wilson replied. Steffens pressed the question again: "Mr. President, do you feel that you achieved here the peace that you expected to make?" Wilson turned and looked at Steffens for a long moment, as though he were thinking through the events of the past six months, all the weary days, the adulation, the tribulations, the victories, the goal always just slightly out of reach. Then he said slowly, "I think that we have made a better peace than I should have expected when I came here to Paris."

For many it was a time to search their hearts. "What use have we made, what use are we making," asked the *Manchester Guardian*, "of an unparalleled victory, an unequalled opportunity? . . . What permanent gain are we securing for the world?" The conference had started upon the making of the peace with such high ideals, hopes, and dreams—and what had happened?

It would be hard, perhaps, fully to explain, still more to justify, but in the six or seven months of discussions and of bargaining among the victors the best fruits of victory have somehow disappeared, and the peace which emerges is not the peace we had promised ourselves or, as the enemy bitterly urges, which we had promised them. The peace we had hoped for would have been one which so far as possible presented elements of finality, which had careful regard, therefore, to the deeper forces by which nations

ARE SWAYED, AND WOULD ENLIST THESE ON THE SIDE OF PEACE AND OF PERMANENCE.

The *Washington Post* agreed that this could not be a lasting peace, but for a different reason. "Peace with Germany is nothing but suspended war and the compulsion of ready force. Germany signs with the settled purpose of treachery to her confession and promises. . . . More than anything else, the Germans will convince themselves that it is their duty to deceive the allies and to defeat the treaty terms in every possible manner."

In the new world of peace, wise men knew that everything must change: "The forces that will direct the affairs of Europe ten—even five—years hence will not be the forces of yesterday or to-day."

31

"And I will bring

them again to this land . . ."

Two men conquered the Atlantic, flying nonstop from Newfoundland to Ireland. The pilot was Captain John Alcock, twenty-seven years old and an RAF veteran of numerous bombing raids during the war, including a long-distance attack upon Adrianople that destroyed three thousand houses, demolished a fort, and blew up an ammunition train. Captured by Turkish forces in September 1917 during a raid on Constantinople, Alcock had returned home in December 1918, at which time he took a job as a test pilot with Vickers Limited, one of Britain's leading aircraft manufacturers. One day a Vickers superintendent had asked Alcock, "How would you like to fly the Atlantic?" "Ripping," Alcock replied. "I am certainly keen on that if you can get the machine ready." The navigator was Lieutenant Arthur Whitten "Ted" Brown, thirty-three, an American citizen who had spent most of his life in Britain. Ever since he was a little boy, Brown had been addicted to mechanical devices. He had learned navigation the practical way—by taking sightings during Atlantic steamer crossings. Brown, too, had been captured during the war while serving as an observer in the Royal Air Force, but he refused to talk to reporters about his twenty-three months in a German camp. Now he was engaged to a British girl, the daughter of an RAF major; the young couple planned to settle in the United States with the aid of Brown's share of the *Daily Mail*'s $50,000 prize.

The machine was a Vickers-Vimy biplane that invariably impressed aviation experts with its strength of construction. The struts, braces, wing frames, and the framework of the rudder were all made of steel. The Vimy was not built for show: the fabric covering the fuselage had changed from white to a dirty gray over the past two weeks, the wings had grown slightly yellow and bore fingermarks all over, and the unpainted metal housing around the engines lacked polish. Except for the tiny Vickers trademark on the struts (invisible from more than three feet away), the plane carried absolutely no markings. It did, however, carry two gasoline tanks with a total capacity of 865 gallons; the smaller tank, on top, was detachable and designed to serve as a life raft in an emergency. With a wingspan of sixty-seven feet and the power of two 350-horsepower Rolls-Royce Eagle VIII engines, the Vimy was larger and stronger than Hawker's Sopwith, although it was still only about half as big as the American NC-4 seaplane. And unlike Hawker's craft, the Vimy carried the most modern wireless equipment, to enable it to notify passing ships of its position in case of trouble.

In the last week of May, the Vimy was assembled at St. John's. Shortly after dawn on the morning of June 14, the head of the Vickers aviation department consented—after considerable urging by Captain Alcock—to allow the voyage to begin in the teeth of a forty-mile-per-hour wind. At the last moment Brown added a small pocket flashlight to his equipment bag so that he could read his instruments if the cockpit lighting system gave out. Each man carried a replica of a big black cat as a mascot; Alcock's was named "Lucky Jim," and had a bit of British bunting knotted about its neck; Brown's was named Twinkletoe. In Brown's wallet was a tiny silk American flag that his fiancée had given him for luck. A canvas sack full of transatlantic air mail was stuffed into a locker at the back of the cockpit. Each of the eight hundred letters bore a special one-dollar postage stamp; the sack was adorned with needlework done by the mother of one of the local postal employees.

At 11:50 A.M., New York time, the port propeller began whirling; twelve minutes later the starboard engine joined in. At 12:10 P.M., Vickers mechanics jerked the chocks from beneath the wheels, and the men hanging on to the wings and tail let go. Trees and fences faced Brown and Alcock just seven hundred feet ahead across the field. The Vimy bounced along the ground for 150 yards and then rose slightly; by the time it reached the first row of hedges, the plane was only one hundred feet above the ground. Then it disappeared into a little hollow and the spectators feared it had gone down, trapped by a sudden, perverse gust of wind. Up it came over the rise, then down again, then up again, now two hundred feet above the ground. For eleven minutes the giant biplane was lost from view. Then it appeared again, heading back toward St. John's with the wind behind it, to allow Alcock to gain control of the plane before rising higher. Local residents, who surely were starting to get used to this sort of thing by now (one farmer complained sourly that the noise of the planes was frightening his hens and inhibiting their production of eggs), ran out of their houses and shops to witness the final departure. The plane flew over Cabot Tower at the mouth of the harbor—then was gone over the Atlantic, lost to view from the ground. Brown (who, incidentally, had never actually navigated a plane under flight conditions before) set a course for Galway Bay, 1,980 miles away.

For nearly the entire journey, the wind was at their backs. But after an hour they ran into dense clouds, one bank at two thousand feet and another at six thousand. Alcock kept trying to climb out of the clouds, but it was no use. Brown could see neither the sea nor the sky to take any bearings. The wind blew the propeller off the generator that drove their marvelous new wireless; now they could send no messages. At the same time, Brown saw one of the stay wires break off in the gale, but he decided not to tell Alcock about it. (Alcock later admitted that if he had known that the stay wire had snapped, he probably would have turned back.) For a while the men spoke to each other through communication telephones, but these, too, broke down after about four hours, and so the men had to shout to each other over the noise of the engines. "Most of our 'conversation,' " said Alcock, "consisted of tapping one another on the shoulder and going through the motions of drinking." They munched on sandwiches and chocolate, although neither man felt like eating much on the flight (they tended to get seasick every time they looked over the side). They did, however, develop an extraordinary thirst, which they tried to quench with the coffee and ale they had brought along.

At about 3:00 A.M. they hit a patch of open sky and Brown got a fix on Polaris and Vega; amazingly, they were only two degrees south of their original course. They ran into an extremely dense fog bank at 4:00 A.M. and were unable to see anything. Sleet poured down upon the plane and jammed the airspeed indicator at ninety miles per hour. The gas gauges were covered with ice. Alcock really had no idea where he was or what he was doing. He looped the loop (by accident) and went into a deep spiral for a few seconds that seemed like an eternity. The dive ended with the plane just fifty feet above the water, flying nearly upside down. Alcock began to climb again, to six thousand feet, then eleven thousand. "We never saw the sun rise," the pilot said. "It was hailing and snowing. The machine was covered with ice. That was about six o'clock in the morning.... My radiator shutter and water temperature indicator were covered with ice for four or five hours. Lieutenant Brown had continually climbed up to chip off the ice with a knife. The speed indicator was full of frozen particles and gave trouble again." Alone, alone, all alone, over the vast, open sea.

At around 9:15 that morning they saw land, the west coast of Ireland. (Alcock: "It was great to do that.") Brown recognized Clifden Bay with its wireless station. They circled the station and Alcock believed he saw a nice soft meadow below and made a perfect landing—but the "meadow" turned out to be a bog instead. After running for about fifty yards, the plane's wheels sank up to the axles, and the Vimy's nose toppled forward. "What do you think of that for fancy navigating?" shouted Brown. (Both men were slightly deaf from the roar of the engines.) "Very good," replied Alcock. They shook hands. They had covered the distance in sixteen hours and twelve minutes, at an average speed of 120 miles per hour. The plane still had nearly three hundred gallons in the fuel tanks.

The first people on the ground to spot the Vimy were an Australian soldier on leave and a farmer's boy tending cattle in a nearby field. When the staff of the wireless station (most of whom were wearing coats and pajamas) reached the plane, they helped the men out; Brown was cut on the nose and mouth from the impact of the landing, and Alcock's face was slightly swollen; both were dazed and unable to walk steadily for several minutes. "This is the Vimy-Vickers machine," Alcock announced in a matter-of-fact tone. "We have just come from Newfoundland." The mail packed into the canvas sack was soaked but still intact. "We didn't do so badly, did we?" Brown asked. Alcock laughed: "I am not at all tired." Brown confessed that he was "a bit fagged out," and so after breakfast he went to bed but, unable to sleep, got back up about an hour later. Alcock went straight out to inspect his damaged plane. He said he wished to borrow an RAF machine to fly over to England immediately; Brown, however, announced that he "had had enough flying for a bit" and planned to return to London by boat and train. The King, who learned of the aviators' success as he was leaving church services at Westminster, sent his royal congratulations, and telegrams poured in from a plethora of politicians. "I cannot find words adequate to express my admiration," cabled Harry Hawker. "I can readily understand the awful strain the flight meant for both airmen, and that increases my immense admiration for such a magnificent performance."

"Yes, I'm glad we did it," Alcock told a correspondent as he relaxed and smoked a cigarette. Asked for his impressions on flying through the night across nearly two thousand miles of water, the pilot thought for a moment and then said, "Well, it is difficult to sum them up. No, there was no sense of remoteness, curious to say. We were too keen on our work. We wanted to get the job over, and we were jolly pleased, I can tell you, to see the coast." King George knighted both men. Northcliffe handed them the

$50,000 prize; Alcock and Brown each kept $20,000 and gave the rest to the workmen who had built the plane so well.

On June 20, in Los Angeles, California, the rules were announced for another air contest: $50,000 to the first aviator to fly across the Pacific Ocean in twelve days or less.

SEVEN

THE DAYS
OF THE
HARVEST

"For they have healed
the hurt of the daughter
of my people slightly, saying,
Peace, peace;
when there is no peace."

32

"Alas! for that day is great,

so that none is like it . . ."

Versailles. Ten miles west of Paris, the name of the town invariably calls up images of Louis XIV and the magnificent palace from which he governed France in the days of its greatest glory. Originally the site of a hunting lodge built for Louis XIII, the chateau had been transformed by Mansard and Le Vau into an imposing residence worthy of the grandeur of the Sun King: the baroque masterpiece of a chapel; the opulent boudoir of Madame de Maintenon; the vast gardens where nearly a century later the court of Marie Antoinette played at being peasants while the nation slid further into revolution; the spectacular fountains whose waters had been silent since 1914. Here Louis XIV had revoked the Edict of Nantes, thereby signaling the renewed persecution of Huguenots; here the treaty recognizing American independence was signed in 1783; here the "Red Guard" bivouacked as Louis XVI and his queen awaited the guillotine; here Bismarck and Kaiser Wilhelm I proclaimed the German Empire in 1871.

On June 24, 1919, the day after the German government formally agreed to accept the terms of the peace treaty, Clemenceau, Wilson, Balfour, and Sonnino journeyed to Versailles to make the final arrangements for the signing ceremony. (Clemenceau had made the journey from Paris in his car in just eighteen minutes. He was not one to tarry in getting from one place to another.) Now that his victory had been assured, the Tiger was in top form, entertaining his colleagues by striding up and down the palatial staircases and corridors, "as if," an amused spectator noted, "he were a strong middle-aged man, talking all the time, and giving a most interesting account of various objects of interest." Clemenceau pointed out the precise spot where he had made his maiden political speech fifty years ago; then, as the guided tour passed through the corridors, someone asked him a question about bathrooms. "In the old days," Clemenceau replied with disarming candor, "ours [was] a dirty nation. They did not wash much, and had disgusting habits." Lord Riddell, who was responsible in part for the press arrangements for the ceremony, asked Clemenceau where the photographers would stand. "In the dungeons, where they can work undisturbed," the Premier chuckled mischievously. In response to a suggestion that the hour for signing the treaty be set at eleven o'clock in the morning, to enable correspondents to send their telegrams at a reasonable time for the afternoon editions at home, Clemenceau shook his head. *"Non, impossible."* One must have lunch first, he explained, in case the ceremony ran late. "If you fix eleven, you will get nothing to eat. It must be two o'clock." The question of whether to invite wives and daughters was left to Balfour. "Of course, if you leave it to me," the ever-gallant Balfour decided, "I vote in favour of the ladies!" It was agreed that in deference to the British Empire delegations, tea would be served after the ceremony from a specially installed buffet. Telephone wires, hitherto unknown to the chateau, were run from Versailles to Paris for the use of journalists.

On June 28, 1914, in the Bosnian capital of Sarajevo, the Archduke Francis Ferdinand was assassinated, setting in motion the train of events that culminated in four years and three months of war, the worst disaster ever wrought by human stupidity.

On June 28, 1919, heavy clouds obscured the morning light; pale sunshine was the best the heavens could do. Solemn, impassive sightseers trudged along the dusty roads to Versailles. An almost unbroken stream of flag-bedecked diplomatic automobiles full of civilian and military officials and their friends and relations started at the hill of the Champs Elysées and wound past the Arc de Triomphe, through the Bois de Boulogne, and out toward the great chateau. Since few of the limousines' occupants seemed to be smiling, it looked more like a funeral procession than anything else. French poilus stood at every crossroads and waved red flags to stop all other traffic and grant the dignitaries the right-of-way. In the gray streets of Versailles, a blaze of color leaped from the flags of all nations draped on every available balcony and lamppost. The elegant, tree-lined Avenue du Château that led up to the palace, the vast square known as the Place d'Armes (by noon a sea of white faces), and the great, cobblestoned Cour d'Honneur beyond the huge gilded gates were all lined with cavalry and a double row of foot soldiers in horizon-blue uniforms and steel helmets (eleven regiments altogether); the infantry stood at attention with fixed bayonets, the mounted troops with upright lances, the sun glistening on the spearheads hung with blue or red-and-white pennants that fluttered in the weak breeze. Someone had tactfully removed the captured German cannon from the courtyard where the guns had been subjected to the scornful gaze of a massive bronze statue of Louis XIV on horseback. Just inside the gates, General Bricker, commander of the United States Sixth Cavalry Division, sat impassively on a chestnut stallion, raising his sword in salute to especially worthy guests.

Approximately four hundred guests had been invited to witness the spectacle in the Hall of Mirrors (Lincoln Steffens had been given a press pass, but decided to stay home and take a bath instead), and thousands more were honored with a place in the gardens outside, where they could watch the ceremonial comings and goings; in years to come they could tell their grandchildren that they stood at Versailles on the day that war had been ended forever. French officials, however, had made the mistake of printing seven different types of admission tickets, each with its own unique commemorative design. Since the guards at the gates were unable to keep track of all the various styles of valid tickets, a number of gate-crashers succeeded in gaining admittance. One American businessman, no more than an idle sightseer, flashed a bright red Pall Mall cigarette case with a coat of arms in gold at the corner, and walked right in. Others gained admittance by using a ticket to the baseball games at Pershing Stadium, or an invitation to a lecture on peace at a Paris salon. At a side entrance, an old woman supported by her two sons, one a major in the cavalry and the other wearing civilian clothes and the Legion of Honor ribbon, pleaded with the guards to let her into the garden: "Just let me inside the courtyard. When the Germans were here, a general was quartered in my house. I shared the defeat; let me share the victory." They let her in.

It was about 1:30 when the first official car struggled through the assembled soldiery and discharged its passengers at the marble stairway leading to the Queen's Apartments and the Hall of Peace. Soon afterward, Harold Nicolson arrived with Sir James Headlam-Morley, the British Foreign Office historian, and immediately Nicolson felt intimidated by the display of military splendor—generals everywhere, including Philippe Pétain, the hero of Verdun—that greeted his eyes: "Headlam-Morley and I creep out of our car hurriedly. Feeling civilian and grubby. And wholly unimportant. We hurry through the door." On every step of the grand staircase inside stood two members of the Garde Républicaine, resplendent in their quaint uniforms, still exactly as they had been designed fifty years earlier, with white breeches and crossbelts, shining breastplates, great crested helmets with long red and black horsehair *crinières*, oversized black riding boots adorned with spurs, and swords held in front, ready for salute. Those swords swung up and down silently as each guest passed by. Behind them, gigantic flags of the Allies were draped over the walls. Nicolson noted dryly that Headlam-Morley made a subtle gesture of dismissal with his hand at all this display: "He is not a militarist."

Marshal Foch, Secretary Lansing, and General Pershing were among the first to arrive. At 2:20 the grizzled face of Georges Clemenceau—smiling smugly once more—could be seen through the windows of a French military car. Spectators in the front gave these three heroes an enthusiastic ovation, and then the lesser lights disembarked: Clemenceau's friend the Maharajah of Bikanir with his splendid turban, Baron Makino of Japan, admirals, more generals in dress uniform, the Italian delegation; from their vantage point in the gardens, the crowd (a happy assortment of shopgirls, officers, aristocratic women, businessmen, and bare-legged actresses) had no idea who most of these people were, so no one cheered until suddenly a truckload of doughboys shouting at the top of their lungs drove up the broad avenue and, instead of proceeding directly to the entrance, swung around the bronze Louis XIV statue and exited by a side gateway. Ten minutes later, a group of Tommies repeated this boisterous performance. Airplanes swooped down from the sky, so low that the firemen stationed on the roof of the palace flinched.

Elegantly attired as always, Arthur Balfour appeared at 2:45, followed by David Lloyd George, who for once wore a silk high hat instead of his customary felt chapeau. At 2:50, Wilson's limousine, bearing his flag—a white eagle on a dark blue background—pulled up to the entrance and the President went inside the palace. By three o'clock the gang was all there, and the avenue stood empty once again.

The German plenipotentiaries, Foreign Minister Hermann Müller and Colonial Secretary Dr. Johannes Bell, had arrived in Versailles late Friday evening in a four-coach train, the engine bearing a British flag hoisted by an overzealous British officer during a stopover at Charleroi. Now Müller and Bell were shown into the palace at Versailles by a side door, to avoid rendering them military honors. Baron von Haimhausen complained bitterly of this humiliating treatment, and so the conference officials compromised by agreeing to have the Republican Guard salute the Germans as they left the ceremony, since by then they would no longer be official enemies of the Allied governments.

Nearby, at the entrance of the Hôtel des Reservoirs dining room (very crowded this day), the elderly aunt of the proprietor stood and watched the pageant from afar, her eyes brimming with tears. She had watched the

Germans dine at her family's establishment the night before the Treaty of 1871 was signed. "And now this," she said softly. "Thank God I have lived for it."

Nicolson and Headlam-Morley, meanwhile, had entered the anterooms, "our feet softening on the thickest of savonnerie carpets. They have," Nicolson thought, "ransacked the Garde Meubles for their finest pieces." In fact, the French government had indeed pulled out all the stops, bringing out of storage every available treasure. Nicolson was certain that Versailles had never looked more resplendent since the Grand Siècle. Disgusted with the ostentatious display, he turned and whispered to Headlam-Morley, "I hate Versailles." "You hate what?" asked the historian, who was slightly hard of hearing. "Versailles." "Oh, you mean the Treaty." "What Treaty?" wondered Nicolson, who could think only of the document signed here in 1871. "This Treaty," Headlam-Morley replied. "Oh," Nicolson said, "I see what you mean—the German Treaty." Not until that moment had Nicolson realized that the treaty would be known not for the city of Paris, where it had been fashioned word by painstaking word during the five long months from January to June, but for the Old World glories symbolized by the opulence of Versailles.

Then they entered the Hall of Mirrors, the Galerie des Glaces, nearly eighty yards long and eleven yards across, adorned with gilded decorations, pictures of Louis XIV on the white walls, elaborately wrought historical furniture, a white marble statue of Minerva (the goddess of war and wisdom), a heavy ceiling frescoed with scenes from France's ancient wars, and the wall of huge ornate mirrors opposite seventeen windows that looked onto the park below. Whoever was responsible for the seating arrangements could not have done a worse job. At one end of the room was a long, horseshoe-shaped table covered with maroon velvet, around which the seventy-two plenipotentiaries would sit, with Clemenceau, Wilson, and Lloyd George at the center. In the open space in front of the table was a smaller table on a six-inch-high dais (looking like a guillotine) where the treaty would be signed. No doubt to Clemenceau's chagrin, it was not the table upon which the 1871 treaty had been signed, that mahogany relic having been spirited back to Berlin by Bismarck himself. The present treaty itself, in a stamped leather case, had been brought into the room at 2:10 by a representative of the French Foreign Office. In the middle of the room were low, red-upholstered benches for the delegates' secretaries, deputies, expert advisers, and distinguished guests. Behind that, at the other end of the chamber, were the seats reserved for the press. Unfortunately, since the seats were not elevated, no one in the back of the room could see anything at all—journalists not being blessed by Providence with the facility for seeing through several rows of human bodies—and once the people in the middle section began to stand up for a better view, the affair turned into a constant shoving match, with photographers and diplomats jostling for standing position. Nicolson complained that the sheer number of people in attendance (about a thousand, counting the various delegations, guests, and reporters) "robs the ceremony of all privilege and therefore of all dignity. It is like the Aeolian Hall." The German correspondents were relegated to an area by a window at the rear of the press section.

As he looked around, Nicolson saw Clemenceau already seated, above him a scroll that read, *Le roi gouverné par lui-même.* "He looks small and yellow," Nicolson thought. "A crunched homunculus." The rest of the room was a sea of military uniforms and black frock coats ("A black frock coat is a dreadful thing," wrote one disgruntled critic), the monotony broken only by an occasional flaming scarlet sash of the Legion of Honor. Even the women who had been granted admission failed to enliven the scene, for most of them were attired in ordinary Sunday or evening dress: Mrs. Wilson wore a frock of pearl gray silk with a gray taffeta turban trimmed on the side with three gray ostrich tips; Margaret Wilson was gowned in a blue tailored dress with a navy blue hat and veil. Premier Paderewski, meanwhile, had his wonderful head of hair mistaken for the fluffy tulle hat of the lady sitting directly opposite him.

Waiting for the ceremony to begin, people began to mill about the room, talking to one another, trying to find their seats, and generally creating a crush of disorder. When Wilson and Lloyd George entered (the little Welshman had to push his way into the hall), a number of delegates rushed up to the front to get autographs from the Big Three.

Out of all the sea of dignitaries, only two groups stood out: one was a guard of grizzled French veterans of the war of 1870–71, who took the place of the Prussian guardsmen of the ceremony nearly fifty years before; the other was a troop of decorated Allied soldiers—fifteen doughboys (all of whom had been assigned to Wilson's Paris residence), fifteen Tommies, and fifteen poilus (Clemenceau went over and shook the hand of each man in the French detachment)—who entered a few minutes before three o'clock and stood in the embrasures of the windows, a few feet away from Marshal Foch.

At three o'clock, everyone finally began to find their seats—the delegates from the minor powers pushing with difficulty through the crowd to get to their places at the head table—but the chattering continued. A number of lesser officials preferred to stand along the walls or sit in the aisles instead of taking their assigned seats. Clemenceau motioned to the ushers, who gave a few warning rounds of "Ssh! Ssh! Ssh!" The chattering stopped, replaced by nervous coughs and the dry rustling of official programs. "Down in front!" shouted the people in the back. This time representatives of the Foreign Office protocol desk walked up and down the aisle and again warned, "Ssh! Ssh!" An absolute hush fell over the room; at 3:07 Clemenceau demanded, *"Faites entrer les Allemands!"* No one stood up to welcome them.

Nicolson recorded the scene:

THROUGH THE DOOR AT THE END APPEAR TWO HUISSIERS WITH SILVER CHAINS. THEY MARCH IN SINGLE FILE. AFTER THEM COME FOUR OFFICERS OF FRANCE, GREAT BRITAIN, AMERICA AND ITALY. AND THEN, ISOLATED AND PITIABLE, COME THE TWO GERMAN DELEGATES. DR. MÜLLER, DR. BELL. THE SILENCE IS TERRIFYING. THEIR FEET UPON A STRIP OF PARQUET BETWEEN THE SAVONNERIE CARPETS ECHO HOLLOW AND DUPLICATE. THEY KEEP THEIR EYES FIXED AWAY FROM THOSE TWO THOUSAND STARING EYES, FIXED UPON THE CEILING. THEY ARE DEATHLY PALE. THEY DO NOT APPEAR AS REPRESENTATIVES OF A BRUTAL MILITARISM. THE ONE IS THIN AND PINK-EYELIDDED: THE SECOND FIDDLE IN A BRUNSWICK ORCHESTRA. THE OTHER IS MOON-FACED AND SUFFERING: A PRIVAT-DOZENT. IT IS ALL MOST PAINFUL.

Müller and Bell took their seats at the side of the horseshoe table, between the delegates from Japan and Brazil. Clemenceau broke the awful silence: *"Messieurs, la séance est ouverte."* The treaty was written; it now needed only signatures. It must, Clemenceau warned, be carried out faithfully by everyone, including the German Republic. "Reich! Reich!" someone shouted at him. Clemenceau corrected himself: it must be faithfully observed by *"le Reich Allemand."* Müller and Bell, who knew that they were supposed to sign the treaty first, leaped nervously to their feet at the conclusion of Clemenceau's brief address, but a minor French official peremptorily waved them back down (as if he were a theater manager, someone said) until Mantoux had translated the Tiger's words into English. (The room was very hot. Riddell opened a few windows in the adjoining chamber to admit more fresh air.) Then a French dignitary escorted Müller and Bell with great solemnity to the table that bore the treaty. In one more cruel twist, one of the Germans found that his pen wouldn't work. One of Colonel House's secretaries stepped over and slipped his fountain pen to the poor fellow. Muller signed at 3:12, Bell at

3:13. In the embarrassment and general disorder, the ceremony lost whatever dignity it might have had in the best of circumstances. General Botha, the Prime Minister of South Africa, surveyed the scene and wrote the following words on his program: "God's judgment will be applied with justice to all peoples under the new sun, and we shall persevere in prayer that they may be applied by mankind in charity and peace and a Christian spirit."

As soon as the Germans had signed, someone gave a discreet signal, and the waters of the great fountains, which had not flowed since 1914, leaped forth into the air.

A minute after Dr. Bell affixed his signature, Wilson approached the table; the Three had decided that the Great Powers would sign in alphabetical order, *les Etats-Unis* first. Wilson affixed his seal with a signet ring, bearing the autograph "Woodrow Wilson," given to him on one of his wedding days. Lloyd George signed with a fountain pen (reportedly this was the first occasion upon which such an instrument had been used to sign a treaty) sent by an admirer in North Battersea; the gold pen bore the Welsh words and a date, *"Nado Lig, 1918,"* and was inscribed with a facsimile of Lloyd George's signature. Bonar Law, Balfour, and the rest of the British and Empire delegates followed—General Smuts signed under protest and filed a written reservation explaining why he believed the treaty was too harsh—then France, Italy, and Japan. Most of the delegates eschewed the box of old-fashioned goose quills provided by the French Foreign Office and sharpened by the expert pen pointer at the Quai d'Orsay, choosing instead to use the modern steel pens that lay alongside a huge inkstand. In all, twenty-seven nations signed the treaty, including—besides the Big Five—Belgium, Bolivia, Brazil, Cuba, Ecuador, Greece, Guatemala, Haiti, the Hedjaz, Honduras, Liberia, Nicaragua, Panama, Portugal, Rumania, the Serb-Croat and Slovene Republic (Yugoslavia), Siam, Peru, Poland, Uruguay, and finally Czechoslovakia. China, still furious over the Shantung decision, refused to attend the ceremony at all. The line moved more quickly than expected. Officials of the Quai d'Orsay stood patiently by, blotting the signatures with neat little pads. Meanwhile, more delegates crowded about the head of the table for autographs. Some tactless souls even approached Müller and Bell for their autographs. A British correspondent left before the ceremony was over; afterward, he told Steffens, "It was an unpleasant sight. I could not stay. All of our victorious statesmen and generals standing over two or three of the defeated Germans, making them sign there. It was—it was so unsportsmanlike. I ran away."

While the pageant continued inside, the guns of St-Cyr, on the southern hill of Versailles, boomed forth the news that the war was finally, irrevocably over. All around Paris, the forts echoed with their own cannon. Once the signing was completed—it was only 3:49—everyone sat down again and a hush of satisfaction and anticipation descended over the room. The guns outside grew silent. Clemenceau rose, said in a husky voice, *"La séance est levée,"* and that was all. The Germans were escorted first from the hall by a side door and went straight back to their hotel. Then the Three strode down the aisle, Clemenceau with "his rolling satirical gait"; a Frenchman sitting near Nicolson rose to congratulate the Tiger. *"Oui,"* Clemenceau admitted, with tears in his wrinkled ancient eyes, *"c'est une belle journée."* Nicolson was not as sure. Far away the French countryside was tranquil.

Clemenceau, Wilson, and Lloyd George walked back down the staircase past the Republican Guard, and at 4:10 they emerged, preceded by a swarm of movie cameramen walking backwards, to the acclaim of the spectators on the terrace. The crowds—about fifty thousand strong—broke through the cordon of troops and swarmed forward, overpowering bodyguards and policemen, bearing their leaders away in a wave of spontaneous—and dangerous—exhiliration. Lloyd George, who was feeling none too well to start with, found the experience quite unpleasant. Finally a platoon of French soldiers forced its way into the melee and rescued the Three, who managed to continue their triumphal progress only slightly impeded, marching side by side by side down the broad gravel pathway between the fountains that gushed forth their victorious spray. (All of the Allied delegates were supposed to make this walk, but the crush of the mob prevented anyone from following the chiefs.) Clemenceau's eyes were nearly closed and his vision blurred, partly from emotion and partly from the dust kicked up by the crowd; Wilson graciously took his hand and guided him the rest of the way. More cannon boomed and a flock of airplanes hummed overhead as the Three turned and walked back to the palace, well-wishers still slapping them on the back. They entered Lloyd George's car, someone thrust a bouquet through an open window, and off they drove through Versailles and then back home to Paris.

"And so ends a dramatic six months," wrote Riddell in his diary.

General Pershing came out, surveyed the scene with dignity (no one ran up to shake his hand), smiled, and got into his waiting car. A doughboy nearby yelled out, "Today is a hell of a long way from Mexico, General." Pershing stiffened, then grinned, and a handful of Americans applauded him. Then he, too, drove away.

Those who had witnessed the ceremony came away with mixed emotions. Shotwell found that the shabby treatment afforded Müller and Bell had earned the Germans considerable sympathy among the Allied delegates. In the end, there had been no exultation of victory inside the room, only a quiet sense of relief that the conflict was at last over—for the time being. Frances Stevenson blamed the persistent aggressiveness of the press for turning the ceremony into a shambles. The relentless crush of photographers and reporters on such formal occasions, she complained, just ruined everything; these callous journalists were "destroying all romance, all solemnity, all majesty. They are," she complained, "as unscrupulous as they are vulgar."

When nearly everyone else had gone, Nicolson found Headlam-Morley "standing miserably in the littered immensity of the Galerie des Glaces. We say nothing to each other. It has all been horrible." They agreed that success, when emphasized as tastelessly as the Allies had done this day, was very beastly indeed.

The Three decided that the blockade of Germany would be raised—not yet, not today, but as soon as the German government formally ratified the treaty of peace.

General Smuts released a statement explaining why he had signed the treaty with reservations:

I SIGNED THE PEACE TREATY, NOT BECAUSE I CONSIDER IT A SATISFACTORY DOCUMENT, BUT BECAUSE IT IS IMPERATIVELY NECESSARY TO CLOSE THE WAR; BECAUSE THE WORLD NEEDS PEACE ABOVE ALL ELSE, AND NOTHING COULD BE MORE FATAL THAN THE CONTINUANCE OF THE STATE OF SUSPENSE BETWEEN WAR AND PEACE. THE MONTHS SINCE THE ARMISTICE WAS SIGNED HAVE BEEN, PERHAPS, AS UPSETTING, UNSETTLING, AND AS RUINOUS TO EUROPE AS THE PREVIOUS FOUR YEARS OF WAR. I LOOK UPON THE PEACE TREATY AS THE CLOSE OF THESE TWO CHAPTERS OF WAR AND ARMISTICE, AND ONLY ON THAT GROUND DO I AGREE TO IT.

Over seven months after the fighting had ceased, peace at last had come. Seven months of decay and despair. One British observer mourned the time and lives forever lost:

ONE HAS ONLY TO LOOK AT THE STATE OF EUROPE, OF ASIA, AND EVEN OF AMERICA, TO REALISE WHAT A DISASTER THE LENGTH OF THE PARIS CONFERENCE HAS BEEN TO THE WORLD. EVERY WEEK'S DELAY HAS BROUGHT FRESH TROUBLE—NEW WARS AND MASSACRES, THE STRAINING OF FRIENDSHIPS AMONG THE ALLIED NATIONS, POLITICAL AND ECONOMIC

CHAOS. IT WOULD BE AN INSTRUCTIVE IF GLOOMY EXERCISE IF ONE OF THOSE STATISTICIANS WHO USED TO DIVERT US WITH ACCOUNTS OF HOW MANY SOVEREIGNS PLACED IN A ROW WOULD STRETCH FROM BUCKINGHAM PALACE TO THE BANK OF ENGLAND COULD CALCULATE THE NUMBER OF CHILDREN WHO HAVE BEEN STARVED IN CENTRAL EUROPE WHILE THE POLITICIANS HAVE BEEN SLOWLY DRAGGING OUT THEIR QUARRELS IN PARIS.

33

"And I will recompense

them according to their deeds,

and according to the works

of their own hands."

The celebrations were most joyous in Paris. Flags, fireworks, music, dancing, torchlight processions, American soldiers and their girls: the grand boulevards were packed thick with humanity. Women donned khaki uniforms and military headgear; soldiers put on any items of feminine apparel they could lay their hands on. Banners with patriotic slogans stretched across the streets. The government allowed the cafés to stay open until one o'clock in the morning, and many patrons paid no attention to any calls for closing time. In front of the Hôtel Crillon, a band of Americans kept singing "Hail, Hail, the Gang's All Here." Bengal lights and the searchlight on the Eiffel Tower and electric and gas lamps everywhere illuminated the city until it might have been midday. Automobile motors and horns and gramophones and sirens all mingled together in the din, and above all there floated the joyousness of the "Marseillaise," over and over again. Nicolson attended an official celebration, drank what he described as "very bad champagne," walked along the boulevards for a while, and then called it a day—or, perhaps more appropriately, an era. "To bed," he wrote, "sick of life."

Britain took the news much more calmly. Standing before a vast throng massed into Trafalgar Square, Mrs. Lloyd George made the official announcement that the treaty had been signed. There were cheers and songs and hymns of thanksgiving and hope (particularly, "O God, Our Help in Ages Past"). Careless boys threw firecrackers and tin trumpets blared forth, but it was nothing like the uninhibited celebrations that had greeted the news of the Armistice in November. After all, this moment came as no surprise to anyone who had been paying the least bit of attention. Besides, as the *Nation* pointed out, "the 'plain people' everywhere were thinking of the approaching winter, with its hunger and cold, of the misery that these six wasted months and this treaty of evil have now made inevitable."

So the bells of Westminster Abbey and St. Paul's Cathedral and all the churches throughout the land rang out joyfully, and people gathered at Buckingham Palace to cheer the King, Queen Mary, the Prince of Wales, Prince Albert, and Princess Mary, all of whom stood on a balcony silhouetted in the darkness against the light from the rooms behind them, and then the people sang the songs of their hearts: "God Save the King" (and for good measure, "God Save the Prince of Wales," always an anticlimax, musically speaking), "The Star-Spangled Banner," "Keep the Home Fires Burning," "It's a Long Way to Tipperary," "When They Wound Up the Watch on the Rhine," "Pack Up Your Troubles in Your Old Kit-Bag," "Kakki Hakki Doolah," and, rather inexplicably, "My Old Kentucky Home." The King and his sons raised their hands and doffed their hats, and every man below did the same. The Berkeley Hotel decorated its restaurant and grill room in the style of the Grand Siècle. At another West End establishment, a woman in evening dress threw roses to the crowd in the street; then she took a bracelet off her arm and tossed it away; then a ring from her finger; then more roses, followed by some ornaments from her hair; then she began crumpling up Treasury notes and flinging them carelessly into the appreciative audience; finally she held up both hands to show that she had nothing more to give. The crowd gave her a rousing round of applause. At a bank in Oswestery, a few rowdies who thought they recognized Admiral von Reuter, the architect of the Scapa Flow scuttle, pelted him with rotten eggs; but they had smeared an innocent man, since Reuter was still safely cooling his heels under Admiralty guard. Official copies of the peace treaty went on sale at His Majesty's Stationery Office, for four shillings apiece, plus postage.

In Ireland, where the British Army had celebrated peace by raiding the Sinn Fein offices in Harcourt Street in Dublin earlier that morning, rebels seized a number of British flags from Trinity College and burned them in the streets, cheering De Valera and singing revolutionary songs as the flames licked high into the night. The president of the Irish Republic was himself in Boston; in a speech at Fenway Park, De Valera called the peace treaty a mockery, claiming that it made "twenty new wars in place of the one nominally ended. A new Holy Alliance," he warned, "cannot save democracy."

One could have walked through the streets of Boston or nearly any other city in the United States and not known it was any sort of momentous occasion at all. In the Senate chamber, where at least a majority of the members opposed the treaty as it presently stood, Wilson's message announcing the peace and asking for quick acceptance of the treaty was greeted with profound indifference. Senator Hitchcock, the senior Democrat on the Foreign Relations Committee, interrupted an appropriations debate to read the text of the President's announcement; then the appropriations debate resumed. One British observer noted the absence of celebrations in America and concluded that "everything that has occurred since the Armistice has tended to numb popular desire to associate with Europe and to confirm the deep habit of distrusting the European way. Men may differ as to whether France should have the Sarre or Britain the bulk of the German colonies, but they agree vaguely that it is not a very inspiring business one way or the other."

In Germany, a heavy rainstorm raged over the land all day and all night. From Weimar, the government issued a manifesto urging its people to carry out every provision of the treaty, vowing meanwhile never to forget those who had been torn from the Fatherland: "They are flesh of our flesh. . . . They may be torn away from the body of our State, but not from our heart." Food riots again wracked Berlin and Frankfurt. A melancholy pessimism settled in over the country. "What we need," said one Berlin newspaper, "is a despot to compel the nation to work. If we are unable to install him, our enemies will send him." Another editorial proclaimed that "salvation is only to be found in a renewal of the old bond of discipline which today is so hated, but is internally glorious." A pan-German journal with the headline REVENGE FOR THE DISHONOR OF 1919 was suppressed by the government.

Müller, Bell, and about fifty other members of the German delegation left Versailles for Berlin at 8:25 on the evening of June 28. To avoid clashes with the celebrating crowds, the Germans were placed in fifteen different cars and sent by a round-about route to Noisy-le-Roi, where they boarded their train at nine o'clock. As the train passed through Compiègne, firecrackers were thrown through an open window into the dining car, creating a momentary panic. When the disconsolate cortege paused for a few hours at Cologne the next day, Müller and Bell invited their British, French, and Italian escorts to join them for lunch. Once more at peace with the German nation, the Allied officers accepted. The train arrived at Potsdammer Station in the quiet of four o'clock on the morning of June 30.

Clemenceau appeared before the French Chamber of Deputies and presented the peace treaty, accompanied by the Rhineland guarantees from Britain and the United States, for the legislature's approval. The Tiger announced that since his work was now finished, he planned to retire as soon as possible, although privately he hoped the people would reward him for his labors by electing him to the ceremonial post of President of the Republic. Huge numbers of sightseers visited Versailles the day after the signing; 42,000 passed through the Hall of Mirrors, where all was as it had been for the ceremony, save for the removal of the inkstands and penholders by Clemenceau for safekeeping.

Lloyd George and Frances Stevenson left Paris on the morning of June 29. "We have had a wonderful time there," wrote Frances, "& we left with many regrets. D. hates returning home. He has been well looked after in Paris—has had every comfort—the best food—the best attendance. He has been able to entertain at will." Riddell stood with Lloyd George as their train pulled out of Paris. "That's over!" the Welshman sighed. "There is always a sense of sadness in closing a chapter of one's life. It has been a wonderful time. We do not quite appreciate the importance and magnitude of the events in which we have been taking part." The Prime Minister, who managed to change his clothes on the train after crossing the Channel, was not expecting a grand reception upon his arrival at Victoria Station in London, especially since Churchill had vetoed a suggestion to line the streets with troops. But shortly before Lloyd George was scheduled to arrive, King George decided to greet his Prime Minister in person at the station. The King's servants tried to dissuade him, telling him that such a royal welcome was unprecedented. "Very well," declared the King, "I will make a precedent." And so he did, accompanied by his two sons. After a brief ceremony at the station, during which the King escorted Mrs. Lloyd George to her husband's coach, the Prime Minister and His Majesty rode back in the same carriage that had taken Wilson to Victoria Station on the last day of the old year; the same scarlet-liveried footmen and coachmen accompanied the procession back to Buckingham Palace, where Lloyd George received the Queen's congratulations on a job well done. Someone threw a laurel wreath into the carriage. It landed on the King's lap, but he picked it up and handed it to Lloyd George, saying, "This is for you." The Welshman gave it to Frances, "& though it will fade," she confided to her diary, "I will keep it all my life."

Before Lloyd George left Paris, Clemenceau had asked him what he thought of Wilson. "I like him," the Welshman replied, "and I like him very much better now than I did at the beginning." "So do I," agreed the Tiger. Lloyd George went over to Wilson's flat after the signing ceremony and told the President that he (Wilson) had done more to bring together the English-speaking peoples than anyone had ever done before. Lloyd George always had been deft with a compliment.

Wilson left Paris from the Gare des Invalides at 9:45 on the evening of

June 28. Prior to his departure he had cabled his private secretary, Joseph Tumulty, in Washington: "All well." Clemenceau ("looking," an onlooker said, "as if he were losing his best friend"), Poincaré, Colonel House, and about a thousand others were at the station to see Wilson off. After all the bitterness of March and April, the President's firm stand against last-minute changes in the treaty had earned him renewed respect among the French public; en route to the station, in the Champs Elysées, a very old Frenchman had jumped in front of Wilson's car and shouted, "Mr. Wilson, thank you for the peace." To the cries of "*Vive* Wilson!" from the crowd at the station, he raised his silk hat. "Deeply happy as I am at the prospect of joining my own countrymen again," the President declared, "I leave France with genuine regret, my deep sympathy for her people and belief in her future confirmed. . . . I take the liberty of bidding France godspeed as well as good-bye, and of expressing once more my abiding interest and entire confidence in her future." Mrs. Wilson threw kisses to the crowd as the train disappeared into the darkness.

They arrived at Brest at 11:40 the next morning. For the last seven or eight miles the railway line was picketed with American troops. The train stopped just fifty feet from the pier. Wilson got out, heard a few scattered cheers from the thousand or so inquisitive Frenchmen who had bothered to come, and saw a parade of Socialists marching down the street, singing the "Internationale" just as the President walked across the quay. Wilson amiably waved his silk hat to the demonstrators. An American Red Cross representative handed Mrs. Wilson (attired in a navy blue tailored dress and a handsome but simple little hat) a bouquet of Brittany roses. An observer thought the President's wife appeared drawn and tired and in a hurry to board the ship for home. The presidential party got into the motor launch that took them to the *George Washington*. "This is America," Wilson said as he stepped aboard the great ship, already full of doughboys returning home at last. The weather was perfect, hardly a ripple in the ocean. As the *George Washington* pulled out of the harbor to the booming farewells of the shore batteries, and as the French warship escort turned around and headed back to Brest, Wilson changed into his comfortable soft cap and stood with Grayson on the bridge, silently watching the shores of France recede into the distance. He never returned.

EIGHT

THE DAYS
OF
DUST AND
ASHES

"We looked for peace,

but no good came;

and for a time of health,

and behold trouble . . ."

34

Nothing is more English than Wimbledon. The smooth, neatly manicured green lawns, the rain delays, the strawberries and cream, the top hats, the prim polite applause from the spectators, all the traditions of Wimbledon call forth memories of the leisurely, prewar society when the ideal of talented amateurism still reigned supreme.

There had been no All-England lawn tennis championships at Wimbledon since the summer of 1914, and so anticipation ran high for the "Victory" Wimbledon that opened on the last week of June 1919. There was a record number of entrants—128—for the gentlemen's singles; according to one cynical commentator, many of these jejune hopefuls entered simply because they wanted to be able to walk about the lawns of their home court, announcing to everyone within earshot, "I say, I found it very difficult to play Ritchie at Wimbledon." Not surprisingly, the governing council of the Lawn Tennis Association had issued a decree in March banning all enemy players from Wimbledon in 1919; the tournament began before the treaty was signed and ended after peace finally had been officially declared.

Observers agreed that the standard of play in the first postwar tournament was generally higher than it had been before 1914. If there were fewer stars, there were more good players. The gentlemen's singles were dominated by Englishmen, Americans, and Australians; when it was all over, the Aussie star G. L. Patterson emerged victorious, routing Lieutenant Colonel A. R. F. Kingscote (the pride of Britain) in only fifty minutes. Indeed, in his relentless march through the challenge round, Patterson lost only one set overall (to Ritchie, as a matter of fact). Most of the excitement, however, was generated by the ladies, and particularly by a twenty-year-old Frenchwoman named Suzanne Lenglen.

Lenglen, who won her first world-class tournament in France at the tender age of fifteen, epitomized—along with Patterson—the new breed of players who unleashed their unabashedly vigorous athletic abilities to break through the cool, stolid veneer of pre-1914 amateur tennis. (By contrast, the traditional "best old English style," of which the unlucky Kingscote was a prime example, was fondly described by one devotee as being a matter of "all-round play without hustle.") Rushing the net to put away her opponent with a vicious volley, smashing a passing shot with her fluid, sweeping forehand, covering the entire court seemingly without effort, Mlle. Lenglen resembled nothing more than a perfect, precise dancer with her hypnotic rhythmical movements on the court. "You can hardly think of her as a woman," wrote one admirer, "—she is a girl who won't grow up. She has no nerves before a crowd. She is wrapped in her art, but she responds like a great actress to the sympathy of her audience. She reminded me much of the divine Sarah [Bernhardt]—splendid eyes, wonderful dark hair, a piquant, expressive face, strongly modelled in nose and chin. . . . Her movements are her greatest physical charm, again with that curious blending of boy and girl. That, too, is the secret of her tennis." Not to mention a marvelous second serve. "I've never played at school and never had a lesson in my life," Lenglen admitted. "I just began to play at home when I was eleven and I've loved the game so much that I've played it ever since."

Dressed in the customary Wimbledon ladies' costume of white hat, white dress, white stockings, and white shoes, Lenglen needed to call upon every measure of her charms and talent in the finals on July 5 against Mrs. Lambert Chambers, already seven times Wimbledon champion. (In those days, the reigning champion received a bye through the challenge round and an automatic berth in the finals.) Before a record crowd of over 10,000, including the King and Queen and Princess Mary, Lenglen and Chambers battled upon the hallowed lawn of center court, the enclosed arena which had been expressly designed to help the performers focus their entire attention upon each other (one veteran player compared it to "playing on a pocket-handkerchief"). After a week's play, the surface at center court had grown so firm that it played more like wood than grass.

The match became a fascinating contrast in styles: Lenglen slight, slim, and strong; Chambers determined, calm, and graceful. Chambers broke the French girl's serve in the first game with a series of forehands to the corner (Chambers's favorite shot); Lenglen, with her "dainty strength," broke right back and then held serve to lead two games to one. A barrage of volleys and smashes earned Lenglen a 5–3 lead, but the English veteran's lobs and drop shots evened the first set at 6–6. After a seesaw battle marked by several excellent baseline rallies, Lenglen finally took the set, 10–8. Chambers then evened the match by capturing the second set, 6–4, taking advantage of numerous errors by Lenglen. So far, the fans were getting more than their money's worth. "The pace had been tremendous," wrote one observer, "even from the standard of men's play."

Chambers retained the momentum by winning the first game of the final set; Lenglen won the next four games with an assortment of driving forehands and volleys. Chambers then took the next three, passing Lenglen at the net time and time again. At 4–4, both women clearly were near the point of exhaustion; even some of the spectators were growing arm-weary just from watching. (One old fellow turned to his neighbor and said, "I don't know how they feel, but I am going to be ill.") Chambers took the ninth game at love, but Lenglen came back and evened it at 5–5 with winners on a volley, a drop shot, and a forehand that hit the baseline. Then it went to 6–5 Chambers, and 40–15 in favor of the defending champion after Lenglen hit a forehand long. At match point, Chambers launched a shot that landed near the baseline to Suzanne's backhand; although her backhand was supposed to be the weakest part of Lenglen's game, she managed to return the shot and went on to win the game. Then Lenglen went ahead 7–6, before Chambers evened it again; but finally the French girl took the third set and the match, 9–7, winning with a cross-court drive that barely skimmed over the net. It was, in the judgment of one longtime tennis writer, "the best match ever seen in women's play."

"The new wine mourneth, the vine languisheth, all the merryhearted do sigh." Although this was not exactly the situation the prophet Isaiah had in mind, much sighing indeed was heard at one minute after midnight on the morning of July 1 (the "thirsty first"), for this was the day wartime prohibition took effect in America. Under the terms of the law, which would remain in force until the nation's armed forces were officially demobilized, the manufacture of alcoholic beverages made from grains, cereals, or fruits had been proscribed since April 1. And now, after the infamous evening of Monday, June 30, 1919, passed into history, it became illegal in the United States to sell or transport across state lines any form of liquor. It was not, however, against the law to take a drink in the privacy of one's own home, if one could somehow obtain a supply.

Wet forces mounted a concerted last-minute legal and popular assault to persuade the government to postpone or overturn the ban. A coalition of New York ironworkers, shipbuilders, longshoremen, hatters, and other assorted unions representing about 166,000 men adopted the slogan "No beer, no work," and threatened to strike as soon as prohibition went into effect. At its annual convention in Atlantic City, the American Federation of Labor voted overwhelmingly against the imposition of the ban on booze, and demanded the annulment of the provision that forbade the manufacture of beer containing 2.75 percent alcohol. (Some tests seemed to indicate that 2.75 beer was, in fact, not intoxicating at all: ten men in a Newark, New Jersey, saloon were given ten very large glasses of the brew, which they drank during the course of a full dinner. Afterwards, a narcotics expert from the city health department examined them and found no trace of intoxication. Their conversation, witnesses testified, was no more foolish than usual; all ten men could walk along a crack in the floor without falling down; and every single one refused to make a speech when called upon to do so.)

But all the protests came to naught. In his annual message to Congress earlier in the year, Wilson had expressed his personal willingness to lift the ban, at least on beer and wines, until the constitutional amendment took effect in January 1920. In the last days of June, though, the President cabled from the decks of the *George Washington* that Attorney General Palmer had advised him that he lacked the legal authority to postpone prohibition at a time when nearly a million American boys were still in uniform. Obviously the army had not been demobilized; thus the nation must go dry. Since Congress had not yet provided specific penalties for violations, however, no one was quite sure how or whether the measure would be enforced. It did seem clear that the government intended to concentrate upon the commercial traffic in liquor instead of harassing individual citizens.

All the confusion notwithstanding, the country entered the dry millenium with a minimum of complaints. There was little evidence in New York City to suggest that June 30 was the last night liquor would be legally available for a long, long time. A few young sailors stood at the corner of Broadway and 42nd Street and pretended they were more drunk than they really were; a stout, elderly lady in a striped gingham frock wandered about the Bowery, shouting in a cracked treble voice that, as for herself, she had never touched the stuff and wouldn't miss it one little bit; and a traffic cop at the Williamsburg Bridge, along the route to the Long Island summer resorts, reported that while he had seen enough booze go by that evening "to float the British navy," there had been no untoward incidents. At midnight, restaurant patrons stopped and waited expectantly for some sign that their lives had changed, but nothing happened, and so they went back to finishing the drinks they had ordered before the clock struck twelve.

At the Methodist centenary celebration in Columbus, Ohio, William Jennings Bryan applauded the burial of "man's greatest enemy"; Bryan refused, though, to act as the grand marshal and ride a camel in the Methodists' Prohibition Day parade, opting instead to maintain his dignity and watch the affair from afar, from the safety of a reviewing stand. In St. Louis, bartenders wore black neckties and mourning bands, and the mirrors in cafés were festooned with black crepe. In Los Angeles, retailers reported the biggest day in the history of the beer and wine business, with an estimated $100,000 worth of liquor sold in the city. At Jack Doyle's famous oasis ("the world's largest saloon"), located in the nearby city of Vernon, California, customers pushed their way up to the two "longest bars in the world"—each one manned by thirty bartenders—to commemorate the passing of John Barleycorn. Police officials throughout the country reported a spectacular one-night jump in the number of drunks thrown into jail to sleep it off, but in the end nothing much else happened.

A few daring restaurateurs in such dens of iniquity as New York and Atlantic City continued to sell drinks after July 1 as if they had never heard of prohibition, taking advantage of city officials' refusal to enforce the law (many politicians at the local level echoed the argument of Mayor Harry Bacharach of Atlantic City that since this was all Washington's idea, enforcement was solely the federal government's responsibility), but most merchants sought to make up their lost profits by raising the price of soft drinks and food. Along Broadway, the price of a small pot of iced coffee rose from thirty-five to eighty cents, and a milk and Vichy water combination went from fifteen to sixty cents; the cost of a glass of lemonade, which never had been very popular in the theater district and still wasn't, remained about the same. But ginger ale jumped from a quarter to a dollar, largely because of its qualities as a mixer: it was not unknown for patrons to bring pocket flasks into restaurants and pour the contents and a bit of ginger ale into a special cocktail glass graciously provided (for fifty cents) by management.

Everyone assumed prohibition would change the traditional American way of life, but no one knew exactly how. Distillers obviously were going to take a terrible beating, especially since there were still approximately forty million gallons of whisky in warehouses in Kentucky, although only the terminally innocent really expected it to stay in storage for long. Hospitals in Philadelphia immediately reported a decrease in emergency and accident cases, particularly during the night shift. Judges predicted a drop in the divorce rate. Bankers expected an increase in personal savings. Publishers urged their authors to delete references to strong drink from their books, and suggested substituting lemonade, sarsaparilla, tea, and milk instead. The price of lobsters fell as demand dropped sharply; as one elderly waiter in a Philadelphia short-dinner restaurant explained, "Folks won't be usin' of many lobsters any more now that booze is gone, because a lobster to booze is like mustard on a ham sandwich. And who've ever eat mustard if they was no sandwich to put on it?" Who indeed?

Dedicated drinkers sought palatable substitutes, most of which proved inadequate and often deadly: bay rum (51 percent alcohol), essence of Jamaica ginger (95 percent), witch hazel (15 percent), or shellac (forget it). Others made their own home brews, putting together stills from tea kettles, earthenware jars, and coils from discarded water heaters. Hundreds of recipes for homemade wines and beer circulated throughout the country. And narcotics officials braced for the anticipated increase in the use of habit-forming drugs.

A blue-ribbon panel appointed in March by the Secretary of the Treasury to investigate the extent of the drug problem in the United States concluded that probably more than a million Americans (out of a total population of about 106 million) were victims of a drug habit; the percentage in some cities ran closer to two out of every hundred. Federal regulation of the drug traffic was based primarily upon the recently passed Harrison Act, which permitted the distribution of limited quantities of certain drugs—including heroin and morphine—to addicts under the care of licensed physicians. Law-abiding doctors across the country reported over 237,000 addicts being "cured" under their supervision, and there were doubtless far more being supplied by unscrupulous physicians whose practice was based solely upon the provision of heroin and morphine to users. A ring of doctors and druggists in New York City, for instance, charged addicts a fee of four dollars per prescription and sixty to seventy-five dollars per ounce of heroin; authorities who broke up the syndicate estimated that each doctor had written about two hundred prescriptions daily. The most commonly used drugs in America in 1919 were, in order of popularity, morphine, cocaine, heroin, opium, laudanum, paregoric, and codeine. Legitimate trade in opium and cocaine was estimated at $20 million a year. More profits, of course, were made in street traffic, but this illicit trade had fallen off since the government legalized prescriptions for habit-forming drugs.

Who was taking these drugs? The Treasury report indicated that the greater part of the addicts in America were native-born citizens, and that men and women seemed equally vulnerable to the habit. Many of the nation's addicts were under twenty-five, including a large percentage of discharged soldiers and sailors. But perhaps the most alarming statistic came from the South, where prohibition had already been in effect at the state and local level for years. "It has been noted," the commission reported, "that in these States the sales of narcotic drugs and cocaine, especially the sale of preparations exempt under the Federal anti-narcotic law have been greatly increased during this period." Physicians in Alabama, for instance, reported 11,690 addicts under their care; the comparable number for Pennsylvania was only 10,202, and just 5,900 in soaking-wet New Jersey. Although the Treasury panel members refused to predict that the Southern trend would overwhelm the entire country during prohibition, it did conclude that "the consensus of opinion of those interested in the subject appears to be to the effect that the number of addicts will increase as soon as the prohibition laws are enforced."

After registering his protest against the treaty signed at Versailles, General Jan Christiaan Smuts of South Africa toured England, explaining the reasons for his stand against the peace terms, and painting in stark and ominous tones the state of the world as he saw it. The predominant feeling at Paris, Smuts said, had been that "we were going into a new world of freedom, an unknown, uncharted world":

> FOR, DOUBT IT NOT THAT WE ARE AT THE BEGINNING OF A NEW CENTURY. THE OLD WORLD IS DYING AROUND US; LET IT ALSO DIE IN US. ONCE MORE IN THE HISTORY OF THE HUMAN RACE WE HEAR THE GREAT CREATIVE SPIRIT UTTER THOSE TREMENDOUS WORDS, "BEHOLD, I MAKE ALL THINGS NEW." OLD IDEAS OF WEALTH, OF PROPERTY, OF CLASS AND SOCIAL RELATIONS, OF MORAL AND SPIRITUAL VALUES ARE RAPIDLY CHANGING. THE OLD POLITICAL FORMULAS SOUND HOLLOW, THE OLD LANDMARKS BY WHICH WE USED TO STEER ARE DISAPPEARING BENEATH A GREAT FLOOD. THE FURNACE THROUGH WHICH WE HAVE PASSED HAS MELTED THE HARD CRUST OF OUR LIFE, AND THE OLD FIXITIES AND CERTAINTIES ARE FLUID ONCE MORE.

Yet, Smuts warned, it clearly would not be easy to navigate a safe course into that new world, for beneath the surface, the foundations of European society had been badly battered. Smuts told his English audiences that he "did not think people here had any conception how sick Europe was." During his fact-finding tour through the territories of the former Austro-Hungarian Empire, Smuts had been "appalled to see how derelict that country had become—governing classes fled, all industries stopped, and this once economic unit carved up into a number of States, all warring against each other and hating each other like poison, the people full of despair, and hungry."

John Maynard Keynes returned to Cambridge and began writing a vicious polemic against the Peace Conference and the treaty. "An inefficient, unemployed, disorganized Europe faces us, torn by internal strife and international hate, fighting, starving, pillaging, and lying," Keynes wrote in *The Economic Consequences of the Peace*. "What warrant is there for a picture of less somber colors?"

Lincoln Steffens stayed behind in Paris after everyone else had left, because, he said, "I wanted to watch the consequences of the treaty. And the consequences of the peace were visible from Paris. There were wars, revolutions, distress everywhere. I challenged a group of war correspondents to name all the wars, big and little, that were going on in the world, and they could not do it. They could not, among them, list more than a score. Real wars, I mean; the economic conflicts were universal." One afternoon, while Steffens was walking near the Crillon, a prostitute approached him. Naturally the prudish Steffens scolded her, and asked why, after he had passed the same way every day for a year, she had chosen this moment to speak to him. "Oh, well," she laughed, "you see the boys are all gone now, and the officers, and the foreigners. So you—so I. Come, I will just walk a block with you, just for fun, just us French." And so they walked and talked about the foreigners who had invaded Paris during the time of the Peace Conference; the girl spoke especially of the Americans, the men "who don't know how to play, to whom everything is business, even love."

The Council of Four went back to being a Council of Ten; of the Big Three, only Clemenceau, who had little choice, remained in Paris to take a personal (albeit desultory) interest in the deliberations of the Peace Conference, which still had to settle affairs with Austria, Hungary, Bulgaria, and Turkey. If possible, the pace of discussions slowed even further after the signing of the German treaty. Clemenceau found it difficult even to schedule a meeting of the Council to fit into everyone's hectic schedule: Tommaso Tittoni, the new Italian Foreign Minister, wanted a late-afternoon meeting so he could have his after-lunch nap; Lansing wanted the meeting held early in the afternoon so he could unwind afterwards with a drive in the Bois and a nap before dinner. "The meeting will be at three," Clemenceau decided with Solomonic wisdom. "Signor Tittoni can sleep before it, Mr. Lansing can sleep after it, and Mr. Balfour and I can sleep during it." Negotiations continued between Dr. Renner's Austrian government (more notes of protest, more notes, more notes) and the Allies.

Bulgaria seemed to have been forgotten entirely. No one could discern any coherent Allied policy toward Turkey, save for the cynical carving up and acquisition of former Ottoman territories by nearly everyone except the United States. An inter-Allied commission had been appointed to settle the boundary dispute between Palestine (Britain) and Syria (France), but only the American members of the commission were actually in the Middle East, gathering facts to make an impartial decision. The Supreme Economic Council went out of business on June 30; the blockade was raised on July 11, and after that it was up to individual nations (i.e., the United States and, more particularly, Herbert Hoover) to transport food to the areas of greatest need.

All the American troops were withdrawn from the Archangel front. Before leaving, each doughboy received decorations for gallantry and efficiency from the local White Russian commander. France, too, reduced its interventionist role in Russia following a mutiny of French naval forces in the Black Sea. Everyone—including most of the Russians themselves—just wanted to go home.

At Weimar, the new government faced a steadily growing railway strike that held up thousands of pounds of food shipments on their way to Berlin. Then the much-vilified Matthias Erzberger, the new Minister of Finance, proposed a system of devastatingly heavy taxes to rebuild the German economy and pay the crushing reparations burden imposed by the peace treaty. "The burden of taxation will reach an absolutely terrible height," Erzberger admitted candidly: a levy of 65 percent on the largest fortunes. "It is the duty of propertied people to achieve an inward conviction as to the necessity of giving up all riches and all that is superfluous." This sort of talk, although essential and actually quite courageous, obviously did nothing to stimulate popular affection for Erzberger personally or the Weimar government generally. Meanwhile, the former Crown Prince, Kaiser Wilhelm's eldest son, vowed once again that he would never stand trial for German war crimes: "The allies can only have my dead body; I will myself decide on my life or death." In fact, for all the blustery talk about prosecuting the Kaiser and German generals, responsible Allied leaders realized that such trials would only create martyrs and accomplish no useful purpose at all.

On July 9 the National Assembly at Weimar voted 208–115, with 96 abstentions, to ratify the peace treaty. Ebert signed the resolution the same day.

Ben Hecht departed Germany and went home to the more rational environs of Chicago. Rejecting offers of assignments to a series of attractive posts around the world, Hecht decided he had seen enough: "A distaste for all politics filled me. . . . Pondering my future, I became aware of likes and dislikes in myself I had not known before. I had never thought I 'preferred' anything. Good and bad food, books, people were much alike to me, as were riches and poverty, importance and unimportance. Now I discovered that I definitely did not want to see Seville, Milan or Peking. I liked Chicago." After the fall of the Kaiser and the so-called revolution of November 1918, Hecht had—for a moment—witnessed a Germany "without a Master. Dreams had flickered in the hearts of its people. Precious hopes for democracy had come to life. With a Master gone, the evil obedience of the German went on a small vacation. He was a man of the world for a day—a dizzy and desperate day. . . . But it was no moral renaissance I saw. It was a recess. The war defeat had not altered a single German characteristic. It had suspended a few, briefly."

In France, the cost of living was nearly four times what it had been in 1910, and still prices kept going up and up. The government promised a decrease of 40 percent in the cost of living; instead, prices rose 60 percent in six weeks. Some consumer items, such as fresh milk, could hardly be found in the cities. New consumption taxes—on gas, electricity, and especially on tobacco—created further irritation, and the nation faced the prospect of additional taxation amounting to over a billion francs to rebuild the shattered French economy. Not surprisingly, the membership of the French Socialist party surged upward from 36,000 in December 1918 to 133,000 in December 1919. With over a million Frenchmen dead in the war, there was the very real possibility of a long-term shortage of labor, especially in the agricultural regions. The only way to ensure sufficient laborers was to abolish conscription. But as long as France continued to rely upon armed force as its only safeguard against a perpetually suspect Germany, conscription could never be abolished. In the manufacturing centers, the shortage of raw materials and the continued disorganization of transport kept French industry crippled. And over it all, reported one astute British observer, hung a spirit of utter pessimism that pervaded the French people through all shades of the political spectrum: "Some of them hate Germany, some of them pity Germany. They are all tired out, and they are all fearful."

After Lloyd George made his official report to Parliament on the proceedings at Paris ("Let us try it," he implored his colleagues when discussing the League of Nations; "I beg this country to try it seriously, to try it in earnest"), he and his family departed for their home in Criccieth, in northern Wales, to fill his doctor's prescription of at least a fortnight of rest.

The whole countryside turned out to greet its most famous son. As the Prime Minister's car wended its way through the mountains toward Criccieth, a delegation of enthusiastic townspeople rushed out to meet it; Lloyd George and his wife were escorted into a wagonette bedecked with gay ribbons and rosettes and towed by admirers the rest of the way up to the town square, past colorful banners of Wales and an ivy-trimmed cottage painted with white letters that read, "Old schoolmate, greeting!" After a few choruses of the stirring Welsh standard "Hen Wlad fy Nhadau" (the Prime Minister standing bareheaded in the wagon, gazing fixedly across the scenes of his boyhood), Lloyd George told his friends—with some difficulty, since he still had a sore throat—"I have come from a very difficult and very anxious task. All I could do was my best for my native land." ("You've done it, too," someone shouted back.) "The deluge of war is over, the beautiful rainbow of peace is adorning the sky. Let us thank God that it is a peace with victory for our native land." Then the wagonette continued up to Lloyd George's house. On the arch over the lane leading back to his unpretentious cottage was the inscription, "Home, sweet home." On the white gates of the house, visitors had penciled random remarks, most of them adulatory—"The man who saved the Empire," "Well done, David!" "Cheerio!" "May he live long!" "God bless him!"—and some rather cryptic, such as "2s. 8d. in the pound," and, underneath, "Sorry! Can't pay today!" The next day the Prime Minister attended a peace thanksgiving service at the Calvinist Methodist Chapel in which all the town's denominations took part.

From Criccieth, the Prime Minister wrote to Frances Stevenson:

MY OWN SWEET DARLING, I HAVE MISSED YOUR LOVING PRESENCE MORE THAN EVER—& MORE THAN EVER I CAN TELL YOU. YOUR LETTER WARMED ME & BRIGHTENED ME UP ON A RAW CHEERLESS DAY WITH A RAW CHEER-LESS FIRE IN THE GRATE. . . . YOU NEEDED A HOLIDAY JUST AS MUCH AS I DID. I SAW IT IN YOUR SWEET TIRED FACE & IT WORRIED ME. THE FACT OF THE MATTER IS THAT NEITHER YOU NOR I REALISE HOW TIRED WE ARE WHEN WE ARE TOGETHER. WE ACT SO MUCH AS A STIMULANT TO EACH OTHER. . . . I HAVE NOT YET HAD MY SLEEP BACK. I SLEPT BADLY LAST NIGHT & I HAVE NOT YET HAD MY AFTERNOON SLEEP TODAY. RAIN OUTSIDE RELIEVED TO A CERTAIN EXTENT BY THE HOWL OF THE WIND.

Frances, meanwhile, was reading the love letters of Abelard and Heloise and supervising the construction of Lloyd George's new house in Cobham, where she had to intervene to prevent the workmen from putting up a picture of Mrs. Lloyd George in the front hall. "How everyone dislikes her," commented Frances in her diary, perhaps with more jealousy than truth. "I have never heard a single person say a good word for her, not even D., who usually finds *some* good points about everyone."

Woodrow Wilson, meanwhile, was still bounding upon the ocean, receiving and signing appropriation bills brought to the *George Washington* direct from the capital in mail pouches via a special transport ship. Never before had a president performed his legislative duties while crossing the Atlantic, and when Wilson addressed the nation via wireless on July 4, it was the first time a president had celebrated Independence Day outside the United States. (Wilson's message, unfortunately, was garbled in transmission.) Nevertheless, the sailors and doughboys aboard the ship heard his words, and reporters captured them for the folks at home. His theme was "The new and enlarged meaning of the Fourth of July": "This is the most tremendous Fourth of July ever imagined," Wilson proclaimed, "for we have opened its franchise to the whole world." Wilson claimed that the war had borne the spirit of American independence into the most remote corner of the earth, earning the United States a tremendous reponsibility to see the creation of a new world order through to a safe and successful outcome. "You cannot earn a reputation like that," he reminded his fellow countrymen, "and not live up to it."

The weather for the crossing was almost perfect, the sea as smooth as a lake under a gentle breeze, and the President passed the time by watching impromptu athletic contests, including games of tug-of-war, between army and navy teams. In the course of an extemporaneous speech to the seamen, Wilson revealed that as a youth he had wished to be a sailor, but his parents had sternly dissuaded him from joining the navy. Charles Seymour, also a passenger on the *George Washington*, spent much of the voyage discussing the President's character with several of his colleagues. They all agreed that Wilson possessed tremendous personal magnetism, which was unfortunately accompanied by a proclivity for alienating people unnecessarily. One of Seymour's friends decided that Wilson was a man "without greatness who will go down in history as great," a leader whose dominant characteristic was "his almost feminine intuition in feeling what the people want and giving it expression in words. A perfect demagogue. Caught the idea of 'self-determination' (stolen by the Bolshevists from the German Socialists) and made it popular. When it came to giving practical effect to the idea in the treaty, he failed." William Allen White, too, believed that Wilson had been defeated by the cynical Old World diplomats at Paris, but he also absolved the President of blame. White compared Wilson to

Prometheus, "bound to the rocks with the vulture forever at his entrails. But they have—those damned vultures—taken the heart out of the peace, taken the joy out of the great enterprise of the war, and have made it a sordid malicious miserable thing like all the other wars in the world." Charles Seymour, on the other hand, believed that Wilson had not failed, that he had in fact "put through a peace which marked a long step in advance, especially as it had written in it the Covenant of the League."

In the United States Senate chamber, the drumbeat of opposition to the League grew stronger every day.

With only a few days remaining before the Willard-Dempsey fight, knowledgeable ring fans remained almost evenly divided in their predictions.

Ring Lardner: "I've got to string with the big fellow. He's got it on Dempsey and ought to win by a knock-out."

Harry Cross of *The New York Times*: "Willard will hold his championship. I will be surprised if he does not win by a knock-out."

Grantland Rice: "My guess is Dempsey inside of six."

Willard Robinson, manager of the Brooklyn Dodgers: "Willard outclasses Dempsey and is too big. Dempsey's only chance is a lucky punch."

Sandy McNaughton, trainer of the illustrious racehorse Omar Khayyam: "I like Dempsey and I'm going to bet that way, too. Dempsey's young. That's all there is to it."

Sam Harris, partner of George M. Cohan: "Looks like Willard. I like Dempsey, mind you, but I don't think he'll ever reach the big fellow."

Benny Leonard, legendary lightweight champion: "Before the florid sun sinks beyond the banks of the placid Maumee Friday afternoon a new heavy weight champion will be crowned. Jack Dempsey will have stripped from the black thatch of Jess Willard the crown. With his pile-driving right and his vicious left, he will have removed the bulky form of Willard from the throne."

Bat Masterson, sportswriter for the *Morning Telegraph*: "Willard should have an easy time beating Dempsey. I can't see how he can lose."

Hype Igoe, of the *New York World*: "Dempsey will knock out Willard. Five rounds should be ample time for him to turn the trick in."

Antonio Scotti, baritone at the Metropolitan Opera House: "I think Willard," with a gesture to the right. "Why? I don't know," with a sweep of his hand to the left. "I think Willard."

Dempsey's father supported Willard right until the end, then finally changed his mind.

Certainly the city of Toledo was going to make a bundle from the bout, no matter who won. As forty thousand prizefight fans (including twelve members of the Wingfoot Walking Club who trekked from Chicago to Toledo) flooded into the town on the shores of scenic Lake Erie, every available inch of floor space was rented for sleeping accommodations. Hotel rooms—usually with two to ten beds in each room—had sold out weeks ago, and the overflow shunted into private rooming houses and vacant stores and office buildings filled with cots for rent starting at five dollars per night. Lunchrooms laid in vast stocks of sandwiches, and enterprising citizens placed signs in their windows announcing, "Meals served here at all hours."

By the morning of July 4 the odds stood at 10 to 8 in favor of Willard; the champion seemed personally offended that he was not a prohibitive favorite. Before the weigh-in, Doc Kearns advised Dempsey not to let any trace of emotion escape as he stood next to Willard. So, Dempsey later recalled, "I made sure that I didn't even look into Willard's face for fear my eyes would give me away. Staring at my own feet was safer. I couldn't take a chance on being psyched out." Willard weighed in at 245 pounds, Dempsey at 187. The champion stood six feet six inches tall, with a reach that exceeded 83 inches; the challenger was nearly five inches shorter, and had a reach of only 78 inches. But Willard was 37 years old, and Dempsey just 24. Damon Runyon began his prefight column with a quotation from chapter seventeen of the first book of Samuel: "And there went out a champion out of the camp of the Philistines, named Goliath, of Gath, whose height was six cubits and a span." Goliath, Runyon wrote, was "the Willard of his time, and we have no doubt that as he went forth, burdened with his battle derby, and the swell duster which weighed 5,000 shekels of brass, the lobby of the Hotel Secor of that period boiled with excitement as his followers shoved around crying: 'Even money on Goliath, even money the big fellow wins.' It must have been a great day. It must have been a day corresponding, in that era, to this day in Toledo, in the dry State of Ohio."

And if Goliath suffered from a terminal case of overconfidence, so Willard appeared not to be rendering Dempsey the respect due the hard-punching challenger. The night before the fight, Willard reportedly downed an entire bottle of gin, dismissing Tex Rickard's concern with the assurance that the bout the next day would be nothing more than mild exercise. Willard even asked Kearns for legal immunity in case he killed Dempsey in the ring.

Rickard's vast octagonal arena stood ready for business on the morning of Friday, July 4. It had taken two months and $150,000 to build; Rickard liked to say that if it all the boards were placed end to end, they would stretch clear from Chicago to New York. The elevated twenty-four-foot-square ring stood five feet above the floor of the stadium. Workmen had wet down the wooden grandstands the night before as a precaution against fire, but there was nothing they could do about the resin and pitch that oozed out of the green timber as the temperature mounted higher and higher. Bayview Park had been the hottest place in the United States on July 3, and it looked like another record would be set on the Fourth. Rickard had priced his tickets too high; although most of the ringside seats were sold, half of the rest of the tickets went begging, leaving scalpers to take a well-deserved financial bath.

It was a motley multitude that assembled at Toledo for the fight. A perceptive correspondent for the *Los Angeles Times* described it as a gathering of "more dips, yeggs, staff humorists, cauliflower ears, wire tappers, plain fish, bottom dealers, round trip tourists, promoters, Texans, case players, Hottentots and sporting editors than ever were herded into this burg before or ever will be again." Two of the most prominent cauliflower ears in town belonged to Oscar Matthew "Battling" Nelson, the former lightweight contender who had wangled an assignment to cover the bout for the *Chicago Daily News*. One of the freer spirits in the fight game, Nelson arose on the hot and muggy morning of the Fourth and decided to take a refreshing bath. He located a likely looking wooden tub filled with what looked like water and jumped in and scrubbed himself clean. As it turned out, the tub was full of lemonade. Since no one except Nelson (and perhaps not even he) was quite certain which vat had been contaminated, those in camp who heard about the incident abstained from drinking any lemonade at all that day. "Tough luck," said Dempsey, for those who didn't know. Beer, of course, was not available—legally.

By noon the thermometer at the press table at ringside had reached 112 degrees. As the crowd sweltered through the preliminary bouts, the mercury hit 120, which was as high as that particular thermometer could go. Every ounce of soft drinks was gone within an hour after the bouts began; the prodigious stocks of ice cream sold out just as quickly; no one even wanted to look at the melted remains of sandwiches hawked by wilted vendors. All physicians in Toledo had registered their services with the police and stood ready to respond to emergency calls if people collapsed from the heat. Outside the arena, Bat Masterson ("a somewhat stocky, spruced-up guy with a curled moustache and carrying a fancy cane," according to Dempsey) and his old crony from Dodge City, Wyatt Earp (who was losing his hair), deputized themselves as official keepers of the peace and insisted that spectators give up their knives and guns before entering the gates. Out by the parking lot, a man paraded about with a sign on his automobile that read I WILL BET THIS MACHINE AGAINST $1,000 ON DEMPSEY. Inside the arena, fans either had to purchase seat cushions or have their pants ruined by the sticky substance oozing from the benches. A brass band made spasmodic attempts to play a few jazz numbers, but the instruments were so hot they burned the musicians' hands. A blind man paid sixty dollars for a ringside seat and sat in the sweltering heat while his friends described the action to him; he could hear the sound of leather against bone, and he remembered what he had seen in past fights before his eyesight had gone forever. Above the arena, Lieutenant Ormer Locklear—the man who had first jumped from one plane to another in midair earlier that year—performed his feats of daredevilry and appeared to be the coolest man in Bayview Park. (Locklear had been barnstorming around the country the past few months, performing his stunts and trying to drum up financial support for a Hawker-style flight across the Atlantic. All he needed, he said, was a plane and a navigator.) One enterprising cameraman taking shots from an army balloon fell into Maumee Bay.

Finally it was four o'clock and time to get down to the real business at hand. The referee was Ollie Pecord, a respected veteran of the fight game from Toledo. ("I don't care who they get to referee this bout with Willard," Kearns had said, "as long as he can count ten.") As the two fighters stood in the center of the newly stretched canvas to pose for photographs and receive their final instructions from Pecord, ringside spectators nudged each other in the ribs and whispered that Dempsey looked nervous and worried. He was. "I saw Ollie Pecord's lips moving and couldn't hear or understand a word he was saying," Dempsey recalled later. "All I knew was that a towering Willard was standing in front of me." It was to be a twelve-round bout, no kidney punches or rabbit punches permitted, with both fighters using the standard five-ounce gloves—actually, Willard's gloves weighed nearly six ounces simply because his hands were so big—with an allowance for soft bandages and a reasonable amount of tape. The custom of having two judges to assist the referee in picking a winner had proved so successful in army and navy matches during the war that it was adopted for the first time in a heavyweight championship bout. The judges selected for this fight were Rickard and Major Anthony J. Drexel Biddle of Philadelphia, president of the Army, Navy, and Civilian Boxing Board. The official timekeeper, who would soon become the object of considerable controversy, was W. Warren Barbour of New York.

Dempsey looked out over the crowd and saw waves of heat rising from the ground. "Ringside was surrounded by a sea of straw boaters and white short-sleeved shirts," he noticed. "I had never seen so many people gathered for a fight before. Not for one of *my* fights." Willard's hair was slicked down with an oily liquid that flashed in the blinding sunlight, and the look on his face—a combination of boredom, arrogance, and annoyance—irritated Dempsey, whose own countenance, tanned to the color of burnt cork, was covered with a three-day stubble of beard to make him look even tougher and meaner than he was (which was considerable). A British reporter wrote that Dempsey's rigid face looked as "black and hard as anthracite coal." Willard bowed and waved graciously to scattered greetings from the crowd; Dempsey stared straight ahead. Pecord's jaws moved furiously as he nervously attacked an innocent piece of chewing gum. Willard wore short, tight-fitting blue worsted trunks with an American flag belt; one reporter decided that the champion looked "as big and impregnable as a metropolitan bank building." Dempsey was attired in loose trunks like those worn by sprinters. Pecord wore a sleeveless white shirt, blue trousers, and a cap. Both corners had erected giant umbrellas to provide the fighters with respite from the sun; Dempsey's was covered with advertisements to turn a few extra bucks, while Willard's was an unadorned dark brown.

"Let's get this thing over," Willard muttered to his seconds.

The bell rang at 4:09. Willard advanced a few steps and Dempsey shuffled forward cautiously; the challenger was not going to take any unnecessary chances. The two men fell into a clinch, Willard leaning heavily against his smaller opponent. Dempsey pushed away and then started to step quickly around the ring. Willard flicked out a pair of left jabs that did no damage. Dempsey moved in and out, finding his range, and then shot a left hook into the champ's midsection. Willard doubled over and winced in pain; as he was stepping backward he launched a feeble one-two combination that fell far short of its mark. Dempsey missed with a right hook but then connected with a hard right to the body. The giant Kansan tried to clinch again, but Dempsey shook him off and moved away, crouching low, his shoulders raised to hide his chin, holding his left slightly out in front. Willard, standing straight up, slugged Dempsey once. Then Dempsey brought out the heavy artillery. The young mauler feinted to the body; Willard went for the fake and lowered his guard; at that moment, Dempsey smashed a terrific left hook to Willard's face. Stunned, Goliath stumbled backwards and finally fell to the canvas, landing on his right side, with his head almost in Dempsey's corner. It was the first time Willard had ever been knocked down. He got up on rubbery legs as the count reached seven. "I saw the look of amazement in his face," Dempsey later said, "as he scrambled to his feet." (Others described the champion's expression as a half-stupid, half-silly look.) The fight was only forty seconds old. Dempsey rushed in to resume the attack as soon as Willard was on his feet. A volley of hooks to the stomach and head put the champion down again.

Seven times Dempsey floored Willard during that murderous first round. The fight would have ended with the seventh knockdown, since Willard failed to rise as Pecord counted to ten, but unknown to anyone in the ring (or to most of the spectators), timekeeper Barbour had sounded the bell to end round one before Pecord finished his count. Apparently part of a piece of rope had gotten wedged inside the gong, muffling the sound. Willard had been saved by the bell; but, unaware of the situation, everyone in the arena went wild, especially Kearns (with his $10,000 bet on a first-round knockout). Fans ran for the exits or pressed toward the ring to congratulate Dempsey, who for a few moments believed he had already won the championship. One of Dempsey's seconds shouted to Kearns, "There seems to be something wrong with the bell!" "Shut up!" bellowed Kearns. "For $10,000, who the hell cares if there's something wrong with the bell! Pecord! Raise Jack's hand! Raise his hand! He's the new champ!" Pecord raised his hand and Dempsey, waving his gloves triumphantly, started to leave the ring, but then Kearns promptly called him back. Barbour, the timekeeper, kept yelling that Dempsey would be disqualified if he didn't get back in the ring immediately.

So on they went into the second round, Willard struggling gamely to launch a few wild, desperate punches. The champion's right eye was cut and stared glassily at Dempsey; his nose and mouth were bruised and bleeding badly. Dempsey carefully surveyed his opponent and stayed out of harm's way, moving in now and then to deliver a quick series of powerful blows to Willard's swollen face. When the bell sounded, Willard had trouble finding his way back to his corner. "Stop the fight!" came the shouts from the crowd. "It's murder!" Then in the third round Dempsey surged to the attack again, even though his arms felt like lead weights. Lefts and rights rained upon Willard's head; defenseless, all he could do was try to cover up. Willard was now nothing more than a giant bloody punching bag for the relentless Dempsey. Again the champion was saved by the bell, but this time it was all over. Before the fourth round began, Dempsey looked over at Willard: "His face was distorted by a broken cheekbone and he was having trouble holding his head up. I felt sick. I hadn't realized that my fury could do so much damage. I couldn't wait for this massacre to end; I was sapped both mentally and physically. I looked at Willard again—I couldn't seem to take my eyes off him. He was a broken man now, he had nothing left." Another witness said that Willard's face looked as if it had been beaten with a baseball bat.

When the bell rang for the fourth round, Willard's trainer threw a bloodstained towel into the ring, signaling his fighter's inability to continue. Never before had a champion failed to answer a bell; never had a champion lost in less than twelve rounds. Never had a challenger risen so far so fast as had William Harrison Dempsey. The crowd booed Willard, but he had absorbed more punishment than any heavyweight champion in such a short time in any fight, and was practically unconscious. With the fight really over this time, fans rushed the ring once more, pushing their way over the reporters vainly trying to telephone or telegraph their story home. Dempsey was rescued by police and hustled off to his dressing room. Now everyone wished to shake his hand. "It felt swell," the new champion admitted. Willard sat in a stupor, neglected, covered with blood, his arms helplessly thrown over the ropes. He said later it took him an hour and a half to clear his head from the devastating left hook Dempsey had thrown in the first round. He dressed himself—his clothes never quite seemed to fit his graceless body—and reportedly staggered, almost blind, along a fence, looking for a way out of the arena. Dazed and confused, he tried to crawl into someone else's car, thinking it was his. Finally Charles MacArthur found the forsaken fighter and led him back to his business manager, Ray Archer, who took Willard first to the training camp in Casino to dress his wounds, and then to the ex-champion's temporary home in an exclusive section of Toledo. As Jess stumbled in, his wife eased him onto a davenport and sat next to him, soothing his closed right eye and his broken nose with iced cloths. Mrs. Willard had witnessed the fight, and was glad it was all over. "I am sorry that Jess was beaten," she told reporters, "but I can truthfully say I am happy that he's no longer champion. It means, now, that we shall be able to live in peace. Jess will become a private citizen again. It was the second boxing contest I had ever witnessed and I do not want to witness any more. I shall be happy when I can take Jess back home to our children."

Dempsey sent a wire to his mother at her home in Salt Lake City: "Your boy made good. Knocked the big fellow out in three rounds." "I am overjoyed," shouted Mrs. Dempsey when she heard the news. Kearns immediately began sifting through the offers to the new champion from vaudeville and circus promoters. Pecord ruled that the fight had ended in three rounds, and officially credited Dempsey with a knockout. As the result of the fight flashed across the country, the Los Angeles bureau of the

Associated Press received a phone call from a sweet-voiced young lady who wanted to know who had won. "Jack Dempsey," answered the editor in charge. There was a pause; then the caller innocently asked, "Well, who lost?"

The Ohio board of censors barred any theater within the state from showing the motion pictures of the fight. "Such human butchery," the chairman of the board announced, "should not be shown where our boys and girls may see it."

That night, Dempsey dreamed the fight all over again. Only this time, in the nightmare, Willard knocked him out. Waking in a sweat, bewildered, Dempsey rushed outside in his bare feet and heard a newsboy shouting, "Extra! Extra! Read all about it!" "Ain't you Jack Dempsey?" the boy asked. "Yeah. Why?" Then Jack saw the paper with his name emblazoned in the headlines as the heavyweight champion of the world. He had no change in his pockets for the paper, but the boy told him not to worry about it. "You don't owe me nothin'—Champ!"

35

"For who shall have

pity upon thee,

O Jerusalem?"

If real or imagined revolutions governed the first six months of 1919, the second half of the year was dominated by strikes and the threat of strikes. *Literary Digest* estimated that there were more than 2,600 labor disputes in the United States in 1919, and that more than four million Americans were on strike at one time or another during the year. No year before or since has even approached those numbers. In early July, seamen were on strike all along the East Coast; machinists walked off their jobs in Chicago, and 100,000 building and street construction workers in that city found themselves locked out; Boston struggled to cope with a strike of its elevated railway employees; and the bakers and telephone operators in St. Louis walked out. Several weeks later, the government's air-mail pilots voted to strike, claiming that they were forced to fly in bad weather in unsafe planes. Citing the frightening statistics of fifteen accidents—two of them fatal—in a ten-day period, the pilots demanded that the government provide them with slower, more stable, better-equipped planes than the Curtiss R-4s they were currently required to fly. The federal government replied, with its usual compassion where labor affairs were concerned, that it would dismiss and then arrest any pilot who went on strike.

It was in Canada, though, that the longest and most bitter strikes took place in this blazing hot summer of discontent. The country had been badly shaken by the introduction of conscription in the last years of the war, and when the soldiers returned in the spring of 1919 they bore little love for the government that had sent them overseas. Officials in Ottawa tried to defuse the discontent by offering veterans six months' extra pay and promising them homesteads and farmland; but the rapidly escalating cost of living—and especially the terribly high food prices—ate up the extra pay, and the land grants turned out to be located far to the north, in the isolated interior. This potentially explosive situation was exacerbated by the combination of veterans' grievances with widespread working-class dissatisfaction over the lack of educational opportunities, and popular resentment at ostentatious displays of wealth by the upper class (anyone who drove an expensive automobile was presumed to be a war profiteer); during the long months at the front, working-class Canadian soldiers had learned at last that material wealth and human worth were in no way related. And above all, there was the growing strength of the radical labor movement in the western provinces, where the IWW dream of "One Big Union" had taken a firm hold on workers' imaginations. It was clear to any perceptive observer that the war had stimulated class consciousness, but obtuse employers refused even to recognize the right of workers to organize, preferring instead to try to smash the trade-union movement wherever it raised its head.

Every major Canadian city was hit by strikes that summer: teamsters, street railwaymen, and metalworkers in Ottawa; shipyard laborers in Montreal; a general strike of eight thousand workers in Toronto. Then all the pressures of social unrest burst into violence in Winnipeg, where for six weeks a general strike paralyzed the city. Food supplies, transport, and communication with the rest of Canada were cut off. The Winnipeg police force, which had organized a union of its own in 1918, was practically the only trade union that opted not to join the general strike; nevertheless, the police were presented by the government with an ultimatum to sign a pledge disassociating themselves from all other trade-union organizations. One hundred and eighty-nine policemen—out of a total force of 198—refused to sign, and were immediately dismissed from their jobs. The government then organized a special constabulary of several thousand citizen volunteers and Northwest Mounted Police, aided by forty-five squads of machine gunners, and pitched battles between these forces and the strikers shook the city repeatedly. Streetcars were wrecked, barbed wire was strung across the streets, shots were fired by both sides, and Main Street became, according to *The Times* of London, "a deserted expanse of asphalt chequered here and there with moving bodies of troops and armoured cars." Twenty thousand strikers sent fraternal greetings to the Spartacists in Germany, conjuring up images in the government's mind of workers' councils and soviets. The mayor of Winnipeg read the Riot Act and declared martial law. Parades and outdoor meetings were prohibited; strike leaders were arrested in the middle of the night and their newspapers suppressed.

When the strike finally ended, more out of exhaustion on both sides than from any clear-cut decision, a royal commission was appointed to investigate the causes of the conflict. In its report, the commission recommended the adoption of a minimum wage; a standard eight-hour day; some provision for unemployment insurance, pensions, and health insurance, all to be funded by the state; and the protection of labor's right to collective bargaining. Taken as a whole, this amounted to a "Charter of Liberty" for Canadian labor, and even though police continued to raid suspected headquarters of revolutionary activity throughout the western prairie towns, the Winnipeg general strike and its brutal repression had succeeded in giving industrial workers in Canada more solidarity and class consciousness than they had ever known before, and launched them on a stormy political future.

To the east, at St. John's, Newfoundland, Captain Frederick Raynham was ready to try again to cross the Atlantic—this time with a new navigator (his original partner had decided that one crash was enough) and a new Martinsyde airplane. On the evening of July 16, Raynham started his run across the landing field from which Hawker had begun his ill-fated flight. The plane rose thirty feet in the air; then, caught by a strong gust of wind, it suddenly stalled and dove back to earth. Neither Raynham nor his navigator were seriously injured, but the plane was wrecked beyond repair. This time, Martinsyde executives decided to call it quits, and Raynham was instructed to return to England by steamer.

On Saturday, July 19, Washington reached the boiling point. For the past month the city had been besieged by a crime wave, the most ominous feature of which was a series of attacks by blacks upon white women on the city streets, usually in broad daylight or in the early evening. Outraged citizens complained that Major Raymond W. Pullman, the chief of police, was so preoccupied with closing down vice operations and catching bootleggers that he was ignoring more serious crimes. (Washington in 1919 was, of course, still very much a Southern city. For instance, no blacks had been added to the police force since 1910, and those who had been hired before that time were gradually being dismissed. In Congress, the nation's representatives regularly introduced resolutions to legalize Jim Crow restrictions on the city's streetcars.)

Shortly after ten o'clock on the evening of July 18, Mrs. Elsie Stephanick, a nineteen-year-old employee of the Bureau of Engraving and Printing, was walking along D Street in the southwest quarter of the city toward her home at 413 Ninth Street, when two black men allegedly accosted her and jostled her back and forth between them. Several of her co-workers who witnessed the incident ran to her aid, and the assailants fled. Police made no arrests at that time.

When a small band of angry sailors and marines learned that Mrs. Stephanick's husband was a soldier, they decided to avenge his wife's sullied honor by taking matters into their own hands. The following day they set out to mobilize every man in uniform who was visiting downtown Washington on leave. Walking up and down Pennsylvania Avenue and Ninth Street, they reportedly told every serviceman they met that "the boys were going to avenge the attack on Mrs. Stephanick tonight," and that "if they wanted to see action they should fall in at Ninth Street and the Avenue between 10 and 10:30 o'clock." At the appointed hour, more than four hundred men, most of them in uniform and armed with revolvers and clubs, assembled and marched off toward the black residential district in southwest Washington for what they promised would be "a general clean-up." Another three hundred civilians joined the procession as it crossed the Mall. Those without weapons picked up heavy pieces of wood from lumberyards along the way. They found one of the men suspected of attacking Mrs. Stephanick and immediately knocked him to the ground and made preparations for a lynching. The black man broke away and, followed by several stray revolver shots, barricaded himself in his house. Frustrated, the mob hurled bricks and chunks of wood at any black person within range; others beat black bystanders with lead pipes. Finally the police ambled over and broke up the crowd without further incident. Major Pullman downplayed the affair, characterizing it as the work of "a few hotheads." Police spokesmen blamed the trouble on black veterans who had become intimate with lower-class white women in France, and who had returned home to spread "vicious" ideas among their friends.

Next evening, a frenzied mob of soldiers and white civilians ranged up and down Pennsylvania Avenue between Seventh and Fifteenth streets, attacking every black person they could find. Most of the men in khaki chose not to use their guns, preferring instead to enjoy the physical satisfaction of beating their victims with fists and clubs, or stones wrapped in handkerchiefs. They commandeered passing automobiles and descended in squads upon black pedestrians when they heard the battle cry, "Here's one." In front of the White House gates, blacks were dragged from streetcars and assaulted. One fearless band of soldiers rushed into Childs' Restaurant in search of a black busboy, and were deterred from their quest only by the complaints of patrons that "too many women were eating." Two marines jumped into a streetcar and pummeled a black man who had been shouting at the crowd outside. Another group of soldiers chased their victim to a corner of the Treasury Building and began beating him; a civilian asked three policeman—standing idly by, twirling their clubs in front of the nearby Washington Hotel—why someone didn't stop the fighting, and the policemen replied, "That is what we would like to know." Police headquarters received scores of calls from blacks who insisted that they could not go home without protection; they didn't get it. As the Sunday midnight army curfew approached and the soldiers drifted away to their barracks, there was defiant talk of assembling again tomorrow evening at nine o'clock to *really* clean up the black districts.

All hell broke loose on Monday night. District blacks had spent the day buying every gun available from any small dealers in Washington willing to sell them arms and ammunition; police estimated that at least five hundred revolvers were sold in the city on that one day alone. Carloads of blacks drove to Baltimore to purchase weapons. Nerves were on edge in the capital all day; late in the afternoon, any noise or disturbance in the downtown area attracted an excited crowd. But even after the warning signs of two nights of rioting and the wholesale purchase of firearms, city authorities still refused to take adequate measures to contain the trouble until it was too late. Instead of calling up additional reinforcements during the day, the city police commissioner contented himself with admonishing law-abiding citizens to keep off the streets at night.

When evening fell, an ugly mob of a thousand whites—nearly all civilians, for military authorities had clamped severe restrictions on leave passes in an effort to keep troublemaking soldiers in camp—ranged across the Mall and then up Seventh Street to H Street, where the shouting, angry crowd was dispersed by a detachment of cavalry hurriedly called out on emergency assignment from Fort Myer. Frustrated, the mob then surged back to the downtown area, once again manhandling every black in sight. But this time the blacks fought back. Confronted by a mob of jeering whites, a black passenger on a streetcar emptied his revolver into the crowd, wounding four men. Seconds later, five bullets from a policeman's gun riddled his body. Another black man who fired at passengers in a crowded streetcar at Fourth and N streets was shot down and clubbed to death.

High-powered cars filled with heavily armed black men seeking revenge speeded through the hitherto sacrosanct white sections in the northwest quarter of the city, firing indiscriminately at bystanders, policemen, and soldiers. (Except for policemen, few of the whites on the streets that evening were carrying revolvers.) One gang in a passing automobile fired eight shots at wounded veterans sitting on the lawn of the U.S. Naval Hospital. Police captured three of these teams of black raiders, but another half-dozen cars and crews escaped. The whole U Street corridor was ablaze with gunfire and littered with the beaten bodies of white men. A marine was shot less than a block away from the White House by a black youth riding a homemade motorcycle; the pool of blood from the wounded man remained in the street until the early morning rain swept it into the gutters.

Now, when they finally bestirred themselves to try to stop the carnage, police found it impossible to keep the streets clear. Only the approching dawn brought an end to the riot. It had been the bloodiest night in the city since the Civil War. Four people lay dead—two blacks, a white civilian, and a policeman shot by a seventeen-year-old black girl—and at least two more were dying. Hospitals reported hundreds of cases of gunshot wounds, broken bones, and lacerated heads. Police arrested three hundred rioters. Frightened congressmen introduced legislation to declare martial law in the capital. "It is the solemn duty of this Congress," shouted Representative Frank Clark of Florida, "to make the streets of Washington safe for the good women of the land." Meanwhile, the good white women whom Congressman Clark extolled were taking matters into their own hands, crossing the river into Alexandria to purchase guns (police stood outside every gun shop and hardware store with orders to refuse entry to blacks) and barricading themselves in their homes.

The next day, President Wilson—who was lying ill in bed, suffering from an attack of acute dysentery during most of the rioting—finally called in Secretary of War Newton Baker and told him in no uncertain terms that this sort of thing simply had to stop. Several hours later, more than two thousand fully armed federal troops were brought into the city to preserve order. This imposing display of armed force, aided in no small measure by a driving evening rainstorm with recurring downpours that sent everyone scurrying for shelter, intimidated both sides into staying off the streets. For the moment, everyone seemed to have had enough violence. There were no more pitched battles in the capital for the rest of the summer; only bitterness and smoldering hatred.

Wilson might have been excused for having other things on his mind as the city tore itself apart outside his door. The Senate Foreign Relations Committee had got its hands upon the peace treaty and the sacred League of Nations Covenant, and as yet there was no clear signal as to when, or in what form, the treaty would emerge from Henry Cabot Lodge's wizened grasp.

As Wilson pondered his strategy for the upcoming battle with the Senate over ratification of the treaty, he grew more and more enamored with the notion of a direct appeal to the people via a cross-country speaking tour. Ever since his days as governor of New Jersey, the guiding principle of Wilson's political philosophy had always been his belief that he personally represented the hopes and dreams of "the people," both in America and abroad. So, if a little group of willful men tried to deny the promise of a new world—the world whose foundations had been constructed so painstakingly in Paris—Wilson would smash them by arousing popular sentiment in their home states until they were compelled to approve the treaty, and the League with it.

The President had received a tumultuous welcome when the *George Washington* docked at Hoboken on July 8. ("Jerseyman though I am," Wilson said, "this is the first time I ever thought that Hoboken was beautiful.") Ten thousand schoolchildren, all dressed in white, greeted the President at the pier; thousands of New Yorkers cheered him as he stood in an open touring car (with Mrs. Wilson sitting next to him, clutching a huge bouquet of American Beauty roses, and bodyguards standing on each running board) along the three-mile route to Carnegie Hall. Tons of confetti showered down from office windows and littered the city's streets, along with leaflets that read, "Everybody's business: To stand by our government. To help the soldier get a job. To help crush bolshevism." Inside Carnegie Hall, Wilson told a standing-room-only crowd that he had considered it a privilege to represent the American people at Paris. The war had led Europe to understand exactly what the United States symbolized, the vision of freedom for which American boys had fought and died in the trenches on the Western Front. Yet Wilson admitted that, unfortunately, there were some people here at home who still did not understand the vision of the new world of 1919: "They do not see it. They have looked too much upon the ground. They have thought too much of the interests that were near them, and they have not listened to the voices of their neighbors."

Wilson returned to Washington at 11:45 that evening. Although his train was nearly two hours late, 100,000 well-wishers—including two lines of lissome yeomanettes and schoolgirls dressed as heralds, waving the flags of all the nations represented at the Peace Conference—greeted the President at Union Station; ten thousand more waited at the White House. "Home at last," Wilson murmured as he stepped out of his car at 1600 Pennsylvania Avenue. Two days later he went down to the Capitol to present the peace treaty to the Senate, although he withheld the special defensive treaty of alliance with France for the moment. "As he was ushered into the Senate Chamber," Grayson observed, "he looked completely well again. His step was elastic, his color good, his eyes bright, his figure erect. His attitude was that of a man who had called his associates in government to reason with them but if they would not reason was ready to fight them to the end." Two senators refused to stand up when the President entered.

Certainly Wilson had no use for any legislator who wanted America to retreat once again into an isolationist shell. "There can be no question," he reminded the senators, "of our ceasing to be a world power. The only question is whether we can refuse the moral leadership that is offered us, whether we shall accept or reject the confidence of the world. . . . Shall we or any other free people hesitate to accept this great duty? Dare we reject it and break the heart of the world? . . . It was of this that we dreamed at our birth. America in truth shall show the way." Later, Wilson's son-in-law, William McAdoo, the former Secretary of the Treasury who was exploring his chances as a Democratic presidential hopeful for 1920, praised the President's inspirational speech but feared that Wilson had been wasting his time, "casting pearls before swine."

With the shock waves from the explosion at Attorney General Palmer's house six weeks earlier still resonating through the tense Washington air, the President was provided with scores of police and Secret Service guards everywhere he went, not excluding Capitol Hill, where he probably had more enemies per square inch than anywhere else in the nation. Yet the protection was not foolproof; as Wilson left the Capitol that afternoon, a bulky package fell out of the crowd and landed at his feet. Wilson hesitated, then made a motion as if to pick it up. Major Pullman and omnipresent Secret Service agent Dick Jervis leaped in front of the President to shield him, and a Capitol policeman grabbed the bundle. It turned out to be harmless, filled only with newspapers.

The President's advisers let it be known that Wilson would accept no reservations to the League Covenant or any other part of the treaty. ("Here I am," Wilson said. "Here I have dug in.") The President believed that any substantive changes in the text would force reconsideration of the treaty by the rest of the signatory powers, and that was something he simply would not allow. He might possibly agree to a Senate resolution expressing in a general way the United States government's interpretation of certain provisions in the League Covenant, but that was all.

Immediately following the President's address to the Senate, Lodge summoned his Republican colleagues on the Foreign Relations Committee to a cloakroom to discuss a plan of action. They decided not to call the President to testify before the committee. Instead, they began their consideration of the peace treaty by having Lodge—accompanied only by a long-suffering clerk—sit in a room and read aloud every one of the treaty's 450 printed pages into the official record. It took him two weeks. Meanwhile, Wilson held a series of conferences with individual senators, explaining the terms of the treaty, answering their questions as patiently as he could, trying to discover exactly how little he needed to change to obtain ratification.

He got nothing for his troubles. Day after day, one senator after another rose in the chamber to denounce some section of the peace treaty. The Shantung settlement drew considerable fire; Senator Lawrence Sherman of Illinois accused Wilson of truckling to the Huns of the East. "It is as plain as the noonday sun," Sherman bellowed, "that the Japanese Government is autocratic and that it will add Chinese province upon province, concession upon concession until an Asiatic kaiser, armed with all the modern implements of scientific destruction in war, will dominate the affairs of Asia and the Pacific Ocean." (Sherman, incidentally, was something of a loose cannon on the Senate floor. He brought considerable embarrassment upon Lodge and his fellow irreconcilables by denouncing the League as a devious plot to restore the Pope to temporal dominion over the world. Since twenty-four of the forty nations who would be League members adhered to the Roman Catholic Church, Sherman reasoned, the Pope would be able to control their votes on economic and political questions. Sherman felt it was no coincidence that the Pope was one of the most ardent supporters of the League: "So far as a layman can discover the Vatican still believes it ought, and would if the power permitted, assume to administer ecclesiastical and civil government.")

When Lodge completed his dramatic recitation of the treaty text, the Foreign Relations Committee began to call a parade of witnesses, most of whom were of course hostile to the treaty, including the thin-skinned William Bullitt and every prominent Irish-American who was willing to testify. So while the hearings droned on, Wilson enjoyed a brief period of rest and recreation, playing golf every day, taking evening drives in the country with his wife, and above all husbanding his strength for the climactic battle that lay ahead.

As major-league baseball passed the halfway mark of the 1919 season, the Chicago White Sox could be found coasting comfortably along atop the American League standings. The Sox were leading the league in hitting with a .275 team average; despite a recent 0–21 slump, Shoeless Joe Jackson led the way with a .354 average, followed by first baseman Chick Gandil at .307 and third baseman Buck Weaver at .300. Eddie Collins, the infield general and peerless clutch hitter, had upped his average to .299. Displaying a rare combination of speed and power, the Sox also led the American League in both stolen bases and extra-base hits. By the end of July, Eddie Cicotte (with the aid of his notorious "shine ball") had already won eighteen games—tops in the majors—against only four losses. And when Cicotte and Lefty Williams, the two aces of the Chicago pitching staff, began showing signs of wear and tear, the Sox picked up little Dickie Kerr (a former bantamweight boxer from the sandlots of St. Louis) and the well-traveled Big Bill James to bolster the mound corps.

Knowledgeable baseball men professed surprise at the ease with which the Sox were dominating the American League, and most experts attributed Chicago's resurgence to the genius of Kid Gleason, "the merry old soul of the diamond." Everyone kept waiting for the Sox to go into a serious slump, but Gleason doggedly refused to let his club fold. Entering the critical month of August, Chicago's chief competition appeared to be the Cleveland Indians, where Tris Speaker had assumed managerial control in mid-season, and the Detroit Tigers. Even with the acquisition of star southpaw Carl Mays—he of the unorthodox submarine delivery—from the Red Sox (the first of many controversial, one-sided deals between the two clubs), the Yankees were fading fast; before an all-time record American League crowd of 33,000 at the Polo Grounds on August 2, the Yanks blew a lead and wound up losing to the Tigers, 14–8, in ten innings. And despite Babe Ruth's torrid home-run pace (on July 28, with over a month to go, the Babe tied Socks Seybold's American League record of sixteen homers in one season), Boston remained mired in sixth place, behind even the lowly St. Louis Browns.

Over in the senior circuit, the Giants and the Redlegs were waging a seesaw battle for first place. Manager John McGraw's boys from Gotham invaded Cincinnati on August 1 for a crucial three-game series, and promptly dropped the first game, 6–2, before a crowd of seventeen thousand raucous fans who unleashed a ceaseless barrage of verbal abuse upon the Giants, singling out McGraw and ex-Red Hal "Corkscrew" Chase for special attention. Fearing an even more violent outburst, management stationed a squad of special policemen in the stands to preserve order for the second game of the series. Intimidated into their best behavior, the 25,000 fans who jammed the stadium on August 2 saw their beloved Reds win once again, this time behind the shutout pitching of Harry "Slim"

Salee. Sheriff Salee's victory was a measure of sweet revenge for the thirty-four-year-old hurler, who had been unceremoniously discarded by the Giants earlier that spring; ever since Pat Moran had picked him up, Salee had done nothing but win games for his new club. The Giants salvaged the third and final contest of the series, but a near-riot ensued after the game when unruly fans surrounded the Giants as they left the field, tagging at their heels and shouting epithets as the New Yorkers disappeared into their clubhouse. Police dispersed the crowd once, but when McGraw became embroiled in a shoving match with a special stadium policeman, the mob closed in again with pop bottles and bricks. Shouting, "We'll be glad to get out of the home of the Huns," McGraw was hustled into a car and driven away to the relative safety of his hotel.

With attendance up and money pouring into their coffers at an unprecedented pace, major-league owners were kicking themselves for their January decision to shorten the 1919 season to just 140 games. Unfortunately, the intense public interest in baseball also promoted increased interest in gambling on the games. Chicago, Boston, and New York were known as especially popular parks for wagering, even though management placed plainclothes detectives at the entrances to keep out professional gamblers, who represented the real danger; hardly a day went by when at least one or two known gamblers were not evicted from the Polo Grounds. But the three-man commission that governed the major leagues refused to take aggressive action to curb the menace, despite the rumors that were by now running rampant about the questionable integrity of the national pastime.

Notwithstanding the unexpected success of the White Sox (and the less said about the Cubs the better), all was not well in Chicago in the summer of 1919. Drawn by the promise of high wages in wartime industries, thousands of blacks had immigrated to the city of broad shoulders and slaughterhouses during the past two years. The influx from the South created a severe housing shortage—eighty thousand blacks were crowded into an area where fifty thousand had lived before the war—and pushed the Black Belt, the five-mile strip that ran through the heart of the South Side, into formerly choice residential districts, creating considerable resentment among white homeowners, who responded by bombing the houses of blacks who dared to cross the line.

To make matters worse, city politicians permitted the underworld a free hand in the Black Belt. There was no limit as long as one cooperated with the syndicate that controlled all the vice in the area. White gangsters purchased saloons and cabarets and put cooperative blacks up front as the ostensible owners. Long after the 1:00 A.M. city closing time for public bars, mixed crowds of both sexes could be seen carousing together in the "black and tan" nightclubs where the infamous "shimmy" got its start, the good-time kids taking in the jazz and gambling until sunrise. Police refused to make any arrests in the Black Belt because they never knew what small-time hood might have enough political influence to get them bounced off the force. There was total disrespect for the law, and conditions were approaching anarchy by the middle of the sultry summer of 1919.

On Sunday afternoon, July 27, a seventeen-year-old black boy named Eugene Williams was swimming at the 29th Street beach, on the shores of Lake Michigan. The beach had long been divided into black and white sections; on this fateful day, young Williams grabbed hold of a railroad tie and floated across the "line." Or at least the white bathers on the beach *said* he had crossed the line, and to enforce their Jim Crow restrictions they promptly began to pelt him with stones. One of the missiles thrown by a white youth appeared to strike Williams. He let go of his makeshift raft, swam for a few feet, then sank beneath the water and drowned. A police-man on duty refused to arrest the white boy who had thrown the stone, claiming that he could not identify him in the crowd. Enraged, the blacks tried to take their own revenge, starting a free-for-all brawl along the beach.

This spark set off the powder keg. All through the next day there was gleeful talk in white neighborhoods of a crusade to "clean up" the stock-yard districts. At dusk the city exploded when black workers were attacked as they walked home from their jobs at Chicago's large industrial plants. For more than five hours the Black Belt was an urban battleground as whites and blacks fought each other with guns, clubs, knives, and razors. A white man was dragged from a truck on 35th Street and stabbed to death; a few minutes later a black chauffeur was killed by whites in the very same block. Blacks looted white stores; police opened fire, aiming low, and a dozen blacks fell. To prevent the rapid dispatch of white police to trouble spots, a band of blacks cut the telephone and telegraph wires in their neighborhoods. A reporter witnessed "groups of blacks formed in football fashion," wielding clubs and razors, charging against whites. Streetlights were smashed everywhere. In the darkness, women battled each other with stones and brooms. At the end of the night, five blacks and two whites were dead.

But all that was nothing compared to the next evening's events. In a series of pitched battles, fourteen more people died, and the fighting spread throughout the city; an Italian neighborhood on the west side was the scene of considerable bloodshed, and even the Loop failed to escape unscathed as two black men and one white were fatally shot in the famous business district. Over 150 people were seriously wounded—stabbed, beaten, or shot—in the city that night. The disorder spread even to the "bull pen" at the city jail, where white and black prisoners took violent exception to each other's presence. Despite assurances from the acting chief of police that he was "very well pleased with conditions," Governor Lowden called in the entire Fourth Regiment of the Illinois militia to restore order.

With three thousand heavily armed troops patrolling Chicago's streets and three thousand more men in reserve, the street fighting gradually abated, though occasional ugly incidents persisted; on its first day in the city, the militia had to step in to rescue one black man who was about to be hanged from a telegraph pole by a white gang at the corner of 63rd Street and Campbell Avenue, and blacks who dared to return to their jobs at the stockyards were beaten, knocked down, and kicked by whites. But since there was little fun in facing a steel wall of fixed bayonets, the rioters changed their tactics and decided to launch a series of incendiary attacks instead. On the evening of July 31 alone, more than thirty-six cases of arson were reported as each side sought to burn out the other. When it was all over, thirty-eight people had been killed (fifteen whites, twenty-three blacks), more than five hundred injured, and a thousand left homeless. Civic leaders began rushing food supplies into the black districts, where four days of arson, looting, and indiscriminate shooting had reduced the population to a state of near-starvation. There was a short-lived exodus of terrorized blacks to the reportedly more hospitable climes of Indianapolis and Memphis. A grand jury was empaneled to investigate the riots, but when the state's attorney persisted in seeking indictments only against black rioters, the grand jury went on strike, demanding that the government present evidence involving white culprits, too.

The Chicago city coroner decided that Eugene Williams had not been struck by stones, but had simply drowned, and so the white youth who had been arrested for his murder was released.

36

_____

"In the land of peace,

wherein thou trustedst,

they wearied thee . . ."

Henri Landru refused to confess. The mountain of circumstantial evidence grew higher every week—a criminologist managed to piece together three human skulls from the bone fragments found at Landru's villa at Gambais—but still Landru withstood the pressure of repeated inquisitions. Threats did not move him, so Monsieur Bonin, the examining magistrate, tried to cajole a confession out of his prisoner. "You look as if a secret weighed heavily on your conscience," he whispered in a low, conspiratorial tone as he leaned his face toward Landru. "Confide in me. What is it?" Landru paused for a moment. Then he slowly raised his head and stared into the magistrate's trusting eyes. "Monsieur le Juge," he replied, "I am heartbroken to think that, thanks to all this scandal, my wife knows that I have been unfaithful to her." Then he clammed up again.

A British novelist and amateur detective, Marie Belloc Lowndes, deemed the Landru case "disappointingly simple from the point of view of the intelligent criminologist," but conceded that it was an excellent example of the way wartime circumstances abetted criminal behavior. "How few persons realize what life in the villages of France has been like during the past five years," Mrs. Lowndes exclaimed. With every able-bodied man gone and every woman in a constant state of agonized suspense over the fate of her husband, lover, or son, not to mention the fate of France itself, it was not surprising to Mrs. Lowndes that no one took any notice of this middle-aged, bearded bourgeois gentleman "who came now with one woman, now with another, to his little house." Lots of Frenchmen were burying or burning their cherished possessions to keep them out of the hands of the marauding Huns, the novelist added, and so the deep holes in Landru's gardens aroused little suspicion. "It is symptomatic," Mrs. Lowndes concluded, "that the one intelligent neighbor of Landru's who studied his strange doings pretty closely, made up his mind that Landru was a spy and actually laid up information against him."

As July droned on, Landru felt a bit under the weather, and so he went to the magistrate to ask a favor. "I have great need of fresh air," Landru pleaded, "and I ask that you liberate me provisionally. I shall go to my house at Gambais, if possible, and I give my word of honor to remain at your disposition, for I am ready to justify myself regarding the flimsy accusations brought against me." Request denied.

"The year 1919, which had been welcomed by credulous souls as an antechamber to the millennium, laboured under a pervasive disadvantage. Too much was expected of it. It was a year of rootless re-beginnings and steadily developing disillusionments. Few people realized this at the time, and I was not one of them," admitted the young British poet Siegfried Sassoon. "Up to the end of June I was actively occupied, confident through success, and insolently healthy with youth and summer weather. But a surprise was in store for me. . . ."

Surprises constantly descended upon David Lloyd George, too, in the summer of 1919. His apparent victories at the Peace Conference behind him, the Welshman now had to settle down and grapple with the perplexing political, labor, and social problems of postwar Britain. It was not nearly so much fun as Paris. As he packed his bags for London after the brief vacation at Criccieth, Lloyd George told Frances Stevenson that, aside from the prospect of seeing her once again, he was not looking forward at all to taking up once again the reins of power: "When I come back I shall be returning to the most fearful welter any Minister ever faced. It appals [sic] me to think of it. I have even had fits of running away & let them clear up their own mess. But those fits soon pass away. I must have a real try & if the public impatience upsets things before I can work out my plans then the fault won't be mine & I shall retire happily to fulfil other plans."

A gradually spreading sense of dissatisfaction with the postwar world kept England in a constant state of agitation in the summer and autumn of 1919. Doubtless much of this was inevitable: promises had been made during the war and then broken with the coming of peace; hopes had been raised that could never be fulfilled in such a short time. With the foreign foe vanquished and the immediate crisis surmounted, England's established interests settled back into a defense of their privileged position. "In the minds of thousands," wrote the *Manchester Guardian*, "the war was to give us a new England and a new Europe. Of those thousands many are dead, having given their utmost to that idea. It still seems, as we think of their hopes and their sacrifices, incredible that the idea should perish." But the politicians seemed to have learned nothing, and many other Englishmen remained unaware, perhaps deliberately, of the rising tides of change. "The result is that in place of building a new Jerusalem we have not yet so much as set seriously to work on the repair of the old jerry-built town," complained the *Guardian:*

WE HAVE OVER A MILLION UNEMPLOYED, PRICES RANGING AS HIGH AS EVER, WORK NO LESS DIFFICULT TO GET DONE, TAXATION (EXCEPT FOR THOSE FORTUNATE ENOUGH TO MAKE WAR PROFITS) MAINTAINED AT THE WAR LEVEL, A FOURTEEN TO FIFTEEN HUNDRED MILLION BUDGET, DEBT STILL BEING PILED UP, ENORMOUS EXPENDITURE INCURRED ON THE ARMY, NAVY, AND AIR FORCE WITH INDEFINITELY GREAT COMMITMENTS IN RUSSIA, AND CONSCRIPTION MAINTAINED TO AN UNCERTAIN DATE. . . . IT IS HARDLY POSSIBLE THAT THIS CONDITION SHOULD CONTINUE FOR ANOTHER SEVEN OR EIGHT MONTHS AS IT HAS CONTINUED SINCE THE ARMISTICE.

Even the official peace celebrations of July 18 and 19 fizzled out in an ignominious display of crankiness. Some towns refused to celebrate at all: in Gloucester, ex-soldiers marched through the streets "in silent procession" as a protest against their grievances; the workers in Trafford Park were so incensed by the government's offer of only one day's holiday that they declined to take any days at all; Stalybridge postponed its celebration of Peace Day until August because the official holiday clashed with the town's annual Wakes; and in Cork, naturally, black flags flew in protest of the continued British occupation of Ireland. "On the whole," muttered a cynical observer, "it seems a very good thing the Government did not postpone Peace Day any further. If many more people had had time to remember their grievances—the cost of coal or clothes, for instance,—and this method of ventilating them, there might have been more protests than celebrations about to-day's programme." Even those who watched or participated in the victory parades found themselves battling the drenching downpour that descended upon the British Isles that weekend.

Undaunted by the rain and the grumbling, King George, Lloyd George, and Marshal Foch made a triumphal procession through the glistening wet streets of London, drawing great ovations everywhere they went. After the parade, a hardy band of loyal Englishmen gathered outside Number 10 Downing Street and endured several hours of soaking rain before Lloyd

George obliged them by coming out and making a little speech. Frances Stevenson found the scene quite touching; "The people *love* him," she wrote of the Prime Minister in her diary, "& he will do his best for them. I think there are very few statesmen who have been as *near* to them as he is." Later in the evening, at a dinner presided over by the Prince of Wales, Marshal Foch—perhaps overstimulated by the generous reception afforded him by the British people—abandoned his usual caution and announced, dramatically and quite indiscreetly, "Germany is ended! There is no Germany now! There are Germans, but no Germany. It is finished!" In relating the story to Riddell a week later, Lloyd George admitted dryly that he was "not quite sure that he [Foch] is right, but he repeated the statement several times."

Virginia Woolf, who sat in a window of her home at Richmond avoiding the processions, was considerably less enchanted by the spectacle. "I fear there will be few people to applaud the town councillors dressed up to look dignified & march through the streets," she wrote in her diary as a steady drip of rain pattered on the leaves outside. "I've a sense of holland covers on the chairs; of being left behind when everyone's in the country. I'm desolate, dusty, & disillusioned." Her servants, though, had enjoyed themselves tremendously: "a triumphant morning. They stood on Vauxhall Bridge & saw everything. Generals & soldiers & tanks & nurses & bands took 2 hours in passing. It was they said the most splendid sight of their lives. . . . But I don't know—it seems to me a servants festival; some thing got up to pacify & placate 'the people'—& now the rain's spoiling it; & perhaps some extra treat will have to be devised for them. Thats the reason of my disillusionment I think. There's something calculated & politic & insincere about these peace rejoicings." (In fairness to the government's efforts to provide popular entertainment, it should be noted here that Woolf was something of a snob when it came to mixing with the multitudes. She once described the London masses as "the usual sticky, stodgy conglomerations of people, sleepy & torpid as a cluster of drenched bees"; on another occasion she decided that a crowd in Hampstead Heath was, at close quarters, "destestable; it smells; it sticks; it has neither vitality nor colour; it is a tepid mass of flesh scarcely organised into human life. How slow they walk! How passively & brutishly they lie on the grass! How little of pleasure or pain is in them! But they looked well dressed & well fed. . . .")

Woolf finally relented and decided to attend the fireworks display the following evening. She set out for a vantage point on Richmond Hill; along the way she passed a woman of obvious wealth dead drunk, carried aloft by two male companions who were only half-drunk. The fireworks themselves proved disappointing, the rain having deadened the chemicals. Then Virginia looked the other way and saw a group of incurably wounded soldiers lying in their beds at the Star and Garter (an old hotel turned into a home for totally disabled veterans) with their backs to the celebration, smoking cigarettes, and only waiting—waiting, and wanting the noise to be over. The thought crossed Woolf's mind that she and the rest of the crowd were nothing more than children who needed somehow to be amused. "So at eleven we went home."

Worse than the rain or Virginia Woolf's misanthropy were the disturbances at Luton, where the town council refused permission for a memorial service to be held in the public park by discharged soldiers. Already angered over other grievances, including niggardly pension allowances, the veterans led a riotous mob that attacked the town hall, broke up the tables and chairs there and threw them out the windows, ripped down the bunting and decorations, and slashed the wires of the electrical illuminations. Amid the melee, the chief constable noted that the women in the crowd behaved quite as violently as the men; he later testified that "he could compare the scene only with what he imagined the French Revolution was like." After destroying the peace decorations, the mob set fire to a pile of papers and documents in the clerk's office and watched the town hall go up in flames. A few impatient spirits raided a nearby garage for extra gasoline to throw on the burning building. Firemen who attempted to put out the fire found their hoses cut; constables who tried to restore order were met with a fusillade of glass bottles. As the town hall collapsed in a heap of ashes, the crowd moved off to loot some stores, appropriating a piano from a warehouse and holding an impromptu sing-along in the night air. Thirty-nine people were arrested and charged with various rioting offenses.

Nor did affairs in England settle down appreciably after the "victory" celebrations. Army discipline was notoriously lax, largely out of a fear of inciting further mutinies among the disgruntled troops. Soldiers on leave in London refused to salute when they passed an officer on the sidewalk. The government had disrupted their lives, and sullen working-class veterans were going to make someone pay for it all. After four years on the Western Front, the prospect of violence no longer frightened them. And labor disputes continued to vex the government. Angered by constantly rising prices, wasteful government expenditures—particularly in the military sector—and blatant profiteering by unscrupulous businessmen ("I'd string up all persons who would take advantage of the sacrifices in blood made by the country," shouted one Labour MP), English workers demanded relief and recognition. "The worst feature of the present situation," lamented Lord Haldane, "is that the working classes refuse to believe anything we tell them." Coal miners, still vaguely dissatisfied with their position, threatened to strike over an interpretation of the Sankey Commission's wage recommendations and the still-unsettled question of nationalization. "There will be no peace in this country," warned Robert Smilie, "until the land belongs to the people. . . . The miner goes down and risks his life, but the bounder who claims the right to own it all never leaves his palace or mansion while night and day his neighbours are working for him in the collieries. It is an abominable state of affairs." Before Lloyd George intervened, 150,000 miners in Yorkshire staged a brief walkout that imperiled the nation's already low stockpiles of coal. Then the Triple Alliance suggested that its members consider a strike to compel the government to abolish conscription and abandon its ill-advised intervention in Russia.

Most ominous of all, however, was the sudden decision by the policemen's union to call a strike on the evening of July 31. The strike was prompted by the government's introduction of a bill that remedied most of the policemen's grievances by raising wages, improving pensions, and substituting a more democratic "national representative body," the Police Federation, for the despised local representative boards. So far, so good; but what alarmed the National Union of Police and Prison Officers was the accompanying provision that forbade policemen to retain membership in any labor organization other than the officially approved federation. Lloyd George and Home Secretary Edward Shortt had maintained all along that they would not permit the police force to establish a conventional trade union, and clearly this bill sounded the death knell for the union.

So the union called a strike on the grounds that policemen were entitled to independent representation. "The Government," the union manifesto thundered, "has dared to persist in its efforts to utilise political machinery to destroy your undoubted right to organise for the legal protection of your own interests. The preservation of your union and the future welfare of your wives and children wholly depend upon the full exercise of the power of your own organisation." The country held its breath as it awaited the coppers' decision.

The first night, only 240 out of 19,000 men in the Metropolitan Police force left their stations. The next day there were 850 strikers in London, most of them from the East End. By August 3 the total had reached 1,041 in London—but it never got much higher. Significantly, most of the strikers were ex-servicemen. The government promptly dismissed every striker and vowed never to reinstate any of them. In Liverpool, however, the strike attracted more support, and unleashed more lawlessness. Fully half of the 1,860 members of the Liverpool force walked out, and for several days the city was at the mercy of hooligans who emerged from the rabbit warrens that were the Merseyside slums and rampaged through the business districts; the looters, searching for the basic necessities of life as well as sound investments for the future, displayed a marked preference for looting clothing, jewelry, grocery, and bootmakers' shops. In all, nearly five hundred shops were attacked. Gamblers plied their games of crown-and-anchor and pitch-and-toss openly in the city streets. Down at the docks along the Mersey, storehouses were plundered repeatedly until the navy sent two destroyers and one cruiser steaming up the river. Loyal troops were dispatched to Liverpool, but the soldiers refused to fire upon the looters; the army's role, they said, was to maintain order, and not to break the strike. (They did, however, stoutly defend two breweries from the depredations of the mob.) To make matters worse, Liverpool tramway workers and London's municipal employees chose this moment to go out on strike themselves, and the Triple Alliance—alarmed at the government's hard-line refusal even to consider a compromise with the policemen's union—made plans for a sympathy strike to force the government to reinstate the striking policemen.

Shortt called the police strike a clear-cut and definite case of mutiny and hinted at a dreadful Bolshevik plot to "hand the country over to the mercy of the criminal classes," while the Dean of St. Paul's Cathedral charged that England's labor unions were engaged in "open brigandage against the community," but these exaggerated warnings were greeted with considerable skepticism, if not amusement, by the public. Doomed by lack of support, the police strike fizzled out, and the union was forced to plead for amnesty for their members. The Cabinet refused to consider any wholesale reinstatement, claiming that there were already more than two thousand applicants to replace the 1,081 members of the Metropolitan Police who had walked out, although the Home Secretary did promise to make exceptions in cases of extreme financial hardship. Never since have British policemen gone on strike.

Confronted with this seemingly never-ending series of revolts and incipient uprisings (now two thousand London bakers were on strike, threatening the nation's daily bread supply), it was all Lloyd George could do just to survive, much less develop any comprehensive, farsighted plans for the future (such planning was never his strong point anyway). "The unexpected is always supervening to occupy one's time and attention," the

Prime Minister complained to a friend. "It is like building a house. You have no sooner started to get out the foundations than a party wall collapses, or the surrounding earth begins to fall in. Before you can proceed with your building operations you have to clear away the debris." Then he laughed. "I am not sure that twelve months of Bolshevism would not be a good thing for this country, so as to clear away a lot of the vested interests which are always stopping progress. . . . It is difficult to move when one is shackled and manacled." To the people Lloyd George continued to preach the virtues of national unity; that theme had worked wonders during the war, but now it rang a bit hollow, and even the Prime Minister seemed to realize this in less guarded moments. "If we all pull in different directions the boat will get on the rocks," he told an audience in Wales, "but if we pull together we shall get clear of the torrents, the reefs, and the rocks, and get into the fairway. Then," he added whimsically, "we can use the oars to beat one another by way of recreation."

Lord Riddell noticed that Lloyd George seemed "quite worn out"; he noticed an underlying "sense of weariness and effort" in the Prime Minister: "Also he seemed physically tired, and I noticed that when he got up from a low couch his face flushed up as if the effort were considerable. He has aged greatly during the past six months." Lloyd George told Riddell he intended to take a month-long vacation in Brittany in September. "I must have peace and quiet," the Welshman sighed. "There is no real peace in this country. I cannot get away from people. There is a fresh crisis every day. Now sometimes we have two in a day." To top it all off, Frances Stevenson came down with influenza in August; Lloyd George, who had a morbid fear of contagious diseases, consoled her from a safe distance.

Lloyd George was exhausted and depressed; no more did anyone else in Britain know quite what to make of the postwar world. From Kings College at Cambridge, John Maynard Keynes gloomily concluded that he no longer believed in the stability of the things he admired. Eton was doomed, he decided, also the governing classes, and perhaps even Cambridge, too. The *Manchester Guardian* found "everywhere, in all classes, a vague disappointment that the victorious England is not the England of August 4, 1914. . . . Something seems to be lost of the spirit which fired us then, and we cannot get it back any more than the parents can get back their sons."

Nor did sexual matters escape the general upheaval. The war had left Britain with a shortage of men: in the summer of 1919 there were nineteen females to every fourteen males—6,542,655 to 4,492,927, to be precise. The disparity was even greater—two to one—among those considered to be of marriageable age (fifteen to forty years old). Obviously a lot of British women in the postwar generation were never going to be married or bear children. The divorce rate, which had doubled in 1918, climbed even higher in 1919 (and in fact kept rising through the early 1920s). A court in Manchester disposed of eighty-six undefended divorce cases in one day alone, with three judges each handling fifteen cases an hour. Bigamy, too, was on the rise. Unwanted illegitimate children seemed to be everywhere; born during the war, they were often forced from their homes and their mothers when soldiers refused to return to unfaithful wives unless the evidence of infidelity—the innocent unfortunate children—was moved out. There was also a perplexing epidemic of police cases involving teen-aged runaway girls, most of whom, when they were located several weeks after their disappearance, claimed they had been led astray by disreputable young men, often of exotic backgrounds. (This sort of thing fed upon itself, of course; reading of other girls' experiences, thrill-seeking young women decided to try it for themselves. And witless parents, reading in the morning paper of runaways found in London, suddenly would be moved to remark, "By the way, I've not seen our Lizzie for about six weeks now.")

For thousands of Englishmen, this was the first August in five years that they had been able to enjoy a vacation at the seashore, where sandbags and sinister rolls of barbed wire had ruled during the war, and the invasion of determined holidaymakers overwhelmed the seaside towns. (Not all these vacationers came attached with a spouse, for the nation had resumed the prewar habit of separate holidays for otherwise quite happily married couples; the trend reflected the increased independence of British women, who were no longer content to tag along behind a husband who insisted on playing thirty-six holes of golf every day, or steering a five-tonner through a North Sea gale.) Every inch of conventional lodging in seashore hotels and inns had been booked for months in advance. Those without reservations were forced to display considerable ingenuity if they wished to sleep with a roof over their heads. Working-class families in resort towns who had never before taken in boarders put extra cots in their bathrooms, and travelers snapped them up eagerly. Other desperate vacationers slept in army huts, on landings, in bathing tents, or in deserted warehouses. Police occasionally permitted women and children to sleep in empty cells at the local stations. "The beaches were black with crowds," wrote Robert Graves, "queues waited outside bathing-machines and dressing-tents for their turn to swim." And there were other inconveniences as well. The Yorkshire miners' strike and the consequent coal shortage meant that many hotels could not provide hot baths for their patrons; the bakers' strike created a bread shortage; and England's waiters and waitresses also threatened to walk out once again.

No matter; it was peacetime and summer and that was enough: "In the bright windy weather, with a blue sky full of white bowling clouds, the visitors took no thought for the morrow."

As part of a major offensive to protect Great Britain's foodstuffs and agricultural properties, Lord Aberconway introduced a Rat Destruction Bill in Parliament to give local authorities additional power to compel recalcitrant property owners to institute effective measures against the rodent population explosion. On the military front, the War Office launched a full-scale assault to clear rats out of army camps throughout the country. The officers appointed to supervise the campaign held a council of war with the experts at the Rat Exhibition at the Zoological Gardens, and came away with the latest scientific advice to further their mission.

To add the coup de grace, the Board of Agriculture proposed a "national rat week" (October 20–27) to inaugurate an effective campaign against the island's rat population before winter set in. Village committees were encouraged to undertake voluntarily to lay bait and arrange trapping and ferreting expeditions, and then award prizes for the most rats destroyed within a given area. Those needing assistance in obtaining anti-rat materials were invited to write to the Rat's Branch of the Board of Agriculture, 4 Whitehall-place, S.W.1.

Trouble was, the rats were getting wise. They, too, had learned from the wartime experience how to organize themselves and cooperate to increase their chances of survival. Eyewitnesses reported that shortly after a military camp in the north of England was evacuated, "a wide and distinct track was observed over a neighbouring railway embankment, where the rats had struck across country to the coal tips." And when a professional exterminator tackled an excess of rats in a coal pit in Wales, miners witnessed "the extraordinary spectacle of an army of rats, several thousand strong, issuing in a compact mass from one of the outlets of the mine on the hillside."

Bathers in America found swimwear both enchanting and expensive in the summer of 1919. Marine-blue taffeta suits with cunning little ruffles and flounces were all the rage that summer, along with stunning satin outfits and the perennial black or black-and-white jersey favorites. Lovely to look at, yes, but the price of a complete bathing outfit had skyrocketed over the past few years. A top-of-the-line bathing suit by itself now cost $35, compared to $2.98 in 1912, but no fashion-conscious American bathing beauty could stop there. She needed a bathing cap to match the suit (another $6); a rubberized scarf ($12.50); a waterproof bag made of the same material as the suit ($6.50); a pair of demure satin bathing slippers ($5); and at least one pair of silk hose ($2.50) to complete the costume. Total cost: $67.50, more than three weeks' wages for most factory workers in the United States.

Any woman who wished to display her charms in the more daring modern fashions, however, was advised to stay away from Atlantic City's beaches. In July, Dr. Charles L. Bossert, the city's chief censor of beach styles, confirmed that his ban on bare knees would continue at least through the 1920 season. "One-piece bathing suits for women," Dr. Bossert admonished visitors, "will not be tolerated so long as I am in charge of the bathing grounds." Female bathers could wear either men's shirts and knickerbocker suits, or skirts that were long enough to conform to the requirements of good taste. Bossert also warned that Atlantic City's rule requiring women to wear stockings on the beach would remain in force. "Atlantic City does not aim to be prudish," the good doctor patiently explained. "It must, however, draw the line somewhere to save appearances." Meanwhile, in sinful New York, young women had finally started to experiment with the Parisian style of bare legs or transparent, "Eve-like" stockings. The new fashion was, in the new slang word from wartime France, positively "chic."

To enhance their sex appeal even further, American women could employ Radir Toilet Requisites, a line of cosmetics allegedly invented by a chemist who had found a way to utilize radium in commercial beauty preparations. "Radium energizes, vitalizes, and rejuvenates all living tissues," claimed the advertisements. "It is the greatest force for betterment of the skin, complexion and facial muscles." Consumers were invited to try Radior face creams and powders, talc, rouge, hair tonic, skin soap, chin pads, or forehead pads. "Try them once. You will prefer them always."

37

"Pray not for these people . . ."

Béla Kun's days were numbered. From the Right he faced the growing boldness of Hungarian counterrevolutionaries who had established their headquarters in the town of Szeged, ninety-six miles southeast of Budapest. From time to time these antiquated, feudal-minded fugitives would attempt a poorly planned and badly organized coup against Kun's Soviet regime; but their incompetent revolts, including one led by the students of one of the military academies in the capital, succeeded only in increasing support on the extreme Left for a wholesale Red terror. Despite Kun's irritation at the reactionaries' provocative behavior (after one unsuccessful coup attempt, he vowed that "blood shall flow henceforth, if necessary, to insure the protection of the proletariat"), he refused to turn power over to radical extremists such as Tibor Szamuely, the infamous "hangman of Hungary." But Kun could not prevent Szamuely from organizing squads of paramilitary "terror troops"—the Freikorps of Soviet Hungary—who operated outside the control of the Red Army.

The food shortage was becoming critical. Despite Hungary's withdrawal from Czechoslovakia, as ordered by the Peace Conference, the Allies were threatening to intensify the blockade, and Budapest was already virtually starving to death. Peasants in the surrounding countryside refused to send food into the city. Coal was nearly nonexistent and so the railroad system broke down, and then the factories that had been working closed again for want of fuel. There was no will to work anyway—why should Hungary be different from the rest of Europe? Army morale plummeted, and some Red battalions had to be disarmed for refusing to fight, but there were almost no munitions in any case. Corruption and graft spread throughout the government, and the Cabinet split into quarreling factions. The commander-in-chief of the Red Army, General Boehm, resigned in protest over the activities of the terror troops. The only saving grace for the Soviet regime was the even greater ineptitude of the White Hungarians. Even that advantage, however, was being lost as Allied and Rumanian military forces drew ever closer to Budapest.

In a last-ditch effort to save the Soviet republic, Kun sent envoys to Vienna to offer concessions to the Allies, and even traveled to the Austrian border himself on a railroad handcar for a personal meeting with Allied military representatives. But the Allies demanded, in effect, the unconditional surrender of the Communists: abolition of the Soviet system and the abdication of Kun himself. At the same time, Paris was secretly negotiating with the Hungarian trade unions, urging them to overthrow Kun and promising recognition and an end to the blockade if they replaced the Communists with a moderate Socialist government. Accordingly, on July 31 a conference of trade-union executives in Budapest presented Kun's government with a request to withdraw and hand power over to the Social Democrats. In despair over the rapidly deteriorating internal and military situations, Kun at last conceded defeat. "Very well," he told the Central Workers' Council in a choked voice, tears staining his face. "If you demand it, I must resign. I made the best fight I could." Ignoring pleas from the left wing not to abandon the revolution, the Cabinet resigned on the understanding that Hungary would be spared further foreign military intervention; Kun said he was "loaning" supreme power to the unions "to avert the pillage of the country by its enemies." The Soviet experiment had lasted 134 days. Predicting a White Terror in Hungary, Kun fled to Austria by plane under a safe conduct from the Allies; there he was interned in Vienna while the Austrian government decided what to do with him. Szamuely was killed near Wiener Neustadt while trying to cross the Austrian border. The board of management of the town's Jewish cemetery refused to allow his body to be buried there, on the grounds that Szamuely had been personally responsible for the murders of at least forty people in Hungary.

Premier Julius Peidl, a very moderate Socialist who had formerly served in Count Karolyi's liberal government, headed the new Socialist Cabinet that immediately applied to Paris for a cease-fire. Imagine Peidl's surprise when the Rumanian armies refused to halt their invasion following Kun's abdication. Instead, seventy thousand Rumanian soldiers marched right into Budapest and, with the White Hungarians from Szegedin by their side, surrounded the National Palace and trained machine guns on its windows while a Cabinet meeting was in session on the afternoon of August 6. They arrested the members of Peidl's government. In its place the Rumanians set up a regime led by Archduke Joseph, scion of the discredited Hapsburg dynasty; Joseph reportedly had been seen begging for food in the streets of Budapest just one month earlier.

The notion that anyone with even a grain of common sense would seriously attempt a restoration of the Hapsburgs through the violence of a foreign-backed military coup astounded American diplomats. Clemenceau sent a series of increasingly outraged notes to the Rumanians, chastising them for entering the capital and forcing a harsh armistice upon Hungary before the Allied generals could arrive. But the Allies had long ago lost any semblance of authority in Central and Eastern Europe; they had gone so long without a coherent policy for the region that now no one paid attention to any commands from Paris. Count Karolyi bitterly indicted the Allies for their stupidity. "The war was terrible," Karolyi said, "but the armistices have quite undone us. That is what they will not understand in the West. While conditions with them have improved greatly since the cessation of hostilities, in Central and Eastern Europe disorganization, anarchy, and uncertainty have been the dominant factors for ten months, and these countries are for the most part industrially, economically, and morally in chaos." The Allied ultimatum to Rumania demanding its immediate withdrawal from Hungary went unheeded.

Now the White Terror began. As in Munich, it was far worse than anything the Communists had done. In the anti-Bolshevik raids led by the Rumanian troops and the new Hungarian police force, more than seven thousand men and women were rounded up and thrown into prison. Shops were plundered, unarmed civilians shot down and their valuables stolen, farm livestock (cattle, hogs, chickens) seized and sent east across the border to Rumania. Herbert Hoover, who by all accounts was not an excessively emotional man, lashed out in a fury at the Rumanians. "Reaction like that in Hungary," he cried, "will revive Bolshevism all over Europe. If we hoped Bolshevism would die a natural death in Russia we have done more to prevent that death by tolerating a Hapsburg than by any other means we could have designed in a hundred years." The Rumanian army, he charged, was stealing food sent for the relief of Budapest, stealing it right before the eyes of Allied representatives and American Relief Commission officers. "Three or four days ago the Rumanians removed all the food, milk and medicine from the Children's Hospital of Budapest," Hoover said. "Eighteen children died the next day because there was nothing to give them. . . . For America to sit supinely by and see this situation is too much for any red-blooded Yankee." But all Hoover could do was suspend food shipments to Hungary until the Rumanians withdrew. Just so powerless were the United States and its Allies in Eastern Europe.

Tin Pan Alley was moving uptown. Formerly located on 14th Street in lower Manhattan, the creative headquarters of America's music factory now stretched along West 46th and 48th streets, on and off Broadway. There, five or six flights up the well-worn wooden stairs, perhaps next to a novelty firm or a bail-bond company, were the offices, each fortified with a half-dozen pianos, where professional tunesmiths banged out one hook-filled melody after another. In the summer of 1919, the hottest tickets were songs about soldier boys "coming back to baby" and sweet chicks "doing the shimmy with Jimmy."

Veteran songwriter (and former headline hoofer) Bert Kalmar, the man who gave the world "Floating Down the Old Green River," "Hello, Hawaii?" and "Where Did You Get That Girl" ("If you can find another, I'll take her home to mother"), explained the populist philosophy that governed life in Tin Pan Alley: "If we got anything that's really clever we cut it out; it wouldn't get across. If we come on something that has what you might call poetry in it, that goes, too. We don't aim to reach the highbrows, or just the Broadway bunch; what we want is something that everybody will understand right away, whether they're hearing it at a movie in some jerk town or on the phonograph in the Philippines." Kalmar, incidentally, later became Fred Astaire; that is, Astaire played Kalmar in the movie *Three Little Words*, the story of Kalmar's songwriting collaboration with Harry Ruby, played in the movie by Red Skelton.

As the welter of jangling sounds from America's musical soul assaulted the ears of pedestrians who pounded the pavements of New York while the city sweltered through August 1919, from the majority of legitimate theaters in the city there were no sounds but silence. Until August 7, this had been the most prosperous season in the history of the American theater—profitable, that is, for the handful of producers and theater managers who exercised virtually dictatorial control over this sector of the entertainment business, which in 1919 was America's fourth largest industry. For the vast majority of actors and actresses, the financial picture was considerably less bright.

Working conditions in the American theater were astonishingly abysmal. Rehearsals for new shows often extended for four or six weeks—some musicals requiring three months—during which time the actors received no wages at all, even though they had to pay for their wardrobes out of their own pockets (the exorbitant price of shoes worked a particular hardship upon poorly paid chorus girls). Managers could fire anyone in a show without notice, or lay off an actor indefinitely, during which time the idle performer was forbidden to work elsewhere. In fact, once a show opened and received good reviews, an unscrupulous manager might dismiss a high-salaried actor and promote an understudy to save money. No one was paid for special matinees given on Sunday evenings or other legal holidays. Often a manager would cancel a Saturday-evening performance, dock the actors for the lost show, and then put on an unpaid Sunday-evening performance instead.

To balance this one-sided business arrangement, exasperated performers had formed the Actors' Equity Association in 1913. Equity's representatives provided expert advice to individual players in their contract negotiations with theater managers; whenever a manager tried to break a contract, which many of them did repeatedly, Equity would take him to court. Between 1913 and 1919, the union garnered $460,000 in legal judgments for its members. It was not surprising, therefore, that when the standard theatrical contract of employment ran out early in the summer of 1919, the managers took a united stand in refusing to recognize or negotiate with the Actors' Equity Association in any new contract. They also refused to submit the question of union representation to arbitration. In other words, they set out to break Equity. Union members—including about 90 percent of the best-known performers in America, led by independently wealthy Equity president Francis Wilson—responded by first affiliating themselves with the American Federation of Labor, and then by calling a strike against "the Prussian bosses of the theatre." On the evening of August 7, the first strike in the history of the American theater got under way with a maximum of publicity. Equity's demands included recognition of the union; minimum engagements of two weeks; two weeks' notice of dismissal; a limited number of performances in a week and regular payment (not even time and a half) for any overtime performances; and a limitation on the number of free rehearsals.

Twelve theaters—nearly half of New York's first-class houses—were forced to cancel their shows that first night; the stricken dozen included the Knickerbocker (*Listen, Lester*), the Forty-Fourth Street Theater (*Gaieties of 1919*), the Schubert (*Ob, What a Girl*), and the Cohan & Harris Theatre, which was currently enjoying tremendous success with George M. Cohan's production of a vacuous but cleverly crafted bit of musical fluff entitled *The Royal Vagabond*. Most theater managers simply refused to accept the possibility that their players would actually fail to show up for a scheduled performance, and so they waited until the last minute before informing capacity audiences that the show had been canceled. Audiences had long walked out on actors; now the actors turned the tables. Unsuspecting theatergoers were bewildered; first they demanded their money back—refunds for this one night alone were estimated at $25,000—and then they wandered out into the streets, blocking traffic as they searched for alternative entertainment: movies, burlesque shows, restaurants and cabarets, or the few plays that Equity permitted to remain open. For the most part, audiences sympathized with the performers' eminently reasonable demands, although muttered epithets against the actors could be heard in the lobbies. "I think I'll go to South America tomorrow," remarked one distressed and disappointed society matron upon leaving the Cohan & Harris Theatre. "That's one place where you can do what you like to do."

Not everyone, it should be noted, was as distressed at the prospect of a prolonged actors' strike. Railing against what he called "the dirtiest business in America," Zionist leader Rabbi Stephen Wise described to the congregation of the Free Synagogue, at a meeting in Carnegie Hall, the baser aspects of a show he had recently attended in one of New York's finest theaters. "It was nothing less than the work of moral scavengers and filth producers," Wise cried. "The stage was filled with half-dressed women—though no more so than the boxes of the theatre itself, or the lobbies of the average hotel. It was the vulgar incarnation of impurity, spun about a display of hosiery and underwear." And Wise wondered why the returning doughboys enjoyed it so.

Equity immediately deemed the strike an overnight smash success. Union officials claimed that 1,200 new members signed up the day after the walkout began, bringing the union's membership to 5,400. Thus emboldened, Equity proceeded to call out the biggest names of Broadway's two premier musical attractions. Eddie Cantor, star of Ziegfeld's Follies, wavered back and forth, but finally joined his comrades in the walkout. "Mr. Ziegfeld and Mr. Erlanger are fine men," Cantor conceded, "and they pay me a lovely salary, but they don't associate with me. The people who associate with me call me 'scab.'" The managers struck back by hiring replacements for the striking actors and reopening three of the previously dark theaters. George M. Cohan hurriedly revised *The Royal Vagabond* and cast himself in two parts; serendipitously, one of his characters was supposed to hold a mortgage in his hand in one scene, and so Cohan wrote the script on the mortgage papers and held on to them for dear life throughout the entire performance, never letting go even while he was singing or taking flying leaps at the proscenium arch.

Few theatergoers were fooled into believing that plays featuring last-minute replacements were "just as good as the original." Picket lines of performers, skipping up and down 44th Street in white knickerbockers in front of the theaters, drew more crowds than the shows themselves. Ed

Wynn, the comedy star of *Gaieties of 1919*, proved especially entertaining with his ad-lib sidewalk patter. Other actors stood outside theater entrances and advised prospective patrons that the entertainment inside was "a bum show." Struck where it hurt the most—their pocketbooks—the producers and managers retained former Secretary of State Bainbridge Colby to initiate lawsuits totaling half a million dollars against the Actor's Equity Association and three hundred of its members for breach of contract. The actors responded by hiring former Attorney General George W. Wickersham to defend them against the suits.

Every management tactic to break the strike failed. Every time the managers hired replacement actors, Equity lured away enough players to wreck the show. When producers tried to bring along new plays, Equity called out its members from rehearsals. Chorus girls formed their own association and elected Marie Dressler its first president. Musicians and stagehands, too, organized and seriously considered a sympathy strike to support the actors. Stars such as John Drew and his nephews and niece— John, Lionel, and Ethel Barrymore—sent expressions of support to Equity. Al Jolson refused to act the scab and replace Eddie Cantor. Theaters were reduced to importing burlesque shows or movies, while the striking actors stood fast, singing their battle cry to the tune of Cohan's "Over There":

> Over fair, over fair,
> We have been, we have been over fair.
> But now things are humming
> And the time is coming
> When with labor we'll be chumming
> Everywhere.
> So beware, have a care,
> Just be on the fair, on the square, everywhere.
> For we are striking, yes, we are striking,
> And we won't come back till the managers are fair.

On a pleasant New England summer afternoon, John D. Rockefeller stopped at a garage outside Portsmouth, New Hampshire, and asked the attendant to put five gallons of gasoline into each of the tanks of his four automobiles. The millionaire watched intently as the tanks were filled with the thirty-cents-a-gallon fuel; finally he called to the owner, Mrs. R. C. Dickey.

"Madam," Rockefeller asked, "are you sure your pump delivers a full gallon to the stroke?"

"Absolutely," replied Mrs. Dickey.

"Would you mind having it tested for me?"

"Not at all," answered the proprietor, willing to humor an old man.

As an attendant filled up a measuring bottle, the millionaire who once had wielded dictatorial power over the American oil refining and distribution industry saw that each pump measured one gallon precisely. Rockefeller smiled, not at all embarrassed. "It's the first pump I've seen for several days which is accurate," he told Mrs. Dickey. "Thank you for measuring it for me."

Rockefeller's contemporary and fellow industrial giant, Andrew Carnegie, was dead at the age of eighty-four. Flags flew at half-mast in the steel city of Pittsburgh. Enfeebled since a bout with pneumonia in 1917, the Laird of Skibo Castle succumbed to another sudden attack of bronchial pneumonia and passed away at his estate in Lenox, Massachusetts, on the morning of August 11. The voice that had struck terror into the heart of American finance, the heart that had given away money freely but judiciously, the mind that had searched for a path to universal peace—was gone. Nor would his like ever be seen again. "Kindly, simple, and human, Mr. Carnegie always remained proud of his humble start in life," recalled the liberal *Nation* in its eulogy to the steel master. "But the future order of society will not permit the duplication either of his career or Mr. Rockefeller's."

Born in the tiny hamlet of Dunfermline, Scotland, in 1835, the son of a weaver who shortly thereafter lost his livelihood to machines, Carnegie reportedly earned his first penny by reciting Burns's lengthy and tiresome poem "Man Was Made to Mourn." In 1848, the Carnegie family emigrated to the United States, settling in Allegheny City, Pennsylvania, just across the river from Pittsburgh. From a start as a lowly bobbin boy earning twenty cents a day in a cotton factory (where a gentleman merchant gave the lads free use of his library, a generosity that permanently instilled a love of books in the impressionable young boy), Carnegie advanced to positions as telegraph clerk with the Pennsylvania Railroad, private secretary to the railroad superintendent, supervisor of the Union government's telegraph communications at the start of the Civil War (he was allegedly the last man on the last train out of Bull Run after the rout began), fledgling investor in a railroad sleeping-car company, and finally leader of the Union Iron Mills company, which the canny Scotsman eventually parlayed into the Carnegie Steel Company. In 1901 Carnegie sold his firm to J. P. Morgan's United States Steel Corporation for a purchase price of $420 million. ("What a fool I was!" Carnegie later admitted to a congressional committee. "I have since learned . . . that we could have received $100 million more from Mr. Morgan if we had placed that value on our property.") He attributed his success in business to the talents of the men he hired; for his own epitaph, he wrote, "Here lies a man who knew how to enlist in his service better men than himself."

Although he made his fortune in steel, Carnegie was a lifelong advocate of disarmament and measures to promote the peaceful settlement of international disputes. He agreed to make armor plate for the United States Navy only at the personal request of President Benjamin Harrison, and scathingly denounced the fearsome dreadnoughts, the most powerful battleships of the early twentieth century, as " 'Dread-everythings'—dread wounds, dread shot, dread drowning, dread savage, hellish passions; dread miserable, tortured, fruitless death."

His one great clash with organized labor came with the bloody Homestead Strike of 1892, which occurred while Carnegie was vacationing in the Scottish Highlands and, he claimed, out of contact with his subordinates. Certainly no one could accuse him of harboring reactionary political sentiments. A staunch advocate of the income tax, Carnegie also supported the establishment of heavy taxes upon inherited wealth. "A heavy progressive tax upon wealth at death of owner is not only desirable," Carnegie declared, "it is strictly just." For his part, Carnegie sought to avoid that problem altogether by giving away as much of his fortune as he could. In a famous article published in *The North American Review* in 1898, the steel baron wrote: "The day is not far distant when the man who dies leaving behind him millions of available wealth, which were free for him to administer during life, will pass away 'unwept, unhonoured, and unsung,' no matter to what use he leaves the dross which he cannot take with him. Of such as these the public verdict will be: 'The man who dies thus rich dies disgraced.' "

Carnegie's attorneys estimated that he had given away more than 90 percent of his estate before he died, a total of $350 million, to libraries, to the Carnegie Institute, to peace societies, to Carnegie Hall, and to many, many others; but never to beggars. His overriding philosophy was to help people help themselves: "I never give a cent to a beggar, nor do I help people of whose record I am ignorant; this at least is one of my really good actions."

Still, Carnegie's fortune totaled over $25 million at the time of his death. After making adequate provisions for his wife and daughter, Carnegie's will left annuities of $5,000 each to the widows of Presidents Theodore Roosevelt and Grover Cleveland, an annuity of $10,000 to former President William Howard Taft, and—much to the British Prime Minister's surprise and delight—a similar amount to the Welsh Wizard, David Lloyd George. He left nothing to Wilson, apparently, except the satisfaction of knowing that one of Carnegie's last letters enthusiastically welcomed the advent of the League of Nations. "I rejoice in having lived to see the day," Carnegie wrote to a friend on August 9, "when, as Burns puts it, 'man to man he world o'er shall brothers be and a' that.' I believe this happy condition is assured by the League of Nations and that civilization will now march steadily onward, with no more great wars to mar its progress."

In Germany the socialist revolution was dead and the dreams buried. In July the Ebert-Bauer Cabinet rejected its own Minister of Industry's plan to socialize German factories, a plan that really was nothing more than the permanent extension of wartime government control over the nation's industrial life via a series of central commissions. This proposal had been the last hope for true socialization, but the government caved in before the violent protests of Germany's manufacturing and commercial interests. The revolution that had begun with such high hopes in November 1918 had, by the end of August 1919, evolved into nothing more than a harmless resurrection of the Manchester school of liberalism. "For a short time after the revolution, anything might have been done," wrote Berlin's leading radical journal, "but the Majority Socialists who then came to power were idealess and helpless." Forced to rely upon the parties of the bourgeois center in the Assembly, Ebert's group now could not afford to disturb capitalism in any way. For the time being, the game of tax-dodging replaced the more sanguinary sport of open rebellion as a popular pastime among discontented German workers. Former Berlin police commissioner Emil Eichhorn, whose refusal to leave office had sparked the January revolt that cost Liebknecht and Luxemburg their lives, slinked into Weimar a fugitive from the Bloodhound's troops, hoping that his position as a member of the National Assembly would render him immune from prosecution.

On August 21, Count Harry Kessler attended Ebert's swearing-in ceremony at Weimar. The tone of the proceedings reminded Kessler of "a confirmation in a decent middle-class home." An organ was playing a solemn tune; the participants, dressed in black jackets, crowded between huge potted gladioli and chrysanthemums, Ebert wearing a frock coat and his gold-rimmed spectacles. Earlier that day, a popular Berlin illustrated magazine had published a photograph of Ebert and Noske in bathing trunks; as he watched the ceremony, Kessler could not get the image out of his mind. Then someone misplaced the text of the oath just as Ebert stepped up to swear allegiance to the Republic. The organ stopped playing; the members of the government searched for a copy of the oath; the audience grew fidgety; then at last someone found the paper, and the ceremony continued on until the end. "This petty drama as conclusion to the tremendous events of the war and the revolution!" exclaimed Kessler incredulously in his diary. "Pondering the deeper significance of it can bring tears very close."

Several days later, Kessler greeted a friend who shared his gloom, and who told him that the workers of Berlin were determined not to let Noske goad them into any more open revolts (although a few roughnecks did assault Noske when he and Ebert visited the Leipzig Fair). "It is my impression too," said Kessler, "that the revolution is provisionally over. Counter-revolution is on the march, with the monarchy clearly in the background. The revolution has come to a dead end through the incapacity of the Social Democratic Government team, the far greater experience and cunning of conservative civil servants, . . . the difficulty of creating socialism in a ruined country, and the physical exhaustion of the famished proletariat. Nothing can stand permanently still, so we shall now have the retrogressive movement, counter-revolution. That will be Germany's real defeat."

At his residence in Hanover, retired Field Marshal Paul von Hindenburg went for a walk every day with his wife and their little dachshund. Wearing a short, rough coat and a collar that barely closed around his thick bull neck, a panama hat on top of his straight-backed head, and poorly cut trousers around his burly figure, Hindenburg might have been a bank manager striding along the sidewalk in any city in Germany. But on August 29 the former hero was called upon to address the youth of Hanover, and his message proved that nothing had really changed. "We must again become what we were when the new German Empire was founded at Versailles, when I was among those able to raise the first cheer to the Kaiser," Hindenburg admonished the boys and girls. "The spirit of that great day must not be lost by us in this false and flabby time. You must take care of that." During the same month, a band of conspirators formed the National Union (*Nationale Vereingung*), an organization dedicated to preparing a military coup d'etat. Its leaders were Captain Pabst, the officer who had ordered the murders of Liebknecht and Luxemburg; an adventurer from East Prussia named Wolfgang Kapp; and General Ludendorff (always in the background, of course). Noske himself reportedly was approached several times by officers who urged him to lead a military revolt and establish a dictatorship, but the time was not yet right for a coup.

In Munich, where martial law kept entanglements of barbed wire in front of hotels, and machine guns in the entrance halls of the city's prominent buildings, the Communists accused of murdering the hostages in the Luitpold Gymnasium in the last days of the Red regime went on trial for their lives. One interested observer was Adolf Hitler, still stationed with the Second Infantry Regiment, working as a political indoctrination official for the Reichswehr (the reorganized German army, formed largely from the various already-existing Freikorps and volunteer units). If the army noticed radical socialist tendencies among any of its units in Bavaria, men like Hitler were dispatched to bring them back to the right way of thinking. Already Hitler was gaining a reputation as an excellent orator who could expound vehemently upon the betrayal of November 1918 and the disgraceful tragedy of Versailles; he was also recognized as an expert on what was euphemistically called "the Jewish problem." Though he was not blessed with a particularly prepossessing appearance ("a pale, small face under an unsoldierly flowing lock of hair, with close-cropped mustache, and remarkable large light blue eyes that shone fanatically"), Hitler's ability to play upon his listeners' deepest fears and dreams and his forceful, guttural style of delivering his message held audiences spellbound. "He commands absolute attention from his listeners, and speaks with total conviction," recorded a witness in Munich. Aside from his duties as a speaker, Herr Hitler was assigned from time to time to investigate some of the bizarre little political organizations shooting forth like weeds from the fetid soil of Munich. At the end of the summer he attended a meeting of the German Workers' Party.

No one was going to catch either the Chicago White Sox or the Cincinnati Redlegs. By the time August was over, the Sox were six games ahead of their nearest rival and coasting home. "Detroit's gone," exulted Kid Gleason, "Cleveland's pitchers are too easy for us, Jimmy Burke has a good ball team [St. Louis] but is too far away, and the rest of the league doesn't worry us in the least. My team is in fine shape now—better than it has been all season. Williams and Cicotte are at their best. . . . There's nothing to it now. There's no chance for us to lose. It's the American League flag and then the world's championship."

Eddie Cicotte's record stood at a sparkling 24–7, followed closely by Lefty Williams's 20–7. (Both pitchers, coincidentally, had been owned and released by the Detroit Tigers several years earlier.) Clark Griffith, long-time manager of the hapless Washington Senators, echoed Gleason's confidence in Chicago's ability to win it all in 1919. "They have a whirlwind attack and a wonderful defense," said Griffith, describing the Sox as "a real, blown-in-the-glass club" that never stopped fighting.

During a series between the Sox and the Philadelphia Athletics, Chicago management, led by club owner Charles Comiskey, asked police to station detectives in the bleachers at Comiskey Park to help control the insidious gambling epidemic. Four men were arrested for betting on one of the games (they were offering odds of 4 to 3 in favor of the home team); the authorities confiscated fifty dollars. The gambling, of course, did not stop.

38

"But I was like a lamb

or an ox that is

brought to the slaughter . . ."

Grayson had persuaded Wilson to delay his swing around the circle to explain the treaty and the League of Nations to the American people, but by the end of August, with the treaty still locked in Lodge's death grip, Wilson knew a cross-country tour was his only hope of rallying public support to the League and forcing the Senate to accept his handiwork without crippling amendments or reservations.

Wilson was plainly in no physical condition to undertake a strenuous campaign. H. H. Kohlstadt, a Chicago editor and close friend of Colonel House, visited the President at the White House and heard him speak about the tour and saw Wilson tired and ill. Kohlstadt told the President he was too sick to make the trip: "The heat will be intense in Ohio, Indiana, Illinois, Iowa and Nebraska. You will break down before you reach the Rockies." Wilson could hardly control the tremor in his hands. "I don't care if I die the next minute after the treaty is ratified," he replied. Kohlstadt sent an urgent message to House—who had been discarded by Wilson during the last month of the conference—and informed him that the President looked wretched and was badly in need of a long, long rest. Visiting Paris at the end of August, there was nothing at all House could do to help.

On August 29 the White House gave out the President's itinerary: thirty cities in twenty-seven states; eleven thousand miles and twenty-seven days. Wilson would leave Washington on the evening of September 3 and make his first speech in Columbus, Ohio; then on through Indiana, Missouri, Iowa, Nebraska, Minnesota, the Dakotas, Montana, Idaho, the Pacific Coast, Nevada, Colorado, Kansas, and Oklahoma.

Grayson made one last effort to dissuade his patient. He walked into the President's study one morning. Wilson sat at his desk, writing. He looked up at the doctor and said he knew why Grayson had come. His words were those of a man perfectly at peace with the prospect of martyrdom. "I do not want to do anything foolhardy," Wilson said, "but the League of Nations is now in its crisis, and if it fails I hate to think what will happen to the world. You must remember that I, as Commander in Chief, was responsible for sending our soldiers to Europe. In the crucial test in the trenches they did not turn back—and I cannot turn back now. I cannot put my personal safety, my health in the balance against my duty—I must go." Wilson stood, still grasping his pen in his hand, and walked to the window and stared silently at the Washington Monument for a few seconds, then turned back to Grayson with tears welling in his eyes. Grayson hesitated and then left the room. He knew.

NINE

THE DAYS
OF THE
THIEF

"There is no hope:

no; for I have

loved strangers,

and after them will I go . . ."

39

Movies are a marvelous teacher of the young. In the spring of 1919, when an Illinois high school history teacher gave her class a test containing the question, "Who participated in great political debates in 1858?" one student answered cheerfully, "Lincoln and Douglas Fairbanks."

Certainly the energetic and acrobatic Fairbanks was one of the world's three most popular film stars in 1919, along with Mary Pickford and Charlie Chaplin. Although much shorter in real life (about five feet five inches in his stocking feet) than he appeared on the screen, Doug could accomplish virtually any daring physical feat humanly possible—and keep the famous Fairbanks smile on his face all the while. "He had extraordinary magnetism and charm and a genuine boyish enthusiasm which he conveyed to the public," Chaplin recalled admiringly. "He had," added one of Fairbanks's favorite directors, "the quality of floating through the air, like Nijinsky."

Fairbanks, fortunately, escaped Nijinsky's madness, but in the summer of 1919 the Hollywood idol had worries of his own. His personal and business affairs were in the process of undergoing a revolutionary turn. Back in January, Fairbanks had joined forces with his good friends Pickford (who was also his lover) and Chaplin, along with celebrated director David Wark Griffith, to form the United Artists Corporation. Western star William S. Hart was also invited to join, but declined rather than invest his own money in the venture. United Artists was primarily a response to a merger planned by the two leading film distribution companies of the time, First National Exhibitors and Adolph Zukor's Paramount Pictures Corporation (which itself had recently merged with Famous Players–Lasky). The movie industry was a tightly controlled operation in those days, dominated by a handful of distribution firms who acted as middlemen between the producers and the exhibitors. Most actors and actresses were treated as salaried employees, who, after the war, were in very real danger of having their wages severely reduced, with no option but to accept management's offer. On the other end, the nation's 25,000 movie exhibitors were forced to take whatever the distributors offered them—which usually included scores of inferior films in the same package with the top box-office draws. If First National and Paramount were allowed to merge without opposition, the movie business was liable to find itself under the thumb of a billion-dollar trust to rival the Carnegie-Morgan combination in the steel industry.

Fairbanks's contract with Paramount was due to expire in early 1919, and he saw absolutely no reason to sit still and watch the profits of his popularity fall into the pockets of a bunch of undeserving business executives. Besides, he had fallen in love with Mary Pickford during the Liberty Bond drives that had taken them across the country in 1917–18. (When Mary—who was still married to her first husband—and Chaplin visited Fairbanks on the weekends at his house in what was then the wilds of Beverly Hills, Charlie would occasionally be awakened at three o'clock in the morning by the sounds of a Hawaiian orchestra playing on the lawn, serenading Miss Pickford; Fairbanks loved that sort of grand romantic gesture.) So Fairbanks, Pickford, Chaplin, Griffith, and Hart decided to dine together one evening at the main dining room of the Alexandria Hotel in Los Angeles to discuss their plans for a joint production-distribution company of their own. The Alexandria, not coincidentally, was at that time playing host to a convention of First National's exhibitors, and the First National–Paramount talks reportedly were approaching a settlement (naturally, Zukor publicly denied all rumors of a merger). Just as the stars had anticipated, the president of First National walked into the dining room that evening and saw, to his astonishment, the five biggest names in Hollywood sitting together, writing astronomical dollar figures on the tablecloth. That looked like a bad sign. He retreated and consulted his associates. One after another, the movie moguls went to the door and saw for themselves. (Quite aware of the stir they were creating, Fairbanks and friends had a wonderful time mimicking their bosses' incredulous reactions.) The seriousness with which the producers treated their proposed venture convinced the stars that it was, in fact, a feasible idea.

The "big five" made no secret of their motives or their plans for United Artists. "The need for the present organization was brought about by the distributors themselves," announced the demure Miss Pickford, who probably had the most hardheaded business sense of any member of the new combine. "We are absolutely on the defensive, fighting with our backs against the wall, so to speak. People ask us why we didn't do this thing long ago. The answer is that we were never forced to do it before. But now, with the possibility of the merger of distributors looming before us—which threatens to dominate the picture theaters of the United States—it becomes necessary for the producing stars to organize as a protection to their own interests." Chaplin and Griffith, especially, looked forward to the freedom to allow their creative sensibilities free rein, unencumbered by financial restrictions imposed by philistine businessmen and accountants who insisted, among other things, that every picture have a happy ending, because movies with happy endings made more money. "We are willing to make certain pictures which we do not expect to make money," Griffith proclaimed pompously. "The reward of fame and glory for advancing the art is sufficient." United Artists' first president, Oscar A. Price, vowed that the company would release its films on the open market, so that every exhibitor could obtain those he wanted without also having to purchase and subject his audiences to a package of unprofitable and unpopular pictures. "We intend to introduce a new and more friendly relationship between the artists and their public," promised Price. (Incidentally, Fairbanks first offered the presidency of United Artists to his friend, William G. McAdoo, the heir-apparent to the Wilson organization within the Democratic party, but McAdoo preferred to stay out of the cinematic spotlight and asked for the post of corporate general counsel instead. Oscar Price had been his right-hand man when McAdoo headed the United States Railway Administration during the war.)

Publicly, Zukor and his associates professed a total lack of concern at this unexpected turn of events. "So the lunatics have taken over the asylum," one film executive scoffed. A reporter asked Zukor if he was downhearted. "No," replied Zukor, "we have a big business and it will go right along." And would they develop new stars? "Yes. . . . We will go on just the same." Privately, Zukor begged the big five to take him, too, into the organization. They refused.

For Fairbanks and Pickford, of course, United Artists also provided a cover for their continuing love affair. During the last months of the war, Beth Sully Fairbanks had finally gotten wise to this behind-the-cameras action; frustrated, Beth held a series of press conferences in the spring of 1918 in which she accused Mary Pickford of wrecking her eleven-year marriage with Doug. Reporters, realizing the import of such charges, refused to mention Mary's name in their stories; the threat of negative publicity hung especially heavy over Pickford, whose pristine image as

America's sweetheart could have been irrevocably damaged by mud slung during a messy divorce. Thus, when reporters questioned Fairbanks about his wife's allegations, he gallantly—and prudently—insisted the story was false: "It is a piece of German propaganda! It's on a level with the report they spread that I was shot." Beth filed for divorce, but even when a New York State Supreme Court judge issued the final decree, the divorce papers mentioned only "an unknown woman" as co-respondent. Beth, who received half a million dollars and custody of their eight-year-old son, Douglas, Jr., in the settlement, promptly married a Pittsburgh financier named James Evans.

Since Pickford and Chaplin still owed First National several more pictures under their old contracts, the burden of sustaining United Artists fell entirely on Fairbanks's shoulders for most of 1919. After turning out a propaganda short, "Knocking Knockers," for the Wilson administration to employ against its critics, Fairbanks started upon United Artists' first feature film, entitled *His Majesty*, co-starring a sweet, natural young starlet named Marjorie Daw. *His Majesty* was the tale of a missing heir (Fairbanks, of course) to the throne of a mythical kingdom in Europe. The film debuted in American theaters in September to the usual critical acclaim: "Doug does nothing essentially different from what has made him famous and familiar as the super-stuntist," wrote one reviewer, "but everything he does happens in more spacious surroundings and with a highly imaginative background, which makes it all." Writing in the *Los Angeles Times*, critic Edwin Schallert explained Fairbanks's appeal to movie audiences:

FAIRBANKS IS AN ESSENTIALLY CAPTIVATING PERSONALITY THAT LIVES AMID THE GLAMOR OF HIS CAPACITY FOR MOVEMENT. HE NEVER STOPS GOING ANY TIME. AND THE MIND ENJOYS RACING ALONG WITH HIM. HE CAN JUMP ACROSS THE GAPS AND CHASMS WHICH YAWN BETWEEN TWO MOUNTAINS OR TWO VILLAGE HOUSES WITH EQUAL APLOMB. HE CAN DIVE THROUGH A WINDOW OR ONTO A MAN'S SHOULDERS AS IF IT WERE THE MOST NATURAL KIND OF HUMAN EXERCISE. IT IS DELIGHTFUL TO WATCH HIM IN MOTION, BECAUSE HE IS LIKE SOME ALL-HUMAN HALF-REAL BEING— WHOSE ANTICS AND CAPERS ARE STIMULUS TO THE IMAGINATION.

By September 1, New York's theater managers had lost $1 million from the Equity strike. Twenty-five first-class theaters were dark; the strike had spread to Boston and Chicago; George M. Cohan's efforts to organize a rival actor's union, the Actors' Fidelity League (nicknamed the "Fidos" by scornful Equity members) fell flat; and Equity was keeping its coffers filled by sponsoring its own all-star variety shows. Feelings ran high on both sides. Embittered by personal attacks upon him and his family, Cohan (who took the strike more to heart than anyone else) resigned his position as reigning Abbot of the Friars' Club; three hundred Friars marched en masse down Broadway to beg him to reconsider, but an angry Cohan took the cigar out of his mouth only long enough to refuse their request. "I am not going to associate as a fellow-club member with actors who insult me and my family," Cohan said. "I am an actor and have always been a friend of the actor. The stage is my life, but I value my manhood above everything else." An uneasy truce governed the actors' and managers' summertime vacation colony at Great Neck, Long Island, where guests at a party were greeted at the entrance by a sign that warned, "Don't talk business."

The deadlock broke when a walkout of performers and over four hundred stagehands on August 28 closed the Hippodrome Theater, known as the world's largest playhouse. Two days later, the Hippodrome's management gave in and signed contracts recognizing Equity and its fledgling sister union, the Chorus Equity Association. Confronted with sympathy strikes by the electricians' and musicians' unions, and anguished by the sight of closed theaters on Labor Day, traditionally the start of Broadway's fall season, the managers swallowed their pride and salvaged their profit sheets by agreeing to virtually all of the reforms Equity demanded. Negotiators hammered out the final settlement in a seven-hour session that ended at 3:00 A.M. on September 6. Once again the Equity contract became the standard agreement between individual actors and managers, although, as a symbolic concession to the managers' association, no actor would be forced to join Equity as a condition of employment. Cohan himself never joined Equity, and never forgot the emotional scars inflicted on him by the strike.

Every day for the past few weeks, the President had been plagued by painful headaches.

At seven o'clock on the evening of Wednesday, September 3, Woodrow Wilson left Washington. He was embarking on the most crucial political tour of his life (he tried to downplay its importance by referring to it as a "little errand") quite unprepared; the press of everyday business in the White House had kept him from composing any of the thirty different speeches he would be called upon to deliver. He would have to rely on notes jotted down as he went along. At Union Station, Wilson heard scattered applause from a small gathering of well-wishers as he walked to his special train. Standing on the platform as the porters loaded all the paraphernalia of a presidential voyage onto the train, Joe Tumulty thought back over all the years since he had first served with Wilson when Wilson was governor of New Jersey; Tumulty decided he had never seen his boss look so weary.

There were seven cars in the special train as it started on its eleven-thousand-mile trek. Most of the space was taken up by reporters (about thirty of them, all men), Secret Service agents, stenographers, and movie cameramen. There was also a diner and a club car; last in line was Wilson's blue private car, the *Mayflower*, complete with double bed and sitting room. The grueling schedule of the voyage meant that most stops were going to be limited to three or four hours at most, and so the President and his party would be forced to sleep on board the train nearly every evening.

Following a brief layover in Baltimore, Wilson headed westward through the night.

Thursday, September 4. Shortly after dawn, the train stopped in the little town of Dennison, Ohio, to change engines. Wilson walked onto the observation platform at the rear of the *Mayflower* and saw thirty or forty people gathered below in the early-morning fog and drizzle to shake his hand and exchange pleasantries. One man came up to him and said, "I wish you success on your journey, Mr. Wilson. I lost two sons in the war; I only got one left, and I want things fixed so I won't have to lose him." Someone else called out that Dennison had voted against Wilson in 1916, but would support him if he ran again in 1920. "Oh, no," Wilson laughed as he shook his head. A group of Red Cross girls were waiting to feed a trainload of soldiers that was following the special; Wilson told them he regretted he would not be on hand to greet Pershing when the general arrived in New York from France later that day.

Eleven o'clock. At Columbus, where a streetcar workers' strike kept many people from reaching the downtown district, Wilson was met by Dr. W. O. Thompson, a former classmate at Princeton and now president of Ohio State University. "I declare, Mr. President, you look younger every time I see you," Dr. Thompson allowed graciously. "Well, I'm feeling as fit as ever," Wilson lied, "and it makes my heart young again to see you." Then the President rode along Broad Street past sparse crowds along the route to Memorial Hall. A company of infantry from the local barracks walked in front of his car, airplanes banked over his head and dropped bunches of flowers, a long string of automobiles snaked out behind, and the chimes of Trinity Church played "America" as he passed. Wilson wore a straw hat and an ordinary business sack suit, Mrs. Wilson a blue dress and sable scarf. At eleven-thirty, Wilson walked onto the speaker's platform at the auditorium as a young woman led the audience in singing "Dixie." The crowd gave Wilson a standing ovation. Mrs. Wilson stood beside him, clutching a bouquet of red roses.

Wilson had originally intended to use this tour to "explain" the treaty and the League Covenant to the people, and not to waste his energy in flailing attacks upon his Senate opponents. Thus he seemed relatively restrained, oratorically speaking, as he told his audience in Columbus that "the League of Nations is the only safeguard against more wars," and "I would rather have every one on my side than be armed to the teeth." The League should be ratified, he said; it would be ratified, it must be ratified to keep faith with the American boys sent abroad to fight the war that must have ended all wars. "If we do not do this thing," Wilson insisted, "we have neglected the central covenant we made to our people." And the President gave his listeners his personal (and biblical) assurance that the treaty of peace was a just and honorable settlement: "If I couldn't have brought back the kind of treaty I brought back, I wouldn't have come back, because I would have been an unfaithful servant."

Trouble was, the people had grown weary of listening to lectures and debates over the League. What they wanted was a good knock-down, drag-out political brawl.

In the afternoon Wilson chatted with reporters in the club car for half an hour. They noticed that he looked relieved to be away from Washington. Wilson hadn't planned to make a lot of rear-platform speeches every time the train stopped for fuel or maintenance checks, but when the people gathered around the *Mayflower* and called out "Woodrow!" or "Woody!" he just couldn't resist the temptation to say a few words. Women implored Mrs. Wilson to come out: "Mrs. Wilson!" they cried, "Show us Mrs. Wilson!" "Very well," the President said, "but she's more shy than I am." So a moment later his wife appeared on the platform bearing a bunch of flowers in her arms. "Speech, Mrs. Wilson!" Blushing, she promptly turned around and fled back inside to safety.

Six o'clock. Indianapolis. The Wilsons were competing with the Indiana State Fair. "This league," the President shouted to a restive audience at the Coliseum, "is the only conceivable arrangement which will prevent our sending our men abroad again very soon. . . ." People in the back of the enclosed elliptical arena couldn't hear Wilson above the unruly crowd, and so they walked out. The undercurrent of noise grew worse. Finally the President had to stop while someone stood up and told everyone either to stay and shut up or leave, and then the police closed and barred the doors. Wilson then continued, using the admonition to the crowd as his text as he defended the League: "If it is not to be this arrangement, what arrangement do you suggest to secure the peace of the world? It is a case of put up or shut up." The League, he said, "is the only thing that can prevent the recurrence of this dreadful catastrophe and redeem our promises," and again he pledged that "when this treaty is accepted men in khaki will not have to cross the sea again. I say 'when it is accepted,' for it will be accepted." Wilson noticed that his fighting phrases earned more enthusiastic applause than his noble expressions of morality. At ten o'clock the train left for St. Louis.

Friday, September 5. Wilson's train arrived in St. Louis at 4:00 A.M.

Rozier Wickard, a former army pilot, was arrested on a charge of threatening President Wilson's life. "Some man would go down in history if he had the nerve to kill that ———," Wickard allegedly said. "I wish I could have the opportunity myself."

The *Washington Post* disclosed that the Senate Foreign Relations Committee was ready to report the peace treaty to the full Senate with four major reservations: first, the United States reserved the right to withdraw unconditionally from the League of Nations upon giving the required notice; second, the United States declined to assume "any obligation to preserve the territorial integrity or political independence of any other country or to interfere in controversies between other nations . . . or to employ the military and naval forces of the United States in such controversies"; third, the United States would decide for itself what matters remained within its own domestic jurisdiction and out of the League's meddlesome purview; and fourth, the United States refused to submit for inquiry or arbitration any issue arising under the Monroe Doctrine. Clearly, the cumulative effect of these amendments struck at the very heart of the League Covenant and rendered American membership virtually meaningless. The *Post* added that events on Capitol Hill over the past few days had made it evident that these reservations would gather an overwhelming majority in the Senate.

In St. Louis, Wilson waved his straw hat to the crowds who pushed through the troops and massed around his car to shake his hand. (The President's choice of hats was causing considerable dismay among the members of the local reception committee. They had been advised that new fall headgear would be *de rigueur* at the luncheon; then Wilson, to beat the heat, appeared wearing a straw kelly.) The President saw signs asking him to TELL IT TO THEM, WOODROW, and assuring him that WE ARE WITH YOU, WOODROW. At several points the procession was disrupted by a car filled with wildly shrieking women; the car evaded police by dodging down side streets and reappearing time and again to confront Wilson with huge placards urging an end to wartime prohibition. Photographers shouted for Mrs. Wilson to turn this way, please. The heat grew worse.

Wilson was finding it harder and harder to restrain himself from bitter denunciations of his senatorial opponents. At a luncheon address to 1,200 St. Louis Chamber of Commerce members, the President declared that any little men who refused to see the noble quest of making peace and a new world through to the end were, in his eyes, "absolute, contemptible quitters." ("Swat 'em!" someone shouted.) Such small-minded men were, Wilson said, incapable of altruistic sentiments themselves and hence could not accept that anyone else might truly be motivated by high moral feelings. Such men would, by their cowardice, make the name of America despised and distrusted among the family of nations. And such men, Wilson charged, were no more than fossils who remained obdurately mired in the muck of the old world that had been swept away by the war and the peace settlement and the magnificent rising tide of public sentiment all over the world. (As a *Post* editorial pointed out, these were fighting words indeed. "A quitter," said the *Post*, "is the 'yellowest' two-legged animal on earth, in the popular conception of the word. He is a mixture of a cheater and a coward, one with pretensions, but lacking the stamina to carry them through; a trimmer, a side-stepper, a four-flusher, a welsher and various other things the names of which may not be found in the dictionary, but which carry real significance among red-blooded men. No adjective is needed to describe a quitter; the whole tribe is contemptible.")

That evening, at the St. Louis Coliseum, where he had received his nomination for a second term in the White House in 1916, Wilson left his audience with no illusions about the League's importance for the future of America: "If we keep out of this arrangement war will come soon. If we go into it war will never come." (Deciding that the President's heat-beating straw hat was a good idea, the entertainment committee had brought out their own boaters for the evening address; Wilson crossed them up again by wearing a cutaway coat and a shining silk hat brought home from Paris.) At 9:15 the presidential party drove down to the train station. Before the special pulled out, Wilson sat for a time on the railing of the observation platform, idly swinging one leg, while hundreds of staring spectators pressed against the iron pickets of the train shed fence a few feet distant. "Hey, Woodie!" they shouted, and called for a speech or a few brief remarks. "Oh, no," said Wilson as he grinned and waved. He refused to say anything more. The *Mayflower* was beginning to look like a conservatory, with all the flowers presented to Mrs. Wilson; she solved the problem by donating most of the bouquets to hospitals along the way. The train left St. Louis at 11:00 P.M.

The *Post* reported that the anti-League forces in the Senate had been strengthened that day by further desertions from the administration's ranks.

Saturday, September 6. Early in the morning the train paused at Independence. Hearing that Wilson was in town, housewives dressed in their rumpled everyday clothes hurried down to the tracks, dragging small children along for a once-in-a-lifetime chance to see the President. Wilson, immaculately attired in a morning coat, came out and shook their hands as dozens of barefoot, freckled boys in overalls scampered about the yard, shouting, "Come on, here he is!" This was Jesse James's old home country, and as the train rolled along to Kansas City, the conductor pointed out to Wilson the scenes of the James Gang's nefarious escapades.

At ten o'clock the Kansas City Convention Hall was suffocatingly hot, the galleries packed to the roof. Wilson's oratory reached fever pitch. The President vowed, mentioning no names, that the "gentlemen" (he was careful not to say "senators") who were fighting against the League for their own private political purposes would "at last be gibbeted, and they will regret that the gibbet is so high." Mere negative criticism of the treaty was nothing but unadulterated Bolshevism, pure and simple, the President shouted in a cracking voice. "Little groups of selfish men must not plot the future of America." (Warned of the President's preference for straw hats in St. Louis the previous morning, the men of the Kansas City welcoming committee had donned their own panamas. Naturally, Wilson wore a brand-new brown fedora when he greeted them at the station.)

Eight o'clock in the evening. The Republican stronghold of Des Moines. Wilson wore a silk hat once more. There was no relief from the headaches. Bishop Longley, of the local Episcopal Church, pronounced the invocation preceding Wilson's speech. Longley prayed "that God might so direct the Senate of the United States that peace may come to this country and to all the world. . . . that those who oppose the Covenant of the League might come out of the darkness in which they dwell and see the new vision which is before the universe." Wilson appeared to be deeply moved. That evening he slept in a suite at the Hotel Des Moines, the first night he and his wife had escaped their railbound prison since leaving Washington; Wilson said he felt like taking three baths to wash away the grit and grime of the train.

Sunday, September 7. A day of rest. The President and his wife attended services at Central Presbyterian Church in Des Moines and took an automobile ride in the afternoon. Grayson was growing more concerned over the President's almost complete lack of exercise, although he told reporters that the day off had done Wilson a world of good.

The train left Des Moines at midnight. So far, the mechanics of the trip had gone off without a hitch. Dick Jervis, the head of the Secret Service contingent, had arranged to have cars awaiting Wilson at the precise point in front of every depot; platforms were cleared before the President's train pulled in; at each luncheon or dinner, seats were assigned to everyone well in advance, and Charles Swem, Wilson's stenographer, was always seated not more than ten feet from the President. And at nearly every stop, someone was waiting to hand Mrs. Wilson another bouquet.

Monday, September 8. The train spent the early-morning hours in a peaceful cornfield near Omaha to give Wilson a few more precious hours' sleep. Then in his scheduled address, Wilson assured an audience of five thousand that reservations to the League Covenant were not necessary; the League would never interfere with American domestic affairs. Holding aloft a copy of the peace treaty, Wilson shouted, "This is the work of honest men." And, he added, "if I felt that I personally in any way stood in the way of this settlement, I would be glad to die that it might be consummated. . . ." Reporters decided that Omaha had provided the smallest crowds and the least enthusiastic reception accorded the President thus far.

In the afternoon, the train rolled through the midwestern cornfields, where the crops were better than they had ever been and prices near an all-time high. One businessman explained that this was the reason for the poor turnout at Omaha: "We are too busy making money out here to care much about the league of nations." Farmers proudly informed Wilson that "there will be enough corn raised in Iowa this year to load wagons with 50 bushels each and stretch a belt westward across the United States, over the Pacific, across Siberia and all Europe, and back to San Francisco. And they would still be loading corn in Des Moines then."

Back in Washington, Senators Borah and Johnson warned Americans that the United States presence in Russia in an "undeclared, undisclosed war" was precisely the sort of military involvement the country could expect under the aegis of the League of Nations. The senators were making preparations for their own cross-country tour as a sort of 1919-style "truth squad," to give the people both sides of the story and allow them to decide whether they wanted "to substitute this super-government of a league of nations for our republic."

The Times of London was amazed at the spectacle of the Senate in revolt against the treaty fashioned so painstakingly at Paris: "That the treaty could be rejected in any circumstances is incredible."

It was raining when Wilson's train pulled into Sioux Falls, South

Dakota, that evening. A Shriner's band led the parade to the Coliseum, where eight thousand awaited the President's words. Mrs. Wilson sat next to her husband on the platform; two small, shy girls walked across the stage and presented her with more roses, and she kissed the girls as the crowd applauded. Republican Governor Peter Norbeck introduced Wilson. The President solemnly recounted the story of a woman who had come to see him at a way stop earlier that day; she took his hand, then broke into tears as she tried to tell him about her son who had been killed in France. This incident had reminded him, Wilson said in a voice deep with emotion and determination, that America had suffered so greatly not just to gain a temporary selfish advantage in its affairs with other nations, but to create a new world where war would never happen again and other women's sons would no longer die in battle.

40

"At that time . . .

they shall bring out

the bones of the kings . . ."

By early September there were an estimated 200,000 British troops in Ireland—more than ever before—and still more were coming over on nearly every boat. The military occupation was costing the British treasury an estimated one million pounds per month. At least six policemen had been shot and killed already this year; no one had been convicted of any of these murders. Day after day, the monotonous litany of rebel raids for arms and government trials for sedition continued. Sinn Fein refused to be intimidated by British threats; as an American critic of British policy saw it, "military rule was irritating without being effective." On the other hand, London certainly was not simply going to hand Ireland its freedom. Lloyd George, who viewed the position of the Ulster Protestants, led by Sir Edward Carson, as akin to the position of his native Wales as a minority enclave within Great Britain, gave repeated public pledges to protect the right of the six counties of Ulster in the north to separate treatment. The notion of partition, of course, was anathema to Sinn Fein, whose leaders refused either to negotiate or launch the sort of full-scale revolt that would give England an excuse to postpone Irish independence indefinitely.

Instead, the dismal cycle of terrorist attacks and reprisals went on and on. Shortly before eleven o'clock on the fine late-summer Sunday morning of September 7, a party of sixteen soldiers from the Shropshire Light Infantry were walking peacefully to morning services at the Methodist Church in Fermoy; they carried their rifles with them, but no ammunition. They passed six men standing by an old motorcar at the corner by the church. Corporal Frank Hudson, in charge of the troops, saw nothing about the men to arouse his suspicions. The British soldiers were about to deposit their rifles at the entrance to the chapel when suddenly a dozen Irishmen—the men from the corner and another group from a second dark automobile (Corporal Hudson thought it was a Ford)—rushed toward them, brandishing revolvers and makeshift weapons. They opened fire on the soldiers without warning. Private William Jones, thirty-four, fell dead with a bullet in his chest. Three more British soldiers were shot; the rest were bludgeoned with wooden staves and spokes torn from wheels; then the assailants stole the rifles and sped away in the waiting cars. The wife of the Methodist minister heard the shots: "I thought it was the military dumping their rifles on the porch, and I went out of the church. . . . Soldiers were scattered around, and one came running towards me bleeding, while men on the opposite side of the road kept pushing things into the car. Other soldiers came rushing up to me, many of them bleeding, and then a motor-car flashed past me going towards Tallow-road." Corporal Hudson ran to a doctor's house for assistance and had the door slammed in his face.

The rebels had planned their escape well. They had cut the telegraph and telephone wires leading out of Fermoy; when a search party tried to follow down the road toward Tallow, they found it blocked by felled trees. Three airplanes went up to survey the surrounding area, but found nothing. Later that night, another military convoy was attacked a few miles outside town by a band of armed civilians who made away with another twenty-five rifles.

It was insult enough to suffer an attack in broad daylight in Fermoy, one of the largest and best-equipped British military depots in southern Ireland, but the verdict of the coroner's jury upon the death of Private Jones proved intolerable to the men stationed in the two strongly garrisoned military barracks in town. The jury condemned the outrage at the church and sympathized with Private Jones's family, but it added its unanimous opinion that the crime of murder certainly was not premeditated, since the raid was designed only to take the rifles, and not to kill anyone.

Deeply angered by what they considered to be the jury's virtual declaration of sympathy with the murderers, two hundred soldiers from the Royal Field Artillery and Hudson's Shropshire detachment marched into Fermoy on Monday evening and proceeded to tear the town apart. For an hour and a half the British troops, armed with iron bars and trench tools, smashed windows and wrecked every shop along Queen's Square, the town's main thoroughfare. More than fifty shopfronts were demolished. An officer with a whistle and a golf club coordinated the orgy of destruction. Nothing else could be heard over the crash of falling glass and the occasional whistle blasts ordering the men to move on to the next row of shops. A mob made up of the local poor followed behind and looted to their heart's content. Over a thousand pairs of boots were stolen from one large store; a jewelry shop belonging to the foreman of the coroner's jury was singled out for special attention. Terrorized citizens telephoned the military barracks for assistance. Finally, after the damage was done, a bugle call sounded "fall in," and the troops marched off in good order back to the barracks. The soldiers threw much of their loot into a nearby river; the next day, there were more than the usual number of fishermen on its banks.

Two days later, the Lord-Lieutenant (Viscount French), the Chief Secretary, and the British commander-in-chief in Ireland issued proclamations warning that Section One of the Crimes Act—which provided magistrates with enhanced summary powers to investigate criminal acts—would henceforth be enforced throughout much of southern Ireland. The next day Lord French declared that the Dail Eireann, the Sinn Fein parliament, was from that time forward to be suppressed as a "dangerous association" and all its meetings prohibited. The government followed up these measures with a series of lightning searches, carried out by troops in full battle gear, of the homes of known rebel sympathizers and the Sinn Fein headquarters in Harcourt Street, Dublin. Two Sinn Fein MPs, duly elected to the House of Commons in November 1918, were arrested and taken into military custody. Crowds gathered around Harcourt Street, shouting, "Up the rebels!" while British soldiers carried away every copy they could find of the Walsh-Dunne report, every copy of the "Affidavits of the Victims of British Atrocities in Ireland" that Sinn Fein sympathizers were compiling, every document relating to Sinn Fein efforts to raise loans in America.

Later that evening, a detective in the Royal Irish Constabulary was shot dead on a dark street just outside a police station in Dublin. Shortly thereafter, authorities announced that officers of the RIC would henceforth be armed with grenades when patrolling "disturbed areas."

And lest anyone think that the troubles afflicted only southern Ireland, on September 17 a band of Orange extremists attacked the homes of their Roman Catholic neighbors in County Down, in the north. When police intervened, the Protestants turned their wrath upon them, pelting the constables with stones and launching a concerted attack upon the barracks at Saintfield.

Eamon De Valera, meanwhile, had been smuggled out of Ireland and into the United States, where he was touring the major cities along the East Coast, drumming up financial support for Sinn Fein and the Irish Republic. His reception was nothing short of spectacular. De Valera was given the presidential suite at the Waldorf; the Massachusetts state legislature received him in a special joint session; forty thousand wildly cheering supporters turned out to hear one of his speeches in Boston; and the press seemed to love him wherever he went. After all, he was excellent copy, and news of English injustices in Ireland always sold plenty of papers. As the *Nation* noted with bemusement, "He gets a front-page spread whenever he wants it, with unexampled editorial kindliness thrown in." The tall, very thin, dark Irishman brought no message of peace and goodwill to the United States, however. Now that the Peace Conference was over and freedom-loving Irishmen still remained enslaved under the British yoke, De Valera told an enthusiastic audience in Providence, "the war front is now transferred to Ireland."

Lord Northcliffe's *Times* noted that the repressive measures adopted by Lloyd George's government in Ireland had produced "a grave effect" in America: "If the anti-British element in America had had their choice of a course of events in Ireland which would help their cause, they could have chosen nothing more effective than what has happened." And in Ireland itself, the new get-tough policy did little more than drive still more of the rapidly dwindling number of moderates into the arms of the radicals. "Coercion advances step by step in Ireland, provoked by repeated outrages," lamented *The Times* in an outspoken editorial following the searches and arrests and the suppression of the Dail Eireann.

THE NEW MEASURE OF THE IRISH GOVERNMENT IS A VERY GRAVE ADVANCE ON THE PATH OF SUPPRESSION. THE PROVOCATION IS EXTREME, AND GOVERNMENT IN IRELAND IS BOUND TO PROTECT ITS INSTRUMENTS; BUT RESPONSIBLE PEOPLE GROW MORE AND MORE ALARMED ABOUT THE END OF IT ALL. THIS IS THE VERY BANKRUPTCY OF STATESMANSHIP. THE GOVERNMENT CANNOT ESCAPE THE GRAVEST RESPONSIBILITY FOR THE STEP THAT THEY HAVE NOW TAKEN. IT OPENS AN APPALLING VISTA OF PROVOCATION AND RETALIATION, EACH VYING WITH THE OTHER IN A CONTEST OF MERELY PHYSICAL ENDURANCE, BUILDING UP A HERITAGE OF THE BITTEREST MEMORIES, BANISHING PEACE AND CONTENTMENT IN IRELAND TO A FUTURE ALWAYS MORE REMOTE.

Conditions for policemen in the United States were no better than those in England. As the cost of living kept rising and trade unions in other lines of work struck successfully for higher wages and better conditions, police in American cities took another long, hard look at their low pay, backbreaking hours of duty, and shoddy treatment by their superiors, and wondered why they, too, should not take direct action to improve their plight. So, in New York, Washington, and Boston, policemen organized unions and explored the possibility of augmenting their own bargaining power by affiliating with the American Federation of Labor. The AFL welcomed them with open arms, but in each case city officials forbade any such association. The commissioners of the District of Columbia went so far as to issue an edict in early September dismissing any policeman who joined a union affiliated with the AFL, but federal court proceedings delayed enforcement of this penalty long enough for labor representatives to alert President Wilson (as if Wilson needed more problems right now); the President, not unsympathetic to the policemen's case, promptly dispatched a telegram temporarily countermanding the commissioners' order until he could return to Washington to look into the matter personally.

Boston policemen were less fortunate. Forbidden to join a union, they had formed an association with the innocuous name of the "Boston Social Club," which fooled absolutely no one; in late July, the city's uncompromising police commissioner, Edwin Upton Curtis, formally notified the men that "I am firmly of the opinion that a police officer cannot consistently belong to a union and perform his sworn duty. . . . I feel it is my duty to say to the police force that I disapprove of the movement on foot." Nevertheless, the Social Club proceeded to apply for a charter from the AFL on August 10, thereby eliciting another objection by Curtis in the form of a new proclamation in the department rules and regulations: "No members of the force shall join or belong to any organization, club, or body composed of present or present and past members of the force which is affiliated with or a part of any organization, club, or body outside the department," except for unexceptionable veterans' organizations such as the venerable Grand Army of the Republic. Undaunted, the militant policemen accepted the AFL charter granted them on August 11 and at once elected a full slate of union officials to represent them against Curtis.

Certainly the Boston police had legitimate labor grievances. The starting salary for a patrolman was $1,100 a year (the maximum for veterans was $1,600), out of which he had to furnish his own uniform and equipment. Men on the day shift worked seventy-three hours a week; those unlucky enough to draw night duty had to put in eighty-three hours. Station houses were infested with a variety of prison-hardened rodents and obnoxious insects. And, like their counterparts in Britain, Boston policemen had no independent channel through which to voice complaints about unfair treatment by their officers.

Unfortunately for the men in blue, their adversary, Commissioner Curtis, was as stubborn a Yankee as was ever raised on cod, baked beans, and Massachusetts winter mornings. A former mayor of Boston (elected in 1895), Curtis was a rather pompous—albeit entirely capable—public servant with more than a little streak of the martinet in his character. Confronted with an open rebellion by his men, Curtis never hesitated in meeting it head-on. When he learned the names of the police union's officials, he immediately charged them with insubordination. The union belligerently replied that any disciplinary action against its leaders would provoke a strike. Curtis then called for a hearing, over which he personally presided as judge and jury, and, to no one's surprise, found the ringleaders guilty; however, he withheld sentencing to allow the union time to change course and withdraw from the AFL. When the rank and file made no move to disengage from the national federation, Curtis suspended the nineteen union leaders on September 8.

That same evening, nearly every policeman in the city of Boston attended a secret meeting to vote on a strike; the final ballot was 1,134 to 2 in favor of a walkout the following day. Sympathetic New England labor leaders decried "the Hunnish attitude of Police Commissioner Curtis," and promised to find new jobs for the striking policemen if they were dismissed. Curtis, who apparently had succeeded in deluding himself that only a handful of men would actually go out on strike, assured Mayor Andrew Peters and Governor Calvin Coolidge that he had the situation well under control. "I am ready for anything," Peters assured reporters. That was a big mistake.

Late on the foggy afternoon of Tuesday, September 9, Boston policemen deserted their stations. In all, 1,117 out of 1,544 cops walked off the beat. As it dawned on the good people of Boston that there were no guardians of law and order on the streets, gangs of rowdies gathered and proceeded to smash store windows, garnering whatever loot presented itself: jewelry, clothing, cigars, shoes. (In one shoe store, thieves became clerks for a day and sat there happily fitting one another with the latest fashions in footwear.) The rioting was worst in the retail district near Scollay Square. Innocent pedestrians were attacked and robbed. Trolley cars were stoned, missiles hurled through the windows of police stations; at a station in Roxbury, boys threw handfuls of mud at departing policemen. Governor Coolidge, trusting Curtis's guarantees and needing his usual twelve hours of sleep anyway, went to bed and gave orders that he was not to be disturbed. By three o'clock in the morning, the entire central part of the city of Boston was under the control of the mobs.

Next morning, groups of young toughs started the day off by throwing paving bricks through shop windows. Trucks were backed up to stores in broad daylight to carry away the loot. The nerves of the city were on edge; fistfights started at the slightest provocation. Secret Service agents watching the railroad stations recognized hardened professional criminals ("old-timers," they called them) arriving on nearly every incoming train. Dice games (which actually attracted more spectators than participants) could be seen on nearly every street, and especially on the Boston Common— anywhere professional gamblers could find patsies with money to lose. Those who won stood a good chance of getting conked on the head and having their roll stolen. Meanwhile, the volunteer policemen who had already been mobilized by the city arrested about 150 looters, many of whom were promptly set free when crowds assaulted the volunteers.

Finally, Mayor Peters called in the Tenth Regiment of the State Guards. Not to be outdone in enforcing law and order (albeit somewhat belatedly), Coolidge mobilized the Eleventh Regiment. By evening, five thousand troops stood ready for action. Despite a light rain, gangs of hoodlums again thronged the city's streets. Cavalrymen ordered a crowd in Scollay Square to disperse; when the people refused, the cavalry charged and a machine gun opened fire, killing one man. In South Boston, guardsmen told looters to move along. The thugs laughed and hooted and continued ransacking the stores, whereupon the guardsmen opened fire; astonished, the mob panicked and trampled those unfortunate enough to fall. A sixteen-year-old boy was fatally wounded. All night long, from two in the morning until dawn, angry crowds—including many women—openly attacked the soldiers with bricks and paving stones, and the troops responded with fixed bayonets and drawn sabers, and occasional rounds from machine guns. By the time it was all over, three people had died.

After witnessing the distressing consequences of the strike, public opinion was almost unanimous in condemning the policemen's action. The verdict of the *Boston Telegraph*, if somewhat overwrought, captured the prevailing anti-union sentiment:

> THE TUMULT AND THE RIOT AND THE DISTURBANCE OF PUBLIC ORDER THAT HAVE DISGRACED THE CITY OF BOSTON FOR THE LAST TWO NIGHTS ARE BUT THE FORETASTE OF THE BITTER FRUITS TO COME IF THE PEOPLE OF MASSACHUSETTS CRAWL BEFORE THE ULTIMATUM OF THE AMERICAN FEDERATION OF LABOR. . . . THE CHALLENGE CONTAINED IN THAT ULTIMATUM IS A CHALLENGE TO STRAIGHT AMERICANISM. IT MUST AND IT WILL BE MET, STANDING—REGARDLESS OF THE COST IN LIFE AND TREASURE. FOR BEHIND BOSTON IN THIS SKIRMISH WITH BOLSHEVISM STANDS MASSACHUSETTS, AND BEHIND MASSACHUSETTS STANDS AMERICA.

Peters and Coolidge had feared that the city's firemen might vote a sympathy strike to support their comrades in blue, but, seeing how poorly the policemen were faring in the public's eyes, the firemen decided to postpone their own strike vote.

Isolated incidents continued to plague the city on Thursday morning. State guardsmen who arrested several dozen gamblers on the Common were jeered and pelted with stones as they marched their prisoners along the street. The troops answered by opening fire, killing one member of the mob (a sailor), and then led a bayonet charge to disperse their tormentors. During the day, several other people who had been wounded in the previous nights' rioting died, bringing the death toll to seven. But with the city resembling an armed camp—6,700 soldiers (many of them veterans wearing their steel trench helmets), six machine guns in front of police headquarters and more mounted in Scollay Square, with Faneuil Hall a military barracks and guardsmen sleeping in full battle gear on army cots in the City Council chamber—the rioting was over. Barbed wire covered the windows and entrances of the larger stores, and armed guards paced back and forth in front of others. Anyone walking the streets at night was told by soldiers to keep moving, and to stay at least three paces away from buildings; window shoppers were ordered away.

Realizing that the police had made a serious error in judgment, John F. McInnes, the leader of the policemen's union, informed Coolidge that his members were willing to return to duty pending further negotiations. Curtis, however—echoing Neville Macready's stand in Britain a month earlier—refused to take back any strikers and announced that he would start immediately to recruit a new force, which would, not coincidentally, be given a $300 raise in pay. Coolidge supported the commissioner. "The action of the police in leaving their posts of duty is not a strike," Coolidge declared. "It is desertion. There is nothing to arbitrate; nothing to compromise. In my personal opinion there are no conditions under which the men can return to the force." And when Samuel Gompers tried to intervene on behalf of the policemen by accusing Curtis of provoking the strike, Coolidge replied with the statement that brought him national recognition for the first time: "Your assertion that the commissioner was wrong cannot justify the wrong of leaving the city unguarded. That furnished the opportunity, the criminal element furnished the action. *There is no right to strike against the public safety by anybody, anywhere, at any time.*" In fact, the entire incident provided Coolidge—previously known as nothing more than a safe, competent, but totally uninspired administrator—with a once-in-a-lifetime opportunity to make the sort of political capital that catapulted him directly into the picture as a leading contender for the Republican presidential nomination in 1920.

Nor was Wilson less forceful than Coolidge in condemning the strike, although for perhaps the only time in their respective lives Coolidge uttered a more memorable phrase than Wilson. Speaking at Helena, Montana, Wilson acknowledged that the policemen's just grievances should be dealt with in the most generous way. But, he added, a strike by the police force of a major city was nothing less than "a crime against civilization."

Dr. Renner, Chancellor of the Austrian Republic, boarded the Orient Express in Vienna on September 5, bound for St-Germain, France, where the treaty of peace between Austria and the Allied and Associated Powers would at last be signed. The train's luggage van was so crowded, however, that officials at the station decided to leave one heavy box behind. It was just three minutes before the train departed that someone realized that Renner's official copy of the treaty was in that particular box, and the precious cargo was rescued just in time.

At 10:15 on the morning of September 10, the signing ceremony began. For a bored English correspondent, the event was supremely uninteresting, "a pale replica of the Versailles ceremony of June 28." French cavalrymen (dismounted) rendered military honors to the Allied delegations as they entered the chateau—the same museum of prehistoric times where the terms had been presented to the Austrians three months earlier. The hall in which the signing was to take place was too small to hold even the few officials who bothered to attend. All five windows were kept tightly closed, with their stone-colored blinds drawn; the heat was oppressive. One disgruntled journalist compared the atmosphere in the ugly room to that of an examination hall. "This academic but not scholarly idea," he wrote in disgust, "was further carried out by the shabby crimson of the velvet covering the tables, and most of all by the cheap moulded glass pen trays and ink wells which were scattered with careful profusion in front of the delegates. . . . Altogether, an examination being held for middle-aged doctors would have been the opinion of any unenlightened ghost who had happened to stray there during the proceedings." Most of the guests were spotlessly dressed young men—attachés and secretaries of the various legations—who spent the half hour before the ceremony gathering autographs from the most famous delegates. Clemenceau, who soon chafed under these repeated intrusions upon his privacy, seemed more interested in the ceremonial inkstand than anything else, asking the omnipresent Paul Dutasta to bring it over to him for closer inspection.

Fully half the people in the room were still standing about chatting when Chancellor Renner entered and was escorted to his seat. Renner looked around amiably, searching for the chairman; when at last he found Clemenceau seated facing the middle window, the Austrian smiled graciously, bowed, and sat down. Without further ado, Clemenceau, in "a perfectly fierce little speech, which was perfectly inaudible," declared the session open, invited Renner to sign the treaty, and then sat down, slapping his hand on the table. Renner arose with alacrity and walked to the Louis XV table (impressively decorated in gilt and bronze, but covered with a worn green leather top that had seen far better days), sat down in a comfortable armchair, picked up a pen, and, after scrutinizing the writing point carefully and testing it on a spare piece of paper, slowly signed his name to the treaty, ending with a vigorous flourish. Then Renner signed the other formal documents (commercial agreements, treaties for the protection of minorities, the Danube Convention, etc.) with almost careless haste. "There was nothing," wrote *The Times*'s correspondent, "to show that the Austrian Chancellor was moved by the dismemberment of what was once the proudest Empire in Europe." A train whistle sounded outside in the distance.

Nor did anyone else seem greatly impressed by the historic occasion. After the Allied delegates had squeezed their way, one by one, to the front of the table and affixed their signatures (America first, Siam last), chatting with one another all the while, Renner left the room; a number of Allied delegates had already strolled out onto the terrace. On the way out, the French cavalry saluted the Austrian delegation and cannons boomed to announce the conclusion of peace with the unfortunate recipients of the Hapsburgs' foolish legacy. Then everyone else left, and by 11:10 a witness realized that "there was nothing to indicate that a momentous ceremony, marking the final dissolution of the great Austrian Empire, had taken place. There had been neither pomp nor circumstance at the mournful ceremony; it was like a funeral at which no one knew the corpse." As he departed, the Tiger received a dutifully enthusiastic response from the villagers gathered outside (no Parisians took the trouble to come out), as did Balfour. Assistant Secretary of State Frank Polk had been delegated to sign the treaty for the United States.

In their infinite wisdom, the Allies had left another open sore upon the body of Europe. Large chunks of indisputably German-speaking territory—particularly sections of Bohemia and Silesia—were wrenched from Austria and handed over to the other successor states of the Hapsburg domains. Nearly three million people of German background, many residing in the Sudetenland, were allotted to Czechoslovakia alone. Despite Renner's repeated protests, Austria was, in the end, saddled with an impossible reparations burden. It was not at all clear how the Allies were going to take cattle from Austria when Hoover had his hands full trying to supply

Vienna with enough condensed milk to keep thousands of children from dying. "If you take Austria by the heels and shake it in the most thorough manner," explained a government official in Vienna, "you can only cause to fall out of the pockets exactly the amount that is in the pockets. If we haven't it, it will be hard to make us pay." With its currency depreciating, with a plague of strikes in nearly every trade and even in some professions hindering economic recovery, and with the fear of famine again dominating everyone's thoughts as another winter approached, Austria appeared to have little chance to survive and prosper on its own.

After bringing its affairs with Austria to a quite unsatisfactory conclusion, the rump peace conference in Paris turned its attention back to Hungary, where it began to perceive the emergence of an ostensibly stable and satisfactory—from the French point of view, anyway—conservative regime.

Archduke Joseph soon realized that the time was not yet right for a Hapsburg restoration, and resigned his position as State Governor after less than a month in office. After all, he had really only wanted to keep a place warm for the ex-Emperor until that august gentleman (whom Joseph loyally, if somewhat obdurately still regarded as the legitimate king of Hungary) could safely return to Budapest. The men who had ridden the Archduke's imperial coattails to power, however, stayed on and led Hungary into a medieval restoration of terror, torture, and murder.

The figurehead who presided over this White reaction was Stefan Friedrich, the owner of a small repair works and a man of no fixed political beliefs, a thirty-five-year-old adventurer who put his boundless audacity and brazen opportunism at the service of Hungary's Rumanian conquerors. But behind Friedrich lay the real centers of power in counterrevolutionary Hungary: the army officer class, its ranks swollen enormously by four years of war, but still inculcated with the old swaggering, strutting, militarist tradition; the dispossessed civil officials of the *ancien regime*, including the unsavory debris of the extensive imperial network of police, spies, and informers; the priesthood, drawn mainly from the peasant class and often barely literate, but thirsting desperately for revenge against the Bolsheviks who had dethroned Roman Catholicism from state and school life; and, of course, the ruthless Rumanian invaders themselves.

Together, these were the creators of the White Terror. As they advanced toward Budapest, the Rumanian troops had nailed placards throughout the countryside ordering the population to report all Bolsheviks to officers of the occupation regime. An orgy of denunciation quickly followed; anyone with a personal grudge could point a finger and accuse his enemy of revolutionary sympathies. Hungarian officers and Catholic students roamed the streets of the capital searching for adherents of Béla Kun's regime; the jails were soon overflowing with prisoners (fifteen or twenty jammed into each filthy cell) who waited weeks for even a preliminary trial and who were beaten indiscriminately and mercilessly in the meantime. Soon even the schools were turned into jails, when the prisons could hold no more. "Disgusting sights were to be seen in Budapest apart from the dreary, interminable processions of arrested men being hauled to prison under armed escort," reported a British witness. "One became almost used to the anguished cries of men being battered and to the sight of bandaged heads, when at length the release of the innocent— i.e., non-Communists and non-Jews—began." Bands of youths wearing the white cross of "Awakened Hungary" stopped streetcars and flogged any victim they chose. Rumanian cavalrymen found it amusing to ride through the streets of Budapest with a prisoner between them tied by a noose; as they rode they would kick him violently, a vicious display designed to terrorize onlookers and discourage any thoughts of revolt. The elements of extreme reaction formed their own mafia, complete with agents provocateurs, detectives, secret tribunals, and executions. On isolated estates in the Hungarian countryside, lynchings of suspected Jews and Reds by the feudal-minded aristocracy were common occurrences.

Throughout the centuries, anti-Semitism has been an almost inevitable companion of political reaction in Eastern Europe, and certainly Hungary in the fall of 1919 was no exception. The only posters approved by the government censors for display on the streets of Budapest were those inciting the population to initiate pogroms. It was necessary, Friedrich told a group of Western correspondents, to spill Jewish blood in order to wipe away the stain of communism. Anyone of Jewish appearance was liable to be savagely beaten on sight. A deputation of priests awaiting an interview with Friedrich watched with open expressions of delight as a rabbi was kicked and bludgeoned in the Castle square; his anguished howls of pain brought forth no display of compassion from the priests. The avowedly anti-Semitic Christian Socialist party, which in its best showing in Hungary's pre-invasion parliamentary elections had managed to win only thirty out of 443 seats, suddenly found itself catapulted into power and promptly initiated a rigid censorship to impose upon the rest of the country the party's bigoted, simplistic creed—a belief that the Jews were responsible for all the evils in the world and the Hapsburgs were ordained by heaven to rule Hungary. All state employees were forced to join the party or face dismissal.

Meanwhile, Rumania continued its systematic despoilation of Hungary's tangible wealth. The soldiers took away the printing presses from newspaper offices (the liberal journals first); they stole factory machinery (parts from lathes, steel furnaces, and borers, and whatever else the troops could find were mixed up at random and piled together in hopeless confusion in railroad cars) and then they exported unemployed workers into Rumania; they took the oxen and bedding from farms; they took the rings from women's fingers; they took the telegraph apparatus from the General Post Office; and then they took the locomotives and railroad cars themselves. Only the very immensity of the crime, the sheer volume of the looting, which blocked every available rail line into Rumania, slowed the plunder.

With winter approaching—heavy snows usually struck the region in late October—Hungary was left naked and once again on the verge of starvation. Stocks of grain, cattle, potatoes, and eggs were far below even what they had been before the terrible winter of 1918–19; the average daily shipment of coal into Budapest had fallen from 7,500 tons to 2,700 tons, barely half of the city's daily requirement, and there was virtually no railway stock left in Hungary to bring in more coal to replenish the depleted stocks. "The working class are without work, without food, without money, and without hope," wrote a British correspondent who charged the Allies with creating a monstrous calamity in Eastern Europe:

THE PRINCIPAL CONTRIBUTORY CAUSE OF THIS LAWLESSNESS AND CONFUSION IS THE SPHINXLIKE SILENCE OF THE ENTENTE, TO PUT IT AS COURTEOUSLY AS POSSIBLE. THE ATTITUDE OF THE CONFERENCE IN PARIS IS ALLOWING TO DEVELOP IN SOUTH-EASTERN EUROPE AN ANARCHIC SITUATION THAT THREATENS TO PLUNGE HUGE POPULATIONS INTO MEDIEVALISM, AND PERHAPS KINDLE NEW CONFLICTS FROM THE GERMAN FRONTIER TO THE BLACK SEA. IF DEFIANCE OF THE ENTENTE IS BECOMING GENERAL IN SOUTHERN AND EASTERN EUROPE, IT IS BECAUSE WITH THE EBBING OF THE TIDE OF THE WORLD-WAR AND THE DEMOBILISATION OF THE GREAT WESTERN ARMIES THE AUTHORITY OF THE ENTENTE IS LOSING REALITY, AND BECAUSE NEW LOCAL FORCES NOT IN SYMPATHY WITH ITS DECLARED AIMS ARE COMING INTO PLAY.

France, whose policy for Eastern Europe centered upon the creation of a *cordon sanitaire* against Soviet Russia, refused to evict the reactionaries forcibly from Hungary; Britain (in the person of Foreign Secretary Balfour, who was preparing to resign anyway) was willing to draft ultimatums but was certainly not prepared to undertake military expeditions against

Rumania or Friedrich; and the United States was getting more and more disgusted with the whole dismal state of affairs. It was not surprising that the news from Eastern Europe gladdened the hearts of those senators who urged America to wash its hands of the entire filthy mess in the Old World.

"For every man that is mad,

and maketh himself a prophet . . ."

Tuesday, September 9. Fifteen thousand people jammed into an auditorium in St. Paul, Minnesota. After listening to Wilson's vivid and graphic descriptions of the devastated lands of France and Belgium, they heard the President ask them flatly whether America should enter the League or stay out. "The roar of affirmative approval," reported Lord Northcliffe's American correspondent, "was like a thunderclap," the biggest and most enthusiastic reception for Wilson thus far.

But now Wilson found himself compelled to divert precious time and energy from the battle to save the League; he had to try to exert the influence of the White House to quell the rising tide of industrial unrest in America. In an address to the Minnesota state legislature, Wilson forcefully rejected the counsels of conflict and blind self-interest that seemed to be dominating both labor and management circles, and insisted that cooperation between management and workers was the one sure means of settling labor disputes while bringing down the rapidly spiraling cost of living. "The interests of capital and the interests of labor are not different, but the same," the President explained, voicing the progressive ideal of a rational human society wherein all men worked together for the common good, "and men of business sense ought to know how to work out an organization that will express that identity of interest. And where there is identity of interest there must be community of interest." But neither side was really listening to him.

Wednesday, September 10. One thousand quiet people sat in a small auditorium in Bismarck, North Dakota. Wilson could see a few colorful sombreros amid the crowd, and several nattily dressed Sioux Indians sporting spotless white collars. Wilson told them all that if the United States rejected the treaty, the world would soon descend into despair and chaos. After hearing the President, one Scandinavian farmer allowed that the "League of nations bane good t'ing if President Vilson bane say so."

Outside of town, Wilson and his wife took a few moments to stroll away from the hubbub of curiosity-seekers surrounding the train, to just walk away and stand quietly where they could see magnificent cascading waterfalls in the near distance.

In Washington, the Foreign Relations Committee finally submitted the peace treaty to the full Senate. The committee's six-page report, which included reservations and amendments but carried no recommendation regarding ratification of the treaty itself, was laden with stinging personal attacks upon the President and sharp rhetorical barbs against the League of Nations: "The committee believe that the league as it stands will breed wars instead of securing peace. They also believe that the covenant of the league demands sacrifices of American independence and sovereignty which would in no way promote the world's peace, but which are fraught with the gravest dangers to the future safety and wellbeing of the United States." The committee also scoffed at the notion that the rest of the civilized world would refuse to alter the treaty to suit the prejudices of a majority of members of the United States Senate. "The other nations will take us on our own terms," Lodge and his colleagues proclaimed with unbounded arrogance, "for without us their league is a wreck and all their gains from a victorious peace are imperiled."

This was going far too far for many disinterested observers of the treaty fight. *The New York Times* assailed the "colossal insolence" of the Senate committee: "This report of the Foreign Relations Committee . . . sets the world back one hundred years. It does destroy the gains of victory, it does annihilate the league of nations, it repudiates not only all that was won by the war, but the declared purpose for which the nations poured out their blood and treasure." The *New York World* was equally indignant. "Senator Lodge's report as chairman of the Senate Committee on Foreign Relations is a masterpiece of misstatement and bad taste," charged the *World*'s editorial. "Never before was any treaty reported to the United States Senate in the scolding, undignified, offensive manner in which the Senator from Massachusetts has presented this most important of all treaties. . . . It is a parody on patriotism, and to put it forth at this time when the whole world is staggering under the wounds of the most terrible war that was ever fought is to degrade Americanism and smear with the slime of partisanship the glorious record of the American people in this supreme tragedy."

At a brief stop in Mandan, North Dakota, where railway workers added a second engine to the presidential train before it began its long hard pull across the Rockies, Wilson told a crowd (which again included many Indians) that a week of travel through the nation had convinced him that the people favored an international guarantee of peace, "to complete what the boys did who carried their guns with them over the sea. We may think that they finished that job, but they will tell you they did not, that unless we see to it that peace is made secure they will have the job to do over again and we in the meantime will rest under a constant apprehension that we may have to sacrifice the flower of our youth again." Full, unreserved membership in the League of Nations, Wilson declared, would fulfill America's highest ideals and its most glorious destiny; "it will be the proudest thing and finest thing that America ever did. She was born to do these things and now she is going to do them."

Wilson's train moved on through a lonely, treeless land, where there was little visible evidence of human habitation. From time to time Wilson would wander out onto the observation platform and wave to a startled rancher or motorist as the train flashed by. The silk hat was put into storage until the party reached the West Coast.

Thursday, September 11. A festival atmosphere in Billings, Montana, with flags everywhere. Thousands of ranchers and their families traveled across hundreds of miles of mountain roads in mud-spattered automobiles to see the President. The crowd awakened Wilson as he slept in the *Mayflower* several miles outside of town. Before the eight thousand who gathered in the arena at the fairgrounds, Wilson stood on a high balcony and spoke of the League of Nations as a star of hope shining in the east, an honest effort to bring an end to all wars, to render unnecessary the terrible human sacrifices of the last five years. Reporters saw red bandanna handkerchiefs flashing in the audience as men and women, many of whom had lost sons of their own in the war, wiped away the tears from their eyes. As the train pulled out of town, three boys, about twelve years old, stood shyly watching Wilson. One boy approached the platform and handed Wilson a flag; the second gave him a flower. Wilson smiled and thanked them. The last boy, shuffling his feet with embarrassment, finally reached in his pocket and, as the train moved slowly away, ran after the President and held out a dime. "Here, Mr. President," he called, "I have something for you, too." He placed the coin in Wilson's hand and Wilson took it. It reminded him of Jesus and the widow who had possessed only a few pennies but had nevertheless given all that she, too, had to give.

In Helena, Wilson turned again to a discussion of labor difficulties. Here it was that he condemned the Boston police strike as "a crime against civilization"; but, like Lloyd George five months ago, he insisted that long-term industrial and political peace could not be established until the Versailles treaty—including the League—was ratified and enforced. The train moved on through drought-stricken pastures and fields. The heat made the steel cars feel like ovens. Wilson's headaches grew more frequent in the higher elevations.

The President again donned his black suit that evening. The others in the presidential party wore their panama hats and Palm Beach suits, causing considerable amusement among the mountaineers. A proud mother handed Mrs. Wilson a baby boy, who promptly let out a fierce wail when the First Lady took him. The father said the child's name was Wilson. The President found it hard to breathe at night; sometimes he slept sitting in an armchair.

Friday, September 12. The train stopped outside of Coeur d'Alene, Idaho—the home of Senator William Borah, one of Wilson's most intractable opponents—and Wilson rode into town in an automobile, led by four horsemen in Western garb. It was raining. Wilson warned the enthusiastic crowd that had gathered in a circus tent that Germany was fraternizing with the Bolsheviks in Russia in an effort to gain strength for a new campaign of world conquest. "Germany wants us to stay out of this treaty," Wilson shouted defiantly, implying in no uncertain terms that Lodge and his cronies were playing directly into Germany's hands. "It was America that saved the world, and those who oppose the treaty propose that after having redeemed the world we should desert the world. . . . If America does not enter the new world arrangement there will be universal disorder, as there is now universal unrest." The audience greeted this dire prediction with complete silence.

Trailing a week behind Wilson, California's Senator Hiram Johnson told a roaring crowd at the St. Louis Coliseum that only "the United States Senate stands between you and the loss of your liberties." The audience hissed whenever Johnson mentioned Great Britain.

Wilson's train went through a chilling drizzle across the state of Washington, then the heat returned at Spokane. Mrs. Wilson distributed a huge box of candy among the reporters on the train that evening.

Saturday, September 13. The busiest day of the campaign thus far. The dawn came foggy and cold. Wilson arrived in Tacoma at 8:55 A.M., took an automobile tour through the city, gave a short talk to high school students at the stadium, then rode to the armory for yet another speech. Amid the tremendous enthusiasm of the people, there were nagging questions about Wilson's plans to run for a third term in 1920; surely, suspicious minds reasoned, the President's first visit to the West Coast since taking office was not unrelated to his personal political ambitions.

At Seattle, where the wounds had not yet healed from Ole Hanson's repression of the general strike in February, Wilson's procession rolled slowly past six blocks of workers and IWW members, radicals dressed in blue denim, standing in silent protest, arms folded, with signs in their hats that read RELEASE POLITICAL PRISONERS. Startled, the President stood in awkward silence for several blocks, then he sat by his wife's side, shaken and pale.

In the afternoon, the Wilsons joined Secretary of the Navy Josephus Daniels and his wife for a review of the Pacific fleet in Puget Sound. (Earlier in the year, the United States Navy had officially been divided for the first time into separate Atlantic and Pacific fleets, an occurrence that generated considerable suspicion and hostility among Japanese militarists.) As the President's naval launch pushed away from the dock, it nearly capsized from the added weight of Secret Service men and reporters. Then, with an inexperienced and nervous pilot at the helm, it shot forward and rammed another boat, jarring the launch's passengers suddenly into their seats. Wilson sat quietly in the rear and just smiled. After the launch finally got under way, the President and Daniels boarded the famous battleship *Oregon*, from which they reviewed the progress of the dreadnoughts, destroyers, and cruisers. When the last ship had passed, Daniels asked Captain Ivan Mettengel, commander of the *Oregon*, "Do we get under way now, captain?" "Just as soon as the destroyers have all passed," Mettengel replied. "The destroyers are hove to," the President called out from the railing; he had always wanted to do that. Mettengel took a look for confirmation, and then touched his cap. "Aye, aye, sir," he said, nodding to the Commander-in-Chief. The sea breezes appeared to invigorate Wilson for a few hours, but after the rigors of a dinner speech and an address at the Seattle Arena, the fatigue returned; following the performance at the Arena, a navy officer turned to Secretary Daniels's son and said that something seemed to be wrong with the President: "He appeared to have lost his customary force and enthusiasm."

After it all, Wilson and his wife sat on the roof of their hotel and saw the lights of the fleet shining in the harbor. For a moment—just as on that day in January at the university in Turin—Mrs. Wilson thought her husband looked young again. For a moment he was young again. . . .

* * *

Sunday, September 14. Wilson received a delegation of labor leaders and listened for more than an hour to their grievances. He asked them to postpone any large-scale walkouts until he could convene a national conference of employers and workers in Washington on October 6. One of the visitors thought the President "looked old—just *old.*"

Monday, September 15: The Senate commenced debate on the peace treaty. In an unprecedented move, it decided to stage its discussions in open session. For the first day, the galleries were filled to capacity; but the spectators saw only lots of bickering, with no prospect of early resolution. Meanwhile, on the other side of the Capitol, the chairman of the House Appropriations Committee revealed that the federal treasury faced a deficit of over $3.5 billion for the coming year, a development that in those innocent times appeared "alarming" to a vast majority of congressmen and promised to bring forth calls for extensive cuts in government spending, particularly in the military sector.

Wilson arrived in Portland. When he appeared on the observation platform in the morning, a railway worker shouted, "Atta boy!" People squeezed through the police lines onto the tracks and started a continuous roar of welcome that kept roaring all the way to the end of the automobile ride through Portland's streets, all the way to the business and professional men's luncheon, where Wilson gave an impromptu address in a smoky room and then left for a sixty-mile automobile trek over the Columbia highway. The cheers pounded in Wilson's head from the thousands of people who had parked their cars along the way. Always there was more noise waiting, and then he heard the raucous yells from those who stood in the small towns through which the procession passed. His head ached so much, so much . . . then crashing cheers came from the enthusiastic crowds in the streets when the President rode from his hotel to the auditorium, where the audience stood and applauded for three minutes when Wilson entered the hall; and more cascades of noise when the mayor presented Mrs. Wilson with a bouquet of roses. Wilson's voice showed obvious signs of strain as he began his speech that night, but he went on and brought another round of applause when he declared that he had "no respect whatever" for his opponents and their "pro-German propaganda."

Before the train left Portland that evening, Wilson paced slowly down the platform (in full view of several hundred curious bystanders), then crossed the tracks to the dark side of the train, away from the station lights; after going about a hundred yards, he turned and ambled back to the

Mayflower. A reporter guessed that it was only the second decent walk Wilson had enjoyed since leaving Washington.

Tuesday, September 16. Wilson slept late and then spent the day traveling, catching up on his correspondence, and chatting with the people who came to see him during the few brief stops as the train labored through the Siskiyou Mountains. Just before the President left Oregon, the citizens of two small towns presented him and his wife with several large deer; the tag on the animal put aboard at Glendale read, "As a token of our high esteem and appreciation of your devoted efforts for the benefit of mankind." At Hornbrook, a few miles over the California line, Wilson took a few minutes to shake the hands or pat the heads of all the schoolchildren who met him in the middle of the afternoon, each child carrying an American flag. A pair of twins, three months old, captured Mrs. Wilson's affection; when their parents started to leave the train, she called out, "Don't take the babies away, please." An old woman told Wilson that all her neighbors were greatly interested in the League of Nations. "Every mother is in favor of the league covenant," Wilson assured her. "Yes, we are," the woman answered. "I wish we could vote on the question forty times for it."

Wilson's special train may have been the latest word in rail travel, but the *Mayflower* paled in comparison to the comfort of a Lawson airliner. The first plane in what aircraft builder Alfred W. Lawson hoped soon would be a fleet of one hundred passenger liners (including some with sleeping berths) alighted at Bolling Field outside Washington, D.C., on the afternoon of September 19. The ship was on the initial leg of the nation's first transcontinental passenger flight; averaging about ninety miles an hour in the air, Lawson intended to complete the entire voyage in thirty-six hours' flying time. The mammoth liner (the largest civilian aircraft in the world, Lawson claimed) stood fifteen feet high and fifty feet long, with a wingspan of ninety-seven feet. Weighing seven tons, it was powered by two four-hundred-horsepower Liberty motors that could, if necessary, push its speed up to 115 miles an hour.

Lawson's liner had left Roosevelt Field on Long Island shortly before nine o'clock that morning, with fourteen passengers aboard. One cautious woman wrote out her will immediately after boarding the plane. The passengers sat in wicker chairs upholstered in green leather; it seemed just like a ride in a Pullman car, only without the jolts and shocks. As the plane passed over New York City they could see the Woolworth Building below, a clean, white toothpick. "This sort of journey gives one a feeling of superiority," wrote Richard Wrightman, one of the passengers and a vice-president of the Aeronautical Touring Association. "The important buildings and affairs of the earth over which you are passing seem very unimportant. You don't care what you are passing over. You don't care where the roads go or where the rivers run or where the tracks are laid." (Wilson really would have benefited from this Olympian perspective.) Upon landing, Miss Felicity Buranelli, voted the prettiest of the airliner's passengers, told reporters that it had all been a wonderful experience so far: "We had lunch while coming down and I would rather travel in the air liner than in an automobile. It was just as though we were floating through the air, and the engines made little noise." The woman who had written out her will tore it up as soon as the plane touched down safely.

Across the Atlantic, two enterprising companies, one British and one French (known collectively as Airco), already had established an air express service between London and Paris. Every day, two Airco planes crossed the Channel (one plane each way), the average flight taking two and a half hours. Only one of the forty-two scheduled flights in the first three weeks of service had failed to complete its run, and that one had been canceled owing to a hurricane carrying one-hundred-mile-an-hour winds and torrential rain. The planes had already gone over ten thousand miles without mishap. Airco's advertisements stressed the speed and reliability of its express parcel service for businessmen with offices on both sides of the Channel; to those merchants and bankers to whom time was money, ten shillings was a small price to pay for same-day delivery of a twenty-five-pound package of documents or perishable goods. Airco's pilots were all experienced ex-servicemen (the *Manchester Guardian* reassured its readers that thus far the "pilots have not lost their way") who, for safety's sake, tried to follow the railway lines across country, so they would never be far from assistance in the event of a forced landing.

Hollywood had a particular affinity for the pioneering aviation industry. Charlie Chaplin and his manager-brother, Syd, were engaged in negotiations with William Wrigley, Jr., one of the owners of Catalina Island, to form an airline service to convey vacationers between Los Angeles and the famous resort community. Director Cecil B. De Mille went Chaplin one better, however, when he established the Mercury Aviation Company to ferry passengers between Los Angeles and Fresno. De Mille, a qualified pilot who had been awarded a commission in the Army Air Corps shortly before the war ended, was convinced that travelers were safer in the air than on the ground. "It is just a question of educating the public into realizing how safe aerial travel is," said the director-general of Zukor's Famous Players–Lasky Corporation. "Fulton had to convince the skeptics with his first steamboat. Stephenson had to do the same with the first steam engine; we all remember how everyone jeered at the first automobile." Mercury's home field was known, modestly, as De Mille Field, located at the intersection of Melrose and Crescent Avenues in Hollywood; from thence over the mountains to Bakersfield took less than two hours by air, compared to six hours by train and five hours by car. De Mille's company charged passengers a dollar a mile for long-distance flights; joyriders who wished to turn an aerial flip-flop were assessed an additional ten dollars.

Despite De Mille's breezy guarantees of the safety of flying, the Travelers Insurance Company announced that it was extending its casualty coverage to include air travel risks. Reportedly the first insurance firm to write such policies, Travelers set its aviation rates for pilots, passengers, public liability, and property damage at about four times the premium for automobile travel.

Back on the ground in Hollywood, De Mille's directorial counterpart, D. W. Griffith, was enjoying a year of memorable, if unspectacular, successes. Having agreed to join Fairbanks, Chaplin, and Pickford in United Artists, Griffith opted to raise his share of the requisite investment capital by signing a deal with First National Exhibitors to make three new pictures for them. His first release in 1919 was the remarkable and largely forgotten melodrama *A Romance of Happy Valley*. Film critic Richard Schickel (who, after all, knows considerably more about movies than this writer) steadfastly maintains that *Happy Valley* was "one of the most fully realized" of Griffith's films, "one for which, even today, so modest and unassuming is it, no explanatory apologies need be made." Perhaps; but to paraphrase Dorothy Parker, it seems more like a modest film with much to be modest about.

Happy Valley, set in the hills of Kentucky, not far from Griffith's own boyhood home along the Ohio River, follows the career of a young inventor named John L. Logan, Jr., (played with appropriate adolescent gusto by Robert Harron), who seeks to make his fortune by creating a mechanical frog that can actually swim. Determined to market his invention in the big city, John sets off for New York, despite the warnings of his mother (who wants to save him from a life of sin), despite the stern advice of his father (who wants him to stay at home and hoe the corn), and despite the tearful entreaties of his sweetheart, Jennie Timberlake (played by the fragile but ever-faithful Lillian Gish), who wants him to stay at home and . . . well, she wants him to stay at home. During John's absence, Jennie consoles herself by embracing a scarecrow garbed in one of her sweetheart's old overcoats; John's father goes deeply over his head into debt; and his mother becomes a religious fanatic. After a series of misadventures, John returns home famous and successful, carrying $10,000 in his pockets. Upon his arrival in Happy Valley, he manages to save the old homestead from the auctioneer's gavel, rescue his father from a life of crime—the old man was about to mug John and steal his money before he realized who he was—and, certainly not least important, save Jennie from a lifetime of standing around in the cornfields, picking straw out of her hair and staring absently at the horizon. To give the film its due, most critics and audiences seemed to love it; the tale, said one review admiringly, "is so simple it seems a tale about one's neighbors, so forceful it seems all life in one white flame." (The movie was believed lost until the late 1960s, when a print was recovered in, of all places, the Soviet Union.)

From this commercial and critical triumph, Griffith went on to release *Broken Blossoms*, a film whose radical technique and tone—it contained a heartfelt plea for interracial understanding—had led the director to shelve it until now. Premiering at George M. Cohan's theater in May, *Broken Blossoms* (some cynics called it *Busted Buds*) gave Griffith another popular success, and Zukor graciously permitted him to buy back the distribution rights for the film and hand it over to his associates at United Artists. In all, six D. W. Griffith movies were released in 1919. And by the end of September, the celebrated director had fulfilled a longtime dream by purchasing his own studio in the East to make pictures the way he knew they should be made.

Over the past decade, Griffith had earned a reputation for innovative camera techniques (he had developed the closeup into a dramatic psychological device, and invented or popularized the long shot, the "iris" effect, the fade-in and fade-out, the soft focus, and the mobile camera) and for creating motion-picture stars from unknown actresses. He was credited with discovering Mary Pickford and Constance Talmadge, among others, and with developing the "shy elusive talent" of the Gish sisters. What, wondered a reporter for *Photoplay* magazine, was his formula for success in selecting an actress? Griffith acknowledged that certain physical equipment was helpful: "For instance, deep lines on the face of the girl are almost fatal to good screening, for on the screen her face is magnified twenty times, and every wrinkle assumes the proportions of the Panama Canal. It is important that her face have smooth, soft outlines. So with the eyes.

Every other physical characteristic is of insignificant importance compared with the eyes. If they are the windows of your soul, your soul must have a window it can see through." But the director steadfastly believed that outward appearances were merely incidental to the real secret of success for an actor or actress. "It isn't what you do with your face or your hands," Griffith argued. "It's the light within. If you have that light, it doesn't matter much just what you do before the camera. If you haven't it—well, then it doesn't matter just what you do, either. Before you give, you must have something to give. . . . The only woman with a real future is the woman who can think real thoughts." As for the relation of movies to real life, Griffith insisted that situations, climaxes, and plots were of secondary importance; a film, like a novel or play, could be successful only insofar as it reflected "the drama of realities—of situations that do happen, not those that don't happen."

In 1914, Gabriele D'Annunzio had proclaimed his readiness to die. Bored with the tedium of mortal existence, the poet allowed himself one more year of life, and then, he vowed, he would annihilate himself in some mysterious fashion, leaving no trace of his corporeal form behind. Fortunately for D'Annunzio, the cataclysm of war changed his plans and gave him a new *raison de vivre:* the glorious military conquest of Italy's ancient archenemy, Austria. Through no fault of the indisputably courageous (some said foolhardy) poet-aviator, that plan didn't work out very well, either. But now, in the autumn of 1919, the fifty-five-year-old, half-blind (he had lost an eye in an airplane accident), delirious genius set out on the greatest adventure of his eccentric life.

Fiume in September 1919: "The greatest temptation in Europe." Clashes between the French and Italian occupation troops during the summer had led an inter-Allied commission to condemn the Italians for provoking trouble. The offending grenadiers were ordered out of the city, their places taken by British soldiers. Before the Italians departed, however, the citizens of Fiume implored them to gather their comrades and return in force to rescue the city from the Anglo-French occupation and the despised Slavs, who, the citizens suspected, were always lurking on the outskirts of the city, poised to attack. The grenadiers dutifully marched to their newly assigned posts in nearby Ronchi and Monfalcone; but several of their officers at once set about fashioning a plot to seize Fiume and force its annexation to Italy.

Word of their plans reached D'Annunzio in Rome. The poet had been considering some sort of extravagant international gesture since the springtime, and had spent the summer fencing with Prime Minister Nitti: first D'Annunzio requested a meeting with the Prime Minister, which Nitti refused; his sensitive feelings wounded, the poet angrily launched a series of scathing personal attacks upon Nitti, demanding his removal from office; Nitti tried to calm him down with a twelve-page personal letter, but D'Annunzio would not be moved. Thus the grenadiers' plot to seize Fiume struck the flamboyant romantic as a masterstroke, a chance to fulfill Italy's destiny (and, not incidentally, his own as well), and to bring down the cowardly Nitti regime. But time was of the essence. Reliable sources reported that the British occupation forces intended to dissolve the National Council of Fiume and disarm the Italian volunteers inside the city on September 12; the same day, a contingent of troops from Malta was scheduled to arrive by sea to take over their peacekeeping duties in Fiume.

So, on the evening of September 10, D'Annunzio—suffering again from a high fever—journeyed by motorbike to Ronchi, where the conspirators had arranged a convoy of forty trucks to convey their forces across the border. The expedition left Ronchi and Monfalcone the following evening, traveling by moonlight, picking up additional supporters at prearranged points along the route. "I led the army as the old healers by faith led crowds," D'Annunzio later explained with characteristic modesty. At dawn the raiders—about 2,600 regulars and 1,500 volunteers, including bands of arditi laden with grenades—reached the Armistice line outside of Fiume, where they were met by General Pittaluga, regional commander of the Italian troops. Pittaluga's orders were to prevent any such filibustering expedition from entering the city. Accordingly, he had erected a barrier and dispatched four machine-gun companies to block the raiders' advance. The poet swept aside such obstacles with ease. Realizing that Pittaluga's men had already begun to fraternize with his own forces at the border, D'Annunzio marched straight up to the general to demand that he step aside and allow them to pass.

Pittaluga: "Thus you will ruin Italy?"

D'Annunzio: "Rather you will ruin Italy, if you oppose Fiume's destiny and support the infamous policy."

Pittaluga: "Then what do you wish?"

D'Annunzio: "A free entry into Fiume."

Pittaluga: "I have strict orders and must prevent an act which may have incalculable consequences for our country."

D'Annunzio: "I understand your words, General. You will order your men to fire on my soldiers, their brothers, but before you do so, order them to fire on me. Here I am, let them first fire on me." Whereupon d'Annunzio exposed his chest, allowing the rising sun to glint off the gold medals of honor he wore.

Realizing that he had been outmaneuvered, Pittaluga saluted the poet and stepped aside. All of Fiume's bells pealed exultantly as the expedition marched into the center of the city at eleven o'clock. British and French flags were hauled down and replaced with the Italian colors. D'Annunzio himself went straight to the commander's palace, disappeared for a moment, then came out on the balcony overlooking the crowd. "I am so ill that I will say but a few words," he began. "In the present mad, cowardly world, there is but one sure thing—our love for Fiume. Fiume stands like a lighthouse over the sea of degradation. . . . I, a war volunteer, and a mutilated fighter, appeal to Victor Hugo's France, to Milton's England and Lincoln's America and, speaking as an interpreter of the whole Italian people, proclaim the annexation of Fiume to Italy." He then unfurled a bloodstained tricolor flag that he had allegedly carried with him throughout the war, and pressed it to his lips while the people cheered madly. Thousands of Yugoslavs prepared to flee the city.

Before departing on his glorious mission, D'Annunzio had sent letters to his favorite newspapers, including Mussolini's *Popolo d'Italia*, to be published upon his entrance into Fiume. "Dear Companion," read the missive to Mussolini, "The dice are on the table. To-morrow I shall take Fiume with force of arms. The God of Italy assist us! I arise from bed with fever. But it is impossible to delay. Once more the spirit dominates the miserable flesh. . . . Sustain the cause without stint during the conflict. I embrace you." For the moment, D'Annunzio's exploits had earned him the undisputed leadership of the extremist wing of the Italian nationalist movement, but Mussolini, standing warily on the sidelines watching his rival garner the adulation of the arditi and the anarchists, would soon see what he could do about that.

In Rome, Nitti stood before the Chamber of Deputies on the thirteenth and denounced the Fiume expedition: "I am filled with humiliation because for the first time sedition has entered the Italian army." This act of "lunatics and traitors," he argued, could only strengthen the Allies' belief that Italy was bent on imperialistic conquests. "Italy," Nitti warned, "is no longer in a position to tolerate a policy of adventure without being brought to a state of anarchy." Perhaps the army would support a nationalist raid today, perhaps a Bolshevik plot tomorrow. The Prime Minister's objections notwithstanding, D'Annunzio's coup aroused tremendous public support throughout Italy, particularly in military circles. Volunteers from Lombardy poured into Fiume to reinforce the raiders; sailors from the

Dante Alighieri jumped ship and swam to join D'Annunzio; the crew of the destroyer *Stocco* mutinied and declared for the rebels; and a squad of arditi concealed themselves in the hold of a steamer laden with provisions and then, after it put to sea, commandeered the ship and diverted it to Fiume. The government attempted to impose a blockade to starve D'Annunzio into submission, but the poet replied by confiscating all foodstuffs in the city, vowing to let the Slavs starve first; besides, committees of sympathetic farmers in the countryside kept the provisions flowing into Fiume. Nitti issued a declaration that any soldier who refused to return to his unit would be considered an enemy of Italy; virtually no one obeyed this command, which D'Annunzio scathingly described as "an infamous order, worthy of a vile government." (In a similar vein, Mussolini wrote scornfully of Nitti's "tangled and slimy net of humiliating understandings" with the Yugoslavs.) Finally the government was reduced to removing vital parts from army airplanes to prevent pilots from taking their machines over to the rebels. (Consequently the aerial postal service between Milan and Rome had to be temporarily discontinued.) Twice every day, D'Annunzio sent wireless messages to Rome calling for Nitti's resignation. When the Prime Minister refused to comply, the poet petulantly announced that he was tired of dealing with the dog. It was not surprising that American diplomats in Washington began to think that the Italian government was losing control of the situation.

Completely frustrated, Nitti called a Crown Council meeting for September 25. It was the first such gathering since 1882; current and former top-level political and military leaders (except Sonnino, who said he was ill but really just wanted to avoid any responsibility for the fiasco) conferred with King Emmanuel at the Quirinal Palace to try to work out a solution that would restore the government's battered authority while avoiding a popular rebellion. Nitti feared, with good reason, that any order to the army or navy to throw the raiders out of Fiume would provoke wholesale mutinies. D'Annunzio, of course, sent his own special appeal to the king imploring him not to abandon Fiume, and hundreds of mothers and widows of men killed in the war sent telegrams to the palace urging Emmanuel to annex the beleaguered city. When the Crown Council failed to devise a viable solution, the issue was thrown into the Chamber of Deputies, where it precipitated a ten-minute free-for-all fistfight between a hundred nationalist and Socialist deputies. The chamber grudgingly gave Nitti a vote of confidence, but the narrow 208-to-148 margin meant that the Cabinet's freedom of action to deal with the crisis would be severely restricted. Finally, Nitti threw up his hands in complete despair. Parliament was dissolved on September 29, and elections for a new legislature were scheduled for November 16.

Having achieved one of his original objectives, i.e., the political embarrassment of Nitti, D'Annunzio still gave no indication of vacating his stronghold. He was enjoying life as Commander of Fiume; almost every day, he and his troops marched through the countryside, shouting defiance at the government. His lieutenants warned that the harbor, the churches, the city hall, the tower, and hundreds of houses in Fiume had been mined to prevent invasion. D'Annunzio openly vowed to blow up the city rather than surrender. Personally, he would deem it a privilege to die for the cause; he had already selected his gravesite in a cemetery, dark with cypresses, on a laurel-covered hill overlooking the sea. "I have risked all, given all, and I have conquered," the poet boasted in Mussolini's journal. "None can dislodge me from here. I hold Fiume; I will keep it while life remains. In any case, we struggle without ceasing. . . . But Fiume is but the solitary peak of heroism where it will be sweet to die, the lips moistened for the last time at the water of its fountains. Up! For six nights I have not slept; the fever devours me, but I am still on my feet. Those who have seen me will tell you how!" D'Annunzio also called Mussolini a coward for failing to come to Fiume to fight alongside him, but Benito deleted that offensive accusation and substituted an invitation for public subscriptions to succor D'Annunzio's forces. On the first day alone, the people of Milan reportedly contributed 102,320 lire (approximately $20,000).

Most of this money never reached Fiume. Mussolini simply pocketed it and used it to finance his own self-promotion campaign. But Benito gained more than lire from D'Annunzio's raid. The spectacle of a few thousand armed and determined men successfully defying a paralyzed government inspired a vision in Mussolini's soul of a future Fascist march on Rome to seize supreme power from the discredited old politicians who would drag Italy's name in the dust. In fact, D'Annunzio apparently suggested such a march—with himself at the head, of course, using Fiume as a launching point—to Mussolini in 1919. But Mussolini discouraged all such talk, urging D'Annunzio to await a nationalist landslide in the parliamentary elections. Privately, Mussolini feared that the poet might bungle the operation and ruin everything. And besides, he knew his own Fascist forces were not yet ready.

One of the more onerous duties of Reichswehr officers in Bavaria was to keep tabs on all the tiny political parties and clubs that infested the beer halls of Munich. Some were so small—only a half-dozen members—that the effort hardly seemed worthwhile. But orders were orders, and so at the end of the summer Adolf Hitler was instructed to set aside his propaganda duties temporarily and investigate an organization that called itself the German Workers' Party: the Deutsche Arbeiterpartei.

On the evening of September 12—the day that had dawned with D'Annunzio's triumphal entry into Fiume—Hitler walked into the back room of the shabby Sternecker beer hall, located on the Herrenstrasse in Munich, to attend his first meeting of the party. (Beer halls were popular sites for political meetings in Bavaria; their bandstands could easily be transformed into speakers' platforms.) An irregular band of twenty-five ragged souls was gathered there; Hitler was definitely unimpressed. Surely, he thought, this was nothing more than just another ineffectual, ramshackle political organization, just like all the others that, he knew, "sprang out of the ground, only to vanish silently after a time." After listening to a long-winded exposition on financial theory by an academic crank, Hitler got up to leave. Then he heard someone in the audience suggest that Bavaria secede from Germany and align itself with Austria instead. At once Hitler jumped to his feet and, for a quarter of an hour, scathingly denounced the disastrous notion of Bavarian secession. Anton Drexler, one of the party's founders, stood at the bar and marveled at Hitler's oratory. "It was a joy to watch," recalled Drexler. "He gave a short but trenchant speech in favour of a greater Germany which thrilled me and all who could hear him." As Hitler was leaving, Drexler pressed upon him a forty-page pamphlet, bound in pink and written by Drexler himself, entitled *My Political Awakening: From the Diary of a German Socialist Worker*, the first official National Socialist propaganda tract. Drexler invited his guest to return the following week for a meeting of the party's inner circle.

Hitler did not rush home and read Drexler's pamphlet. He went to bed. But before he closed his eyes, he set out—as was his habit—some crumbs for the mice who shared his room. Before dawn, unable to sleep (in part because of the mice scurrying about the floor), Hitler began to leaf through the pamphlet. To his surprise, he found it extraordinarily sympathetic to his own awakening political beliefs, particularly the sections in which Drexler expounded upon the Jewish threat to Western civilization.

Already his superiors in the Reichswehr considered Hitler an expert on the "Jewish question"; when one of them had received a request from a junior member of the army's political branch for advice on the military's attitude toward Jews, the officer gave the letter to Hitler to answer. On September 16, Hitler sent the following reply—his first significant political statement:

IN GENERAL THE JEW HAS PRESERVED HIS RACE AND CHARACTER THROUGH THOUSANDS OF YEARS OF INBREEDING, OFTEN WITHIN VERY CLOSE FAMILY RELATIONSHIPS, AND HE HAS BEEN MORE SUCCESSFUL IN THIS THAN MOST OF THE PEOPLE AMONG WHOM HE LIVES. THUS WE ARE FACED WITH THE FACT THAT THERE LIVES AMONG US A NON-GERMAN, ALIEN RACE WHICH DOES NOT WANT AND IS NOT IN A POSITION TO SACRIFICE ITS RACIAL CHARACTERISTICS OR TO RENOUNCE THE EMOTIONS, IDEAS, AND ASPIRATIONS PECULIAR TO IT, YET NEVERTHELESS POSSESSES THE SAME POLITICAL PRIVILEGES THAT WE DO. THE EMOTIONS OF THE JEWS REMAIN PURELY MATERIALISTIC, AND THIS IS EVEN MORE TRUE OF THEIR IDEAS AND ASPIRATIONS. . . .

THEY CORRUPT PRINCES WITH BYZANTINE FLATTERY. NATIONAL PRIDE, THE VIGOR OF A PEOPLE, ARE DESTROYED BY THEIR DERISION AND THE SHAMELESS INCULCATION OF VICE. THEY USE THE WEAPONS OF PUBLIC OPINION, WHICH IS NEVER REPRESENTED BY THE PRESS, ALTHOUGH THE PRESS CONTROLS AND FALSIFIES IT. THEIR POWER IS THE POWER OF MONEY. . . .

To eliminate the threat posed to *aer Volk*—the German people—by these insidious creatures who were constantly working to undermine the nation's moral strength from within, Hitler recommended "a methodical legal struggle against them and the elimination of the privileges they possess, which distinguish them from other aliens living among us. . . . The final aim must be the deliberate removal [the German word meant deportation to a faraway place] of the Jews. Both are only possible through a government of national strength, not a government of national impotence." And clearly, for Hitler, the Weimar Republic of Ebert, Scheidemann, and Bauer was incapable of solving the problem. "Only the rebirth of the moral and spiritual strength of the nation can bring this about," Hitler concluded; it was a rebirth that required "the ruthless intervention of national personalities possessing leadership and profound inner feelings of responsibility."

Herein lay the germ of the Holocaust.

As yet Hitler had no intention of employing the Deutsche Arbeiterpartei as the vehicle of his ambitions; in fact, he may not yet have entertained any great political ambitions at all for himself. Nevertheless, on the sixteenth—the same day he wrote out his solution to the Jewish problem—Hitler received official notification of his membership in the German Workers' Party, along with an invitation to attend the party's executive committee meeting two days hence. Grumbling to himself about the utter futility of getting involved with losers such as these, Hitler nonetheless betook himself to another seedy beer hall not far from the Sterneckerbrau on the evening of September 18. There, in another back room, by the light of a sputtering gas lamp, he saw four people sitting at a table. Drexler introduced Hitler to Karl Harrer, cofounder of the party, and ostensibly its national chairman. "There was nothing here, really positively nothing," Hitler recalled in *Mein Kampf*. "Not a soul in Munich knew the party even by name, except for its few supporters and their few friends." But General Ludendorff himself specifically requested that Hitler remain inside the German Workers' Party to help it grow, to shape it into a useful instrument of the Reichswehr's will. And so he did.

Meanwhile, the six Communists charged with the murder of the hostages in the Luitpold Gymnasium in the last days of the Bavarian Soviet were found guilty and sentenced to death. The case had reopened old wounds. Once more in September unrest seethed just below the surface in the working-class districts of Munich. The authorities feared a renewed outbreak of violence; in fact, they claimed to have uncovered a Spartacist plot to murder a number of Reichswehr officers in their sleep. Thus, after the court pronounced the death sentence, police hustled their prisoners back to jail in motor vans under a strong military escort; the condemned men were then placed in separate cells under close guard, and the prison was surrounded by artillery, machine guns, and trench mortars. On September 19 all six prisoners were shot. Still to come were the trials of Count Anton Arco Valley, the slayer of Kurt Eisner, and the Viennese butcher Alois Lindner, who had been extradited from Austria, whence he had fled after his attack upon Herr Auer in the Bundestag.

Wednesday, September 17. Wilson's headache was continuous, his discomfort apparent to reporters on the train. At San Francisco, fourteen thousand people—far more than the hall could comfortably handle—gathered to hear his evening address. The audience was hot, impatient with the crowded accommodations, and angry at the hecklers who held up Wilson's speech for fifteen minutes by drowning out his words with whistles and jeers. "Sit down!" called the President's supporters. "Put them out!" The disorder did not end until Wilson concluded his speech.

Thursday, September 18. Three cities and three more speeches. To a gathering of 1,500 at a San Francisco businessmen's luncheon, Wilson predicted that American rejection of the League of Nations would isolate the United States and create such an atmosphere of distrust abroad that

American commercial interests would be severely damaged. What the world needed, Wilson insisted, was "a settled peace" that would permit Eastern Europe and Russia to rebuild their shattered economies.

Across the bay to Berkeley for a talk in the Greek Theater to the faculty and students of the University of California. Then there was a meeting at an Oakland auditorium that night, where, for the first time on the tour, Wilson was introduced by a woman, Dr. Aurelia Reinhardt, president of Mills College. As Wilson rose to speak, someone in the crowd called out, "Are we with him?" "Yes!" came the answer in shouted chorus. Wilson's voice broke several times during his speech, and he appeared to be suffering from a slight cold.

Back in Washington, the *Post* reported that federal warrants had been issued for the arrest and deportation of anarchists Emma Goldman and Alexander Berkman. In Pittsburgh, leaders of the union campaign to organize America's steel and iron workers announced plans for a nationwide strike to begin September 22.

Friday, September 19. After sixteen days of travel, Grayson insisted that Wilson preserve what was left of his health and his voice; he forbade any more impromptu speeches from the observation platform of the *Mayflower* during the train's frequent stops for fuel and maintenance.

At 8:15 A.M., there was a fifteen-minute stop in Santa Barbara, where the crowd vainly endeavored to induce Wilson to talk; then at Oceanside, an old man told Wilson that he supported the League: "I am a Republican, but I voted for you last time and I will vote for you again." Wilson laughed at the idea of a third term in the White House. "No, I am not hankering for trouble," he said. "Well," continued the old man, "it looks like you are the only one who will stand for American principles, and you have already borne more trouble than any other man." Wilson just smiled and looked up to see a group of boys sitting on top of a nearby freight car. "Hello, gallery," he called to them.

At 11:25 the train pulled into Los Angeles, en route to San Diego. As railroad crews switched the cars from the Southern Pacific to the Santa Fe tracks, a thousand people rushed the barrier of policemen around the *Mayflower*. Wilson stepped down to the vestibule entrance, and an engineer from a Santa Fe train reached his greasy hand up to the President, who graciously gave it a firm shake. "Good morning to you," Wilson said. Then a Mexican ("bareheaded and begrimed," remarked the *Los Angeles Times*'s correspondent) reached up, and Wilson accepted his hand, too. Finally the police, realizing the situation was hopeless, formed an avenue for people to pass through, and in ten minutes Wilson shook nearly a thousand hands. Then, his body aching, he turned and clattered down the *Mayflower*'s steps for a brisk walk around the station. A reporter at the scene saw the President as a man "slightly under six feet in height, [who] wears his clothes rather snug-fitting, and wears a jaunty cap for travelling. His eyes are clear and bright, his skin has a ruddy glow, and his handshake is like that of a wood-chopper." Wilson felt terrible. The crowd called for Mrs. Wilson to come out on the platform. After repeated entreaties, the First Lady at last emerged, only to duck back inside quickly when she sighted the battery of newspaper cameras awaiting her. As the train pulled out for San Diego, Wilson stood on the rear platform of his car, bowing and waving.

San Diego greeted him with shrieking factory whistles and a drive through the fairgrounds. At the mammoth San Diego stadium, Wilson stood sweltering in an enclosed glass platform from which a not-very-effective loudspeaker system (audio technology was still in its infancy) carried his words to a small part of the crowd. In the middle of the stands sat several hundred schoolgirls, arranged so that their white dresses spelled out the word WELCOME to the President. The stadium held forty thousand, but many more stood in the aisles and on the terraces at the start of the speech. Everyone carried a small American flag. In pleading for acceptance of the treaty and the League, Wilson quoted from a magazine article written by Theodore Roosevelt in 1914, in which the former President supported the concept of an international peacekeeping body; but since hardly anyone except the people in front could hear Wilson's words, much of the audience drifted away before he was finished.

Senator Hiram Johnson abandoned his cross-country tour after less than a week, pleading that his presence was needed more in Washington than on the road attacking Wilson.

Saturday, September 20. Mayor Meredith Snyder asked every citizen of Los Angeles to "set aside all business and pleasure and be prepared to lend his assistance" to a spectacular California welcome for Wilson. This was precisely what the President did not need, of course. So, instead of arriving at the Santa Fe passenger station in Los Angeles shortly after noon as planned, Wilson's train pulled in at 9:00 A.M. to allow the President to slip quietly into town and get a few extra hours' rest at the Hotel Alexandria before the parade scheduled for 11:30. Upon seeing a thousand raucous Angelenos awaiting him, however, Wilson's aides decided instead to back the train onto a remote siding, where the President could rest for another hour. At 10:10, Wilson left for the hotel. After settling into the Imperial

Suite (dining room, two bedrooms, baths, parlor, private pantry, and serv-ants' quarters) at the Alexandria, Wilson plunged into a waiting pile of correspondence that required his immediate attention. (The presidential party took over most of the Alexandria's seventh floor; Joseph Tumulty had the privilege of staying in D. W. Griffith's private suite—reportedly one of the most luxurious in the world—recently renovated at a cost of $15,000.) Then came the pounding, earsplitting torture of the parade. All the whistles in the city were tied wide open, and the *Los Angeles Times*'s siren screamed as the President's car set off on the fifty-block route from First Street to Broadway to Seventh Street, then west to Hope Street and Twelfth, along Twelfth to Main, and then back to Spring Street. Young girls in blinding white dresses tossed red roses in Wilson's path. A solid wall of people shouted and cheered all along the route; police estimated the crowd at 200,000, the largest ever to witness a parade in Los Angeles. Flags waved in the President's face.

During luncheon at the hotel, a police security cordon kept the usual hangers-on and lounge lizards from entering the lobby. Wilson himself requested the menu: olives, radishes, and almonds as hors d'oeuvres; casaba melon; broiled chicken à la President; corn sauté au beurre; spinach; salade moderne (romaine lettuce, asparagus tips, avocados, and mayonnaise dress-ing with chopped pimiento and chives); peach ice cream; charlotte russe; and coffee brewed in a glass bowl over an alcohol flame. Wilson compli-mented the chef on "the best salad I tasted since I left Washington." There followed a quiet afternoon in his hotel room, no visitors allowed. A few minutes before six, the presidential party stepped into the elevator and descended to the banquet room on the mezzanine. Wilson entered through an arch of grapevines and tiny electric bulbs that gave the effect of glow-worms in a garden. Five hundred fifteen invited guests stood and cheered; after a hurried meal, Wilson was introduced as "the greatest constructive genius the world has ever known." He told a story he had heard recently of former President McKinley, who, the day before he was assassinated, appeared to have a prophetic vision. McKinley had spoken that day of the need for America to end its isolation, to take a hand in urging other nations to adopt arbitration as a means to end war. "It would look," said Wilson sympathetically, "as if the man had been given a vision just before he died—one of the sweetest and humane souls that has been prominent in our affairs. . . . His intelligence was beginning to draw the lines of the picture which has now been completed. . . ." Once America joined the League, Wilson vowed, every boy who fought overseas could say not merely that he had defeated Germany, but "that he redeemed the world."

At the Shrine Auditorium, people had gathered as early as nine o'clock that morning to obtain seats for the President's evening address. By 6:30 P.M., every alley and street leading to the hall was jammed. Police estimated the crowd at fifty thousand people; the auditorium held only six thousand. A stampede ensued when the doors were finally thrown open. Blaring horns announced Wilson's imminent arrival. When the President walked across the platform, everyone in the audience stood and cheered themselves hoarse for minutes; when Wilson waved his hands for silence, the shouts only grew louder.

Sunday, September 21. A presidential breakfast of tip-top California melon, toasted shredded wheat for Wilson, soft-boiled eggs (medium), crisp bacon, and coffee, and then the President slipped quietly away to visit an old family friend living on a back street in the city. To forestall another crush of curious spectators, Tumulty deliberately refused to announce which church service the Wilsons would attend. (The ensuing uncertainty caused considerable consternation among the city's pastors, each of whom prepared an especially learned sermon in case the President should decide to grace his particular church.) Since Wilson was a Presbyterian, the Immanuel Presbyterian Church optimistically roped off and reserved a large space in the center of the church. But Wilson and his wife, an Episcopalian, took turns attending each other's churches while traveling, and this week it was her turn. So precisely at 11:00 A.M. a large automobile pulled up at the entrance to St. Paul's Procathedral and the Wilsons and Grayson emerged and were ushered to the few remaining empty benches in the front of the congregation. There they listened attentively to Dean William MacCormack's sermon based on the Old Testament text, "And he requested for himself that he might die."

42

"Remember me, and visit me

and revenge me of my persecutors;

take me not away

in thy longsuffering . . ."

As the White Sox and Redlegs tuned up for their imminent confrontation in the World Series, Babe Ruth shattered every home-run record in major-league baseball history. The modern record was twenty-four, set by Gavvy "Cactus" Cravath of the Philadelphia Phillies in 1915; but Cravath had hit nineteen of his homers that year over a notoriously short fence at home (the Phillies played in the friendly confines of the old Baker Bowl in those days). The Babe broke Cravath's record on September 5, appropriately enough in Philadelphia, off an undistinguished hurler named Wynn Noyes, who had a lifetime record of eleven wins and fifteen losses. Number twenty-five, incidentally, came in the second game of a doubleheader; Ruth had been the starting pitcher and scored the winning run in the first game. Fifteen of Ruth's 25 homers had come on the road, proving his ability to hit the ball out of any park. But even this herculean feat was not enough to satisfy the Babe's detractors, who pointed out that back in 1899, a Washington Senators outfielder named John "Buck" Freeman had hit twenty-five home runs. So, on September 8, Ruth smashed that record too, when he hit number twenty-six into the right-field seats at the Polo Grounds. (The fan who retrieved the ball promptly returned it to Ruth and refused the proffered twenty-five-dollar reward; Ruth said that he would donate the souvenir to the St. Mary's Industrial School for Boys in Baltimore, the orphanage where he had been raised.)

Then someone discovered a dusty record of twenty-seven home runs, set by Edward Nagle "Ned" Williamson of the late, unlamented Chicago Colts, all the way back in 1884, when many pitchers threw underhanded and the Colts had played in a stadium with a right-field fence only 215 feet from home plate. Not surprisingly, Williamson had hit twenty-five of his homers at home that year. Undaunted, Ruth proceeded to clout number twenty-seven off Lefty Williams on September 20. The most spectacular thing about the record-tying shot was that Ruth, a left-handed hitter, smashed it over the left-field fence off an excellent left-handed pitcher. Buck Weaver, the Sox third baseman, came by between games to congratulate Ruth on "the most unbelievable poke I ever saw"; Williams, too, stopped in to express "his horrified disbelief."

Four days later, the Babe hit number twenty-eight out of the Polo Grounds—literally *out*, over the stadium roof, the longest clout anyone at *The New York Times* sports desk could remember. (Shoeless Joe had once hit a ball onto the roof, but apparently no one had ever hit one out of the Polo Grounds altogether.) Ruth finished with twenty-nine home runs in 130 games, a truly spectacular accomplishment. Nevertheless, the Red Sox finished a distant sixth, twenty-one-and-a-half games behind Gleason's White Sox. As the season ended, Boston manager Ed "Wheel" Barrow pledged to press Ruth to cut down his swing next season and raise his average to .400 (Ruth hit only .322 in 1919). "No, he will not be trying to knock the ball out of the lot after this season," Barrow promised. "He will be content with his record, because it will be far and away out of reach of any other batter the game is likely to develop."

By the end of September, star White Sox right hander Eddie Cicotte and first baseman Chick Gandil had met at least twice with professional gamblers in a New York hotel room.

Charles Spencer Chaplin: The man who made more people laugh than anyone else in history. In fact, Chaplin himself once estimated that "I am known in parts of the world by people who have never heard of Jesus Christ." (Chaplin probably had more justification than John Lennon, who later made a similar statement, although, strictly speaking, both entertainers may have been correct.)

Born in south London in 1889, the son of a pair of temperamentally unstable vaudeville performers—his father drank heavily and deserted the family shortly after Chaplin was born; his mother eventually went half-mad—Chaplin drove himself to success as a pantomime comedian, landing a film contract with producer Mack Sennett in 1913 after touring America with an English comedy troupe. By 1918, Chaplin's immense popularity with movie audiences had already earned him a $1-million contract with First National Exhibitors for eight pictures; for the first time in his career, Chaplin was able to control the entire creative process in his films—

writing, acting, directing, and producing. The first two movies Chaplin made under this agreement, *Shoulder Arms* and *A Dog's Life*, were quite successful, but both took longer than expected, and so back Chaplin went to First National for more money. The company refused. ("Exhibitors were rugged merchants in those days," Chaplin wrote several decades later, retaining a trace of bitterness, "and to them films were merchandise costing so much a yard.")

This philistine attitude antagonized the artist in Chaplin, and left him willing and ready to join his Hollywood friends in the United Artists venture, for he was a notorious perfectionist who insisted upon getting each frame exactly right. It was not unusual for Chaplin to spend weeks shooting a single scene, or to discard 95 percent of the film shot on a production (or even, in extreme cases, to throw out all of the film and start over from scratch) to create precisely the effect he desired. His costars usually were nothing more than mimics who followed his instructions down to the tiniest detail. The combination of Chaplin's artistic vision and his immense self-confidence allowed him to carry off these dictatorial tactics successfully: "You have to believe in yourself—that's the secret," he once told his son. "I had that exuberance that comes from utter confidence in yourself." He was certain that he knew, from years of observation in theaters and on the street, what made people laugh. "Even funnier than the man who has been made ridiculous is the man who, having had something funny happen to him, refuses to admit that anything out of the way has happened, and attempts to maintain his dignity," Chaplin explained in 1918. "I am so sure of this point that I not only try to get myself into embarrassing situations, but I also incriminate the other characters in the picture."

But in early 1919 Charlie experienced a severe creative crisis. Embittered as he was by First National's refusal to give him the funds he felt he needed to make his pictures, the spark of inspiration deserted him, and he found himself at a loss for comic ideas to complete his current production, *Sunnyside*. The daily studio reports eloquently bespoke his inertia:

February 21	Did not shoot. Mr. Chaplin cutting
February 22	Did not shoot. Mr. Chaplin cutting
February 23	Did not shoot. Mr. Chaplin cutting
February 25	Did not shoot. Looking for locations
February 26	Did not shoot. Mr. Chaplin not feeling well
February 27	Did not shoot. Mr. Chaplin cutting
February 28	Did not shoot.

March 1   Did not shoot. Filmed sunset, 100 feet.
March 2   Did not shoot. Talked story
March 4   Did not shoot. Talked story

Chaplin eventually completed *Sunnyside*, but it was neither a commercial nor an artistic success. Almost its only distinguishing feature was a dream dance sequence inspired by Nijinsky's *L'Apres-midi d'une Faune*; Nijinsky and his company had visited Chaplin's studio shortly before the dancer settled in St. Moritz and began his final descent into insanity. Chaplin's next feature, *A Day's Pleasure*, was equally undistinguished. *Photoplay* magazine sneered that " 'Sunnyside' was anything but sunny; 'A Day's Pleasure' certainly was not pleasure," and an article in *Theatre Magazine* wondered, "Is the Charlie Chaplin Vogue Passing?" Nor could Chaplin find solace in his personal life. In 1918 he had married a sixteen-year-old girl, Mildred Harris, who convinced him that he had gotten her in trouble. By the time Chaplin found out Mildred was not, in fact, pregnant, the couple was already married, albeit none too happily. "Charley is like a whole lot o' other fellers," joked a homespun comedian, "he kin make ever' buddy laugh but his wife." The death of their malformed baby boy several days after it was born in July 1919 did not strengthen their relationship; a long, long time afterward, Mildred still remembered that "Charlie took it hard . . . that's the only thing I can remember about Charlie . . . that he cried when the baby died."

A four-year-old boy rescued Chaplin from this slough of artistic despair. In the spring of 1919 the comedian had attended a show at the Orpheum that featured an unusual dance act by one Mr. Jack Coogan and his young son. The boy obviously impressed Chaplin, for when he ran into the Coogan family again at the Alexandria Hotel a day or two later, Charlie asked if he could speak with little Jackie for a few minutes. For three-quarters of an hour the world's greatest comedian (who was even shorter than Fairbanks, standing only five feet four inches tall and weighing about 130 pounds) and the little boy sat and played together on the floor of the Alexandria's lobby. Chaplin asked the boy what he did; "I am a prestidigitator who works in a world of legerdemain," Jackie replied nonchalantly. Now the wheels of inspiration started to turn once again in Chaplin's mind. "This is the most amazing person I ever met in my life," Chaplin told the Coogans when he returned Jackie. When summer came and Charlie started work on a film tentatively titled *The Waif*, he began to think of what he could do with Coogan in the title role. Discovering that the child was not yet under contract to any studio, Chaplin signed him up with alacrity and spent August and September working on the movie, now given its final title, *The Kid*.

Jackie Coogan, claims film critic David Robinson, was "the most perfect actor" with whom Chaplin ever worked, simply because "Jackie's genius was as a mimic. When Chaplin showed him something, he could do it." The two had a relationship that was very special: the boy was both a surrogate son for Chaplin and a playmate when Charlie indulged the streak of childlike whimsy that so endeared him to movie audiences. Their affection for each other was obvious. "In leisure moments at the studio," reported the *Los Angeles Times* on September 15, "Charlie delights in petting the youngster and in listening to his amusing prattle. . . . Chaplin has not only developed a deep affection for the small lad, but he believes he will some day be a very clever comedian." He already was; Robinson maintains that "no child actor, whether in silent or in sound pictures, has ever surpassed Jackie Coogan's performance as The Kid, in its truthfulness and range of sentiment."

But in 1919 the vision of history's most famous comedian extended beyond the personal and professional trials he had recently suffered, beyond the promise of more complex, innovative cinematic masterpieces for the future. With the war finally over, Chaplin understood that this pivotal year marked a new beginning for the rest of the world as well: "One thing was sure, that civilization as we had known it would never be the same—that era had gone. Gone, too, were its so-called basic decencies—but, then, decency had never been prodigious in any era."

On every side, Comrade Lenin saw his enemies closing in. In the south, the rough-hewn reactionary General Anton Denikin stormed through the Ukraine with his volunteers and Cossacks; in the blistering summer the southern front extended nearly eight hundred miles, from the mining districts around Petrovsk on the Caspian Sea to the dreary steppes surrounding Tsaritsyn, just east of the Don, and every day the front shifted like the mist into a new and equally impermanent configuration. Denikin captured the city of Kharkov, then Yekaterinoslav on the Dnieper. So Lenin diverted Red reinforcements to counter Denikin. Then from the east Admiral Alexander Kolchak's armies swept hundreds of miles across the plains from their base in Omsk, taking full advantage of the depleted Soviet defenses in the path of their march toward Moscow. Kolchak's victories persuaded the Allies in Paris to recognize him as Supreme Ruler of Russia pending his pledge to reconvene the representative Constituent Assembly, which had been so rudely interrupted by the Bolshevik coup in

1917. From the west came the White General N. N. Yudenich, aided by Baltic nationalists, threatening Soviet control of Petrograd. The Bolsheviks offered a reward of 500,000 rubles for Yudenich, alive or dead. Thus threatened, Lenin obviously could spare no forces at all to save Béla Kun and the beleaguered Hungarian Soviet Republic from its foreign enemies as Kun's experiment collapsed late in July.

Lenin had hoped the first six months of 1919 would be "our last difficult half-year," but it was not. The second half was worse. From his office in the Kremlin, Lenin dispatched a multitude of telegrams giving orders to shift the Red armies to meet the most immediate threat, exhorting his commanders to employ every physical and psychological resource to save the Revolution. Decency, which had never been prodigious in Russia in the best of times, disappeared in the crucible of civil war. The imperative of terror bothered Lenin not at all. "Civil war is civil war," he announced philosophically to a Norwegian journalist. "It writes its own laws. It is like this: Either the proletariat governs or capital rules. There is no other alternative. There are some who are not pleased with our dictatorship. I say to them, 'Go to Siberia [where Kolchak ruled] and see if the dictatorship is better there.' " In Siberia the peasants hung Red prisoners head downward in huge holes and then slowly, methodically threw dirt into the holes to fill them up, watching their victims' agonies and wondering who would be the last to die. "I think," wrote Maxim Gorky in despair, "that the Russian people have an exclusive sense of cruelty (as exclusive as the Englishman's sense of humour), cold-blooded, as if testing by exact experiment how much pain human beings can endure. In Russian cruelty one feels a diabolical inventiveness, refined and recherché." Gorky asked some soldiers if they felt no despair at the relentless killing and suffering. "No, not at all," they replied. "He has a rifle, so have I. That means we are equal. Let us kill each other. Thus the earth will be disencumbered." "We have so many people, such bad agriculture," a Soviet soldier explained to the famed author. "Well, so we burn down a village. What does it matter? It would have burned down in any case some time."

But the wanton destruction wrought by the White armies in the lands they conquered, accompanied by the reimposition of harsh feudal land-holding laws in the regions they governed, aroused violent discontent among the peasants, who knew that the Bolsheviks at least had given them their own small portions of land to farm. Although Kolchak himself did not necessarily desire to reinstitute the most repressive features of the Czarist regime, the conservative militarists and great landowners who supported him certainly did. "What can Kolchak bring you," cried a streetcorner orator in Moscow, "but new whips to drive you back to your kennels?" From his exile in Paris, the liberal Alexander Kerensky warned the Allies that Kolchak was "merely an instrument in the hands of unscrupulous reactionaries. . . . I cannot understand," Kerensky added, "how the nations of the West, professedly democratic as they are, can bring themselves to the rehabilitation of tyranny in Russia, or expect any good to come from substituting a White Terror for a Red Terror. How can they fail to see the inevitably disastrous effects upon themselves as well as upon Russia of such a regime?" Meanwhile, in the Ukraine, Denikin's bands of irregulars instigated wholesale pogroms. It was nothing less than the organized genocide of the Jewish population: in some villages every male over twelve years of age was slaughtered; people were buried alive; Jewish quarters were razed to the ground, leaving only smoking ashes behind. By the end of August approximately 90,000 Jews reportedly had been killed in southern Russia alone.

For a time the only cheerful news that reached Lenin came from the north, where the Allied military intervention had suffered an ignominious collapse. By the end of June, no American fighting forces remained in the Archangel sector. Despite Churchill's reluctance to abandon what he saw as a grand crusade, the British government announced on September 11 that it, too, would withdraw its troops from the Archangel and Murmansk regions as soon as an evacuation could be safely carried out. French sailors already had mutinied in the Black Sea. Both British and French workers were exerting political pressure at home against further military expeditions against the Bolsheviks. Restive Czechs serving with Kolchak decided they preferred to return to their newly independent homeland, which had its hands full fending off its own enemies in the Balkans. The Japanese, who extended recognition to Kolchak's government in return for acknowledgement of their predominance in Manchuria and Mongolia, posed no threat to the Russian heartland. By the end of the summer, Finnish and Estonian troops concluded that they held all the Russian territory they desired, and most of them deserted Yudenich's assault upon Petrograd.

Indeed, no sooner did the Allies agree to recognize Kolchak than the admiral's forces fell back before the Red armies' determined assault in August. Behind his lines, angry peasants cut off Kolchak's supply of provisions and ambushed his soldiers. By the end of the summer, Kolchak's supporters found themselves reduced to arguing whether the admiral had retreated eight hundred miles or only four hundred. The Reds claimed to have captured his entire southern army, nearly 45,000 men. On September 16, the Supreme Allied Council decided to write an end to the whole sordid chapter of military intervention, voicing unanimous opposition to any new "Russian adventures." Yet, following what *The New Republic* termed "the indefinable but irresistible impulse which drives the Allies and America to bet on the wrong horse in Russia" (an impulse that later would be extended to China as well), the United States continued to ship extensive stores of arms and ammunition to Kolchak's forces even as they fled eastward for their lives into Siberia; such aid was imperative, State Department spokesmen argued, to give the White armies a boost in morale.

But to save Moscow from Kolchak, Lenin had stripped his defenses in the south and the west. So, even without extensive Allied support, Denikin and Yudenich were able to resume their threatening advances. "The second half of 1919 was more difficult than the first," recalled Lenin's wife, Krupskaya, nearly twenty years later. "Especially difficult were September, October, and the beginning of November." The Whites set their sights directly on Moscow and Petrograd, the twin centers of Soviet power. Yudenich, commanding about 17,000 men against 27,000 Red defenders, launched a final assault on Petrograd on September 15.

Inside Moscow, Lenin faced dissension within the Bolshevik ranks and rising opposition from counterrevolutionists emboldened by the White successes in the field. Communist Party officials debated violently a motion to expand the practice of employing veteran military officers from the old Czarist regime to train, discipline, and lead the Red Army (a practice that already had, surprisingly, produced spectacularly successful results); the Eighth Party Congress, opting for expediency over the strictures of Bolshevik theory, voted overwhelmingly in support of the proposal. But the Red Army still needed more men; commanders on the southern front demanded more troops to hold Denikin at bay; at the same time, the defenders of Petrograd insisted that they deserved highest priority on reinforcements. Trotsky found himself clashing more than once over questions of strategy with a hardheaded, practical-minded, and extraordinarily ruthless young party official known by the pseudonym of Josef Stalin, "a man of infinite resource" who already had begun to display a psychopathic obsession with the agents of treason he saw lurking behind every expression of opposition to his personal will. (Stalin had successfully organized the defense of Petrograd in May, and then was transferred to the southern front to battle Denikin; still, he found time to plot assiduously in Moscow to undermine Trotsky's relationship with Lenin.) For his part, Lenin found Stalin's brutality in the service of the Revolution a useful weapon at a time when enemies continued to stalk the Bolshevik regime behind the lines. On September 25 a bomb planted by anarchists exploded at the headquarters of the Moscow Committee of the Party, killing a number of Communist functionaries. Lenin's reply to the rising tide of troubles was to step up the pace of his own exertions, to redouble his dedication to the vision that he saw more clearly and believed in more passionately and faithfully than anyone else. "He worked from morning till night," wrote Krupskaya, "and out of great anxiety he could not sleep. He would awake in the middle of the night, get out of bed, and begin to check by telephone: had this or the other of his orders been carried out? . . . In those busy months I saw him less than usual, we almost never took walks. I hesitated to go to his office since I had no business there: I was afraid to interfere with his work."

Monday, September 22. Wilson's train swung eastward at last, speeding through small California towns—Merced, Turlock, Modesto—and past disappointed crowds waiting at every station to catch a glimpse of the President. A ten-minute stop had been scheduled for Stockton at 10:45 A.M., where the town fathers optimistically had erected a special speaking platform near the track, but the weary Wilson refused to make a speech. Frustrated spectators pressed forward to try at least to shake his hand, engulfing a member of the presidential party in the swirling throng and forcing the unfortunate man away from the train until two Secret Service agents came to his rescue. When Wilson finally leaned over the platform to say a few words as the train prepared to pull away, the din of the crowd's shouting drowned out his weakened voice.

At Sacramento, Wilson consented to address the twelve thousand enthusiastic admirers—mostly women and children—who had gathered at the station. The train's departure was delayed when the crowd surged across the tracks in front of the engine. A six-year-old boy who kept yelling, "I want to shake hands with the President," was picked up and passed over the heads of the crowd until he reached Wilson, who grasped his hand, patted him on the head, and passed him back. On through the Sierras, where acrid black smoke from forest fires raging through the mountains billowed through the steel coaches; time and again the *Mayflower* passed within a few feet of flaming trees; once the train was stopped to make certain there was no danger to the tracks from a blaze blackening the sky ahead. At Midas, near the Nevada border, Wilson and his wife walked along a precipice overlooking a canyon through which the American River flowed. The sudden changes in altitude exacerbated the President's asthma. There was a pronounced nervous twitching in his face almost all the time. Pain writhed through his head. His wife often found him leaning forward, resting his head against a chair as he sought to sort out his thoughts through the pain.

Angered at reports from Europe that Clemenceau and Lloyd George were willing to grant Italy additional concessions in the Adriatic, Wilson released a statement reiterating that he had not altered his position on Fiume, Signor D'Annunzio's successful invasion notwithstanding.

The train reached Reno at 8:05 in the evening. Without pausing for rest, Wilson and his party climbed into waiting automobiles for still another parade through streets densely packed with cheering spectators. Two thousand people awaited the President at a theater; Wilson's speech was relayed via telephone lines to three other theaters where several thousand more people heard his words. "This treaty was not written, essentially speaking, in Paris," Wilson told them all. "It was written at Château-Thierry, in Belleau Wood and in the Argonne. Our men did not fight with the purpose of coming back and having the same thing happen again. They fought with the purpose of seeing the thing through, and we are going to see it through."

Tuesday, September 23. Dry, hot, dusty desert towns. A one-hour drive through Ogden, where the people's cheers rang through the scorching air. At another stop, someone asked the President how the tour was going. "Well," he replied, "I am having a wonderful trip, with gratifying results." He delivered an evening speech at the Tabernacle in Salt Lake City, where President Grant of the Mormon church already had come out in favor of the League of Nations. Fifteen thousand people packed tightly into the Tabernacle; rumor had it that Wilson was going to unleash the verbal fireworks against Lodge this evening, and so the temple hummed with the anticipation of a knock-down, drag-out political fight. Instead, Wilson stood tall and pale on an elevated platform, his shirt soaked with perspiration, his tortured lungs breathing the close, stale air with terrible difficulty; his wife passed him a handkerchief soaked in lavender smelling salts. After two hours of heartfelt pleas to save the League, rewarded only by polite applause, the ordeal was over for another night, but Tumulty tartly advised the President that his speech had seemed weak and listless.

Wednesday, September 24. The train swept across sparsely settled territory with no one there to see it pass. Wilson slept late. At Cheyenne, near the end of the afternoon, he vowed to condemn any substantive senatorial reservations to the League Covenant as the equivalent of total rejection of the treaty. The question of whether the League would have the heart cut out of it, the President added in the appropriate Western phrase, must soon come to a "show-down."

Wilson admitted privately to his wife that he felt sick and very, very tired, but he could not rest, he could not abandon the fight now. "I have caught the imagination of the people," he said. "They are eager to hear what the League stands for. I should fail in my duty if I disappointed them." He promised her, half seriously, that they would take a vacation together after they returned to Washington.

Denver was ablaze with special lights strung up by the local gas and electric company as the presidential train arrived at eleven o'clock that night. At the hotel Wilson met his beloved cousin Harriet, to whom he had once proposed marriage, and they talked for an hour; even then, exhausted as he was, he could not fall asleep at once.

Thursday, September 25 to Sunday, September 28. The President arose early for a parade from the state capitol to the Denver City Auditorium. Wilson entered the hall to the cheers of eleven thousand people and the booming, throbbing chords of "Onward, Christian Soldiers," played on a huge pipe organ. The speaker's podium, adorned with a white cover and the emblems of the United States, stood ten feet above the heads of the rest of the people on the platform. Charles Grasty, *The New York Times* correspondent traveling with the President, noticed that Wilson looked shaky as he rose to speak at 9:56, but seemed to gather strength as he went on. The President repeated the charge that the League's enemies were pro-German; outside of the Senate, Wilson charged, the only people who opposed the treaty were those who had favored Germany in the late war. He promised to resist all crippling amendments to the League Covenant: "There is no question of reservations or amendments to the treaty. The issue is flatly acceptance or rejection." A demonstration erupted in the audience as people jumped on their chairs and shouted, "You bet, Woodrow!" and "We're with you, old boy!" A woman called out, "You are God's chosen spokesman, thank God!" Now Wilson was throwing everything he had into the fight. Acceptance of the League meant "insurance against war," he promised, "and that's worth the whole game." He held himself personally responsible to the mothers, wives, and sweethearts of America to prevent another war in the next generation. "The children," he promised solemnly, "are my clients."

Back on the train, the President had little appetite for lunch. He wanted to cancel the planned parade to the fairgrounds at the next stop, in Pueblo, but finally consented to drive past the assembled crowd; as he heard the cheers through the haze of pain in his head, he waved his brown fedora in vague reply. There was one step at the entrance to the auditorium in Pueblo where Wilson would make his last speech. He stumbled and nearly fell, but was steadied by a Secret Service agent. Wilson sat in the middle of the platform, only a few feet from newspapermen who noticed that his expression seemed somehow different. Mrs. Wilson was visibly anxious. Just before he rose to speak, a few minutes after three in the afternoon, Wilson turned and, in a low voice, jokingly said to the reporters who had been traveling with him across the country, "You fellows must be sick and tired of this." It was the fortieth speech of the tour. Grasty noticed that Wilson appeared to be in some distress as he began his address: "he did not look about the audience and smile in the usual way." Wilson's voice was unsteady, and for the first time during the tour he seemed to lose the thread of his thoughts. "Germany must never be allowed . . . A lesson must be taught to Germany . . . The world will not allow Germany . . ." His wife grew pale, and the reporters glanced at one another and at Mrs. Wilson. Then he recovered and went on. Wilson spoke of the men who had died in the war—the men whom, he could never forget, he as Commander-in-Chief had sent abroad to meet their deaths on the Western Front—and he spoke of the white crosses in France, and he spoke of America as the savior of the world. He spoke of "the moral obligation that rests upon us not to go back on those boys, but to see the thing through . . . to the end and make good the redemption of the world." Men and women wept openly in the audience; standing before them on the platform, Wilson wept, too. And then the final plea: "Now that the mists of this great question have cleared away, I believe that men will see the truth, eye to eye and face to face. There is one thing that the American people always rise to and extend their hand to, and that is the truth of justice and of liberty and of peace. We have accepted that truth and we are going to be led by it, and it is going to lead us, and through us the world, out into pastures of quietness and peace such as the world never dreamed of before."

It was a magnificent summation of an ideal that had driven one of the world's great men to the brink of self-destruction. Wilson would never again have the strength to deliver such a speech.

Twenty miles outside of Pueblo, en route to Wichita, the train stopped as it passed through the upper valley of the Arkansas River. Wilson, his wife, and Grayson descended and walked briskly along a dusty country road. An old man dressed in farm clothes stopped his car when he recognized Wilson; he gave the President some apples and a cabbage for dinner. After thirty minutes they turned and headed back to the train. On the way back, Wilson—his own words still swirling through his head with the pain—saw a young man, obviously ill, dressed in a private's uniform, sitting on the porch of a nearby house. Wilson climbed over the fence and shook hands with him and talked of small things. The boy's parents and brothers came out and spoke briefly with the President. Wilson and Grayson jogged the last hundred yards to the train.

A crowd had gathered at Rocky Ford where the train made a brief stop, and Tumulty pressed the President to go out and shake hands, but Grayson kept Wilson inside until the train was ready to leave. As it pulled away, Wilson stood waving to the people receding into the distance. . . .

At 11:30 P.M., Wilson called to his wife: "Can you come to me, Edith? I'm terribly sick." She went into his bedroom and saw him sitting on the edge of the bed. "I can't sleep because of the pain." His head rested on the back of a chair. "I'm afraid you'd better call Grayson." The minutes ticked by. Grayson arrived and discovered that the President was "on the verge of a complete breakdown." He couldn't lie still on his own bed; he had to get up and move about, and so he dressed himself and went to his office, in terrible constant pain and unable to rest, until finally, at five o'clock, he fell into an uneasy sleep seated in a chair cushioned with pillows. His wife stared at his face and decided that this was the beginning of the end.

Soon Wilson arose and started to shave himself in preparation for the day's activities at Wichita. Grayson alerted Tumulty and told him of the President's condition and the two men hurried through the *Mayflower* and argued with Wilson; he refused to cancel the tour, insisting that "I must go on. I should feel like a deserter. My opponents will accuse me of having cold feet should I stop now." Grayson replied that he must exercise his authority and order the train back to Washington immediately, for the sake of the country, for Wilson himself, and for his family. Wilson looked at Tumulty, his devoted aide for nearly a decade, and said, "My dear boy, this has never happened to me before, I don't know what to do." Wilson could not move his left arm or leg. "I want to show them that I am not afraid. Just postpone the trip for twenty-four hours and I will be all right." He looked to Edith for support.

No. She explained to him that if he tried to carry on the glorious fight in this condition, everything would surely be lost. Persuading her husband to give it up on this lonely morning was, she said later, the hardest thing she ever did in her life. "I suppose you are right," he said sadly, and tears flowed down his cheeks. "This is the greatest disappointment of my life." In years to come, Wilson believed that his cause might have triumphed if he had only died that day.

Tumulty and Grayson informed the reporters on board that the President had suffered "a complete nervous breakdown" and would be returning to Washington at once. The train stopped on the outskirts of Wichita; to allow the President to eat breakfast, they said at first. But then came the announcement that the scheduled speech was canceled. Fifteen thousand people waiting in the auditorium took the news in bewildered silence and filed out slowly while a quartet sang "Smile Awhile." There was no parade. Grayson's public bulletins insisted that the President's condition was "not alarming" and that he could have continued the tour, but only at the risk of further damage to his health. "The trouble," Grayson explained, "dates back to an attack of influenza last April in Paris from which he has never entirely recovered. The President's activities on this trip have overtaxed his strength and he is suffering from nervous exhaustion." What his patient needed most, he added, was complete rest and fresh air. Curious onlookers surrounded the *Mayflower* at the Wichita train station before it left at eleven o'clock. Over the heads of the Secret Service cordon, they could see Wilson moving about in his private car, his wife at his side. Soon Mrs. Wilson pulled the curtains across.

Grasty filed a story with the lead sentence, "The wonder is not that President Wilson has come to the end of his physical resources now, but that he did not come to the end of them long ago." The image that would remain with the people of the West, *The New York Times* reporter wrote, was "that of a man burning with a restrained passion for a great purpose, for the accomplishment of which he would gladly lay down his life."

Crowds gathered at every station along the way, hoping to catch a glimpse of the stricken President, but the train rolled relentlessly eastward at top speed. Railway officials cleared the tracks for miles ahead. Unannounced, the train slipped in and out of St. Louis, where it changed engines at four o'clock in the morning. Wilson could not sleep at night, drifting off only toward dawn and then sleeping until noon. Grayson moved into a spare compartment in the *Mayflower*. Word leaked out that the President looked "all in," utterly exhausted. Grayson mumbled something about nervous indigestion. No newspapers or telegrams reached the President. The train dashed across Indiana at fifty miles an hour. Relays of locomotives waited at frequent intervals; the train roared through some cities without stopping at all; gangs of men were lined up at maintenance stops to perform their duties with the speed and precision of a well-drilled military unit. People still stood at every station platform late into the night, cheering, cheering. Another restless night for the President. Tumulty announced that all engagements were canceled and that no others would be made.

The *Washington Post* canvassed opinion on Capitol Hill and found that "the indications so far are that the situation is just about where it was when the President began his trip. No single vote, so far as can be learned, has been influenced one way or the other." Republican Senator Miles Poindexter of Washington (who coveted his party's nomination for President in 1920) told a partisan audience at a Long Island gathering that Wilson was "the world's greatest menace" and "the greatest pro-German in the country."

The President complained that the train was going too fast, the jolts and bumps over switches and around curves jarring his head and making the pain worse. At Pittsburgh it slowed its frantic pace. "He still suffers from headaches and nervousness," Grayson explained, though the doctor said Wilson was progressing "as well as could be expected." Everyone urged the President to rest, but how could he rest when the League lay in danger of death? Worry stalked his mind day and night; "his whole being," a perceptive journalist realized, "is wrapped up in the league of nations."

At 11:05 on the morning of September 28, after traveling nearly ten thousand miles—1,700 since Wichita—the train returned to Washington's Union Station. Margaret Wilson, alerted by Grayson, met her father at the station. He walked under his own power, smiling to the few people who came to see him. (Alice Roosevelt Longworth, a close friend of Senator Lodge, stood among the people and silently invoked an Irish curse upon Wilson.) He stepped into his automobile. Along the way to the White House, he waved his hat to the people on the sidewalks . . . but no one was there.

43

"Let him hear the cry

in the morning,

and the shouting at noontide . . ."

Movie mania held Great Britain contented in its celluloid grasp in 1919, just as it had done since Charlie Chaplin's comedy shorts (not to mention his baggy pants) first brought a welcome wave of laughter to the country in the dark days of 1915, when the war was going quite badly for the Allies. Still wildly popular four years later, Chaplin was, according to Robert Graves, "the main cause why half the population of Britain in 1919 went to the pictures twice a week." Chaplin's female counterpart in the hearts of British audiences was one of his United Artists partners, "the world's sweetheart," little Mary Pickford. Even on the muggiest London summer evenings, long lines formed in front of movie theaters (not yet air-conditioned) as early as six o'clock for seats to the opening eight-o'clock show. Nor was the cinema regarded as the exclusive province of the common folk; elegantly attired scions of Britain's most noble families frequented movie palaces in the West End, and Queen Alexandra often had given royal film parties—by invitation only, of course—at Marlborough House. Movies even invaded the inner sanctums of the British government when an American propaganda film exposing the impending Bolshevik peril was shown to two hundred MPs in the House of Commons on August 12.

Although the British moviemaking industry, its growth stunted by the war, lagged far behind Hollywood in quantity and quality of productions, there was no shortage of films imported from America. Graves complained that the movies that found their way across the Atlantic were "admittedly 'not much class' "; but, he added, "to see photographs really moving about on a screen was still such a novelty that audiences were uncritical." On the whole, British authorities took far less interest in censoring movies than did their counterparts in America (where most states had their own boards of censors) or on the Continent. In Illinois, for instance, the guardians of public morality objected to the presence of naked natives in *Adventures Among the Cannibals*, and permitted only an expurgated version to be shown. Other states placed a time limit upon the duration of screen kisses—usually seven seconds.

Italian censors, on the other hand, allowed filmmakers to portray nearly any sort of lurid behavior on the screen, but insisted that they treat religious subjects with considerably more circumspection. French authorities approved D. W. Griffith's masterpiece *Intolerance* only after they snipped out scenes of strikes (which they felt would stir up the working classes), the persecution of Huguenots (bad memories), and the life of Christ. And in Germany, where, as we have seen, the Weimar government had abolished the Kaiser's censorship office, cinema patrons took matters into their own hands. While German audiences may not have known much about art (the classic *Caligari*, for instance, was not a great popular success when it was first released), they certainly knew what they didn't like. Outside the sophisticated, decadent environs of Berlin, the tidal wave of sexually oriented films that deluged the country in 1919 began to provoke violent reactions. At Düsseldorf, hundreds of people watching *A Vow of Chastity* objected to the film's explicit depictions of unchaste behavior, and forced the theater to suspend the performance. When the projectionist tried to resume the showing, enraged patrons rushed forward and literally destroyed the screen.

On September 22, four days before Wilson reached Pueblo for his final speech, executives of the Colorado Fuel and Iron Company stood at the main gates of the town's steelworks, waiting for the morning shift of employees to arrive for work. The men showed up, all right, but not for work. Out of 6,500 workers at the plant, only three hundred walked through the plant entrance that morning. The rest stood outside, on picket duty. The nationwide steel strike of 1919 had begun.

Labor organizers in the United States had never faced a tougher foe than the steelmasters of America. The whole weight of the steel industry's history in the United States militated against cooperative management-labor relations. As the industry quickly matured in the decades following the Civil War, it had suffered the rigors of excessive competition, which drove out less efficient concerns and forced the survivors to cut costs to an absolute minimum. No one epitomized the spirit of economy in operations more fully or successfully than Andrew Carnegie himself; "Carnegie never wanted to know the profits," recalled a former associate. "He always wanted to know the cost." Naturally, the constant desire to cut operating costs led steelmakers to keep wages low and working hours long. In 1910, 30 percent of the workers in America's steel mills put in a seven-day week, and approximately 75 percent worked at least twelve hours a day—sometimes two twelve-hour shifts were scheduled back-to-back, and workers would be forced to spend a continuous twenty-four hours in the mills. Early attempts to unionize the industry and alleviate these disgraceful conditions perished at Homestead, Pennsylvania, in 1892, in the bloody confrontation between the army of Pinkerton detectives hired by Carnegie's company and desperate strikers armed with rifles and revolvers.

As the titans of finance capitalism, led by J. Pierpont Morgan, muscled into the steel industry at the turn of the century and brought order (i.e., mergers and trusts) out of the chaos of unrestrained competition, management's attitude toward labor grew considerably more enlightened, if not charitable. To operate his United States Steel Corporation, the combination that quickly came to dominate the steel industry to an extent hitherto unknown in America, Morgan brought in a corporation lawyer named Judge Elbert H. Gary as chairman of the board of directors. (Gary had earned the "Judge" in his name through a brief stint as a county court magistrate in Illinois early in his career.) A handsome, gray-haired man of unassailable dignity, Judge Gary was a devout Methodist and teetotaler—H. L. Mencken once called him "the Christian hired man"—whose executive talents earned him the enviable distinction of being the first man in America to receive a salary of $100,000 a year (that being the price Morgan paid to lure him away from his corporate law practice). Now, as "the commanding general of the largest industrial army in the world," Gary set out to restore peace to the troubled iron and steel business.

Gary's industrial philosophy eschewed conflict and competition in favor of cooperation; the Judge sought to promote a "community of interest" between employers and workers, and among the individual corporations as well. In the area of labor relations, this attitude promoted the growth of welfare capitalism. U.S. Steel, for instance, instituted a profit-sharing plan for employees in 1903, in which the company loaned money to workers to allow them to purchase homes, or provided company houses at low rents; and it paid bonuses for "long and faithful service." As Gary exhorted his colleagues in January 1919, management had an obligation to "make the Steel Corporation a good place for them to work and live. Don't let the families go hungry or cold; give them playgrounds and parks and schools and churches, pure water to drink, every opportunity to keep clean, places of enjoyment, rest and recreation."

But paternalism also brought certain distinct disadvantages, too, for labor. First, the company tended to offer generous benefits exclusively to skilled workers, ignoring the mass of unskilled laborers who had no bargaining power and who management assumed (not unrealistically) could be hired and fired at the company's convenience. Second, paternalism created deep psychological resentment among workers who envisioned themselves as equal partners with management in the great industrial enterprise of building America; obviously, this attitude had been reinforced by the wartime experiences of men who had served in the trenches abroad and those who had fueled the stepped-up production effort at home—these men, too, took to heart Wilson's grand words about human dignity and true democracy and the supreme worth of the common man. Finally, there was no place in Judge Gary's paternalistic scheme for trade unions in the steel industry, although the Judge bore no personal animus against unions per se. Rather, he firmly believed that enlightened, benevolent management knew what was best for the workers, and insisted that management must remain omnipotent and unshackled to be able to operate for the good of the entire industry. An ill-advised and unsuccessful strike against U.S. Steel in its early days, when the new combination was still struggling to get on its feet, only strengthened Gary's determination never to negotiate with union officials.

Nevertheless, in early 1919 labor representatives were organizing steelworkers at a record pace. Management's refusal to abandon the twelve-hour shift and the seven-day week created considerable discontent, as did the skyrocketing cost of living (which often meant that real wages were declining) in the spring and summer of the year. To slow the unions' growth, some steel company officials fired any employees they caught engaging in unionizing activities. For his part, Judge Gary preferred to leave the union men themselves alone; any one of his employees was welcome to join a union, he repeatedly said, but no one could make *him* recognize the unions or negotiate with them. In most steel towns, where the welfare of the entire community depended upon a healthy, prosperous steel company, public opinion naturally sided with management against any disruption of the status quo. Labor organizers found themselves unable to obtain permits for parades; no one would rent them a meeting hall; ministers and newspaper editors denounced their mission; and often the sheriff and his men broke up their gatherings and drove the leaders off to jail. When Rabbi Stephen Wise proposed to come to Duquesne, Pennsylvania, to speak in favor of the union, the city's mayor refused point-blank: "Jesus Christ himself [a quaint analogy to use to a rabbi] could not speak in Duquesne for the A.F. of L." Occasionally these strongarm tactics backfired, as they did in Homestead in August when police threw the crusty, eighty-nine-year-old, legendary labor agitator Mary Harris "Mother" Jones in jail for telling a union meeting that "we are going to see whether Pennsylvania belongs to Kaiser Gary or Uncle Sam. . . . Our Kaisers sit up and smoke seventy-five-cent cigars and have lackeys with knee pants bring them champagne while you starve, while you grow old at forty. . . . If Gary wants to work twelve hours a day let him go in the blooming mill and work. What we want is a little leisure, time for music, playgrounds, a decent home, books, and the things that make life worth while."

As membership in the steel unions surged through the summer of 1919—over 100,000 workers had joined the drive by the end of August—it gradually dawned on union leaders that the heated rhetoric that fueled the organizing drives had also helped create an insistent demand for immediate action among the men. The national committee established to coordinate the unionizing activities polled the members of the various steel unions and found that approximately 98 percent of the men were in favor of "stopping work should the companies refuse to concede . . . higher wages, shorter hours, and better working conditions." On August 26 a deputation of union leaders marched into United States Steel's New York City headquarters at 71 Broadway and asked to speak with Gary. The Judge refused to see them. On September 5, Samuel Gompers wired President Wilson and asked him to intervene, to use his influence to persuade Gary to meet with the union. Wilson dispatched Bernard Baruch to reason with Gary; still the Judge refused to meet with the officials of any steelworkers' union. Gary insisted that since the union leaders represented, in his view, only a small minority of his workers, they did not deserve recognition. He repeated his assertion that he had no objection to his workers joining the union; he simply would not recognize it or negotiate with it under any circumstances. Wilson believed these stonewalling tactics were intended to cover up labor abuses by employers. "They are wrong," the President charged, "and dare not talk things over." Unfortunately, Wilson had other things on his mind at the time.

The unions threatened to strike unless Gary consented to meet with them. Gary refused to budge. From the *Mayflower*, Wilson pleaded with the union leaders to postpone any strike for three weeks, until he could convene a national labor-management conference in Washington on October 6. The unions refused, citing, among other reasons, persistent management persecution and intimidation of union members and activists through the use of brutal repressive tactics—allegedly including the murder of

union men in McKeesport, Pennsylvania, and Hammond, Indiana—that
recalled "the days of Homestead and the reign of despotism in Russia."
The steelmakers' treatment of labor, said one labor leader, was the "rotten
apple of the industrial situation." Union officials also informed Wilson that
they feared the steel mill owners were preparing to cut wages and return
to the old, despotic system of labor control. "Mr. President," they concluded, "delay is no longer possible. We have tried to find a way, but
cannot. . . . If delay were no more than delay, even at the cost of loss of
membership in our organizations, we would urge the same to the fullest
of our ability, notwithstanding the men are firmly set for an immediate
strike. But delay here means the surrender of all hope."

In an effort to win public support, the unions published a list of their
twelve demands, including the right of collective bargaining (i.e., recognition of the union); an eight-hour day; one day's rest in seven; abolition of
the twenty-four-hour shift; increases in wages "sufficient to guarantee
American standards of living"; and double time for overtime and Sunday
and holiday work. Gary countered by releasing for publication an open
letter to the heads of his subsidiary companies, explaining the rationale
behind his position. "It is the settled determination of the United States
Steel Corporation and its subsidiaries," Gary noted, "that the wages and
working conditions of their employees shall compare favorably with the
highest standard of propriety and justice." He defended his refusal to meet
with union officials with a ringing endorsement of the open-shop principle:
"A conference with these men would have been treated by them as a
recognition of the 'closed shop' method of employment. We do not combat
labor unions as such. We do not negotiate with labor unions, because it
would indicate the closing of our shops against non-union labor; and large
numbers of our workmen are not members of unions and do not care to
be. The principle of 'open shop' is vital to the greatest industrial progress
and prosperity. It is of equal benefit to employer and employee." This last
statement was, to say the least, open to argument; while J. P. Morgan sent
a telegram from London publicly applauding his lieutenant's stand ("Heartiest congratulations on your stand for the open shop . . . I believe the
American principle of liberty deeply involved and must win out if we all
stand firm"), certainly the thousands of steelworkers who walked out on
strike on September 22 found Gary's arguments altogether unconvincing.

Although the union leaders' better judgment told them that labor was
not yet ready for a full-scale strike, and that the walkout was a quixotic
gesture at best, steelworkers responded to the strike call with unexpected
solidarity in many cities. In Lackawanna, Youngstown, Wheeling, Johns-

town, Cleveland, Milwaukee, and even Gary itself (the Indiana city built by U.S. Steel in 1905 and named after the Judge), plants were forced to shut down when virtually every worker stayed away. David Brody, the author of the definitive history of the 1919 steel strike, has estimated that about 250,000 men joined the walkout—half of the industry's work force. The strike, he wrote, "exceeded in magnitude and scope anything in the nation's experience: a quarter of a million or more steelworkers across the country simultaneously on strike! America had never seen the like of this."

And America did not like it one bit. Following close upon the heels of the Boston police strike and the labor uprisings that had plagued the country in the spring and summer, not to mention the Seattle general strike back in February, the steel strike looked like one more radical attempt— and an extremely ominous one—to launch a social revolution in the United States. The fact that many of the most fervent union supporters among the rank-and-file steelworkers were foreigners merely provided additional ammunition for the growing legion of nativists and Red-baiters in America. *The New York Times* called the strike leaders "radicals, social and industrial revolutionaries"; the *New York Tribune* warned that it was "another experiment in the way of Bolshevizing American industry. Its motive is political; its leaders have mobilized industrial alienism for a disruptive purpose; and its purpose is un-American"; and the *Chicago Tribune* thundered that "the decision means a choice between the American system and the Russian— individual liberty or the dictatorship of the proletariat." Judge Gary encouraged such sentiments by advising a businessmen's dinner in New York that "if the strike succeeds it might and probably would be the beginning of an upheaval which might bring on all of us grave and serious consequences."

Actually, most of the violence during the strike came from management's hired guns. In western Pennsylvania's Allegheny County (which encompasses the area around Pittsburgh), the sheriff deputized nearly five thousand men—paid and armed by the steel companies themselves—to preserve order and enforce the law. At Homestead, mounted troops of the state constabulary rode roughshod through union meetings, swinging long, heavy clubs at anyone—men, women, and children—within their reach. Union sympathizers were jailed and held without any formal charges filed against them; when they were finally brought to trial, they received outrageously stiff sentences for minor offenses. In Lackawanna, police on horseback charged strikers who refused to disperse from street-corner gatherings. Steelworkers in Duquesne were given the choice of returning to work or going to jail. Local and state officials, including

Governor Sproul of Pennsylvania, refused to acknowledge union complaints of brutality by thugs cloaked in the mantle of responsible authority. Federal officials were barely more sympathetic.

But as the strike entered its second week (Wilson had just returned to Washington), and its third, and then its fourth, neither side gave any indication of giving up the struggle. The steelmasters reopened as many mills as they could operate with strikebreakers protected by armed guards, and managed to produce about two-thirds of the nation's normal supply of iron and steel. The union, meanwhile, discovered that its members were grimly determined to see the battle through to the bitter end. The steelworkers who were veterans of the Great War saw the strike as a continuation of the fight against Prussian autocracy; the foreign-born strikers displayed a rock-solid tenacity that pleasantly surprised the union leadership. A Polish steelworker explained his pro-union stand: "For why this war? For why we buy Liberty Bonds? For mills? No, for freedom and America—for everybody. No more [work like] horse and wagon. For eight-hour day."

"We're no more afraid of the Cincinnati Reds than we are the other teams in the American League," crowed Kid Gleason. "It is no even money bet. The Sox should win the series easily." Fans in New York made the White Sox early 7-to-5 favorites to take the World Series; hometown Chicago bookies gave odds of 8-to-5. Gleason's cockiness seemed perfectly justified; his well-oiled baseball machine was still humming along in perfect order at the close of the regular season, while Cincinnati had stumbled a bit nearing the finish line, owing to a late-September hitting slump. Connie Mack, manager and owner of the Philadelphia Athletics (with whom Eddie Collins had played four World Series before being sent to Chicago when his salary demands got too high), predicted the Sox would win the Series because of their superior all-around talent; Cincinnati's pitching was deeper and the Reds may have had more overall team speed, but in a short series Mack preferred the White Sox bats (six regulars finished the season with batting averages over .290), and the arms of Cicotte (who had been driven from the mound by the St. Louis Browns in the pennant clincher) and Lefty Williams. Yankee manager Miller Huggins also liked Chicago's chances, although he added, diplomatically, that the Reds were far from pushovers.

In an effort to recapture some of the profits lost with the shortened regular season, major-league owners voted—over the vociferous opposition of Charles Comiskey and the White Sox—to extend the World Series to nine games this year. Meanwhile, Cincinnati club executives, taking advantage of rabid fan support—this was the city's first appearance ever in a World Series, ending a drought of fifty years without any sort of league title—raised ticket prices for the series to the limit, charging five dollars for seats in the lower grandstand and three dollars for the privilege of sitting in the temporary bleachers erected beyond the outfield fence in Redleg Stadium.

Events in Washington had already convinced Lloyd George that the League of Nations was a failure. "One of its main objects was the reduction of armaments," the Prime Minister reminded several of his colleagues at the end of the summer, "yet what do we find? America, the protagonist of the League, is about to increase her navy and army to an enormous extent. The League is to apply to every nation but America. The League is not to interfere with American affairs, but America is to have a voice in the affairs of Europe. A strange position!"

Unlike Wilson, Lloyd George managed to enjoy at least a measure of respite from the cares of office during his vacation at Deauville, across the Channel in Brittany, in late August and early September. But two weeks after his return to London on September 12, the Prime Minister found himself face-to-face with a labor crisis of his own, even more threatening than the steel strike that Wilson had been powerless to prevent.

During the war, the British government had operated the nation's rail system; to keep the trains running efficiently, railway workers had been granted substantial wage increases. But wartime inflation ate up these gains and kept real wages only slightly higher than they had been in 1914; and, as we have seen, prices continued their upward spiral throughout 1919. Following the wintertime strikes in London, the government had pledged to maintain railway workers' wages for the rest of the year, but negotiations between the Cabinet and the National Union of Railwaymen (which insisted upon a minimum wage of sixty shillings a week for its members) dragged on for six months through the spring and summer—while Lloyd George was away in Paris—and by the end of August there still was no agreement on future wage scales. The long months of inconclusive negotiations, along with the government's repression of the policemen's union and its rejection of any nationalization schemes for the coal industry, created an atmosphere of distrust that made the NUR leaders extremely wary of the Cabinet's intentions. So when two of the chief government negotiators (Bonar Law and Sir Eric Geddes) made some offhand remarks in mid-September that led union officials to believe that the Cabinet was planning to make a final offer that would actually reduce the real wages of several grades of railway workers, the railwaymen's executive committee suddenly broke off negotiations and called a lightning strike, to begin at midnight on the evening of Friday, September 26.

With only a few days' warning, citizens scrambled to lay in a stock of provisions, and hurried to get to or from their holidays at the seashore before the trains came to a standstill. Promptly at the appointed hour, the rails fell silent all over England. A passenger on a train coming into London from the north remarked that the occasion "had a queer resemblance to the days in the trenches waiting for 'zero' "; railwaymen in stations throughout England stood with their watches in their hands waiting for the moment when they would go "over the top" and off their jobs. The government and the press treated the strike as a full-scale national emergency—September 27, the first full day of the walkout, was dubbed "Black Saturday" by one hysterical journal—and indeed the last nation-wide rail strike, in 1911, had caused tremendous inconvenience to the country in the course of only two days. This time the government immediately reimposed strict wartime food rationing of meat, bacon, sugar, butter, and margarine; newspapers carried official pleas to the population to reduce consumption of coal, gas, and electricity; the government started to recruit a Civilian Guard to maintain order and keep vital supplies moving; demobilization was suspended and all military leaves canceled; soldiers guarded train stations to protect the railwaymen who decided to report for work (but since the strike was nearly a hundred percent effective, the troops really had nothing to do); and authorities called upon the citizenry to contribute every available motor vehicle to carry England through the crisis. "Every citizen must do his part," ran the official appeals. "Help by working. Help also by saving petrol, light, coal, food. Don't use the TELE-PHONE, TELEGRAPH, or other postal service more than you can possibly help. Keep in good spirits. Make the best of things. . . . Fight for the life of the community."

Lloyd George, who, as Chancellor of the Exchequer, had played a prominent role in settling the 1911 strike, condemned the railwaymen's action in no uncertain terms. Everyone knew, the Prime Minister said, that he had never lacked sympathy with the working class, but this walkout was a threat to the community—"an anarchist conspiracy"—that he could not countenance. "I have come to the conclusion," Lloyd George announced on September 28, "that in a long and varied experience I can recall no strike entered into so lightly, with so little justification, and with such disregard for the public interest." He vowed to fight the strike "with all the resources at the disposal of the State." On this occasion *The Times* supported the Prime Minister to the fullest, taking the opportunity to castigate trade-union leaders—both those of the NUR and their comrades in other trades—as Bolshevik conspirators. "There is no doubt," asserted *The Times* in a lead article, "that the present temper of large bodies of workpeople in many trades is ugly. . . . There are active men in all trade unions—some hold influential and responsible positions in them—who wish to see the overthrow of the present system of government in this country and the substitution for it of some undefined scheme which may be modelled on the Soviet system." Even the normally placid, liberal *Manchester Guardian* worked itself up to a minor frenzy, characterizing the strike as a look "over the edge into the abyss of social revolution."

If true, the abyss proved to be neither as deep nor as dark as the nation feared. On the first morning of the strike—a Saturday—there was no violence and no chaos, only an endless procession of commuters on rusty tandem bicycles, in charabancs, on motorcycles with sidecars, in victorias, and, of course, on foot. Two silk-hatted gentlemen heading into the City—London's financial quarter—considered themselves fortunate to obtain a ride among the barrels on a brewer's dray. Able-bodied veterans, used to catching rides on the quick, had no trouble hopping onto buses and trucks that were already in motion, pulling up less experienced and less nimble women after them. Airplane companies started special commuter services (London to Leeds for fifteen guineas, eight passengers per plane). Somehow people managed to get to their favorite shows at the theaters and movie houses, and spectators refused to forgo their weekend football games (30,000 trekked to the stadium at Highbury, and 20,000 more showed up to watch the contest at Upton Park; 470,000 attended the scheduled matches of the principal Association Leagues). Probably the strike fell hardest upon the last contingents of soldiers to return to England from Russia; eager to return home, the men who arrived just as the strike began were forced to kill time in local quarters for the duration of the crisis.

The unexceptionably peaceful character of the strike, along with an unprecedentedly successful public-relations campaign run by the union, made a mockery of the government's predictions of anarchy and social catastrophe. Most of the credit for the pacific demeanor of the strikers went—and deservedly so—to J. H. Thomas, the general secretary of the NUR. Thomas, a Welshman and a Labour member of Parliament with a flair for the dramatic, enjoyed a well-earned reputation as a moderate trade unionist who eschewed the weapon of "direct action" (that is, strikes to obtain political rather than economic objectives). In fact, earlier that summer, when Lloyd George had sought advice from some responsible labor leader who could tell him "what the working-classes really want," he thought first of Thomas.

Right from the start, Thomas was fully a match for Lloyd George in generating favorable publicity. The union placed full-page advertisements in newspapers stating its position in calm, measured tones, and made a film of Thomas patiently explaining the railwaymen's case that reached thousands of cinema-goers across the country. Thomas advised his men from the start that if they kept their heads, made no mistakes, and refused to be drawn into provocative behavior, victory was inevitable. There was no doubt that rank-and-file union members did feel considerable hostility toward the government; the workers were convinced that the future of trade unionism itself was at stake (and in fact many Conservative MPs did wish to use this occasion to deal the trade-union movement a fatal blow), and speakers at union meetings bitterly denounced the government for promising "a country fit for heroes to live in" and then proposing to cut the workingman's wages. Nevertheless, cooler heads maintained control and there were no outbreaks of open violence during the entire nine-day strike.

As the strike entered its second week, however, there were ominous signs that it might develop into a full-scale conflict. Other unions threatened to join the NUR in sympathy strikes, and newspaper printers, rebelling against their employers for the first time anyone could remember, refused to print material condemning the railwaymen. But since neither Thomas nor Lloyd George wished to crush the other or escalate the conflict into armed repression or rebellion, negotiations resumed on October 3 and a compromise settlement was reached two days later. The government agreed to maintain the present railway wage rates through September 1920 (even if prices fell), and guaranteed a minimum of fifty-one shillings per week. The union seemed to have won two-thirds of its objectives, and Thomas called the terms "honourable to both sides." For his part, Lloyd George exulted over detaching the railwaymen from the Triple Alliance, since the union pledged, as part of the agreement, not to strike for any reason for one year. When it was all over, the railway strike had made it perfectly clear that British labor would not abandon its wartime wage gains without a bitter fight; at the same time, Conservatives noted with satisfaction that labor appeared to be abandoning its short-lived postwar devotion to revolutionary political objectives and was returning to the more conventional battle over economic questions; and everyone else rejoiced that they would not have to walk to work the next day.

* * *

Of all the chilling scenes of human cruelty enacted during the year of 1919, none surpassed in sheer hatefulness the hellish actions of the citizens of Omaha, Nebraska, on the evening of Sunday, September 28. Three nights earlier, a black man named William Brown allegedly had held up a young white couple on their way home from a theater performance. According to police reports, Brown robbed them both and then held off the white man—a cripple—at gunpoint while he dragged nineteen-year-old Agnes Loebeck into a ravine.

On the strength of a positive identification by Miss Loebeck, police arrested Brown the next night (he was already the object of considerable hostility in the community for living openly with a white woman); at that time, deputies had to call in reinforcements to keep their prisoner out of the hands of a mob of self-appointed guardians of law and order bent on lynching Brown. But on Sunday night all hell broke loose. Shortly after six o'clock, an angry crowd—mostly young men and boys, but many women, too—gathered in front of the courthouse where Brown was being held. Within a very short time they had worked themselves into a state of mass hysteria, seizing control of the town, looting pawnshops and hardware stores and stealing every available gun and load of ammunition. Policemen on the streets were attacked and beaten, their clubs and pistols taken for a murderous task.

Outside the jail, three thousand people stood and shouted for Brown. But instead of Brown, Mayor Edward Smith emerged with a pistol in his hand, and announced that they could not have the prisoner. Outraged, the frenzied crowd promptly seized the mayor and beat him nearly into unconsciousness. They placed a rope around his neck. Somehow he struggled free, so they seized him again and put the rope around his neck again. "I'll give my life if necessary, but I'll not surrender the Negro," they heard him say. "I'm going to enforce the law." They looped the rope around a lamppost and started to lift Smith from the ground, when police finally charged the mob and the rope was cut. Then the rioters burned his automobile. Unconscious, the mayor was taken to a hospital, where he kept repeating deliriously, "You shall not take him."

Deprived of one victim, the mob spread gasoline on the first floor of the courthouse and set it afire to burn out their prey. Hundreds of shots were fired through the windows, accompanied by occasional bricks and stones. As the flames licked through the building, Sheriff Michael Clark and his deputies removed all the prisoners—about sixty men and a dozen women—to the roof of the courthouse. From below came the howls, "We want Brown!" "Give us Brown!" A captured German cannon, presented to the city by the War Department, was used to batter down the barricaded door. Shots were fired indiscriminately from the ground and from snipers on the tops of nearby buildings into the confused and frightened mass of policemen and prisoners on the courthouse roof. At this point, Clark turned his women prisoners loose to make their way to safety. Fire and dense smoke billowed from the airshafts, making it almost impossible for the men to breathe. The roof was scorching under their feet. Firemen arrived but were beaten off by the mob. A number of prisoners began to pray; others cursed their tormentors. The mob worked its way past the flames up to the top floor. Someone pushed Brown, who, witnesses said, had been the coolest man through the whole fifteen-minute firestorm on the roof, into the arms of the mob. They bore him down triumphantly, tore every bit of clothing off his body, put a noose around his neck, and hoisted his body about six feet off the ground, then riddled it with fire from revolvers and shotguns. The shooting continued for ten minutes. By the end, Brown's body had been dismembered.

But the mob was not done. They took down what was left of the corpse, tied it to a police patrol wagon, and dragged it through the main streets of town and through the black district. Then they poured kerosene and gasoline on railroad ties and other discarded lumber and threw the body onto the blaze. They stopped passing cars and drained off their gasoline and added that to the flames. Photographs showed girls laughing in the crowd, and one young woman standing, smiling, within five feet of the burning body. People crowded close for grisly souvenirs; after a while the torso was taken off the pyre and kicked around the streets like a football.

When it was all over, with three people dead and fifty-eight seriously wounded, when federal troops had arrived the following day to maintain order, when twenty-five black prisoners had been removed from the city jail and taken to Lincoln for safety, and when civic leaders had called for punishment of the murderers, the women of Omaha expressed their satisfaction at Brown's fate. Society matrons believed the lynching would teach "a great lesson" to the blacks and help make the city safe for women, and teenaged girls laughed and bragged about taking part in the murder. The mother of Agnes Loebeck declared, "I am glad the brute was killed." Agnes herself said she, too, was glad Brown had been punished. Street fights between blacks and whites in the city the following day were dispersed by troops with shrapnel helmets and armed with fixed bayonets, and by the force of a heavy downpour; from the hospital bed where he was recovering, Mayor Smith attributed the rain to divine intervention.

A New York State sheriff, touring the country's jails and prisons to offer suggestions for improving housing conditions for prisoners, returned to the East and reported that blacks in the South and Southwest were quietly and systematically arming themselves in preparation for further outbreaks of racial violence.

44

"So the captain

of the guard gave

him victuals and a reward,

and let him go . . ."

For several days after his return to Washington, Wilson seemed to be slowly regaining his strength. Grayson forbade him to do anything more strenuous than signing routine legislation and dictating a few letters. In the afternoons the President and Mrs. Wilson went for long automobile rides into the countryside, far away from the White House. The scheduled state visit of the King and Queen of Belgium was postponed indefinitely. Former New York Congressman Jefferson Levy went to the White House; although he could not get in to see the President personally, Levy left the message that the venerable estate of Monticello (Thomas Jefferson's home, which Levy now owned), just outside of Charlottesville, Virginia, was at Wilson's disposal if the President elected to get away from it all and enjoy a long vacation with clean mountain air.

On Wednesday, October 1, Wilson displayed symptoms of restlessness. He had not slept well Tuesday night; on Wednesday afternoon the weather in Washington turned sharply colder and the automobile ride under overcast skies and through a cutting wind was curtailed. "Few persons realize that the President has had very little rest since the beginning of the war, or even since he went into office," the *Washington Post* reminded its readers. "During the first few years of his term he had summer vacations in Vermont, but from the time of the entry of the United States into the war he has been at his desk almost continually. His only opportunity for relaxation was aboard the *George Washington* on his trips to and from Paris."

That evening Wilson played billiards, watched a movie in the East Room, and read to his wife from a khaki-covered Bible just like the ones the army had provided for the doughboys. Then he wound his watch and went off to bed, leaving the watch behind him. Mrs. Wilson, who also had been unable to sleep well since their return to Washington, looked in on her husband several times during the night. Everything seemed normal as morning approached.

As Wilson slept that night, Kid Gleason wondered where it had all started to go wrong.

The day had started off so well: the club came together for a team breakfast at the Sinton Hotel in Cincinnati, then several hours later sprinted through a brief workout at Redlegs Stadium. No opening-game jitters for his veterans, who ran through the practice session with the loose good humor of seasoned professionals. In fact, while the underdog Reds had spent the previous afternoon working out at the stadium, the supremely self-confident White Sox had enjoyed a team excursion to the racetrack. The weather for the first game of the 1919 World Series was perfect, eighty-three degrees at game time (more like June than the first day of October), and wispy clouds in a brilliant blue sky. Thirty-one thousand fans—including two elderly members of the legendary, undefeated 1869 Cincinnati Red Stockings, who had left their homes in the city early that morning and walked, very slowly, to the stadium—jammed the freshly painted wooden grandstands, standing shoulder to shoulder (and stepping on one another's feet) in the temporary bleachers in right and left fields, looking out with nervous anticipation onto the neatly manicured playing field. All the wood in the stands had been sprayed with water the night before to guard against fire. There were legions of dignitaries in attendance: Governor Cox, Senator Warren Harding (who had reserved the entire bridal suite at one of the city's leading hotels), and dozens of present and former governors and congressmen from the Midwest and the South. Pictures and banners proclaiming the greatness of the Reds covered Cincinnati's streets; after fifty years of dwelling in the baseball darkness, the city finally had emerged into the sunlight and nothing could quench the excitement of the moment.

Nevertheless, Cincinnati fans seemed extremely reluctant to back up their braggadocio with hard cash. Sportswriters covering the series commented on the fact that up until the morning of the first game, virtually no money had been bet upon the Reds. Chicago backers offered odds of 7 to 5 for the Series, but few Redlegs fans were willing to take up the challenge. "It is doubtful," wrote one reporter, "if there ever has been a series in which so few bets have been made. Everyone seems to want to take the White Sox." (Rumor had it, though, that Lenin and Trotsky were quite willing to bet two-to-one on the Reds.)

A standing ovation greeted the home team as it took the field for batting practice at 12:20. When the White Sox emerged from the runway at 12:45, the brass band parading around the field swung into "Hail, Hail, the Gang's All Here." Pat Moran and Kid Gleason shook hands and exchanged pleasantries while cameras clicked and whirred and the roving musicians played "The Wearin' of the Green." Half an hour before game time, the crowd fell silent as an elderly man dressed in the uniform of a U.S. Navy lieutenant walked slowly across the field toward the band, which responded with the opening notes of "The Star-Spangled Banner." The old man stood at attention until the national anthem was over, then took the baton with a dignified bow and lifted it; this was the venerable John Philip Sousa, leading the band through "The Stars and Stripes Forever," and when the march was over the stands rocked with thunderous cheers and applause.

Suddenly, just before the game began, there was a rush to put down money on Cincinnati.

In a surprise move, Moran started "Dutch" Ruether, a twenty-six-year-old left-hander who before this year had won only three major league games. But Ruether had rung up a 19–6 record in the 1919 regular season, and the young southpaw justified Moran's confidence by setting the White Sox down in the first without any trouble. Eddie Cicotte, chosen by Gleason to pitch the first game for the Sox, fared not nearly so well. Cicotte hit the first batter he faced, second baseman Morrie Rath, squarely in the back; Rath eventually came around to score, giving the Reds a 1–0 lead after one inning. Chicago tied the game in the second, as Joe Jackson reached on an error and scored when Cincinnati shortstop Larry Kopf misplayed Chick Gandil's bloop behind second base. But everything fell apart for Cicotte in the bottom of the fourth. Reds centerfielder Eddie Roush flied out, then young Pat Duncan cracked a single to right center. Kopf sent a sharp grounder right back to the mound. Cicotte grabbed it and turned to throw to Swede Risberg to start a double play; but the throw was delayed for a split second because Risberg—who had become an excellent defensive shortstop during the last few months of the regular season—was not yet on the bag. When Swede finally got there, Cicotte's throw was high and Risberg stumbled, and the best he could do was get the force at second. Instead of the Sox being out of the inning free and clear, there was a man on first with two out. Then Reds rightfielder Earl Neale hit a bouncer right through the middle; again Risberg just missed the play by inches as the ball trickled under his glove and out into center field. Catcher Ivy Wingo sent a shot to right, scoring Kopf. That brought up Ruether, and Cicotte still could have gotten out of the inning with only one run against him if he had just managed to retire the opposing pitcher. But, inexplicably, Cicotte grooved one right down the middle of the plate and Ruether sent it deep to left center for a two-run triple. The crowd went absolutely wild; when the exhausted Ruether arrived at third base, coach Sherry Magee suggested that he sit down on the bag for a moment to catch his breath. Eddie Collins walked to the mound to try to calm Cicotte, then Gandil and Buck Weaver did the same, but nothing helped. Morrie Rath smashed a run-scoring double down the left-field line, then first baseman Jake Daubert brought him home with a single. That was all for Cicotte—Gleason was furious at his star pitcher's sudden attack of ineptitude—but it was enough. The Reds scored five runs in the inning, and went on to a 9–1 victory.

Sportswriters called it "an utter rout," "a crushing defeat." "Never before in the history of America's biggest baseball spectacle," said the front-page story in *The New York Times*, "has a pennant winning club received such a disastrous drubbing in an opening game as the far-famed White Sox got this afternoon." J. V. Fitz Gerald of the *Washington Post* wrote that Cicotte had suffered "one of the worst beatings in his career with the White Sox. The defeat chalked up against him is one of the most crushing a pitcher ever has suffered in a world's series contest. Few teams have ever been as decisively routed in the annual series between the pennant winners of the two major leagues as Chicago was this afternoon." Fitz Gerald added that there never had been a worse pitching performance in a World Series game than Cicotte's dismal outing that day. Publicly, Gleason said he couldn't understand it. "The Sox didn't play their game, neither defensively nor offensively," he muttered afterwards. Gleason pointed to the botched double play by Cicotte and Risberg in the fourth as the key to the game: "The Sox failed to make a double play they can make ninety-nine times out of a hundred and it left the opening for the entire mess." It was, Gleason said, a "bad break."

What actually happened has never been established with complete certainty. Conflicting evidence, stories that changed from day to day, confessions that were later retracted, all muddy the water sufficiently to keep many of the exact details shrouded in a fog of mystery. But the basic outlines are clear. Several weeks before the World Series began, White Sox first baseman Chick Gandil, one of the most hard-bitten characters in the history of major-league baseball, met with a small-time Boston gambler named Joseph "Sport" Sullivan in a Boston hotel room and offered to throw the Series for $80,000. Gandil had already approached Cicotte, Swede Risberg, utility infielder Fred McMullin, and Lefty Williams, all of whom had indicated they might be willing to participate in a fix if the price was right. These men were all badly underpaid, even by the penurious standards of that time; Charlie Comiskey was notoriously tightfisted with players' salaries and traveling expenses, going so far as to send his team onto the field in mud-stained uniforms to save a few dollars on cleaning bills. Lefty Williams, for instance, made less than $3,000 in 1919, far below the salaries earned by many mediocre pitchers on less successful clubs. So the Sox, the best team in baseball, also were the most embittered and resentful, and ripe for plucking if some enterprising gambler should wave thousands of dollars in front of them. (The team was also riddled with dissension and cliques; Eddie Collins and Ray Schalk—straight-arrow types who also happened to be the highest-paid players on the club— headed one faction, and Gandil, Risberg, and centerfielder Happy Felsch led the other.) To assure the deal, Gandil then brought in Jackson, Buck Weaver, and Felsch. On the evening of September 21 the eight players met in Gandil's room at the Hotel Ansonia in New York to discuss the fix in detail.

Enter "Sleepy" Bill Burns, a former ballplayer turned Texas oilman and mining executive who had been known to place a few wagers on sporting events in his day. Burns had heard rumors of a possible fix, but apparently was unaware that the Sox already had a bona fide offer to throw the Series. So after running into Cicotte at the Ansonia, Burns met with him and Gandil and offered to find a banker for the deal. Never one to miss a chance to make an extra buck, Gandil promptly upped the ante to $100,000, to be paid in advance. Burns then tried to get Arnold Rothstein, a professional gambler and prominent member of the New York underground sports scene (the wealthy Rothstein was known on the street as "a walking bank"), to bankroll the deal. Rothstein refused, believing the scheme was unworkable and doomed to failure. But soon thereafter one of Rothstein's lieutenants, ex-prizefighter Abe Attell, told Burns that the boss had changed his mind, and that Burns should go ahead and arrange the fix. Attell was lying; he simply saw the deal as a way to make a bundle for himself by betting on Cincinnati. Apparently he never had any intention of paying the players more than a token fee for their services. Meanwhile, Sport Sullivan, too, had visited Rothstein to see if the big man would be interested in putting up the front money to finance the deal. By now Rothstein was starting to believe there was something to this crazy idea, after all, and so this time he said yes and gave Sullivan a $40,000 down payment, with the other $40,000 to follow once the Series was lost. As October 1 approached, Rothstein and his associates quietly began laying heavy bets upon Cincinnati to win the Series.

Two days before the World Series began, Sullivan handed Gandil $10,000. Where, Gandil asked angrily, was the rest of the promised cash? Sullivan told the first baseman he would receive it soon. (Actually, Sullivan had already used nearly $30,000 of Rothstein's money to place his own bets.) Furious, Gandil had little choice; he took the money and put it all under Eddie Cicotte's pillow, to guarantee the cooperation of the opening-day starter.

Now the second team of gamblers returned to the stage. (As the cast of characters kept expanding amid all the confusion and deceptions, the World Series was starting to resemble a Shakespearean comedy.) The evening before the first game, Burns and Atell visited with seven White Sox players (Gandil, Cicotte, Williams, Felsch, Risberg, McMullin, and Weaver—Joe Jackson was not present) in a room at the Sinton Hotel. Burns said he had lined up the money to handle the fix, and gave the players the name of the man whom Burns thought was bankrolling the venture: Rothstein (who actually was financing Sullivan, but not Burns and Atell, although Burns apparently did not know this at the time). Attell told the Sox he would pay them $100,000 if they lost five games—$20,000 after each loss. The players wanted it all in one lump sum, but Attell refused, and so Gandil accepted the installment plan (which was better than nothing, and besides, in the unlikely event that both sets of gamblers paid off, the players would earn the princely sum of $180,000). Attell said he didn't care which of the games were thrown, as long as he knew ahead of time when the Sox were going to lose. Gandil and Cicotte agreed that the first two games should be thrown; Cicotte reportedly said, "I will throw the first game if I have to throw the ball clear out of the Cincinnati park." Since Cicotte and Williams were the scheduled starters for games one and two, and probably for games four and five as well, the fix seemed assured. Cicotte did ask that he be allowed to win one Series game to help in his contract negotiations next year. (Eddie was bitter about losing out on extra money in 1919; Comiskey had promised Cicotte a bonus if he won thirty games during the regular season, but he ended up winning only twenty-nine.) This, the players promised Burns and Atell, would be a "made-to-order" World Series. Of the seven White Sox in the room that day, only Buck Weaver later reneged on the deal and played every game of the Series to win.

Now Cicotte's dreadful pitching performance and the missed double play in the fourth inning made perfect sense. But gamblers never could keep secrets, and as soon as the first game was finished the word spread quickly that the fix was in. Before the night was over, the Reds became 7-to-10 favorites. "The complexion of the betting situation in the world's series," wrote a bemused *New York Times* correspondent from Cincinnati, "changed as suddenly and completely as the complexion of a shop girl between the time of arising from her couch and emerging from her room." Gleason, too, had heard the ugly rumors. That evening he confronted Cicotte and Risberg in the lobby of the Sinton. "You think I don't know what you're doing out there? Cicotte, you sonovabitch!" A Chicago sportswriter pulled Gleason away before he could do anything else.

Shortly after eight o'clock the next morning, Wilson collapsed.

His wife had seen him resting comfortably as dawn came quietly to the still, hushed White House. She went back to sleep until eight, and when she looked in again she found Wilson sitting on the edge of his bed, trying to reach a water bottle. His left hand dangled loosely at his side. "I have no feeling in that hand," he told her. "Will you rub it? But first help me get to the bathroom." He moved slowly, in obvious pain. She asked if he would be all right for a moment while she called Grayson; he said yes. She went to a private telephone line that bypassed the White House switchboard and its eavesdropping operators and asked Ike Hoover, the chief usher, to alert Grayson at once. "The President is very sick," she whispered. It was ten minutes before nine. Hoover called Grayson and sent a car to bring the doctor to the White House. When Mrs. Wilson returned, she found her husband lying, unmoving, on the bathroom floor. She pulled a blanket over him to keep him warm; he stirred and asked for a drink of water. She put a pillow beneath his head to ease the pain.

Ike Hoover went upstairs to see if there was anything else he could do to help. Everything was unnaturally quiet, all the doors shut. Grayson arrived and knocked on the President's door. Mrs. Wilson let him in and together they carried Wilson back to bed. Ten minutes later, Grayson emerged and told Hoover the President was "paralyzed"; he asked Hoover to get another doctor—a specialist—and the nurse who had ministered to Wilson's first wife all through her final illness. A little more than one hour had passed since Edith Wilson had entered the President's room.

As the clocks slowly ticked away the minutes of that awful day, more doctors were called in—including a Philadelphia neurologist of international reputation—for hurried consultation. No one outside the room could find out what was happening. In the late afternoon, Mrs. Wilson admitted Ike Hoover to help Grayson and the nurse rearrange the furniture in the room. Hoover entered and saw the President "stretched out on the long Lincoln bed. He looked as if he were dead. There was not a sign of life. His face had a long cut about the temple from which the signs of blood were still evident. His nose also bore a long cut lengthwise. This too looked red and raw. There was no bandage." Someone told Hoover that Wilson had fallen in the bathroom and cut himself; Mrs. Wilson later vehemently denied that her husband had been cut, and claimed that Hoover must have seen the President with shadows falling across his face.

The White House became a hospital. Grayson and his medical colleagues issued a bulletin at ten o'clock that evening: "The President is a very sick man. His condition is less favorable today, and he has remained in bed throughout the day." The bulletin contained no hint of the real problem; the newspapers guessed it was nervous exhaustion. But the consensus from the specialists who examined Wilson was that the President had suffered a cerebral thrombosis—a clot, but not a rupture, in a blood vessel in the brain. His entire left side was paralyzed. Looking back on his collapse in Paris in April, it now became clear that the illness Grayson had incorrectly diagnosed as influenza probably had been a minor thrombosis, aggravated at the end of the Western tour in September. (Although Grayson did not rank among the world's most learned physicians, he should not be blamed too harshly for missing the diagnosis in Paris. Some of the physical symptoms of a thrombosis, including intestinal difficulties, resembled the symptoms displayed by flu victims, and with everyone's mind on influenza at the time, Grayson's was an understandable, if regrettable, mistake.)

For several days Wilson lay dangerously near to death. His sixty-two-year-old body had never been hardy even in the best of times, and now complications from the thrombosis threatened to kill him. His doctors and his wife kept all news of the nation's affairs from him—and kept all news of the President from the nation, save for bulletins that hid more than they told. No one, not even the members of the Cabinet, knew whether the President was in a coma, insane (the Philadelphia neurologist was also a specialist in mental disorders), or the victim of some dread, unnamed disease. Secretary of War Baker admitted to a Cabinet colleague, "I am scared literally to death." Joe Tumulty suggested to Secretary of the Navy Daniels that "we must all pray." And that was what America did. The blind chaplain of the House of Representatives, Reverend Dr. Henry Couden; rabbis celebrating Yom Kippur; the bishop of Atlanta, at services in the Bethlehem Chapel of the Washington Cathedral; all across the country, people prayed for the stricken President.

In England, the Victorian biographer *par excellence* Lytton Strachey sent a letter to his friend John Maynard Keynes, who earlier that summer had read Strachey a draft of his polemic attacking the betrayal of Wilsonian idealism at the Paris conference. "I seem to gather from the scant remarks in the newspapers," Strachey wrote on October 4, "that your friend the President has gone mad. Is it possible that it should be gradually borne in upon him what an appalling failure he was, and that when at last he fully realised it his mind collapsed? Very dramatic, if so. But won't it make some of your remarks almost too cruel?—Especially if he should go and die."

As the starting time for the second game approached, the White Sox conspirators had not yet received their initial $20,000 payment from Burns and Attell. The gamblers reassured them, telling them that the money was still out on bets; as soon as the pigeons paid off, the players would receive their money. Just get Williams to be a little more subtle than Cicotte had been in the first game, they said. So Lefty Williams went out and lost the second game 4–2. Williams, one of the premier control pitchers in organized baseball, constantly fell behind in the count to the Redlegs' hitters, and ended up either walking them or grooving a pitch down the middle. The most damaging blows once more came in the fourth inning, when Williams—displaying a most uncharacteristic wildness—walked three men, and then allowed light-hitting shortstop Larry Kopf to smash a hanging curve into left center, knocking home two Cincinnati runs. The White Sox had their chances to break the game open, but twice Chick Gandil failed to hit the ball through a drawn-up infield; once Jackson was called out on strikes with Weaver at second base; and in the ninth, Risberg bounced into a double play and McMullin grounded out weakly to end the game. Risberg, in fact, came up three times with men on base and failed to drive anyone home.

Publicly, Gleason professed to be baffled by the startling turn of events. "I never saw such bad breaks as we got today," he muttered, "and I don't think it can occur again." He shook his head when he thought about Gandil's failure to drive in runs, and Williams's sudden loss of control. Nor could he explain Happy Felsch's failure to catch Kopf's shot in the fourth inning. "That ball should have been caught," Gleason argued. "Not the way Felsch was playing it, but he was in the wrong spot, and I don't know how it happened. He was playing well over toward the right side when he should have been stationed toward left center. Had he been there it would have been an easy catch and the Reds would have counted only once in that inning." In the privacy of the Chicago locker room, White Sox players had to restrain Gleason from throttling Gandil. Later, under the grandstands, a smoldering Schalk called Williams aside and suddenly started swinging at his battery mate, landing several solid punches before teammates intervened.

Counting up his profits after the game, Attell now openly informed Burns that he had no intention of paying the players. All he would give them was $10,000, which he had hidden under a mattress in his hotel room. So when Burns met the conspirators in the Sinton and paid them only the ten thousand (Risberg took the money into the bathroom to count it), Gandil and the others realized they were being double-crossed. Attell had suggested that the Sox win the third game, since by this time so many people had heard rumors about the fix that it was nearly impossible to get anyone to bet on Chicago. (*The New York Times* remarked that even the very tempting odds of 4½ to 1, offered after the second game, failed to elicit any Chicago backers. "It was just as if the earth had opened and swallowed them up," the *Times* chuckled mischievously.) A White Sox victory in game number three, the gamblers figured, might stop the talk and loosen up the odds a little. Dickie Kerr was scheduled to pitch for the Sox that day, and the conspirators grumbled about winning for "a busher" like Kerr while Cicotte and Williams took the losses, but they agreed to play to win. The third game would be played in Chicago.

Waiting in the Redlegs' hotel lobby late that evening for the taxis that would take the team to the station for a late-night train to the Windy City, star Cincinnati outfielder Eddie Roush was approached by a man who asked if Roush had heard of the Schalk-Williams squabble after the game that afternoon. He told Roush that Schalk had accused Williams of throwing the game. The story made Roush wonder if some of the rumors about his own teammates being approached by gamblers were true after all.

On the morning of October 3, Burns called Gandil to confirm the setup, but now Gandil told him that the third contest would go down just like the first two. Then the Sox went out and won, 3–0, behind a magnificent performance by Dickie Kerr, as baseball fan Jack Dempsey sat watching admiringly from a box seat behind home plate. (Judge Kenesaw Mountain Landis, the target of one of the May 1 mail bombs and the man who would later play a major role in the aftermath of the World Series scandal, was at the game that day, too.) Shoeless Joe went two for three, and only a magnificent play by Daubert took away a third hit. Risberg handled ten chances flawlessly. "The Sox," observed one sportswriter with marked understatement, "showed a lot more pep today. It was somewhat lacking in their two starts in Cincinnati." What had happened was, simply, that the players met in secret that morning and decided to pull their own double-cross by luring the gamblers into betting on Cincinnati and then going all out to win the game. Again, Joe Jackson did not attend the conspirators' meeting.

Afterwards, Gandil met Burns at the Warner Hotel at 9:30 that night and told him that he and most of the others were sick and tired of being played for chumps; now they were through with the whole rotten mess. (Risberg, desperately hoping for some payoff, allegedly held out and said that he was going to go ahead and throw the rest of the games anyway.) Burns tried to persuade Gandil to string along for a little while longer, but the tough first basemen simply turned and walked away. Then, completely by coincidence, Sport Sullivan reestablished contact with Gandil the following morning. Gandil gruffly demanded an immediate payment of $20,000 to proceed any further with the fix. After scrambling all morning, Sullivan managed to raise the money.

Cicotte started the fourth game and pitched magnificently before a standing-room-only crowd at Comiskey Park. But in the fifth inning he made two flagrant fielding errors: on a weak bouncer back through the box, Cicotte knocked the ball down; it trickled slowly toward third base, but instead of letting Buck Weaver handle it, Cicotte grabbed the ball and heaved it wildly over Gandil's outstretched glove. Then, after Kopf knocked a single into short left field, Cicotte moved to cut off Jackson's throw to the plate; the ball deflected off his glove and rolled wildly to the backstop, allowing Duncan to score from third. A second Cincinnati run came across when Neale lifted a long fly ball over the head of Jackson, who was playing unusually shallow in left. That was all the Reds needed, as the White Sox failed to score against Cincinnati starter Jimmy Ring. Final score: Cincinnati 2, Chicago 0. After this debacle, the odds immediately shifted further in favor of the Reds, and gamblers were seen plying their trade openly in Chicago hotel rooms. Sullivan handed Gandil $20,000 that night, and the first baseman divided up the spoils among his teammates: $5,000 each for Risberg, Felsch, Williams, and Jackson. Cicotte would get nothing more, Weaver had taken himself out of the deal, and McMullin, who only batted twice in the entire Series, would be lucky to get anything.

Rain forced a postponement of the fifth game until Monday, October 6. Pat Moran had planned to start Hod Eller that day, but before the game Roush went to the Reds' manager and said, "I've been told that gamblers have got to some of the players on this club. Maybe it's true and maybe it isn't. I don't know. But you sure better do some finding out. I'll be damned if I'm going to knock myself out trying to win this Series if somebody else is trying to throw the game." Moran hastily assembled the entire team for a pregame meeting and confronted Eller point-blank. "Hod," said Moran, "I've been hearing rumors about sellouts. Not about you, not about anybody in particular, just rumors. I want to ask you a straight question and I want a straight answer." "Shoot," said Eller. "Has anybody offered you anything to throw this game?" "Yep," Hod replied laconically. (You could have heard a pin drop in the room, Roush said.) "After breakfast this morning," Eller continued, "a guy got on the elevator with me and got off at the same floor I did. He showed me five thousand dollar bills, and said they were mine if I'd lose the game today." "What did you say?" asked Moran. "I said if he didn't get damn far away from me real quick he wouldn't know what hit him. And the same went if I ever saw him again." Moran stared at Eller for what seemed like an eternity. Finally he nodded. "Okay, you're pitching. But one wrong move and you're out of the game." Spotting his "shine ball" (the pitch that made Cicotte famous) to perfection, Eller pitched a masterful shutout and the Reds won game five, 5–0. The usually sure-handed Felsch made two terrible defensive plays in center field. Gleason was beside himself with frustration. Now Cincinnati led the Series four games to one. The White Sox had failed to score in two straight games. There were no longer any odds, official or otherwise, on the Series; nobody was willing to bet anything on Chicago's chances. "Looks to me as if Moran could pitch himself and stop those birds," muttered one disgusted fan.

But now it was Sullivan's turn to stiff the White Sox. There was no $20,000 payment waiting for Gandil at the Sinton Hotel in Cincinnati before the sixth game as promised. Furious at being double-crossed yet another time, the Sox proceeded to take out their financial frustrations upon the Reds, winning a second game for Kerr. Gandil himself knocked in the deciding run as the Sox won in ten innings, 5–4. The next day Gleason sent Cicotte to the mound again and watched his ace spin a masterpiece, holding Cincinnati to just one run as the Sox won, 4–1. Cincinnati still led the Series four games to three, but the White Sox were building up an impressive head of steam. Bettors who had heard rumors that the fix was off now rushed to lay down their money on Chicago.

Faced with the prospect of losing hundreds of thousands of dollars in wagers, Rothstein called Sullivan and asked Sport to come see him. The banker told Sullivan to make certain that the Series ended at once, before any further damage was done. Sullivan called an associate with a reputation for getting things done, no questions asked. That same evening, a stranger stopped Lefty Williams on a dark Chicago street and informed him that he should lose the game tomorrow. If he didn't, something might happen, something quite unpleasant, to Williams—or to his wife. To make sure there were no mix-ups, Williams was ordered to lose the game in the first inning.

And that was what he did. Throwing a steady diet of fastballs that the Reds pounded all over the park, Williams lasted only fifteen pitches. Three runs scored before an apoplectic Gleason yanked the left-hander. Christy Mathewson, writing a syndicated column about the Series, described the Reds' hitting as a "Dempsey-like attack," but Willard never threw a championship fight. The final score was Cincinnati 10, Chicago 5; Hod Eller had won his second game of the Series, and the Redlegs were world champions. "I tell you those Reds haven't any business beating us," Gleason screamed in the locker room when it was all over. "We played worse baseball in all but a couple of games than we played all year. I don't know yet what was the matter. Something was wrong. I didn't like the betting odds. I wish no one had ever bet a dollar on the team!"

A day or two later, Sullivan handed Gandil the remaining $40,000. Risberg got another $5,000 and took $5,000 more to give to McMullin. Gandil kept the rest for himself. He went home to his wife and daughter in California and never played major-league baseball again.

To counter the rumors still swirling through hotel lobbies and locker rooms, Charles Comiskey announced on the evening of October 10 that he would pay a $20,000 reward for solid evidence that any of his players had deliberately tried to throw any of the World Series games. "There is always some scandal of some kind following a big sporting event like the world's series," Comiskey blustered. "These yarns are manufactured out of whole cloth and grow out of bitterness due to losing wagers. I believe my boys fought the battles of the recent world's series on the level, as they have always done." Shoeless Joe Jackson tried to get into Comiskey's office to discuss "a personal matter" with the owner after the Series, but Comiskey stubbornly refused to see the greatest hitter who ever lived, so Jackson went on home to his own folks in South Carolina for the winter. He later said his wife cried when he showed her his share of the money from the fix.

TEN

THE DAYS
OF
DREAMS

"The harvest is past,

the summer is ended,

and we are not saved . . ."

45

"Woe is me, my mother,

that thou hast borne me a man of strife

and a man of contention to the whole earth"

October . . . November . . . No one saw Wilson except his immediate family, his doctors, and a small circle of White House staff members who helped him through his daily routine. Two weeks after the collapse, Wilson suffered a prostatic obstruction that threatened to kill him; the doctors begged his wife to let them operate, insisting that without surgery the President would die of uremia. But Grayson told her that her husband's body probably could not stand the strain of an operation, and so she told the specialists they could not have him. Wilson recovered, but the crisis left him in an even more weakened condition. He made little jokes to relieve the tension: when his wife propped him up and fed him a small bit of soup with a spoon, he turned to Grayson and whispered, "A wonderful bird is the pelican; his beak can hold more than his belly can. He can take in his beak enough food for a week; I wonder how the hell he can." The President could not shave himself and no barbers were allowed into his room, and so he grew a white mustache and beard. One day the doctors offered to give him a shave; after all, they said, surgeons used to be barbers, too. Whereupon Wilson muttered from his bed, "They are barbarous yet."

Mrs. Wilson forbade any explicit public statements on the President's true condition. So the rumormongers had a field day: Wilson had contracted a veneral disease in Paris; his brain had degenerated into senility; the President was hopelessly and dangerously insane—he spent the day spouting nursery rhymes about pelicans; his doctors put bars on the White House windows to keep him from throwing himself out. (Actually, there were bars on one section of White House windows. They had been put up to keep Teddy Roosevelt's children from breaking the glass when they played ball.) Mrs. Wilson was spitefully dubbed "the Iron Queen" and "the Regent"; Senator Albert Fall of New Mexico, who several years later would go to jail for his role in the Teapot Dome scandal, shouted hysterically in the Senate, "We have petticoat Government! Mrs. Wilson is President!"

Of course she wasn't, and the country managed to limp along somehow with an almost totally incapacitated man in the White House. As autumn deepened into winter, Wilson recovered enough strength to sign several documents every day, at first with his wife steadying his hand, then by himself. But the frustration of knowing that he was unable to discharge his duties effectively any longer, that he could not lead the nation as he once had done so magnificently, that he could not even govern his own thoughts or speak more than a few sentences without losing the thread of an argument—all this brought Wilson to tears, and very often he wept.

Anyone having business to transact with the President first worked his way through the fringes of power until he reached Mrs. Wilson, who alone decided what matters warranted her husband's attention. (She also decided what items should be kept from him, to ensure that he was not unduly agitated.) From her years of intimate familiarity with the President's thoughts and dreams, the First Lady usually could tell a visitor right away what Wilson wanted to do in any given situation. In unusual situations, she took the questions to the President himself; he tried to give her some vague indication of his decision, and she relayed the message back to the visitor.

Nothing much got done; but then nothing of substance had gotten done since the end of the war anyway. Wilson had always been the only real driving force within the administration (his Cabinet being composed primarily of second-raters), and ever since he had gone to Europe at the end of 1918, the country had experienced a profound lack of effective leadership from the Executive Branch. In this regard, Wilson ill in the White House was not much worse than Wilson abroad in Paris, and fortunately there were no pressing domestic crises for the next eighteen months. At the end of October the President received the King and Queen of Belgium; shortly thereafter the Prince of Wales, on a tour of Canada and the United States, stopped in to pay his respects. And in mid-November, Senator Hitchcock called twice, to discuss the fate of the peace treaty.

Everyone who could count to fifty knew that a majority of the Senate steadfastly opposed the treaty without reservations. Hitchcock gently proposed that the President accept a compromise with Lodge. Wilson acidly suggested that Lodge take the first step. Wilson would not betray the plan for the world's future that he had fashioned at Paris; Lodge's reservations, he warned Hitchcock, cut "the very heart out of the Treaty," and if the

United States bowed to the will of these small-minded men in the Senate, it would suffer the righteous contempt of the world. But, fearful of the effect on her husband if the Senate rejected his treaty outright, Mrs. Wilson, too, implored him this one time to "accept these reservations and get this awful thing settled." Tired, Wilson took her hand and said, "Little girl, don't you desert me; that I cannot stand. Can't you see I have no moral right to accept any change in a paper I have already signed? It is not *I* who will not accept it; it is the Nation's honor that is at stake. Better a thousand times to go down fighting than to dip your colors in dishonorable compromise." He thereupon released a statement to the Senate urging rejection of the treaty with the Lodge amendments: "I sincerely hope that the friends and supporters of the Treaty will vote against the Lodge resolution."

On November 17 the Senate did the President's bidding and defeated the treaty with the Lodge reservations by a vote of 55 to 39. Then it turned around and defeated the treaty without the Lodge reservations, 53 to 38. Moderates on both sides resumed their efforts to find a reasonable compromise. When his wife brought him the news of his treaty's initial defeat, Wilson gave no visible sign of emotion, but quietly said, "All the more reason I must get well. . . ."

Lloyd George sat and talked of the halcyon, bygone days of the Peace Conference. He told Riddell he had truly regretted leaving Paris when it was all over at the end of June, and he spoke of his sorrow at looking out the window of his flat in the Rue Nitot to see Wilson's house closed up tightly after the President's departure. "Strangely enough I like Wilson and was more sorry to leave him than I anticipated," the Welshman admitted. "He is more likeable than Clemenceau. Clemenceau is hard." But the French Chamber of Deputies ratified the treaty of peace by a vote of 372 to 53.

America: By the end of November the steel barons had won. Gradually the strikers drifted back to work; skilled workers, who had more to lose in the first place, and who were never really comfortable acting in cooperation with immigrants and radicals, came back first. Then the unskilled laborers returned in droves, after management began hiring blacks to replace them. Union leaders voted to try to hold out a little longer and meanwhile sought intermediaries to arrange a negotiated settlement with Gary, but the Judge refused to compromise.

In Boston, city officials recruited a new police force. None of the striking policemen were permitted to return to their old jobs. Governor Calvin Coolidge won reelection by a landslide, prompting someone in the White House to send him a telegram saying, "I congratulate you upon your election as a victory for law and order. When that is the issue all Americans stand together." Massachusetts Republicans made plans to nominate Coolidge for the presidency at the 1920 party convention.

John R. Shillady, secretary of the NAACP, went down to Austin, Texas, to investigate reports that the local branch of his organization had been subjected to harassment by the authorities. He explained to the assistant attorney general of Texas and a special "court of inquiry" that the goal of the NAACP was to end racial hatred and *not* immediately to enforce social equality of whites and blacks. When Shillady, a white man, disregarded pointed warnings to leave town immediately, he was attacked and brutally beaten in broad daylight on a main street in Austin; among the mob that beat him was a county judge.

In the House of Representatives, Congressman James Byrnes of South Carolina accused the IWW and other radical organizations of stirring up racial hatred in the United States and inciting riots like those that had shaken Washington and Chicago. Arguing that the Bolshevist movement was gathering strength among blacks in America, Byrnes charged that "these radical leaders of the negro race are urging their followers to resort to violence in order to secure privileges they believe themselves entitled to and the recent riots indicate that they are accepting this advice." (In 1945, President Harry S Truman appointed Jimmy Byrnes Secretary of State.)

A Department of Justice investigation into the links between radicalism and racial unrest concluded that "at this time there can no longer be any question of a well-concerted movement among a certain class of negro leaders of thought and action to constitute themselves a determined and persistent source of a radical opposition to the Government, and to the established rule of law and order." As evidence of this dangerous attitude, the government report cited the black leaders' "ill-governed reaction toward race rioting," "the threat of retaliatory measures in connection with lynching," and "the more openly expressed demand for social equality in which the sex problem is not infrequently included."

The Surgeon General of the United States warned the nation to expect another invasion of influenza in the winter of 1919–20. Dr. Royal S. Copeland, Commissioner of Health for New York, agreed: "I have no doubt but that we will have another epidemic this year, though infinitely less violent than last year's when practically every person was affected." Doctors prescribed plenty of outdoor exercise, and advised their patients to sleep with the windows open, wash their faces and hands with soap and water several times a day, and, above all, stay away from anyone who had a cold or the flu.

In an open letter to an official of the Ohio state Republican Committee, Senator Warren G. Harding announced his candidacy for the 1920 presidential nomination. But the senator preferred not to announce any platform or propose any program, leaving such matters to the Republican Party convention. "One thing that should be stated," Harding boldly declared, "we are all agreed that a thing worth doing at all is worth doing with all one's might. . . . This undertaking is not without encouragement beyond the borders of our State, and we must play a worthy part, assuring our fellow Republicans of our utter good faith and that it is ever our belief that party success is of first importance when Republican restoration is so vital to the nation. . . ." (It was precisely this sort of vacuous utterance that prompted William McAdoo to describe Harding's speeches as "an army of pompous phrases moving over the landscape in search of an idea; sometimes these meandering words would actually capture a straggling thought and bear it triumphantly, a prisoner in their midst, until it died of servitude and overwork." More succinctly, H. L. Mencken likened Harding's speeches to "a string of wet sponges.") The field for the 1920 Republican nomination was already getting crowded, as Governor Frank Lowden of Illinois, Major General Leonard Wood, and Senator Miles Poindexter of Washington had already announced their eagerness to serve as the party's standard-bearer.

Alarmed at the growth of antiradical opinion in the United States and in deep despair over its rapidly declining membership, the Socialist Party held an emergency national convention in Chicago. But a left-wing faction led by John Reed, disgusted with the party leadership's failure to adopt a truly revolutionary stance, walked out of the convention and established its own political body, the Communist Labor Party. (The Communist Party of America was holding its convention at the time, too, but wanted nothing to do with Reed and his comrades.) Reed's party approved the principles of Lenin's Third International, declared that its ultimate goal was the dictatorship of the proletariat, called for a general strike in the United States, sang revolutionary songs ("All who right and justice seek / Burst your bonds, no longer weak / Unite and join the Bolshevik / Rise, rise, rise") and adopted the emblem of the Soviet Republic of Russia: a scythe and hammer surrounded by a wreath of wheat (a suggestion that a torch be added to the emblem was voted down). Before the year was over, Reed secretly boarded a ship bound for Sweden, whence he made his way into Finland, and then once more into Russia for a meeting with Lenin, who had written the introduction to Reed's masterpiece of historical journalism, *Ten Days That Shook the World*.

"For one year," wrote Walter Lippmann on the first anniversary of the Armistice, "we have tried to drift somehow back to some kind of peace footing. Instead we have drifted into a severe internal conflict." The approaching domestic disaster, Lippmann believed, was due not to the agitation of Bolsheviks, blacks, or radicals, but to the ineptitude of the nation's elected officials, "who have been too absent-minded to behave like a government. They have refused to look ahead, refused to think, refused to plan, refused to prepare for any of the normal consequences of a war. The attack on the government is nothing as compared with the paralysis of the government." Lippmann saw that America's leaders were frightened, and what was worse, they showed their fear. Lost in terror, they had magnified a few minor political and industrial conflicts into an imaginary revolution. "Let our leaders put aside this opera bouffe revolution with themselves cast for Marie Antoinette," Lippmann urged. "Let history make its legends if it must. But let us stop living in a legend. Life today is grim and difficult enough without complicating it further by behaving as if it were half melodrama, half nightmare."

Looking back to the world of August 1914, Winston Churchill was convinced that the intervening years had transformed civilization "into a sphere infinitely lower than that which existed before Armageddon." In a speech in London on November 24, the Minister of War painted a devastating picture of the state of the world at the end of 1919: "Never has there been a time when people were more disposed to turn to courses of violence or show such scant respect for law and custom, tradition and procedure. Never has there been a time when a more complete callousness and indifference for human life was exhibited by the great communities all over the world. All over Europe we see the seething scene of misery, torment, and malevolence, which is not for the moment dangerous only because it proceeds on a basis of exhaustion such as the world has never recorded in all its history."

Adolf Hitler persuaded Drexler and his comrades in the German Workers' Party to embark upon an intensive campaign to expand the membership of the party by holding more frequent—and better publicized—meetings in larger and more reputable halls. At first Hitler typed or wrote out and distributed the invitations to the meetings himself; later he employed a mimeograph machine and, when the party's growing funds permitted, placed advertisements in the newspapers of Munich to attract even more followers. The audiences grew from less than a dozen to 110, 130, then two hundred; and soon more than four hundred sat and heard Hitler denounce the Jews and the shame of Versailles and the *Dolchstoss*. "The misery of Germany," he proclaimed, "must be broken by Germany's steel. That time must come." Hitler reorganized the party's structure to make it an effective political weapon instead of a "tea club." He was appointed as the party's new chief of propaganda. By the end of the year, he and Drexler had formulated an official party platform of twenty-five points, which Hitler vowed would someday rival the theses Martin Luther had nailed to the church door at Wittenberg. And Hitler now brought into the movement his comrades from the army, men who he knew possessed the "indomitable will" and "brutal ruthlessness" that he believed were essential if the party was "to sweep aside any obstacles which might stand in the path of the rising new idea. For this only beings were fitted in whom spirit and body had acquired those military virtues which can perhaps best be described as follows: swift as greyhounds, tough as leather, and hard as Krupp steel."

Germany: In the countryside, peasants resumed with grim determination the centuries-old autumn tasks of the harvest. Perhaps this year the earth's bounty would surpass the reduced harvests of wartime. In the villages, the arches of pine branches—inscribed in another day, in another time, with slogans to greet the men returning from the front (*Willkommen zu unseren siegreichen Soldaten*, "Welcome to our victorious soldiers"; or *Mit Stolz and Liebe erinnern wir uns an unsere Verblichene*, "We hold in loving remembrance those who died")—now stood bowed and bedraggled, battered by the harsh, chilling storms of November. An American visitor to Germany found it difficult to describe in words "the blank pessimism which is all but universal in Germany today. People are hopeless, without faith in God, themselves, their rulers, the Allies, or the neutrals; in capitalism or Bolshevism; in democracy, revolution, or monarchy. And they are too tired and half-starved to care." The American heard few complaints about the peace treaty; instead, the people seemed to have accepted it "with a curious combination of fatalism and conviction that it cannot endure. You find no intention to resist it, simply a calm assumption that it cannot possibly be executed."

Germany lacked sufficient coal stocks to warm the nation's houses and supply the factories for the entire winter; one or the other would have to suffer. While food supplies were increasing, prices remained prohibitively high. But the people were desperate: the first shipment of chocolate to reach Berlin in years sold out quickly at five dollars a pound. And sometimes things were not as they seemed. Sausage makers were discovered using cat meat instead of pork, and distraught consumers rebelled when they learned they had been eating "whipped cream" made of soapsuds and sugar. This sort of deception might have seemed relatively harmless, but beneath the surface the working classes remained bitterly discontented. Traveling through Germany's cities on his way back to Washington, Stephen Bonsal saw "men, women, and children, all thinly clad, standing around or wandering aimlessly about, pale and hungry. Few if any of them seemed to be sustained by the thought that now the war was over the future promised better things; all they knew was that they were cold and hungry—and winter was coming on. . . ." But whenever trouble threatened to flare anew, Noske dispatched a few companies of his volunteer corps, whose membership now numbered a half-million. "I will oppose with all my energy any attempt to introduce the Russian system into Germany," Noske barked. "If it is a matter of staking the life of a couple of thousand mad persons in order to save a hundred thousand peaceable citizens, I will act as I did in Berlin, Hamburg, Bremen or Munich."

At the start of December, the Freikorps officers accused of murdering the sailors at Moabit Prison in March went on trial. On December 6, Berlin's official state of siege, declared on March 3, was finally raised.

In Berlin the shadows fell earlier in the afternoon as winter approached. The sky took on a curious opalescence, the yellow leaves scuttled down the Unter den Linden. In a first-class restaurant, wealthy patrons enjoyed a choice of eight meat dishes (including mutton, pork, veal, and beef) and sparkling wines, as the band played *Lohengrin* or a Strauss waltz. Outside the door, a crippled veteran, armless, lay trembling with shell shock on the pavement. It really was too bad, someone said upon entering the restaurant, that the fellow should be allowed to make such an exhibition of himself.

Verzweiflungsrevolution: a revolution born of desperation.

Ex-Kaiser William Hohenzollern purchased a fourteenth-century estate of over 1,300 acres at Doorn in the Netherlands for a price of nearly $250,000. Arrangements were made to buy twenty houses nearby for his retinue. By the end of the year he was ready to leave Amerongen.

When Premier Ignace Jan Paderewski dared to propose a program of drastic land reforms in Poland, conservative landowners and a reactionary military clique joined forces in Parliament to defeat the measures. On December 9 the Premier resigned his office.

* * *

Lest anyone think that famine and malnutrition had ended their reign over Central and Eastern Europe, Dr. Hilda Clark of the American Friends' Service Committee reported from Vienna that 60 percent of the children of the better working classes in the city suffered from severe rickets, and hardly any of them were completely free of the disease. "The toddlers of one to five years are hardly seen in the streets," she wrote, "for they can hardly toddle, and unless you undress them and ask their ages you would not realize what had happened." Statistics revealed that there were 52,000 more deaths in Vienna in 1919 than there had been in 1914, and 69,000 fewer births. Over the past four years, the terrible rate of infant mortality had produced a loss to the population of 121,306 souls. "The bread ration in Vienna," reported Hoover, "has already been reduced to three ounces per day and bread is 60 per cent of the people's food." The Austrian government arranged to distribute Christmas gifts of one loaf of bread for each person; it promised the bread would be of slightly better quality than usual. (Physicians in Austria had to cope with an epidemic of intestinal diseases caused by bad bread.) People had long ago eaten their pets; now they hunted rats. Horsemeat was a luxury few Viennese workers could afford. The American relief mission in Vienna prepared to feed 200,000 children on Christmas Day. "Never in history," wrote an American observer, "has Europe had such a black Christmas as this."

Unable to obtain even the minimal government ration of coal to heat their homes, the citizens of Vienna already had stripped the city of every combustible article: signboards, park benches, wooden fences. Every morning a grotesque army of gaunt, pinched women and children and old men, armed with axes, saws, and hatchets, poured out of the city and scoured the countryside for fuel, cutting down shade trees along the highways and fruit trees in the orchards, denuding the forests of aristocrats' estates. Chancellor Renner implored the Supreme Allied Council to rush food and fuel to his desperate country.

A Swiss mission visiting Budapest declared that hundreds of thousands of children in the city lacked boots or clothing, and hundreds had already suffered frostbitten feet that had to be amputated.

On November 14, Rumanian troops finally evacuated Budapest. They were replaced by the White Hungarian troops of Admiral Miklos Horthy, a representative of the reactionary landed aristocracy. An Allied commission investigating affairs in Hungary in December found the dead bodies of sixty-two Communists hanging from trees in a patch of woods outside of Budapest. Austrian Socialists charged that over 1,500 suspected radicals had already been executed in the counterrevolutionary rampage in Hungary, and the Austrians begged the Allies to help stop the slaughter.

Horthy condemned the citizens of Budapest for having "dragged the Holy Crown and the national colors in the dust," and promised to forgive the capital only "if it turns from the false gods to the love of our fatherland . . . if it reveres the Holy Crown once more. . . ." Allied pressure forced Horthy to accept a coalition government until new parliamentary elections could be held; but after the army arrested the leaders of the Social Democrats and forbade Communists to vote at all, no one was surprised when the new National Assembly, meeting under the eyes of the military hierarchy on March 1, 1920, decided to make Horthy "Regent Governor of the Kingdom of Hungary," an office he held until 1944. During Horthy's reign, the government repealed most of the social and political reforms passed during the reigns of Karolyi and Kun in the year after the Armistice. Power returned to the prewar aristocracy, which bided its time until it found an opportunity two decades later to avenge Hungary's humiliation at the hands of the Paris Peace Conference and the Rumanian thieves.

When Herbert Hoover returned to the United States in the autumn of 1919, he vowed that he would never again return to Europe. The experience of dealing with the vicious, chaotic postwar world had instilled in the future President a deep inclination toward isolationism. As Hoover wrote several years later:

I CAME OUT OF ALL THESE EXPERIENCES WITH ONE ABSOLUTE CONVICTION, WHICH WAS: AMERICA, WITH ITS SKILL IN ORGANIZATION AND THE VALOR OF ITS SONS, COULD WIN GREAT WARS. BUT IT COULD NOT MAKE LASTING PEACE. I WAS CONVINCED WE MUST KEEP OUT OF OLD WORLD WARS, LEND OURSELVES TO MEASURES PREVENTING WAR, MAINTAINING PEACE AND HEALING THE WOUNDS OF WAR. I CAME TO THIS CONCLUSION BECAUSE OF IRRECONCILABLE CONFLICTS IN CONCEPTS AND HISTORIC EXPERIENCE BETWEEN THE NEW WORLD AND THE OLD WORLD. THEY REACHED INTO DEPTHS OF OUR INTERNATIONAL RELATIONS, GOVERNMENT, SOCIAL AND ECONOMIC LIFE. THEY CONFRONTED ME DAILY DURING THE WAR, THE ARMISTICE, AND IN THE CONFUSION OF MAKING PEACE. THE TWO WORLDS WERE INDEED STRANGERS TO EACH OTHER. WE HAD DRIFTED FARTHER AND FARTHER APART OVER THREE HUNDRED YEARS.

46

"The heart is deceitful

above all things,

and desperately wicked . . ."

"It takes you a long time to learn how to deal with all the sorts of rats there are—the big black Norway rats that come in ships, sewer rats, farm rats, house rats, and lots of others," explained Jack Jarvis, a professional English rat-catcher and a member of the fifth generation of a rat-catching family. "No one knows how long a rat lives, but it certainly keeps on learning things all the time." In London, he said, the favorite haunts of well-educated rodents were the Tube system and the railways; they got plenty to eat there, and since no one had the job of getting rid of them, they scurried about all over London to their hearts' content, emerging at whatever stations took their fancy.

Britain's National Rat Week proved a great success. Authorities advised neophyte rat-killers that the best bait was bread, the best gas sulphur dioxide, and the best poison a combination of squill extract and barium carbonate. The chief medical officer of London also reported encouraging results with varnish traps, wherein the victims' feet and tails stuck fast to the varnish, "and the more they struggle the faster they stick. Rats caught during the night are always dead in the morning, and it is a very remarkable thing that if two rats get on to the varnish together one of them kills the other. Evidently each thinks that the other is holding him."

Nevertheless, some localities refused to participate in Rat Week, giving rise to fears that rodents driven from one town might simply migrate to another, more slovenly region and breed a new generation. Moreover, experts noted with considerable forboding that the old English black rat and the common brown rat (more repulsive but less dangerous), hitherto mortal enemies, appeared to be laying aside their age-old enmity and learning to live together in the same room in a state of peaceful, albeit uneasy coexistence.

* * *

At a tension-filled meeting of the Royal Society and Royal Astronomical Society on November 6, as the learned audience of astronomers and physicists gazed with a combination of sympathy and nervous anticipation upon a portrait of Sir Isaac Newton behind the speakers' platform, Sir Frank Dyson, the Astronomer Royal, announced that a detailed analysis of the photographs taken during the solar eclipse by the expeditions to Sobral and Príncipe in May appeared to verify Herr Einstein's calculations, providing overwhelming evidence to support the German physicist's theory of relativity. The photographs showed that rays of light did indeed bend when they passed the sun on their way to the earth. Following Dyson to the podium, Dr. Crommelin of the Greenwich Observatory confirmed that the system of Newtonian physics apparently no longer adequately explained the actual workings of the universe; space did not extend indefinitely in all directions, Euclid's straight lines were actually curved, and two "parallel" lines would eventually meet.

"These are not isolated results that have been obtained," concluded the president of the Royal Society, Sir Joseph Thomson. "It is not the discovery of an outlying island, but of a whole continent of new scientific ideas of the greatest importance to some of the most fundamental questions connected with physics." Indeed, Sir Joseph ventured to describe Einstein's theory of relativity as "one of the greatest—perhaps the greatest—of achievements in the history of human thought." (Five years later, Bertrand Russell declared himself in complete agreement with Thomson. The theory of relativity, Russell wrote, "is probably the greatest synthetic achievement of the human intellect up to the present time. It sums up the mathematical and physical labors of more than two thousand years.")

Nevertheless, before anyone got too excited, Sir Joseph confessed to the November 6 gathering of Britain's leading scientists that "no one has yet succeeded in stating in clear language what the theory of Einstein really is." Thomson predicted that while the new Einsteinian concepts would surely dominate all other previous systems of physics, the next generation of mathematics professors were in for a most difficult time in trying to explain it all to their students. Einstein himself, in offering his most recent research to his publishers, had warned that there were not more than twelve people in the whole world who would truly understand it.

From his library on the top floor of a comfortable Berlin apartment house, Dr. Einstein tried to summarize his conclusions in plain English for a *New York Times* reporter. "The term relativity refers to time and space," the professor explained. "According to Galileo and Newton, time and space were absolute entities, and the moving systems of the universe were dependent on this absolute time and space. On this conception was built the science of mechanics. The resulting formulas sufficed for all motions of a slow nature; it was found, however, that they would not conform to the rapid motions apparent in electrodynamics." So Einstein and a Dutch colleague developed the theory of special relativity, which "discards absolute time and space and makes them in every instance relative to moving systems. . . . Till now it was believed that time and space existed by themselves, even if there was nothing else—no sun, no earth, no stars—while now we know that time and space are not the vessel for the universe, but could not exist at all if there were no contents, namely, no sun, earth, and other celestial bodies."

In later years, constantly badgered for even more simplistic summaries, Einstein used homely little anecdotes to get his point across. If you were talking to a pretty girl for two hours, he explained, the time would pass so quickly it might seem more like two minutes. But if you were sitting on a hot stove, two minutes would seem like two hours. That, he explained, was what relativity was all about.

Even though virtually no one really understood the new physics, the notion of relativity caught the public's fancy at a time when moral and spiritual absolutes were breaking down in Europe and the United States (in large measure because of the devastating psychological trauma inflicted by the war). In Britain, Robert Graves observed that "the word 'relativity' now came to be commonly used, out of the context of Einstein's theory, to mean that a thing was only so if you cared to assume the hypothesis that made it so. Truth likewise was not absolute. . . ." The blossoming revolution in sexual mores gathered further momentum from this notion in the 1920s, leading the young to reject the taboos that had presumably (although not necessarily) inhibited social behavior in the decades before the war.

In less tolerant quarters, however, Einstein's theories were seen as just one more wave in the rising tide of antiestablishment radicalism that threatened to engulf civilization. At Columbia University, a slightly hysterical professor of celestial mechanics querulously rejected the theory of relativity as cheap claptrap and charged that:

FOR SOME YEARS PAST THE ENTIRE WORLD HAS BEEN IN A STATE OF UNREST, MENTAL AS WELL AS PHYSICAL. IT MAY BE THAT THE WAR, THE BOLSHEVIST UPRISING, ARE THE VISIBLE OBJECTS OF SOME DEEP MENTAL DISTURBANCE. THIS UNREST IS EVIDENCED BY THE DESIRE TO THROW ASIDE THE WELL-TESTED METHODS OF GOVERNMENT IN FAVOR OF RADICAL AND UN-

TRIED EXPERIMENTS. THIS SAME SPIRIT OF UNREST HAS INVADED SCIENCE. THERE ARE MANY WHO WOULD HAVE US THROW ASIDE THE WELL-TESTED THEORIES UPON WHICH HAVE BEEN BUILT THE ENTIRE STRUCTURE OF MODERN SCIENTIFIC AND MECHANICAL DEVELOPMENT IN FAVOR OF METHODOLOGICAL SPECULATION AND PHANTASTIC DREAMS ABOUT THE UNIVERSE.

At a gathering of the Midland Institute in Birmingham, England, to celebrate the two-hundredth anniversary of James Watt's birth, Sir Oliver Lodge spoke of the vast potential storehouse of energy contained within tiny atoms of radioactive matter. "If you were able to use mechanically the energy contained in an ounce of matter," Sir Oliver predicted, "you will find enough energy to raise the German Navy [from the bottom of Scapa Flow] and pile it on the top of a Scottish mountain." Reflecting upon the potential consequences for humanity of such a discovery, however, Lodge admitted that it was perhaps a good thing that the Kaiser's Germany had not possessed the knowledge that would release the power of atomic energy, and he hoped that the human race as a whole "would be equally unsuccessful until it had brains and morality enough to use it properly, for if such a discovery were made before its time and by the wrong people the very planet would be unsafe."

Shortly after he moved back home to St. Paul, Minnesota, F. Scott Fitzgerald received word from Scribner's editor Maxwell Perkins that the publisher had accepted for publication his first novel, now entitled *This Side of Paradise* (the title drawn from a poem by Rupert Brooke). Fitzgerald naturally wished to have the book appear as soon as possible (by Christmas, he suggested), since "I have so many things dependent on its success—including of course a girl," but Perkins assured him that the late winter or early spring of 1920 was a much more realistic publication date. By the end of the year, *The Smart Set*, a magazine edited by H. L. Mencken and George Jean Nathan, had accepted a short story and a one-act play by Fitzgerald, and the young author was preparing for a trip to Montgomery to rescue his engagement, which Zelda had broken off in June. By February 1920, all was well between the lovers once again.

Ernest Hemingway spent the summer on the shores of a northern Michigan lake, and lost his virginity in a brief affair with a woman several years older than he. Then he set off for Toronto, as a hired companion to the son of a top executive of the F. W. Woolworth Company.

John Dos Passos was discharged from the army and spent the rest of the year traveling through France and Spain, gathering material and polishing several manuscripts. What he had seen since the Armistice convinced him that "a false idea, a false system, and a set of tyrants, conscious or unconscious, is sitting on the world's neck at present and has so far succeeded in destroying a good half of the worthwhile things in the world. Do you realize," he asked a friend, "what it means to have half a continent in ashes and starving?" The year 1919, Dos Passos decided, was "a time to save what we can of the things worthwhile and to decide damn quick what things are worthwhile and what are not."

Dorothy Parker was fired from her job at *Vanity Fair* for writing several uncomplimentary reviews of Broadway plays, including one production that starred Billie Burke, the wife of Florenz Ziegfeld—who just happened to be one of *Vanity Fair*'s most generous advertisers. Messrs. Benchley and Sherwood marched into Frank Crowninshield's office and informed him that if Miss Parker went, they, too, would leave the magazine. Crowninshield, who was not terribly enthusiastic anyway about the work the trio had been doing, replied that that arrangement suited him fine, and so the three newly unemployed writers spent the afternoon at the Algonquin, joking to keep their spirits up.

T. E. Lawrence returned to England and settled in at Oxford, where he had been awarded a fellowship to continue his research into Near Eastern history. Lawrence spent the rest of the year working on the manuscript of his masterpiece, *Seven Pillars of Wisdom*. He told a friend that he had lost the first draft (with which he had apparently been dissatisfied) on a train between London and Oxford in the fall of 1919, and so on December 2 he began the second draft. Lawrence did most of his writing while living a spartan existence in a furnished attic in Westminster; "I work best utterly by myself," he insisted, "and speak to no one for days." During the days he slept, and at night he came alive to write. "He refused all service and comfort, food, fire or hot water," recalled the architect who provided Lawrence with the room. "We who worked in the rooms below never heard a sound; I would look up from my drawing-board in the evening sometimes to see him watching, gnomelike, with a smile; his smile that hid a tragedy." Later, Lawrence came to believe that this lonely attic room "was the best and freest place I have ever lived in. . . ."

In the Middle East, events moved toward a confrontation between the Zionists and Arab nationalists in the last months of 1919. The British military administration in Palestine attempted to stem the tide of Jewish immigration into the region, but the pressure of Jews fleeing the pogroms in Central and Eastern Europe proved too strong; the desperate refugees ignored all barriers and flooded into Constantinople on their way to the Promised Land. At a world conference of Zionists, Lord Curzon (who had replaced Arthur Balfour as Lloyd George's Foreign Secretary) reaffirmed the British government's commitment to the establishment of a national home for the Jewish people in Palestine. Early in 1920, after Britain and France finally agreed upon a division of the Middle Eastern spoils—the treaty allotted Syria to the French sphere of influence, much to the dismay of Faisal—Britain received a League of Nations mandate to administer Palestine. Deprived of Damascus, Faisal was soon turned out of Arabia as well by the forces of the rival Sa'ud dynasty, and had to be satisfied with the British gift of Iraq as a consolation prize.

In Palestine itself, Arab nationalist emotions—aroused by the war, fed by Faisal's pretensions to suzerainty over a sovereign pan-Arab state, and alarmed at the exaggerated Zionist rhetoric that confidently predicted the birth of a Jewish state in the near future—clashed with the growing strength of the *yishuv*. At first, Arab hostility displayed itself in a refusal to sell land to the Jews pouring into Palestine, or to cooperate in the economic development of the region. But in the early spring of 1920, a series of riots in the Jewish Quarter of the Old City of Jerusalem left nine people dead and over two hundred wounded. Most of the victims were Jews: children, women, and old men.

Nonetheless, the backbreaking work of colonizing the land went relentlessly on. In November 1919, David Ben-Gurion stood at the pier of Jaffa harbor and embraced his wife, whom he had not seen for nearly two years, and his fourteen-month-old daughter, whom he had never seen. The family stayed in a hotel until their residence, in a new socialist quarter of Jaffa, was completed. Before their arrival, David had promised his wife that she and their daughter would lack none of the normal comforts of home while living in Palestine: "I will supply eggs and milk, not only for drinking but for bathing our baby, if you so desire. . . . I promise you, my Paula, that Ge'ula will have all the comforts that exist in Brooklyn and the Bronx, at least until she wants to go to the Metropolitan Opera House."

Russia: In October, the White armies at last appeared to have victory in their grasp. Denikin was storming toward Moscow from the south; in the face of the determined assaults of Yudenich upon Petrograd's defenses, Lenin prepared to abandon the city (known as "the birthplace of the revolution") and move the line of defense closer to Moscow. He was dissuaded from doing so only by the force of Trotsky's will. The mercurial

Commissar for War went to Petrograd himself to direct the city's defense. By throwing thousands of new working-class recruits into the front, Trotsky blunted Yudenich's advance and forced the White general to retreat into Estonia, where he promptly disappeared; he was presumably arrested and thrown into prison by the Estonian government.

Denikin, meanwhile, had overextended himself badly. The peasants behind his lines sabotaged his campaign; he could find no reliable new recruits to match the Red reinforcements. Attacks by the wildly unstable and unpredictable anarchist leader Nestor Makhno in the Ukraine forced Denikin to divert precious manpower from the advance upon Moscow. By the beginning of November his army had started to unravel, morale plummeted, and the retreat began. By the end of the year Denikin realized his cause was hopeless; he hopped a British ship bound for Constantinople and made his way to France, where he lived in peaceful retirement (writing a five-volume set of memoirs) until his death in 1947. Kolchak was less fortunate. Captured by Soviet forces at Irkutsk in January 1920, the admiral was sentenced to death and executed by a firing squad on February 7. They pushed his body under the ice of the frozen Angara River.

On December 5, 1919, Lenin confidently informed the Seventh All-Russian Congress of Soviets that "the chief difficulties are already behind us." But Lenin had no intention of abandoning the Terror. "Terror and the Cheka are an absolutely necessary thing," he insisted again and again. "We did not paint sweet pictures for our peasant, that he could abandon the capitalist system without the iron discipline and a firm government of the working class." Nor could Lenin relax his own iron self-discipline as starvation and typhus continued to ravage the country in the bitter Russian winter of 1919–20. Lenin carried logs to heat the Kremlin; Lenin refused all invitations to concerts ("Of course, it's very pleasant to listen to music, but imagine, it affects my mood. Somehow, I cannot bear it"); Lenin had no time for anything that did not bear directly upon the great struggle.

Lenin knew that the Russian workers were hungry and freezing as 1919 came to an end at last, but he also knew that the civil war was effectively over. Now he had to consolidate his rule over a devastated and exhausted nation.

The government in Tokyo proposed a vastly expanded military budget, to construct dozens of new warships, improve Japan's island defenses, and augment the strength of the Imperial Army. To neutralize opposition to the buildup, newspapers controlled by the nation's military party began screaming loudly and regularly about the "white peril of cruel, ambitious

America" that allegedly threatened both Japan's legitimate interests on the continent of Asia and the Japanese homeland itself.

Italy: The parliamentary elections of November 16 resulted in a resounding triumph for the Socialists (particularly in the industrial centers of northern Italy); Socialist representation in the Chamber of Deputies jumped from fifty-one to 156. None of Mussolini's Fascist candidates won. A parade of leftists in Milan carried through the city streets a casket containing a dummy of Mussolini surrounded by burning candles. The procession made certain that it passed Mussolini's house and finally, amid crude jests and ribald laughter, tossed the effigy ("a political corpse") into the canal that ran through the center of the city. "I faced, and all of us faced, complete defeat," Mussolini wrote several years later. "It was tragic, our record, but in the passage of time it is amusing and may be remembered by all losers." He attributed the Fascists' defeat to the masses' misplaced faith in Bolshevism as a panacea for the social discontent that continued to sweep across Italy through the end of 1919. For a brief moment, Mussolini considered giving up the struggle and taking up again his craft as a mason—or becoming a pilot or a wandering musician (he played the violin) or a writer of novels that he planned to fill with tales of madness, murder, and incest.

But on the day after the elections, frustrated arditi threw a bomb into a Socialist parade in Milan. (This was a traditional arditi method of relieving pent-up frustration.) Not surprisingly, police responded by searching the offices of Mussolini's newspaper for weapons; even less surprisingly, they found a cache of guns and grenades. Mussolini was arrested, but twenty-four hours later the government released him, partly because it did not want to make him a martyr to the nationalist cause, and partly because army officers sympathetic to the arditi movement exerted high-level pressure on his behalf. Determined to rebuild his shattered political organization, Mussolini set to work at once to capitalize upon the growing uneasiness of conservatives and the middle class following the Socialist victories at the polls. He also waited patiently for the inevitable disillusionment among Italian workers when the Socialists proved unable to carry out their own rash, ambitious campaign promises of a proletarian utopia. But nobody said it was going to be easy; from time to time Mussolini found it necessary to stiffen his colleagues' resolve. "Don't fear," Benito told them. "Italy will heal herself from this illness. But without our watchfulness it might be deadly. We will resist! Resist! I should say so! Indeed, within two years I will have my turn!" Nitti's latest Cabinet survived a vote of confidence in late December, but only by a slim margin of 242 to 216.

Meanwhile, the city of Fiume grew restless under the autocratic rule of Gabriele D'Annunzio. A plebiscite in December resulted in an 85-percent majority in favor of a government proposal to substitute Italian regulars for D'Annunzio's forces, but the poet refused to accept the people's verdict. He insisted that Nitti's guarantees regarding the city's future were insufficient to induce him to leave, and he vowed once again to resist every attempt to dislodge him from his stronghold.

In August, General Dyer finally filed his report on the Amritsar disturbances. When reliable indications of the true scope of the disaster at last reached London in October, the government appointed a commission of inquiry, headed by Lord Hunter (lately Solicitor-General for Scotland), to investigate both the causes of the disorders and the measures taken to suppress them. The eight members of the Hunter Commission (five Englishmen and three Indians) began taking testimony in India on October 29. On November 19, General Dyer appeared before the committee and told them exactly what he had done. The tone of his testimony revealed that he still harbored no doubts that his actions at the Jallianwala Bagh had been both necessary and proper. Shortly thereafter, while traveling on a night train from Amritsar to Delhi, Jawaharlal Nehru found himself in a sleeping compartment with a number of British military officers. In the morning, he heard them talking: "One of them was holding forth in an aggressive and triumphant tone, and soon I discovered that he was Dyer, the hero of Jallianwala Bagh, who was describing his Amritsar experiences. He pointed out how he had the whole town at his mercy and he had felt like reducing the rebellious city to a heap of ashes, but he took pity on it and refrained. . . . I was greatly shocked to hear his conversation and to observe his callous manner. He descended at Delhi station in pyjamas with bright pink stripes, and a dressing gown. . . ."

In England, two men—one Liberal, one Conservative—discussed the Amritsar massacre. The Liberal remarked that such an incident would have been quite impossible twenty or thirty years earlier. Or even five years ago, replied his friend: "It is the war that has made such things possible. For four and a half years men have been shooting one another down, blowing one another to bits, bombing houses, and sinking ships, and after that do you suppose the normal regard for life is left intact?" Perhaps, thought the Liberal; but perhaps the decline of civilized behavior between men and between nations had begun even before the war; perhaps the war was merely one manifestation of a retrogressive movement characterized by the renewed ascendancy of barbarism in human life. "It is characteristic of such movements," the Liberal thought, "that they are self-accelerating. Each advance that they make facilitates a still further advance, constitutes a precedent, and makes resistance more difficult. This is not the ordinary nor perhaps the most natural view," he admitted. "It seemed reasonable to think that a consummated tragedy like the Great War would purge the mind of civilisation, prove to it by an experiment on the grand scale the true results of trusting to violence, and 'accomplish through pity and terror the purgation' of the latter of those passions. It has not been so. The war has settled nothing, and left the victors at least more disposed than ever to settle all difficulties by [in Brigadier General Reginald Dyer's words] 'shooting well.' "

Early on the afternoon of December 19, Sir John French, Lord-Lieutenant and Viceroy of Ireland, returned to Dublin from a weekend visit to his country house in Roscommon. He arrived at Ashtown Station shortly after one o'clock and got into his armored motorcar. Escorted by a military guard, the Lord-Lieutenant started for the Viceregal Lodge, about a mile from the station. Before they had gone fifty yards, the motorcade met an obstacle in the road by Kelly's Corner: an overturned two-wheeled farm cart blocking their path. As the cars slowed down, a barrage of bullets and grenades rained down upon them from assassins hidden behind a dungheap by a public house and the stone hedges on either side of the road. The second car, in which French normally traveled, was riddled with bullets. But this day the Viceroy had decided to ride in the lead car, which now sped past on the side of the road. ("We are in it now," shouted one of the soldiers to the driver. "Go on like the devil!") Four bullets struck French's car, but none of them penetrated the armor. His guards killed one of the attackers, a grocer's assistant named Martin Savage. That evening the Lodge issued a statement reassuring everyone that Viscount French was "quite well and never had been better." The coroner's jury that sat in inquest on the death of Savage returned a verdict that read more like a challenge to British authority: "We find that Martin Savage died from a bullet fired by a military escort and we beg to tender our sympathy to the relatives of the deceased."

It was the first attempt on a viceroy's life in Ireland since 1886, and it confirmed Lloyd George in his belief that something must be done about the Irish controversy, which, in his words, resembled an "old family quarrel which had degenerated many times into a blood feud." But all his Cabinet could propose was a limited Home Rule bill that created two parliaments: one for the Protestant north and another for the Catholic south. In presenting the measure to the House of Commons on December 22, Lloyd George again steadfastly refused to consider any proposal that coerced Northern Ireland into joining the Catholic majority in the south: "It would be an outrage to the principle of self-government to place her under alien rule," the Prime Minister declared, to the ringing cheers of the Conservative backbenchers. Lloyd George's bill eventually received Parliamentary approval a year later, but it made no difference. Events in Ireland had already moved far beyond the control of any such pale remedies by the end of 1919.

Sir John Alcock, the English aviator who had conquered the Atlantic in June, crashed while flying in a thick fog twenty-five miles north of Rouen, a week before Christmas. En route to an international airplane exhibition in Paris, Alcock was piloting a Vickers hydroplane that was due to be one of the featured exhibits. Witnesses said that Alcock had been flying low to the ground due to the extremely poor visibility; one of his wings struck a tree during a turn, and the plane dropped suddenly to earth. Alcock was dead before the ambulance arrived from the military hospital at Rouen.

Attorney General Palmer escalated his war on America's Reds. On November 7, Department of Justice agents raided suspected Bolshevik headquarters in eleven cities; many of the aliens seized in the wholesale sweep were held for weeks without benefit of counsel. It was time, Palmer said, to start deportation proceedings in earnest against as many of these radicals (he put the number of dangerous, foreign-born Reds in America at sixty thousand) as possible. Anti-Bolshevik hysteria in the United States rose another notch a week after this first wave of Palmer raids, when four members of the American Legion, marching in an Armistice Day parade in Centralia, Washington, were shot and killed by assassins firing from hotel windows. (Since the American Legion had vowed to drive the IWW out of Washington, suspicion naturally fell first upon members of that radical labor organization. Forty-four suspects were arrested, and an outraged mob lynched "Brick" Smith, the secretary of the IWW.) Working closely with the Attorney General in this campaign to clean up America was the director of the Justice Department's General Intelligence Division, a twenty-five-year-old ex-librarian named John Edgar Hoover, who had compiled a remarkably detailed, cross-referenced index card system containing information on every known radical organization in the United States.

Nominees for deportation—allegedly the intelligentsia of the radical movement—were sent to Ellis Island, where they were held virtually incommunicado. They were joined in December by Emma Goldman and Alexander Berkman, two of America's most famous and feared foreign-born revolutionaries. (Emma later described her quarters at Ellis Island as "the worst dump I have ever stayed in," which was saying a lot.) Goldman and Berkman had been arrested during the war for interfering with the draft, and now Commissioner General of Immigration Anthony Caminetti decided that they, too, should be sent out of the country. So, several hours before dawn on the bitterly cold morning of December 21, 249 alien radicals were taken aboard the old five-thousand-ton steamer *Buford*, which had carried troops to Cuba in the Spanish-American War, and ferried doughboys across the Atlantic during the war to end all wars. Now it was laughingly rechristened "the Soviet Ark."

Awaiting the passengers was a crew of 250 military guards armed with rifles and revolvers. J. Edgar Hoover came just to say goodbye. As the ship pulled out shortly after six o'clock in the morning, Emma Goldman reportedly shouted, "This is the beginning of the end of the United States. I shall be back in America. We shall all be back. I am proud to be among the first deported. The Czar, in all his career, never treated his subjects as we are being treated." "We're coming back," muttered Berkman defiantly, "and we'll get you." Opening his sealed orders after he was safely at sea, the captain of the *Buford* set a course for Finland. While the ark was en route to Scandinavia, the State Department released its official explanation of the deportation order:

THESE PERSONS, WHILE ENJOYING THE HOSPITALITY OF THIS COUNTRY, HAVE CONDUCTED THEMSELVES IN A MOST OBNOXIOUS MANNER; AND WHILE ENJOYING THE BENEFITS AND LIVING UNDER THE PROTECTION OF THIS GOVERNMENT HAVE PLOTTED ITS OVERTHROW. THEY ARE A MENACE TO LAW AND ORDER. THEY HOLD THEORIES WHICH ARE ANTAGONISTIC TO THE ORDERLY PROCESSES OF MODERN CIVILIZATION. . . . THEY ARE ARRAYED IN OPPOSITION TO GOVERNMENT, TO DECENCY, TO JUSTICE. THEY PLAN TO APPLY THEIR DESTRUCTIVE THEORIES BY VIOLENCE IN DEROGATION OF LAW. THEY ARE ANARCHISTS. THEY ARE PERSONS OF SUCH CHARACTER AS TO BE UNDESIRABLE IN THE UNITED STATES OF AMERICA AND ARE BEING SENT WHENCE THEY CAME.

After twenty-eight days the ship docked at the port of Hango, whence the deportees were taken across the border into Russia. The Soviets treated them as heroes—at first. Goldman found her friend John Reed, and together they talked of the future of the revolution.

Back in New York, authorities prepared a second Soviet ark for departure. But Palmer had an even more spectacular surprise planned for the new year.

"And the vessel that he made of clay

was marred in the hand of the potter . . ."

Harry S Truman ended 1919 on an upbeat note. On June 28—the day the peace treaty was signed at Versailles—Captain Truman married Bess Wallace; the couple drove to Chicago for their honeymoon, then went on to Detroit and the lakes of northern Michigan. (Presumably they did not run into Ernest Hemingway during the summer.) In November, Harry and an old army buddy, Harry Jacobsen, opened a haberdashery on Twelfth Street in Kansas City, Missouri. Both men put in long days of hard work to make the venture a success, and their efforts were well rewarded. Money poured in, they said, "by the basketful."

France: For those who could afford it, the first peacetime Christmas celebration in six years provided an occasion for unrestrained revelry along the boulevards of Paris. The weather was perfect, clear skies after weeks of rain, with temperatures that brought back summer for a day. On Christmas Eve, thousands of wealthy Parisians (many of them war millionaires) flocked into the great cafés, which took advantage of the festive spirit by doubling their prices. The cost of a traditional holiday dinner of oysters or snails, turkey and sausages, and dried fruits and dessert, with champagne, reached nearly seventy-five dollars for a family of four. Although the cost of living in Paris was higher than ever before, shopkeepers reported their stocks of luxury gift items exhausted in the week before Christmas; jewelers had to strip their window displays to meet the demand. To some observers, the uninhibited flaunting of wealth by the profligate nouveaux riches brought to mind Louis XIV's ominous prediction: *"Après moi, le déluge."*

Beyond the glitter of diamonds and champagne, all was not well in France at the end of the year of peace. The skyrocketing cost of living and the new taxes imposed by Clemenceau's government on necessities such as bread and sugar, and increased levies on the postal service, telephones (the rates increased by 70 percent), and telegraph service wrought severe hardships upon the working classes of France. Railway fares rose even higher; the government prepared to withdraw the subsidy that had kept the price of basic foodstuffs at a reasonable level; coal was still in short supply, and all the available firewood had been bought up weeks before. Christmas brought no relief. The price of dolls for children's presents— even simple rag dolls—was more than six times what it had been in 1913. Already there were disturbing signs of social discontent: at the opening of a new dance hall, attended by the cream of Paris high society, a surly crowd gathered in the street to jeer the arrivals, growing more and more threatening until police arrived to disperse the mob. And on Christmas Eve itself, the spectacle of wild spending in the midst of so much misery provoked severe disturbances in the Place Pigalle. To avoid any more incidents on New Year's Eve, the prefect of police reversed his earlier decision to allow cafés to remain open all night.

In a small room in the Rue des Gobelins, a young Vietnamese immigrant worked quietly, restoring old photographs; he was not very successful and was often unemployed, so he spent a great deal of time talking politics with the leading radical Socialists in the city. Small, frail, delicate, with a gaunt face and large eyes and a funny little hat perched precariously on top of his head, he had adopted several pseudonyms since leaving Indochina. Now he was known as Nguyen ai Quoc, or "Nguyen the patriot"; he would later change his name again to Ho Chi Minh.

For thousands of Parisians, midnight Masses at the city's great churches on Christmas Eve held more attraction than the garish scenes along the boulevards. At eleven o'clock, the doors of the Madeleine had to be closed because more than six thousand people had filled the magnificent cathedral. At Rheims Cathedral—devastated by German artillery fire, the church doors closed since the Armistice—the work of reconstruction paused long enough to allow the celebration of a Christmas Mass under a temporary roof that protected half of the interior.

One British visitor to the battlefields on the Western Front found that a year's growth of weeds had given the land an air of battles won and lost long ago. Starving dogs crawled forlornly around the deserted villages; the only signs of human life were the laborers who searched for graves and collected the last remains of the heroes. "These areas," wrote the visitor, "are the altars on which mankind has established a quantitative record in human sacrifice. . . . The rolling downs are now like a gigantic rabbit warren, where woods, fields, farms, villages have been reduced to one dead level of colour, save where a wavering band of poppies, appropriately red, marked the fresh soil of a recently levelled trench." Trenches still filled with decomposing gas masks . . . rusting food tins and weapons alongside a deep, jagged hole in the ground . . . a shallow covering of earth over a reclining figure whose presence was betrayed by an upright boot, the toes gnawed by mice . . . a jaw protruding from the soil, half-hidden by the weeds grown in the summer of peace, now turning brown and dry.

Just before he left Europe, Herbert Hoover paid a call upon Georges Clemenceau. He found the wise, cynical old Frenchman in a gloomy mood. "There will be another world war in your time," the Tiger warned Hoover, "and you will be needed back in Europe." Clemenceau was discovering that peace brought a bittersweet triumph. France's parliamentary elections in the fall had produced an overwhelmingly nationalist—and conservative—Chamber of Deputies, including many army veterans. During the campaign, the nationalists had played upon Clemenceau's personal popularity to gain their majority; "I have become a regular fetish," the Premier told Lloyd George during a state visit to London in December. "Even the priests and the Roman Catholic ladies have taken me up. I am like those little charms that the ladies put on their breasts. They have no hesitation in putting me there nowadays. At my age I am not dangerous!" But now, the election won, his political allies turned on Clemenceau out of fear that the unpredictable Tiger might jeopardize their plans for the future of France. They reminded the new deputies, many of whom were Roman Catholics, that Clemenceau held notoriously anticlerical sentiments. When the Tiger proposed a more equitable system of taxation, with heavier levies on accumulated wealth, the conservatives made certain that his remarks were given the widest circulation among the upper classes.

Thus the old man did not achieve his one remaining political ambition. Late in the year, a conference of the combined nationalist parties rejected Clemenceau's bid for the presidency, and on January 17, 1920, a safer candidate, Paul Deschanel, was elected President of the French Republic. Stung and terribly hurt by the insult, Clemenceau immediately handed in the resignation of his Cabinet and retired from political life.

In Berlin, too, Christmas came only for the rich in 1919. The tiniest candles for a Christmas tree cost twenty-five cents, a box of tasteless crackers two dollars, and there were no cheap toys at all for parents to hang on the tree, the price of dolls and trains being twelve to twenty times higher than before the war. Christmas trees themselves were scarce and prohibitively expensive. "In short," cabled an American correspondent, "Germany's Christmas this year will be a Christmas for the war profiteer." At Amerongen Castle, the former Crown Prince arrived just in time for the Christmas banquet. The ex-Kaiser himself personally arranged the Yule celebrations, distributing gifts from the huge pine tree in the great hall of the Bentinck castle.

In New York, where widespread prosperity raised the prices of gifts to similarly distressing heights, shoppers slogged through the slush on the city sidewalks and streets to spend their cash on train sets that cost $150, or on "the simplest, punk little dolls with dresses that any little girl could make for herself" that retailed for twenty-five dollars. But the most popular item for Christmas gifts in Manhattan in 1919 seemed to be Ouija boards. All of New York high society was captivated by the craze; debutantes consulted their boards at every opportunity to peer into the future, and society girls never made a move without first consulting their spiritual chaperones. Mysticism became the refuge of disappointed and disillusioned Americans who had somehow expected a world more exciting, more daring, more—shining—upon the arrival of peace.

Christmas dinner at Folsom Prison, California: roast pork with sage dressing, celery gravy, boiled sweet potatoes, mince pie, sugar-coated cookies, oranges, and coffee with cream and sugar. The usual work tasks for inmates were suspended for the day.

At the White House, the President and Mrs. Wilson celebrated a quiet Christmas; Margaret came to visit her father for a few days. Wilson ate his dinner, including turkey, in his room, served by his wife. During the day, Mrs. Wilson went alone on the traditional errands to distribute Christmas gifts to friends of the family, and to the children who lived along the route to the Virginia country club where the President used to play golf. Wilson spent some time looking over the thousands of cards and telegrams he received.

Britain: Lloyd George was in a pensive mood. "The world is very sordid," he informed Riddell in the course of a rambling conversation. "Fifty years hence, when the people of those days look back on these times, they will be appalled at the social conditions under which we are living. As I walked through a factory the other day, I thought how dark and gloomy it all was and that even the sunshine was shut out by the smoke." Much against the

Prime Minister's wishes, the House of Commons attempted to abolish unemployment insurance, despite the fact that by Lloyd George's own estimate there were still approximately 300,000 people—many of them discharged soldiers—who could not find work. Lloyd George himself finally rejected the coal miners' demand for nationalization and proposed instead a halfhearted reform measure that included the nationalization of royalties and the amalgamation of all collieries within each area, to be operated by a single company subject to a limitation on its profits. When the Miners' Federation angrily rejected this sop and charged that they had been "deceived, betrayed, duped" by the Sankey Commission, the government responded by dropping all plans for reform and the matter returned to the status quo of January 1, 1919.

British women looked back upon the year with mixed emotions. Parliamentary approval of the Sex Disqualifications Removal Act opened to women a wide range of government positions from which they had previously been barred. In an unprecedented step, seven women were appointed justices of the peace, and Lady Astor became the second woman elected to Parliament (after the Irish revolutionary Countess Markiewicz), and the first ever to sit in the House of Commons. (On her first day in Parliament, Lady Astor almost ruined everything for England's other female aspirants to high political office: when Lloyd George introduced her to the House, she talked all the way during the walk up to the register—it is against the rules to talk on the floor of the House—and when she got to the table she almost forgot to sign the register in her eagerness to engage Bonar Law in conversation. Then she wanted to chat with the Speaker. Lloyd George was obviously relieved when it was all over.) On the other hand, most high-level government positions remained closed to women, and they continued to suffer the loss of their wartime jobs. Employers and trade unions alike seemed to be engaged in a conspiracy to force women back into domestic service. Some acquiesced meekly; others refused to go quietly back to their prewar economic servitude.

Frances Stevenson met the Prince of Wales, who seventeen years later abdicated the throne to marry Wallis Simpson. "He is a dear thing," she wrote in her diary, "with beautiful eyes, but such a boy."

For many families, Christmas Day brought the first true family reunion in six years. For others, it served as the occasion for a pilgrimage to the Cenotaph, the simple monument in London that served as a symbol of the human suffering caused by the late war. Hundreds of new wreaths were laid upon the monument. Many bore simple notes of grief, like the one that read, "To dear Jack—We are thinking of you this Christmas time—Peggy and Baby." A column of Australian and American nurses walked past and quietly placed their holly wreaths on the steps. Reunited army companies marched silently around the Cenotaph after paying tribute to their departed comrades. The Welsh Guards asked a widow to place their wreath on the monument, and the crowd stood at attention, bareheaded, as a bugler sounded "Last Post."

Lloyd George spent a quiet family Christmas at Criccieth. Riddell, who was rewarded with a peerage for his service in supervising the government's arrangements with the press during the war and the Peace Conference, visited the Prime Minister several days later and noticed that Lloyd George seemed much taken with his granddaughter Margaret. "At mealtimes he takes her on his knee and feeds her with tit-bits, and is perpetually walking hand in hand with her about the house." Riddell was struck by the tremendous contrast between their life in Paris during the Peace Conference—in the millionaire's flat in the Rue Nitot—and the simple cottage in Criccieth. Lloyd George, he thought, was "very adaptable. When one sees him here, one would never imagine that he had ever lived under any other conditions. Full of fun with his wife and children. To-day he was much perturbed about the health of his small nephew, and descanted at length upon the diet which should be provided for the small boy."

On December 28, Wilson celebrated his sixty-third birthday. Grayson reported that his patient was "most remarkably improved and is steadily mending." Tumulty lied and said, "I never saw the President look better in my life than he did today." In the mornings Wilson would dress himself and have a quiet breakfast. ("It was a sight I shall never forget," said a member of the White House staff, "the President using only his right hand and going so slowly and qui :tly through the meal.") Then his wife would read him the headlines fro11 the newspapers, after which he would be taken, wrapped in blankets, in his wheelchair to the South Portico for some fresh air. He would have lunch in his study, then a nap, and perhaps an hour's work in the afternoon; then dinner. Just before Christmas, Douglas Fairbanks had sent Wilson a movie projector as a gift. The East Room thus became a movie theater, and every morning at eleven o'clock the President would see a new film—he preferred Westerns, with the wide-open spaces and magnificent vistas that liberated his spirit from the close confines of his daily existence in the White House.

Gradually Wilson learned to walk again.

Harry Grabiner, secretary of the White Sox, reported that an investigation had revealed that rumors of Chicago players deliberately throwing games in the recent World Series were nothing more than hearsay. Gary Herrmann, president of the Cincinnati Redlegs, announced that he, too, had found such charges to be groundless. "Why start another investigation of moth-eaten rumors?" Herrmann asked. "I am confident that if any real sport had knowledge of any irregularities, he would have been only too glad to have informed the proper officials. Show me any real ground for action and I will be the first one to insist that it be sifted to the bottom."

A French syndicate offered Jack Dempsey $200,000 and 25 percent of the movie revenues for a match with European heavyweight champion Georges Carpentier. Jack Kearns, Dempsey's manager, said he'd think about it.

Six months of the dry regime: In Los Angeles, authorities surveyed the effects of the first half-year of prohibition. Anti-liquor forces had predicted a sharp decrease in crime, and sure enough, there had been far fewer arrests for petty offenses since July 1. But serious crime—including murders, rapes, and burglary—showed a marked increase. As foretold, the use of narcotics had also risen rapidly. The rate of divorce had not slowed, but judges attributed many cases of incompatibility to the general postwar spirit of unrest. Personal savings accounts had grown, as had the percentage of home ownership. Doctors reported no change yet in the health of the city's citizens, but they believed the physical benefits would show up eventually. Clergymen professed to see an improvement in the general standard of spiritual life, while the city librarian confessed that, from her vantage point at least, the advent of prohibition had not made the public noticeably more studious.

On a more deadly note, sixty people in New England were fatally poisoned when they drank what they thought was whiskey; the concoction turned out to be composed largely of wood alcohol—"coroner's cocktails."

"We are at the dead season of our fortunes," wrote John Maynard Keynes in *The Economic Consequences of the Peace*, which appeared in British bookstores just before the end of the year. "The reaction from the exertions, the fears, and the sufferings of the past five years is at its height. Our power of feeling or caring beyond the immediate questions of our own material well-being is temporarily eclipsed. The greatest events outside our own direct experience and the most dreadful anticipations cannot move us. . . . We have been moved already beyond endurance, and need rest. Never in the lifetime of men now living has the universal element in the soul of man burnt so dimly."

And yet, Keynes believed,

WE MAY STILL HAVE TIME TO RECONSIDER OUR COURSES AND TO VIEW THE WORLD WITH NEW EYES. FOR THE IMMEDIATE FUTURE EVENTS ARE TAKING CHARGE, AND THE NEAR DESTINY OF EUROPE IS NO LONGER IN THE HANDS OF ANY MAN. THE EVENTS OF THE COMING YEAR WILL NOT BE SHAPED BY THE DELIBERATE ACTS OF STATESMEN, BUT BY THE HIDDEN CURRENTS, FLOWING CONTINUALLY BENEATH THE SURFACE OF POLITICAL HISTORY, OF WHICH NO ONE CAN PREDICT THE OUTCOME. IN ONE WAY ONLY CAN WE INFLUENCE THESE HIDDEN CURRENTS,—BY SETTING IN MOTION THOSE FORCES OF INSTRUCTION AND IMAGINATION WHICH CHANGE OPINION. THE ASSERTION OF TRUTH, THE UNVEILING OF ILLUSION, THE DISSIPATION OF HATE, THE ENLARGEMENT AND INSTRUCTION OF MEN'S HEARTS AND MINDS, MUST BE THE MEANS.

48

"The prophet which prophesieth of peace,

when the word of the prophet shall come to pass,

then shall the prophet be known . . ."

New Year's Eve, Paris. Fed by the heavy rains of December, the Seine again rose ominously above its banks: ten inches, twelve inches, twenty inches higher in the last twenty-four hours. The stone Zouave on the Pont d'Alma stood in icy water up to his waist. The Marne had long ago overflowed its banks. The swiftly rising tide swept away a large heap of sand from the front of the Quai d'Orsay. Floodwaters filtered through into the electric railway between Versailles and the Invalides. River traffic came to a standstill; Paris faced a paralyzing shortage of coal. The city braced for the worst.

New Year's Eve, London. Sixteen hundred diners filled the Savoy's banquet rooms; four thousand dancers swirled across the floor of the Albert Hall; at the Ritz, dancing to the music of jazz bands went on long past midnight. After dinner, those who chose not to dance congregated in the streets of the West End and gradually drifted eastward, toward St. Paul's Cathedral. This year there was hardly a khaki uniform to be seen among the crowd. The men of other nations who had welcomed the new year twelve months ago had departed for their own lands. At 9:45 the bells of the cathedral began to chime; only a single light in the lantern of the dome illuminated its ancient gray outlines. As midnight approached, more and more people arrived, descending from buses, taxicabs, and automobiles, wearing masks, blowing horns and bagpipes, singing and laughing, dressed in fashionable evening clothes, furs, and brocades. The streets were now impassable. Bells from a nearby church made everyone jump; "Hurry up," someone shouted, "it's an air raid." This year everyone laughed. Then, at the hour, the great clock struck midnight. There was no respectful silence or community singing; a few people ran halfheartedly through "Auld Lang

Syne" and there were scattered cheers for the new year; but mostly there was just a continuance of the babel. "A year of torture has passed," said the *Manchester Guardian* in commemorating the death of 1919; "that is all that at the moment can be positively affirmed. A new year is beginning. . . . Nothing is more certain than that the arrangements now made or about to be made in Europe and the Near East cannot stand."

New Year's Eve, New York. It seemed that nearly every man who entered a restaurant or hotel dining room was carrying a satchel, a suitcase, or some sort of mysterious package that, once inside, revealed a bottle or flask of forbidden liquor; others had sent their booze ahead via limousine. Café proprietors earned a small fortune by charging "corking" and "cooling" fees, but the hotel barrooms that in other years had witnessed so many uninhibited celebrations were as dark and silent as morgues. Throughout the evening, Broadway remained unnaturally quiet, no more crowded or disorderly than on any ordinary Saturday night. Once again the street vendors (there were far fewer than in previous years) did a disappointing business in horns and confetti, and went home in disgust with much of their stock unsold. At Madison Square Garden, a chorus of one thousand voices sang hymns to welcome in the spirit of the new year; from the churches came the soft chants of midnight services. As the last minutes of the old year died, the great golden globe began its annual slide down the pole atop the Times Building as someone in the crowd shouted, "There she goes!" When it reached the bottom, the numerals "1920" shone forth above a flame of red fire on the roof. . . . "The year just past," proclaimed *The New York Times*, "to which so many of us looked forward as the portal of enduring peace, and of a prosperity more deeply grounded in righteousness, has seemed a devil's garden. . . . The whole world has seemed to be in jeopardy, trembling perhaps on the brink of ruin. It is not only a material debacle that has threatened; the decline from the moral and spiritual mood in which we won the war has been even more alarming." Looking back to 1913, the serene world before the war seemed in retrospect a Golden Age, "cheered by the warmth of a declining sun." But whatever else 1919 had brought in its wake, the past twelve months had at least served mankind by laying open to plain view the strains and decay that had for so long been working beneath the surface to undermine that halcyon prewar age of Victorian false confidence; now the people everywhere knew they faced a formidable task in creating a better world. "It is always so," concluded the *Times*, "when a new age is born."

* * *

New Year's Eve, Los Angeles. Rowdy sailors cruised down the city's main streets, sweeping everything before them. Automobile horns blared and whistles shrieked; sidewalks were buried deep under towers of confetti. Red and yellow fire illuminated the tops of the mountains surrounding the city. At the Alexandria Hotel, a giant book hanging over the orchestra opened to reveal the martial figures of Pershing, Foch, and Haig, the men who had led the Allied armies to victory. In nearby Venice, revelers tossed an effigy of the old year off a pier; at that moment, 1920—in the person of a beautiful young society girl—arose from the ocean like a goddess.

And 1919 was gone.

EPILOGUE

"As for me, behold, I am in your hand:

do with me as seemeth good and meet unto you . . ."

Jess Willard returned to California after losing his title to Jack Dempsey. All the rest of his life, Willard claimed that Dempsey's gloves—or at least the left glove—had been filled with some hard substance, such as plaster, for the July 4 fight. In later years, fight experts who reviewed films of Willard's bouts decided that the Kansas giant had been an excellent boxer after all, and named him one of the most underrated heavyweight champions of all time. Willard died in Los Angeles in 1968 at the age of eighty-six.

Jack Dempsey successfully defended his title five times between 1920 and 1926. On September 23, 1926, Gene Tunney defeated the champion in a ten-round bout at Philadelphia. ("I just forgot to duck," Dempsey explained after the fight.) One year later, in Chicago, the two men fought again; in the seventh round, Dempsey—who had been taking a terrible beating up to that point—knocked Tunney to the canvas. Dempsey, who had a nasty habit of standing over his fallen opponents to start pounding them again as soon as they got to their feet, neglected to go to a neutral corner as required by a new boxing commission regulation. The referee stopped his count over Tunney to push Dempsey to the corner. Then the count started again. At nine, Tunney was back on his feet. The total elapsed time during which Tunney had been down was somewhere between fourteen and seventeen seconds. Tunney eventually won the fight on points, and Dempsey retired at the age of thirty-two, never to know whether he might have won the fight of "the long count."

On January 2, 1920, in the climax of the anti-Red drive that had begun after the May 1 bomb scare, Attorney General A. Mitchell Palmer launched a carefully coordinated series of raids against suspected radicals in thirty-three American cities. Invading private homes, meeting halls, and union offices, Palmer's agents arrested over four thousand people. (Many of the meetings had actually been set up by Justice Department undercover agents acting on J. Edgar Hoover's instructions.) The suspects were held on the general charge of attempting to overthrow the government by force and violence, even though there was no specific evidence at all to support the accusation in the vast majority of cases. Prisoners were denied food, forced to sleep in grossly unsanitary cells and hallways, and deprived of legal counsel. Most were found innocent and released weeks later. Historians have generally viewed Palmer's actions on January 2 as the worst wholesale violation of civil liberties in American history.

Despite the hysteria, Palmer's net caught few real revolutionaries. His political reputation began to suffer when he predicted another radical bomb plot for May 1, 1920. Nothing happened; people began to laugh at Palmer. Within the Department of Labor, a few courageous high-level officials challenged the Attorney General's authority to deport alien radicals without fair legal hearings. By the end of 1920 the Great Red Scare was over, the victim of the Roaring Twenties' preoccupation with pleasure. "Too much," declared President-elect Warren G. Harding, "has been said about Bolshevism in America." Palmer himself lost even more public support when he failed to make good on his pledges to bring down the high cost of living by prosecuting antitrust law violators. He did not receive the Democratic presidential nomination in 1920, and subsequently retired from politics to enter private law practice. He died in May 1936 of complications following an operation for appendicitis.

John Reed was arrested by Finnish authorities when he tried to leave Russia in 1920. Returned to the Soviet Union, he died of typhus in October of the same year. He was thirty-three years old.

Ole Hanson resigned as mayor of Seattle, claiming that he needed a rest, and set off on a lecture tour to warn America of the imminent Bolshevist menace. Hanson, too, failed to obtain any nomination to high office in 1920, and several years later took his family to California, where he went into the real-estate development business. He was one of the original founders of the city of San Clemente.

On January 10, 1920, Clemcenceau, Lloyd George, and a German delegate signed the Protocol ratifying the peace treaty. From that time on, the world was governed by the Treaty of Versailles.

Public pressure forced the Senate to reconsider its first rejection of the peace treaty. Lodge made a halfhearted effort to reach a compromise with his Democratic opponents in the Senate, but Wilson remained adamant against any substantive changes in the treaty. Wilson understood that America must give the world a clear, definite guarantee that it would stand by the League and the treaty arrangements. But America was not ready to do so, and would not be ready until the nation had gone through another world war.

On March 19, 1920, the Senate voted for a second time on the peace treaty with the modified Lodge reservations. Uncompromising to the end, Wilson instructed his supporters to reject the amended document. Twenty-one Democratic senators rejected the President's pleas and voted in favor of the treaty, giving it a forty-nine-to-thirty-five majority; but the treaty still fell seven votes short of the required two-thirds majority. The United States eventually signed a separate treaty of peace with Germany.

Senator Warren G. Harding won the 1920 Republican presidential nomination; his running mate was the governor of Massachusetts, Calvin Coolidge. The Democrats, disunited and leaderless, nominated Governor James Cox of Ohio on the forty-fourth ballot of a fractious convention that also chose Franklin D. Roosevelt as its vice-presidential nominee. Wilson had hoped to make the campaign a clear referendum on the League, but the issues were far too complicated for that. On election day, Harding and Coolidge won thirty-seven of the forty-eight states; the Republican presidential ticket won an astounding 61 percent of the popular vote. Harding died of a cerebral embolism on August 2, 1923, during a tour through the Western states. After serving the rest of Harding's term, Coolidge then soundly defeated the Democratic candidate, John W. Davis (nominated on the 103rd ballot of a badly deadlocked convention), in the 1924 presidential contest.

Henry Cabot Lodge enjoyed a brief period of control over Harding's foreign policy in the early days of the Republican administration, but soon the President grew restless under the overbearing presence of the Massachusetts senator, and Lodge's influence declined rapidly. Known to his critics as "the Magnificent Negation," Lodge barely won reelection to the Senate in 1922; his statewide margin was less than eight thousand votes. After his refusal even to consider President Coolidge's plan for American participation in a World Court, Lodge lost all influence within the Republican Party. He was practically an outcast at the 1924 convention; delegates pointed up to his seat in the balcony and shouted, "Down with Lodge!" and "Put Lodge out!" He died of a stroke at the age of seventy-five, several days after the 1924 presidential election.

On August 26, 1920, the women's suffrage amendment was officially adopted as the Nineteenth Amendment to the United States Constitution. It was, said National Woman's Party chairman Alice Paul, the high point of her life. Ms. Paul at once set to work drafting an equal-rights amendment; she spent the next fifty years campaigning for sexual equality in the United States and abroad. Meanwhile, the advent of women's suffrage had little noticeable effect on American political life.

Ignace Paderewski retired from active political life and moved to an estate in California in February 1922. Later that year he returned to the concert stage. When the Nazis invaded Poland in 1939, Paderewski launched a series of appeals in America and Europe to raise funds for his starving countrymen. In January 1940 he was named President of the Polish Parliament-in-Exile. Paderewski died in New York on June 29, 1941, at the age of eighty, while participating in yet another humanitarian fund-raising drive.

Douglas Fairbanks, the most spectacular star of silent movies, helped make United Artists one of the most successful and profitable companies in

Hollywood with films such as *The Mark of Zorro*, *Robin Hood*, and *The Three Musketeers*. He married Mary Pickford on March 28, 1920, after Pickford received a divorce from her first husband. Fairbanks's career began a long decline with the advent of talking motion pictures; his last film was *The Private Life of Don Juan*, in 1934. He and Mary were separated and divorced in 1935, and the following year Fairbanks married Lady Ashley, another former actress. By the time he retired, his investment in United Artists had made Fairbanks a very wealthy man. But sometimes in reflective moments he considered himself an artistic failure, nothing more than "an acrobatic clown," far from the serious Shakespearean actor he had started out to be. Fairbanks died in his sleep of a heart attack early on the morning of December 12, 1939, at the age of fifty-six. His death pushed the war off the front pages of British newspapers; on the streets of London, newsboys shouted, "Doug's dead!"

D. W. Griffith, honored in later years with the title of "king of Hollywood directors," produced or directed nearly five hundred films before he retired in 1931. Two years later he sold his partnership in United Artists and faded into obscurity to work on his memoirs. He died in Los Angeles in 1948.

T. E. Lawrence emerged from his Oxford retreat and served for a year as a political adviser on Near Eastern affairs at the Colonial Office, during which time he helped his friend Prince Faisal establish himself on the throne of the new Arab kingdom of Iraq. His work done, Lawrence then resigned from civilian government service and, craving anonymity, joined the Royal Air Force in August 1922 under the pseudonym of Shaw. He soon changed his name again, this time to Ross. After he was discovered and discharged, he enlisted in the Tank Corps, again under the name of T. E. Shaw. (His official designation was Aircraftsman T. E. Shaw 338171; he was known to his friends as "338.") He rejoined the air force in 1925, and was discharged again ten years later. In 1927, *Seven Pillars of Wisdom* was published in a limited edition of 110 copies, for Lawrence's friends alone. On May 13, 1935, shortly after his final discharge from the air force, Shaw (his legal name when he died) was riding a motorcycle along a quiet Dorset road when he collided with a butcher's boy on a bike. T. E. Shaw died from his injuries six days later.

In March 1920, a military coup led by Freikorps commander Walter von Luttwitz, whose troops (wearing swastikas on their helmets) had savagely dispatched scores of Spartacists in the Berlin and Munich uprisings of 1919, drove the Ebert government out of Berlin and into hiding in Dresden.

Before they fled, however, the Majority Socialists called upon the citizens of Germany to launch a general strike to resist the rebel troops. The strike movement proved nearly a hundred percent effective; the entire city of Berlin was shut down as the middle classes joined the workers in opposition to Luttwitz. Frustrated, the soldiers marched back out of the capital, firing machine guns at civilians as they went, and Ebert returned to take power again. Luttwitz fled to Hungary, where he was welcomed by the White reactionaries; he received a pardon from the German government in 1925.

Matthias Erzberger, vilified for signing the November 1918 Armistice and then for instituting heavy new taxes upon the German people in the wake of the peace treaty, survived several assassination attempts in 1919 and 1920. Finally, in August 1921, he was shot and killed while walking through the Black Forest.

Philipp Scheidemann, who always carried a pistol in self-defense, also survived several assassination attempts, although one assailant scarred him with prussic acid. In 1933, when the Nazis came to power in Germany, Scheidemann fled to Czechoslovakia and never returned to his homeland.

President Friedrich Ebert found himself beset by scandals within his government and libeled by critics outside. By 1925 he was suffering from severe abdominal pains. His doctors recommended surgery; under terrible political pressure from all sides, perhaps no longer capable of rational judgment, Ebert refused to abandon his office even to undergo an essential operation. He died soon thereafter of peritonitis at the age of fifty-four.

Gustav Noske went to the well once too often. Faced with a Communist uprising in the Ruhr Valley in the aftermath of the 1920 general strike, the Bloodhound sent German troops into the area to reestablish order. But since the Ruhr had been designated neutral territory by the peace treaty, Noske's action technically was a violation of the treaty terms. Forced to resign his position as Minister of Defense, Noske was later appointed to the ceremonial post of president of the province of Hanover. He survived the terrors of the Nazi regime until 1944, when he was arrested on suspicion of complicity in an assassination attempt against Hitler. He spent part of the next year in a concentration camp. When the Allies liberated Berlin at the end of World War II, they found Noske in Moabit Prison—the site where so many Spartacists had been executed in 1919. The old man died of a heart attack in November 1946, just as he was planning to emigrate to the United States.

General Erich Ludendorff involved himself in several unsuccessful military coups—including the abortive 1920 Luttwitz fiasco and the infamous "beer-hall putsch" led by Hitler in Munich in November 1923—and, as a consequence, suffered the unrestrained ridicule of the German populace. He descended into the worship of ultra-Teutonic gods, which obsessed him until his death in 1939.

For many years, his wife, Romola, was the only person Vaslav Nijinsky would allow to come near him. Nijinsky was treated for schizophrenia at a private hospital for the insane in Kreuzlinger, Switzerland; when World War II came, he and Romola moved back to her native Hungary. In 1947 he went to England for further treatment. In his last years he showed encouraging signs of recovery. The end came in London in 1950; just before he died, Nijinsky made the sign of the cross and whispered goodbye to his wife and relatives at his bedside.

Sergei Rachmaninoff never returned to Russia. Angered by his open opposition to the Communist regime, in 1931 the Soviet Union banned all performances of his works. In February 1943 he became an American citizen and purchased a home in Beverly Hills. He died less than two months later.

Cast aside by Wilson, who suspected him of dealing with Clemenceau and Lloyd George behind the President's back, Colonel House retired to private life after the Paris Peace Conference. He returned to national prominence only briefly during the early days of the Roosevelt administration in 1933, when he acted as an unofficial adviser to the first Democratic President since Woodrow Wilson.

Sir Barton, the first Triple Crown winner in horseracing history, suffered a slump in the spring of 1920, but came back strong to win the Saratoga Handicap on August 2, defeating the legendary Exterminator by three lengths. It was perhaps the greatest race of his magnificent career.

Lieutenant Ormer Locklear moved to Hollywood in February 1920, where he originated many of the airplane stunts used in movies. (He was also the first aviator charged with reckless driving in the air, when he looped the loop over a public park in Los Angeles in April.) In the summer of 1920 he was working on a film called *The Skywayman*; the last stunt was supposed to be a shot of a pilot plunging to his death with the plane in flames. Just before he ascended to film the sequence on the evening of August 3, Locklear turned to his friends and said, "I have a hunch that I should not fly tonight." Spectators on the ground watched and marveled at the stuntman's skill. Then they suddenly saw the plane only two hundred feet from the ground, struggling to right itself. It crashed in flames. Locklear died instantly; the farewell letter to his mother that he always carried with him when he flew was found undamaged.

After suffering three strokes, Vladimir Ilych Lenin died on January 21, 1924. Trotsky spread the rumor that Stalin had poisoned Lenin. Trotsky subsequently was banished from the Soviet Union after losing a prolonged power struggle and eventually settled in Mexico City, where he was brutally assassinated by one of Stalin's agents in 1940. By 1929, Stalin had consolidated his position atop the Party hierarchy, and until his death in 1953 the dictator governed the Soviet Union by a far greater terror than Lenin had ever employed. He also succeeded in dragging the nation into the twentieth century through a policy of forced industrialization, albeit at an appalling cost in human life.

Alvin C. York settled down on the farm on the Wolf River that the state of Tennessee gave him in 1919 and spent the rest of his days hunting, raising crops, blacksmithing, and teaching Sunday School. He took the Springfield rifle he had employed on that memorable day in October 1918 and hung it over his bed and let it stay there. In 1936 the Prohibition Party nominated York for Vice-President, but he rejected the offer, preferring to spend his spare time helping with the industrial and agricultural school he founded for the badly undereducated children of the mountains. Watching Europe slide toward war in the late 1930s, York declared, "Hitler and Mussolini jes' need a good whuppin', and it looks like Uncle Sam's gonna have to do it." In 1942, Gary Cooper won an Academy Award for his portrayal of America's most famous hero of the Great War.

After serving as Secretary of Commerce under Calvin Coolidge, Herbert Hoover received the Republican nomination for President in 1928 and defeated the Democratic candidate, Al Smith (who had started his first term as governor of New York in 1919), in a landslide. Less than a year later the stock market crash spun the nation into the Great Depression. Many impoverished Americans held Hoover personally responsible for their desperate plight; in a cruel twist of fate, the great humanitarian of 1919 now was vilified as a cold, uncaring man shut away in the isolation of the White House. When another difficult problem of postwar relief faced the world in 1945, however, President Harry S Truman called upon Hoover's expertise once again. Hoover died at the age of ninety in 1964.

* * *

Viscount John French survived the rest of his tenure in Ireland without serious incident and resigned his position as Lord-Lieutenant in May 1921, whereupon he was created Earl of Ypres.

The violence in Ireland grew worse throughout 1920 as the British government unleashed the "Black and Tans"—a volunteer force composed largely of ex-soldiers, recruited to support the Royal Irish Constabulary in suppressing the increasingly bold (and deadly) Sin Fein guerrilla movement. Terror and torture reigned throughout the island, leading finally to Bloody Sunday, November 21, 1920, when Irish rebels murdered fourteen British officers (some in the presence of their wives); the Black and Tans responded by driving their trucks into Croke Park, Dublin, where a crowd was watching a soccer game, and opening fire upon the spectators. Twelve people were killed and sixty wounded. As the British public grew disgusted with the barbaric behavior of both sides, Lloyd George's government pressed negotiations with the rebels. In December 1921, Sinn Fein representatives led by Michael Collins concluded a treaty with Britain that granted southern Ireland limited independence (i.e., dominion status), but also gave Northern Ireland the right to remain out of the newly created Free State. A diehard faction led by Eamon De Valera, who steadfastly opposed partition, rejected the treaty and plunged Ireland into another year of civil war—Catholic rebels against Catholic rebels. Collins was killed in an ambush before the war ended. In 1937 the Irish Republic gained its complete independence from Great Britain. The island remains partitioned.

By the end of 1921, Conservative backbenchers (the rank-and-file of the party in Parliament) decided that they could safely dispense with the mercurial, unpredictable Lloyd George and nominate a safer, more reliable man in his place. For its part, Lloyd George's Cabinet seemed to have forgotten that the real base of its power lay well on the right wing of the political spectrum. Accordingly, in October 1922 the Conservative majority carried out a series of partisan maneuvers that ousted the Welshman from office and put Bonar Law in his place. A general election in November returned another overwhelming Conservative majority. Bonar Law died less than a year later; Stanley Baldwin was named Prime Minister and governed Britain for most of the next fifteen years. Winston Churchill took office as Chancellor of the Exchequer, where he remained until 1929; from that time until the next war came, he held no Cabinet office.

* * *

After his resignation in January 1920, Georges Clemenceau traveled for a while through the Near East—Egypt, India (where he shot several tigers)—and then returned to his homes in Paris and the Vendée, where he wrote a biography of Demosthenes, several books of philosophy, and his memoirs. In November 1929 Clemenceau fell seriously ill. Doctors gave him morphia to ease his pain. He lay in a coma, stretched out on a low couch in a little blue and gray room in his ugly little house in the Rue Franklin in Paris, wearing his favorite field service cap that had accompanied him on his visits to the trenches during the war.

On the evening of November 23 gusty winds and a hard rain blew against the windows of the house. Outside, a small band of Frenchmen stood watch at his doorway. At 1:40 the next morning, Clemenceau slipped almost imperceptibly into death. Those who came to pay their respects thought they noticed a slightly ironic smile on the Tiger's face. Crowds walked past the house on the opposite side of the street in silent tribute. Friends brought little bags of earth from the site where Joan of Arc had been burned, to be mixed with the soil of Clemenceau's grave. The Armistice battery fired the same salvo it had done on November 11, 1918. Ever the iconoclast, Clemenceau had explicitly asked to be spared the pomp and ceremony of a state funeral, and so he was laid to rest in a simple ceremony, next to the grave of his father at Mouchamps in the Vendée.

In 1923, William Christian Bullitt married Louise Bryant Reed, the widow of John Reed. Ten years later, Bullitt was chosen by President Franklin D. Roosevelt to be the first American ambassador to the Soviet Union. Disillusioned by what he saw of the Soviet system, Bullitt resigned and was subsequently made ambassador to France. In 1949, he publicly advocated American intervention in China to aid the forces of Chiang Kai-shek. Switching his allegiance to the Republican Party in the 1950s, Bullitt supported the political ambitions of Senator Robert Taft and Vice-President Richard Nixon. He withdrew from active political affairs after 1960.

After the Sopwith aviation works closed, Harry Hawker acquired part of the plant as a factory for the production of an improved type of motorcycle. He and his wife were blessed with another daughter whom they named Mary, in honor of the humble Danish steamer that had rescued Hawker from the Atlantic. In 1920, while test-driving a powerful experimental car, Hawker swerved off the track at a high speed and the car shattered against an iron fence; Hawker emerged unscathed and nonchalantly posed for photographs. Early on the evening of July 12, 1921, Hawker took off from the airfield at Hendon in a Nieuport plane for a practice flight in preparation for the British Aerial Derby four days hence. Witnesses on the ground said they saw the plane burst into flames and then go into a nosedive, turning over two or three times before it crashed in an open field. Hawker either jumped or fell (an old man said he thought he saw Hawker jump) from the plane during the descent. They found Hawker's lifeless body two hundred feet from the spot where the plane landed.

The urbane, polished German diplomat and author Count Harry Kessler made a lecture tour of the United States in 1924, during which he pointed out the deficiencies of the Versailles Treaty, and urged Americans to help reestablish an atmosphere of international goodwill and mutual trust. Kessler served as the first minister of the German Republic to Warsaw; in 1922 he was named Consul General to Petrograd. Upon Hitler's accession to power in 1933, Kessler exiled himself to France, where he died at Lyon in December 1937.

General William Groener resigned his position as commander-in-chief of the German army in protest against the Versailles Treaty, but took no part in the military coups that threatened the Ebert regime. In 1928, in the face of bitter conservative opposition, President Hindenburg appointed his old comrade Minister of Defense. In 1931, Groener was also made Minister of the Interior, making him responsible for both the army and the police forces of the German nation. He promptly outlawed the Nazi storm troops who had begun to ravage the land. In 1932, Groener lost both positions in a Cabinet shakeup; Hitler later allowed the general to retire quietly to private life. He died in May 1939, shortly before World War II began.

Field Marshal Paul von Hindenburg was pressed into political service by a coalition of Conservative and Nationalist parties following Ebert's death in early 1925. Hindenburg won the presidency in a runoff election, but disappointed his supporters (and surprised his opponents) by refusing to embark upon a full-scale reactionary program. In the course of a relatively moderate eight-year reign, President Hindenburg deemphasized the cult of personalities and focused attention on the essential tasks of reconstruction and the restoration of national unity and order. In the early 1930s, Hindenburg (who never bothered to conceal his distaste for the leader of the Nazi movement) repeatedly rejected Hitler's bids for power, and was rewarded with reelection to the presidency in 1932 by a majority of more than six million votes. But after three Cabinets fell in quick succession, he had no choice but to turn the government over to the Nazi-Nationalist coalition headed by Hitler on January 30, 1933. Hitler soon deprived Hindenburg of all powers and assumed dictatorial control of Germany himself. By the time Hindenburg died on August 2, 1934, "the Old Man," as he was affectionately known—the loyal soldier who had stood beside Kaiser William I at Versailles in 1871—was very, very tired.

Kaiser William II lived out his life in isolation at his estate in Doorn in the Netherlands; he was popularly known as "the Hermit of Doorn." His first wife died in April 1921, and William remarried eighteen months later. The government of the Netherlands refused to surrender him voluntarily, and so he never stood trial for any crimes of war. He spent his days sawing wood, playing with his collection of toy soldiers (he had soldiers of every German regiment, in both peacetime and wartime uniforms), studying architecture, writing a book about the Gorgons, and contributing to local charities. When Nazi forces invaded Holland, they detoured around Doorn; Hitler ordered them to observe the privacy of the Kaiser's estate and posted an honor guard at the entrance. (Nevertheless, the Nazi press castigated William for failing to lead Germany with sufficient severity during the Great War.) William followed the movements of the armies with considerable interest, tracking their progress with colored pins stuck in a huge map propped against a statue of his idol, Frederick the Great. He died on June 4, 1941; his attendants dressed his corpse in the gray field uniform of a German field marshal, and placed a cross of forget-me-nots on the bedstead.

F. Scott Fitzgerald married Zelda, of course, and the couple moved to the French Riviera, where Scott wrote his masterpiece, *The Great Gatsby*. Zelda went mad and was placed in an asylum in 1930. Fitzgerald became an alcoholic, moved to Hollywood to write screenplays, and died in 1940. Zelda lived for seven more years.

Ernest Hemingway won the Pulitzer Prize for Fiction in 1953, for *The Old Man and the Sea*. The following year he was also awarded the Nobel Prize. On July 2, 1961, he shot himself with a shotgun at his home in Ketchum, Idaho. He was wearing a robe and pajamas when he died.

John Dos Passos, praised by Jean-Paul Sartre as "the best novelist of our time," completed a brilliant trilogy, *U.S.A.*, that chronicled American life between 1898 and 1929. (The middle volume of the series was entitled *1919.*) In the 1930s he began to break away from his Communist friends as he witnessed the terror in Russia; he returned further disillusioned from the Spanish Civil War in 1937. In the 1960s, Dos Passos became a fervent supporter of Barry Goldwater and William F. Buckley, Jr., and contributed articles to the conservative journal *The National Review*. He died of heart trouble in 1970.

Ben Hecht's first novel, *Erik Dorn*, published in 1921, earned him a national literary reputation. His 1930 play, *The Front Page*, which he cowrote with Charles MacArthur, was a critical and commercial success, as was their follow-up, *Twentieth Century*. Hecht became a much-sought-after screenwriter, and wrote or collaborated on more than sixty films, including *Wuthering Heights*, *Gunga Din*, and a remake of *A Farewell to Arms*. An ardent Zionist, Hecht supported the terrorist activities of Menachem Begin's Irgun irregulars in the war for Israeli independence in 1948. Hecht died at his home in New York in April 1964 at the age of seventy.

Béla Kun was permitted to leave Austria and return to the Soviet Union, where he became a high-level Comintern bureaucrat. In 1934 he began to move away from Stalin when the dictator decided to seek an accommodation with Nazi Germany. Three years later, Kun was denounced for his "subversive" attitudes and was arrested, imprisoned, and tortured. During his twenty-nine months in jail, Kun reportedly went insane. He was executed on November 30, 1939, over twenty years after he had fled Hungary. He was fifty-three years old.

Chancellor Karl Renner of Austria resigned his office in late 1919 in protest against the Versailles Treaty, but remained a member of the National Assembly from 1920 to 1934. As a Socialist leader, Renner was imprisoned briefly by the right-wing terrorist Dr. Engelbert Dollfuss in 1934. After his release several months later, Renner remained politically inactive until the *Anschluss* in March 1938, at which time he apparently began to work in the anti-Nazi underground movement. Upon the establishment of the second Austrian Republic in 1945, Renner was elected President and held office until his death on December 31, 1950.

In December 1920, Italy and Yugoslavia reached an agreement to make Fiume an independent sovereign city. Refusing to accept this compromise, Gabriele D'Annunzio declared war on Italy. After one day of bombardment by the Italian navy (one well-aimed shell hit the Government House), D'Annunzio declared that the Italian people were not worth fighting for (he said they were more interested in their Christmas dinners than in his crusade, which by this time was probably true); the poet surrendered and retired to his villa at Gardone on the Lake of Garda. In 1924 King Victor Emmanuel made him Prince of Monte Nevoso ("the Snowy Mountain"). A strong supporter of Mussolini's Fascist government, D'Annunzio converted his villa into a museum full of war relics, pictures of saints, and assorted pagan and Renaissance symbols. He frequently expressed intentions of committing suicide, usually in some bizarre and grandiose manner. In October 1936, the poet cut himself off from the rest of the world, refusing to see even his closest friends, and spent most of his time sitting in a windowless and doorless cell, eating virtually nothing. He died while working at his desk on March 1, 1938, with the quill pen he always used still in his hand.

Benito Mussolini watched with considerable interest as a half-dozen Cabinets passed through the revolving doors of power in Rome. It seemed that no one could govern the chaotic postwar Italian state. In 1922, Mussolini began his advance with a new attack on Fiume; when the government failed to move against him, he ordered terrorist strikes on other vital Italian cities. Frightened by Socialist rhetoric, the middle classes were ready to welcome anyone who could restore public order; so was King Victor Emmanuel. On October 24, 1922, Mussolini held a mass meeting of Fascists at Naples and launched the final drive to power. His thugs attacked opposition newspapers and occupied government offices all over Italy. This time the government was ready to move forcefully against him, but the King refused to let the army take part in what he feared would be the first stage of open civil war. Instead, on October 29, Victor Emmanuel invited Mussolini, by now an open rebel against the government, to become Prime Minister. Mussolini ruled Italy until he was arrested by the army in July 1943, when Allied troops were pressing hard upon Rome. Rescued from his "prison"—a ski resort in the Apennine Mountains—by a daring Nazi commando raid, Mussolini was restored to power by Hitler as head of a puppet government in northern Italy. On April 28, 1945, as his German protectors retreated into Austria, Mussolini disguised himself as a Luftwaffe officer and tried to hide among a group of German soldiers. Communist partisans discovered his identity and executed him at once, with American troops just a few hours away. His body was taken back to Milan, where it was strung up by the heels in the Piazzale Loreto to be cursed by the mob.

* * *

Vittorio Orlando outlived all the other members of the Big Four. A confirmed anti-Fascist, Orlando retired from political life in 1925 and became a senior partner in a major international law firm. He remained a fervent nationalist, however, and complained bitterly (again) about the treatment Italy received at the hands of the victorious Allies after World War II. In his later years he became a respected elder statesman, and was remembered with great affection by the Italian people after his death on December 1, 1952, at the age of ninety-two.

In November 1921, after a month-long trial, Henri Landru was condemned to death by the Versailles Assizes for the murders of ten women and one boy; all the other alleged victims had been accounted for. The indictment ran to fifty thousand typed pages and included seven thousand documents. Since all the evidence was circumstantial, however—not one single body was ever recovered to prove Landru's guilt—the jury added a recommendation for mercy. (It should be pointed out that the French system of jurisprudence presumes an accused man guilty until he proves his innocence.) In a virtually unprecedented action, the jury's recommendation was refused; President Millerand decided the death sentence must be carried out. Landru himself never gave anyone a clue as to whether he was really guilty or not. At six o'clock on the morning of February 25, 1922, all appeals exhausted, Landru walked, unassisted, the few paces from the prison door at Versailles to the guillotine. At 6:05, just as the first rays of dawn brightened the sky, his head fell into the basket. Church bells sounded his passing.

Landru's wife, who had loyally stood by him at the start of the investigation, initiated divorce proceedings in November 1919 and petitioned the court to change her name. The villa at Gambais was sold for five times its nominal value and was opened to the public as a museum; a fee was charged for admittance. Landru was buried in an unmarked grave, where his wife and his two children placed a small cross that read simply "Henri Désiré."

In May 1920, the Hunter Commission filed a 176-page report of its conclusions. The majority (the Englishmen) found General Dyer to have committed grave errors in judgment by not giving the crowd at Jallianwala Bagh a chance to disperse before opening fire, and by allowing the fire to continue as long as he did. Moreover, the commission criticized Dyer's attempt to use the Amritsar massacre as an object lesson to overawe the rest of the Punjab into submission, describing his misbegotten strategy as "a mistaken conception of his duty." The minority report used much stronger language in condemning Dyer's actions. Both factions, however, joined in denouncing the infamous "crawling order," which, the majority claimed, "has continued to be a cause of bitterness and racial ill-feeling long after it was recalled." The army commission that reviewed these findings supported the decision of the commander-in-chief in India to remove Dyer from his command in the Punjab and bar him from further service in India. On July 7, Minister of War Winston Churchill announced in the House of Commons that Dyer would be suspended from the army on half-pay. Conservative forces in England were outraged at this shabby handling of a hero of the Empire. The *Morning Post* took up a public subscription for "The Man Who Saved India," and collected over £26,000. On July 20, 1920, the House of Lords adopted a resolution deploring the government's treatment of General Dyer. In November 1921, Dyer suffered a stroke that left him partially paralyzed. He retired to a quiet civilian life, out of the spotlight of publicity, in the West Country of England. Shortly before he died on July 24, 1927, he reportedly said, "I only want to die and know from my Maker whether I did right or wrong."

Sir Michael O'Dwyer, the Governor-General of the Punjab during the massacre, lived to be seventy-five years old, and was assassinated in England in 1940 by a survivor of the Jallianwala Bagh.

India received its independence from Great Britain in 1947. On January 30, 1948, while on his way to the prayer grounds outside his home, Mohandas K. Gandhi was shot and killed by a Hindu fanatic.

Charlie Chaplin created several film masterpieces, including *The Kid*, *The Gold Rush*, *Modern Times*, and *The Great Dictator* (the last a satire on Hitler). In the late 1940s, as a second Red Scare gathered momentum (led, of course, by Senator Joseph McCarthy of Wisconsin), Chaplin was denounced in America as a dangerous left-wing radical. While Chaplin was on his way to England for a visit in 1952, the Attorney General of the United States announced that the actor could not reenter the U.S. unless he could prove his "moral worth." Outraged, Chaplin spent the rest of his life in Europe, mostly at his estate in Switzerland. In 1972 he returned briefly to the United States to receive a special Oscar from the Academy of Motion Picture Arts and Sciences. Chaplin was knighted by Queen Elizabeth in 1975, and died at the age of eighty-eight on Christmas Day, 1977.

* * *

In early January, 1920, Babe Ruth—who was threatening to hold out again if Harry Frazee didn't raise his salary—was sold to the New York Yankees in what was undoubtedly the worst deal in baseball history. The Yankees promptly doubled Ruth's salary to $20,000. Ruth hit fifty-four home runs that year, a magnificent achievement when one considers that George Sisler came in second with nineteen. The Yankees finished third in 1920, but in 1921 they won the pennant and began a forty-five-year domination of the American League. Ruth's record of sixty home runs in a single season (1927) stood until Roger Maris hit sixty-one in 1961. Acknowledged by most to be the greatest baseball player who ever lived, Ruth died in New York on August 16, 1948.

The Chicago White Sox finished second in 1920, two games behind the rejuvenated Cleveland Indians. Cicotte won twenty-one games, Lefty Williams won twenty-two, and little Dickie Kerr added another twenty-one victories. Joe Jackson hit .382 and drove in 121 runs. In late September, the 1919 World Series scandal began to unravel. A grand jury empaneled to investigate gambling in baseball called Eddie Cicotte to testify; Cicotte confessed everything. Joe Jackson and Lefty Williams followed Cicotte to the witness stand, and they, too, confessed, although they later retracted their confessions. As Shoeless Joe left the grand jury room on September 30, a small boy reportedly tugged at his sleeve and begged him, "Say it ain't so, Joe. Say it ain't so." "Yes, kid, I'm afraid it is," replied Jackson. "Well, I never would've thought it," said the kid. In the summer of 1921, a jury found the eight White Sox players innocent of the charge of deliberately defrauding the public. Nevertheless, Judge Kenesaw Mountain Landis, who had recently been appointed commissioner of baseball in an effort to clean up the mess and restore the integrity and reputation of the sport, banned all eight men—including, unfairly, Buck Weaver—from any further participation in organized baseball.

Buck Weaver retired to run a drugstore, and died in 1956. Eddie Cicotte became a Michigan state game warden. Swede Risberg ran a tavern in Oregon. Lefty Williams moved to Laguna Beach, California, where he operated a garden nursery. Happy Felsch bought a tavern in Milwaukee. Chick Gandil worked as a plumber and then retired to the Napa Valley of northern California. Fred McMullin died in Los Angeles in 1952. Kid Gleason managed for several more years, but the spark was gone, and he shut himself off from the baseball world after his retirement in 1923. He died ten years later. Shoeless Joe Jackson went home to Greenville, South

Carolina, where he later opened a liquor store. For the rest of his life, Jackson steadfastly maintained his innocence of any wrongdoing. He applied for reinstatement in 1933, but Landis rejected his plea. He kept in touch with the game through sandlot baseball and became a respected member of the community. He died of a heart attack in December 1951.

After his resignation as Prime Minister in 1922, David Lloyd George never again held any Cabinet office. He remained the Liberal member of Parliament from Caernarvon for another twenty-three years, "admired, distrusted, unused," and watched silently as Britain descended into depression and war. In May 1940 he helped overthrow the government of Neville Chamberlain, whom he accused of bumbling and leading the nation into a war for which it was utterly unprepared. He rejected Winston Churchill's offer of the ambassadorship to the United States later that same year. In 1941 his wife fell gravely ill with influenza at their home in Wales. Lloyd George was in London when he heard the news; desperately trying to reach her before she died, he traveled through a raging blizzard; twice his car needed to be dug out of snowdrifts that blocked the roads. Friends tried to clear the mountain passes that led to Criccieth, but the snow piled up again before Lloyd George could get through. She died before he could reach her. Two years later he married Frances Stevenson. David Lloyd George made his last speech in Parliament in January 1943; for the rest of his days he preferred to sit in his study and stare out at the countryside. In early 1945 the little Welshman was made an earl. He died on March 26, 1945, at the age of eighty-two.

Mrs. Woodrow Wilson survived until 1961, occasionally taking part in official Democratic Party functions. During John F. Kennedy's inauguration, she stood on the reviewing stand next to former President Harry Truman. She died on the one hundred fifth anniversary of Woodrow Wilson's birthday.

After leaving the White House in March 1921, Woodrow Wilson moved into a house at 2340 S Street in the northwest section of Washington, D.C. He spent his days receiving occasional visitors, going for long automobile rides with his wife, and gazing out the window of his third-story room, from where he could see the Capitol dome, the White House portico, and the Washington Monument; and beyond the river there was the Arlington National Cemetery and the Tomb of the Unknown Soldier. Beyond that rose the hills of Virginia, where he was born. Every Saturday night he attended Keith's Theater in downtown Washington and sat in the last chair on the extreme left-hand aisle.

At the end of January 1924, Wilson's strength began to fade quickly. "His present illness cannot be attributed to any one malady," Grayson announced. "His whole physical being is broken." On February 1, Wilson uttered his last sentence: "I am a broken piece of machinery. When the machinery is broken—I am ready." The following day, Grayson told the public that Wilson was "making a game fight, but realizes the great battle is over." When his wife left his side for a moment that afternoon, Wilson whispered, "Edith." He slipped into unconsciousness later that evening.

The sun was warmer in Washington on February 3 than it had been for weeks, the air mild and still; people noticed the unusual calmness of the day.

At 11:05 A.M., Wilson opened his eyes once. His wife, his daughter Margaret, his brother Joseph, and Admiral Grayson were at his side. Ten minutes later Wilson stopped breathing.

Grayson wept as he read the announcement to the people, more than a thousand, waiting outside. They knelt for a moment of prayer and then walked silently past the house. Cars in nearby streets stopped and passengers descended to pay tribute to Wilson. An old woman walked up the steps to the door, paused, and then walked back down. "I only wanted to stand on the threshold of Woodrow Wilson's home," she said. "I think he is one of the greatest men that ever lived. Next to my son, I love him better than any man." A five-year-old boy brought a single pink rose.

There was no light in the third-floor room that evening.

NOTES

Throughout these source notes of quoted material, newspapers and periodicals are identified by the following abbreviations:

CSM: CHRISTIAN SCIENCE MONITOR
ES: BALTIMORE EVENING SUN
LAT: LOS ANGELES TIMES
LT: THE TIMES (LONDON)
MG: MANCHESTER GUARDIAN
NAT: NATION (U.S.)
NR: THE NEW REPUBLIC
NYT: THE NEW YORK TIMES
PI: PHILADELPHIA INQUIRER
SUN: BALTIMORE SUN
WSJ: THE WALL STREET JOURNAL
WP: WASHINGTON POST
WSN: WASHINGTON STAR-NEWS

All dates for newspapers and periodicals refer to the year 1919 unless specifically stated otherwise.

PROLOGUE

PAGE

xi "the most successful visit . . .": *LT* Jan. 2.

xiii "the most unintelligent . . .": Nicolson, *Peacemaking 1919*, 19.

xiii "I could not bear him . . .":

PAGE

Rose, *King George V*, 232.

xiii "Wilson with his high . . .": Lloyd George, *Memoirs of the Peace Conference*, 140.

PAGE

xiv "the eight days I spent . . .":
LAT Jan. 5.

xv "the most wretched . . .":
NYT Jan. 1.

xv "the greatest criminal . . .":
Rose, 229.

xv "He was both shy . . .":
Kessler, *In the Twenties*,
51–52.

xv "never get me alive.": *WSJ*
Jan. 14.

xvi "lay across the eastern third
. . .": Dos Passos, *Mr.
Wilson's War*, 374.

xvii "Tens of governments . . .":
Fischer, *The Life of
Lenin*, 336.

xvii "a very large country . . .":
Manchester, *The Last
Lion*, 676.

xvii "the real dictator . . .": *LT*
Jan. 7.

xviii "I know of nothing greater
. . .": Fischer, 329.

xix "The earth must have
looked . . .": *LT* Jan. 6.

xix "The destruction of . . .":
NYT Jan. 2.

xix "The German method
. . .": Ibid.

xix "The French want me
. . .": Bailey, *Woodrow
Wilson and the Lost Peace*,
115.

xx "a people with the heart
. . .": Nicolson, 24.

xx "brutes they were . . .":
Ibid.

PAGE

xx "Clemenceau, with a . . .":
Lloyd George, 140.

xxi "America is very far . . .":
NYT Jan. 1.

xxi "coming on the heels . . .":
Dos Passos, 452.

xxi "the dawn of a New Year
. . ." etc.: *LAT* Jan. 1;
NYT Jan. 1; *Sun* Jan. 1.

xxii "offensive against decency": *Sun* Jan. 6.

xxiii "To the exploiters . . .":
LAT Jan. 1.

xxiii "a part of the plot . . .":
NYT Jan. 1.

xxiv "this is America . . .": *PI*
Jan. 1.

xxiv "We are holding him . . .":
Ibid.

xxiv "There is a lamppost . . .":
Ibid.

xxiv "and instantly . . .": *MG*
Jan. 1.

xxv "which perhaps to-morrow
. . .": *LT* Jan. 6.

xxv "The last day . . .": Kessler,
47.

xxv "Another thing . . .": *ES*
Jan. 1.

xxv "those same principles . . .":
Sun Jan. 2.

xxvi "I have the helmet . . .":
Ferrell, *Dear Bess*, 286–
87.

xxvi "rose to the occasion . . .":
NYT Jan. 1.

xxvii "At a given signal . . .":
LAT Jan. 1.

PART ONE: THE DAYS OF VANITY

PAGE

3 "Mere anarchy is loosed . . .": Yeats, *The Poems of W. B. Yeats*, 187.

4 "Europe is in revolution . . .": *MG* Jan. 2.

4 "Mankind are on the march . . .": Lord George Riddell, *Lord Riddell's Intimate Diary*, 7.

4 "there was throughout the world . . .": *Papers Relating to the Foreign Relations of the United States. Russia: The Soviet Republic, 1919*, 13.

4 "The Revolution came and went . . .": *LT* Jan. 3.

5 "In Hungary no one . . .": Ibid.

5 "The plain fact is . . .": *CSM* Jan. 17.

5 "almost impossible to digest.": *LT* Jan. 28.

5 "there is a constant menace . . .": *Sun* Jan. 8.

8 "quite incapable of taking . . .": Mayer, *Politics and Diplomacy of Peacemaking*, 212.

8 "Imperialism is the . . .": Max Gallo, *Mussolini's Italy*, 62.

8 "one day Italy . . .": Ibid., 6–9.

10 "We cannot undertake . . .": *NYT* Jan. 8.

11 "I tell you the past . . .":

PAGE

Sandburg, *SelectedPoems*, 84.

12 "It was most fortunate . . .": *MG* Jan. 4.

13 "There's no wood . . .": Fischer, 321.

13 "locomotive of history": Payne, *The Life and Death of Trotsky*, 221.

14 "We were never dealing . . .": Lloyd George, 215.

14 "Liberate Eddie Moore . . .": *PI* Jan. 2.

14 There is every evidence . . .: Paraphrase of interview in ibid.

15 I don't know a thing . . .: *PI* Jan. 4.

15 "probably frustrated . . .": *PI* Jan. 6.

15 BOLSHEVIK GROWTH ALARMS . . .: *PI* Jan. 7.

16 "mental disease carriers . . .": *Sun* Jan. 2.

16 "The strikers . . .": Kessler, 51.

16 "all the inhumanity . . .": Hecht, *A Child of the Century*, 269–70.

18 "Hey, Joe . . .": Ritter and Honig, *The Image of Their Greatness*, 67–68.

19 "It is inconceivable . . .": *Sun* Jan. 6.

20 "perhaps fifteen years older . . .": *NYT* Jan. 19.

21 "If he is found guilty . . .":
All senators' comments
are from *Sun* Jan. 5.

22 "The practical danger . . .":
Sun Jan. 6.

23–25 The narratives of the
Spartacist revolt are
taken from eyewitness
accounts from the fol-
lowing sources: Jan. 4:
Friedrich, *Before the Deluge*, 39; *LT* Jan. 6 and 7.
Jan. 5: *LT* Jan. 8;
Kessler, 52. Jan. 6:
Kessler, 52–54; *MG* Jan.
8; *NYT* Jan. 8.

26 "My problems . . .": *LT*
Jan. 7.

26 "His country did well . . .":
Ibid.

26 "Among radicals and regulars . . .": *NYT* Jan. 7.

26–27 The Hoar story is quoted
in ibid.

27 "Mr. Wilson and his . . .":
Dos Passos, 432–33.

27 "The first expression . . .":
Krock, *Memoirs*, 109–10.

27 "Being free . . .": *Sun* Jan.
7.

27 "The thoroughfares . . .":
Ibid.

28 "I cannot find words . . .":
NYT Jan. 7.

28 "How young and virile
. . .": Dos Passos, 455.

28 "Looking back on . . .": *LT*
Jan. 8.

28–29 "Waiting for peace . . .":
Sun Jan. 16.

29–31 See the following: Jan. 8:
Kessler, 54; Hecht, 285–
86; *LT* Jan. 8 and 9. Jan.
9: *NYT* Jan. 10; *LAT*
Jan. 10; Kessler, 55–56;
Sun Jan. 11.

32 "Feel I should . . .": U.S.
Department of State, vol.
2, 711.

32 "old men and women . . .":
Villard, *Fighting Years*,
398.

32 "Especially in Berlin":
U.S. Department of
State, vol. 3, 142–43.

33 "To him the greatest danger . . .": Ibid., 159.

33 "fat as a seal . . .": Seymour,
Letters, 104.

34–35 Jan. 10: *NYT* Jan. 12; *LT*
Jan. 9 and 14.
Jan. 11: *LT* Jan. 13; *NYT*
Jan. 13; Kessler, 56.
Jan. 12: *NYT* Jan. 14; *Sun*
Jan. 14.
Jan. 13: *NYT* Jan. 15; *LT*
Jan. 15.

36 "The Government has
chosen . . .": *MG* Jan. 16.

36 "it will be a terrible thing
. . .": Kessler, 57.

36 "All my brothers . . .":
Friedrich, 41.

37 "I shall never forget . . .":
Ibid., 45–47.

37 "Regrettable as is . . .":
NYT Jan. 18.

PAGE

37 *"Wir sind alle . . ."*: Payne, *Life and Death of Lenin*, 525.

38 "only about four days . . .": *NYT* Feb. 6.

39–40 Nicolson's account of his meeting with Wilson is in his *Peacemaking*, 234–37.

40 "Anyhow I had the most pleasant dream . . .": Ferrell, 290.

40 "It is a myth . . .": Seymour, *Letters*, 89.

40–41 "It's my opinion . . .": Ferrell, 293.

41 "We want civvie suits.": Mowat, *Britain Between the Wars*, 22.

41 "arrest the mutineers": Manchester, 671.

PAGE

42 "I am afraid your case . . .": *LT* Jan. 13.

42 "I am afraid there will be . . .": *LT* Jan. 6.

42 "in areas where large numbers . . .": *MG* Jan. 22.

43 "I still had the Army habit . . .": Graves, *Good-bye to All That*, 287.

43 "Good night, isn't there any . . .": *LAT* Jan. 17.

43 "The rain of tears . . .": *Sun* Jan. 19.

43 "which up to now . . .": *NYT* Jan. 21.

45 ". . . somewhere in sands of the desert . . .": Yeats, 187.

46 "stones crackling on the roof . . .": *LT* and *MG* April 17.

PART TWO: THE DAYS OF GREAT RAIN

PAGE

49 "Now I will dance . . .": Buckle, *Nijinsky*, 407.

49 "It was tragic . . .": Ibid.

50 "I want to live a long time . . .": Nijinsky, *The Diary of Vaslav Nijinsky*, 161–62.

51 "He looks calm . . .": *NYT* Jan. 19.

51 "Well, they've made . . .": Ibid.

52 "as midwife I several times . . .": Crankshaw, *Bismarck*, 296.

PAGE

52 "You hold in your hands . . .": *MG* Jan. 20.

53 "Like a machine gun": Nicolson, 242.

53 "I was told . . .": Ibid., 245.

53–54 "the allied Governments . . .": *NYT* Jan. 18.

54 "artificial and even repellent . . .": Villard, 386–87.

55 "I must say . . . that Clemenceau . . .": Nicolson, 257.

PAGE

55 "O, we'll appoint . . .": Seymour, *Letters*, 155–56.

55 "really the best fun . . .": Ibid., 155.

55 "What! You mean to tell me . . .": Dillon, *The Inside Story of the Peace Conference*, 63.

56 "tangled and thorny . . .": Lloyd George, 142.

56 "That settles it . . .": Villard, 388.

56 "a truth which has . . .": Lloyd George, 152–53.

57 "Lloyd George believes himself . . .": Bailey, 159.

57 "Clemenceau followed . . .": Lloyd George, 140.

58–59 "The Bolshevik danger . . .": U.S. Department of State, *Russia*, 21.

59 "One of the things . . .": Ibid.

59–60 Two slightly different versions of Lenin's encounter with the bandits may be found in Payne, *Lenin*, 526–27, and Fischer, 322–23.

61 "Our chief characteristic . . .": *Sun* Feb. 10.

61 "One day . . .": *LAT* Feb. 2.

61–62 "terrifying still, short days . . .": Sholokhov, *The Don Flows Home to the Sea*, 72.

62 "What happened in the ruthless . . .": Lloyd George, 200.

PAGE

62 "abysmally ignorant": White, *Autobiography*, 560.

62 "If the Bolsheviki . . .": *NYT* Feb. 9.

63 "Why, don't you know . . .": *NYT* Jan. 21.

64 "As undramatic . . .": Kessler, 60.

64 "Berlin is lucky . . .": *LT* Jan. 20.

64 "have been raging like Huns . . .": *MG* Jan. 22.

65 "For centuries the German people . . .": *NYT* Jan. 29.

66 "I am going to ask . . .": *NYT* Jan. 18.

66 "I've had actors . . .": *Sun* Jan. 22.

66 "the most natural and graceful . . .": Smelser, *The Life that Ruth Built*, 64.

67 "Any player who . . .": *NYT* Feb. 6.

68 "a bomb in each hand . . .": Gallo, 65.

68–69 "For a few minutes . . .": Mayer, 219–20.

69 "And what peace . . .": Ibid., 222.

69 "into an awful spiritual crisis.": Mussolini, *My Autobiography*, 61–62.

70 "Those most familiar . . .": *LAT* Jan. 5.

70 "I want to teach . . .": *LAT* Jan. 17.

70 "an awful time . . .": Seymour, 105–6.

71 "Some of the hotels . . .": Villard, 398.

71 "said no to nobody . . .": Ibid., 399.

71 "two of the worst-looking . . .": Ibid., 399.

72 "It was a forest . . .": White, 555.

72 "I balked at snails": Ibid., 555.

72 "but they look better.": Seymour, *Letters*, 120.

72 White's account of the dinner is in his *Autobiography*, 556.

73 "The shortage of milk . . .": *NYT* Feb. 2.

73 "as rarely seen . . .": Dillon, 13.

73 "One of them has . . .": Ferrell, 294.

74 "Gee! This is a . . .": *Sun* Feb. 3.

74 "were guests and not . . .": White, 572.

74 "I had never before met . . .": Ibid., 573.

74 "limited democracy . . .": *NYT* Jan. 28.

75 "President Wilson is deceiving . . .": *LAT* Feb. 3.

76 "a huge doll . . ." and "has forgotten, or else . . .": *NYT* Feb. 10.

76 "It is not the women . . .": *Sun* Feb. 11.

76 "having a most demoralizing . . .": *NYT* Feb. 8.

76 "It is the way . . .": *NYT* Feb. 10.

77 "There has resulted . . .": *Sun* Feb. 16.

78 "time to think . . .": *MG* Feb. 17.

78 "displayed unexpected readiness . . .": *LT* Feb. 3.

78 "a vicious spirit . . .": *MG* Jan. 21.

79 "Clouds are gathering . . .": *LT* Jan. 18.

79 "Belfast is like . . .": *NYT* Jan. 29.

80 "Do ye no' think . . .": *MG* April 15.

81 "the Jewish tailor . . .": *LT* Feb. 3.

81 "The proceedings in Belfast . . .": *LT* Jan. 30.

81 "We are all disposed . . .": *MG* April 12.

81 "pale, hollow-chested . . .": *NAT* March 8.

81 "I had thought of slums . . .": Sassoon, *Siegfried's Journey*, 197.

82 "It was as if . . .": Dangerfield, *The Damnable Question*, 61.

82 "What did you expect?": *NYT* Jan. 31.

83 "absolutely forlorn . . ." and "a separate, distinct . . .": see the excellent discussion of party politics in James, *The British Revolution*, 406.

84 "a definite revolutionary . . .": *LT* Feb. 4.

PAGE

84 "We are in chaos . . .":
James, *Revolution*, 415.

84 "On the whole . . .": *LT*
Feb. 8.

85 "Well.": *NYT* Feb. 9.

85 "for the satisfaction . . .":
LT Feb. 8.

86 "Heaven knows I wish
. . .": Villard, 399–400.

86 "not getting anywhere
. . .": Seymour, *The Intimate Papers of Colonel House*, 274.

86 "geography, ethnography
. . .": Dillon, 102.

86 "desultory and unconvincing . . .": Nicolson, 249–50.

86 "Halloa . . .": Ibid., 248.

86–87 Accounts of the meeting
are in Nicolson, 251–56
and Seymour, 133–34.

87 "the half-smile . . .": Ibid.,
256.

87 "The worst of Clemenceau
. . .": Ibid., 258.

88 "Germany and Austria
. . .": *Sun* Feb. 25.

88 "The emancipated races
. . .": Lloyd George, 200.

88 "in Austria, especially . . .":
MG Jan. 20.

89 "Hell has been to this place.
. . .": Herbert Hoover,
Memoirs, vol. 1, 429.

88 "The appearance of the
children . . .": *MG* April
12

89 "Factories are stopped . . .":
NYT Feb. 5.

PAGE

90 "I saw young girls . . .": *LT*
Feb. 3.

90 "the most starved looking
lot . . .": Herbert
Hoover, 406.

90 "Of course, the Conference
. . .": Seymour, *Letters*,
137.

91 "The North Russia . . .":
NYT Feb. 10.

92 "making a valiant stand
. . .": *Sun* Feb. 18.

92 "a heavy reckoning . . .":
NYT Jan. 30.

93 "in a torrent . . .": *ES* April
5.

94 "the hot-bed . . .": *NYT*
Feb. 7.

96 "any man who attempts
. . .": *NYT* Feb. 7.

96 "We have 1,500 police
. . .": *LAT* Feb. 8.

96 "The sympathetic revolution . . .": *NYT* Feb. 9.

96 "a great array . . .": *NYT*
Feb. 8.

96 "only four of the strike
. . .": *LAT* Feb. 8.

96–97 "an attempted Bolshevik
revolution . . .": *Sun* Feb.
11.

97 "never got to first base
. . .": *NYT* Feb. 15.

97 "The employee in a public
utility . . .": *LAT* Feb. 11.

97–98 "arrest, try and punish
. . .": *LAT* Feb. 10.

98 "An enormous revolution
. . .": Seymour, *Letters*,
132.

PAGE

98 "The proceedings against
...": *LAT* Feb. 11.

99 "we don't need the cuffs
...": *NYT* Feb. 10.

99 "anarchists and wild-eyed
theorists ...": *Sun* Feb.
7.

99 "the time has come ...":
LAT Jan. 26.

99–100 "hard, grueling ...": *LAT*
Feb. 1.

100 "get a job ...": *LAT* Feb.
13.

100 "The entire arrangement
...": *Sun* Feb. 7.

101 "the general effect produced ...": *LT* Feb. 8.

101 "We have done forever
...": Ibid. and *LAT* Feb.
8.

PAGE

101 "Well, anyhow ...": *LT*
Feb. 13.

101 "A few telegrams ...": *WP*
Feb. 21.

101–02 "There are no eggs ...":
LAT Feb. 7.

102 "This unrest ...": *Sun* Feb.
25.

102 "He smiles all the time
...": *NYT* Feb. 3.

103–04 "It is definite ...": *Sun* Feb.
15.

104 "It was a great moment
...": Dos Passos, 468.

104 "Dear Governor ...": Mee,
The End of Order, 96.

104 "It would perhaps ...": *Sun*
Feb. 10.

104–05 "While all are speaking
...": *Sun* Feb. 16.

PART THREE: THE DAYS OF THE SHADOW OF DEATH

PAGE

109 "Once more the storm is
hid ...": Yeats, 188–
90.

110–11 "Now, therefore, we ...":
Dangerfield, 302.

111 "Fools. What good is a revolution ...": *NAT*
March 22.

112 "Ireland wants freedom
...": *Sun* Feb. 24.

112 "justice, freedom and right
...": *Boston Globe* March
4.

112 "Can it be possible ...":
Boston Globe March 17.

PAGE

113 "what he doubtless is ...":
Bonsal, *Suitors and Sup-
pliants*, 45.

113 "his voice seemed to
breathe ...": Nicolson,
142.

114 "the lines of resentment
...": Ibid., 142.

114 "The Arabs have long
enough ...": *NYT* Jan.
22.

114 "Listening to the Emir
...": Bonsal, 45.

115 "a land crying out ...": Litvinoff, *Weizmann*, 120.

PAGE

115 "I tell you . . .": Meir, *My Life*, 68.

115 "a place where our . . .": *Sun* Jan. 4.

118 "Yes, I am slightly touched . . .": *NYT* Feb. 20.

119 "*Ce n'est rien.*": Ibid.

119 "As I ran . . .": *Sun* Feb. 20.

119 "Accomplice!": *Sun* Feb. 21.

119 "to get rid of the man . . .": *MG* Feb. 20.

119 "an integral anarchist . . .": *NYT* Feb. 20.

119 "I have dodged . . .": *NYT* Feb. 20.

119 "Dear, dear . . .": Bonsal, *Unfinished Business*, 64.

119–20 "Horrified . . .": *CSM* Feb. 20.

120 "I am shocked . . .": *MG* Feb. 20.

120 "Government and people . . .": *NYT* Feb. 20.

120 "The Paris criminal . . .": *NYT* Feb. 22.

121 "or it will break . . .": Lash, *Eleanor and Franklin*, 234.

121 "he was sure he could convince . . .": *Sun* Feb. 24.

121 "the evil thing . . .": *NYT* March 8.

122 "a reign of terror . . ." and "I think it is impossible . . .": *Sun* Feb. 25.

122 "They loathe the League . . .": Nicolson, 260.

PAGE

122 "What swine these people are": Seymour, *Letters*, 124.

122 "They are behaving like children . . .": Nicolson, 265.

122–23 "the attempt to combine . . .": Ibid., 167.

123 "there is a definite inarticulate . . .": Ibid., 269.

123 "We are not worrying . . .": *NYT* March 5.

124 "I want Jackson . . .": *WP* Feb. 20.

124 "If there is one thing . . .": *Chicago Tribune* March 18.

125 "In these days . . .": *MG* March 26.

125 "*In neun Tagen* . . .": Villard, 405.

125 "a wreck, the cars dirty . . .": Ibid., 410.

125 "had not been without . . .": *NAT* April 12.

125 "incredible coffee . . .": Villard, 412.

126 "I was the same . . .": Ibid.

126 "Now they are all here . . .": Ibid., 414.

126 "You'd better get away . . .": *NAT* April 12.

126 "Down with the revolution . . .": *NYT* Feb. 22.

127 "I have seen terrible things . . .": *NAT* April 12.

127 "There's another chap . . .": Ibid.

127 "Comrades! . . .": Ibid.

PAGE

128 "the torn and disrupted . . .": *MG* Feb. 24.

128 "A reckless lack of dignity . . .": Ibid.

129 "I am a lazy man . . .": *Sun* Feb. 22.

129–30 Clemenceau's story is recounted in Bonsal, *Unfinished Business*, 69–71.

130 "a gang of jackasses": Ibid., 65.

130 "I am better . . .": *NYT* Feb. 25.

131 "We have just won . . .": Bonsal, *Unfinished Business*, 67.

131 "It feels like . . .": Ibid., 65.

131 "The man we must fit today . . .": *LAT* Feb. 6.

132 "DARLING HEART . . .": Bruccoli, *Some Sort of Epic Grandeur*, 96.

133 "at the earliest possible . . .": *WSN* Feb. 18.

133–34 "Two weeks ago this morning...": *WP* April 6.

134 "I don't care if it is the beach. . . .": *WP* Feb. 24.

135 "complicated machine . . .": *Sun* Feb. 24.

135 "national murder conference": *WP* Feb. 25.

136 "packed with people . . .": Lash, 235.

137 "warm regards and sympathy.": *WP* Feb. 25.

137 "There was a got-back-home twist . . .": *NYT* Feb. 25.

137 "in the clear, incisive twang . . .": Ibid.

137–38 Wilson's speech is recorded in *NYT*, *WP*, and *Sun* Feb. 25.

138–39 Nijinsky, *Diary*, 97–187, *passim*.

140 "What an appalling record!": *Sun* Feb. 27.

140 "One had only to open . . .": *MG* March 5.

140 "Our children die . . .": *LT* March 12.

141 "the food ordinarily given . . .": *LAT* March 9.

141 "I found the children . . .": Ibid.

141 "Our inmates are all dead.": *MG* March 7.

141 "although I have seen . . .": *NAT* March 8.

141–42 "At the present moment . . .": *LT* March 4.

142 "Too many men . . .": *NAT* Feb. 8.

142 "their historic rights . . .": U.S. Department of State, vol. 4, 162.

142 "in the name of a million Jews . . .": Ibid., 165.

143 "a fine chance . . .": *ES* March 18.

143 "The Zionist organization . . .": U.S. Department of State, vol. 4, 169.

143 "there is not the slightest . . .": *ES* March 3.

143 "We do not aspire . . .": *LT* March 1.

PAGE

144 "deepest sympathy" and "We will do our best . . .": *MG* March 7.

144 "if the views of the radical . . .": Bonsal, *Suitors*, 56.

144 "It would be a great grief . . .": *NYT* March 12

145 "Every time I see you . . .": Roberts, *Jack Dempsey*, 51.

145 "a stripling compared to . . .": *Sun* Feb. 16.

146 "becoming to those who possess . . .": *Illustrated London News*, Jan. 18.

146–47 "I understand the French gowns . . .": *NYT* Feb. 27.

147 "seemed to me to be altogether . . .": Gandhi, *An Autobiography*, 456.

148 "You can wake a man . . .": Ibid., 458.

148 "evidence of a deep-seated . . .": *LT* March 12.

149–50 "Isn't it awful . . .": Lago and Furbank, *Selected Letters of E. M. Forster*, vol. 1, 300.

150 "their hands are capable . . .": *WP* Feb. 23.

151 "personally, I would sooner . . .": Riddell, 23.

151 "The other day . . .": *NAT* March 1.

152 "Some months ago . . .": *NYT* Feb. 28.

153 "has left electors . . .": *NYT* March 17.

PAGE

154 "I have dined": Sorokin, *Leaves From a Russian Diary*, 220.

154 "our existence was filled . . .": Ibid., 222.

155 "If only it were not . . .": Ransome, *Russia in 1919*, 62–63.

155 "triumphed not only . . .": Payne, *Lenin*, 530.

156 "It was a long time . . .": Ransome, 221.

157 "By taking cognizance . . .": Kennan, *Russia and the West*, 127.

157 "a most striking man . . .": Fischer, 353.

157 "An open, inquiring face . . .": Steffens's account of his meeting with Lenin is in his *Autobiography of Lincoln Steffens*, 796–98.

158 "We can afford to starve . . .": Ransome, 232.

159 "all the Balkan peoples . . .": *NYT* Feb. 22.

159–60 "To prevent a collapse . . .": *NYT* March 15.

160 "America was once told . . .": *NYT* March 13.

160 "and whatever promotes . . .": *MG* March 2.

160–61 "East of the Rhine . . .": *NYT* March 13.

161 "So far, not a single . . .": Lloyd George, 193–95.

163 "They must all . . .": *ES* March 19.

PAGE

163–64 "Take it from me . . .":
LAT March 8.

164 "Units of twenty-five men
. . .": Hecht, 291.

164 "They were shooting behind . . .": ES March 17.

164–65 "What on earth else . . .":
LT March 22.

165 "The truth is . . .": NAT
April 12.

165–66 "its achievement during
this time . . .": MG Feb.
20.

166 "Such apprehension . . .":
NYT March 19.

166 "conquered, abased . . .":
Sun Feb. 24.

166 "You can starve us . . .":
Sun March 18.

PAGE

166 "Germany will soon repent
. . .": NYT Feb. 26.

166 "Not in years have such
beautiful . . .": LAT Feb.
9.

167 "Well, Mr. President . . .":
Sun Feb. 27 and 28.

167 "as if I had been . . .": Daniels, The Time Between the
Wars, 26.

168 "It is a notice . . .": NYT
March 4.

169 "the sweetest and best
behaved . . .": Chicago
Tribune, March 5.

169–70 Wilson's New York speech
is in NYT March 5.

170 "He is tired, of course . . .":
NYT March 5.

PART FOUR: THE DAYS OF DARKNESS

PAGE

174 "I have ridden . . .": NYT
March 5.

175 "The change in his appearance . . .": Mee, 141–43.

176 "My hide is too thick . . .":
LAT March 15.

176 "we shall never get . . .":
Riddell, 32.

176–77 "everything must hang on
. . .": Taylor, Lloyd
George, 172.

177 "I won't budge . . .": Watson, George Clemenceau,
345.

177–78 "It appears that things . . .":
MG March 19.

PAGE

178 "Day by day . . .": MG
March 2.

178 "There has seldom . . .":
NYT March 22.

179 "I may say that . . .": NYT
March 4.

179–80 "Do Americans fully realize . . .": NYT March 5.

181 "as few engagements . . .":
LT March 31.

181 "The old boy . . .": Riddell,
36–37.

182 "I thank you . . .": LT
March 7.

182 "Rarely has a crime . . .":
Sun March 15.

PAGE

183 "they have beautiful costumes . . .": Ferrell, 297.

183 "standing in the doorways . . .": *NYT* March 16.

183 "There are considerable dumps . . .": Seymour, *Letters*, 196–97.

184–85 "Yet in his talk . . .": Nicolson, 275–76.

185 "If your house is warm . . .": Barker, *Marcel Proust*, 261.

187 "My ship may be . . .": Riddell, 33.

188 "to put in the hardest . . .": Ibid., 36.

188 "There is a sense . . .": *LT* March 21.

188 "I thought the British . . .": Pruessen, *John Foster Dulles*, 34.

189–90 "entirely frustrated the efforts . . .": *LT* March 21.

190 "*Das ist mir ganz egal*": Mayer, 547.

191 "We knew that conditions . . .": Seymour, *Letters*, 185.

191 "we are losing the peace . . .": Nicolson, 288.

191 "There is no peace . . .": *LT* March 24.

191–92 "We are certain . . .": Fischer, 339.

192 "what happened in Hungary . . .": *NYT* March 25.

192 "Intervention, intervention . . .": *LAT* March 28.

193 "It was important to avoid . . .": Mayer, 725–26.

193 "a curious business . . .": Ibid., 726.

194 "not since Mr. Parker . . .": *Sun* March 18.

195 "I am yielding to men . . .": Bonsal, *Unfinished Business*, 153.

195 "These changes . . .": Ibid.

197 The police report on Mussolini is in Delzell, *Mediterranean Fascism*, 4–6.

197–98 "the ones that came . . .": Mussolini, 68.

198–99 Mussolini's speech is quoted in Delzell, 7–11.

199 "I have the feeling . . .": Gallo, 70.

199 "If Italy does not get . . .": *WP* April 3.

200 "Scott, you've been . . .": Bruccoli, 97.

201 "Just as soon as we can . . .": *NYT* April 11.

202 "of all the tyrannies . . .": James, *Churchill: His Complete Speeches*, III, 2771.

202 "too much of the war . . .": *MG* April 10.

202 "by rolling forward . . .": James, *Speeches*, 2725.

203 "One day our regiment . . .": Zhukov, *Memoirs*, 49–50.

PAGE

203 "As long as the British
    . . .": Kennan, 128.

203 "There was some sugges-
    tion . . .": Ibid., 129.

204 "I have been over . . .":
    Steffens, 799.

204 "Like the ancient mariner
    . . .": White, 563.

205 "does not lie in mistaken
    . . .": NYT March 19.

205 "many lawless things . . .":
    NYT April 2.

206 "a peril we all must face
    . . .": LAT March 22.

206 "I would take away . . .":
    LAT March 22.

206 "a very small calibre man.":
    Link, Wilson, 462.

207 "I cannot interpret . . .":
    LAT March 5.

207 "The slogan of Europe
    . . .": Sun March 19.

207 "putting brass rails . . .":
    Seymour, Letters, 188.

207 "it is of course . . .": Bonsal,
    Suitors, 248.

207–08 "Give me time . . .": Gray-
    son, Woodrow Wilson, 85.

208 "I have sat at the feet . . .":
    Ibid., 248.

208 "I think that the Confer-
    ence . . .": Seymour, Let-
    ters, 189.

208 "A most unpleasant scene":
    Taylor, 177.

208 "Those men this morning
    . . ." and the rest of the
    meeting: Grayson, 76–
    78.

PAGE

209 "We go on feet . . .": WP
    March 30.

210 "D[avid] had a complete
    . . .": Taylor, 177.

210 "D. thinks it better . . .":
    Ibid.

210 "If Poland does not receive
    . . .": NYT April 8.

210 "What everybody in Paris
    . . .": NAT April 12.

211 "At a moment when . . .":
    LT April 3.

211 "He is worse today . . .":
    Taylor, 178.

212 "He hasn't a bluffing . . .":
    Mee, 170.

213 "a State whose principal
    object . . .": MG April 7.

213 "weak-kneed as well as . . .":
    Kessler, 92.

213 "the German Republic
    does not . . .": LT March
    27.

214 "it would, at any rate . . .":
    MG April 3.

215 "The atmosphere is fraught
    . . .": NYT April 15.

215 "Do not submit . . .": ES
    April 1.

215 "For of what use . . .": NYT
    March 19.

215 "Noske guards everywhere
    . . .": Kessler, 93.

216 "sheer waste of time . . .":
    Ibid., 94.

217 "It makes no difference
    . . .": ES April 15.

217 "Nothing in Germany
    . . .": NYT April 4.

PAGE

217 "if the peace terms . . .": *ES* March 18.

217 "it is a question whether . . .": *NYT* March 26.

217 "Only one thing . . .": *NYT* April 5.

217 "With Russia on our hands . . .": James, *Speeches*, III, 2772–73.

218 "Munich is hungry . . .": *MG* Feb. 25.

219 "The quietest and most orderly . . .": *ES* April 10.

219 "the theme song . . .": Hecht, 300.

220 "because these dogs have not . . .": Watt, *The Kings Depart*, 326.

221 "a frightened middle-aged man . . .": *ES* April 12.

221 "I will not enter into such a . . .": Ibid.

222 "Munich will be compelled . . .": *NYT* April 11.

223 "Great rats, small rats . . ." from Robert Browning, "The Pied Piper of Hamelin," quoted in *ES* April 7.

224–26 "The suburban trains . . .": Nicolson's account of the Smuts mission is in *Peacemaking*, 292–307.

226 "It was a world . . .": Taylor, 178.

226 "The Big Four are rushing . . .": Seymour, *Letters*, 193.

227 "looking thin and pale. . . .": Mee, 170–71.

PAGE

227 "everything is being rushed . . .": Nicolson, 308.

227 "The doings of the Council . . .": Riddell, 48–49.

228 "It is extraordinary . . .": Nicolson, 309.

228 "It just shows you . . .": Taylor, 179.

228 "old and worn. . . .": Mee, 172.

228 "more sincere than he had done . . .": Riddell, 51.

229 "until the League is seasoned . . .": Bonsal, *Suitors*, 216.

232 "is no small thing. . . .": Fischer, *The Life of Mahatma Gandhi*, 177.

233 "I have received . . .": *LT* April 16.

233 "The situation was . . .": *LT* April 19.

233 "Remember, there is another . . .": *NYT* May 30, 1920.

234 "much excitement and disturbance . . .": *LT* April 14.

235 "I think it is quite possible . . .": *LT* Dec. 15.

235 "It was a horrible duty . . .": Ibid.

235 "No, certainly not. . . .": Ibid.

236 "I shall never forget . . .": Swinson, *Six Minutes to Sunset*, 53.

236 "It remains for the Governor-General . . .": *LT* April 19.

PART FIVE: THE DAYS OF WRATH

PAGE

239–40 "I have seldom seen . . .": Bertensson and Leyda, *Sergei Rachmaninoff*, 217.

240 "Metaphorically speaking . . .": Ibid., 219.

240 "Even the air . . .": Seroff, *Rachmaninoff*, 187.

240–42 For summaries of, and comments on, Lloyd George's Parliamentary speech, see *MG* and *LT* April 17.

242–43 "the gold, blue and red glories . . .": Mowat, 32.

243 "the mean, unpaved streets . . .": *MG* April 14.

244 "Well, if it does . . .": Riddell, 49.

245 "You are a great little man . . .": Ibid., 52.

246 "I am sorry that when I . . .": Fischer, *Gandhi*, 179.

246–47 "The enormity of the measures . . .": *MG* July 9.

247 "The only exciting thing . . .": *LAT* March 21.

248 "I do not even know . . .": *WP* March 26.

248 "was in those days . . .": Dempsey and Piatelli, *Dempsey*, 102.

250 "that when the victims . . .": Smith, *Mussolini*, 36.

253 "Revolution cannot be made . . .": Leviné-Meyer, *Leviné*, 107.

253 "The dark city . . .": Hecht, 311.

254 "We were not ready . . .": Leviné-Meyer, 107.

254 "Inventors appeared . . .": Ibid.

256 "Nobody can watch . . .": *LT* April 19.

258–59 "ARRIVED IN CAMP MILLS . . .": Truman's telegram and letter are quoted in Ferrell, 297–98.

260 "We shall conduct ourselves . . .": De Valera, *Speeches*, 91.

260 "The week which has passed . . .": Forester, *Michael Collins*, 100.

261 "traditional English hatred . . .": the speaker was the Irish Nationalist leader, John Devlin, *LT* April 4.

261 "is the sight of . . .": *LT* March 4.

261 "the most unique and beautiful . . .": *LT* April 2.

263 "Perhaps, however . . .": *MG* May 12.

264 "It is as difficult . . .": Ellmann, *James Joyce*, 454.

264 "A writer should never write . . .": Ibid., 457.

265 "Nobody is going to get . . .": *MG* April 12.

266 "If Italy gets Fiume . . .": Seymour, *Letters*, 203.

266 "looks like hell in orchids.": Nicolson, 314.

PAGE

266 "We were assisted . . .": *WP* April 20.

267 The account of the April 19 Council of Four meeting is in U.S. Department of State,vol.5, 80–94.

268 "who, when he was bitten . . .": Bonsal, *Suitors*, 101.

268 "D. very tired . . .": Taylor, 181.

268 "our peace must be a peace . . .": *NYT* April 20.

269–70 The account of the April 20 Council meeting is in U.S. Department of State, vol.5, 95–101.

271 "It is the same with me . . .": Riddell, 55.

271 "How I would like to retire . . .": Bonsal, *Suitors*, 102.

272 "as a result of the declaration . . .": *MG* April 24.

273 "Well, the fat . . .": Riddell, 56–57.

273 "I am taking this . . .": Bonsal, *Suitors*, 112.

273 "The people must decide . . .": U.S. Department of State, vol. 5, 212.

273 "You may be still fonder . . .": Bonsal, *Suitors*, 113.

274 "we would go just the same. . . .": *MG* April 25.

275 "as long as you can . . .": Baker, *Hemingway: Letters*, 21–24.

276 "Italy, great and victorious . . .": *MG* April 28.

276 "I was never prouder . . .": *MG* April 26.

PAGE

277 "whether the Government . . .": *MG* April 28.

278 "Do you not hear? . . .": *NYT* May 6.

281 "I trust Washington . . .": *NYT* May 12.

282 "Any spring is a time . . .": Leuchtenberg, *Perils of Prosperity*, 69–70.

282 "had all the iridescence . . .": "My Lost City," in *The Crack-Up*, 25–26.

283 "As I hovered . . .": Ibid.

283 "Amid a silence that hurt . . .": Manchester, *American Caesar*, 127–28.

284 "all those ladies . . .": Nin, *Linotte*, 213.

284 "Develop the decorative sense . . .": *ES* March 19.

284 "like a giant grapefruit. . . .": *NYT* April 6.

285 "to see a jazz band . . .": *MG* April 21.

285 "This, too, was the Paris . . .": Ludington, *John Dos Passos*, 175–76.

287 "I shall never forget . . .": Seymour, *Letters*, 220.

287 "a man with a bad cut . . .": Shotwell, *At the Paris Peace Conference*, 303.

287–88 "There was an army kitchen . . .": Ibid., 304.

288 "only a duck . . .": *MG* May 2.

288 "The trade unionists . . .": *MG* May 3.

288 "saw against the sky . . .": Shotwell, 305.

PAGE

288 "I did not wish . . .": *MG* May 5.

289 "Now that the time has come . . .": *ES* May 8.

290 "The most remarkable . . .": *NYT* May 7.

291 "The hardest part . . .": *Sun* Feb. 26.

291 "Miss Keller was so . . .": *Sun* Feb. 25.

293 "old men and women . . .": *NYT* April 7.

293 "Japan's position . . .": *CSM* April 16.

293 "With all of her mighty army . . .": *WP* April 21.

294 "Russia! Russia! . . .": Manchester, *Last Lion*, 673.

295 "the benevolence of his eyes . . .": Seymour, *Letters*, 222–23.

295 "From where I could see . . .": Shotwell, 307–8.

295 "I have done my best . . .": *NYT* May 6.

295 "And why, Monsieur . . .": Nicolson, 327.

PAGE

296 "We were fond together . . .": Mack, *A Prince of Our Disorder*, 272.

297 "the right touch of iciness . . .": *MG* May 2.

297 "We have a feeling . . .": *Sun* May 7.

297 "He must be a German . . .": *MG* May 5.

298 "Nobody knows what is doing . . .": *Sun* May 7.

298 "There was nothing . . .": Riddell, 70.

299 "a coffee-room . . .": Ibid.

300 "looking very much . . .": Ibid., 71.

300 "a stiff, precise, industrious . . .": Ibid.

300–03 The narrative of the session is from accounts in *NYT*, *LT*, *MG*, and *Sun*.

303 "I think that beats . . .": Riddell, 75.

304 "quite exhausted with emotion . . .": Taylor, 183.

304 "Because we are accustomed . . .": Riddell, 76.

PART SIX: THE DAYS OF THE WHIRLWIND

PAGE

309 "It is a terrible punishment . . .": *NYT* May 8.

309 "If these are . . .": *ES* May 14.

309 "Everyone seems delighted . . .": Taylor, 183.

309 "I am much troubled . . .": quoted in Mee, p 209

PAGE

309–10 "I was awakened . . .": Herbert Hoover, 461.

310 "It is an imperialistic . . .": *ES* May 14.

310 "For the first time . . .": Mee, 212.

310 "Would it not be better . . .": *MG* May 8.

310 "We had such high hopes
. . .": Noggle, *Into the
Twenties*, 137.

310–11 "These conditions represent . . .": *MG* May 9.

311 "The situation created . . .":
Lippmann, 114.

311 "a mockery . . .": *Sun* May
13.

311 "These conditions are no
thing else . . .": *MG* May
10.

311 "The big issue . . .": *NYT*
May 9.

311 "The acceptance of these
terms . . .": London
Daily Telegraph, quoted
in *MG* May 8.

311 "It is unbearable . . .": *MG*
May 10.

312 "The policy of reducing
. . .": Keynes, *Economic
Consequences of the Peace*,
225.

312 "What is Poethlyn?": *MG*
March 29.

313 "in deep distress . . .": *MG*
May 10.

313 "Away with this murderous . . .": *Sun* May 14.

313 "If this treaty comes to pass
. . .": *Sun* May 13.

313 "and reaction is restlessly
. . .": Ibid.

314 "we are not a defeated people . . .": *ES* May 13.

314 "Whatever comes now
. . .": *ES* May 14.

314 "Perhaps we will sign . . .":
ES May 8.

314 "It is wonderful . . .": *ES*
May 13.

315 "It is not necessary . . .":
NYT May 6.

317 "need not remain . . .":
NYT March 17.

317 "to defend the constitutional . . .": *LAT* May 14.

317 "to which it was not without kinship . . .": Cash,
Mind of the South, 344.

317–18 "Here in ghostly rides . . .":
Cash, pp. 345–6

318 "Scott, my darling . . .":
Bruccoli and Duggan,
*Correspondence of F. Scott
Fitzgerald*, 44–45.

321 "American women will go
without . . .": *LAT* May
16.

321 "*Les notes!* . . .": *MG* May
16.

321 "on essential points . . .":
MG May 12.

321–22 "In the course . . .": *MG*
May 15.

323 "in the best spirits . . .":
Mee, 224.

323 "I see some defects . . .":
Bonsal, *Suitors*, 271.

323 "The Germans had suc-
ceeded . . .": U.S. De-
partment of State, vol. 3,
975.

323 "By reestablishing militarism . . .": *MG* May 13.

PAGE

324 "which descend upon us . . .": Nicolson, 355.

324 The Talleyrand analogy is from Bailey, 293–94.

324 "a whited sepulchre.": The description is Robert Benchley's, quoted in Gaines, *Wit's End*, 36.

325 "They were always sneaking up . . .": Keats, *You Might as Well Live*, 44.

325 "an erudite and witty man . . .": Ibid., 46.

328 "the most perilous airplane flight . . .": *NYT* May 19.

328 "People have flown . . .": *NYT* April 16.

329 "Do not take property . . .": *ES* April 23.

329 "There will be no Red terror . . .": *ES* May 12.

329 "I was greatly impressed . . .": Mayer, 737.

330 "We are not at war . . .": *ES* April 10.

330 "the Allies intend . . .": *ES* April 23.

330 "*Ne vous enervez pas. . . .*": Mayer, 746.

331 "We are now at the worst . . .": *WP* April 27.

331 "If you drew a line . . .": *MG* May 21.

331 "What impressed me most . . .": *MG* June 9.

331 "Austria presents a peculiar . . .": *LAT* May 1.

332 "What do we want . . .": This account is from *MG* May 28.

PAGE

332–33 "This is how . . .": From "In the Penal Colony," in Kafka, *Complete Stories and Parables*, 140–67.

333 "I am very sad . . .": Leviné-Meyer, 141.

335 "It seemed as if . . .": *MG* May 21.

336 "You will be received here . . .": *MG* May 16.

336 "like a typical commercial man . . .": *MG* May 16.

336 "I hope I may go away . . .": *LAT* May 15.

337 "incessant ill temper . . .": Nicolson, 351.

337 "More than ever . . .": Ibid., 335.

337 "There, (in that . . .)": Ibid., 328–29.

337–38 "very white and worn . . .": Seymour's comments are in his *Letters*, 224–26.

338 "Oh, no, you can't . . .": Nicolson, 333–34.

338 "It is appalling . . .": Ibid., 337.

338 "those three all-powerful . . .": Ibid., 342.

339 "It is like hunt the slipper . . .": Ibid., 351.

339 "looked around angrily . . .": Seymour, *Letters*, 250.

339 "Why, I have not come . . .": Nicolson, 351.

340 "There is no speed limit . . .": Taylor, 186.

340 "but it was the most ragged . . .": Shotwell, 323.

PAGE

340 "The *Daily Mail* are making . . .": Taylor, 185.

341 "Russian events have shown . . .": Riddell, 79.

341 "It is hard, is it not . . .": Ibid., 81.

341 "Bonar Law cares . . .": Seymour, *Letters*, 227.

341 "there is not a single person . . .": Nicolson, 359.

341 "I know I should not . . .": Taylor, 186.

341 "the President looked wretched . . .": Bonsal, *Suitors*, 277.

342 "I was the only older man . . .": Steffens, 802.

342 "Inexperienced as we were . . .": Berle and Jacobs, *Navigating the Rapids*, 14.

342 "It is my conviction . . .": Mee, 226.

342 "the food is getting on . . .": *LAT* June 7.

343 "Saved hands Sopwith aeroplane.": *MG* May 26.

344 "when, to our great relief . . .": *MG* May 27.

344 "I thank you for your kind greeting . . .": Ibid.

344 "Nothing has stirred the imagination . . .": *MG* May 26.

345 "I want to . . .": *MG* May 28.

345 "this exploitation of the air . . .": *MG* June 2.

PAGE

348 "little more than a mob . . .": Miller, *Khyber*, 318.

350 "Having regard to the . . .": *MG* May 6.

350–51 "We recognize the necessity . . .": *MG* May 30.

351 "in such a state of scepticism . . .": *MG* April 5.

351 "let me know . . .": *MG* June 2.

353 "The powers that be . . .": *WP* June 3.

354 "The outrages of last night . . .": *LAT* June 4.

355 "It doesn't matter . . .": *Chicago Tribune* March 7.

355 "shapeless blue calico . . .": *NYT* Feb. 16.

355 "There is a definite . . .": *NYT* March 2.

355 "I would not want . . ."; "Women know nothing . . ."; "I think 999 . . .": *WP* June 4.

356 "to sweep out of the way . . .": *NYT* March 22.

356 "the great majority of women . . .": *NYT* March 24.

356 "an outrage upon our form . . .": *WP* June 4.

358 "What you did . . .": *ES* May 26.

358 "I couldn't hardly miss 'em . . .": Ibid.

358 "What ah like best . . .": Sergeant York's homecoming is reported in *LAT* June 1 and 5.

359 "like a ghost . . .": Ibid.

PAGE

359 "may be beaten, but [they] will . . .": *ES* June 18.

359 "There are days . . .": Ibid.

363 "the tragic remnant . . .": *ES* June 10.

363 "What a terrible disappointment . . .": *LAT* June 7.

363 "All has been taken from us . . .": *WP* June 5.

363 "German Austria is in no wise . . .": *MG* June 19.

364 "when taken in all its provisions . . .": Seymour, *Letters*, 269.

364 "the curious, the humorous . . .": Ibid., 252.

364–65 "We ought not to be sentimental . . .": Ibid., 255–56.

365 "our treaty violates none . . .": *MG* June 7.

365 "I ought to tell you . . .": Keynes, ix.

365 "I cannot quite understand him . . .": Riddell, 93.

366 "We've had enough of fighting . . .": *LAT* May 21.

366 "To suspect it of intrigue . . .": *MG* May 26.

367 "never uttered a revolutionary . . .": *ES* June 6.

368 "its deep regret . . .": *MG* May 24.

368 "They all look good . . .": *Sun* May 11.

369 "I felt that if I ever fell

PAGE

down . . .": Dempsey, 103.

369 "That June was the hottest . . .": Ibid., 106

369 "June 1919 . . .": Ibid., 110.

370 "He made me sit . . .": *ES* May 29.

373–74 "The [German] reply . . .": *NYT* June 17.

374 "another revolution . . .": *ES* May 30.

375 "Plundering, death, and murder . . .": Watt, 460.

376 "It is hard to conceive . . .": *WP* June 18.

376 "It would be best . . .": *NYT* June 16.

376 "Rather the end . . .": *NYT* June 19.

376 "It was like 1914 . . .": Kessler, 102.

376 "Desultory work . . .": Nicolson, 362.

378 "She cannot rise until . . .": *NYT* June 20.

379 "Nobody cares for Orlando . . .": *MG* June 20.

379–80 The account of the generals' meeting with Noske is drawn largely from Watt, 480–83.

380 "God does not desert us . . .": *WP* June 21.

380 "High-brows, Cabinet officers...":*ES* June 19.

381 "the Prussian people": quoted in Watt, 485

381 "Beyond Sollingen . . .": Shotwell, 377.

PART SEVEN: THE DAYS OF THE HARVEST

PAGE

403 "as if he were . . .": Riddell, 98–99.

405 "Headlam-Morley and I . . .": Nicolson, 366.

406 "He is not a militarist.": Ibid., 366.

407 "And now this . . .": *NYT* June 29.

407 "our feet softening . . .": Nicolson, 366.

408 "robs the ceremony . . .": Ibid., 367.

408 "He looks small . . .": Ibid., 367.

408 "A black frock coat . . .": *MG* June 30.

409 "Through the door at the end . . .": Nicolson, 368.

410 "God's judgment . . .": *MG* Sept. 29.

410 "It was an unpleasant sight . . .": Steffens, 788.

411 *"Oui, c'est une* . . .": Nicolson, 369–70.

411 "Today is a hell of a . . .": *NYT* June 30.

412 "destroying all romance . . .": Taylor, 187.

412 "standing miserably . . .": Nicolson, 370.

PAGE

412 "I signed the Peace Treaty . . .": *NAT* July 5.

412–13 "One has only to look . . .": *MG* June 30.

414 "To bed, sick of life.": Nicolson, 371.

415 "the 'plain people' . . .": *NAT* July 5.

415 "twenty new wars . . .": *MG* July 1.

416 "everything that has occurred . . .": *MG* June 28.

416 "They are flesh of our flesh . . .": *MG* June 26.

416 "salvation is only to be found . . .": *MG* June 30.

417 "We have had a wonderful time . . .": Taylor, 187.

417 "That's over! . . .": Riddell, 101–2.

417 "Very well . . .": Taylor, 187.

417 "I like him . . .": Lloyd George, 145.

418 "looking as if he were . . .": *NYT* June 30.

418 "Mr. Wilson, thank you . . .": *NYT* June 30.

PART EIGHT: THE DAYS OF DUST AND ASHES

PAGE

422 "You can hardly think of her . . .": *MG* July 7.

422 "I've never played at school . . .": *WP* Sept. 8.

423 "the pace had been tremendous . . .": *MG* July 7.

PAGE

423 "I don't know how they feel . . .": *LT* July 7.

423 "the best match ever seen . . .": *MG* July 7.

426 "Folks won't be usin' . . .": *ES* July 19.

PAGE

427 "It has been noted . . .": *LAT* June 2.

427 "the consensus of opinion . . .": *ES* May 24.

427 "we were going into a . . .": *MG* July 7.

427 "For, doubt it not . . .": *MG* July 18.

428 "An inefficient, unemployed . . .": Keynes, 249.

428 "I wanted to watch . . .": Steffens, 803.

429 "The burden of taxation . . .": *WP* July 10.

429 "The allies can only . . .": *WP* July 7.

430 "A distaste for all politics filled me . . .": Hecht's feelings are revealed in *A Child*, 318–19.

430 "Some of them hate Germany . . .": *MG* June 27.

430 "Let us try it . . .": *MG* July 4.

431 "I have come from a very difficult . . .": *MG* July 7.

431 "The man who saved . . .": *MG* July 9.

431 "My own sweet darling . . .": Taylor, *My Darling Pussy*, 26–27.

432 "How everyone dislikes her . . .": Taylor, *Diary*, 188.

432 "This is the most tremendous . . .": *WP* July 6.

432 "without greatness . . .": Seymour, 276–77.

PAGE

433 "bound to the rocks . . .": Noggle, 136–37.

433 "put through a peace . . .": Seymour, *Letters*, 277.

433 The opinions of the ring experts are from *ES* July 2, and *WP* June 29, July 3, and July 4.

434 "I made sure . . .": Dempsey, 112.

434 "the Willard of his time . . .": *WP* July 4.

435 "more dips, yeggs . . .": *LAT* July 4.

435 "a somewhat stocky, spruced-up guy . . .": Dempsey, 113.

436 "I don't care who they get . . .": *LAT* June 30.

436 "I saw Ollie Pecord's lips . . .": Dempsey, 116.

437 "Ringside was surrounded . . .": Ibid., 115.

437 "as big and impregnable . . .": *WP* July 6.

438 "There seems to be something wrong . . .": Dempsey, 118.

438–39 "His face was distorted . . .": Ibid., 119.

439 "It felt swell": Ibid.

439 "I am sorry that Jess . . .": *WP* July 5.

440 "Such human butchery . . .": *WP* July 7.

440 "Ain't you Jack Dempsey?": Dempsey, 121.

442 "a deserted expanse of asphalt . . .": *LT* June 16.

PAGE

444 "the boys were going to . . .": *WP* July 20.

444 "a few hotheads.": *WP* July 21.

445 "That is what we would like to know.": Ibid.

446 "It is the solemn duty . . .": *WP* July 23.

447 "Jerseyman though I am . . .": *WP* July 9.

447 "Everybody's business . . .": Ibid.

448 "As he was ushered . . .": Grayson, 93.

448 "There can be no question . . .": *WP* July 11.

448 "casting pearls before swine.": Smith, *When the Cheering Stopped*, 57.

448 "Here I am . . .": Bonsal, *Suitors*, 277.

449 "It is as plain . . .": *ES* July 17.

449 "So far as a layman . . .": *ES* July 20.

453 "very well pleased . . .": *WP* July 30.

454 "You look as if . . .": *LT* June 19.

454 "disappointingly simple . . .": *WP* July 13.

455 "I have great need . . .": *LT* July 8.

455 "The year 1919 . . .": Sassoon, 239.

455 "When I come back . . .": Taylor, *Letters*, 30.

455–56 "In the minds of thousands . . .": *MG* June 7.

PAGE

456 "On the whole it seems . . .": *MG* July 19.

457 "The people *love* him . . .": Taylor, *Diary*, 188.

457 "not quite sure . . .": Riddell, 106.

457 "I fear there will be . . .": Woolf, *Diary*, 292.

457 "the usual sticky, stodgy . . .": Ibid., 292.

457 "detestable; it smells . . .": Ibid., 267.

458 "he could compare the scene . . .": *MG* July 31.

458–59 "I'd string up all persons . . .": *ES* Aug. 9.

459 "The worst feature . . .": *ES* April 25.

459 "There will be no peace . . .": *MG* July 3.

459 "The Government has dared . . .": *MG* Aug. 1.

460 "open brigandage . . .": *NYT* Aug. 1.

460–61 "The unexpected is always . . .": Riddell, 107.

461 "If we all pull in different . . .": *MG* July 17.

461 "Also he seemed . . ." and "I must have peace . . .": Riddell, 107.

461 "everywhere, in all classes . . .": *MG* June 27.

462 "The beaches were black with crowds . . .": Graves, *Weekend*, 24.

463 "a wide and distinct track . . .": *MG* Sept. 30.

464 "One-piece bathing suits . . .": *ES* July 23.

PAGE

465 "blood shall flow . . .": *ES* July 21.

466 "Very well . . .": *NYT* Aug. 2.

466 "to avert the pillage . . .": *ES* Aug. 7.

467 "The war was terrible . . .": *LT* Aug. 12.

467 "Reaction like that in Hungary . . .": *NR* Sept. 3, and *ES* Aug. 25.

468 "If we got anything . . .": *ES* Aug. 12.

468–69 For working conditions in the theater generally, see McCabe, *George M. Cohan*, 147–48.

469 "the Prussian bosses . . .": *NYT* Aug. 2.

470 "I think I'll go . . .": *ES* Aug. 8.

470 "the dirtiest business . . .": *ES* May 12.

471 "Over fair . . .": McCabe, 149–50.

471–72 Rockefeller story is from *ES* July 19.

472–74 Carnegie quotes are from

PAGE

NYT Aug. 12, *NAT* Aug. 16, *ES* Aug. 28, and *WP* Aug. 29.

474 "For a short time after . . .": Statement in *Freiheit*, quoted in *ES* July 19.

474 "a confirmation . . .": Kessler, 108–10.

475 "We must again become . . .": *LT* Sept. 1.

476 "a pale, small face . . .": Toland, *Adolf Hitler*, 115.

476 "He commands absolute . . .": Payne, *The Life and Death of Adolf Hitler*, 129.

476 "Detroit's gone . . .": *ES* Sept. 2.

476–77 "They have a whirlwind attack . . .": *ES* Aug. 30.

478 "The heat will be intense . . .": Gene Smith, 59.

479 "I do not want to do anything foolhardy . . .": Grayson, 95.

PART NINE: THE DAYS OF THE THIEF

PAGE

483 "He had extraordinary magnetism . . .": Chaplin, *My Autobiography*, 199.

483 "He had the quality . . .": Herndon, *Mary Pickford and Douglas Fairbanks*, 170.

484 "The need for the present

PAGE

organization . . .": *LAT* Jan. 16.

485 "We are willing to make . . .": Ibid.

485 "We intend to introduce . . .": *ES* April 10.

485 "So the lunatics . . .": Herndon, 181.

PAGE

485 "No, we have a big busi-
    ness . . .": *LAT* Jan. 16.

486 "It is a piece of German
    . . .": Herndon, 175.

486 "Doug does nothing essen-
    tially . . .": *LAT* Sept. 9.

486 "Fairbanks is an essentially
    . . .": Ibid.

487 "I am not going to associate
    . . .": *NYT* Aug. 13.

487–94 The account of Wilson's
    tour is taken from the
    following:
    Sept. 4: *ES* Sept. 4, 5, and 6;
    WP Sept. 5; *LAT* Sept. 5;
    Smith, 61–64.
    Sept. 5: *ES* Sept. 5; *WP*
    Sept. 5; Smith, 64–65; *LT*
    Sept. 8.
    Sept. 6: *ES* Sept. 6; *WP*
    Sept. 7; Smith, 66.
    Sept. 8: *WP* Sept. 9; *ES*
    Sept. 8; *LT* Sept. 8.

496 "I thought it was the mili-
    tary . . .": *LT* Sept. 9.

498 "He gets a front-page
    spread . . .": *NAT* July
    12.

498 "the war front is now trans-
    ferred . . .": *ES* Sept. 13.

498 "If the anti-British element
    . . .": *LT* Sept. 15.

498 "Coercion advances . . .":
    Ibid.

499 "I am firmly of the opinion
    . . .": Fuess, *Calvin Coo-
    lidge,* 206.

499 "No members of the force
    . . .": Ibid., 207.

PAGE

500 "the Hunnish attitude . . .":
    Ibid., 216.

500 "I am ready for anything
    . . .": Ibid., 218.

501 "The tumult and the riot
    . . .": *Boston Telegraph,*
    quoted in *ES* Sept. 12.

502 "The action of the police
    . . .": *ES* Sept. 12.

502 "Your assertion . . .": *WP*
    Sept. 15 (emphasis
    added).

503 "This academic but not
    scholarly . . .": *MG* Sept.
    11.

504 "There was nothing to
    show . . .": *LT* Sept. 11.

504 "there was nothing to indi-
    cate . . .": Ibid.

505 "If you take Austria . . .":
    ES July 31.

506 "One became almost used
    to . . .": *MG* Oct. 7.

507 "The working class . . .":
    MG Sept. 10.

507 "The principal contribu-
    tory cause . . .": *MG*
    Sept. 23.

509–15 The account of Wilson's
    tour is taken from the
    following:
    Sept. 9: *LT* Sept. 12; *WP*
    Sept. 10.
    Sept. 10: *ES* Sept. 10 and
    11; *WP* Sept. 11.
    Sept. 11: *ES* Sept. 11; *WP*
    Sept. 12.
    Sept. 12: *WP* Sept. 13; *ES*
    Sept. 12.

PAGE

Sept. 13: *WP* Sept. 14; Smith, 72–73.

Sept. 14: Smith, 74; *WP* Sept. 15.

Sept. 15: *WP* Sept. 16; *ES* Sept. 15 and 16.

Sept. 16: *LAT* Sept. 17.

515–16 "This sort of journey . . .": *WP* Sept. 20.

516 "We had lunch . . .": Ibid.

516–17 "It is just a question . . .": *LAT* May 11.

517 "one of the most fully realized": Richard Schickel, *D. W. Griffith*, 381.

518 "is so simple . . .": *Sun* May 11.

518–19 "For instance, deep lines . . .": *Current Opinion* Jan. 19.

520 "I led the army . . .": *LT* Sept. 30.

520–21 There are different versions of the confrontation between d'Annunzio and Pittaluga; this account is taken from *MG* Sept. 17 and *ES* Sept. 15.

521 "I am so ill . . .": *LAT* Sept. 19.

521 "Dear Companion . . .": Mussolini, 79.

522 "tangled and slimy net . . .": Ibid., 80.

523 "I have risked all . . .": *LT* Sept. 27.

524 "sprang out of the ground . . .": Toland, 119.

524 "It was a joy to watch":

PAGE

Orlow, *History of the Nazi Party*, 14–15.

525 "In general the Jew has preserved . . .": Payne, *Hitler*, 129–31; Payne's book also contains an excellent discussion of the letter.

526 "There was nothing here . . .": Hitler, *Mein Kampf*, 354.

526–30 The account of Wilson's tour is taken from the following:

Sept. 17: *ES* Sept. 17 and 18.

Sept. 18: *WP* Sept. 19; *LAT* Sept. 19.

Sept. 19: *LAT* Sept. 20; *WP* Sept. 20.

Sept. 20: *LAT* Sept. 21; *WP* Sept. 21.

Sept. 21: *LAT* Sept. 22.

532 "I am known in parts of the world . . .": *NYT* Dec. 25, 1977.

533 "Exhibitors were rugged merchants . . .": Chaplin, 221.

533 "You have to believe . . .": *NYT* Dec. 25, 1977.

533 "Even funnier than the man . . .": Ibid.

533–34 Shooting schedule quoted in Robinson, *Chaplin*, 249.

534 " 'Sunnyside' was anything . . .": Gehring, *Charlie Chaplin*, 30.

PAGE

534 "Charlie is like . . .": Ibid., 29.

534 "I am a prestidigitator . . .": Robinson, 252–53.

534 "This is the most amazing . . .": Ibid., 252.

535 "In leisure moments . . .": LAT Sept. 15.

535 "no child actor . . .": Robinson, 255.

535 "One thing was sure . . .": Chaplin, 225.

536 "our last difficult . . .": Fischer, 343.

536 "Civil war is civil war . . .": ES April 17.

536 "I think that the Russian people . . .": Hare, 102.

536 "No, not at all . . .": Ibid., 103.

537 "merely an instrument . . .": MG May 17.

538 "the indefinable but irresistible . . .": NR Aug. 23.

538 "The second half of 1919 . . .": Fischer, 343–44.

539 "He worked from morning . . .": Ibid., 344.

539–45 The account of Wilson's tour is taken from the following:
Sept. 22: LAT Sept. 23; Ross, Power With Grace, 191.
Sept. 23: LAT Sept. 24; ES Sept. 24; Ross, 191; Walworth, Woodrow Wilson, 369.
Sept. 24: WP Sept. 25; Gene Smith, 80.

PAGE

Sept. 25–28: ES Sept. 25 and 27; Gene Smith, 81–85; Walworth, 370–71; Grayson, 97–100; WP Sept. 27 and 28; ES Sept. 28 and 29; Ross, 195.

546 "the main cause why . . .": Graves, Weekend, 123.

546 "admittedly 'not much class' ": Ibid.

547 "Carnegie never wanted to know . . .": Brody, Labor in Crisis, 13. My account of the steel strike in general is greatly indebted to Brody's excellent history.

548 "the Christian hired man": Ibid., 19.

548 "the commanding general . . .": MG Oct. 24.

548 "make the Steel Corporation . . .": Brody, 78.

550 "we are going to see . . .": Ibid., 93–94.

550 "They are wrong . . .": Ibid., 104.

551 "Mr. President . . .": WP Sept. 19.

551 "It is the settled determination . . .": LAT Sept. 18.

552 "exceeded in magnitude . . .": Brody, 113.

552 Newspaper editorial comments are in ibid., 129.

552 "if the strike succeeds . . .": ES Sept. 26.

553 "For why this war? . . .": Brody, 157.

554 "One of its main objects . . .": Riddell, 118.

PAGE

555 "had a queer resemblance . . .": *MG* Sept. 27.

555–56 "I have come to the conclusion . . .": *MG* Sept. 29.

556 "There is no doubt . . .": *LT* Sept. 29.

556 "over the edge . . .": *MG* Oct. 6.

557 "what the working classes really want . . .": Riddell, 110.

559 "I am glad the brute . . .": *ES* Sept. 29; *WP* Sept. 29.

562–63 "It is doubtful if there ever has been . . .": *WP* Oct. 1.

564 "Never before in the history . . .": *NYT* Oct. 2.

564 "one of the worst beatings . . .": *WP* Oct. 2.

566 "I will throw the first game . . .": *NYT* July 20, 1921.

567 "The complexion of the betting situation . . .": *NYT* Oct. 2.

567 "You think I don't know . . .": Asinof, *Eight Men Out*, 72. My account of the Series and the scandal is based on newspaper reports in the *Washington Post* and *The New York Times* and on Asinof's excellent study.

567 "I have no feeling . . .": Gene Smith, 95.

568 "stretched out on the long Lincoln bed. . . .": Irwin Hoover, 102.

568 "I am scared . . .": Gene Smith, 97.

569 "I seem to gather . . .": Holroyd, *Lytton Strachey*, 374.

569 "I never saw such bad breaks . . .": *WP* Oct. 3.

570 "It was as if the earth . . .": *NYT* Oct. 3.

570–71 "The Sox showed a lot more . . .": *WP* Oct. 5.

571–72 "I've been told that gamblers . . .": Roush's account is in Connor, *Baseball for the Love of It*, 187–88.

573 "I tell you those Reds . . .": Asinof, 119.

573 "There is always some scandal . . .": *NYT* Oct. 11.

PART TEN: THE DAYS OF DREAMS

PAGE

578 "We have petticoat Government! . . .": Gene Smith, 112.

578 "the very heart . . .": Grayson, 102.

579 "Little girl, don't you . . .": Gene Smith, 120.

579 "All the more reason . . .": Ross, 212.

PAGE

579 "Strangely enough . . .":
Riddell, 108.

580 "I congratulate you . . .":
Fuess, 238.

580 "these radical leaders . . .":
LAT Sept. 1.

580 "at this time there can no
longer . . .": *NYT* Nov.
23.

580 "I have no doubt . . .": *ES*
Sept. 3.

581 "One thing that should be
. . .": *LAT* Dec. 17.

581 "an army of pompous
phrases . . .": Leuchten-
berg, 90.

582 "For one year . . .": Lippmann, *Letters*, 270–73.

582 "into a sphere . . .": James,
Speeches, 2875.

583 "The misery of Germany
. . .": Toland, 126.

583 "indomitable will . . .": Hitler, 356.

583 "*Wilkommen zu unseren*
. . .": Bonsal, *Unfinished
Business*, 260–61.

583 "the blank pessimism . . .":
NAT Sept. 27.

584 "men, women, and children . . .": Bonsal, *Unfinished Business*, 261.

584 "I will oppose . . .": *WP*
Sept. 21.

585 "The toddlers . . .": *NAT*
Oct. 11.

585 "Never in history . . .":
NYT Dec. 25.

586 "I came out of all these ex-

PAGE

periences . . .": Herbert
Hoover, 473.

587 "It takes you a long time
. . .": *MG* Oct. 25.

587 "and the more they struggle . . .": *MG* Jan. 1,
1920.

588 "These are not isolated results . . .": *NYT* Nov. 9.

588 Russell's opinion is in *NYT*
April 19, 1955.

588 "no one has yet succeeded
. . .": Frank, *Einstein*,
140–41.

588–89 "The terms relativity . . .":
NYT Dec. 3.

589–90 "for some years past . . .":
Frank, 143.

590 "If you were able to use
. . .": *LT* Sept. 18.

590 "I have so many things
. . .": Kuehl and Bryer,
Dear Scott/Dear Max, 21.

591 "a false idea, a false system
. . .": Ludington, 176.

591 "I work best . . .": Mack,
283–84.

591 "He refused all service
. . .": Ibid.

592 "I will supply": Bar-Zohar,
Ben-Gurion, 42–43.

593 Lenin's Dec. 5 speech is in
Fischer, *Lenin*, p. 375.

593 "Of course, it's very pleasant . . .": Ibid., 345.

593–94 "white peril of cruel . . .":
LAT Dec. 15.

594 "I faced, and all of us . . .":
Mussolini, 82.

PAGE

594 "Don't fear . . .": Ibid., 87.

595 "One of them was holding forth . . .": Norman, *Nehru*, 51.

595–96 "It is the war . . .": *MG* Dec. 20.

596 "We are in it now . . .": *MG* Dec. 20.

596–97 Lloyd George's Irish proposals are summarized in *NYT* Dec. 23.

598 "This is the beginning of the end . . .": *LAT* Dec. 22.

598 "We're coming back . . .": Ibid.

598 "These persons, while enjoying . . .": *NYT* Dec. 24.

600 "by the basketful.": Truman, 83.

601–02 "These areas are the altars . . .": *MG* Sept. 12.

602 "There will be another . . .": Herbert Hoover, 482.

PAGE

602 "I have become a regular fetish . . .": Riddell, 152.

603 "In short, Germany's Christmas . . .": *NYT* Dec. 24.

603 "the simplest, punk little dolls . . .": *LAT* Dec. 25.

603 "The world is very sordid . . .": Riddell, 135.

604 "He is a dear thing . . .": Taylor, *Diary*, 194.

605 "At meal-times he takes her . . .": Riddell, 155.

605 "most remarkably improved . . .": *LAT* Dec. 28.

605 "It was a sight . . .": Ross, 206.

606 "Why start another . . .": *LAT* Dec. 21.

606–07 "We are at the dead season . . .": Keynes, 296–97.

609 "A year of torture . . .": *MG* Jan. 1, 1920.

609 "The year just past . . .": *NYT* Jan. 1, 1920.

SELECTED BIBLIOGRAPHY

Most of the material in this book comes directly from eyewitness accounts of the people and events of the year 1919. To give the reader a vivid sense of reliving the year, I have relied heavily upon articles in contemporary newspapers, including *The New York Times*, the *Los Angeles Times*, the *Manchester Guardian*, and *The Times* (of London), among others as cited in the footnotes. Anyone who does a substantial amount of historical research in journalistic sources soon realizes that one should not, indeed, believe everything one reads, and so I have attempted to cross-check and verify any information that seemed to be even slightly dubious. I have avoided hearsay articles ("We have received reports from Moscow that Lenin has jumped off a cliff . . .") altogether. On the other hand, when a correspondent—identified with a byline—states that he saw Woodrow Wilson shake hands with Lloyd George on the steps of the Quai d'Orsay on such-and-such a day, I have generally accepted his word for it. I would like to point out to diehard skeptics of journalistic veracity that the newspaper accounts I examined often proved more accurate in terms of the chronology of events than secondary works; I discovered numerous instances of a reputable historian placing an event in the wrong month of 1919, and sometimes even in a different year altogether.

The most valuable collection of official documents for the Paris Peace Conference is the U.S. Department of State's *Papers Relating to the Foreign Relations of the United States, Paris Peace Conference,* published in eleven delightful volumes.

The works cited below are those I found most interesting and useful in giving me the behind-the-scenes stories unavailable in either daily newspapers or official documents. I would like to take this opportunity to express my profound gratitude to everyone who kept an intimate diary or wrote revealing letters during 1919; there are few things more interesting to a historian than reading someone else's mail.

Asinof, Eliot. *Eight Men Out: The Black Sox and the 1919 World Series*. New York, 1963.

Baker, Carlos, ed. *Ernest Hemingway: Selected Letters, 1917–1961*. New York, 1981.

Bailey, Thomas A. *Woodrow Wilson and the Lost Peace*. Chicago, 1963.

Barker, Richard H. *Marcel Proust: A Biography*. New York, 1958.

Bar-Zohar, Michael. *Ben-Gurion: A Biography*. New York, 1979.

Ben-Gurion, David. *Letters to Paula*. Pittsburgh, 1968.

———. *Memoirs*. New York, 1970.

Berle, Beatrice B., and Travis Beal Jacobs, eds. *Navigating the Rapids, 1918–1971: From the Papers of Adolf A. Berle*. New York, 1973.

Bertensson, Sergei, and Jay Leyda. *Sergei Rachmaninoff: A Lifetime in Music*. New York, 1956.

Birkenhead, Lord. *Rudyard Kipling*. New York, 1978.

Blum, John Morton, ed. *Public Philosopher: Selected Letters of Walter Lippmann*. New York, 1985.

Bonsal, Stephen. *Suitors and Suppliants*. Garden City, New York, 1946.

———. *Unfinished Business*. Garden City, New York, 1944.

Brody, David. *Labor in Crisis: The Steel Strike of 1919*. Philadelphia, 1965.

Bruccoli, Matthew J. *Some Sort of Epic Grandeur: The Life of F. Scott Fitzgerald*. New York, 1981.

Bruccoli, Matthew J., and Margaret M. Duggan, eds. *Correspondence of F. Scott Fitzgerald*. New York, 1980.

Buchan, John. *Memory Hold-the-Door*. London, 1940.

Buckle, Richard. *Nijinsky*. New York, 1971.

Burner, David. *Herbert Hoover: A Public Life*. New York, 1979.

Campbell, John. *F. E. Smith: First Earl of Birkenhead*. London, 1983.

Casals, Pablo. *Joys and Sorrows*. New York, 1970.

Cash, W. J. *The Mind of the South*. New York, 1969.

Chaplin, Charles. *My Autobiography*. New York, 1964.

Connor, Anthony J. *Baseball for the Love of It*. New York, 1982.

Crankshaw, Edward. *Bismarck*. New York, 1981.

Curtiss, Mina, ed. *Letters of Marcel Proust*. New York, 1949.

Dangerfield, George. *The Damnable Question*. Boston, 1976.

Daniels, Jonathan. *The Time Between the Wars*. Garden City, New York, 1966.

Daniels, Josephus. *The Life of Woodrow Wilson*. New York, 1924.

De Valera, Eamon. *Speeches and Statements*. Edited by Maurice Moynihan. Dublin, 1980.

Delzell, Charles F. *Mediterranean Fascism, 1919–1945*. New York, 1970.

Dempsey, Jack, with Barbara Piatelli Dempsey. *Dempsey*. New York, 1977.

Dillon, E. J. *The Inside Story of the*

Peace Conference. New York, 1920.

Dos Passos, John. *Mr. Wilson's War.* Garden City, New York, 1962.

Downes, Randolph C. *The Rise of Warren Gamaliel Harding, 1865–1920.* Columbus, Ohio, 1970.

Draper, Alfred. *Amritsar.* London, 1981.

Ellmann, Richard. *James Joyce.* New York, 1982.

Ellmann, Richard, ed. *Selected Letters of James Joyce.* New York, 1976.

Falk, Candace. *Love, Anarchy, and Emma Goldman.* New York, 1984.

Ferrell, Robert H. *Dear Bess: The Letters from Harry to Bess Truman, 1910–1959.* New York, 1984.

Ferris, Paul. *The House of Northcliffe.* New York, 1971.

Fischer, Louis. *The Life of Lenin.* New York, 1964.

———. *The Life of Mahatma Gandhi.* New York, 1950.

Fitzgerald, F. Scott. *The Crack-Up.* Edited by Edmund Wilson. New York, 1956.

Forester, Margery. *Michael Collins: The Lost Leader.* London, 1971.

Frank, Philipp. *Einstein: His Life and Times.* New York, 1972.

Freedman, Ralph. *Hermann Hesse: Pilgrim of Crisis.* New York, 1978.

Friedrich, Otto. *Before the Deluge: A Portrait of Berlin in the 1920's.* New York, 1972.

Fuess, Claude M. *Calvin Coolidge: The Man from Vermont.* Westport, Conn., 1968.

Gaines, James R. *Wit's End: Days and Nights of the Algonquin Round Table.* New York, 1977.

Gallo, Max. *Mussolini's Italy: Twenty Years of the Fascist Era.* New York, 1964.

Gandhi, Mohandas K. *An Autobiography: The Story of My Experiments with Truth.* Boston, 1957.

Gehring, Wes D. *Charlie Chaplin.* Westport, Conn., 1983.

Goldman, Emma. *Living My Life.* Garden City, New York, 1931.

Graves, Robert. *Goodbye to All That.* Garden City, New York, 1957.

———, and Alan Hodge. *The Long Weekend.* New York, 1963.

Grayson, Rear Admiral Cary T. *Woodrow Wilson: An Intimate Memoir.* New York, 1960.

Grey, Ian. *Stalin: A Man of History.* Garden City, New York, 1979.

Hare, Richard. *Maxim Gorkii: Romantic Realist and Conservative Revolutionary.* London, 1962.

Hart, William S. *My Life East and West.* New York, 1929.

Headlam-Morley, Sir James Wycliffe. *Memoir of the Paris Peace Conference, 1919.* Edited by Agnes Headlam-Morley. London, 1972.

Hecht, Ben. *A Child of the Century.* New York, 1954.

Herndon, Booton. *Mary Pickford and Douglas Fairbanks: The Most*

Popular Couple the World Has Ever Known. New York, 1977.

Hicks, Granville. *John Reed: The Making of a Revolutionary.* New York, 1937.

Hitler, Adolf. *Mein Kampf.* Boston, 1971 edition.

Holroyd, Michael. *Lytton Strachey: A Critical Biography.* Vol. 2. New York, 1968.

Holt, Edgar. *The Tiger: The Life of Georges Clemenceau.* London, 1976.

Hone, Joseph. *W. B. Yeats.* New York, 1962.

Hoover, Herbert. *The Memoirs of Herbert Hoover.* 2 vols. New York, 1951.

Hoover, Irwin Hood. *Forty-Two Years in the White House.* Boston, 1934.

Jackson, Kenneth T. *The Ku Klux Klan in the City, 1915–1930.* New York, 1967.

James, Robert Rhodes. *The British Revolution, 1880–1939.* New York, 1977.

———. *Churchill: A Study in Failure, 1900–1939.* New York, 1970.

———, ed. *Winston Churchill: His Complete Speeches.* Vol. 3. New York, 1970.

Jean-Aubry, G. *Joseph Conrad: Life and Letters.* Garden City, New York, 1927.

Kafka, Franz. *The Complete Stories and Parables.* Edited by Nahum N. Glatzer. New York, 1983.

Keats, John. *You Might as Well Live: The Life and Times of Dorothy Parker.* New York, 1970.

Kennan, George. *Russia and the West Under Lenin and Stalin.* New York, 1960.

Kessler, Harry. *In the Twenties: The Diaries of Harry Kessler.* New York, 1971.

Keynes, John Maynard. *The Economic Consequences of the Peace.* New York, 1971.

Kirk, H. L. *Pablo Casals.* New York, 1974.

Kracauer, Siegfried. *From Caligari to Hitler.* Princeton, 1947.

Krock, Arthur. *Memoirs: Sixty Years on the Firing Line.* New York, 1968.

Kuehl, John, and Jackson R. Bryer, eds. *Dear Scott/Dear Max: The Fitzgerald-Perkins Correspondence.* New York, 1971.

Lacouture, Jean. *Ho Chi Minh: A Political Biography.* New York, 1968.

Lago, Mary, and P. N. Furbank, eds. *Selected Letters of E. M. Forster.* Vol. 1. Cambridge, 1983.

Lash, Joseph P. *Eleanor and Franklin.* New York, 1971.

———. *From the Diaries of Felix Frankfurter.* New York, 1975.

Leuchtenberg, William E. *The Perils of Prosperity, 1914–32.* Chicago, 1958.

Leviné-Meyer, Rosa. *Leviné: The Life of a Revolutionary.* Farnborough, England, 1973.

Link, Arthur. *Wilson: The Road to the White House.* Princeton, 1947.

Lippmann, Walter. *Public Philosopher: Selected Letters of Walter Lippmann.* Edited by John Morton Blum. New York, 1985.

Litvinoff, Barnet. *Weizmann: Last of the Patriarchs.* New York, 1976.

Lloyd George, David. *Memoirs of the Peace Conference.* New Haven, 1939.

Longford, the Earl of, and Thomas P. O'Neill. *Eamon De Valera.* Boston, 1971.

Ludington, Townsend. *John Dos Passos: A Twentieth Century Odyssey.* New York, 1980.

McCabe, John. *George M. Cohan: The Man Who Owned Broadway.* New York, 1973.

Mack, John E. *A Prince of Our Disorder: The Life of T. E. Lawrence.* Boston, 1976.

McTague, John J. *British Policy in Palestine, 1917–1922.* Lanham, 1983.

Manchester, William. *American Caesar.* New York, 1978.

———. *The Last Lion: Winston Spencer Churchill, Visions of Glory, 1874–1932.* Boston, 1983.

Markiewicz, Constance. *Prison Letters of Countess Markiewicz.* London, 1934.

Mayer, Arno J. *Politics and Diplomacy of Peacemaking: Containment and Counterrevolution at Versailles, 1918–1919.* New York, 1969.

Mee, Charles L., Jr. *The End of Order: Versailles, 1919.* New York, 1980.

Meir, Golda. *My Life.* New York, 1975.

Messick, Hank. *John Edgar Hoover.* New York, 1972.

Meyers, Jeffrey. *Hemingway: A Biography.* New York, 1985.

Miller, Charles. *Khyber: British India's North West Frontier: The Story of an Imperial Migraine.* London, 1977.

Monkhouse, Allan. *Moscow, 1911–1933.* Boston, 1934.

Mowat, Charles L. *Britain Between the Wars, 1918–1940.* Boston, 1971.

Mussolini, Benito. *My Autobiography.* New York, 1928.

Nash, Jay Robert. *Citizen Hoover.* Chicago, 1972.

Nicolson, Harold. *Peacemaking 1919.* New York, 1965.

Nijinsky, Romola, ed. *The Diary of Vaslav Nijinsky.* Berkeley, Calif., 1936.

Nin, Anaïs. *Linotte: The Early Diary of Anais Nïn, 1914–20.* New York, 1978.

Noggle, Burl. *Into the Twenties.* Urbana, Illinois, 1974.

Norman, Dorothy, ed. *Nehru: The First Sixty Years.* Vol. 1. New York, 1965.

O'Brien, Conor Cruise. *The Siege.* New York, 1986.

Orlow, Dietrich. *The History of the Nazi Party: 1919–1933.* Pittsburgh, 1969.

Pachter, Henry. *Weimar Etudes.* New York, 1982.

Pais, Abraham. *"Subtle Is the Lord . . .": The Science and the Life of Albert Einstein.* New York, 1982.

Pandey, B. N. *The Break-Up of British India.* London, 1969.

Payne, Robert. *The Life and of Adolf Hitler.* New York, 1973.

———. *The Life and Death of Lenin.* New York, 1964.

———. *The Life and Death of Mahatma Gandhi.* New York, 1969.

———. *The Life and Death of Trotsky.* New York, 1977.

Pruessen, Ronald W. *John Foster Dulles: The Road to Power.* New York, 1982.

Rachmaninoff, Sergei, as told to Oskar von Riesemann. *Recollections.* Freeport, N.Y., 1934.

Ransome, Arthur. *Russia in 1919.* New York, 1919.

Riddell, Lord George. *Lord Riddell's Intimate Diary of the Peace Conference and After.* London, 1933.

Ritter, Lawrence, and Donald Honig. *The Image of Their Greatness.* New York, 1979.

Roberts, Randy. *Jack Dempsey: The Manassa Mauler.* Baton Rouge, 1979.

Robinson, David. *Chaplin: His Life and Art.* New York, 1986.

Rose, Kenneth. *King George V.* New York, 1983.

Ross, Ishbel. *Power with Grace: The Life Story of Mrs. Woodrow Wilson.* New York, 1975.

Rossi, A. *The Rise of Italian Fascism, 1918–1922.* New York, 1966.

Rowland, Peter. *David Lloyd George: A Biography.* New York, 1975.

Sandburg, Carl. *Selected Poems of Carl Sandburg.* Edited by Rebecca West. New York, 1926.

Sassoon, Siegfried. *Siegfried's Journey, 1916–1920.* New York, 1946.

Schickel, Richard. *D. W. Griffith: An American Life.* New York, 1984.

Seaton, Albert. *Stalin as Warlord.* London, 1976.

Seroff, Victor I. *Rachmaninoff.* New York, 1950.

Seymour, Charles. *Letters From the Paris Peace Conference.* Edited by Harold B. Whiteman, Jr. New Haven, 1965.

———, ed. *The Intimate Papers of Colonel House.* Boston, 1926.

Shirer, William L. *The Rise and Fall of the Third Reich.* New York, 1960.

Sholokov, Mikhail. *And Quiet Flows the Don.* New York, 1966.

———. *The Don Flows Home to the Sea.* New York, 1966.

Shotwell, James T. *At the Paris Peace Conference.* New York, 1937.

Smelser, Marshall. *The Life that Ruth Built.* Chicago, 1975.

Smith, Dennis Mack. *Mussolini.* New York, 1982.

Smith, Gene. *When the Cheering Stopped: The Last Years of Woodrow Wilson.* New York, 1964.

Smith, Robert. *Babe Ruth's America.* New York, 1974.

Sorokin, Pitirin. *Leaves From a Russian Diary.* New York, 1924.

Steffens, Lincoln. *The Autobiography of Lincoln Steffens.* New York, 1931.

Stewart, Desmond. *T. E. Lawrence.* New York, 1977.

Stewart, Rhea Talley. *Fire in Afghanistan, 1914–1929.* Garden City, New York, 1973.

Swinson, Arthur. *Six Minutes to Sunset: The Story of General Dyer and the Amritsar Affair.* London, 1964.

Taylor, A. J. P., ed. *Lloyd George: A Diary by Frances Stevenson.* New York, 1971.

———. *My Darling Pussy: The Letters of Lloyd George and Frances Stevenson, 1913–1941.* London, 1975.

Toland, John. *Adolf Hitler.* New York, 1976.

Truman, Margaret. *Bess W. Truman.* New York, 1986.

Ulam, Adam. *Stalin: The Man and His Era.* New York, 1973.

U.S. Department of State. *Papers Relating to the Foreign Relations of the United States, Paris Peace Conference, 1919.* 11 vols. Washington, D.C., 1942–7.

———. *Papers Relating to the Foreign Relations of the United States, Russia, 1919.* Washington, D.C., 1937.

Villard, Oswald G. *Fighting Years: Memoirs of A Liberal Editor.* New York, 1939.

Walworth, Arthur. *Woodrow Wilson.* New York, 1978.

Watson, David R. *Georges Clemenceau: A Political Biography,* New York, 1974.

Watt, Richard M. *The Kings Depart: The Tragedy of Germany, Versailles and the German Revolution.* New York, 1968.

Wells, H. G. *Experiment in Autobiography.* New York, 1934.

Wexler, Alice. *Emma Goldman: An Intimate Life.* New York, 1984.

White, William Allen. *The Autobiography of William Allen White.* New York, 1946.

Woolf, Virginia. *The Diary of Virginia Woolf.* Vol. 1. Edited by Anne Olivier Bell. New York, 1977.

Yeats, W. B. *The Poems of W. B. Yeats.* Edited by Richard J. Finneran. New York, 1983.

Zhukov, Georgi. *The Memoirs of Marshal Zhukov.* New York, 1971.

INDEX